D0910302

AN EVERGLADES PROVIDENCE

env ronmental
h story
and the
amer can
south

SERIES EDITOR

Paul S. Sutter, University of Georgia

ADVISORY BOARD

Judith Carney, University of California–Los Angeles

Robbie Ethridge, University of Mississippi

Ari Kelman, University of California–Davis

Jack Temple Kirby, Miami University of Ohio

Shepard Krech III, Brown University

Tim Silver, Appalachian State University

Mart Stewart, Western Washington University

An EVERGLADES

The University of Georgia Press ATHENS & LONDON

2258740221697 3341

QH
31
.D645
D38
2009

PROVIDENCE

Marjory Stoneman Douglas
and the American Environmental Century

JACK E. DAVIS

DISCARDED

NORMANDALE COMMUNITY COLLEGE
LIBRARY
9700 FRANCE AVENUE SOUTH
BLOOMINGTON, MN 55431-4399

NOV 0 4 2009

© 2009 by the University of Georgia Press

Athens, Georgia 30602

www.ugapress.org

All rights reserved

Designed by Erin Kirk New

Set in 11 on 16 Minion Pro by

   Graphic Composition, Inc., Bogart, Georgia

Printed and bound by Maple-Vail Book Manufacturing Group

The paper in this book meets the guidelines for
permanence and durability of the Committee on
Production Guidelines for Book Longevity of the
Council on Library Resources.

Printed on 100% post-consumer processed chlorine-free paper.

Printed in the United States of America

13   12   11   10   09   C   5   4   3   2   1

Library of Congress Cataloging-in-Publication Data

Davis, Jack E., 1956–

An Everglades providence : Marjory Stoneman Douglas and the American environmental century /
Jack E. Davis.

         p. cm. — (Environmental history and the American South)

Includes bibliographical references and index.

ISBN-13: 978-0-8203-3071-6 (hardcover : alk. paper)

ISBN-10: 0-8203-3071-x (hardcover : alk. paper)

1. Douglas, Marjory Stoneman. 2. Conservationists—Florida—Biography. 3. Feminists—United
States—Biography. 4. Authors, American—20th century—Biography. 5. Nature conservation—
Florida—Everglades—History. 6. Environmental degradation—Florida—History. 7. Wetland
conservation—Florida—History. 8. Environmental policy—Florida—History—20th century.
9. Environmental policy—United States—History—20th century. I. Title.

QH31.D645D38 2009

333.72092—dc22

[B]   2008049073

British Library Cataloging-in-Publication Data available

FOR WILLA

providence (noun): the foreseeing care and guidance of God
or Nature over the creatures of the earth

Contents

Foreword

Nineteen-forty-seven was a watershed year in the history of Florida's Everglades. On December 6, President Harry S. Truman dedicated Everglades National Park, the culmination of a decades-long campaign to protect a portion of this unique watery wilderness. Many people, then and since, have rightly seen this moment as emblematic of a turn toward ecological significance as a core standard for national park preservation. As importantly, few moments better symbolized the transformation of American attitudes about wetlands. Once vilified as a dangerous and pestilential swamp that needed to be drained and "improved," the Everglades had come to be valued as a beautiful place, the home of a distinctive flora and fauna, and a vital provider of what we have come to call ecosystem services. The creation of Everglades National Park thus constituted a signature moment in American environmental history.

But not everyone had turned the corner on Everglades appreciation. A series of hurricanes and tropical storms drenched South Florida in 1947, and while the critical dikes and levees that protected human life held, the resulting flooding did untold economic damage to the booming region, revealing, in the minds of some people, the inadequacies of an antiquated water-management infrastructure. Buoyed by postwar confidence (which might retrospectively be called hubris), the U.S. Army Corps of Engineers stepped in with an aggressive plan—the Central and Southern Florida

Project for Flood Control—to replumb the region. Just as a portion of the Everglades had been preserved in perpetuity, then, the corps embarked on a massive engineering project that would, over the following half century, profoundly upset the Everglades' ecological integrity.

Just a month before the park dedication, Rinehart published, as part of its Rivers of America series, Marjory Stoneman Douglas's *The Everglades: River of Grass,* a volume that still stands as the definitive appreciation of the Everglades. It was hugely popular from its first appearance, and it both enhanced Douglas's reputation as a skilled writer and foreshadowed her role as an influential environmental advocate. In addition, Douglas's landmark book gave readers a new way of understanding what the Everglades were and how they worked—not a stagnant swamp but a vast and flowing "river of grass," unique and worthy of protection. "There are no other Everglades in the world," her now-famous first sentence read. *The Everglades: River of Grass* joined a small group of other seminal environmental books of the late 1940s—including Fairfield Osborn's *Our Plundered Planet* (1948), William Vogt's *The Road to Survival* (1948), and Aldo Leopold's *A Sand County Almanac* (1948)—that together charted a transition from the concerns of the early conservation movement to those of postwar environmentalism. With *River of Grass,* as her volume came to be popularly known, Douglas placed South Florida at the center of this pivotal—though thus far underappreciated—moment in American environmental thought and politics. In so doing, she soon found herself there as well.

But as significant as it was, 1947 represented for Douglas but a brief moment in a long and rich life. As Jack Davis's superb biography demonstrates, Marjory Stoneman Douglas, more than any other single writer or activist, embodied the American environmental century—that period from the closing of the frontier to the end of the twentieth century during which environmental concerns rose to the fore in American politics and society. While other well-known figures such as John Muir, Aldo Leopold, and Rachel Carson have come to define the environmental activism of the Progressive, interwar, and postwar eras, respectively, Douglas's remarkable life and career spanned all three. Born in 1890, the same year that the decennial census suggested that an identifiable frontier line had ceased to exist, Douglas came of age during the era of Progressive conservation. Having moved to South Florida in 1915 to join her father, Frank Stoneman, the cofounder of the *Miami Herald,* she spent the next several decades building an impressive career as a writer and becoming intimate with the landscape and history of her adopted city and its wild hinterland. Douglas was fifty-seven when *River of Grass* appeared. While it was surely a climactic moment in her life, what followed can only be described as a hell of a denouement, for Douglas had another five decades in front of her. She remained active in environmental and other causes into the 1990s, when the frailties of advanced age caught up with her. She died in 1998 at the auspicious age of 108. Few other figures can claim to have been alive, let alone active and lucid, for such a sweeping and formative period in America's environmental history.

Just as importantly, Douglas's life and career bounded a critical century in Everglades history for which 1947 was but a fulcrum. She was a teenager (although not yet living in South Florida) when plume hunters murdered game warden Guy Bradley in the Everglades in 1905, an event that reenergized the national Audubon movement. Bradley's murder came just a few months after the Florida Federation of Women's Clubs had first suggested the idea of an Everglades national preserve. And Douglas lived through the planning stages of the Comprehensive Everglades Restoration Plan, which President Bill Clinton signed into law in the waning days of his second administration, just two years after Douglas's death. Many observers have hailed the restoration plan as a fitting continuation of the work started with the creation of Everglades National Park, but Douglas and her allies understood that it was, in its emphasis on technological fixes and its efforts to assuage the powerful agricultural and development communities, but another chapter in the Corps of Engineers' half century of ruinous meddling with Everglades hydrology. As Davis so eloquently shows, Marjory Stoneman Douglas's life was inextricably interwoven with a century of Everglades preservation battles.

And yet, until this book, Douglas enjoyed the ignominious distinction of being arguably the most important modern environmental figure not to have been the subject of a major biography. Jack Davis has not only stripped her of that distinction but has given us a book that will stand for a long while as authoritative. But this book is more than a biography of Douglas; as Davis explains in the "Author's Note," he was not long into this project when he realized that he could not tell Douglas's life story without inserting the modern history of the landscape as well. The happy result is a dual biography, one in which Everglades environmental history receives equal billing with the woman who came to personify the region. One virtue of this approach is that it gives readers a rich context within which to understand Douglas's life and work. But another, more surprising virtue is that readers get a sense of how Douglas, over her long life, flowed in and out of the picture of Everglades activism. It would be easy, in a conventional biography of someone of her stature, to inflate Douglas's importance at the expense of others. Instead, Davis provides a remarkably balanced assessment of her relative importance at different moments in time. It is a rare biographer who can give supporting characters substantial time in the spotlight, but Davis does precisely that. He contends as well with what he calls the myth of Marjory Stoneman Douglas, the notion that this "Grande Dame of the Everglades" was always at the center of South Florida environmental politics. In the process, *An Everglades Providence* offers a tremendous amount of information about those, such as Mary Barr Munroe, Ernest Coe, and Joe Browder, who were sometimes more important than was Douglas in protecting the Everglades. By the time you put this book down, you will understand that Douglas would have wanted it this way.

Several other remarkable aspects of Douglas's life and Davis's treatment of it deserve brief mention. Marjory Stoneman Douglas embodied not only the American environmental century but a century of American feminism as well. As Davis shows so compellingly, few other lives better brought together these two sweeping historical movements. Indeed, Douglas was an environmental activist who was committed to political and social justice more broadly. Douglas's life story also intersected with a remarkable century in the history of Miami and South Florida. Settling in Coconut Grove, one of the city's most distinctive neighborhoods,

Douglas watched Miami grow from a small frontier and vacation town into a sprawling modern metropolis. In many ways, Douglas was, as Davis depicts her, a strikingly urban creature. She was uninterested in the strenuous wilderness immersion that so many of America's other (usually male) environmental heroes practiced. More to the point, Davis insists that Douglas was preeminently a regionalist. For Douglas, the Everglades, Miami, and the entirety of South Florida formed a single unit whose value lay in a balance between wildness and adaptive, sustainable human habitation. In this sense, *An Everglades Providence* offers impassioned testimony to how a distinctive person and region together shaped the environmental history of the nation and the world.

Paul S. Sutter, *University of Georgia*

Author's Note and Acknowledgments

I had not long been exploring the possibility of writing the biography of a busy, fascinating woman who lived during busy, fascinating times—and indeed, for a long time—when I learned something surprising. Marjory Stoneman Douglas, a writer by profession, did not leave behind a comprehensive diary, journal, or great cache of letters that would allow for a classically constructed biography. Excavating those kinds of rich materials makes the venture of a biography more pleasant for both the biographer and the reader. Fat books that give a blow-by-blow account of an individual's life and activities, especially details that affirm or disprove juicy speculation and innuendo, make some of the best reading around, in my opinion. This book is fat, to be sure, and I hope, in light of the labor required to write and read it, that it contributes to knowledge and facilitates the memory of an important person, with a juicy tidbit or two thrown in. It offers as complete a biography as my limited energies and the available sources allow. It is more comprehensive than Douglas's eloquent autobiography (and corrects a few of the mistakes she made in her account), and it provides a historical context for her life not found in her own writing.

This book is not solely a biography but is also a comprehensive history of the Everglades. It is as much one as the other. To date, many books have been written about the Everglades, including Douglas's 1947 landmark

The Everglades: River of Grass. Relying on original research, this volume covers much of the same ground as the others. That simply cannot be avoided. But to write about a woman whose life was so wrapped up with the Everglades without telling the full story of the Everglades simply does not make sense. This seems expressly true since no individual had a more enduring relationship with the Everglades, tracking the busiest years in their history from the decades of tenacious exploitation to the beginning of atoning ecological restoration. Unlike other Everglades books, this one emphasizes the literary and the conservation/environmental-activist sides of the Everglades narrative, the sides to which Douglas belongs. It is written to capture the subject's perspective of the Everglades, taken from numerous angles in multiple shades of light, from the reflective to the witty to the didactic, and across a long arc of time. Even outside her Everglades labors, Douglas led a full life, and this book explores in depth all its dimensions. Yet so much of her life beyond the Everglades was really not that far beyond the Everglades. It was the yeasty pretext of her rise as a multilayered scribe of her region, and it prepared her for the realistic transition (for her at least, although it came at a time when others her age had long been retired) to the sobering and full-time commission of environmental activism. It also helped her realize that in the Everglades was Nature's providence, offered not just to the creatures and green growing things but to fellow folly-prone humans.

In short, then, this book is two books in one: a biography of a woman and a biography of a place, both of surprising endurance, and the story of the mutually beneficial relationship they forged with one another.

My journey across the sometimes disquieting but always rewarding landscape of biography and geography was assisted by many selfless individuals. The journey began almost twenty years ago, when I was in graduate school and my classmate, Jill Bennett, and I pursued independent readings in environmental history with David Hackett Fischer. David is not known as an environmental historian professionally but as the Pulitzer Prize–winning author of hefty books on early America. He knows the history and historiography of environmentalism, though, and Jill and I spent two stimulating semesters dissecting books and articles with him, never in the dim confines of his office but always rattling about the back-streets, sauntering through wooded paths, or roaming across the hillside cemetery of Waltham, Massachusetts, with Fischer stopping to explain the cultural history of a "privy bush" (without its privy) or a crumbling race in the Charles River. Jill, brilliant in so many particulars, possessed an enthusiasm and knowledge that humbled me daily. During these adventure-filled semesters, we read Douglas's *River of Grass*. A Floridian, I had known about but had never read her. And in the first environmental history course I taught a few years later, I assigned her book; later, I began assigning her short fiction. After she died in 1998, I decided to write this book or something like it.

The late Helen Muir, one of Douglas's oldest and closest friends, told me at the outset of this project, "I don't envy you the chore, because this is not an easy character." I could not have even attempted the chore without the kind help of more people than I can thank here. Among the first to get me started were Muir's son, William "Toby" Muir, Douglas's attorney, and the late George Rosner, her estate's executor, both longtime friends of Douglas. They granted me special access to her papers, which were closed to the public for five years after her death. Those papers are housed at the University of Miami's Otto G. Richter Library, and the staff in special collections—in particular, William Brown, Maria Estorino, Marcia Evanson, Craig Likeness, and Ruthanne Vogel—could not have been more accommodating over the many years. Today, Marcia still greets me with a smile and hug. Bertha Barahona of the Historical Museum of Southern Florida in Miami was unfailingly pleasant and attentive. Dave Nelson at the Florida State Library in Tallahassee always had materials pulled and waiting when I arrived, and he shared some of his excellent research with me. Across town at the Claude Pepper Library at Florida State University, John Nemmers epitomized courtesy and assistance. He maintained those qualities when he moved to the P. K. Yonge Library of Florida History at the University of Florida in Gainesville. He is in good company there with Jim Cusick and Flo Turcotte, who were always eager to help. Way up at Carleton College in Minnesota, Eric Hillemann dug up obscure records for me on Frank Stoneman, Douglas's father, and the staff at the University of Minnesota provided additional materials. The staff of the Edmund S. Muskie Collection at Bates College in Maine was ready for my visit. Susan Watkins of the Red Cross Archives in Virginia sent a copy of Douglas's records. Trudy Laframboise in special collections at Rollins College affirms the spotless reputation of librarians and archivists, as does the staff at the Taunton (Massachusetts) Public Library and at the Welles-ley College archives. I give a nod also to the staff at the Newark Public Library and New York Public Library.

Numerous nonlibrarians, too, went out of their way to share relevant documents or to help in some productive way. Kelly Crandall transcribed oral history interviews for me, and Bridget Bihm-Manuel made order out of the chaos of the manuscript's endnotes. Boyd Stephens and Pete Runyan kept my computers from crashing or retrieved the data when (#%*+#@!) they did. Chris Larson of the worthy Florida Rural Legal Services photocopied and sent a dissertation about her organization. Michael Chenoweth and Pam Pierce at Friends of the Everglades helped me with important documents, as did the late Bob Kelley at Tropical Audubon in Miami. I am grateful to Cindy Thorner for saving and sharing materials on the early American Civil Liberties Union's Greater Miami chapter, and to Ray Mohl, a friend and former colleague at the University of Alabama at Birmingham, who let me use his Elizabeth Virrick papers and other relevant research. Every few weeks for the last several years, Gary Mormino has faithfully sent a care package, a nine-by-twelve-inch manila envelope stuffed with newspaper and magazine clippings and other useful items. He's a true friend, still sending things (Lynn, how do you stand it?), and they remain as invaluable as when I was writing the book. Former senator Bob Graham graciously opened up his daily notebooks to me. Estus Whitfield, who worked for Graham when he was governor and for other governors, persisted with a temperamental fax machine until I received valuable documents, and he graciously answered numerous subsequent e-mails. Joe Knetsch copied and sent a bundle of state papers on Douglas's house. Michael Munroe and Carl Kesser gave me DVD copies of Douglas documentaries they produced. Alice Knight and Chris Meindl were kind enough to send copies of memos, letters, and such in their possession. Julian Pleasants shared a transcription of a Douglas talk and pointed me to several oral histories at the Samuel Proctor Oral History Program at the University of Florida. Horacio Sierra selflessly provided me with all sorts of materials he dug up while researching Douglas, and his published materials have been an inspiration. Tom Swihart and Bob Mooney were always eager to provide help and information. Martha Hubbart, one of Douglas's former assistants, gets special thanks for entrusting me with several boxes of original Douglas papers, which will now go to the collection at the University of Miami. This surprising and invaluable gift added much to this book.

As I met more of Douglas's friends like Hubbart, it became clear how much Douglas was loved and respected. I hope that I have captured something of the individual they cherished. They were all kind and generous with their time and materials, and my debt to them is enormous. I don't know how to thank Toby Muir, who not only opened the Douglas papers to me but patiently answered my e-mails with offerings that turned into some of the best stories in the book. Joe Browder offered similar e-mails and recollections in interview. Without him, the biographical and historical sections of the book would have been much less complete. He generously shared from his treasure trove of personal papers and over many years answered what must have been hundreds of questions, always persisting in helping me get the facts right. I feel as though he reached out into the swirling waters and pulled me into the lifeboat more than once, and for that I can never repay him. Lili Neale entrusted me with her wonderful diary and scrapbook from the 1970s and with her husband, Andy, gave me a place to stay when I was in South Florida. Rosalie Leposky dropped everything when I called or e-mailed with a question, and she steadfastly helped me hunt down people and facts. She's a wonderful sleuth, and she created and maintains an invaluable Marjory Stoneman Douglas online bibliography. Sharyn Richardson offered her memories and excerpts from interviews she conducted with George

Rosner. Johnny and Mariana Jones copied Florida Wildlife Federation papers for me. Sallye Jude gave me a cherished tour of Douglas's house, and Theo Long invited me down to the Marjory Stoneman Douglas Biscayne Nature Center.

The manuscript has benefited from the discerning eyes of others who gave freely of their time to offer comments. Paul Sutter, one of the anonymous readers (though not so anonymous) and the editor of the series to which this book belongs, combed over every chapter of the penultimate draft. His perspective and vast knowledge are impressive, and I agreed with virtually every suggestion he made and apologize if I've failed to live up to expectations. The other reader, who remains anonymous, saved me from a number of embarrassing errors in the natural history parts. Lee Irby, a buddy and a talented novelist who deserves a major audience, boosted my confidence to keep me moving forward. I take full responsibility if anyone thinks he should have stopped me instead. Gary Garrett, another talented writer and an Everglades native, read parts of the manuscript and kept me honest. Chris Warren, a friend to the end, unfailingly answered my questions and sometimes researched answers for me. Steve Whitfield and Ray Arsenault remain mentors and scholars to emulate as well as treasured friends. I owe Ray my professional life, though he would surely prefer his own. Although I'm long removed from graduate school, I still think of Jackie Jones and Christine Heyrman as model writers and historians and almost daily reflect on their teachings. I must also acknowledge University of Florida graduate students Tom Berson, Bridget Bihm-Manuel, Steve Griffin, Leslie Poole, Dan Simone, and Roger Wiblin, who have listened to me chatter on about parts of the book and even its structures. I benefited considerably from our conversations.

For as long as my partner, Sonya Rudenstine, has known me, she has known Marjory Stoneman Douglas. Although she looked at me askance when I allowed three other book projects and three house renovations to distract me from this project, she never wavered in support of the other woman in our lives. Like Douglas, she too has made a compact with social justice. Sonya graciously read most of the chapters in early draft with such an eye and more, never failing to rein in my prose and to force me to prioritize clarity over all else. And she created a welcome distraction when she gave birth to our beautiful and lively daughter, Willa. Sonya and I look forward to sharing Douglas's books for young readers with Willa, and we hope for the future on this green earth that Douglas desired for all generations.

PART ONE

CHAPTER ONE

Journey's End

Everglades National Park Ranger Sandy Dayhoff squinted into the still-rising sun of late spring. Scanning the grand uniformity of the wet prairie, she made her way through shin-deep water, under which she felt the familiar pull of muck around her jungle boots and at the stab of her walking stick. Shuffling through the same a few feet ahead was park superintendent Richard Ring, who fixed his gaze down past a square sift-proof box he carried in his hands. Trailing behind was ranger Craig Thatcher. He had piloted the airboat that brought the three out to a place where the water flowed freely and the media and public would not find them. On foot, they made their way deliberately, lost in separate thoughts but mindful of their shared task. Dressed in their summer-issue gray and green uniforms, they had put on the Park Service's signature flat hat in a gesture of respect for the contents of the box in Ring's possession. Inside were the ashes of Marjory Stoneman Douglas.[1]

They would soon be left to commingle with the last besieged fragment of a primeval wetland, which, much to Douglas's credit, persisted as a national treasure. Other Everglades conservators existed, to be sure, but she was the genius loci, the protective spirit of the place. Congress had confirmed as much. Six months earlier, it had designated 1.3 million acres, approximately 86 percent of Everglades National Park, as the Marjory Stoneman Douglas Wilderness Area. Ceremonial acknowledgment coincided with the park's fiftieth-anniversary celebration at Everglades City. Douglas had attended the park's dedication in 1947, when beneath a cloud-studded December sky, President Harry S. Truman spoke of the importance of conservation. But she was too frail to attend the anniversary affair in 1997. Secretary of the Interior Bruce Babbitt and Vice President Al Gore, stopping off en route to an international global-warming conference in Japan, performed the honors of inducting the largest wilderness area east of the Rocky Mountains into the national system. The event put Douglas in the company of fifteen select individuals who bore recognition as namesakes for one of nearly seven hundred national wilderness areas. "Nobody," said Gore, "has had a greater understanding of the Everglades' importance than Marjory Stoneman Douglas."[2]

Scientists and other activists certainly knew as much and more about the ecological matters of the Everglades. But no one had known the country's greatest wetland for as long and from as many intimate vantage points—from that of an early South Florida resident, a writer of fiction and nonfiction, and an advocate of Everglades restoration. For this reason, in 1972, Dayhoff had invited Douglas to teach in the seasonal-training program for park rangers. She was eighty-two at the time, and she returned every year until she was nearly one hundred. An early photograph set in pine flatwoods shows her surrounded by a score of rangers, all of them young and comparatively tall and most wearing civilian clothes—jeans, cotton shirts, and head bandanas—suited for the scrubland of outdoors. Douglas stands out among the others not only for her age but for her printed dress, her string of white pearls, and one of her signature wide-brim hats—on this occasion, a natural straw-colored one. She loved to visit the park, remembered Dayhoff, and always came nicely dressed, as if she were visiting an old friend.[3]

If the rangers in the seasonal-training program thought her attire was an odd choice for the wilderness environment, they had to admire her work as a writer and activist. They had been assigned to read her *The*

Everglades: River of Grass, which was by then a classic. Its 1947 publication had convinced Americans that a place called a swamp, once seen as a vulgar, immutable wasteland, was actually a biological masterpiece of many vital environments, including cypress strands, wet prairies, tropical hardwood uplands, and pine flatwoods and none so evocative as sawgrass marsh possessed by flowing water. The book appeared in stores four weeks before President Truman dedicated Everglades National Park, and forever after, the Everglades were known as the River of Grass. "That was her genius," said fellow writer Helen Muir: Douglas transformed the country's most menacing swamp into its most cherished wetland. She opened the book with her revelation: the Everglades "are unique also in the simplicity, the diversity, the related harmony of the forms of life they enclose. The miracle of the light pours over the green and brown expanse of saw grass and of water, shining and slow-moving below, the grass and water that is the meaning and the central fact of the Everglades of Florida. It is a river of grass."[4]

The book was destined to stay indefinitely in print, a credit to Douglas's eloquent and enduring warning against civilization's headlong sprawl into a life-giving natural area, a providence of Nature. Beginning in the 1960s, activists embraced the book as the green Bible of Everglades environmentalism, comparing it with Rachel Carson's *Silent Spring* and Aldo Leopold's *A Sand County Almanac.* As long as Dayhoff had been with the National Park Service, every new park superintendent had wanted to meet the book's author. When Dade County, Douglas's home, relocated its public library to a new building in 1985, the last several hundred books were transported by a human chain. Douglas's *River of Grass,* the last of them all, was carried like a torch by a runner. The gathering reverence for the book signaled shifting attitudes in the American environmental century, an age of inexorable ecological ruination countered by a maturing environmental ethos. Pivotal moments in Everglades history fell within this age (roughly the twentieth century), and Douglas found herself shaping the environmental ethos as a writer and activist. For her, the most profound measure of its progress was the ecological well-being of the magnificent wetland that reached across the tip of the Florida peninsula.[5]

Douglas's life more or less shared chronological bookends with the environmental century. "She was here at a good time," said Muir. Dayhoff believed so, too, though she hated to see Douglas's own time come to an end. Before it did, Douglas had made clear her desire to have the Everglades as her final resting place. Fulfilling that wish was the task of the rangers. As they gathered at the appropriate spot, a small but disquieted assembly of red-winged blackbirds began calling from a nearby bay head. Checking the wind's direction, Dayhoff took the box from Ring's hands and began mutely broadcasting ashes, finishing as the birds fell silent. She later told reporters that her friend "was put to flowing with the river she loved."[6]

Two weeks earlier, Douglas had passed away quietly at home in bed in the small hours of May 14, 1998. The phone rang early that morning at the house of William T. "Toby" Muir, Douglas's lawyer. The caller, a hospice nurse substituting for Douglas's regular aide, was delivering news that was not wholly unexpected but was nonetheless sad. Douglas had been part of Muir's life since she visited his mother in St. Francis Hospital at his birth. She and his parents had shared a "firm and committed friendship," as Helen Muir put it. Douglas and Toby Muir's father, Bill, had long ago coauthored a play, *Storm Warnings,* and both she and Helen were newspaper, magazine, and book writers. Toby Muir broke the news to his mother and the rest of his family and then phoned George Rosner, the executor of Douglas's estate, and a number of others close to her. After Muir finished dressing, he went outside and down the block to Douglas's house. It was a tidy little structure built in the style of an English country cottage, though with a tropical garden that had crowded around it in the seventy-two years Douglas lived there. Muir let himself in through the front door, its solid mahogany weight steadfastly familiar to him. As a boy, he had bounded down the street and entered through that door countless times to visit "Jarjee," as he had always called Douglas. She was fun, interesting, and a source of worldly wisdom and gingersnap cookies.[7]

This time, his entry was greeted by the nurse. Douglas's final moments had passed peacefully, she told Muir. He excused himself to pay his last respects to his old friend, withered and tiny, in the small twin bed in the efficiently small bedroom, painted flamingo pink many years earlier. After the solemn coming and going of the funeral-home van and after the nurse had completed her duties and moved on, an unfamiliar quiet settled in. The house had always produced energy; the momentum of Douglas's life had always been a matter of fact. The ominousness of the quiet made the end feel too abruptly complete and seemed at odds with the largeness of the event. Breaking the spell, the old rotary phone rang at Douglas's desk. Muir would spend much of his day there. A news van, laden with telecast equipment, arrived around noon. The major Florida newspapers, USA Today, the New York Times, and national news services called to confirm the death. The cause, Muir told them with resigned simplicity, was that "the years caught up with her."[8]

Six weeks earlier, Douglas had turned 108. In the last years, her mind slipped between periods of impressive lucidity and placid vagueness. The downturn began after she was hospitalized with swallowing problems when she was 101. A few years earlier, she would have been up, dressed, and sitting at the big desk in her equally big living room qua study, her small self swallowed up by a white canvas-covered chair. Though by then blind and nearly deaf, she would have been working with her literary assistant, Sharyn Richardson, on the endless revisions of her massive biography of William Henry Hudson. Or she would have been dictating to her secretary, Martha Hubbart, a letter to the governor or to the water-management district about some matter related to the repair of the Everglades. When she was 106, she experienced a heart flutter, fainted, and went into the hospital again. Expected to die, she rebounded instead and went home a few days later. Kathy Gaubatz, part of the group of local Wellesley College alumnae who cared for their oldest sister, was at the time stopping in frequently to read to Douglas, who was mostly confined to bed. Gaubatz would look over at the white halo of hair, the ashen skin sunken into hollow cheeks, the blind eyes staring from skeletal sockets, and the ossified fingers laced peacefully across the near-motionless chest. Gaubatz could not tell whether she was looking at a lifeless or living form. One day, she walked in and asked a question to which she did not really expect an answer: "Marjory, what is that beautiful red-flowering tree in your front yard?" "*Phyllocarpus septentrionalis*," responded the corpse-like figure, sharp and clear and with unfaltering diction.[9]

That's how she was when a few days after her last birthday, Joe Browder came to town from Washington. His visits were always a reason for Douglas to be alert and engaged. A dear friend, he was the principal who some thirty years earlier had convinced her to start an environmental organization to save the Everglades. She was in bed and weak but wanted to talk. He fed her ice cream—vanilla, the flavor she preferred, believing others excessive. Browder and Douglas avoided conversation about politics and the wetland they both loved, instead talking about other current events, his work, and his two sons, by then grown men. She knew people across generations and took an interest in them. Yet it was hard sometimes, outliving family, one's own generation, and nearly another. Before Browder left, she said she loved him. Reciprocating her feelings, he was brought to tears. It was a rare display of emotion by Douglas; she was clearly saying good-bye.[10]

A few weeks later, on May 21, Toby Muir and George Rosner met Richard Ring at the funeral home. To avoid the possibility of conflict between groups and friends who maintained a proprietary claim to Douglas's memory, the lawyer and executor gave the superintendent possession of the ashes with the request that they be spread in an undisclosed location by only the necessary number of rangers. Two days later, more than 650 Douglas mourners, some of whom had never known her personally, paid their respects at a public sunset memorial tribute Muir and Rosner organized with the national park. Florida's lieutenant governor, members of Congress, local officials, heads of environmental organizations, friends, and admirers gathered at the head of Anhinga Trail at Royal Palm Hammock, an islandlike clump of subtropical vegetation. At one end of the speakers' platform, two rangers stood sentinel on either side of an easel cradling a large photograph of Douglas in a wide-brim hat. Several of those in attendance wore similar hats in worshipful remembrance of the deceased. The ceremony's organizers asked the few speakers to keep their comments short, but as one politician with only a tenuous connection to Douglas droned on, Browder stirred uneasily. Ever since Everglades protection had become popular, people seeking personal gain had materialized from all corners to pledge their friendship to Douglas. To Browder's pleasure, a black crow started cawing and interrupted the speaker. Browder amused himself with the thought of the bird as Douglas reincarnate, upbraiding the man for his long-windedness. When Browder's turn to speak came, he recited one of Douglas's poems, published in the 1920s, celebrating the unacknowledged beauty of buzzards. Friends who knew the poem believed that the author, who considered herself physically unattractive, had composed the verse during a moment of self-reflection. But to Browder, the poem represented her "perfect understanding of what nature can help us know about ourselves."

> I never knew how beauty grew
> From ugliness, until you flew.
>
> .   .   .   .
>
> Oh brother buzzard, you whose sin
> On earth, is to be shackled in
> To horror, teach me how to go
> Like you, to beauty, sure and slow.

Ring followed with a letter from President Bill Clinton, who said that Douglas strove "with vigor and passion, to teach us the lessons of conservation and to save America's wild places." Bowed and uplifted heads paused for a final moment of silence. One magazine journalist rhapsodized, "As the setting sun cast a warm glow over the river of grass, Marjory passed easily into immortality."[11]

During Douglas's long life, friends had sometimes amused themselves with the idea of her literal immortality. They often speculated about the reason for her longevity, looking for hints in her daily habits. She had always been a late-night worker, sometimes writing into the morning hours, and a late riser, at times staying in bed until nine or ten. "This getting up early is always a mystery to me," she wrote when she was thirty-two. "People make such a fetish of it." She brewed tea as soon as she awoke and ate a light breakfast. For much of her life, she read several newspapers a day and several books a week. When macular degeneration impaired her sight in her eighties, she took up listening to audio books, and she often depended on the eyes of a secretary or friend. The redbrick patio outside the back French doors of her house had always been her favorite spot to sit with a lapboard to write and to watch, smell, and listen to the mass of living things. She could identify all the birds, the trees, and the plants and even the various lizards that skittered across the brick. Eventually, she lost visual contact with nature, although she never became fully disconnected. Sunlight still penetrated the blur.

The enduring tropical sun had enamored her since childhood. Her first memory of it was during a brief visit with her parents to Florida en route to Cuba from the Midwest. Twenty years later, when she saw it again, she was unsettled and depressed after fleeing her husband for an uncertain life in Miami with her estranged father. The sun's white light met her arrival before anything or anyone else, first startling her before warming her from her melancholy. The sun always remained her connecting spirit to South Florida, drawing her back time and again from sojourns in New England and Europe.

Failing vision slowed her, but she adjusted without complaint. By her late eighties, she had stopped dancing and swimming, two of her favorite pastimes, and began spending most evenings at home. Save for one abortive attempt when she was young, she never drove a car and was spared the trauma of giving up a driver's license. She never owned a television and so never missed that either. Talk radio became a new companion; people who spoke their minds impressed her, even if their politics irked her. She took her evening meal regularly at 5:30 P.M. Her calendar had previously been full of dinner dates with friends, but when going out and cooking at home became too trying, the Miami Wellesley Club delivered dinners to her house. She drank tea rather than coffee and ate simply—typically mashed potatoes, turkey breast, vanilla ice cream, and angel food cake, what friends christened her "white diet." Her desires were actually more varied, though not by much. When writing out instructions for the Wellesley Club, Rosner, Douglas's longtime friend and custodian in later years, explained, "Food to Marjory is limited by self-imposed restrictions of 'Don't,' 'Won't,' and 'Can't.' . . . She won't eat vegetables, salads, fruits . . . because they don't appeal. Other dont's include eggs (cholesterol). . . . Citrus is a can't because it affects her hiatal hernia." Despite her spare diet, she was knowledgeable about cooking: "She even swaps menus and recipes in fluent French with a French *maitre d'*." But her culinary abilities had been limited by a kitchen equipped with little more than a hot plate and toaster oven. "A friend teases," Rosner added, "saying Marjory learned *haute cuisine* by avoiding cooking."[12]

She learned also to take two aspirins daily to keep her blood flowing and to subscribe to relaxation. She had loved "buzzing around in a public way," said Helen Muir. "Oh, it was her life. You bet she buzzed. And people loved it." Yet one of the great pleasures of her senior years was that she had left behind the hurried compulsion to achieve, allowing her to pursue interests and goals at a more reasonable pace. By observing her beloved cats, who typically arrived as strays, she made something of an art of relaxation. "They always say that a cat watcher lives longer because a cat knows how to relax," she said a month before she turned 103.[13]

One favorite way to relax was with a drink. Friends swore that her passport to old age was stamped with the label of Desmond and Duff scotch, which she drank with soda. They would give her bottles of scotch at Christmastime, in part because they wanted her to live longer. She was no lush, but she did become a bit louder when alcohol was in her. She had mocked Prohibition in the 1920s and remained unapologetic about her ritual evening cocktail. "Five o'clock is an excellent time for a drink," she was quoted as saying when she was 104. Although she was not above perching her small frame atop a barstool, she usually took her drink at home—hers or someone else's—and preferably in the company of a good conversationalist. "There was one period a few years ago," recalled Helen Muir in 1999, "when we would drink sherry in the afternoon, and then I would walk her home, and then she'd walk me back, and we would have another sherry. What fun she was."[14]

Anyone who knew her was privy to that fun side, another certain source of youthfulness. When she was writing a daily column for the

Miami Herald in the 1920s, she charmed readers with her hallmark sense of humor. She could hold her own with the day's political satirists. Unsatisfied with the candidates during the 1920 presidential campaign, she wrote, "Now is the time for a good Ouija board to come to the aid of the parties." A ready wit and laughter were "part of her magic," said Judy Wilson Lawrence, a friend for forty years.[15]

Outspokenness similarly formed part of her being. "Marjory was never afraid to say the obvious," recalled fellow activist Joe Podgor. "That's her salient feature." "She was very opinionated," said Helen Muir, but "with great style. It was peculiarly hers. Debonair, chivalrous, thought provoking, and in a strange way composed." Former governor Bob Graham remembered that she would come to cabinet meetings to convey "one simple, blunt message: We would safeguard the health of the Everglades, and if we didn't, we would all spend an uncomfortable afterlife in hell." At her corporeal peak, she stood five feet, two and one-half inches. The media took pleasure in presenting this diminutive woman of implausible age as a fierce heavyweight who, with perfect diction and supreme eloquence as well as a vast knowledge of the issues at hand, stood firm before stammering policymakers. She spoke with a Julia Child accent, a product of her Victorian Massachusetts upbringing, and with a voice that commanded a potency belying her physical attributes. A journalist friend dubbed her the Elocutioner. "I studied elocution at Wellesley College," she told him, "and I've been going around elocuting ever since." When engaged in negotiations or being interviewed by a journalist, she could be unabashedly caustic. She believed that there were indeed such things as fools and dumb questions. If undisciplined speech were spoken, it deserved correction with schoolmarm abruptness. She preached against compromise and espoused pigheadedness. Protecting the Everglades required stubborn resolve.[16]

She was equally pigheaded about friendships. The closer ones were a "force" in her life; they filled a void. She never had siblings or children. When she was a child, her parents' marriage fell apart after her mother became mentally ill. Marjory went to live with her maternal grandparents and an aunt, pious and stern people who could have stifled her creative mind. In early adulthood, she experienced her own truncated marriage, which at the time stifled her restive ambitions. Although she had other brief flirtations, she jealously guarded her independence, fearing men's domineering nature despite her strong will. Whatever her fantasies and illusions about marriage, she could not both love a man and have a career, and she would not sacrifice the latter for the former.[17]

As much as the past shaped her private and public character, she never dwelled on it, not when the present needed tending. And because the present required so much of her attention, she categorically rejected the proverbial pasture of old age. "Don't begin to think about your age," she wrote when she was eighty-one. "That has nothing to do with it." People who acted old left her bewildered. Life offered too much to sit about waiting for death. Paraphrasing Robert Browning, Douglas said, "The last of life is supposed to be the climax." When she was ninety-one, she told a reporter, "Old age isn't boring, not by a long chalk." When she was ninety-five, she decided to brush up on her French, speaking it whenever possible with visitors who were fluent. When she was ninety-seven, she published her autobiography. She kept three part-time secretaries busy reading and dictating letters and assisting with personal business and the operations of her environmental organization, which reached a peak membership of seven thousand. Keeping one's mind busy and enlarging one's exposure to the world of ideas was not the exclusive province of youth. "In spite of people saying that the old cannot learn anything new," she wrote in 1985 to her few remaining sisters from Wellesley's 1912 graduating class, "I have found that by attending very closely to listening I can indeed learn new things."[18]

Douglas maintained that having purpose was perhaps the most important necessity of a long life. "Do you realize," she asked a newspaper reporter when she was eighty-three, "I have practically no life expectancy and so many things left to do?" Her journey in search of purpose began in 1915, when she took a risk and boarded a train to Florida, a place as foreign and bucolic to an urbane New Englander as Texas or even Alaska. From the moment she saw Miami, she fell in love with the living landscape illuminated by the tropical light. She was twenty-five, Miami was still a teenager, and both were poised at the doorway of change.[19]

Her 1915 journey fulfilled a personal quest for professional accomplishment and greater self-worth. Both required that she leave the Northeast and her husband, a possessive man perpetually stalked by trouble. As a child, she had a preordained sense of herself as a writer, and marital dissolution and geographic relocation enabled her to execute her vision. For eight decades thereafter, she consecrated her life to writing. She started out at the *Miami Herald,* where her father was the founding editor. After she quit the newspaper in 1923, twenty years of writing short stories for the *Saturday Evening Post* and other popular serials followed. She then went on to produce several works of fiction and nonfiction. South Florida's transplanted residents and visitors, variegated characters without need of writerly embellishment, emerged on her typed pages. Her fictional creations imbibed the impulses she felt from the wet, green setting of her subtropical world and pursued its promises, experienced disillusionment, and clung to hope.

Douglas never stopped writing or composing through dictation, whether producing an article or a book. Her most ambitious personal project in later life was a biography of the turn-of-the-century author William Henry Hudson. The Argentine-born naturalist made a fitting subject. His classic, *Green Mansions,* had long ago provided her with a fundamental characterization of nature that she refined in her writing. Nearly three decades of labor, including research trips to South America and Britain when she was in her eighties and nineties, went into the biography. The book was to be her magnum opus next to *River of Grass.* When she died, her possessions included a two-volume, two-hundred-thousand-word unpublished manuscript, "W. H. Hudson and the Green World." Despite her doubts that the book would ever find its way into print, she stuck with the project, noting, "I think the original excitement and enthusiasm carries on if the idea is a good one."[20]

Good ideas also drew her to selfless purposes with the goal of improving society. The examples of her Quaker forebears, Wellesley College professors, and Florida club women reddened the embers of a social consciousness. Writing was her torch. In her twenties, she began producing articles and editorials challenging pin-striped government leaders to hold in check their preoccupation with economic growth and development and to give attention to social welfare problems. Her most abiding sense of mission was that of putting women on an even playing field with men. Invitations arrived to join other women in the meeting halls and lobbies of political action. *Herald* readers came to know her as a suffragist and supporter of the first Equal Rights Amendment. Later, as a fiction writer, she crowded her stories with gutsy women who usurped male domination and asserted a strong presence in the world. When the Equal Rights Amendment resurfaced in the 1970s, her senior authority gave a new generation of activists a link to the historic roots of their striving.

By that time, she had been drawn to a new purpose that had taken form after many pieces fell into place over many years. She matured as America modernized and as Florida, one of the nation's fastest-growing states, developed. She watched as meandering rivers disappeared into undeviating drainage canals, as jade-green bays devolved into sewage basins, as a bird-filled sky lapsed into empty space, and as an open frontier transformed into a crowded megalopolis, and she listened as the grunting and bellowing of wild places fell silent beneath the interminable roar of automobiles and construction equipment. These changes challenged her convictions, which deepened as she evolved intellectually, ethically, and spiritually toward the solemn commitment that consumed her late senior years: reversing the century-long abuse of the South Florida environment, especially that of the Everglades. Between ages seventy-nine and one hundred, she worked as a full-time, unpaid founder and head of an environmental organization, stumping the state, writing articles, giving interviews, and berating policymakers for a new environmental ethos. On the strength of these efforts, she and others compelled the nation to adopt a more benign attitude toward the Everglades.

The public canonized her as the environmental saint of the River of Grass. Upon the publication of her book in 1947, her life began to carry the weight of Everglades history and eventually obliged her involvement in the emerging environmental movement. By the 1980s and 1990s, one could hardly think about the country's most remarkable wetland and not

think of the person whom the national press variously dubbed the grandmother, the matriarch, and the grande dame of the Everglades. "She was
an iconic figure because of the book," said Browder, and she was an environmentalist because she was an iconic figure. She had not planned
things this way. Writing had always been her first love. It lay on the career
path she had plotted as a teenager, and while she was a writer by ambition, she was an environmental activist by fateful invitation.[21]

Douglas recognized that fate is not born of chance alone. She saw fate
as the convergence of opportunity and preparation. The opportunity
came from Browder's invitation to start an organization. She could accept
the invitation because she was prepared, with expanded knowledge of
government and science and the ways of people, with a trained speaking
voice that captured audiences, with a historical claim to the region, and
with a writing portfolio that complemented the cause. Writing provided
her strongest link to nature, always more of a subject and character than
backdrop. A literary affinity for trees, birds, and the white light trained
her seeing eye on the Everglades and guided her toward a scientific appreciation of nature's importance.

Seemingly oddly, Douglas resisted the label *nature writer*. To friends,
she also confessed that she was not an environmentalist. Browder agreed:
"She was so much more." Her concern, whether expressed in print or
from a speaker's podium, lay with humanity and what it was doing to itself. "We run the risk," she said, "of forgetting that action without intelligence is nothing but idiocy." She saw such idiocy, or the lack of basic
pragmatism, in Western civilization's historic relationship with the nonhuman world. And to speak out in witness of a social or moral wrong was
part of the old Quaker social gospel, bequeathed to her from her father's
lineage. Why, she would ask, bulldoze a lot clean to build a house or a
parking lot when trees provide energy-saving shade and comfort? Why
block cooling ocean breezes and the public's view with rows of hotels and
condominiums? What social value lay in needless preying on plant and
animal life? Humans were no less creatures of nature and no less dependent on nature's providence than were birds and alligators. Destroying
nature was equivalent to rejecting its dispensation and turning one's community or home to ruin.[22]

Her intercourse with nature challenged the profile of a conventional environmental activist. Said Podgor, "She was an armchair, living room environmentalist." This interpretation is perhaps a bit unfair. In the 1920s, she spent considerable time with friends sightseeing and fishing in the Everglades, and she bird-watched in the region with some of the great ornithologists of the time. During the 1930s, she took an extensive excursion—by boat, foot, and dirigible—in the wetland multiplex when she worked with the association created to form a national park. In the 1940s, she accompanied scientists on research trips into the Everglades when she was writing *River of Grass.* Podgor knew her in her later years, when her closet featured no hiking boots next to the dress shoes she wore out to Dayhoff's ranger-training sessions. Even if she criticized it, Douglas exhibited a comfortableness with civilization. Her inclination was to leave buggy and wet places to themselves and to go where the tourists went, where accommodations awaited the not-too-adventurous. That meant the boardwalks at the national park. Her favorite was the Pa-Hay-Okee Overlook. "It's the silence that's so wonderful," she said. "You hear the wind rustling in the grass and maybe a bird in the distance. You get the sense of the sawgrass and the openness and the island hammocks." To find a similar fulfillment, she did not have to trouble someone to drive her to the park. She could stay on her back patio. "Unlike other wilderness areas where the naturalist is a hiker, camper, and explorer, the naturalist in the Everglades must usually appreciate it from a distance. I saw great flocks of birds—amazing flights of thirty thousand to forty thousand in one swoop—coming from their sandy coasts to their rookeries."[23]

Of course, countless environmentalists learned to appreciate the Everglades by trekking through them, and Douglas might be accused of rationalizing her preference for avoiding rugged engagements with the wild. Despite this avoidance, she understood that the evening journey of birds passing over her backyard epitomized the interconnectedness of the Everglades ecology with the rest of the world. She and her cohorts sought to pass a central message along to others: the Everglades were part of a complex ecosystem that extended beyond the shining vastness of sawgrass, hammocks, and cypress swamps and beyond the national park. Whereas other naturalists risked setting themselves apart from the

general population as wilderness snobs, Douglas showed that enlightenment required no special hobbies. Her message could be received by
looking only as far as the sky above.

For some of the more famous forebears of American environmentalism with literary credentials, the sky beheld something that Douglas denied: a higher power that was hardly knowable from nature. Quaker William Bartram and transcendentalists John Muir, Ralph Waldo Emerson,
and Henry David Thoreau (all of whom except Thoreau sauntered into
wild Florida) valued "an absolute freedom and wildness" in nature as a
source of the divine. When Muir looked at mountains, he saw the "terrestrial manifestations of God." Douglas held her Quaker heritage close,
and she appreciated the writings of the early transcendentalists, but she
neither felt a godly connection to nature nor believed in its divine origins.
Although raised in the Methodist and Episcopal Churches, she took little
if any moral direction from the experience, found in it no framework for
understanding human existence. When she looked at her mountains of
South Florida—cumulus clouds rising above the Everglades, which she
called cloud mountains—she made no association with a power higher
than the physical. She did not dismiss the idea that such a power existed,
but she professed not to know. She knew nature's providence, not divine
providence.[24]

Her agnosticism did not preclude a "spiritual appreciation" of nature,
however. Those who knew her best described her as spiritual even if she
worshiped no god. She approached life as an explorer and inquisitor. In
knowledge gained through personal experience and education and possessed within the inner self, she found the animating force of life. What
she sought in the world—knowledge—brought her closer to all living
things. A cyclorama of beauty, simplicity, order, balance, action, and interaction, nature lent itself to curiosity and discovery, but it served as a
biological, physical source of knowledge as much as a metaphysical one.
All wisdom, Douglas wrote, emanated from a personal kinship with the
earth, an intimation with both its mysteries and its revelations. A passage
from her writer's notebook describing the experience of reading while
looking out across Biscayne Bay fairly illustrates her spiritual relationship with nature:

Yesterday the view lay across a gentle slope to the bay; across tall grass and flowering weeds fragrant in the sun; across a tangle of weedy growths, and past the fountains of glitter which were palm trees in the sun, and so out across the blue, bright waters of the bay to the faint clear line of Cape Florida and the outer sea, and so at last to the sky. That long reach of vision is a lifting up, a lifting out, mentally as well as visually, and I am beginning to believe that such liftings out have a real effect on one's inner life; and I hope a permanent one. . . . It is a sort of physical confirmation of one's belief that thought will more and more be lifted up and out, as one's gaze is. Certainly there must be some such idea behind our use of the word "vision" to mean, not just seeing with the eye, but a sort of plunge and fright of the mind, which can distance everything but time.[25]

A lifelong appreciation of learning gave Douglas an appreciation of the Everglades. And science, social and physical, evolving in its sophistication across the American environmental century, taught her pivotal lessons about humans and nature. In the 1920s, she became an impassioned subscriber to the social-scientific concept of regionalism, promoting her subtropical corner of the state as the potential source of a unique and inspiring culture that fostered a wholesome mutual relationship with its natural surroundings. At the region's center lay the unique feature, the Everglades. A few lines of verse she composed in the 1920s capture her vision:

I have seen the force of the tremendous everlasting Everglades.
I have seen the black force and the sun force of its soil
Casting forever new forces among the assemblages of nations.
Through them I have seen the meaning of the new Florida.[26]

She eventually learned about the wetland's biological significance apart from the aesthetic and became acquainted with all the important scientists associated with Everglades study during her lifetime. She first got to know the Everglades in the days before ecosystem study, when the physical scientist intellectually connected to nature was the naturalist. A Darwin-type practitioner of Victorian-era science and values, he—or

occasionally she—was an ardent finder of specimens and keeper of tax-
onomies who emerged from the wilderness and shipped extracted and
carefully cataloged discoveries off to a repository of natural history or
to a wealthy patron. Then he plunged back in for another round of collection. He saw nature as a world unto itself to which humans did not
belong. More often than not, he referred to nature as a mother, a be-
witching bacchante worth protecting for her beauty and specimen stores,
but could marshal no real scientific argument in defense of her protection. He rarely premised his science on an understanding of the interconnected universe, leaving, therefore, the fate of landscapes mostly outside
the jurisdiction of scientific testimony.

By midcentury, however, environmentalism's intellectual base in natural
science had begun conceding to a new field of study. Ecology turned the
naturalist perspective on its head by introducing an empirical authority
that transcended conflicting and subjective judgments about the necessity of species preservation and about what accounted for beauty—that
is, beauty not in the aesthetic but in the living. As the physical allure
came to matter less, biology or biological communities came to matter
more. According to a dictum of ecologists, nothing on earth, not even
humans, dwelled in isolation from the rest. By the last decades of the century, those who would alter the environment were increasingly forced, in
varying degrees, to answer to science.

When Douglas began the research for *River of Grass* in the 1940s, she
had little more than an elegiac fascination with nature. But her mostly literary mind had always had a scientific side. That side expanded as she listened to and read the work of scientists concerned with the natural world.
As their ecological insights evolved, as environmentalism evolved, so too
did her own environmental commitments. As environmentalists began
equipping themselves with valuable ecological truths, so too did Douglas
the activist. Her historical significance lies not only in the history-making
initiatives she undertook, such as reconceptualizing the Everglades as a
river, but mainly in the events that intersected her sweeping life and that
fell within her writer's gaze and her activist impulse. Her transformative
journey in the environmental century is the story of a changing America

and national temperament, including a new collective awareness of the human-nature nexus. Her experiences and observations in human life and in the natural world amount to a biography of the Everglades, a history of the environmental century, and more.

Marjory Stoneman Douglas's life is also the story of how the perennial forces of nature and history reshaped environmentalism. As a writer, historian, and activist, she recognized nature's starring role in both the human experience and her own. In her backyard context were the Everglades. Living in South Florida required an awareness of them, even if they were not perceived as a thing of beauty or as a biological link to human existence. "Without the Everglades," Douglas wrote in 1959, "the whole nature and history of south Florida would be utterly different." Even as parts were being "walled about with titles, loans, mortgages, papers, trivialities," the Everglades regulated the local climate, fed the wells and rivers from which people took their drinking water, shaped the urban development along the coasts, and provided habitat for the spectacular wildlife that decorated the landscape. And nature engaged life—at least Douglas's—beyond sustenance and the aesthetically or spiritually evocative. She always said that the Everglades ultimately came to her, not she to them, first as a writer and then as an activist.[27]

With the confidence that others would carry on her activist work, with her unpublished manuscript in the hands of her competent assistant, and in spite of her rejection of an afterlife, Douglas was in the end relaxed about her mortality. She was compelled to contemplate death in part because her longevity had become an object of public curiosity. The divine soul was a "fiction of mankind," she concluded. From the fear of death, people created the hope of an afterlife and that of a god who would receive them. For her, it seemed a shame that a preoccupation with a "dual universe" diverted so many people from living "vividly" and "intensely" in the present world. In the end, she met death believing in heaven only in a poetic sense, not in a religious one. She considered herself a metaphysical monist, the meaning of which she researched before identifying herself as one in her autobiography. There was a single universe; nothing lay on the other side of the proverbial veil. Death was the final punctuation, and the commencement of nothing more.[28]

True to her beliefs, she insisted on a nonreligious memorial service.[29] When that time came, the news of her passing generated an outpouring of sympathy that, according to the *Miami Herald,* was "worldwide." Environmentalists, women's rights advocates, and both Democratic and Republican policymakers remembered her presence as a center, a truth, a hope, and a light. Offering his regrets while traveling in Germany, President Clinton, who had awarded her the Presidential Medal of Freedom five years earlier, called her "both an inspiration and mentor for a generation." Florida's Democratic governor, Lawton Chiles, concurred, hailing her as a "prophet who . . . inspired us to save our environment for our children and our grandchildren." Republican speaker of the U.S. House of Representatives Newt Gingrich asked that "we remember the founding mother of the Everglades." Secretary of the Interior Bruce Babbitt said that "her voice and her spirit are not stilled." Attorney General Janet Reno, a fellow Miamian, described Douglas as "one of the truly great ladies of the world."[30]

Douglas never overestimated her impact. "No one is satisfied with their life's work," she said during the week she turned 104. "There is always the need to carry on. The most important thing is to prepare competent people to follow you." No matter how fearful the odds, she was never despairing. Yet she was also never tempted to claim victory. On her 105th birthday, schoolchildren gave her a cake decorated with a Wonder Woman motif, designed by portrait artist Menden Hall. They thanked her for saving the Everglades. She corrected them: They're "not saved yet."[31]

CHAPTER TWO

River of Life

It's unclear when Douglas first learned about the Everglades. She conceivably knew of them when a child, living in the North. Much popular literature of the time told tales of the strange jungles and swamps of Florida, and as soon as she was old enough, Marjory read virtually everything that came into her hands. People talked, too, about faraway places they wanted to visit or where they wanted to resettle. Still, she apparently formed no early impression of the Everglades. She lived in Miami for five years before first seeing them. On one Sunday afternoon in 1920, she and friends went off on a fishing adventure, with Marjory stealing the time from the column that needed to be written for the *Miami Herald*'s Monday edition. They drove west beyond the city limits to the end of Tamiami Trail, still eight years away from becoming the first roadway to ford the Everglades. For now, the blacktop stopped where the water of the Everglades washed the creeping edge of civilization. Facing the open distance, her back turned against the developed fields of Dade County, Douglas was elevated by what unfolded before her. "The grass and the islands of hardwoods stood alone in the light and the beautiful air," she recalled years later. She also remembered the Everglades as "completely untouched." This impression was not quite accurate, however. She and her friends were, after all, fishing from the spillbank of an Everglades drainage canal.[1]

People with restless dreams and ambitions had been tampering with the watery province since the nineteenth century. The region was to be for them what the Republic had been for others, a grand experiment in cultural unity and universal social and economic progress. How the natural endowments of the Everglades fit into this history is how nature was asked to fit everywhere in the nation—that is, as a symbol and source of democratic greatness. The Everglades therefore could not be kept in their original form, an unbounded sodden land. They were to be drained to bring a merchantable commodity to the surface. But like the region's remaining Seminole resisters, residing not far from where Douglas and her friends fished, the enemy water would not be slain easily or completely. Land merchants had to settle for dry enclaves: to keep them dry, they diverted the water with dams, dikes, canals, and building-size electric-powered pumps, doing so with a mind toward growth.

By the last years of Douglas's life, the number of people living in South Florida had grown to six million, and the Everglades ecosystem was a great pumping heart at risk of arrest. In the name of flood control, state bureaucrats and the Army Corps of Engineers pumped 1.7 billion gallons a day from the Everglades watershed to the ocean, contributing to a 70 percent decline in downstream flow. One of the world's most expansive and expensive water-control systems gave the corps near complete mastery over the wetland. The results were a boon for agribusiness and developers and a disaster for animal and indigenous plant communities and Everglades National Park, America's rarefied subtropical park, consistently ranked as the most threatened in the national inventory. Humans were also imperiling the subtropical life they coveted. The region's moderate climate and plentiful rainfall were the gift of the Everglades. Beginning with Frank Stoneman, Douglas's father, experts had periodically warned that the gift would be withdrawn if Providence suffered irreparable harm.[2]

The Everglades were a prime example of the human relationship with the environment gone awry. Just as Americans were achieving the upper hand over nature, they began to feel the effects of depleted and polluted resources. Beginning in the 1980s, a mildly contrite state legislature enacted into law one ecological restoration plan after another, all bringing minimal results. "Florida has made great strides," Douglas wrote, "but the degradation of the environment has become institutionalized, embedded in the nature of things." Finally, in 2000, Congress gave fervid bipartisan approval to the Comprehensive Everglades Restoration Plan, which carried an estimated $7.8 billion price tag and a thirty-year timeline for completion. In terms of cost, logistics, bureaucracy, and science, the plan was portrayed as the most ambitious effort ever to bring an ecosystem back to a full and vibrant existence. Nullifying the historic rejection of the archetypical wetland with a reaffirmed belief in its ecological worth seemed the appropriate punctuation to the American environmental century as well as to Douglas's life.[3]

For hundreds of years, people had thought of the Everglades as a forbidding abyss. Standing where Sandy Dayhoff spread Douglas's ashes, one might agree. Wet prairie stretches in all directions to the luminous horizon, its linear purity interrupted only by occasional hammock islands, dollops of subtropical growths on a golden-brown Andrew Wyeth landscape. It is not intuitive to think of the Everglades as a river, as Douglas did. Rivers are not typically grassy and 60 miles across. The Mississippi, the great superwaterway of America's rivers, is just over 4 miles at its widest. Rivers slice through the earth, creating a channel that can carry people and commerce, but few people have dared to travel the Everglades from headwater to broad mouth, and in prelevee days, no banks distinguished the River of Grass's boundary. Looking again, one will swear this river does not flow. Yet it does, for 120 miles, leaving Lake Okeechobee on an unhurried pilgrimage of a few feet per minute. The journeying water sprawls westward to the Big Cypress Swamp and southward, quietly reaching a belt of mangroves that rise on tangled roots in a brackish environment along the shorebird-swept Florida Bay. Wrapping the peninsula's west end, the mangroves form the Ten Thousand Islands lying between Chokoloskee Bay and the Gulf of Mexico. This is the river's end, a three- to four-month flow from the beginning. Within the River of Grass are numerous smaller rivers, some called sloughs, such as Taylor Slough and Shark River Slough. The Everglades once commanded 6,200 square miles of emphatic flatness. Water control and human habitation have pared them down to 52 percent of their original size, and they continue to give battle to diasporatic populations that have congealed into bloated metropolises on Florida's east and west coasts.[4]

In the early years of exploration and settlement, most people could not see the river for the swamp, and no one conceived that the Everglades were part of an ecosystem that begins far to the north. The wellspring is Lake Okeechobee, which in Seminole language means "big water." That is a lyrical description. In dramatic terms, the lake is 730 square miles, the second-largest body of freshwater wholly contained within the contiguous United States. The lake carries the eye to the visible end, where silver-gray water rises up to blue sky. At the lake's southern shore, turning away from the water brings a view cluttered with wearisome houses, shopping centers, paved roads, and cropland. All are protected by a blasted-limestone dike, so tall that the lake cannot be seen from the other side of the barrier. Before the Army Corps of Engineers impounded the lake with its stout levee, before drainage canals connected the lake to the Gulf of Mexico and the Atlantic, before pumps pushed obliging water to retention areas or to the sea, water spilled over the southern rim during wet months. The water then opened out across a 150,000-acre swamp of pop ash and custard apple trees, canopied by a flowering tangle of moonvines, which impressed early botanical explorer John Kunkel Small as "more beautiful than words can describe," and swept into a brimming sawgrass marsh. After the contraptions of civilized progress were in place, economic interests seized the custard apple swamp and upper portions of the sawgrass marsh and slowly amassed a nearly one-thousand-square-mile enclave of agricultural land.[5]

On the lake's north side, the ecosystem leads into the Kissimmee River. The river feeds Okeechobee's gentle depths with water gathered from a twenty-five-hundred-square-mile wetlands basin, including a chain of lakes, in the central region of the state. By the mid–twentieth century, cattle ranches had diffused across much of the Kissimmee basin, and to create more grazing land, army engineers by the 1970s had bypassed the laconic snaky river with a blueprint-perfect drainage canal. Rain washed livestock feed, dung, and crop fertilizer into the canal and other rivers, stimulating eutrophic conditions in the lake and the growth of invasive nutrient-loving cattails. Engineers sent the contaminated Okeechobee water into a latticework of additional canals, each cut with calculated directness and conducted along sugarcane fields, truck farms, and ranchland to the remaining Everglades, the sprawling cities, and the mangrove-filigreed coastlines.

Indians called the Everglades Pa-hay-okee, or "grassy water." A nineteenth-century explorer called them a "sea of grass." Douglas immortalized them as the "River of Grass." These are poetic allusions (not illusions) whose creators nevertheless recognized the multifarious sum of the region's ecology. Scientists and others today generally take exception to Douglas's river metaphor, preferring instead to think of the Everglades as a freshwater confection of marl prairies, sawgrass marshes, tropical hammocks, cypress swamps, pinelands, sloughs, and lakes. They also ignore her plural standard ("They are") by referring to the Everglades in singular verbiage ("It is"), and they quibble with her when they clarify that sawgrass is not grass but a sedge. Douglas, however, knew its true state: "It is not grass at all so much as a fierce, ancient, cutting sedge." Before accepting her river conception, she cleared it with the first hydrologist to make a thorough study of the Everglades, and while she was a grammar snob who heeded the rules of subject-verb agreement, she was originally torn over the appropriate form before settling on the plural. She wanted readers to value the singular living mosaic that was singularly unique with "subtlety and diversity, a crowd of changing forms, of thrusting teeming life." "There *are* no other Everglades in the world," she wrote in the oft-quoted first line in her book.[6]

She was technically correct. Although similar wetlands exist in Brazil and the Yucatán, more than one thousand plant and nearly four hundred animal species make the Everglades, to quote one biologist, "one of the most distinctive wetland complexes" on the planet. They are a "world so empty and so crammed with wonders," says the narrator in Douglas's novel *Alligator Crossing*. Observers have recorded more than one hundred fish species in Florida Bay and three hundred kinds of birds (including migrants) throughout the Everglades. Those enhancing the region's wondrousness include stick-legged wading birds with a narrow habitat range: herons, egrets, roseate spoonbills, ibises, wood storks, and others. The birds interact as prey and predator with some of the area's sixty-five known species of reptiles, including snakes, alligators, turtles, and the American crocodile. Among the twenty-five native mammals are the endangered Florida panther, West Indian manatee, and black bear.[7]

When John James Audubon wanted to see some of these animals and sailed from Key West to Cape Sable at the southern end of the Everglades in 1832, he described the region as tropical. Later in the decade, Congress followed suit with a corresponding designation in legislation. But in reality, the Everglades lie at a latitude where temperate and tropical elements converge, and what Audubon and others were observing was by strict definition a subtropical environment. Douglas wrote, "This land, by the maps, is in the temperate zone. But the laws of the rain and of the seasons here are tropic laws."[8]

South Florida, in other words, is an ecological hybrid. Unlike the tropics, the region has wide tracts of pinelands, yet the majority of the Everglades' vascular plants, including the gumbo-limbo and West Indian mahogany, have tropical origins. These tropical hardwoods prefer hammock areas, as in the tree islands of the wet prairie, where "exceedingly vigorous" vegetation grows in fertile humus soil raised atop a limestone swell. Hammocks were the favorite oasis of early naturalists, and their decimation by looting plant thieves, feckless developers, and drainage-related fire was the naturalists' greatest lament. For its more-than-nominal part, the sawgrass sustains a fecund, primary-level ecology. Having adapted to the natural flooding and dry cycles, including burns, it has lived in the region for more than four thousand years as the most persistent plant. In the south, it yields to wet prairie lying over peat and marl. The Atlantic coastal ridge, the geological foundation of the present-day urban centers, girds the Everglades in the east. A great cypress swamp, host to flowering air plants and ferns, forms the western boundary in what is today the twelve-hundred-square-mile Big Cypress National Preserve, much of which was lumbered at one time or another and half of which has become encircled by ranchland and houses.[9]

Water is the core element of this once boundless ecosystem. It arrives from three sources: the Kissimmee River–Lake Okeechobee system, groundwater springs, and rain. The Everglades began taking geologic form approximately five thousand years ago after the end of the Wisconsin ice age, when the rising sea lifted the fresh groundwater beneath the peninsula to the surface. A new wetland system gradually replaced the existing dry landscape. By 2700 B.P. (before present), it had produced the distribution of flora species that exists today. All was dependent on rain. Surface water and seawater evaporation and plant transpiration increased area precipitation to the modern-day per-annum average of fifty-eight inches.[10]

"Here the rain is everything," *River of Grass* declares. Rain is the determinant of the abundance or dearth of life in the water and sky and on land, all interlocked in an exquisite chain of existence. The heaviest rains come between June and October, a period that is frequented by hurricanes, some awesome enough to influence the course of history. During the remaining months, the water level in the Everglades runs low. In a region where the four seasons lose their meaning, early settlers were quick to note only two essential climatic divisions, rainy and dry. The wildlife learned to live with these conditions, finding sustenance aplenty in the right places at the right times. But humans began tampering with the water flow, fouling up the whole system: things became dry when they should be wet and wet when they should be dry. Wildlife began starving or drowning or abandoned the premises altogether.[11]

Beneath all the water and a layer of peaty muck—the rich soil agriculture reclaimed—is the Everglades' shallow underbelly, pocked limestone rock. "To understand the Everglades," Douglas wrote in 1947, "one must understand the rock." Through its permeable mass, surface water recharges the aquifer on which Florida floats and its population depends.

The rock slopes southward at a gradient of less than three inches per mile, which is why the river creeps. Along the peninsula's perimeter, the rock spoons upward to form a natural barrier between salt water and freshwater. In places, engineers dynamited away that barrier and installed motorized locks that allow water to be released when it risks flooding agricultural lands and city streets.[12]

In *River of Grass,* a black ink illustration shows a mammoth rearing back from a crouching saber-toothed tiger. Sabal palms lean against the background sky, and a vulture perched rapaciously in the foreground waits for its carrion repast. Except for the palm trees, this scene could have been witnessed by the first humans who inhabited Florida some fifteen thousand years ago, when megafauna roamed an unshapen peninsula that was arid, windswept, and at least twice its current width. Another two thousand years passed before hunter-gatherers spread down into South Florida. Six thousand or more years later, they mysteriously disappeared. The Everglades had yet to take form. The wetland would be anywhere from two hundred to seven hundred years old before people again inhabited South Florida. A century after the disappearance of these hunter-gatherers, white settlers stumbled on ancient remains half hidden in the bristly outlands.

In the nineteenth century, exploring and even excavating the sites of lost civilizations was an adventurous and manly art largely restricted to wealthy or well-connected men. Just such an individual, a lieutenant colonel in His Majesty's military named Charles D. Durnford, generated the first professional interest in archeological research in Florida. Durnford went to Naples in early 1895 to catch tarpon, and resident whites told him about buried artifacts. After gathering a cache of "fish netting and pins, wooden billets and bowls, and carved conch cups," he went to Philadelphia to show his find to experts at the University of Pennsylvania.[13]

Among them was Frank Hamilton Cushing, "one of the most brilliant and original ethnologists of his day," according to Douglas. Her approving description was not prompted simply by an appreciation for Cushing's eventual pioneering contribution to Florida's pre-Columbian history. He was, to be sure, brilliant. At age nineteen, he assumed the position of curator of the Department of Ethnology at the National Museum in Washington, D.C.; by the time he met Durnford in Philadelphia, Cushing had established a reputation as one of the foremost authorities on aboriginal cultures. His duties of late had confined him mostly to stale indoor laboratories. A sickly, waiflike fellow, he tended to feel better when working in the field, dressed as always in Victorian convention in a pressed wing-collar shirt (his sleeves rolled up), black tie, and suit vest. By late May 1895, he was in South Florida and the welcoming outdoors, excavating the coast and coastal islands courtesy of Phoebe L. Hearst, wife of William Randolph Hearst. Before his return to Washington a year later, a particularly triumphant day of collecting prompted him to record in his journal, "Greatest day in my life in exploration."[14]

His boss, John Wesley Powell, head of the Smithsonian Institution's Bureau of Ethnology, was similarly impressed, announcing that Cushing had discovered a "new culture." Cushing referred to the creators of the pottery, cooking utensils, tools, masks, and other carved wood, bone, and shell objects he troweled from the earth as "key dwellers." They were part of the Glades culture, and the root to understanding them was planted in their natural surroundings. Cushing explored that connection in a seven-hundred-page manuscript he produced after the expedition, although his untimely death prevented him from publishing the treatise. His discoveries were nevertheless, Douglas wrote in 1947, "the basis of present-day knowledge of those prehistoric Glades people."[15]

Much of their life indeed had been excavated by midcentury. Scholars determined that three groups representing the Glades culture had emerged along a rough geographic distribution. The Mayiami occupied the southern vicinity of Lake Okeechobee, the Calusa the west side of the Everglades, and the Tekesta the east. In *River of Grass,* Douglas devoted considerable space to the Calusa, about whom scholars knew the most. Aside from the archeological record, a useful written record had been provided by Spanish explorers and would-be settlers who came into contact and conflict with the fierce Calusa in the sixteenth century. Douglas wrote admirably about their society and leader Carlos, as the Spanish called him, who took a brave though fruitless stand against his European counterpart in Florida, Pedro Menendez de Aviles.

Unlike most historians of the day, Douglas criticized the Spanish, who redrew the map of Everglades history by setting the indigenous landscape and its people on a course of irreversible change. From both secular and religious teachings, Europeans subscribed to the great chain of being, believing that humanity should hold rank over "inferior" nature and that "superior" humans should hold rank over "lesser" ones. In the cataclysmic clash between Old World and New World societies, Christians armed with technologically advanced weapons felt justified in subjugating those presumed to be heathen and savage, people who had not civilized wilderness. Europeans demeaned themselves to no one except their god, and they measured the value of a natural place by its utilitarian gifts—social, aesthetic, intellectual, and commercial. Exploitation for the enrichment of one's blessed monarch—and, not incidentally, the monarch's charge— was both a worthy endeavor and a cause. Both the labor and environments of New World people were to be seized. Under rule dictated by these beliefs, untold numbers succumbed, including an unsubmissive Carlos.[16]

His was a wasted act of murder by the commercially minded. Menendez ultimately rejected South Florida as "very poor land, subject to inundation." It held neither precious metals nor agricultural promise. Spanish maps ventured the words "El Laguno del Espiritu Santo" (The Lagoon of the Holy Ghost) across an empty outline of the peninsula's end. South Florida was terra incognita. Menendez turned his attention to the north, where he hoped to develop commercial agriculture. He also possessed dreams of discovering a natural water passage across the peninsula to serve as a profit-making alternative shipping route to the storm-risky Bahama Channel. The conquistador never found his natural passageway, however, and the development of a world-market agricultural colony never materialized. His dreams had to wait for the technology of future generations, which converted once-forsaken South Florida into an agrarian success story and carved out a corridor for a cross-state shipping canal to the north.[17]

Although Menendez eventually ignored them, the Glades people were not left in total isolation. The stealth diseases of the Europeans contaminated the Glades people's world, reducing their population, destabilizing their society and traditions, and weakening their security defenses. What "was to affect them more deeply than any invasion," Douglas wrote, was the white man's "yellow fever and small pox and measles." Over the course of a century, the Calusa lost an estimated 80 percent of their population, a catastrophic development that left the largest and strongest of the Glades groups exposed to hungry slavers and Catholic missionaries. Historians commonly believe that by the time the English assumed control of Florida in 1764, after the Seven Years' War, the last of the peninsula's indigenous people had fallen to disease and warfare, escaped to lands elsewhere, or surrendered to enslavement. South Florida was subsequently an "empty" land, a condition that, although suitable to whites, proved only temporary.[18]

Douglas sympathized with the Glades people, though not as victims of brutal invaders. She admired them for the complex civilization they had developed, having done so as a sedentary, hunting and gathering culture. Scientists at the time she was writing *River of Grass* averred that stability and "progress" were the hallmarks of agrarian cultures — to wit, cultures not unlike that of the scientists making the judgments. Douglas was dubious. The Glades people flourished in part because they did not think in terms of new markets and commercial agriculture, as did Europeans. Their basic wants remained reasonably compatible with what the natural environment could render. Everywhere about the land, coastal waters, inland lakes, and the River of Grass were the elements of the Glades people's thriving existence. They hunted deer in pine flatwoods, grubbed around in scrubland for root plants, and harvested turtles, bivalves, lobsters, whales, sharks, manatees, and the now extinct West Indian monk seal from fresh- and saltwater habitats. Tools and utensils were made from bones and shells, houses from palm and grass thatch, and netting and ropes from palm fiber.[19]

The trail of clues left behind for field researchers such as Cushing represented the environmental imprint of the Glades people. They were master mound builders. Their discarded shells grew into waste heaps, or mid-dens, and they moved earth to create places for their dead and their pos-sessions. They dug canals to facilitate travel and constructed jetties and conch-shell seawalls to protect harbors and landings from storms. The people living around Lake Okeechobee promoted burning to foster the propagation of wild staples. The land and the water easily bore all these demands, however, and in the absence of a natural disaster or the incur-sion of a more demanding ecological relationship, like that of Europeans, the environment likely would have sustained them indefinitely.[20]

In *River of Grass,* Douglas offered the first comprehensive study of the indigenous Glades culture suitable for a general readership. Their archive was housed in the earth and water, but Douglas was not the type to dig around in natural elements for historical evidence. She preferred research in libraries and conversations with experts. Her principal expert on the Glades people was a Cushing-like scholar, John Mann Goggin.

Goggin grew up in Miami after his family moved there from Chicago on the eve of the cacophonous land boom of the 1920s. He spent countless blissful boyhood hours exploring the Everglades and befriending local Indians. Before going off to college in Gainesville and then New Mexico, he assembled a meticulously documented collection of eight thousand South Florida tree snails and began to locate and excavate archeological sites. By the time he entered graduate school at Yale, he had published eighteen papers on native cultures of the Southwest and Florida. He was part of a last generation of naturalists who carried guns into the field, os-tensibly as protection against snakes, but he abandoned the practice as he and colleagues grew self-conscious of the paradox. After completing his doctorate, he took a position at the University of Florida as the state's first university-appointed anthropologist. An affable, bespectacled, bald-ing professor with one bad eye and a penchant for drink, Goggin was a favored colleague and teacher who made field research an educational ad-venture. In fifteen years at Gainesville, he turned Florida into one of the premier and most thoroughly documented places of anthropological re-search. When he died in 1963, at age forty-seven and at the peak of his ca-reer, the discipline's main journal, *American Anthropologist,* remembered him with a ten-page obituary.[21]

Douglas met Goggin when he was not yet thirty. No academic knew more about the life and material culture of Glades Indians than he, and few were as generous. He shared "whole-heartedly from the store of his own scholarship," she wrote in her acknowledgments, "and patiently checked and rechecked my presentation of his intricate and fascinating subject." Because his approach combined history, ethnology, archeology, and ecology, so did hers. Braiding together the biographies of people and land, she logically recognized Euro-Americans' simultaneous domination of people and the natural world. Her voice turned critical when she discussed white incursions into native life by way of enslavement, contagion, alcohol, land claims, religious conversion, and environmental degradation. To her, the tragic drama of powerful people dominating both less powerful people and compliant nature ran like an unbroken thread throughout the history of Western civilization, with repeat performances played out in the Everglades. Her insights here prefigured the idea of environmental justice, which came to life comparatively late in the environmental century.[22]

During the 1800s, not only did whites bear responsibility for the native depopulation of South Florida, but their exercise of force bore responsibility for the reestablishment of Indians in the Everglades. The Creeks of Georgia and Alabama first became familiar with the geography of Florida when they descended into the Spanish colony on slave raids, working in collusion with Carolina slave traders. Thinning populations of commercial game in the lower British colonies, partly of the Indians' making, also sent them into Florida on hunting expeditions. Eventually, the white appetite for land crowded out the eastern bands and pushed them into territorial conflict with each other. Permanent migration to North Florida began in the 1740s and continued into the next century. Separating from the Creek Confederacy, Florida's new arrivals became collectively known as Seminoles.[23]

Even the name *Seminole* reflects an unwanted imposition by whites. It came into common use in the 1760s during the British occupation of Florida and was likely adopted from the Spanish. Douglas did not care for it. "At worst, to the contemptuous white man," she wrote in *River of Grass, Seminole* meant "runaway" or "outlaw." Another translation offers the more benign "seceder." Douglas favored a meaning with dignity and Muskogee origins, "free people of distant fires." In an acknowledgment of Indian agency, she offered the qualification that Seminoles preferred to speak of themselves as "*Ikaniuksalgi,* the people of the peninsula."[24]

Soon after moving to Miami, she encountered Seminoles for the first time, seeing them in an unflattering pose. As the city evolved into a tourist destination, they began daily commutes down the Miami River and assumed the role of roadside attraction, selling crafts and wrestling alligators before quietly retreating back into their real Everglades world as darkness gathered. Goggin too first saw the Seminoles this way. When working on her book, Douglas again relied on Goggin, who remained an outsider among the Seminoles even as he became a friend: he never learned their language or practiced their ways. Instead, almost as if he were studying a lost civilization, he looked to interred material culture to learn about his subjects' origins in Florida.[25]

Seminoles at first established an agricultural way of life in North Florida. But before inevitably settling on a policy of total removal, incoming white settlers drove the Indians deeper into the peninsula. The Treaty of Moultrie Creek, signed two years after the United States acquired Florida from Spain in 1821, forced Seminoles onto reservations south of expanding American settlements. Seven years later, President Andrew Jackson set out to cleanse the East of all but whites and useful slaves by brandishing the Indian Removal Act, which set aside territory west of the Mississippi River as the land of the exiled. Florida Indians resisted removal in the longest sustained white-Indian conflict in American history, the Second Seminole War (1835–42) and the subsequent Third Seminole War (1854–58). Ultimately, close to four thousand men, women, and children were sent to Arkansas, but many Seminoles confounded their would-be removers by escaping into the naturally fortified recesses of the Everglades. When military officials declared an end to the conflict in 1858, perhaps one hundred Seminoles had eluded U.S. soldiers and their bloodhounds and resided mostly undisturbed in the Ten Thousand Islands, the Big Cypress Swamp, and the Everglades. If nothing else, the watery gambit impressed the pursuers: one Indian fighter called South Florida a "most hideous region."[26]

Using wetlands as a defensive strategy was as old as one of the first white-Indian conflicts in North America, Metacomet's War in colonial New England. Emerging from hiding places in the swamp, Indians devastated white settlements and killed one of every sixteen militiamen. The natural defenses no doubt heightened Puritan fears of treachery lurking in a dark environment and reinforced their moralistic characterizations of good and evil. Whites perceived the savage swamp as an environment natural to Indians, suitable only for the Other. Lodged in the social memory of nineteenth-century whites fighting in Florida, if not the institutional memory of the army, may well have been the specter of vicious New England swamp wars. "No country I have ever heard of bears any resemblance to it," noted one soldier of the Everglades. "It seems . . . expressly intended as a retreat for the rascally Indian."[27]

Dating back to Old Europe, people used words such as *hideous, dismal,* and *evil* to describe the naked wilderness as a whole. During the romantic period in the nineteenth century—the days of Washington Irving, James Fenimore Cooper, and Henry David Thoreau—forests, mountains, and rivers attained recognition as sublime places, sanctuaries of soulful reflection and emotional regeneration. Only a semblance of that exalted status was accorded to wetlands and even then not until the twentieth century, when attitudes toward the Everglades began to change. Before Douglas redefined them as a river, they were abhorred, perceived as a vile swamp crawling with poisonous "serpent life," evil things and evil doings. Civilization's view of the River of Grass when it was still metaphorically a swamp moved Douglas to wax poetic: "Off and on for . . . four hundred years the region now called The Everglades was described as a series of vast, miasmic swamps, poisonous lagoons, huge dismal marshes without outlet, a rotting, shallow, inland sea, or labyrinths of dark trees hung and looped about with snakes and dripping mosses, malignant with tropical fevers and malarias, evil to the white man."[28] White cultural prejudices against swamps allowed the last of the Florida Seminoles safe harbor. While Americans were preoccupied by civil war during the 1860s and Reconstruction thereafter, Everglades Indians adopted a habit of living with the land and water that resembled the tendencies of the Calusa, thereby leading a stable existence. Yet whatever fortunes existed with isolation were gone within a generation. The Everglades embodied too large a territory for expansion-minded Americans to ignore.

If the great wetland was worthless in its natural state, whites would simply divine a method of converting it into something that suited their desires. By the time of Marjory Stoneman's birth in 1890, Indians had witnessed several expeditions of frequently exasperated white men traveling into the depths of the Everglades, trudging along in heavy, cowhide leggings through wet muck and portaging supply-laden watercraft through head-high sawgrass. They were civilization's landing force, scouting the course for drainage crews that came later with odd-looking steam-powered dredges. The explorers carried compasses, sextants, tilting levels, and guns—always guns. And they were not alone. Seminoles also met white hunters, commercial and sporting, who were developing a similar relationship of conquest with the once-forbidding environment. They shot virtually anything that moved, sometimes even one of their own, and left behind little that remained alive. Long before Douglas saw the Everglades for the first time, surveyors, drainage engineers, and hunters had all left their footprints.

CHAPTER THREE

Lineage

When Douglas composed her autobiography in the late 1980s, she offered some unblushing confessions. She revealed that she had had sex only with her best-forgotten divorced husband, most recently in 1915. She held back from laughing during their first time together, never came to understand all the fuss made about sex, and never missed having it. Although she was glad for the experience, she was equally glad to get it out of the way. In nearly the same breath that she demeaned an inviolable American indulgence, she questioned the importance of a sacred but frail American institution: the family. Many of society's ills grew out of dysfunctional relationships at home, she honestly claimed. Properly run orphanages provided a more salutary environment than some families she had known.[1]

The ninety-seven-year-old autobiographer made this observation while reflecting on the saddest part of her life, her childhood. She was an only and sometimes lonely child. When she was six or seven, her mother was grievously incapacitated by a mental breakdown. Her parents soon separated, and her father dropped out of her life for eighteen years, leaving her to be raised by Victorian-stiff grandparents who offered distressingly little familial vitality. She suffered constant rejection from boys and came to believe she was ugly, an impression from living in a household of attractive women. She had no wholesome parental attachment to which to cling for emotional succoring, nurturing molds of personality development, or answers to what the future might hold for her and how to approach it.

In place of the immediate, she looked to family ancestors as the vessel for the ingredients of self. When she spoke French, she felt a connection to the native land of her maternal grandmother's family. When she looked across the ocean or smelled the salt air, she felt keenly the seafaring spirit of her maternal grandfather's predecessors. She had a special affinity for the Quaker forebears on her father's side and their commitment to social justice. She became a living repository of the family's history. She sketched out a Stoneman pedigree chart, frequently answered relatives' questions regarding their heritage, and wrote stories about her ancestors. She discovered venerable figures worthy of emulation. Family history ultimately contained clues to who she was and what she might become. In looking back, she was in some ways looking at herself and at the qualities she came to embody.

The American roots of Douglas's maternal line went back seven generations to Henry Trefethen of Cornwall. By 1678, when he was forty-seven, Henry had left Britain and assumed the life of a shipwright in New Castle, New Hampshire. The Trefethens produced five more generations of able men of the sea who lived on the rocky coast and islands of Maine and New Hampshire. As weighty as the family's seafaring tradition was, Douglas's grandfather, Daniel Augustus, broke from it after his father advised him that a mariner's profession no longer paid reasonable dividends. A determined young man still in his teens, Daniel set out from the family home in Kittery, Maine, in the 1840s to find a new calling. He began with an apprenticeship as a brass maker in Attleboro, Massachusetts. The trade lacked the glamour of life at sea, but he fulfilled his obligation before moving to Taunton, Massachusetts, for journeyman's work.[2]

When he arrived, just over ten thousand people lived in Taunton, less than one-tenth as many as lived in Boston, thirty-three miles to the north

by the Old Colony Railroad. Leaving the train, Daniel would have encountered the smell, noise, and black smoke of a thriving industrial town,
telltale signs of opportunity from the young man's perspective. Flowing
through the middle of the city, the Taunton River brought waterpower to
the manufacturing plants and carried their waste downstream to Mount
Hope Bay in Rhode Island. Taunton was a city of heavy manufacturing
and metals, a center for brass, copper, and silver works. Whether Daniel
prearranged employment is unclear. He may have wandered the streets
in search of work, as Douglas speculated, and come upon a position at a
small brass foundry owned by Pierre Parady in the northwest section of
town. Daniel took the job.[3]

Within a few years, he married Parady's sister, Florence, bought a
house a few blocks from the foundry, and settled into the routine of an
artisan. When his boss and brother-in-law died a few years later, Daniel
assumed control of the foundry. As the owner of a small manufacturing
concern, Daniel rose early, ate fried potatoes and an omelet prepared by
Florence, and walked to work, his bobbing gait and derby hat a familiar
sight to those en route. On Thursdays, with "his umbrella well rolled, his
hat brushed, his shoes polished, his watch chain heavy gold across his
vest," he boarded the eight o'clock train to Boston to call on customers.
A man of serious demeanor and few words, Daniel lacked the salesman's
talents, but he always spoke with truth and certainty. Before returning
home, he would take his evening meal at the Faneuil Hall Market restaurant. He never left a tip.[4]

Florence too did not believe in gratuities for service. Douglas always
referred to Florence as her French grandmother, a nod to her French
Canadian birth and her preferred language, the tongue of her ancestral
Normandy. Florence had vague knowledge that her family were exiled
Bonapartists and Protestants who came from a village on the Seine River
near Rouen, a place of tradesmen who soldered and forged brass vessels
and utensils. As Douglas always understood the story of her grandparents' meeting, cobbled together from conversations with family members, when Pierre and Florence were still young, the Paradys relocated
from French Canada to Vermont. Sometime in her teens, Florence fell in
love with a local man. Her troubled parents sent her to live with her older

brother in Taunton and to apprentice in a millinery shop. She then met the quiet, young, but slightly older man from Maine working for Pierre.[5]

Census and genealogy records tell a slightly different story. Florence was born in 1824 or 1825, one of the seventeen children of Antoine and Marie Josephte Roy Paradis of St. Jean. In 1844, Florence married Joseph duPont of that city. Nothing more is known about duPont or the marriage. If Florence's parents were spiriting her away to Taunton to keep her from a man, he may well have been her husband, and she was older than her teens. A divorce also would not have been out of the question. Alternatively, she may have been widowed and seeking an environment in which to recover from her grief. When she married Daniel in September 1854, she was around thirty years of age, while Daniel was twenty-five.[6]

Leaving a grandchild ignorant about the previous marriage of a grandparent would have been consistent with the day's social conventions. Florence nevertheless frankly acknowledged that she had had a love interest before Daniel. According to Douglas, her grandmother often longed for the taller and more handsome man she had once loved. Florence was an attractive woman, with high cheekbones, well-formed eyebrows, and a soft smile that gave her an alluring vivacity. She was "dramatic, voluble, fascinating" and perhaps a tad flirtatious. Daniel, by contrast, was introverted and hardly taller than she, apparently unlike the previous man in her life in many exciting ways. Contrasts though may have been an attraction, and Daniel had his own qualities. His granddaughter remembered deep blue eyes, a "melodious" speaking voice—both traits of Trefethen men—and "beautiful teeth."[7]

His character, the true measure of a man in Daniel's belief, ensured steady companionship and a stable home life. Daniel did not shirk community responsibilities, serving for a time on the Taunton board of aldermen as a "rock-ribbed Republican." More important than public service was family. The foundry provided a stable means of support, but for all Daniel's hard work, it never made him rich, a circumstance that lessened Florence's esteem for him. The family lived frugally but without wanting for necessities. Daniel never paid for a shave, insisting that a man should save his money and groom himself. Florence made his shirts from "carefully washed flour sacks, with her delicate precise hand hemming."

If unrelenting thriftiness suggested a struggling existence, it also allowed access to certain middle-class comforts. "Our street had always had the very strong hold of respectable gentility," Douglas reflected after growing up in Taunton. The Trefethens were the first on their street to have an indoor bathroom with running water, a marble basin, and a bathtub. Daniel also paid for music lessons and instruments, including a piano, for the couple's three girls and two boys born over an eleven-year span.[8]

Florence assumed primary responsibility for raising the girls, exuberant and chirpy, and Daniel the boys, pensive and quiet. The middle daughter was Lillian, Marjory's mother. She was born Florence Lillian in 1859. Along with her siblings, she had musical talent. On occasion, she displayed her perfect pitch, setting up glasses on the dining table and tapping out a tune for family and guests. Although she could play any stringed instrument, her favorite was the violin. Problems with one of her eyes abbreviated regular schooling, and her parents sent her to study music under Julius Eichberg, a German-born composer and founder of the Boston Conservatory of Music. Despite her talent, Lillian was not destined for a musical career but for the traditional role of a woman, which revolved around a man.[9]

The first man at the center of her life was her younger brother, Charles. He possessed his father's mechanical aptitude, although much of his training came not from an apprenticeship but in the classroom. He attended the Massachusetts Institute of Technology but left before completing his degree to take a teaching job at the University of Minnesota. When Charles moved to Minneapolis, Lillian went with him.

One of the first new people they met was Frank Stoneman, a tall, angular man who was outwardly conventional in a way that exemplified the plainspoken vigor of the region. Members of his family had lived in Minneapolis since the Civil War, arriving as part of a migration of Quakers that originated in England and followed the expansion of the American frontier.

Douglas believed that her great-grandfather, Joshua, was the first Stoneman to come to America from a place of limited opportunities for hopeful young men in the south of England. She was off by one generation. Joshua was born in 1772 in Grayson County, Virginia. His father, James, was the true founder of the American line, having sailed from England, near London, to Pennsylvania. He married Sarah Freeman, and the couple migrated to Virginia, as did many Pennsylvania Quakers. The third of their six children, Joshua was born outside the mountain town of Galax. As a young man, he apprenticed with a physician before starting a practice as an itinerant doctor serving the Quaker colonies in southern Virginia and northern North Carolina. His first wife, Elizabeth, gave birth to some fourteen children, the last of whom, Mark Davis Stoneman, born in 1815, became Marjory's grandfather. Elizabeth died four months after he entered the world.[10]

Mark too became a physician, possibly studying with his father, and developed a respectable professional reputation.[11] Aras B. Cox, who as a young man read medicine under Mark Davis Stoneman, remembered him as "an able physician and esteemed friend." Mark made his home near Galax in Blue Ridge country. To the west of town, the earth reared up to fifty-seven hundred feet, making Grayson County the highest point in Virginia. The steep countryside added to the toil of getting crops to market, forcing farmers to cultivate wheat and tobacco and avoid heavier produce such as corn. But the burden was a fair exchange for what the locals perceived as the divine beauty surrounding them in the cool green valleys and in the woodlands that turned to brilliant shades in fall. On the east side of the range, toward Galax, the spring thaw fattened creeks and rivulets draining into the New River, given its name in 1749 by Thomas Jefferson's father. A river that flowed through geological time, it was one of the oldest on the continent, rising from its source in North Carolina and tumbling northward over rocks and past flatlands along an elevation of nearly two thousand feet to what later became West Virginia.[12]

Mark was part of a large Quaker community that extended into North Carolina. His first wife—and first cousin—was from Guilford County, across the border. She died less than two years into the marriage at age twenty from complications related to childbirth. Two years later, in 1843, Mark moved to Indiana. He likely took the popular Magadee route, striking up the Virginia Turnpike to the Ohio River and then heading west to Indiana. He almost certainly went with other Quakers, including his late wife's family, but it appears that no other Stonemans accompanied him. In June, he was received by the Duck Creek Monthly Meeting in Henry County. Three years later, he married Ann Iddings, and in another four he was twice a widower.[13]

Mark was thirty-three years old, the father of at least one child, and he did what he was expected to do—he married again. His new wife was sixteen-year-old Aletha C. White. Over the ensuing twenty years, Aletha bore six children. The first died. In the days before advanced medical science and a full understanding of germs and sanitization, disease and environmental conditions made childhood a perilous time. As a physician, Mark routinely witnessed the beginning and end of life; it was a routine common to his personal experience, too. Nine of his whole and half siblings died at birth or in childhood, two of his wives failed to live to age thirty, and he lost at least four of his children.[14]

Migration was another of life's conventions for Mark and for Friends generally. The Ohio River Valley had been a veritable magnet for Quakers since the passage of the Northwest Ordinance in 1787. The families of Mark's three wives migrated from Pennsylvania to North Carolina and then to Indiana, situating themselves in the same general area. Migrating Quakers from Virginia tended to settle in Ohio, while those from North Carolina clustered in Indiana. By the second quarter of the nineteenth century, Quaker colonies had formed in several of the counties around Indianapolis. By one estimate, one-third of Indiana's 1850 population—more than three hundred family names—had roots in North Carolina.[15]

Like other American pioneers drawn to new lands, Quakers moved in the great chase for fresh soil and opportunities. Indiana's rolling land was less rugged than that in the New River Valley and consequently was easier to reshape by hand, tool, and beast for cultivating wheat and corn. Still, the migrants from the Southeast found in this part of the West more that was familiar than not. The annual rainfall and the length of the growing season were similar, and the trees—sycamore, pin oak, juniper, bald cypress, and bigtooth aspen—were reminders of those they had cleared in the South. With few exceptions, settlers in Indiana even plowed under the same varieties of grasses—bluestem, brome, and dropseed.

Mark and Aletha Stoneman bought property and made a home in Washington, a township founded by North Carolina Quakers in the 1830s. The migrants then cleared trees for houses and fields, organized monthly meetings, built schools, and opened a post office and general stores. Mark continued his medical practice, traveling from township to homestead to township, his horse following the cut of narrow roads that had originated as traces blazed by hunters. These rural pathways led to rural places, where people lived spread about and worked the land.[16]

Mark's Quaker patients were as engaged in the market economy as were non-Quaker farmers, but many Friends in America had taken lessons about husbandry from the Indian relationship with nature. During the quietist period of the early eighteenth century, Quakers turned closer to God by putting aside worldly desire and personal pride in favor of self-restraint. The refined Quaker dictates rejected the hierarchy of humans over other humans, whether whites over enslaved blacks or men over women. Complete humility required the humbling of oneself to the land as well as to all that walked and lived on it. Seeking harmony with God's whole creation pointed the way toward earthly grace. The earth belonged not to humans but to God, and those who sowed the soil were to serve as the earth's stewards. No one embodied this triangular spirit more than Pennsylvanian Anthony Benezet. In the mid–eighteenth century, he provided fuel for the Quaker abolitionist fire, using his platform as a teacher and writer to condemn acts of racial and social injustice. He was equally adamant that the human domination of nature amounted to a sinful act. Benezet adhered so closely to the belief of all living things as divine that he could not bring himself to squish the life out of a bug. "He who made us," the otherwise doughty Quaker preached, "made the bird and the fish . . . and loves to do them good."[17]

In this ethic, Douglas would have discovered a human-nature relationship of considerable appeal. But she never showed an awareness of this side of Quaker life. Being duty bound to nature's stewardship was not necessarily an article of faith for all Friends. In the experiences of her Stoneman ancestors and so many of their neighbors, nature's presence was unmitigated, and it was probably less a welcome companion than an intrusion or annoyance. The natural conditions of the frontier confounded American settlers, and they therefore changed it, sometimes ruthlessly and always dramatically and with little awareness of environmental consequences. Douglas's writings give no indication of whether the Stonemans were more American or Quaker in their relationship with the natural world. Only her father seems to have left her with ideas about thoughtful land use, but such ideas were based primarily on economic pragmatism and common sense rather than a particular land ethic. The pattern of going westward and converting the frontier was part of Frank's makeup. He was born on one frontier, and he lived on two others. Economic and social imperatives more than the allure of a landscape prompted each change of venue.

Because of whom they brought and what they found, Quakers recreated old ecological and familial environments in Indiana. They did not encounter or reconstruct the same political environment that had existed in the East, however. The distinguishing element left behind in the old system and unwelcome in the new, and increasingly a wedge dividing the country, was slavery. The Quakers' stand against slavery most affected Douglas's social sensibilities.

For Quakers of the East, slave society reinforced the westward pull of economic opportunity and independence. According to abolitionist Addison Coffin, "If the question is asked, Why did Friends emigrate from North Carolina? It can be answered with one dark, fearful word SLAVERY, than which a darker is not known." Quakers came to the cause of abolition gradually. By the end of the eighteenth century, a growing number had begun to believe that being a part of the system of slavery, whether by holding other humans in bondage or by acquiescing to the practice, corrupted the humanist values that "made Quakerism a distinctive faith." Although the issue divided meetings around the country, the Society of Friends contributed a considerable share of the people engaged in the abolitionist movement. Thousands of Quakers left the South. Some had

prospered, even owned slaves, but they had received the abolitionists'
moral message, and fear of the "ruin of their posterity" trumped material temptation.[18]

As Douglas understood, the desire to avoid raising children in a slave
state was the primary impetus for her grandfather's decision to abandon
a successful medical practice for a uncertain future in Indiana. She took
great pride in the resolve of her ancestors, showing a particular affinity for Levi Coffin. The reputed president of the Underground Railroad
who sheltered as many as two thousand runaway slaves was Douglas's
great-great-uncle by marriage, the husband of Mark's third wife's aunt.
Douglas's debt to Coffin is unmistakable. She wrote an unpublished
story commemorating his antislavery pursuits, and in her autobiography she embraced him as a "great inspiration to me as a free thinker and
activist."[19]

But she did not have to look so far out to a grafted branch of the family tree to find a role model of similar measure. Coffin was joined in his
efforts by approximately two thousand fellow Indiana Quakers, including Mark's in-laws, the Whites. Beyond offering their blessing, there is no
evidence that Mark and Aletha gave active assistance to the movement.
But Aletha's siblings and parents made enough of a name for themselves
to be remembered in state and local history books. Only one-tenth of the
state's Friends were activists, but their initiatives gave a strong boost to
the cause. The Whites and others chanced arrest and confrontation with
slave hunters for violating the federal Fugitive Slave Act, doing so in a
state where the white majority preferred to restrict the number and opportunities of free blacks.[20]

There is no uncertainty about the considerable risk Mark's mother-
in-law, Lovica White, took.[21] She owned an inn in the Quaker township
of Westfield and operated it as a station on the central route of the Underground Railroad. On one occasion, conductors brought a female runaway
to Westfield, only to have the security of White's inn compromised when
two slave hunters stopped to take lodging. They were without suspicion,
but they had been tracking the woman, and their presence alone portended danger. Wanting to get her to safety, White dressed the woman

in the soft linen of a free person, concealed her hair and dark skin with a bonnet and veil, and conducted her past the slavers sitting in the parlor and along to the house of White's oldest son.[22]

Such actions secured Quakers a place in the fellowship of American social reformers. Abolitionism was only the beginning. Quakerism, in both its spiritual and cultural dimensions, supported work in woman suffrage, immigrant aid, child welfare, education reform, peace movements, and social justice. Douglas took notice. As an agnostic, she could not share in the Friends' obedience to a god whose light shone equally on all. But she recognized an intellectual dimension that advanced her secular humanist beliefs. Quaker abolitionists were voracious readers and well-informed people, she often said, and they approached their cause against slavery with great deliberation. She identified with what she called the Quakers' "stiff-backed breed." Of the various religious groups that came to America, she insisted, none was more fiercely independent and stubborn than Quakers. Although in some people these could be ugly qualities, in Quakers they fortified altruist behavior.[23]

The Quaker closest to her was her father. The third child of Mark and Aletha, Frank Stoneman was born into a free society, as his father had wished, on June 26, 1857. Douglas said her father was raised in the Quaker township of Spiceland in Henry County, Indiana. But Mark and Aletha were married two counties away in Hamilton and the township of Washington, and available evidence indicates that they lived there until they moved to Minneapolis.

At the time of Frank's birth, the sectional conflict was testing Quakers' ardent pacifism. The ancestors of many Indiana Friends had taken up arms in North Carolina and Virginia during the American Revolution. These so-called Fighting Quakers became legendary among Friends, who looked back on this reference during each succeeding conflict. Many Indiana Quakers justified voluntary military enlistment in the effort to destroy the tyranny of human bondage, an end just as virtuous as defeating the tyranny of the British monarchy. Despite the righteousness of the Union cause, many people must have struggled with the decision to fight.

The distance between a doctrine-quoting pacifist and an armed warrior was vast, and only a minority of men ultimately joined the fight. Quaker periodicals and yearly meetings continued to emphasize nonviolence as the virtuous path to salvation. Even the passionate Coffin refused to stray from doctrine, although he finessed the matter by allowing his home to become an assembly place for volunteers ready to enlist.[24]

One can only guess whether Mark struggled with his conscience. The day after Indiana's governor called on the men of his state to volunteer their services, Hamilton County sent its first company to camp under the command of Captain John D. Edwards, an abolitionist and a Quaker. Mark's brother-in-law and friend, Mordecai White, joined Indiana's 147th Regiment and was promoted to sergeant. At forty-three, Mark was twelve years older than White, not of good age for the physical demands of regiment life. Yet off to war he went, not to fight but to serve as a military surgeon. At Shiloh, however, where the Confederates took on the enemy with sixty-two cannons, he was wounded.[25]

Removed from the theater of action, he was transferred to Fort Snelling at St. Anthony, Minnesota. In the winter, the sun retreated far to the distant south and the arctic winds blew hard and brutal, but he liked what he saw. The diamond-shaped fortress of limestone rock, completed in 1825 to prevent Indians from trading furs with the British, overlooked the Mississippi and Minnesota Rivers. The prairie around the fort opened out to wooded wilderness, where remnants of the Dakota dwelled. Having recently gained statehood, Minnesota supported a scant population of 172,000, smaller than the number of residents in Indiana when Mark moved there and where 1.5 million people now lived. At Fort Snelling, he was back on the frontier. Yet across the Mississippi and downstream a bit was Minneapolis, a city of energy and promise.[26]

After his release from military service, Mark returned to Indiana and discussed with his family the prospects of living in Minnesota. In the spring of 1863, he and Aletha left Hamilton County with their three children and Mark's daughter by his second wife. Mordecai came, too, with his mother, Lovica, now sixty-five and a widow. In Indiana, the family had lived on a plot of land denoted by survey measurements of rods and quarters. In the St. Anthony district of Minneapolis, Mark bought a home on a numbered street and worked from an office on Central Avenue. He identified himself as a dental surgeon. Aletha bore two more children.[27]

Although Minneapolis had a Quaker community, the Stonemans did not belong to meeting. Even so, as Douglas put it, Frank had a "strict tradition to guide him, the tradition of 'Yea and nay,' the tradition of plain living and clear and independent thinking." Frank was a tall, lanky boy with hazel brown eyes, sandy-colored hair, big ears, and a Roman nose inherited from his father. He was precise in speech, manner, and dress, and, like his mother, his face invariably wore a serious look and his gaze remained direct, features that belied an unfailing politeness. The woodlands and the rivers and streams lured him and his older brother, Orville, into spending much of their leisure time hunting and fishing. More outgoing than Frank and unmindful of Quaker teachings of pacifism, Orville was perpetually getting himself into brawls with other boys. Frank sometimes came to his aid, although he was more disposed to reading than to fighting. His bookish ways earned him the nickname Ben, for Benjamin Franklin. He read the *Iliad* and the *Odyssey,* Josephus, *The Prince of the House of David, Incidents of the French Revolution,* and *The Report of the English Commission on the White Slaves of England.*[28]

Although Frank failed to stand out in school, he entered the University of Minnesota sometime before he was seventeen.[29] Unlike the institutions of higher education in the East, those in the West were coeducational, and Frank's fifteen-year-old sister, Kate, attended the university as well. Orville too gave college a try, but neither he nor Frank completed a term. In September 1874, Frank took the train sixty miles south to Northfield and enrolled in the second class of the Preparatory Department at Carleton College, a Lutheran-affiliated liberal arts school. He was one of eighty-two students, including twenty-nine young women, honing their skills to qualify for college-level work. Frank's overall performance was slightly above average; he received his lowest marks in ancient languages and his highest in deportment.[30]

Douglas said that the religious zealotry on campus encouraged Frank to leave Carleton after the winter term. But in a story common at a time when living conditions—from underdeveloped medical science to dangerous workplace conditions to unsanitary cities—kept the average individual's tenure on earth short, Frank seems to have terminated his studies primarily to go to work to help the family. His father died in 1875 at age fifty-three, changing the family's prospects. Frank never returned to school, and his daughter said that his lack of a degree made him feel inadequate. He read so voraciously and extensively that, she offered in his defense, he was nevertheless "as scholarly a man as I've ever known."[31]

Frank was also industrious. Before and after Carleton, he was employed for a few years as a pressman for a printer and binder. He then moved on to take a similar position with a weekly newspaper, the *Citizen*. Setting type became second nature, and for the rest of his life, the visual memory of his hands in motion helped him remember difficult word spellings. Although he did not stay with this trade, the experience left him with a self-assurance that helped ready him to go into the newspaper business more than twenty years later in Florida. By 1878, Frank had begun working as a grocery clerk, a job he held until the mid-1880s while living at home with his mother and younger siblings. For extra money, he and the rest of the family spent their evenings cutting cabbage for sauerkraut. Douglas said that her father also taught school in a Swedish-immigrant community. Frank's oldest sister, Kate, taught school as well, and his youngest sister, Stella, eventually entered the profession.[32]

By 1884 or so, Frank had grown restless, wanting to become something more than a grocery clerk in a midwestern city. His employer, Luther Johnson, agreed to set up his son, Fred, and Frank in the grocery business in Billings, Montana. The two rode the Northern Pacific Railroad across the Dakota Territory and on to Montana, where the track ghosted the Yellowstone River. The territory they saw from their windows, starkly beautiful open range and sheer mountains, had once belonged to the Sioux, Cheyenne, Crow, and Blackfeet. Railroads, like the one that took the two young Minnesotans to Montana, conveyed and symbolized white America's manifest destiny and both human and non-human native America's demise.[33]

Stoneman and Johnson were foot soldiers in continental expansion, and in their own small manner they brought civilizing ways to the unfettered western landscape. They opened their store, the first in Billings by Douglas's calculation, on a dusty street. They sold staples and supplies to cowboys, mountain men, immigrant pioneers, copper miners, and Indians resigned to living with the influx of newcomers. Frank took time to explore the South Dakota Badlands and, lacking a Quaker veneration of nature, hunted some of the last bison on the prairie. In Billings, he joined the Masons, becoming a member of one of those civic/social organizations that were part of the institutional fostering of American civilization.[34]

He and Fred lived at the back of the store, where after hours they talked about the day's receipts, the inventory on the shelves, and their dream of great profits. On many nights, Frank played checkers with a variety of local characters who had their own reasons for being in Billings. One was a retired artillery officer, a genuine Indian fighter with a bit of bluster in him whom people called Bean Belly Brown. Frank was no match for him at the checkerboard, and time and again the old man ventured, "Well, Stoneman, I admire your courage but damn your judgment." Frank took those words as an admonition for life — courage without judgment was not enough. They also summed up his experience in Montana. He might have become a permanent settler of the West had its promises come through for him. Despite his and Fred's initiative, the store failed. As Douglas put it, the initial economic boom in the Northwest petered out. The store's closing marked the beginning of a succession of disappointing ventures that would plague Frank until he moved to Miami. Over and over again, his judgment, or at least his timing, proved wrong.[35]

The defeated Frank returned to Minneapolis and moved back in with his mother. Before Frank left for Montana, his older brother, Orville, had gone into the real estate and loan business, and he offered his prodigal brother a position in his firm. Orville lived in his own house and served on the city's board of aldermen, and in 1889, he had one of the city's few residential telephones, an accouterment of economic status. Orville had accomplished what Frank had not. Frank may have been too much the intellectual with too "subtle a personality"—a go-getter but not a glad-hander—to achieve early success like his brother. Frank joined the Episcopal Church rather than the Quaker meeting when he was eighteen, but he always retained "that Quaker touch," remembered Douglas, the "plainness of speech, his hatred of profanity and gaudy statements, his unpretentiousness, even his grey suits." He remained tangled in his Quaker roots at the same time that he reached for the gritty, somewhat fashionable life of enterprise and entrepreneurship of the Gilded Age and Progressive Era, when technology, development, investments, and cities increasingly eclipsed land as the source of moneymaking opportunities, when personality was nearly as important as a strong work ethic. Frank occupied a sometimes punishing place in life, suspended somewhere between a reserved tradition and bourgeois seductions, with only nebulous road markers to happiness.[36]

He nevertheless remained a persistent competitor in the race for middle-class stability, if such a condition existed. Social status increasingly became tied to an expanding and always unpredictable market economy, and few people knew that better than Frank. He worked with Orville for a year or so before landing a job as manager of the loan department at the American Building and Loan Association. It was not the same as being self-employed, but it was a respectable position with one of the most recognized firms in Minneapolis. His office was downtown in the Bank of Commerce Building, where the busy hallways, lobby, and sidewalks outside transported the staccato sounds of business and commerce in action.[37]

Minneapolis was also bustling with recent arrivals, bringing new people within Frank's orbit. He and his youngest brother, Edward, had moved out of their mother's home and were living at a boardinghouse when another resident, a diminutive New Englander with a boyish face, introduced himself and his sister as Charles and Lillian Trefethen.

CHAPTER FOUR

Mr. Smith's "Reconnoissance"

The New York City police officer did not know the man who passed out in the cold street one January day in 1871. He carried no identification, or someone had stolen it. As far as the officer was concerned, the man was just another street drunk, another reason for the pious temperance folks to continue their crusade against demon drink. The man was different from most drunks, though. He was well dressed and clean shaven, a man of apparent means. Still, the officer locked the man in a cell to sleep it off before seeing the judge. But the man did not regain consciousness, so he was moved to Bellevue Hospital. Doctors there determined that he had collapsed not from too much drink but with a bad heart, and there in the hospital he died. But the hospital staff also could not identify the man, and they sent his body to the city morgue. The staff there had no choice but to prepare the body for interment with those of the other street derelicts in Potter's Field in the Bronx. Then at the last minute, someone looking for a missing friend identified the body as that of sixty-year-old Thomas Buckingham Smith, a resident of New York City and St. Augustine, Florida.[1]

In that instant, the derelict became a gentleman. He was a graduate of Cambridge law school at Harvard College, a past member of the Florida territorial legislature and secretary to the territorial governor, a former U.S. legation secretary in Mexico and Spain, a distinguished historian of Spanish explorations, and a founder of the Historical Society of Florida. A widower, he had lived with his mother until she died. They had been slave owners in St. Augustine but then sided with the North and President Abraham Lincoln during the Civil War. When Smith's executors located his will, lost for a period, like his identity, they discovered that he had left a life interest in land to one of his former slaves and one hundred dollars to each of three other former bondspersons. The remainder of his real property was to be used to set up a charitable organization for St. Augustine's aged and invalid blacks. Two years after his death the Buckingham Smith Benevolent Association was founded, and by the middle of the twentieth century it had become one of the wealthiest charities in St. Johns County.[2]

Even more abiding than Smith's charity was the policy he had shaped for Everglades drainage. In addition to his other public service, the man who nearly went to his grave anonymously had in 1847 been appointed to execute the U.S. government's first survey to ascertain the practicability and expediency of reclaiming the Everglades. He had no outstanding qualifications for the project. His background was in law and history, and he could claim no expeditionary experience. But he apparently wanted the appointment, and he had the political connections to get it.[3]

Under the commission of U.S. Secretary of the Treasury Robert J. Walker, Smith embarked on his Everglades "reconnoissance," as he called it, exactly one hundred years before the release of Douglas's *River of Grass*. He sailed to Fort Dallas, a military outpost on Biscayne Bay established during the final Seminole War, assembled a crew of men and boats, and headed up the Miami River, where only Indians and Indian fighters had previously traveled, into open country. America's great wetland offered him no visceral compensation for the drudgery of swamp exploration. Born on Cumberland Island, Georgia, Smith lived in St. Augustine for a time before moving with his sister and widowed mother to Taunton,

Massachusetts. The reedy saltwater marshes on the Georgia and north-eastern Florida seacoast, teeming with shore and wading birds, resembled the sawgrass landscape of South Florida. Yet unlike the seemingly infinite Everglades, the coastal marshes merely accented heavily forested terra firma in one direction and bays, bayous, and inlets commingling with the Atlantic Ocean in the other. For centuries, the serene beauty of this blended landscape—in particular, the extraordinary live oaks with their ample buntings of Spanish moss—excited rhapsodic commentary from travelers. This was Smith's bailiwick, and it was not the same as the Everglades. Having read the eighteenth-century journal of William Bartram, the Quaker naturalist whom the Seminoles called Flower Hunter and whose depictions of North Florida reemerged in the works of latter-day poets, including Coleridge and Wordsworth, Smith acknowledged that a romanticist mind would likely discover something "poetic" in the Everglades that "indulges his fancies." Although bookish himself, Smith had no time for such effete intellectuals. He was interested in men "of practical, *utilitarian* turn of thought," who, he said, would be struck by the Everglades' "*utter worthlessness*" to civilized society. They were suitable only for the "haunt of noxious vermin; or the resort of pestilent reptiles." Opinion of the day hardly disagreed with him. Two years earlier, Florida's first state legislature had proclaimed the Everglades "wholly valueless."[4]

But they were not beyond redemption. Smith was convinced that the swamp could be "rendered healthy" and civilized, much like other "insalubrious" places "in southern latitudes." Two years before Smith's expedition, magazine editor John Louis O'Sullivan gave the label "manifest destiny" to the spirit of western migration. The term validated, in the name of civilization, America's expanding empire and ultimately the despoliation of new lands. In Smith's opinion, the "march of civilization" should turn toward Florida. His report evidences an intense faith in his culture's superiority to both nature and other cultures. Smith reminded his solicitors that the trans-Mississippi West had once been regarded as "irreclaimable" and fit for only bison and "savages." South Florida may have lacked the grand stretches of the West, but in Smith's mind it possessed unique potential as an agricultural region.[5]

By the time of the U.S. territorial period, Florida's agricultural economy had hardly begun to turn the corner to profitability. Its soil had two
extremes, sandy and swampy. Rooting white culture in it, turning wealth
out of it, had been difficult since the time of the Spanish. But something
in the human spirit kept directing the ambitious to Florida, and statehood in 1845 and the relocation of all but a few Seminoles brought a new
round of possibilities to the attention of the nation. Like the unsettled
West, Florida represented regeneration and independent living for urban
dwellers in the overcrowded North and farmers on worn-out land in the
East. Competing directly with the western states and territories, Florida's promoters used advertisements, publicity schemes, and land deals
to create a propaganda dike that would divert a stream of the transcontinental migration to the peninsula.[6]

People in the business of agriculture knew that the most productive
agricultural soil was found in bottomlands, where the earth was renour-
ished by the seasonal flooding of rivers or streams. By extension, Florida's agricultural promoters believed that soil that had been fermenting
for eons beneath the nation's largest wetland would be unsurpassed. One
of Douglas's literary characters expressed the prevailing mood: "They
ain't rich land like this nowhere. Old sea bottom, rotted rich way down.
Why you could spread this soil for fertilizer."[7] Still, the soil was mere an-
aerobic muck until it was drained and worked. Only then could it release
its nutrients to cash crops and deliver promised economic benefits. That
potential would have been lost if idealists such as Smith, steeped in the
commercial ethos of nineteenth-century America, had not looked out
over the sawgrass and imagined a land of profit making, just as Americans were doing on the Great Plains of the marvelous West. And Florida's heavy annual rainfall foretold a more promising Arcadia than the
dry trans-Mississippi. Turning the sodden Everglades wilderness into
a fruitful Eden would require more effort at greater expense than did
plowing under the West's indigenous grasses, but Florida had the advantage of already being a state—and a slave state at that. Unlike the western
territories, it would not become a lightning rod in the brewing national
conflict.

The chief political force behind Everglades development, Senator James D. Westcott, surely knew of Florida's advantageous situation. If not for his efforts, the Smith expedition might not have happened. Westcott had joined other ambitious migrants in relocating from New Jersey soon after Spain ceded its parasitic possessions—West Florida and East Florida—to the United States. A Jacksonian Democrat who had once dueled with a fellow member of the territorial council, Westcott professed that his sympathies lay with independent, white yeoman farmers. To that end, he gave his blessing to the government's campaigns against the Seminoles and worked to seek official corroboration for the popular conviction that the Everglades could be cheaply drained. At Westcott's request, Secretary Walker commissioned Smith to undertake his exploration.[8]

Smith did not disappoint. The right initiative, Smith maintained in his report, would bring South Florida drier prospects in the near future. Drainage not only was practicable but could be accomplished with modest resources and with a handsome return on investment. Such conclusions relied heavily on correspondence between Smith and military officers who had fought Indians in the region and had been the first white men to experience the raw physicality of the Everglades. Appended to Smith's report, their letters suggest that memories of the keenly agonizing realities of the swamp had given way to new perspectives, the most common of which was the idea that reclamation could be accomplished with reasonable effort. Basing his findings largely on this testimony, Smith calculated that drainage would yield one million arable acres, and he considered his estimate that the job could be completed for five hundred thousand dollars generous and "beyond question." Congress, though, need not worry about even that modest cost; Smith maintained that the money would be recouped in the appreciated value of reclaimed land alone. Infinite profit making would then begin with the first harvest of commercial crops. Noting incorrectly that the Everglades lay "entirely below the region of frost," Smith spoke of a great tropical agricultural empire that could supply the nation with "valuable productions," such as sugarcane, coffee, and a variety of fruits. He then dangled the carrot of American self-reliance: domestic production would reduce the dependence on imported products from European-controlled lands.[9]

Based on Smith's findings, the Senate Committee on Public Lands recommended that Congress pass legislation to proceed toward the twin goals of drainage and cultivation. As an apparent added inducement, the committee echoed the sixteenth-century hope of Spanish conquistador Pedro Menendez de Aviles by proposing that drainage canals could also serve as a cross-Florida shipping passage. The South's leading business journal, J. D. B. DeBow's *Commercial Review,* calculated that each year the storm-haunted Florida Straits sent a million dollars in cargo to the ocean floor.[10]

Amid the assurances and positive predictions, no one seemed to notice or to care that Smith's "reconnoissance" had been anything but a reconnaissance. His expedition was cut short when it was "frightened back" by seemingly impassable sawgrass, the same fate that would befall military soldiers pursuing the last intrepid Seminoles a few years later. From a scientific and engineering standpoint, his report is amateurish and impressionistic, a convenient truth to please prodrainage interests. Douglas, who admired Smith as the first historian of Florida and later wrote a preface for a reprint of one of his most important Spanish translations, described the report as "magnificently written" as a political document but sadly flawed from a factual perspective. To Smith's credit, he restrained from portraying himself as a scientist or engineer, but this willingness to humble himself must have lent a degree of credibility to his report's findings. What gave them unusual force was their affirmation of prodrainage claims about gravity, water flow, and arable muck soil. Thirty years later, John Wesley Powell's *Report on the Lands of the Arid Region of the United States* argued against the accepted gospel that the western plains could sustain the traditional farming practices of the more humid East. As director of the U.S. Geological Survey, Powell carried indisputable credentials, yet his recommendations were shelved for fifty years. Both Smith's credentials and his optimistic precepts were disputable, yet his report resonated with the expansionist mood in Congress and endured as the foundation for Everglades policy for the next century.[11]

Smith's affirming influence did not stop at the Florida border. Draining swampland was a subject of national debate, especially since most wetlands within the states were controlled by the federal government. In late 1848, Senator Westcott attached Smith's report to a Senate bill mandating that the federal government cede the Everglades to the State of Florida. Westcott's bill failed, but Smith's document provided encouragement for others in and outside Washington. If a government report concluded that a swamp the size of the Everglades could be drained with relative ease, then, by implication, so could wetlands in other states. Handing over those lands would be a judicious nod to state sovereignty and a huge boon to Florida and other eastern states that hoped to stem the tide of western migration. Some of these arguments were floating about when Congress passed the first Swamp Land Act in March 1849. Targeting the terrifically fertile riparian bottomlands in Louisiana, the new law conveyed federal wetlands to the state with the requirement that it finance drainage and levee construction with proceeds from the sale of swampland and then use the expanded real estate tax base to fund education.[12]

Following the Louisiana land grant, Congress considered a more comprehensive bill that put the question of the purpose and meaning of swamps before its members. Most heeded the traditional miasma theory, which portrayed swamps as rotting and putrid environments that breathed noxious gases, themselves the source of yellow fever and malaria outbreaks common in the South. But the benefits of wetlands—siphoning away water to keep other areas dry, recharging groundwater repositories, and providing habitat for wildlife—were also fairly well known at the time. At least one congressman talked about the flood-control properties of wetlands. Still, the image of the fetid swamp was too deep-seated to allow an alternative perception to prevail, and even when natural benefits were acknowledged, the full utilitarian value of nature was assumed lost without human-induced improvements. As Smith put it, "latent and dormant resources" awaited reclamation. Congress ultimately styled its proposed bill with "Swamp Lands" in quotation marks, broadly defined swamps as land "wet and unfit for cultivation," and allowed the states to use their discretion in platting inundated areas.[13]

The law succeeded in September 1850, with Westcott playing no small role in its passage. A windfall to all the states, the Swamp and Overflow Land Grant Act proved a bonanza for the second-wettest state. Florida ultimately acquired more than thirty thousand square miles of federally held lands, more than any other state. Douglas concluded ninety-seven years later that "much Florida history is based" on the 1850 legislation. The law nearly doubled the land mass belonging to the state and opened the way for railroad and agricultural expansion, the spectacular land boom of the early twentieth century, and new private and state drainage projects. All of these developments boded ill for the Everglades, the multi-million-acre grand prize in the congressional giveaway. The gloom of the Civil War and Reconstruction initially delayed reclamation efforts, and, from a practical standpoint, a proper and thorough reconnaissance still needed to be conducted.[14]

After the Civil War, people made a lot of noise about agrarian utopias and the fulfillment of the American experiment in the Great West. The region had achieved mythic status in the popular imagination, and it ultimately welcomed hordes of settlers. The South, meanwhile, struggled to regain its status, lost with the war, as a place of opportunity, and freshly drained real estate helped it to do so. For its part, Florida was beginning to generate excitement as the region's land of enchantment. Minnie Moore-Willson, who moved to Kissimmee from the Midwest in the 1880s with her husband, a real estate developer, compared "Florida's Scenic Wonders," in particular the Everglades, with California's Yosemite Valley, Wyoming's Yellowstone, and Arizona's Grand Canyon. Writing to his son at home in the North a few years earlier, newly transplanted L. D. Huston said of Florida, "So far it is a perfect Eden." A California newspaper tempted readers with correspondence from a Manatee River citrus grower, Samuel C. Upham, who claimed, "The rivers are overflowing with fish, and the forests are overrun with game. . . . The climate is delightful— sort of an earthly Paradise."[15]

Travel writer Edward King was one of the first to evangelize Florida's natural wondrousness and agrarian possibilities, which seemed to go hand in hand. In 1872, he and illustrator James Wells Champney embarked on an excursion of the South underwritten by *Scribner's Monthly,* a new periodical looking for subscribers. Other magazines, including *Harper's* and *Century,* sponsored similar projects, but King and Champney's twenty-five-thousand-mile journey was the most exhaustive. King's hefty report appeared as a series in the magazine, and he later compiled his writings into a book, *The Great South.* King began with the premise that where paradise had been lost to the disruption of war, it could within time be regained through agricultural development. It was an idea best befitting the southernmost state. "The fitness of Florida for the growth of tropical and semi-tropical fruits is astonishing," King wrote. Although travel writers were known for expansive, flourishing prose and King could romance with the best, he soberly and blandly described the potential of citrus agriculture. He explained that ten years of careful planting and cultivating a grove of orange trees almost certainly assured a personal utopia: "income for life." King predicted that with proper infrastructure development—railroad and canal construction—Florida would be supplying the North "with oranges of more delicate texture than any it has yet seen."[16]

In such an atmosphere of enthusiasm for utopian futures, expeditions to the Everglades commenced—no fewer than nine in the late nineteenth and early twentieth centuries. In the midst of these expeditions, the supervisor of the U.S. Census announced that the frontier had closed and with it presumably the days of the explorer. Florida therefore stood as a remnant of a powerful American experience. If the Everglades happened to be good for nothing else, they offered a last opportunity for men with a wistful hunger to be explorers without the burden of traveling abroad— "puny adventurers," as Jack London might have called them, "bent on colossal adventure." Everglades exploration in fact acquired the patina of swashbuckling romanticism. Alonzo Church, who joined one of the first exploring parties, described the Everglades as "endowed with that glamour that unexplored regions shroud themselves in and which to an ardent fancy have all the attractions that the imagination can bring forth." Hugh L. Willoughby, whom Douglas called an "adventurous gentleman," compared his 1897 Everglades crossing with blazing the Amazonian wilderness. William Krome, who never quite outgrew his preadolescent fascination with the knighted Henry M. Stanley, accepted an Everglades surveying expedition as a reputable substitute for plunging into the African wilds.[17]

All of these men had come of age in an era in which the likes of Theodore Roosevelt, an explorer in his own right, and newspaper editor Horace Greeley encouraged young men to develop their mettle on the rugged borderlands of the American continent. In the absence of war, the traditional proving ground of nations and men, the physical and mental challenges encountered in a wilderness allowed the demonstration of manhood. "If a man is a dude," Church concluded, "a trip through the 'Glades is the thing to cure him."[18]

The unchallenged fact that only Indians had traversed the hazardous terrain gave greater legitimacy to the Everglades as a proving ground for Anglo manhood. In the words of the *New Orleans Times-Democrat,* which sponsored two expeditions, this "region hitherto concealed from the white man" was as mysterious as the "center of 'the dark continent.'" Church got a sobering reply when he asked an Indian woman how long it would take to cross the Everglades to Miami: "Indian two days, white man ten, fifteen days." A similar exchange later showed up in Douglas's final *Saturday Evening Post* story between a Seminole woman and the young white protagonist, Harvey, who rises to the occasion when a man who is to lead him across proves ill suited to the task. The woman's observation underscored the desperate feat for those who would be admired for accomplishing it. Whites regarded Indians as inferior beings but superior wilderness travelers, and to succeed at what only they could do enhanced a white man's and an expedition's reputation.[19]

The Seminole woman knew that the gravest challenge facing the white men was the muck and sawgrass that for generations had protected her people from outsiders. The "wide brown mud-and-grass-and-water world" that the fictional Harvey and his companion entered was all too real for expedition parties. As the "sawgrass closed in about them," Harvey set a "flaming match to it." After the smoke cleared, the "ground underfoot was black and still smoking, but it was easier to get ahead, except for the low places, where he sank again to his hips and had to go on with that extraordinary tiring process, drawing out one leg, thrusting it hip-high and forward as far as he could, stepping on it, and so down and down into the oozing, bottomless muck."[20]

Both Douglas's fiction and her nonfiction profited from the notebooks of Archie Williams, who led the two *Times-Democrat* expeditions, and James Ingraham, who commanded Church's group. The Ingraham expedition's west-east ford was so grueling that, by Church's estimation, "many a man in our party wished he had swapped his valor for . . . discretion." Traveling southward from Lake Okeechobee into the heart and heat of the Everglades, Williams's group at first made an easy passage, floating through the cooling shade of the custard apple swamp. Soon enough, however, the vessels that conveyed them and their supplies became their burdens. The party's dozen men struggled to push five canoes and two provision bateaux through muck and mosquitoes underneath an unmitigated sun—and then they encountered the sawgrass. With no other humans or wildlife in sight and no sounds other than those of their making, the men were entombed in what Williams described as a stony "death-like stillness." For twelve days, the sawgrass held them hostage. Covering a single miserable mile required a whole day of steady toil. The sawgrass shredded the hull of one of the bateaux, forcing the party to abandon the boat and some of the provisions. The men cooked in the canoes and lived off rations that were running short, and at "night they slept cuddled up in the boats the victims of millions of mosquitoes." The situation had grown desperate, the men pressed fatally close to submission, when the ordeal ended as suddenly as it had begun. The bedraggled explorers found their exit at the head of Shark River Slough and in comparatively short order sailed south to White Water Bay, the gulf, and sweet civilization.[21]

Sawgrass could sometimes be avoided, but other hazards could not. Ingraham's party was told by a local that they were about to enter an implausible domain of "mosquitoes, red bugs, alligator fleas, *wampee,* and a thousand other horrors, known and unknown." Of the known horrors, none was more insufferable and ubiquitous than mosquitoes, "one of the most serious obstacles," Krome admitted. Each member of an exploring party slept under a cheesecloth bar, or netting, their only armor against the ravenous insects. In the daytime, when the temperature topped sixty degrees, the air thickened with insects. The adventurers' worries also included alligators and snakes. "I was glad that the moccasin that I stepped on turned out to be a bullfrog," wrote A. W. Dimock, who explored the Everglades in 1907.[22]

When confronting such threats, explorers were not generally as passive as Dimock's remarks suggest. Men armed themselves heavily against dangerous wildlife and carried with them an attitude of total conquest. Expedition leaders often took military titles, such as captain or major, officially acquired or not. In battle, men followed rules of war, but when the enemy was nature, no rules applied. Expedition parties conveyed the instruments required to conduct geodetic surveys, which employed the stars to give peaceful definition to the amorphous swamp. Yet survival was the most important outcome for the men, and for that they provisioned themselves with knives, machetes, and firearms. While a kill-or-be-killed psychology was inevitable under these circumstances, the explorers took the notion to a cold-blooded extreme. Like Cub Scouts gathered around a campfire telling stories to frighten themselves, party members shared morbid tales about a beast that dragged off one of their kind into the dark night, coloring their wild surroundings with evil. Nothing was sacred; nothing was to be protected or conserved. They killed for food and to protect themselves, but mostly they preyed on wildlife for the excitement of taking a life or to practice their aim. Anything wild was fair target for the impulse to shoot, burn, hack, or otherwise destroy. At one point in their journey, the men aboard one of the *Times-Democrat* boats complained that the lead boat had left them only with dead alligators to shoot.[23]

Yet despite the aura of evil and potential death, the Everglades managed to hold a few white intruders in pleasant awe. They had entered the wilderness with that cold, hard bias Americans held against wetlands, unprepared to be enchanted and surprised. One early explorer referred to the Everglades as a "Delightful Country." Dimock said that no description "can possibly convey any true idea of their beauty and their charm." A

Florida publication that supported ongoing reclamation efforts conceded that the Everglades offered one of the few remaining spots in the country "where one can be alone amid the beatitudes of nature." Even the water was a surprise—rather than a dark and motionless "vast morass," it was "limpid," "pure," and "flowing." After a difficult trek across the southern portion of the Everglades, Willoughby related a remarkable discovery: "The popular impression has always been that the Everglades is a huge swamp, full of malaria and disease germs. There was certainly nothing in our surroundings that would remind one of a swamp. Around the shores of the little islands the mud may be a trifle soft, but pure water is running over it, and no stagnant pools can be found."[24]

The early explorers clearly recognized the Everglades as a body of flowing water. Their records, which Douglas read when preparing *River of Grass,* may well have planted the seed for her deductions. Willoughby, for example, wrote that he endeavored to show in the account of his expeditions "that the word swamp, as we understand it, has no application whatever to the Everglades; that it is a country of pure water; that this water is moving in one direction or the other, depending on the natural topography of the country."[25]

At the time Willoughby was writing, however, Americans were not ready for a radical rethinking of the Everglades. Even if they were scenically arresting, there was nothing soft about a direct encounter with them. Nor was there anything soft about the determination to tame them. Douglas identified the era of exploration and conquest as "white man's return." The expeditions were not organized merely to affirm white American manhood; they were motivated by the conventional predilection to develop uncharted land. A character in one of her short stories expressed the matter succinctly: "Don't you see, it's not just the last frontier. It's the very end of the limit of speculation." The Ingraham/Church party was sent out to survey a potential train route for Florida railroad pioneer Henry Plant. "Should our expedition be successful," said Church, "it may result in good to the whole country, for if this land can be rendered fit for cultivation it will be the most productive of any in this state." Krome was part of a similar delegation for Plant's fellow mogul, Henry

Flagler, who considered the possibility of directing the Florida East Coast Railway from Homestead to Cape Sable and then across Florida Bay and the Florida Keys. Before organizing its two expeditions, the *Times-Democrat* thought that the Everglades were a "territory which will soon be thrown open to settlement and cultivation."[26]

The expeditions ultimately were intended to verify what a coldly confident Buckingham Smith had surmised decades earlier: the Everglades could be cheaply drained. The leader of the *Times-Democrat* parties, Williams, initially confirmed the newspaper's prediction about South Florida's great commercial potential. The "richness of the soil" in the Everglades had no equal "within the boundary of the United States." That appraisal followed the first expedition, which merely skirted the fringe of the northwestern part of the Everglades, where farming had already begun. After entering the belly of the swamp on the second expedition, his optimism evaporated. His new report lacked the celebratory zeal of the first; it told a dramatic tale, but its tone was now grave and blunt, undoubtedly irking state officials and investors who pined for the future development of the region. The Everglades lacked potential beyond a "vast and useless marsh," Williams concluded, following with his bombshell: drainage "is utterly impracticable." Even running a telegraph line through the Everglades seemed unrealistic. His newspaper sponsor, once an enthusiastic champion of Everglades conquest, no longer wanted to be an accomplice to the grand folly, lamenting that the "world" had been "encouraged into the mistaken belief that the Everglades could be redeemed."[27]

This inferred swipe at Smith hardly removed the bloom from Everglades enthusiasm. If anything, the newspaper's opinion was waved aside. Americans remained hell-bent on freeing the wetland from the "bondage of inundation." No explorer other than Williams questioned the majority opinion that humans could overcome the obstacles a wilderness set before them. In the end, the first Everglades drainage operation did not wait for the completion of a comprehensive survey. Dredges dug canals at the same excruciating moment that explorers were losing their way through the sawgrass. After his punishing second crossing, Williams must have wondered whether popular delusion was propelling the dredges, which he observed at work during his first expedition, and whether they were digging their way toward defeat. His editorial colleagues in New Orleans ventured that the canals would "probably increase the depth of water in the glades." These notions seem less wild in light of the fate of that drainage project and its unfortunate principal.[28]

CHAPTER FIVE

Birth and Despair

Minneapolis was a bustling western city in the late nineteenth century, a conduit between the lands to the east and the west. Early in the century, the settlement had risen up on the ancestral territory of the Ojibway and Dakota Indians around the Falls of St. Anthony and the confluence of the Mississippi and Minnesota Rivers. Like the region's axial city, Chicago, Minneapolis was a metropolis of nature. The Mississippi was the steady-running engine that connected the local economy with those in other regions. In the surrounding forests, lumberjacks—German, Irish, and Scandinavian immigrants—who in their dangerous work communicated with hand gestures, nods, and a logger's pidgin language, felled two-hundred-foot white pines and red pines, named not for particular characteristics of the trees but for the hue of the dressed wood they became. Removed to river's edge, they were rafted down the currents and over the falls to be run through water-powered blades in the metropolis's sawmills. The fresh-cut lumber was still green when it went up into balloon-framed houses, a new architectural design that put a heavy demand on the locally harvested wood for the expanding city's construction industry. The rest went on barges and paddle-wheel boats to commercial markets downstream.[1]

The sawmills did not monopolize the Mississippi's economic benefits. The wheat grown in the hinterlands combined with the river's hydropower eventually turned Minneapolis into the nation's leading flour-milling center. The most prominent names in the business belonged to self-made men such as Charles Pillsbury and Cadwallader Washburn, the founders of Pillsbury and General Mills, respectively. They shared the great water resource with metal foundries, machine shops, furniture manufacturing, and paper and woolen mills. Together, these businesses formed the well-spring of the industrial effluence carried downstream to gather with that from St. Paul, Cairo, St. Louis, Memphis, and New Orleans before draining into the Gulf of Mexico, creating within a century an oxygen-sapped dead zone the size of Massachusetts.[2]

Before the Mississippi began moving the power wheels of manufacturing, it had moved people's emotions and imagination. An important tourist trade took hold around the Falls of St. Anthony when Minneapolis was still a nascent city. With a mere sixteen-foot drop, the falls were quaint when compared with the breathtaking Niagara Falls back east, but they were the Mississippi's only cataract and an "astonishing work of nature," in the words of an early British visitor. In the 1830s, Americans began taking "fashionable tours" up the Mississippi to the falls. The patriarch of western landscape painting, George Catlin, conceived the tours, and joining one early junket was a short, bearded Transcendentalist from Concord, Massachusetts, Henry David Thoreau. A habitué of nature for soulful nourishment, he remembered the falls in his essay, "Wild Apples."[3]

But if tourists expected to see pristine nature or a benignly imposed pastoral against a helter-skelter wilderness, they were sometimes disappointed. The plethora of logs on the river, resembling a cattle drive, according to one local, increasingly fouled the scenery. Industry created another problem. So much water was being diverted to power local factories that the rocks on the falls were exposed to constant freezing and thawing, resulting in erosion. The falls' sandstone foundation was washing away, and boulders were tumbling down from the crest. The natural attraction was in danger of turning into commonplace rapids, jeopardizing not simply a landmark but also local industry's power supply. In one of its first preservation projects, the Army Corps of Engineers in 1876 built a dike, a timber apron, and two small dams to protect the falls. But timber bosses continued to send more and more logs over the falls—4.5 million feet in 1879 alone. In 1887, the apron could no longer withstand the onslaught and collapsed.[4]

That was the year that Charles and Lillian Trefethen took the train west, trundled through the great city of Chicago, and ultimately arrived at the University of Minnesota campus, downriver from the falls. Located on eighty-foot limestone and sandstone bluffs on the Mississippi's east bank, the university had been established by the territorial legislature in 1851 and reorganized in the 1860s with a congressional land grant. Its mission, typical of state universities of the West, was to provide a "practical" education that integrated classical and technical curricula. Charles was hired to teach metalworking in a new school of mechanics and design.[5]

From the perspective of the young man from the East, Minnesota was a world away from Massachusetts. It was colder for one. The first frost came earlier, and the ground thawed later. Sometimes the Falls of St. Anthony would freeze over, bristling white like a giant ice sculpture under the winter sun. The West was also full of wide, open spaces, a reminder that in both time and geography, Minneapolis was not far removed from the frontier. Yet the city was already modern. There was its landmark suspension bridge, with twin Elizabethan towers. A hundred yards away stood an odd 257-foot tower built by the power company as a monument to the city's new electric streetlights. With 165,000 people, Minneapolis was more than six times the size of Taunton. People came from all over, and they were less settled. Many were on their way to somewhere else, maybe not tomorrow but next month or next year. The university was young and dynamic, too, although it was not yet very big.[6]

Charles was one of twenty-six faculty, including two women, teaching fewer than a thousand students. In a university photograph, he appears to be the youngest of his colleagues. He has grown a mustache, perhaps to convey his faculty status or a level of maturity he had not yet acquired. Only twenty-one, he looks more like a student than a teacher. He in fact still suffered from childhood asthma. His family hoped that the dry western air would ease his condition. Daniel and Florence also insisted that he have "mature companionship," so with him they sent the older and more "sophisticated" Lillian. Small—a half inch above five feet—she had inherited her mother's French beauty and vitality. The hair was black, the eyes velvety brown, and the mouth endowed with her father's fine teeth. Remarkable for the day, she had not yet married although she was twenty-eight years of age.[7]

Charles and Lillian took rooms at 40 Eastman Avenue in a neighborhood just south of the main business district, an easy trolley ride from the university. The location was also convenient to the American Building and Loan Company, where fellow boarder Frank Stoneman worked as a manager.[8]

The circumstances of his and Lillian's courtship have not been recorded. It is not known what the attractive woman from the East, who had been exposed to the sophisticates of the classical music world, thought of the businessman who had romped around on the frontier or what he thought of her. A year or so after meeting, they went to Massachusetts, where Frank was introduced to the rest of Lillian's family—the chatty, animated sisters, the emphatic French mother, and the taciturn father. On June 12, 1889, the couple married in Malden, Massachusetts, just outside Boston.[9]

The newlyweds then returned to Minneapolis. Ten months later, on April 7, Lillian gave birth to a twelve-pound baby girl, whom her parents named Marjory. In later years, when Douglas was a well-known environmentalist, 1890 seemed to be a befitting birth year. Congress granted a wish of John Muir, future founder of the Sierra Club, when it set aside fifteen hundred square miles of forestland that would soon constitute Yosemite National Park; the General Federation of Women's Clubs, an important player in the early conservation movement, was founded; and the U.S. Bureau of the Census reported that a distinct boundary no longer existed between the unsettled and settled parts of the West.

By 1893, the Stonemans were living at 2121 Bryant Avenue, south of downtown. Their house was a recently built, large, two-story structure with a steep gabled roof in the Victorian mode, with street-side bay windows overlooking up- and downstairs porches. The Stonemans remained in Minneapolis and at that address for two more years. Later, as an adult, Douglas confessed to having no recollection of Minneapolis beyond the family's home address.[10]

Her earliest clear memories were in fact of Florida. In 1894, by her recollection, she traveled with her parents to Havana so that Frank and Uncle Forrest Rundell, who was married to Frank's sister, Katie, could investigate a business venture. The two families took the train south to New Orleans, where they boarded a Plant Line steamer bound for Cuba via Florida. The ship crossed the choppy Gulf of Mexico, rounded Pinellas Point, and steamed northeast into Tampa Bay. It berthed for a night at the long wooden pier of the two-million-dollar Tampa Bay Hotel, built a few years earlier by developer and transportation mogul Henry Plant. His friendly rival on the other side of the state, Henry Flagler, precipitated a rush in grand resort building in Florida in 1888 when he opened St. Augustine's Ponce de Leon Hotel, a magnificent structure of poured concrete and coquina with windows designed by Louis Comfort Tiffany. Constructed of red brick, the five-story Tampa Bay Hotel was famous for the Moorish spires that towered from its corners above the sabal palms planted on landscaped grounds.[11]

From Tampa, the party sailed on to Havana and back, while Marjory's unetched mind absorbed first images. Not surprisingly, her most prominent memories were produced by extreme events, such as succumbing to seasickness and then falling from an upper berth to the stateroom's steel deck. She also remembered torchlight processions moving "up and down the Prado" in Havana, when Cuba was a discontented colonial remnant of a long-ago Spanish empire inching toward war. Of Tampa, her memory centered on someone lifting her to pluck an orange from a tree in the hotel's garden, creating a still-life scene that would have delighted Florida citrus growers. Nothing left a more enduring impression than the source of the golden fruit's existence: the sun. While she was recovering from seasickness, the stateroom filled with a profusion of white tropical light that soon brought her renewed vigor. She had never seen this light in the disenchanting skies at home, which in the winter melded with the landscape in monochrome shades. After returning to Minneapolis, she looked in vain for that white sunlight, but she would not see it again for two decades.[12]

The potential of Cuba had failed to appeal to the brothers-in-law. Popular agitation may have caused them concern about imminent conflict, and they instead relocated east to Providence, Rhode Island. Douglas later said that the Panic of 1893 had forced the families to leave Minneapolis. The economic downturn hit especially hard in the midwestern states, which depended heavily on railroad commerce. Banks closed their doors, and railroads—the engines of the economy—went into receivership. The bottom fell out of the grain market, and in Minnesota mills and other businesses faltered and collapsed. Worker strikes became a regular occurrence. Some were led by socialists, who were beginning to make inroads into American politics. In the hinterlands, by contrast, lumberjacks were willing to work for nothing more than food and shelter. Farmers, in an uproar over falling market prices, growing debts, and outrageous shipping rates, organized the People's (Populist) Party and ran candidates for office, including Iowan James B. Weaver for president in 1892. Frank was apparently laid off from his loan manager's job, and the family moved out of the Bryant Avenue house. In 1894, Frank was living in the Victoria Hotel, no longer able to keep up appearances, and Lillian and Marjory had evidently gone to stay in Taunton until Frank arranged housing in Providence.[13]

Built on the bones of a colonial settlement, Providence was an industrializing city with roughly 140,000 residents. It was more compact physically than Minneapolis and architecturally older, with narrow streets and smallish houses and commercial buildings. It had a river, too, though the Providence, which emptied into beautiful Narragansett Bay, was far less magisterial than the Mississippi. Providence was also similarly a mill city, with textiles the economic mainstay, and it was increasingly a city of immigrants—primarily recently arrived European Jews and Italians.[14]

Why the brothers-in-law chose the Rhode Island capital remains unclear. Providence was no more immune than any other city from the most severe economic depression the country had seen. The decision may have come mainly from Rundell, whom Douglas described as something of a schemer and inveterate promoter. Her stocky, bearded uncle had been born in upstate New York, and he may have had business contacts in Rhode Island. In Providence, he started a loan and building firm, the New England Investment Company, serving as president while Stoneman worked as a manager.[15]

From a child's perspective, life in Providence was at first normal. A diet heavy in cream and butter had made Marjory into a healthy, plump child with a cherub face. She had mouse-colored stringy hair, and by the time she was three, she had been fitted with a pair of gold-rimmed glasses to correct a crossed left eye, inherited from her mother. A tumble left Marjory with a slight crook in her nose and a restricted breathing passage that bedeviled her for the rest of her life. She entered kindergarten in Providence, but her real education came from home, filled with music and books.[16]

The Stonemans initially lived in a comfortable two-story duplex at 43 East Manning Street. A small white-brass enamel bed was set up for Marjory in a correspondingly small bedroom off her parents' room. The third bedroom was occupied by Mary McCabe, an Irish immigrant from Dublin whom Lillian's mother lent to the Stonemans as a nanny. McCabe easily won Marjory's affection with both her Irish lilt and her chocolate-frosting drop cakes. McCabe's singing taught Marjory the wistful tone common to Irish ballads. Lillian, too, made music an integral part of the home. In the parlor downstairs, she would arrange chairs in a square and hold spontaneous recitals for receptive guests, usually with a visitor on piano accompanying the professionally trained Lillian on violin. Evening repertoires would begin with a Brahms lullaby or some type of soporific melody to put Marjory, upstairs in bed, to sleep.[17]

Books soon became an equally important part of her life. When at home, her father spent much of his time in the living room—the front room upstairs—where she would see him working silently at his desk or reading in an overstuffed armchair, his books arranged on a narrow bookcase nearby.

In the upstairs sitting room, her parents frequently read to her. She remembered being introduced to *Alice in Wonderland* and Longfellow's *The Song of Hiawatha*. When her father first read from chapter 7 of *Hiawatha*, "Give me of your bark, O Birch tree! . . . I a light canoe will build me," she cried at the thought of the tree sacrificing itself. In later years, Douglas devotees interpreted this outburst as evidence that she had an innate compassion toward nature; however, a similar search for precocious sensibilities could also lead to the conclusion that because Longfellow and by extension his readers anthropomorphized the birch tree, Douglas was actually revealing a predisposition toward social justice. Douglas remembered the incident as nothing more than "childhood sensitivity."[18]

As popular as Longfellow was in his day, he could not compete with the manifest importance of the Good Book and its teachings in American middle-class households. The Stonemans' was no exception. Lillian, who had been raised Methodist and joined the Episcopal Church with Frank, took on the role of moral conservator, as society expected of wives and mothers. She taught Marjory the Ten Commandments, the Apostles' Creed, the Lord's Prayer, and other prayers. Lillian offered lessons in faith, divine truth, and memorization, whereas Frank emphasized inquiry, skepticism, and careful analysis.[19]

Marjory developed an inquisitive, rational mind that eventually led her away from her mother's religious teachings. At the outset, that mind revealed itself in a youthful logic that sometimes spoiled popular childhood fantasies. When she first listened to *Alice in Wonderland*, the idea of a frocked rabbit with a pocket watch seemed sensational to her. Even the greatest of childhood myths came under suspicion. One evening after Christmas, she tried to imagine Santa Claus shimmying down every child's chimney, pulling a bloated sack of toys behind him. At the time, she was standing in her nightgown at an upstairs front window, looking out across frost-covered rooftops and chimneys, while her father sat in his armchair with a book. She turned around and declared her doubt about the existence of Santa Claus. Frank accepted her deduction, allowing her to develop independent thought at the expense of the joys of make-believe.[20]

The incident says as much about Frank as Marjory. Throughout their relationship as father and daughter and later as boss and employee at the *Miami Herald,* he granted her the latitude to think freely, never pressuring her to conform to his way of seeing things. The relationship was liberating, giving her intellectual license to explore the universe of her ideas and opinions. She always appreciated her father's treatment of her in what she called the "Quaker fashion": his valuing of the female mind as much as the male.[21]

At precisely the moment that her childhood myths began to unravel, so too did Marjory's real world. Once again, business success eluded Frank. The building and loan business failed to take off. Rundell stayed on as president, but Stoneman left to sell oil (probably for heating and for kerosene lights, which were being phased out in favor of electric lights), a vocation that ill suited his personality. The family moved to a smaller house across the street from Uncle Forrest and Aunt Katie, who had a son who was a year older than Marjory and who was her constant tormentor. Frank's mother, Aletha, also lived with Forrest and Katie.[22]

Life seemed normal at first. Marjory and Lillian were inseparable. In the fading light of dusk, the two took walks around the neighborhood hand in hand or arm in arm, sharing pleasure in watching people going about their business inside their houses. At home, Lillian spent hours sitting and looking through windows from the other direction, a habit she passed along to her daughter. One can imagine her young imagination at work, fables from her books being played out against the backdrop of her Providence neighborhood or original stories taking shape in her mind.[23]

But for Lillian, what may have begun as voyeuristic fun evolved into an early and undetected symptom of the mental illness that would remove her physically from Frank and psychologically from Marjory. Happiness eventually deserted Lillian and consequently the family. The Stonemans had moved at least four times in five years, and debts kept the family at the distressing edge of privation. No matter how hard Frank tried, his perseverance had not brought the kind of security and sense of permanence that Lillian had known in Taunton. One dreary failure after another was simply too much for her to handle. There is no evidence that Frank was anything but hard working. There is plenty that he had bad luck, and through no fault of her own, Lillian seems not to have been emotionally equipped for the unpredictability of the entrepreneur's life.[24]

To make matters worse, she never got along with her mother-in-law, living just across the street. According to Douglas, Aletha, who had experienced frontier life, civil war, and death as a condition of daily existence, apparently never accepted Lillian's eastern bourgeois upbringing. The two women were simply cut from different cloth. The traditional coif Aletha wore daily in staid obedience to an almighty god was a literal reminder of that difference. To Marjory, the sum of a frightening mortal was that coif framed around dark deep-set eyes and a perennial glowering cast. Grandmother Aletha was "one of the most disagreeable women," Douglas recalled decades later. Lillian, who could be gay and funny and who appreciated the latest Victorian fashions, never conquered her aversion for her mother-in-law.[25]

One afternoon, when Marjory was playing on the side porch of the house, Lillian revealed that aversion in a lurid way. Looking up, Marjory saw her mother in a struggle with Forrest Jr. Lillian had said something hateful about Aletha, and Forrest had fallen upon Lillian with his fists. He was likely seven or eight years old, nearly as tall as Lillian, and protective of his grandmother. Gripping his skinny wrists, Lillian twisted her head to the side and released an unearthly, possessed laugh. Marjory had never before heard such a sound come from her mother. Ninety years later, it still haunted her.[26]

Lillian began straddling a narrow line between sanity and madness. On another occasion, Marjory awoke in her small bed to find her father trying to calm her mother, frantic and inconsolable over the incredible idea that Frank wanted to kidnap their daughter. Another day, while Marjory was again on the porch playing, her mother approached hurriedly with Marjory's hat and jacket. She was carrying a suitcase, too, and again seemed out of sorts. Frank had pleaded with Lillian to stay, but she insisted that she and Marjory leave immediately for Taunton. They arrived later that day at dusk.[27]

In the course of an afternoon, Frank's world emptied. He could expect little sympathy from his family, and Lillian's relatives blamed him for her illness. Daniel and Charles soon arrived from Taunton in a large wagon to retrieve the furniture and carpets from the house. Frank now had nothing to keep him in Providence, and in 1896 he left for Florida for a new go at life in a completely unfamiliar place with vastly different weather and landscape and with few physical reminders of his previous life.[28]

Marjory learned that nature could be an emotional ballast in the storm of family troubles. Partly through precociousness and partly through circumstance, she began forging an ameliorating connection with the world outside her door. When in Providence, she escaped her increasingly bewildering and unhappy home by venturing to a small nearby lake. Flashes of white ripples on the water brought the distant, northern sun closer. The reflected light was a palliative. In Taunton, in a big house of little joy amid the vicissitude of her childhood, she continued to find nature a sheltering place—and she began to write about it.[29]

CHAPTER SIX

Suicide

When a wealthy Yankee gentleman in the 1880s announced that he was undertaking a million-dollar Everglades drainage scheme, idle groups that routinely gathered at barbershops and general stores probably responded with a dismissive cluck or two. Since the Yankee had been the beneficiary of inherited wealth, disdainful utterances may have also been audible in the finely appointed smoking parlors of some self-made men. Private opinions aside, public pronouncements overwhelmingly expressed confidence about the prospects for creating a fruitful Arcadia in the Everglades. The feasibility of draining them was congressional fact, surmised decades earlier from Buckingham Smith's 1848 report. People had always been willing to undertake such a project, but the opportune moment had not yet arrived. A succession of compelling distractions, including most recently the state's insolvency, had repeatedly deferred reclamation. Thirty years after the enactment of the 1850 Swamp Land Act, the state was solvent again, and surveying parties were exploring the Everglades. It was time to get back to the business of progress.

The man putting the first dredges to work in the Everglades was Philadelphia industrialist Hamilton Disston, one of those conspicuous capitalists surely mocked in private conversation. Though wealthy, he lacked the safety net of an aristocratic line, so his social status depended on his merit as a moneymaker. In spite of his considerable resources, he had a constant restive need to succeed in business. He cultivated fruitful relationships with powerful men in Florida, and even though an outsider, he quickly made his influence felt. His legacy ultimately reached far into the future to include a school, a town, and neighborhoods named for him. These honors came after his Florida ventures failed and his life ended, and they likely would have seemed implausible to him, even if he had hoped for such things. His success in Florida had depended on nature submitting to his will. Instead, it broke him.

Hamilton Disston's wealth arose less from his unsparing drive than from his father, Henry Disston, who raised his son in easy comfort and provided a daunting example to follow. Henry had emigrated from England in 1833, when he was fourteen, with his father and sister. When the father died not long thereafter, Henry's sister went to live with friends, and he apprenticed with a saw manufacturer. After completing a seven-year obligation, he opened his own firm, which weathered a series of setbacks before fortune arrived from selling guns, swords, and armor plate to the U.S. government during the Mexican and Civil Wars. The company was best known for the Disston handsaw, which became the standard by which all other saws were measured. By the late twentieth century, saws with the Disston name had become collector's items.[1]

Like many sons of self-made men, Ham, as friends and family called him, wanted to forge his own reputation, not inherit it. He duly served an apprenticeship at the saw factory, which was abbreviated by service in the U.S. Army during the Civil War. His father twice intervened and paid for substitutes when Ham attempted to answer President Abraham Lincoln's call for volunteers. After finally giving in to his son's determination, Henry used his money to ensure that Ham and the self-styled 100 Disston Volunteers were properly equipped. After the war, Ham returned to the saw factory and a partnership with his father. Henry died thirteen years later, and the thirty-four-year-old Ham took charge of the family business. His first responsibility was to oversee the completion of a new factory and the expansion of operations begun when his father was still alive. But Ham was building on someone else's dream, and the frontier offered men of high ambition the opportunity to create something of their own. Disston's Florida hunting and fishing companion, Henry Sanford, a retired Union general and former high official in the Lincoln administration, was just such a man. As a civilian, he owned more than fourteen thousand acres in Central Florida. The opportunity for Disston to control his own sweep of land, one so large that it might allow him to lead Florida's march from frontier to civilization, came in 1881, when the state's governor, William Bloxham, pitched an attractive land deal to him. At the time, the state was anxious to unburden itself from debt.[2]

Florida owed approximately one million dollars to creditors as a consequence of the Swamp Land Act of 1850. Five years later, to comply with the federal requirement to drain and sell the submerged land, the legislature created the Internal Improvement Fund, with the governor, comptroller, treasurer, attorney general, and commissioner of agriculture serving as its trustees. The trustees had authority to execute land grants and guarantee loans to promote railroad and canal development. By the end of the decade, they had offered most of the land under their purview as collateral to guarantee more than three million dollars in railroad construction bonds. It was an unfortunate venture. Economic depression and the Civil War followed, and the railroad companies defaulted on their loans. The state subsequently could not cover the interest payments, bondholders petitioned to seize the fund's fourteen-million-acre inventory of land, and the federal courts ordered the fund into receivership.[3]

Florida's assumption of the role of guarantor for private railroad companies, despite the risks involved, was a common undertaking for a public entity in the nineteenth century. Locomotive technology was key to accessing new territory, converting wilderness into settled areas, and bringing rural products to the marketplace, and railroads were ravenous for land. Exploiting these imperatives, they reaped huge dividends in federal and state land giveaways amounting to approximately two hundred million acres, a cumulative acquisition approximately 5.3 times the size of Florida. The decade of the Internal Improvement Fund's birth was the first of great railway expansion, when track nationwide increased from nine thousand to thirty thousand miles, though little of it reached the southernmost state. At the beginning of the 1850s, Florida had one mule-drawn railroad running on thirty-three miles of track and at the end only four hundred miles more, even though the fund had granted railroads five hundred thousand acres of land. Major expansion did not come until later in the century, when Disston's fellow capitalists Henry Flagler, William Chipley, and Henry Plant undertook railroad ventures.[4]

As the first big corporations, railroads not only drove the economy of the new industrial era but also introduced a "new capitalist logic" to virgin land. Accompanying that logic was a hardened indifference to indigenous landscapes. In the American West, rail expansion led to the denuding of forests, the mass killing of bison, and the replacement of drought-resistant plains grass with drought-sensitive staple crops. In Florida, expansion, however sluggish, translated into wetlands destruction. In both regions, frontier land went not to family farmers, in accordance with the Jeffersonian dream, to which Republicans like Disston claimed an ideological allegiance, but primarily to speculators and corporations. By the turn of the century, the Internal Improvement Fund had deeded to railroads more than nine million acres of swamp and overflowed land.[5]

Within days of moving into the Ionic-columned governor's mansion, Bloxham boarded a train to Philadelphia to meet with Disston. Douglas described Bloxham as a "country gentleman interested in all the new talk of railroads and mindful again of that forgotten idea of reclaiming the Everglades." Disston apparently possessed that idea, too. Following Bloxham's visit, Disston agreed to buy four million acres of swampland for one million dollars. The *New York Times* described the transaction as history's largest private land purchase by an individual. As if to live up to such billing, Disston authorized marketing maps that suggested he owned two-thirds of the state of Florida.[6]

In exchange for the state's largesse, Disston promised economic renewal, a promise that the state's newspaper editors generally found credible. Others were less enchanted with the land baron's deal making. Signed before the four-million-acre purchase and based on a proposal initiated by Disston, a separate drainage contract applying to another parcel of land awarded Disston ownership of one acre of land for every two that his Atlantic and Gulf Coast Canal and Okeechobee Land Company drained in the east/northeast corridor of the Everglades watershed. He and his partners could obtain up to twelve million acres in fulfilling the provisions of the contract. Not surprisingly, squatters and homesteaders were astonished when they saw strange men running surveying lines across land they had long settled and improved. Some held their claims under the Armed Occupation Act of 1842, which had been passed to push Seminoles out of the area. Now those who had opened the Florida frontier, risking their lives against Indian attack, were being pushed out. If Disston's agents could show that the property was submerged, which through various creative ways they often did, the land was Disston's.[7]

His engineering plans for drainage were comparatively unembellished. He would excavate canals and channelize part of the Kissimmee River to drain the Kissimmee basin into Lake Okeechobee. From there, the water would run down new canals leading to the Atlantic and down a deepened Caloosahatchee River on the lake's west side to the Gulf of Mexico. Like so many men before and after him, Disston's vision included a waterway running from gulf to ocean across the state. By the end of 1882, he appeared to be making good progress on his drainage plans. Work crews had blasted away limestone rapids, dredged their way up the Caloosahatchee River, and connected a string of smaller lakes to Okeechobee. The otherwise putrid muck horsed up by Disston's dredges had the sweet smell of success.[8]

To keep things from going foul, Disston needed land sales to pay for his operations. Each winter during the 1880s, sunny Florida drew some 150,000 visitors, many of them wealthy and each representing a potential investor. National publications developed a fascination with the state. Each article provided free publicity, and the timing was perfect for Disston. In 1884, when all was going well for him, *Harper's Weekly* published an eight-page spread that highlighted Disston's operations, proclaiming them the state of the art.[9]

Another opportunity to grab headlines arrived with President Chester A. Arthur, who joined the winter flock going to Florida in 1883. His entourage of course included the national press. Disston arranged, probably through the politically connected Sanford, to have the president cruise down the Kissimmee River and out to Lake Tohopekaliga. The excursion was a grandly orchestrated promotion of Disston's Arcadian vision of Florida. One can imagine him standing on the main deck of the paddle steamer *City of Philadelphia* inducing his guests to imagine the sawgrass panorama converted into not brown but black earth that would give its fertility to fruitful harvests. Gesturing to the southwest, he could affirm that sugar cane was germinating on recently reclaimed land. A year later, he was able to boast that samples from the first harvest beat out entries from Louisiana, Mexico, and Cuba to win the top prize in yield and quality at the Cotton Centennial Exposition in New Orleans, the biggest regional event since the Civil War.[10]

Disston's enterprise seemed assured of a bright future. To cover his installments to the state, Disston promptly sold two million acres to Sir Edward Reed, a British naval architect and owner of a Florida railroad, for $600,000. To fund his drainage operation, he offered to sell smaller parcels of land for a minimum of $1.25 an acre. In leaflets and advertisements circulating throughout the United States and Europe, he promoted his territory as a farmers' paradise. He truly believed in the area's potential. Other entrepreneurs took notice, and Disston's ventures stimulated a minor land boom. One historian maintained that "every section of the state from Key West to Pensacola was benefited by the action of Mr. Disston."[11]

From the beginning, his plans included a personal agricultural empire. In 1887, he bought a half interest in the St. Cloud sugar plantation, located in the Kissimmee basin and on reclaimed land with a fertility that, according to fund investigators, "can not but impress the most casual observer." He experimented with rice, peaches, grapes, and an assortment of vegetables, but sugarcane prevailed as his crop of choice. St. Cloud in its first year yielded a record five thousand pounds of granulated sugar per acre. For the coming season, Disston built a $350,000 mill with its own railroad spur and a cane-crushing capacity nearly twice the national average. Tourists included Disston's plantation on their lists of places to see. One latter-day observer characterized it as a "cross between an old southern planter's domain and a northern factory—flavored with a frontier rusticity." Disston hired the ablest of sugar men from Louisiana to run St. Cloud. He also donated land for the establishment of a U.S. Department of Agriculture sugarcane laboratory, for which he lobbied, and he added thirty-six thousand acres to the plantation, which he reorganized as the Florida Sugar Manufacturing Company. In 1890, Congress imposed a two-cent-per-pound bounty on imported sugar, which was paid to domestic producers. Disston had invested in anticipation of this windfall.[12]

His goal was to make Florida into a sugar kingdom that surpassed the dominance of Louisiana. But success in growing sugarcane depended on the success of drainage, and that endeavor was proving troublesome. In 1884, Disston reported to the Internal Improvement Fund that his company had drained more than two million acres of land, and the trustees in turn conveyed to him his requisite half of the total. Critics of Florida's land policies balked. His canals, they charged, were nothing more than stagnant "mosquito ditches," and drought, not dredges, had created the land he had allegedly reclaimed. The complaints were not unfounded. Disston had dug only two canals, one connecting Lake Okeechobee with the Caloosahatchee River and running three miles, and one extending a short way south from the lake, with no outlet. Governor Edward Perry appointed an investigative committee that confirmed the worst: perhaps fifty thousand acres truly could be judged as reclaimed. The most damaging evidence against Disston originated from a contract stipulation that required him to lower Lake Okeechobee: its water level remained unchanged.[13]

The report undoubtedly stung, but Disston responded with gentlemanly aplomb. He agreed to improve his canals and to pay twenty-five cents per acre for any new land he reclaimed. Yet all subsequent efforts at drainage brought minimal results. Disston's canals were too narrow and too shallow, and they failed to drop along the necessary grade to carry water away. His product was defective and his science and engineering rudimentary. By 1889, Disston had suspended his drainage operations and refocused his energies on sugar.[14]

But misfortune followed misfortune, and the would-be agriculturalist eventually had to submit to another defeat. Cane borers penetrated the sugar crop and reduced yields, and high turnover among plantation managers undermined efficiency. Devastation struck with the economic panic of 1893, the same crisis that uprooted the Stoneman family from Minneapolis a thousand miles away. Putting up the Philadelphia saw factory as collateral, Disston took out a two-million-dollar mortgage on his Florida holdings. Then in 1894, a September storm inundated South Florida, and farmers claimed that his canals backwashed water onto their land. Not long thereafter, Congress lifted the sugar bounty. Just when it seemed Disston's luck could get no worse, freezes in December and February stunned Florida agriculture. It was the last of too many misfortunes.

By early 1896, he had laid off nearly all his Florida employees. A few months later, his creditor called in the loan. The son of a self-made man who circulated in a world where a man's peers determined his reputation apparently could not accept failure. On the evening of April 30, Disston sat in a bathtub in his house on North Broad Street in Philadelphia and shot himself. This is the tale, at least, of Disston's demise. Some contemporary researchers argue that political rivals planted the story of suicide and that Disston actually died, like Buckingham Smith, from heart failure. Perhaps so, but in the weeks before his death, he increased his life insurance by $600,000, giving him coverage totaling $1,094,825, according to one source, with the risk shared by thirty-three companies.[15]

Disston's death left no punctuation mark in the larger Everglades narrative. The values at the foundation of his enterprise had an abiding history. They were rooted in the cultures of the Old World, when civilizations set themselves apart from and above the nonhuman world and first began to conceive of nature's offerings as commodities for the enjoyment and monetary benefit of humans. Conservationist Aldo Leopold called this abstraction the "Abrahamic concept of land." Economic desires and designs would master nature: land would give itself to agriculture, fur-bearing animals to markets, rivers to transportation and hydropower, forests to timber, and mountains to mining. Exported to America, this faith in nature's largesse formed a cornerstone to the collective ideals and purposes of a people living amid seemingly boundless natural resources to be exploited in the name of God or profit—or both.[16]

At the time of Douglas's childhood, Florida was graced by more wetland acreage (in absolute and proportional measurements) than any other state; before she turned eighty, 46 percent of Florida's surface water, give or take a swamp or two, was gone. Disston's efforts to make land from water may have come to naught, but others carried those efforts into the future. In 1905, the same year that Marjory Stoneman entered high school, the state succeeded private interests, attempting to reclaim Everglades land in a desperate kind of public project. Watching closely was the project's most ardent newspaper critic, Frank Stoneman.[17]

CHAPTER SEVEN

Growing Up

When a teenager settled into a routine of life at her grandparents' home in Taunton, Marjory spent occasional summer weekends with her high school friend Madeleine Beers at Lake Assawompsett. These weekends were a New England summer pastoral. Madeleine's parents owned a place at Nelson's Grove, a regionally familiar waterside colony of shaker-shingle seasonal cottages. Assawompsett was the largest body of freshwater in Massachusetts, contoured by silver birch, hemlock, and beech trees climbing sloping banks and connected to bogs and reed marshes littered with lichen-matted granite boulders and draining into the Taunton River. Though big, the lake could feel intimate when the air was quiet and the water settled, when words and sound—a paddle bumping the side of a canoe—carried across the glassy surface. But this was New England, where weather often hastened an about-face.

During one weekend retreat, Madeleine's parents returned to Taunton, leaving Marjory and Madeleine looking for something to do on a "calm sunny morning."[1] They decided to take out the small sailboat that belonged to Madeleine's brother. Neither girl had experience at the tiller, but Madeleine had watched on countless occasions as her brother trimmed and eased the sail to adjust the boat's speed and direction according to the wind. Their confidence was equally likely steeled by Marjory's seafaring heritage. Madeleine took the tiller as the boat languished in breathless air. Then a brisk full wind blew up, snapping the sail tight. Marjory moved the panic-stricken Madeleine aside, and as she recalled, "I had the tiller, gloriously, for the first time in my life and we brought her around and sailed her home before the sharp wind, with my ancestors' blood boiling in my excited veins." It was all so instinctual, a maneuver that would have made New England mariners proud.[2]

Not her grandfather, though. Daniel eventually learned of the adventure, and he boiled inside. Marjory's encounter with the water and weather without the assurance of experience, in his estimation, amounted to foolishness, and in his quiet but severe manner he said as much. One night at the supper table, "he folded his napkin and cleared his throat" and turned to Marjory. Resorting to the "double negative purely for emphasis and not of custom, 'Don't you never take liberty with the sea,' he said, and got up and left."[3]

The lake experience and Daniel's admonishment might have fatally turned an adolescent's malleable mind against a certain kind of place and a dangerous natural event. Not Marjory. The brush with threatening wind rewarded her with an exultant thrill and the rush of ancestral blood. She remembered the lake incident in an unpublished story she composed as an adult, when she was as likely to revel in a picture-perfect day as in a foul-weather day. Climate, weather, flora, fauna, topography, and light had as much a role as did local culture in defining her sense of a place and her attachment to it. She found deep personal meaning in physical settings, and she was aware of how they could inspire her as a writer, nourish her political sensibilities, and serve as an antidote to sadness. A mere change in physical surroundings could alter her emotional response to life's circumstances.

Place also provided a reference to her personal history, a connection to memories good and bad. In Massachusetts, she had lost her mother, first to the horrible disease that afflicted her mind and ultimately to cancer. During that time, Marjory had no contact with her father, forever

banished by her mother's family. Marjory had to start her childhood over
in the disenchanting home of grandparents and an aunt who were traditional in their habits and exacting in their expectations. They created a
confining and generally cheerless milieu that censured even modest gestures to nonconforming behavior, as in a girl taking the tiller. Years later,
Douglas described the region's general ethos: "There was the respectable,
important, grown-up New England life of the neighborhood, which insisted that you go to Sunday School and learn your lessons and do your
practicing and never inquire into things which it was not nice for a little
girl to know. It was life which admitted nothing about any other lives, or
possible lives."[4] Yet Marjory also had another world—of books. Her story
fits the convention of writers who reacted to some childhood discomfort
by retreating into the printed page. She also had close friendships, school,
and the natural setting. Unlike an unexpected rebuke from her grandfather, an unexpected weather change on a placid lake provided sustenance for her mended soul.

Many locals thought of Taunton in terms of firsts. It was the first settlement in New England to be founded by a woman, Elizabeth Poole, who
in 1637 bought a swath of land on the Taunton River from Indians. A
town was organized and, as was fashion, named for an Old World city.
Settlers generally came from the original Taunton and nearby counties
in southwestern England—Somerset, Devon, Dorset, and Gloucester.
When Taunton, Massachusetts, incorporated as a city, it adopted a seal
with the Latin words *dux femina facti* (woman leads the way). By the
1650s, the first successful ironworks in the colonies had begun operations
beside the river, serving as a start for the various metal industries that
came to identify Taunton. In the next century, Robert Treat Paine, son
of Thomas Paine, sashayed into town, intending to ease into a quiet life
before duty called him to lead the local revolutionary committee. On the
Taunton green, the Sons of Liberty unfurled the colonies' first flag bearing the words *Union and Liberty*.[5]

A slightly elevated circular 1.5-acre common in the middle of town, the
green formed Taunton's physical and civic center. The main roads through

town radiated out from the green, and the business of and with the city was conducted in its vicinity. On the edge of its street-wrapped perimeter stood a granite Romanesque building with an overstated patina dome, the Bristol County Courthouse. In keeping with the prevailing customs of nineteenth-century municipal landscaping, "very dignified" elm trees, as Douglas remembered them, encircled the green and arced over neighborhood streets and sidewalks, including Harrison Street, where her grandparents lived. By the third quarter of the twentieth century, the trees would be lost to Dutch elm disease (the victims of a vulnerable sylvan monoculture unwittingly created by city planners in the Northeast and Midwest), leaving the sidewalked streets without their canopy and Taunton's craggy granite courthouse to lord over a stark, bald green.[6]

Within a ten-minute saunter to the northwest of the green, past churches and wood-frame houses, was an enclave of small manufacturers. In place of trees and grassy space were brick and pavement, the dark stains of industry. Here, the air smelled of metallic residue, and hollow buildings broadcast the percussive sounds of manufacturing. In the midst of all this was Daniel's foundry, described in the 1899 city directory as the manufacturer of a "full line of plumbers' brass retinues" and castings in German silver, bronze, aluminum, and composition. Douglas remembered the foundry as a "place of strange drama," of liquified metal, hammering, and heat—always heat—even in the dead of the New England winter. Never so big or so productive as to receive a name or to require the employment of more than a few men, the foundry was really a tradesman's shop. Taunton had many small proprietorships, commissioned to do outsourced or overflow work for the larger firms or contracted to complete small individual jobs. These establishments allowed men such as Daniel who neither fished nor farmed for a living the ownership of their own labor. Yet all over the country, the small proprietor shops were disappearing in the tumult of rapid corporate growth, making self-sufficient men and their offspring dependent workers. Daniel's son, Charles, worked for corporations rather than for himself.[7]

Daniel avoided this transition, continuing to operate his foundry until he could no longer work. A creature of routine and tradition, he had discovered his vocation early in life, married his boss's sister after securing a means of support, bought the house in which he spent the rest of his life, and raised a family with Florence. Three of their children married, moved away, and gave Daniel and Florence grandchildren. When Lillian returned to live in Taunton with Marjory, Daniel was in his late sixties and Florence in her early seventies. Both were healthy, and Daniel still kept his vigorous work schedule, but neither had anticipated raising another child.

Their house had plenty of room for the newcomers. Fanny was the only Trefethen sibling living at home at the time.[8] Alice had moved to Connecticut and raised a family. Charles had returned after spending only a year at the University of Minnesota but eventually married and settled in Providence. The family house was a three-story Victorian on a broad lot and fronted by an ample porch with a white-painted railing of lathe-turned balusters. The attic had been converted into a third floor, with a room for Mary McCabe, the housekeeper who had been with the Stonemans in Providence, and a larger room for Florence and Daniel with blue and white rosebud wallpaper and a view overlooking the back garden. Lillian and Marjory were put in a front bedroom on the second floor. It was tastefully furnished with walnut and marble-top furniture and a double bed for mother and daughter to share.[9]

Behind the house were two outbuildings. Every fall, the lawn furniture was stored on the upper floor of one of the buildings. After her daughter and granddaughter settled in, Florence told Marjory that she could do anything she wanted on that floor short of burning the building down. It became the perfect sort of hideaway where an only child in a house full of adults could lose herself in play or daydreaming, where the wooden steps in the boxy stairwell sounded the footfalls of approaching intruders.[10]

Marjory remained close to her mother, but Lillian was slipping deeper into her mental morass. The family speculated that Lillian's mental problems had a hereditary component: a paternal uncle had apparently gone insane. But Fanny and Florence also continued to blame Frank for Lillian's condition, and Lillian grew resentful of her mother and quarreled incessantly with her sister, who could be prickly and insensitive. Lillian tended to withdraw from the past and her marriage, however. She cared only about the present, a place in which she functioned poorly.[11]

The Trefethens resigned themselves to sending Lillian away for treatment. The Massachusetts state hospital for the mentally ill was located in Taunton, but Lillian entered the Butler Hospital for the Insane near Providence. The state hospital was a grim, sprawling affair, and many of its 900 "inmates" were assigned to crews that worked the hospital's 140-acre farm or kept the swampland around it drained. "Useful employment" was regarded as a "remedial agent in the treatment of mental diseases." Butler was by all comparisons a superior facility. Founded in 1847 largely as a consequence of the efforts of Dorothea Dix, arguably the country's most influential social reformer for the treatment of the mentally ill, Butler incorporated the latest treatment practices and facilities design of progressive European institutions and maintained a maximum patient capacity at a manageable 180. Whatever her treatment (there are no institutional records of her commitment), its benefits were minimal. After she returned home, her disconnects from reality and her vicious clashes with Fanny and Florence continued.[12]

The disequilibrium around Marjory was often too great for her to manage alone. Although Daniel sometimes gave comfort in his clumsy, taciturn way, Florence and Fanny were not always loving. Marjory could not cleave to either as she did her mother, although she found that connection more difficult as Lillian's malady worsened. Florence at times lacked the patience for a child in the house, and while Fanny could be lively and musical and funny, she was all too often dictatorial and humorless. Their undisguised animosity toward Marjory's father added to the child's despair. For years, she experienced bad dreams from which she awoke screaming, and on occasion, she awoke after walking about in a half sleep, her arms twisting in the air, overcome with a fearful dread of something having exploded next to her left ear.[13]

Marjory eventually adjusted to her new surroundings, although the nightmares continued, and the family itself adjusted, however grudgingly, to her presence. Dimensions of a normal childhood gradually evolved. She entered school, went to church, celebrated holidays and birthdays, and made friends. Her mother regained some of her mental faculties, although she remained mostly listless and sometimes sat alone on the front porch with her back to the street, holding a conversation with only herself. The mother-child relationship became reversed, with Marjory trying to look after Lillian. They played card and board games together and resumed their leisurely strolls in the evenings, while Marjory peppered her mother for stories about Frank's years growing up in Minnesota.[14]

Florence and Fanny became surrogate mothers to Marjory. Florence was a woman of ranging intensity, from a temper that could turn a room cold to a mirthfulness that could warm it up again. A stout individual with excessive energy, she had infectious passions. The few blocks to St. Thomas Episcopal Church on Sunday mornings with her were always taken like an excursion. She was not one to walk down the sidewalk; she bounded, though elegantly and smoothly, and without slowing she would in her usual manner of incessancy encourage Marjory to take in the surroundings—the colors, sounds, and smells—of beloved New England. Sewing was her greatest passion. She made clothes for the entire family. Any dress of Marjory's that had not been handed down from a neighbor had come from Florence's sewing room, a big sun-drenched space on the second floor. Marjory spent hours there with her grandmother, not to learn her handicraft but to listen to stories taken from books. Dickens was Florence's favorite, and he became Marjory's favorite. Florence talked about Daniel, too, seeing him as a man of simple ambition, a state of affairs that depressed her, and she was often superior about her potential had society allowed a woman the same opportunities that many men squandered. If she were in charge, the foundry would be a factory and the family would be living in fine comfort. Marjory's first political sensibilities about women's rights came from Florence, an early suffragist. To her, "life for women was precarious at best," Douglas later remembered. Florence raised her granddaughter to believe that a "woman had to be able to support herself."[15]

Fanny followed this path. She shared her mother's temper, humor, and inquisitive mind. Music, though, was her propensity. She played virtually any string instrument and gave lessons most of her adult life. She also kept the books for the foundry and a local family-owned bank. One of her greatest joys was belonging to a female cycling club. Bicycles were the rage, and Fanny threw herself into the pastime with vigorous devotion. After Marjory got a bicycle, Fanny took her niece on rides in the country, gathering nuts en route, and in December they would pedal out to cut a Christmas tree for home. Fanny also introduced Marjory to astronomy, a hobby that suited Fanny's somewhat solitary existence. An attractive woman, she had many men callers, yet she perceived none as her equal. Her high standards were likely inherited from Florence and in part were calculated to save herself from later disappointment. After her two sisters married, societal pressures consigned her to the role of sacrificial female offspring, as Douglas put it, conscripted to stay at home to care for aging parents. Marjory knew of thirteen so-called old maids living on Harrison Street, and she estimated that sixty thousand Massachusetts women remained single because so many men had perished in the Civil War and so many others had journeyed west. She was consequently exposed early to a "very female society" in which single women found ways to express their independent selves—in art, writing, or social activism, for example. Many managed to enjoy fulfilling lives (a "respectable spinsterhood"), as would Marjory later. But Fanny's was a different story. Despite her pleasures in cycling and astronomy, her social enthrallment was devoid of much joy. Self-fulfilling forces may have been at work here. Fanny once gave her niece the unsavory advice to avoid making friends: they were too untrustworthy.[16]

This crucial bit of cynicism seems to have come from Daniel, who indeed had no friends. Douglas remembered "Grampa" as the placid center in the "excitable, talkative, unpredictable household." When rare nighttime thunderstorms sent Florence rushing about creating her own tempest, ordering the family to dress and sit separately in individual rooms downstairs in the event of lightning, fire, or some other disaster, Daniel slept soundly in his feather bed in the cooled-down attic air. After Lillian was sent to the hospital, he was the only person she allowed to come visit. He went on the designated visiting day, Sunday, spent the allotted hour with her, and returned home, trying to put the best face on things. Only the death of his youngest child, Walter, at age seven, in the diphtheria epidemic of 1876, grieved him more. Florence coped with the loss by weaving screens for climbing roses from the wires of discarded hoop skirts. Daniel planted trees in the yard. Over the years, he put in five pear trees, a cherry tree, an apple tree, and a tulip tree. He built a small pagoda-peaked summer house in the backyard and planted roses around it. In the summer he picked the fruit from his trees, and in the fall he raked their leaves with the paid help of a Portuguese immigrant boy who lived nearby, building a fire that would catch Marjory's attention through the window of the sewing room before luring her out to join them. Daniel rose before the sun and before everyone else in the house. On summer mornings, the metallic clink of his hoe issued from the backyard and entered Marjory's sleep as he turned up the hard ground for a bed of beans, corn, and squash. Sailing was his one indulgent pastime. He bought Charles a longboat with a mast stepped through the forward seat and taught him how to sail like his forebears. After Charles moved to Providence, he got a cottage at Field's Point on Narragansett Bay. He and Daniel went out on the water on Sundays and holidays when the weather was good, and they frequently took Marjory with them. She was struck by how the two men eased into an otherworld without conversation, effortlessly communicating with few or no words as they wandered the bay. They never taught her how to sail, yet she observed enough to turn about the little boat belonging to Madeleine's brother.[17]

The family neglected to pass along other skills to Marjory. She gained some elementary knowledge about gardening, mainly from watching her grandfather work, but she did not learn to sew, cook, or sail. Florence had ensured that each of her children mastered a musical instrument, and for a while she insisted that Marjory practice the piano every afternoon and on Saturday mornings. "Not the most golden and green Saturday morning in the world was exempt from a whole hour of misplaced sharps and forgotten flats," she recalled some twenty years later of her lack of an ear and a passion for music. If translating "black dots on bunches of five lines" was a "thing of torment," reading the written word on a page was pure pleasure. The Taunton house had plenty of books and a space called the writing room, but Marjory learned to read and write only after entering the first grade.[18]

School offered Marjory more than a release from the confinement of home. Barnum Street Primary School was a long walk away from Harrison Street. But after Florence enrolled Marjory, she adapted immediately to this unfamiliar and exciting environment and prepared herself to absorb every amazing new thing she could. Long thereafter, she acknowledged this special, fleeting moment when a child's mind contained the "gem-like flame" of eagerness and curiosity. "Every day is a new adventure and the whole scope of the world which one can touch and see and taste and smell and learn is an expansion of one's being, so that, with such a mind, the child is really the possessor of a life so full and rich and varied and beautiful that no riches of his adult days can equal it." These words may have reflected her nostalgia, but even in her youth she embraced school as the foundation of knowledge with which she could fill the emptiness in her childhood.[19]

Douglas remembered Barnum's teachers—all of them female—as devoted. They embodied a universe of ideas that impressed her, even if some of those ideas made little sense to her. She never mastered math beyond the most basic principles, and her pragmatic mind formed perspectives that sometimes contradicted a teacher's lessons. In her few years on earth, life experiences had already shaped her way of knowing; the dislocation of her family made her into a skeptic. The permanence of ideas and fact carried little weight with her, and her difficulties with math probably stemmed from a distrust of prescribed absolutes. Although Barnum's teachers were disinclined to suggest the existence of alternatives to conventional wisdom, Marjory often conceived of alternatives. Early on, she learned the power of both knowledge and dissent, with the latter reinforced as she became acquainted with her Quaker ancestry.[20]

For her, knowledge was best obtained through books. Soon after learning to read, she could reach the final pages of books long before the rest of the class. When the first grade moved up to the second, she was advanced to the third. She raided the reading room at home, where she found the *Encyclopaedia Britannica,* various histories, Byron, Dickens, and a calf-bound volume of the complete Shakespeare. She also borrowed books from the public library, opened in 1904 with a sixty-thousand-dollar gift from Andrew Carnegie and housed in an impressive Indiana limestone building of beaux arts design with inviting light-filled rooms. She immersed herself. On Sundays after church, she consumed two or three books at a sitting. Even on days when she stayed home from school sick and nestled in a blanket by the radiator, she read. As an adult, she was a snob about reading, contemptuous of those who said they lacked time for books and of those who apologized for their failure to read: "Why should anyone apologize if he does not like a wider experience, a broader panorama of his world, adventures without hazard and treasures without cost? At least, it is not to the world in general he should apologize. It is to himself."[21]

Books led to writing, and she was in stellar company when it did. Marjory liked to read *St. Nicholas,* one of the day's most popular children's magazines. Its contributors included Robert Louis Stevenson, Mark Twain, Louisa May Alcott, L. Frank Baum, and Rudyard Kipling. The magazine's St. Nicholas Club invited young readers to send in stories and poems. Their contributions were then judged, and along with being awarded gold or silver badges of recognition and cash prizes, the winners became published authors. F. Scott Fitzgerald, William Faulkner, Ring Lardner, Eudora Welty, Edna St. Vincent Millay, and Rachel Carson were among those who made their literary debuts in *St. Nicholas.* So did Marjory. After a number of rejections, she won a gold badge for a literary puzzle she called "Double the Headings and Curtailings." She was sixteen and inspired.[22]

Six months later, the *Boston Herald* awarded her a junior writing prize for a short story. Published in June 1907, "An Early Morning Paddle" tells the tale of a boy who wakes early in his tent before other campers and canoes out to the middle of a lake to watch the sun rise. The seventeen-year-old author, struggling with descriptive language, cluttered her prose with superlatives:

Then a little breeze began to blow which wrinkled the water and began to thin the mist. The east became tinged with pink, which was reflected in the water around him.

Gradually the mist disappeared, the pink streaks became red, then copper-colored and bright gold, until, with a burst of song from the throats of countless birds, the sun itself rose from behind the trees and flooded the pines, the sandy beach, the water and the canoe with a deluge of sunshine.[23]

Words offered Marjory a new way to connect with nature, which had first entered her consciousness on the trip to Florida and Havana. In place of the white sun of southern latitudes, she reveled in New England's intense seasons. Fall spoke to her with its pronounced colors, and spring announced its approach with the scent of cherry, apple, and pear blossoms from her grandfather's trees. Brilliant May baskets crafted by her mother and the ritual run of herring up the Taunton River, where locals had built a fish ladder, provided other spring excitements. When Marjory was a senior at Wellesley College and living in a dorm overlooking Lake Waban, she left the window open year-round to bring the outside in. In late winter, she loved to hear the rolling plaint and crack of the breaking ice when the weather began to warm.[24]

The canoe story probably derived from Marjory's summer visits to Nelson's Grove with Madeleine Beers and from her camping excursions to New Hampshire with the family of Margaret Blaine. Marjory had many friends who vitalized her life outside the home. She fell in with a stable of five girls of like interests, forming close companionships and going together to parties and dances and sometimes to the foundry to watch Daniel's workers pouring hot liquid metal. Marjory and Edith Siebel, the other intellectual in the bunch, occasionally spent quiet afternoons lounging about reading. Ideas for the group's other social activities typically originated with Marjory. She spoofed herself in the "classifieds" section of her high school journal: "Miss Marjory Stoneman, Professional Entertainer and Wholesale Dealer in Ideas for Parties, Club Meetings, and Social Gatherings of all kinds . . . ideas by the dozens or the hundreds."[25]

Boys were not expected to answer her solicitation. She liked them, but in their eyes, personal charm and humor rarely substituted for pretty faces. She first felt their rejection during high school dances, when she was left to stand as a wallflower outside the circle of stepping couples. Only one boy ever asked her to dance, none to go on a date, and she sensed why. Later in life, she looked back and described herself as having been a "greasy fat girl with one crossed eye" who wore clumsy glasses and giggled too much. The realization that she had not inherited the French beauty of her mother and aunt caused her lasting disappointment. But she learned to accept, if she also lamented, that the social rewards for being a swan were not available to a duckling.[26]

She compensated with female friends, books, writing, mirth, and school. During her high school years, she started to find her center, increasingly habituated by the way she saw the wider world through maturing eyes and by her pursuit of those identifiable things that gave her pleasure. She was simultaneously extroverted and introspective, fun loving and serious, settled and adventurous. Her world for now remained localized, although it was somewhat expanded when she entered Taunton High School, housed in a massive Elizabethan-style edifice with a grand tower and observatory over the front entrance. The teachers there enlarged her universe through books and lessons. They struggled to strengthen her math skills yet found an able student in Latin. "Mary Hamer was undoubtedly the greatest teacher I ever had," Douglas wrote to an old classmate, Helen Tucker Betagh, in 1988. "Her Latin classes were the foundation of whatever education I've ever had." The French teacher promoted her to the front seat. English and American literature were like candy to her. She devoured *Ivanhoe,* Shakespeare, Tennyson, and Washington Irving. Beyond her lessons, she developed a trademark personality. The school's journal offered a tongue-in-cheek description of Marjory: "Age: Giggling; Peculiarity: Sense of humor; Ambition: To be champion featherweight; Occupation: Reading penny dreadfuls; Demeanor: Appalling." She indulged in the occasional amiable prank, even with the most unlikely persons. Once when she and Helen were walking home from school, she gave Helen her hat, coat, and glasses, and Helen walked into the Trefethen house. "Hello, Grandma," she said to Florence as Marjory stood outside the door laughing.[27]

She also wrote. The school journal published one of her stories, "Waiting for a Train," a first-person account of a girl who sets aside her book to watch hurried passengers at a train station. Distracted by so much activity, the narrator ultimately must rush to make her own departure. The story betrays the witty, mirthful style that later became evident in Douglas's newspaper and magazine writing. She remained forever indebted to two of her English teachers, Blanche Grant and Florence Stone. They helped her adopt a writer's mode and develop the practical skills of research and the artistic component of voice. As with mature writers, her temperament was already ranging across the emotional spectrum, the drag of life's burdens keeping her at one end as she reached against it to the other. In the high school journal, she revealed to her classmates, "I have always more need of a laugh than a cry, being somewhat disposed to melancholy in my temperament." Privately, she thought of her few published pieces as "inadequate" and "faintly embarrassing," but seeing them in print gave her a "secret glow." They affirmed her course in life. From the vantage point of an established author, she described her venture into writing in a way that suggested a cosmic calling: "There was no decision to become a writer. The becoming was all."[28]

Despite the self-criticism, her writing skills were recognized when she was called to compose the "parting ode" for her June 1908 high school graduation ceremony. True to her demeanor, she wrote of the struggles and joys of climbing up the academic ladder and of coming of age intellectually. There was sadness in saying good-bye to those who had prevailed together, but they had been well prepared for the new challenges that lay ahead. Marjory graduated magna cum laude, and she was heading to college and away from her grandparents' home.[29]

CHAPTER EIGHT

Frank's Journey

In 1896, Frank Stoneman was on a train bound from Jacksonville to Orlando. He had taken a lonely passage from the Northeast a week or two earlier after he was certain that Lillian's departure to Taunton with Marjory was permanent. With neither job nor family keeping him in Providence, he set out for new surroundings. Why he chose Florida is not altogether clear. Prone to developing pneumonia, he may have been following a doctor's advice to seek a warmer climate, and having grown up on the frontier, his daughter explained, he had always felt the pull of an "unfinished place." The Florida frontier was different from that he had known in the West. A landscape with no discernable roll, wetlands straddling the horizon's broadness, and weather that could be as serene as heaven and violent as Hades would remove him geographically and thus emotionally from his past. No doubt, too, Frank read some of the countless newspaper and magazine articles that depicted Florida as an agricultural promised land and resort empire. At the very moment he was contemplating his future, wealthy capitalists were building railroads and big hotels down both of Florida's coasts, opening America's tropics—though really subtropics—to visitors, settlers, and entrepreneurs. People, in other words, were going to Florida.[1]

And going to Orlando was a reasonable choice. Others before Stoneman had seen potential in Central Florida, and they were creating new opportunities for latecomers like himself. Lush and green and located at the edge of the watershed of the great Everglades system, Orlando was the largest city in the peninsula's interior. A century before Walt Disney World, the bright placid beauty around a chain of lakes made Orlando, including the exotic-sounding cities of Altamonte Springs and Winter Park, a popular wintertime retreat. Henry Plant, a Connecticut Yankee turned Confederate tariff collector turned southern railroad magnate, completed a rail line from Jacksonville to Orlando in 1880 to service leisure travelers and the area's expanding citrus industry, known for the temple orange. The *Atlanta Constitution* described Plant—with his steamer line, railroads, and eight new resort hotels—as the man who "revolutionized nature." Nature was Florida's business, and Plant and other capitalists soberly exploited it.[2]

Stoneman took a Plant steamer from New York to Jacksonville and then climbed aboard Plant's South Florida Railroad to Orlando. At age forty, Stoneman was starting life over, in some ways an exciting prospect but one dampened by what he had to leave behind in the previous life. Sometime along the way, he decided that law would provide a suitable new profession. He settled temporarily outside of town and raised chickens as an income-generating sideline to preparing for the bar. After his admission, he moved to Orlando and hung out his shingle. He rented the room in which he lived from Martha Virginia Eppes Shine Greetham, a great-granddaughter of Thomas Jefferson who, with her late husband, Thomas Shine, had been a pioneer settler of Orlando. Also living with Greetham was her thirty-year-old daughter, Lillias Shine, and she and the new boarder caught each other's eyes.[3] But Stoneman was still legally married, and he and Shine did not act officially on their mutual attraction for seventeen years.[4]

The law profession was ultimately no better to Stoneman than real estate and oil had been. With his prospects for marriage on hold and his legal practice foundering, he pursued an opportunity to go into the newspaper business. In 1900, he and an acquaintance named A. L. La-Salle, the printing department foreman at the weekly *Orlando Sentinel,* purchased a flatbed press from a defunct newspaper in Avon Park, a citrus community that had gone bust after the same 1894–95 freezes that did in Hamilton Disston's St. Cloud sugar enterprise. After hauling the press to Orlando on an oxcart, the two prepared for several months to give the city its first daily newspaper. On January 1, 1896, they ran the inaugural issue of the *Daily Herald.*[5] Central Florida's economy continued to languish, however, while much was happening in the state's southern parts, which had escaped the freezes. Miami, for one, was begot in their aftermath when Henry Flagler extended the southern reach of his Florida East Coast Railway. The railroad dominated the city's affairs—in Douglas's words, an "almost invincible political power." Wanting to unshackle Miami from Flagler, an antirailroad faction called for a new newspaper to represent its interests. Stoneman and LaSalle answered the summons by moving their printing plant to Miami in August 1903.[6]

Miami was a budding city of only two thousand people at the time. The first train had trundled into town in April 1896, when Miami was still a pioneer settlement called Fort Dallas. Some locals said that Standard Oil millionaire Henry Flagler and his railroad were responsible for the existence of Miami and that weather had brought him there. As the story went, following the 1894–95 freezes, a local woman, Julia Tuttle, convinced Flagler that extending his tracks to balmy Biscayne Bay would be a worthy investment. "It is the dream of my life," said Tuttle, who owned sizable parcels of land, "to see this wilderness turned into a prosperous country and where this tangled mass of vine, brush, trees and rocks now are to see homes with modern improvements surrounded by beautiful lawns, flowers, shrubs and shade trees." In exchange for a section of her land and for land from other private and commercial interests, Flagler ran his line south, and Miami was born at its terminus. In most particulars, including a population of 480, Miami remained a wilderness settlement when it incorporated three months later. Locals nicknamed it the Magic City.[7]

Douglas always said that when she moved to Miami in 1915, South Florida was still a frontier. Beyond the propagating masses in the city, her observation was credible. The Everglades were as wild a country as existed anywhere in late-nineteenth-century America, and they would remain in some state of wildness throughout Douglas's long life. Miami's geographic proximity to the Everglades meant that the city—its expansion, economy, weather, and image—would always be attached to them. Wedged between Biscayne Bay and the Everglades, Miami had its "peculiarities of situations," wrote Will Davenport, an early resident. At "its back door [lay] a jungle with serpents, saurians [alligators] and aborigines while its front door swung open on the [Hotel] Royal Palm's pageant of cosmopolitan civility." Unlike the "artificially beautiful Palm Beach," declared the 1904 city directory, Miami was "the most glorious picture that Dame Nature has printed," a "land where the finger prints of God linger on every flower," a "paradise regained." The seeming ugliness of the dominant scrubland was sufficiently offset by the bay, the sunshine, the delicious trade winds, and the hammocks with lush fortifications of live oaks, figs, mahoganies, satin leaf, pigeon plum, several kinds of palm trees, and the red-licorice-like gumbo limbo. Culturally, too, Miami was a city in between, where pioneers, northern retirees, and dreaming businessmen mingled, where Yankee accents and energy sometimes collided with southern drawls and steadfast customs. From its inception, Miami began evolving as a winter playground, offering tourists diversions in "fishing, driving, riding, cycling, golfing, bathing and yachting." Before Miami had public schools, it had a yacht club and a championship golf course. Sightseers could glimpse the peculiar juxtaposition of civility and wilderness by taking rides around the bay and up the Miami River on the "observation boat" *Marjorie,* from which they viewed the "wonderful water front" and the "wonderful Everglades."[8]

The *Marjorie* took the sightseers past Flagler's Hotel Royal Palm. Like his Florida west coast rival and friend Henry Plant, Flagler located winter resorts, including the Royal Palm, along his train routes. To build the hotel, he hired one of Disston's former employees, John Sewell, who used black and leased convict labor to do the construction. To accommodate the 450-room hotel and resort (which included a billiard room, swimming pool, and casino), "John Sewell's gang," as Douglas called them, cleared guava, coconut palm, banana, key lime, and ironwood trees (a South American invasive called *quebracho* [ax breaker] that was dynamited out). To build a 578-foot veranda, the crew leveled and looted an ancient seventy-five-foot burial mound left by the Tekesta Indians at the mouth of the Miami River. The hotel stretched nearly the length of three football fields when it was completed in 1897. Its grand long red mansard roof above five yellow stories could hardly escape notice as the altarpiece of the leisure class.[9]

The city's founders would have incorporated under the name Flagler City if the mogul had let them do so. Men on Flagler's payroll stacked the city council. One was his lawyer; another went on to manage his Colonial Hotel in Nassau, Bahamas; and the first mayor was an agent for one of his land companies. Sewell laid out Miami's streets and became a three-term mayor. Flagler persuaded Congress to help finance the channeling of the shallow Biscayne Bay to promote water commerce among Miami, Havana, and the Bahamas, where he had hotels. He extended electricity to the city from the Royal Palm's power plant, paid for Miami's water mains and sewage system, and started the first newspaper, which took the hopeful name *Miami Metropolis*.[10]

Flagler was also connected to Miami's first water-pollution problem. The city originally pumped potable water from Slaughter Creek, which flowed out of the Everglades. No one found anything ominous about the name of their water source until an "inquisitive" newspaperman named Stoneman discovered that the creek drained the blood-soaked land where animals were killed and dressed for the market. Flagler's people warned Stoneman not to publish the discovery. He resisted the pressure and went to press with his findings in hope of bettering the town. People took notice, and artesian wells were dug.[11]

But if people winced at the thought of effluent running red down a vital creek, if they fretted over how cutting a bay channel and removing whole swaths of mangroves and coral reefs depleted fish and bird populations, if they grieved over the way clearing verdant hammocks left the land devoid of wildlife, only a few said anything. Embarking on his canoe trip down the southeast portion of the Everglades in 1897, Hugh Willoughby noted, "What a change has been made in this place since last year! . . . Of course, its splendid big hotel, with every modern convenience, will prove a great boon to the tourist, but for me the picturesqueness seemed to have gone; its wildness has been rudely marred by the hand of civilization." Although Willoughby regretted the change, he conceded that "we must not look upon these things from the sentimental point of view. The romance and poetry must be suppressed for the sterner, material welfare of our fellow-man."[12]

Here, from someone who felt at home in the wild, was testament to the priority humans accorded their own lifeless artifacts over nature's animations. In the early nineteenth century, Americans reminded their European rivals that the young republic had landscapes and vistas that had no counterparts in the world. America's first great painters and photographers, creating a new national tradition, made their reputations in the landscape genre while finding inspiration on the frontier, including Florida. But as technology and the economy modernized and Americans achieved greater sophistication in the construction of things, they increasingly became refugees from nature. After the Civil War, beauty was redefined by an emerging cultural narcissism. Beauty became less associated with the beholder than with something manufactured or designed by technology, a product of human conjuring that was imposed on society. In Florida, that change dates to the 1890s, when Flagler completed construction of the last in his chain of grand hotels at the mouth of the Miami River. His endeavors were welcomed, praised, and celebrated for many decades to come. The 1904 city directory aptly if melodramatically captured the enduring mood: "Guided by the enterprise and liberality of Henry M. Flagler" and "before the weapons of civilization, wielded by an army of energetic men, the almost impenetrable tropical growths melted away, and in its place the hand of progress set its mark."[13]

Flagler's cities foreshadowed the hurried development that routed the Florida environment for the next century and beyond. His exalted status signaled the power that local governments surrendered to developers and real estate agents, many of whom voters sent to serve in the state legislature and the governor's office. These stewards of the built environment, with their myopic vision of progress and contrived beauty, eventually drew Douglas's derision after she joined her father's newspaper. Yet here too was a weakness in the strategy of conservationists of the time who evangelized beauty. As long as purveyors of progress believed that human know-how and talent could improve on nature's beauty, they had the advantage. In 1940, Frank Stoneman spoke of the "beautiful islands" out in Biscayne Bay with their "hundreds of beautiful residences" that were "once merely submerged acres, and were 'made lands,' . . . land that was originally pumped up from the bottom of the bay."[14]

By rule, agents of progress held a winning hand when playing the beauty card. When Willoughby set out on his Everglades junket, he observed, "In all Florida I have never seen a more beautiful spot than where this deep, narrow river suddenly opens into Biscayne Bay." When Douglas arrived eighteen years later, she never saw the mangroves that he had seen lining the river's banks or the water's tannin color. She saw a river reduced to a drainage ditch for the besieged Everglades. The city directory, for all its elation for the native aesthetic, was wrong on one point: Miami was in fact turning artificial, like Palm Beach.[15]

Nature would not be allowed to stand in the way of future prosperity. Boosters believed that nature should be reshaped to maximize its potential as a resource, whether, in Douglas's words, by dynamiting the "great dark jungle along the bay front" to build hotels or by stripping the indigenous pines and palmettos to plant ornamental "gardens of coco palms, date palms, oranges and grapefruit, and a few enormous banyans." What was true for the city was true for the wet hinterland to the west. In the fraternity of profit-minded men, drainage constituted a regular topic of conversation. When the governor announced that he would resurrect Disston's idea of draining the Everglades, boosters sounded no complaints about the state entering into matters of private enterprise.[16]

William S. Jennings had been in Florida only a relatively short while before winning the governorship in 1900. Fifteen years earlier, he left his native Illinois to open a law practice in the Florida citrus and farming community of Brooksville. He climbed remarkably quickly through the ranks of the state Democratic Party as an anti-Bourbon—meaning anti-railroad—populist. When he married a local, May Mann, in 1891, he did so for love, but he also helped secure his political footing. May's father, Austin, was a combative state legislator who had served on the committees investigating the Disston purchase. He also reigned as the "silver-tongued orator" of the state Farmers' Alliance and organized its historic 1890 national convention in Ocala. May too emerged as a highly skilled lobbyist and arguably the most important suffragist and conservationist in early twentieth-century Florida. Jennings's family had its own distinguished politician and the greatest of orators in the person of William's cousin and lifelong friend, William Jennings Bryan. Relatives said that the two men resembled each other in appearance, temperament, and political talent, though not in public speaking abilities. When Jennings ran for governor, he brought the Great Commoner to Florida, where he gave a rousing speech from the balcony of the Jennings home in Brooksville.[17]

After winning the election, Jennings essentially stumbled on what would become his political legacy. On a trip to California for a governors' convention in August 1902, he stayed over in Colorado to observe federal irrigation projects. Jennings later described the stop as a pivotal moment in his public service career. Congress had authorized the Bureau of Reclamation earlier that year, and in Colorado bureau engineers were bringing water to arid land, where it was wanted for agriculture. Florida's problem was just the opposite, Jennings noted; it had too much water where it was unwanted. He reasoned that if government could solve the problems of irrigation in the West, it could do the same with drainage in Florida. Years later, the *New York Times* commented that drainage in Florida "is almost as important as irrigation in the Southwest." Jennings would have taken issue only with the word *almost*.[18]

The irrigation projects gave him an idea for what to do with the Internal Improvement Fund land that had languished since the failed Disston venture. From his hotel, he dispatched a letter with instructions to his aides in Tallahassee to sort out the state's landholdings. By the time

he arrived home, the work was well under way. An engineer's survey revealed that the federal government had never turned over a sizable piece
of Everglades territory. Jennings had been hoping to find just this sort of
prize, and he immediately petitioned Washington for the parcel. When
he was told that the land belonged to the Seminoles, he countered that
Indians had "no rights under the treaties to any lands in the Everglades."
The argument failed to generate a land grant, so Jennings traveled to
Washington in 1903 to meet with the secretary of the interior. This was
the same year that Stoneman moved to Miami; it was also the year that
South Florida farmers watched late-spring floods wash away seeds and
plantings from poorly drained fields. Jennings's trip paid off. President
Theodore Roosevelt offered a grant of 2,862,280 acres of submerged land.
Jennings had also wanted Congress to pay for the construction of drainage canals and dikes to relieve inundated farms, but he was content to
receive the land alone, wet or dry. That conveyance represented the final
federal parcel in the Everglades, except Seminole territory, as well as two-
thirds of the remaining unoccupied land on the peninsula.[19]

Unfortunately for Jennings, a one-term limit for governors left him
without the time to set drainage operations under way. When he left office in 1905, he shifted over to the role of special council to the Internal
Improvement Fund. He sought to keep state land from conveying to railroads, which sued in search of their own windfall; Flagler's Florida East
Coast Railway, for example, claimed that it was entitled to two million
acres in return for laying track from Jacksonville to Key West. Jennings
passed the mantle of drainage to his successor in the governor's mansion, Napoleon Bonaparte Broward; down in Miami, Stoneman monitored these developments.[20]

The inaugural edition of Stoneman and LaSalle's *Miami Evening Record*
appeared on September 15, 1903. LaSalle served as president of the newspaper and Stoneman as managing editor. Four years later, they absorbed
the *Miami Morning News* and changed their masthead to the *Miami
News-Record*. As the newspaper's editorial writer, Stoneman turned his
skills in analytical reasoning and the full spectrum of his knowledge into

a way of life. From nearly the first publication, he criticized the cozy company that railroads kept with Florida's politicians. Using corporate power for the private interest of a few men at the expense of the community and for accruing power rubbed against his convictions.[21]

Stoneman believed that his first duty as a newspaperman was to give his readership factual information and well-informed opinions. For the first time, he valued his vocation, and Miami's strange amalgamation of pioneer town and resort city on the cusp of transition suited him nicely. But in an all-too-familiar personal scenario, the *News-Record* struggled financially and within a few years went into receivership. Douglas always believed her father's editorial attacks against Flagler were responsible for drying up advertising revenue, but Stoneman had eased off the railroad issue. His chief competitor, Bobo Dean, publisher and editor of the *Miami Metropolis,* was a greater Flagler antagonist. Unceremoniously dubbed the Bobonic Plague by the railroad crowd, Dean championed a successful campaign to change shipping rates that discriminated against small farmers. According to one source, Dean's anti-Flagler position stimulated advertising revenue, stealing it away from Stoneman. Stoneman attributed his newspaper's decline not to Flagler-bashing but to the economic crisis of 1907, which wiped out several local businesses and the city's leading bank. A prelude to the national crisis was an October hurricane packing one-hundred-mile-per-hour winds that claimed 164 human lives and left economic ruin in Miami. Stoneman was facing yet another business failure when Frank B. Shutts, an Indiana attorney recently relocated to Miami and working for Flagler, stepped in to rescue the newspaper. With a loan of twenty-nine thousand dollars from Flagler, Shutts took control of the *News-Record* in 1907 and changed it to a morning publication with himself as publisher and Stoneman as editor. In 1910, when Marjory was entering her junior year in college, they renamed the newspaper the *Miami Herald.*[22]

Stoneman's editorial interests had assumed a new focus after Broward became governor in 1905, and they did not change under Shutts's stewardship. The new governor wasted little time trying to make good on his campaign promise to reclaim the Everglades. Early South Floridians put their stock in agriculture, believing that Miami would one day be "indebted" to the Everglades for "wealth and increase of population." Stoneman recognized this connection and initially supported the governor but soon found reason to regard his leadership with suspicion. "Father was from the West where [too little] water was a problem," said Douglas. He was uncomfortable with policymakers who cavalierly treated the resource as the enemy of civilization and who allowed a populist initiative to degenerate into a scheme to further enrich a few already wealthy men. Stoneman blamed Broward. As governor, Internal Improvement Fund head, and chief engineer and decision maker, he had anointed himself sovereign of Florida drainage.[23]

CHAPTER NINE

The Sovereign

Even when its boiler was cold and dormant, the one-hundred-foot-long floating dredge was an imposing rig. The superstructure straddling the thirty-eight-foot beam was a small factory, pungent with the smell of grease and rotting Everglades detritus. When lit off, the boiler roused the dredge into a belching hulk of steel cables, pulleys, and I beams in repetitive motion. A mechanical sigh sounded with each in-and-out, turning move of the boom, controlled like a giant grasshopper leg on puppet strings by an operator pulling at levers. Assisted by an onboard crew of twelve, he could plunge the dredge's bucket twenty-two feet into the water, swing it out seventy feet, and disgorge 4.5 cubic yards of muck, enough to cover the infield of a baseball diamond.

One lover of wild Florida called these creatures of human invention "steel behemoths." They were earthmovers in the grimmest sense of the term. In 1908, the trustees of the Internal Improvement Fund purchased two of them from the Marion Steam Shovel Company of Ohio, one for $22,000 and another, with a shorter boom, for $19,941. Over the next several decades, they and other dredges crisscrossed the Everglades, excavating more than seven hundred miles of canals. In their day, the dredges were a masterwork of engineering. In Florida, they attempted to create yet another kind of engineering marvel—the reclaimed Everglades.[1]

The initiative was a bold one. The project's domain encompassed as much earth as sky, with no end to either. Running out to all points of the compass, through the sawgrass and marsh, around the hammock islands, and through the cypress strands, was water. To convert so much water into land required technology that did not yet exist. The attempt, though, required only blind faith in human capacity. Dredges were that faith manifested.

One had been under way in the New River outside of Fort Lauderdale since July 1906, and it yielded positive results. The freshly exposed muck soil, reported the *Miami Metropolis,* was "creamy black and ranging anywhere from three to five feet thick." Cultivated fields took form as quickly as the land was dried out, rendering "good, big healthy" fruits and vegetables. Additional land would be made available as the dredge, later joined by one of the new Marion machines, continued carving out the river, which was turning from a mere drainage outlet into a bustling avenue of commerce. A flotilla of launches, workboats, and other craft plied the placid waters; truck farmers and citrus growers built new homes along the precisely carved banks; and entrepreneurs opened new businesses. Here was Florida's very own land of milk and honey, a "tale from the Arabian Nights," said one Florida magazine.[2]

The reports of the *Metropolis,* whose editor, the partisan Bobo Dean, had traveled to Fort Lauderdale to survey the work, were more than encouraging for the future of drainage. Dean's assessments of agrarian success made the people living around Biscayne Bay eager to hear the machine noise of progress and to see the signs of "thrift and prosperity." Seven months before the Internal Improvement Fund placed its order with the Marion Company, Governor Broward received a petition from Miami citizens requesting a dredge to convert the loping Miami River into a busy canal linking their city to reclaimed land.[3]

Broward liked the idea. Before making a trip to inspect the progress on the New River in early 1908, he sent word to the petitioners that he would be in Fort Lauderdale and available to discuss their request. A delegation of sixty businessmen subsequently huddled with him in the meeting hall above the store of Frank Stranahan, a pioneer merchant who enjoyed a lucrative trade with Seminoles and the local reclamation crews. Broward told the Miami men that if they purchased forty thousand dollars worth of Internal Improvement Fund land, the state would buy a new dredge and dig the canal they wanted. The delegation agreed to the terms. According to the *Metropolis,* the meeting was a veritable "love feast," and Broward was the gracious host extolling the feasibility of drainage with what had become his trademark refrain: "Water will run down hill."[4]

When the promised dredge arrived in early 1909, people celebrated in the streets. Delivered from its assembly site in Tampa, the *Miami* was the state's gift of progress to the dredge's namesake city. The editor of the *Miami News-Record* had a different response to the dredge. Never one to indulge in sentimental reverie, Frank Stoneman showed front-page contempt for the hoopla: "Probably in the whole United States it never before occurred to any set of people to celebrate the advent of any one of the thousands of dredges now at work in this country." One of the most vocal critics of Broward's drainage efforts, Stoneman was a disliked man in Tallahassee, and he was risking yet another business by criticizing a popular program and a governor who held grudges. But canal boosters were proving to be reckless purveyors of progress. Stoneman perceived their dynamiting of the Miami River's rapids as the "first great impetus toward the" unrestrained "upbuilding" of South Florida, and the river itself had been turned into a dead, silt-laden channel that fouled the blue-green waters of Biscayne Bay.[5] It is not accurate, however, to idealize Stoneman as an oracle of Everglades preservation and model for his daughter's future environmentalism: Stoneman and Broward were actually ideological cousins on the issue of land use. A child of the transitional frontier and an individual of ambition, Stoneman saw wetlands and arid lands as in need of improvement, and he supported bringing land "into subjection to the plow." One of his articles claimed that 120 million acres of desolate spaces were "lying waste in America." The United States lagged behind other countries, even unassuming Argentina, in making progress in reclamation. In the tone of Horace Greeley and Theodore Roosevelt, he linked nationhood and world leadership to the exploitation of natural resources: the "American people cannot rightly claim to have measured up to their opportunity until the deserts and the swamps have been replaced by vistas of prosperous farmsteads."[6]

Stoneman, in other words, supported the concept of Everglades drainage. But he was not willing to be foolish about it. He found cause for concern in Broward's eagerness to charge ahead with an unproven plan bankrolled by public monies. The celebrants in Miami's streets, he lamented, were "hysterical enthusiasts" duped by bureaucrats and speculators. "Only after . . . searching investigation do wise men enter upon great undertakings," he wrote, and Broward was too hasty and heedless to be wise.[7]

Many years later, Douglas followed her father's lead. She inherited his robust suspicion of people who denied the possibility of failure. The Browards of the world were slaves to their inner drive and averse to any other rationale but their own. Listen they would not, and argue they would always. The argument for drainage, she wrote, was based on nothing more than a "school boy's logic." Drainage was a "dream, a mirage of riches that many men would follow to their ruin."[8]

Broward blamed others for trying to ruin him and his project. Whenever someone registered a demurral, he was convinced that railroad interests, his staunchest opposition during the gubernatorial campaign, lay behind the effort. In the previous century, public outrage over the state's land giveaways (including that to Hamilton Disston but mainly that to railroads) led a sizable faction of the Democratic Party to cleave off to form the Populist Party. Broward believed himself to be the enduring embodiment of this popular dissent. Railroads were Florida's largest landowners, the "prime ogres of the farmers," as one historian of the era noted. One of Broward's supporters complained that some railways were "built on nothing more substantial than blue-print paper," and they held a disputed claim to every Everglades acre the governor wanted for the hardworking husbandmen. The railroad claims had little to do with drainage (a venture the railroads preferred to avoid), since new settlers on reclaimed land translated into new customers. But the railroads were unwilling to relinquish potential profits from selling the land to farmers and developers. "They not only want the biggest half of the cake," Broward growled, "but they don't want anyone else to have any cake at all."[9]

Broward was never one to allow his critics to thwart his ambitions. He judged men like himself and even the luckless Disston, men of unlimited self-assurance, differently than did Stoneman and Douglas. In 1907, Broward wrote to one of his detractors, "It might be said of me, and perhaps of every other man who has a desire to accomplish something for the good of mankind, that he belongs to that class 'who rush in where angels fear to tread.' This land would have remained a wilderness and would have been inhabited by the Indians until the dawn of the millennium had those who preceded us been as weak as the majority of those who quibble now . . . instead of plunging in and doing something."[10]

Broward was a proud and sometimes bellicose plunger. Six feet, two inches tall, with broad shoulders and a stout walrus mustache, he drew the reflexive looks of other men when he entered a room. His temperament matched his bearish anatomy; he insisted on getting his way. The son of a wealthy plantation owner broken by the Civil War, Broward was orphaned at age thirteen and lacked the head start in life that someone of his social pedigree might have expected. He first tried his hand at farming; when that failed, he rafted logs down the St. Johns River. At age eighteen, he began work on riverboats and sailing ships, eventually earning his license as a river pilot. In 1895, he oversaw the construction of *Three Friends,* a seagoing tug that he, his brother, and a third partner employed in a wrecking and towing business. During the Cuban campaign for independence, the men converted their vessel into an armed blockade-runner and smuggled munitions and patriots to Cuba.[11]

Before winning the public's admiration as a minor war hero, Broward made his debut on the political scene. The *Jacksonville Florida Times-Union* at first regarded him as a man of "integrity, honesty, courage, and above all absolute sobriety." His career in public service began in 1888 as sheriff of Duval County, a post to which he was twice appointed and twice elected and from which he was once removed after he was accused, probably accurately, of using the power of his office to interfere in a county election. In 1900, he overcame the controversy and made a successful bid for the state House of Representatives. Four years later, he ran for governor as an anticorporate, antirailroad candidate.[12]

Everglades drainage provided the "most dramatic factor" in Broward's campaign, said Douglas. He promised to create six million acres of new farmland and do so with a mere thirty miles of canals. Maps of his plans, which he carried on the campaign trail, indicated his support for independent farmers, whom he promised would "tap the wealth of the fabulous muck." In a public letter circulated after his election, he declared the challenge of draining the Everglades to be a "simple . . . engineering feat." If humans could control the "mighty Mississippi River" and the "turbulent Nile," they could reclaim the Everglades. With a single sentence, he tapped into the voters' sense of human superiority, invoked natural law to validate the simple logic of Everglades drainage, and portrayed opponents of his plan as enemies of reason: "Shall the sovereign people of Florida supinely surrender to a few land pirates and a few purchased newspapers and supinely confess that they cannot knock a hole in a wall of coral and let a body of water obey a natural law and seek the level of the sea?"[13]

After becoming governor, Broward needed money for drainage. In his first message to the legislature, he urged lawmakers to create the Everglades Drainage District. The district would be run by a board of commissioners—the trustees of the Internal Improvement Fund. To pay for drainage, they would be endowed with the authority to tax property owners within the district. By May 1905, the legislature had given Broward everything he wanted. As their first order of business, the commissioners set up a drainage district around Lake Okeechobee and established a five-cent-per-acre tax. One of the larger Everglades landholders, the Southern States Land and Timber Company, promptly sued, and the U.S. circuit court issued an injunction protecting the company. Broward and his legal counsel, William Jennings, reasoned that the commissioners could still tax landholders not protected by the injunction. Again, the court rejected the commissioners' actions. The decisions represented an infuriating setback, but Broward still had approximately four hundred thousand dollars in fund reserves.[14]

Jennings kept busy fending off corporate land grabbers while Broward purchased the state's first dredges. The fund trustees readily deferred to his expertise. He was actually more studied in the principles of engineering than his rhetorical claim that water would always run downhill implied. Broward's background as a shipbuilder and tugboat pilot gave him the mechanical know-how for the job, and his intensity was even greater. Very much at home around machines, he knew how they worked, and he knew how to work them. The minutest details in the design of the dredges caught his attention, and on more than one occasion he traveled to the manufacturing plants to inspect the assembly of his machines, spotting flaws and recommending changes. He approached canal work in similar fashion, and he was something more than a meddlesome politician when he visited a construction site. The chief engineer on the New River project, who had been the chief engineer of *Three Friends,* regularly sought the governor's counsel. Broward was sufficiently admired as an authority on canals to be elected president of the National Drainage Congress in 1907.[15]

Before excavation got under way in Florida, the governor considered a number of plans and canal routes for Everglades reclamation. The first to tempt him included a canal from Lake Okeechobee to the St. Lucie River, which emptied into the Atlantic Ocean at the village of Stuart, followed by a connecting canal to the St. Johns River. The watery axis would create a circuitous cross-Florida waterway running from the port of Jacksonville, up the northward-flowing St. Johns, up the St. Lucie, across Lake Okeechobee, down the Caloosahatchee River, and out into the Gulf of Mexico. But in 1906, Broward opted to appease political allies and in early July put the first dredge at the headwaters of New River near Fort Lauderdale. In a grand ceremony, he reportedly stood on the bow of the *Everglades,* regarded as the "largest and finest dredge boat south of Philadelphia," made "a lordly wave of his right arm" toward an outsize sawgrass plain, and exclaimed, "'There, boys, is Lake Okeechobee. Go to it!'"[16]

Broward's biographer notes that the governor had no "definite technical survey to follow." Other observers agree that an engineering party faced the northwest; forged ahead of the dredge through sawgrass, muck, and angry clouds of mosquitoes; and hastened out a course with stakes. When the new dredge *Okeechobee* was launched in the big lake, it was expected to meet its counterpart somewhere to the southeast. Based on data gathered by Buckingham Smith and the plans of Hamilton Disston, the task was uncomplicated. The dredges would connect Lake Okeechobee, twenty feet above sea level, to the Atlantic and the gulf and let the water run out until the lake dropped six feet.[17]

The luminous simplicity of Broward's drainage science irked Stoneman. It was an affront to hardworking taxpayers and would-be Everglades farmers. In Quaker fashion, his daughter would later say, he believed that true nation building required not only the practical matter of reclaiming wastelands but also the political matter of the occasional grassroots challenge to power brokers—profiteering politicians and greedy corporations. One of the requirements of citizenship was policing those who took positions of leadership. "He had an Episcopalian sense of grace and formality in human relations," Douglas remembered, "at variance with the fiery, emotional tone of" his abolitionist forebears.[18]

The watchdog editor went to press with one challenge that the governor surely had not anticipated. Listening to science, Stoneman made the remarkable claim that draining the Everglades would likely alter the local climate in serious ways. That humans could manipulate weather conditions was not a new idea. But human impact typically was associated with positive change, especially within a culture that believed in its manifest destiny. In the late nineteenth century, for example, whites settling the arid West believed that rain would follow once they converted the indigenous grasslands into pastoral farmlands—precisely the sort of tragic optimism that worried Stoneman. In the case of Everglades drainage, he warned of drought and cooler winter weather. He reminded readers how farmers near bodies of water had been spared the ravages of the 1894–95 freezes, which devastated Florida agriculture and ruined Disston, and Stoneman asked whether it was wise to eliminate the Everglades. South Florida, he said, was the only place in the country producing "tropical fruits," which were "commanding large prices." Alfred Newlander, a civil engineer from St. Augustine who identified himself as a veteran of drainage projects, had originally suggested these dire prospects to Stoneman. After visiting the New River site in 1906, Newlander dispatched a letter to Stoneman advancing this theory of microclimate change and indicting Broward's economic and planning discrepancies. Stoneman reprinted the letter in its entirety on the front page of the *News-Record*.[19]

The two men were attaching a biological and social value to the Everglades in its raw, unaltered state, denying the equation of swampland with wasteland. Stoneman's daughter adopted this argument in her campaigns sixty years later. Although she reflected on her father's opposition to Broward, she remembered fair government, hasty planning, and good economics as the issues that concerned him. In *River of Grass*, she noted, "To the intricate and subtle relation of soil, of fresh water and evaporation, and of runoff and salt intrusion, and all the consequences of disturbing the fine balance nature had set up in the past four thousand years—no one knew enough to look." Yet some years before Newlander's warning, conservationists had begun including the calamities of climate change in their arguments to protect forest watersheds, which in the heyday of logging were disappearing with ever-increasing alacrity. Douglas was not entirely off base, however. Early scientists were more interested in the quality of Everglades soil than anything else, and they took the subtropical climate for granted. Her father's editorial would be long forgotten by the time other people began giving the Everglades their full ecological due.[20]

Defending practical economics alone, much less something as foreign as climactic change, brought Stoneman into an editorial scrap with his chief news rival, the *Miami Metropolis*. He and the pugnacious Bobo Dean had an established history of disagreeing, often exploding trivial differences into major rifts. Moreover, Dean had been a faithful Broward supporter from the first. Few readers would have been surprised when the *Metropolis* accused the *News-Record* of having a dim-eyed view of the "prevalent [positive] sentiment in this country" toward Everglades drainage.[21]

Yet many other editors in the state were on the same page as Stoneman. The *Orlando Democrat* wrote, "Some men believe the Everglades should be drained while others urge the annexation of the moon." The *Jasper*

News sounded a blunt echo: "Of all the foolish ideas that ever entered the brain of man the draining of the Everglades is the most nonsensical." The *Bradenton Herald* noted presciently, "Saw-grass muck is a peat bog that will burn down to bedrock when drained." The most anguished complaint was that the governor's "pet scheme" would drain the state treasury before draining the Everglades. Broward's hometown newspaper, the *Jacksonville Metropolis,* ran a front-page cartoon showing the governor poking holes in a money bag and letting streams of specie flow out. That same year, Stoneman claimed that Broward and the state had "plunged into enormous expenditures . . . without any previous investigation as to the character of the land to be drained, the ultimate cost of the operations, or any preliminary surveys preparatory to locating the canals." Stoneman called for the governor to "open the books" and to commission "experts and scientists" to conduct a careful "examination of the subject."[22]

Broward was proposing a plan that would use progressive approaches—the power of the state and scientific knowledge, however suspect and manipulated that knowledge—to fulfill a populist promise. By the same token, he was turning the enterprise of drainage into a giant and unproven public works project. Granting such a degree of authority to the government might normally have contradicted the doctrines of the day's liberals, who feared too much centralized power. Broward was identified as a liberal, but he was leading a developing state during a transitional period in American politics, and in practice he represented a not-so-strange amalgamation of progressivism, populism, and liberalism. Even among the voices of protest, regardless of their position on the political spectrum, the burning question was not whether the state should pursue an endeavor better left to private oversight; rather, critics wondered who stood to receive the spoils of this public project and whether it was economically feasible or even likely to work.[23]

Largely based on his observations as a river pilot, Broward deployed science that was indeed questionable. Just as he could take the helm of his tug and turn the wheel to port and starboard, commanding *Three Friends* to follow, he would direct the force of gravity to move unwanted water into his canals, commanding it to the southwest and the Gulf of

Mexico or to the southeast and the Atlantic. As simple as his engineering seemed, it was in sync with the philosophical context of the day's more credible engineering methods. Given his affinity for things mechanical, Broward may well have seen nature as did the philosophes of his ances-tral homeland in Europe—that is, as a machine in tune with the mathematical laws of motion. If humans could build and dismantle a machine, they could deconstruct nature, God's machine. Nature could at times be maddeningly unpredictable, but so could machines. When and where a steam-powered vessel would break down was anybody's guess.

The sixteenth-century European discovery of the laws of motion had reduced chaotic nature to predictable science and eventually ushered in the Age of Reason. Intrepid nature could no longer keep at bay once-fearful humans armed with new understanding. Into the vacuum left by fear poured a sense of superiority, an inclination to control, and a desire to possess. At the very least, humans needed to denaturize nature. Francis A. Hendry, a South Florida cattle king who gave his name to the county where Florida's sugarcane industry would grow up, articulated as well as anyone of his and Broward's generation this idea about the Everglades. "Old Dame Nature," he wrote in 1906, "has been fixing up this trick for decades. She never does it all, but always leaves something for man to do. It is here she temptingly invites man to roll up his sleeves and pitch in."[24]

In another corner of Broward's expansive sparring ring, political power, not science or land, was the divisive matter spurring on his opponent. The growing national interest in South Florida stirred up a sectional rivalry between upper parts of the state and the developing peninsula. North Florida politicians were heirs of the Confederacy and the prewar agrarian tradition, which continued to dominate state politics and policy for many decades. Broward was trying to perpetuate that tradition in the southern part of the state, but he was pursuing that end in populist fashion, and populism did not sit well with white-columned planters of the Panhandle. Moreover, they watched as the peninsula filled up with Yankees, mere carpetbaggers like Disston, with offensive cosmopolitan ways. As a son of North Florida and a paternalistic purveyor of peninsula growth, Broward tried to bridge the political chasm between the two regions. More often, however, he simply got caught in the crossfire. His rivals in the north did not want their political power diluted either by large landholders or by small farmers in the south—and certainly not by city dwellers.

Despite taking unfriendly fire from all flanks, Broward persisted as an implacable force. He had the fighting spirit of a gladiator. He was invigorated by thoughts of reducing his opponents to "weeping and gnashing of teeth." He must have felt such a charge when at one point he turned directly on Stoneman. According to Douglas, the governor, in a moment of apparent vindictiveness, refused to validate Stoneman's election to a circuit court judgeship. For some years, he had combined running the newspaper with a seat on the municipal court bench; Broward's actions ensured that Stoneman would never rise to a higher court. Uncowed, Stoneman continued to write pieces opposing Everglades drainage, while Broward forged ahead with his project even after it erupted into a national controversy that involved squabbling bureaucrats in Washington.[25]

CHAPTER TEN

Wellesley

The paean for new horizons in Marjory's "parting ode" at her high school graduation in 1908 concealed a personal ambivalence. Her excitement at starting college that fall was equaled by her misgivings about leaving her invalid mother. Marjory was Lillian's one true love, and everyone worried about the dismal toll her daughter's absence would take on Lillian. Lillian wanted Marjory to have a college education, though, as did her grandmother and aunt. Having consulted teachers, friends, and the family, Marjory was inclined to a liberal arts education at a women's school that would push her to grow intellectually, artistically, and emotionally. The Northeast's inventory of such schools was large—Vassar, Bryn Mawr, Smith, Mount Holyoke, and Wellesley. To lessen the pain of separation from her mother, she chose the closest school, Wellesley, an hour and a half away by train.[1]

With the choice made, the family had to consider whether it was affordable. The tuition at Wellesley was $175 a year, and if Marjory lived frugally, a convention as familiar to her as her mother's illness, expenses for room, board, books, and other essentials would still run as much as $400 (less than half of what some girls spent at Wellesley). Daniel's foundry was not generating enough business to pay for that sum, so the family decided to let out the front bedroom to a boarder. Funds still ran short. If not for Aunt Fanny's generosity, Marjory would have had to settle for a lesser alternative—living at home, taking the trolley each day to Framingham Normal School, and feeling grimly hemmed in and miserable. Fanny had for years had a secret bank account, stashing away her earnings from music lessons and bookkeeping. When Fanny announced that she would pay for Wellesley, Marjory was overcome by the generosity. She assured Fanny that Wellesley would be well worth it.[2]

The college had the track record to suggest as much. When Wellesley opened in 1875, its founder, Henry Durant, a wealthy lawyer, businessman, lay preacher, and philanthropist, expected his school to rise quickly to the vanguard of higher education, to emerge as the female equivalent of Harvard. He spent nearly two million dollars to give it a head start in that direction. Near where he lived in West Needham, Massachusetts, he located an idyllic spot for a campus, a grassy knoll overlooking a sweeping lake-centered pastoral. He then commissioned the construction of College Hall at the crest of the knoll. This grand edifice would represent an intriguing amalgamation of Gothic and Second Empire architecture with a column-and-wainscot interior finished in polished wood. To match the architecture, he recruited an edifying and energetic female faculty and assembled a library with one of the best reference collections in the country. The school's curriculum emphasized elocution and science, and no male college had better student laboratories than those at Wellesley. No other women's college had Wellesley's laboratories, library, or founding vision. Durant sought, as he put it, to empower Wellesley students to "revolt against the slavery in which women were held by the customs of society."[3]

Marjory experienced an overwhelming feeling of liberation when she left Taunton, despite her worries about her mother. To help with the move, Fanny rode with Marjory on the train up to busy, noisy Boston, where they changed lines for the quiet village of Wellesley (the name under which West Needham had incorporated in 1881), thirteen miles to the west. Every fall, the village's sidewalks and street crossings perked up with the jittery excitement of the freshman class, whose members traditionally looked for residences off campus. Fanny and Marjory found something suitable to budget and taste, renting the cheapest room in a house where seven young women would ultimately reside. Marjory would live alone in the attic and in the one room that had not been wired for electricity, but she nevertheless found her accommodations cozy and wonderful. From the window she had a grand view of the garden and trees, and she had no roommate with whom to contend. On her first night, she lit an oil lamp and put off sleep until she finished reading Brander Matthews's *English Composition*.[4]

A few days later, she applied his lessons to her first writing assignment, twined with her own style, and got exciting results. Undertaken for Frances Perry's advanced composition course, the assignment required the students to compose a letter to their families. Marjory wrote about the aura of the campus clothed in crisp fall colors. Perry was looking for something restrained and ascetic and thought Marjory's composition showed too much literary flair. Perry had Marjory read the piece to the class as an example of how not to write a letter. When she finished, the students broke into applause. From that first exercise, her classmates knew her as a writer, and she found immediate confirmation for her choice of schools.[5]

The ideal fit for her desire for intellectual interaction, understanding companions, and independence, Wellesley gave her a new sense of belonging and self-worth. Women's colleges generally offered an uplifting social and academic environment for those who felt awkward and nervous around the opposite sex. Many of the professors at Wellesley had themselves been self-conscious girls who needed to be turned out of their shells. They were ready champions of the Wellesley philosophy that the transformative force of the college experience should extend to the student's personality, making diffident girls into self-confident women with ideas, ambitions, and the know-how to get things done. Marjory appreciated Wellesley as much for its confidence building as anything else. It was an "Adamless Eden," to borrow a description from a Wellesley historian. Free of the "bewildering presence of boys," Douglas reminisced, the classroom at Wellesley provided her with a protected domain where young women could express opinions and challenge those of others without having to tolerate the persecuting looks and snickers of male students. In their absence, she no longer felt self-conscious about her looks. The sanctuary of residential living similarly insulated students from the day-to-day scrutinizing of brothers and fathers that went on in many homes. "Despite ourselves," Douglas remembered, "here and there our minds were opened, absorbing beyond our wills, material with which in years to come we might try to answer the eternal question, 'Who am I? What is life?'"[6]

If discovering one's individual place in the world outside the family was central to the Wellesley mission, thought offered the route to discovery. Marjory and the other girls learned that the mind was their most important asset and that success and true happiness depended on exercising the mind like the lungs, by freely absorbing and expending knowledge and ideas. Thought, Douglas wrote for the alumnae magazine sixty-five years after graduating, "had been shown to us as the central force in the experience of the human race . . . the supreme activity of human living." This concept bordered on the heretical during her college years, which were not far removed from the days when education experts and male physicians divined that rigorous intellectual activity deflowered women by pulling blood to the brain and away from vital reproductive parts. Plenty of people still believed that higher education was wasted on members of the female sex, who were most vital to society as mothers and wives. But Marjory did not see waste at Wellesley. She saw a resource, and she valued the school most for what it was: an institution for women run by women, who wrote books, made scientific discoveries, and blazed trails into male-dominated fields.[7]

During Marjory's years there, Wellesley had a prized faculty. She declared her major in English composition, perhaps the school's premier department. More than half its faculty were poets, and not surprisingly, many of them subscribed to the idea that humanist values could be realized through literature, and in analyzing texts they emphasized the method, if not the politics, of social criticism. The most famous faculty member was Katherine Lee Bates, the author of "America the Beautiful" and an activist in labor reform and the settlement movement. Never a student of Bates but very much aware of her presence, Marjory took her advanced courses with the department's chair, Sophie Chantal Hart. Willowy and distinguished and partial to wearing expensive clothing and long, cascading capes, she resembled, in the words of one historian, a "medieval lady out of a French tapestry." Some students remembered her as being acerbic and difficult. Yet under her leadership, the department taught more students than any other and sent more of them on to earn doctorates than did any other women's college English department.[8]

Marjory had no plans to pursue a Ph.D. Even though her family expected her to find her vocation in the classroom, she wanted to write rather than teach. Wellesley provided the kind of intellectual and academic support desired by an aspiring writer; it also offered material for two of Marjory's early stories. Spring brought the traditional annual pageant hosted by the freshman class, which planted a tree on the college green before a gathering of the entire campus community. Marjory wrote a story about the event and sent it to Taunton for publication in the journal published by her old high school. In her junior year, she was elected to the editorship of the senior yearbook, *Legenda*. The ascension followed her publication of "Lost Balls" in the *Wellesley Magazine*. Douglas was disinclined to structured exercise and in lieu of gym classes chose a more languid option, golf. Using the sport to write a fanciful story was in keeping with her skills on the links. Told in first-person narrative, the tale is about a wayward golf shot that leads to adventurous encounters with storybook-type characters, including a wood sprite. The protagonist's odyssey quickly transports the reader from pastoral golf links to a Gothic forest.

> Your golf bag safely cached, you may at last listen to the call of the gipsy wind rollicking over the sunny slopes, to the seductions of the little path that disappears among the pines, to the whole mellow, gloriously golden autumn day. And hark, don't you hear? Beneath the humming and buzzing of the insects in the tawny meadow of

grass, beneath the rustle of the birch leaves beside you, beneath the sudden "caw" of the crow floating overhead, like the tang of wood smoke on the pine-laden air, comes a suggestion of far-heard melody, sweet and shrill and joyous. What care we for scores of bogeys? These are the pipes of Pan.[9]

In classical mythology, Pan is the lord of the woods. Marjory had to imagine his fabled world as she might the disappearing American wilderness, an environment that increasingly few of her generation had the opportunity to see or know. The nature of her real-life domestic setting—the colors, sounds, and animation—provided her with a window into a primeval place with which she had no firsthand experience. Indeed, she developed images of the story's setting more successfully than she did its characters. Decades later, she constructed similar conduits between that which she witnessed in the daily course of life and a certain lost wilderness to which she had little practical exposure, the Everglades. Before she gained an empirical knowledge of this extraordinary ecosystem, she developed an intuitive sense about an extraordinary place. She eventually combined the intuitive with the empirical, and the poetic grace and scientific exactness of the Everglades together fed her passion as an environmentalist.

Wellesley guided her toward that exactness, providing the basis for understanding evolving scientific knowledge. She took courses in zoology and geology. Geology had a greater impact on her in part because of the professor, Elizabeth Fisher, one of the earliest female graduates of the Massachusetts Institute of Technology. Fisher's expertise was sufficiently impressive to land her a commission as the first woman to conduct a geological field exploration for an oil company and to be appointed by the czar to study rocks in Russia. In the classroom, she lectured in front of a dozen or so maps and incorporated geography, anthropology, meteorology, and archeology into her courses. One of her most attentive students, Marjory learned to think of geography as a basic science, and on numerous later occasions she credited "dear Miss Fisher's course" with rousing her interest in the scientific workings of the natural environment.[10]

Marjory was also quite fond of and forever indebted to Malvina Bennett, who taught elocution. The vigorous, persistent Bennett taught her students to stand erect, discard their regional accents, pronounce their consonants, and throw their voices across the school auditorium without shouting. Marjory took to the lessons so well that she was elected class orator. "My dear," Douglas later told a reporter, "It was duck soup. I went around . . . elocuting all over the place." And she never forgot those lessons. The refined patrician diction and stentorian voice that impressed audiences and politicians when she was stumping for the Everglades decades later carried over from two years of courses with Bennett.[11]

Wellesley held up plenty of role models with vital voices. Marjory's college years paralleled the height of the Progressive Era, when growing numbers of women were putting their skills into practice within the public sphere. Reformers of multiple stripes were angling for change in government, business, education, and society. Outside the classroom, the Wellesley faculty actively participated in numerous arenas of reform. At every turn, students ran into professors hurrying to speak at labor rallies, organizing to expand suffrage rights, petitioning for improved public education, and drafting declarations for poor relief. Inside the classroom, faculty were unapologetic about orienting students toward public service, reminding them that civic responsibility was more noble than the attainment of personal wealth or social status. The ideal Wellesley product accepted the private act of academic achievement as no less a selfless one, and she went off after graduation to work toward bettering society.[12]

Many Wellesley professors attained national reputations for such undertakings, and none more so than Emily Greene Balch, Marjory's social economics professor. A refined woman of independent wealth but frugal habits, Balch joined the Religious Society of Friends in 1920 when she was establishing the world headquarters for the Women's International League for Peace and Freedom. A year earlier, during a time of inflamed patriotism, the trustees of Wellesley had fired her after twenty years of teaching for opposing U.S. involvement in the world war. She refrained from claiming poetic justice in 1946, when she won the Nobel Peace Prize for her work in the peace movement, making her the first Quaker and third female laureate. When still a professor, Balch cofounded and presided over the Boston Women's Trade Union League and denounced social-class exploitation. She was famous for taking her students on field trips to prisons, factories, welfare agencies, saloons, and slum neighborhoods in Boston's North End. Hers were among the most popular and eye-opening courses at Wellesley, and although she worked hard to avoid imposing her values on students, her message about social inequities was unambiguous. Marjory had never seen the underbelly of America, never thought of it as an abject appendage of wealth and privilege. That Balch's courses gave "form and stability" to a "developing social consciousness," as Douglas often said, received salience from an incisive comment she made nine years after leaving Wellesley: "The people who have quantities of leisure generally have taken it from others who have none."[13]

Putting that consciousness into practice began with securing women the right to vote. Few within the college community doubted that women had an important role to play in civil life outside the electoral process, and a boisterous many argued that women could be much more effective as participants in that process. Combined with this civic sentiment was the feminist impulse to improve women's social and economic status. Many Wellesley professors talked about and exemplified "symmetrical womanhood," the philosophy that marriage should not be the dominating ambition of an educated woman, since marriage by convention translated into a commitment that privileged male power over female. If marriage were the chosen path, the woman should avoid allowing spousal loyalty to circumscribe her intellectual faculties, which should be used to have social impact. Marjory was fully on board, put there originally by her suffragist grandmother, Florence. A suffragist did not alone make a feminist, but Marjory leaned in the more radical direction, believing that without the right to vote, all other rights for women and the disfranchised were left to the vagaries of a single sex. She was one of six in her class to join a suffrage club that a classmate founded as the student equivalent to the faculty's Wellesley Woman's Suffrage League, a club that hosted talks with Alice Paul and Anna Howard Shaw. With suffrage as her starting point,

Marjory agitated for women's issues off and on for the rest of her life, giving her last formal speech on the subject at age ninety-nine.[14]

Friends were an equally enduring and important offering of college life. Marjory made many, but most important was the fast and salutary relationship forged with Carolyn Percy, who arrived at Wellesley the same year as Marjory. A resident of Hoosick Falls, New York, tall and stout with a big-city persona and wardrobe, but with no hint of pretentiousness, Carolyn had known Marjory since she was twelve. Carolyn's cousin, Pauline Starrett, lived in Taunton and was a friend of Marjory's, and before college, Carolyn and Marjory corresponded about their future alma mater. They became housemates during their freshman year and later moved to accommodations in the coveted College Hall, where they had rooms close together and overlooking the beautiful campus lake. The two developed a sibling love in a friendship that lasted until Carolyn died sixty years later. Each consoled the other during emotionally difficult times, and on one such occasion Marjory moved to be close to Carolyn; on another, Carolyn established a part-time residence to be close to Marjory.[15]

One place to which Marjory did not follow Carolyn was into teaching. Marjory was more hostile to that career choice than before, a fact that continued to strain familial bonds. In her senior year, she decided to announce her true ambitions to her family and anguished over the response to come. She expected accusations of betrayal from those who had sacrificed to give her an education. Fanny and Florence were indeed inconsolable when Marjory broke the news. Marjory could not possibly support herself and would "die in a garret," Florence sneered. She was "firm in her knowledge of Grub Street," Douglas once recalled. Despite Florence Trefethen's strong convictions about female independence, she could also be frustratingly closed minded at times. She made no ultimatums, but her response ruined any prospect of Marjory wanting to return to Taunton after graduation.[16]

Convinced that her mother was holding her own and compensating for their separation by sending daily postcards, Marjory limited her visits to breaks and holidays. On rare occasions, Aunt Fanny came to Wellesley, but no one else. Then in her junior year, Marjory feared that her mother had cancer after she found a lump in her left breast. Doctors confirmed the diagnosis. Surgery followed, and Lillian seemed to edge toward recovery.[17]

Commencement exercises for the Class of 1912 were held outside on the green, passing with the customary processions and speeches, congratulations and good-byes, and hugs and tears. Fanny attended, as did Marjory's Connecticut cousin, Pauline Hopson, the daughter of Lillian and Fanny's sister, Alice. After the ceremonies were over, Fanny and Pauline dropped a bombshell: Lillian's cancer had spread to her spine. Marjory rushed to Taunton. Within a couple of weeks, Lillian slipped into a coma and died. She was fifty-two. Marjory made the funeral arrangements, while someone else sent word to her father, who, sixteen years separated from his wife, did not travel from Florida to attend the service. Three days later, Alice died unexpectedly. The Trefethens had lost two daughters in a single week.[18]

It was the blackest period of Marjory's life. She had lived for years in constant apprehension of her mother's death, even as she tried to deny Lillian's frail and failing condition. After prayers for the restoration of her mother's health went unanswered, Marjory began to question the existence of God. She had been raised in a household where the Bible and the church were embraced for the sake of the moral being and the eternal soul. Florence was a devout Episcopalian who had ferried Marjory off to church every Sunday, and Daniel faithfully attended Methodist worship twice a week. Early on, Marjory committed parts of the *Book of Common Prayer* to memory, and she acknowledged its influence on her writing style. Although Wellesley encouraged an active religious life, she preferred to sleep in on Sunday mornings and then replenish herself by reading books. Standing next to God had never been her desire, and after her mother's death she never again entered a house of worship to divine providence. She later confided in her diary, "The arrogance of religious belief is the only one still considered ethical. Must be because religion fulfills most fundamental childish inadequacies of [the] individual."

She eventually came to believe that religion, God, and the eternal soul were fictions of the human mind, abstract responses to unknowns and fears about life and the afterlife. None of these things had a part in her existence. She unlearned the fiction, and despite adversities and morbid uncertainties, she decided to accept life without the "crutch" of worship and prayer. She always missed her beautiful mother, but she never missed God, never returned to him, even when she needed a savior during her failed marriage.[19]

CHAPTER ELEVEN

Reports

In her first novel, *Road to the Sun,* Douglas wrote of the proverbial abstract "they": "'The Empire of the Everglades' they
kept on saying, pointing and sweeping their arms so that all
listening heads swept around with them. [Governor Napoleon Bonaparte] Broward had drained the Everglades at last,
they said. . . . The crops they would raise would make them
all rich. That's what everybody said. The future looked wonderful." In fiction and nonfiction forms, including in *River of
Grass,* Douglas constantly debunked the myth of agrarian success under the Broward plan. A near-spellbinding allure, se-
ducing trusting investors from across the country, drainage
had been an insidious charade, she said, the work of land companies and Broward, master promoters of the storied Florida
dream.[1]

Broward also knew how to outmaneuver those such as
Frank Stoneman who censured him. To mollify hesitant land
purchasers, Broward sought a feasibility study of drainage
from the U.S. Department of Agriculture (USDA). For help
in obtaining the agency's cooperation, he called on Congressman Stephen Sparkman to meet with agriculture secretary
James Wilson in 1906, and Sparkman twice did so. Broward

followed up with his own visit and entreaty to Wilson on July 11, just a few days after the New River christening of the dredge *Everglades*. Broward sought nothing more than official validation for construction that was well under way. He was willing to answer critics with a third-party study, but he would not go so far as to suspend drainage operations until feasibility had been determined. "I will be dead by that time," he said. "The state will be poor. . . . We can sell some land to build dredges and if my friends will hold the knockers in check, we can make a convincing ocular demonstration." Such demonstrations rarely proved more convincing than controversial, but the USDA offered its full cooperation in the interim.[2]

Broward's request found its way to the desk of Charles G. Elliot, chief of drainage investigations in the USDA's Division of Irrigation and Drainage. With twenty-five years of experience as a drainage engineer, mainly in agriculture, Elliot possessed a national reputation. He had written the USDA's first bulletin on drainage, had published an important book on the subject, and went on to write three others. He had also spent time in the eastern Everglades to advise the Bureau of Plant Industry at Miami about how to establish a small agricultural experiment station on marshland. Instead of trying to contain the vast untamed wetland, Elliot proposed creatively building a dike around the agricultural area to protect it from outside sources of inundation. It was an innovative but unconventional concept that drew few adherents.[3]

Two years later, Elliot went to Tallahassee to confer with Broward on the governor's concept. Elliot subsequently told a colleague that Broward "has a sort of plan of his own and is evidently the engineer as well as the promoter and pusher of the whole drainage scheme." Elliot, like Stoneman, thought Broward was moving "forward in a very energetic and possibly arbitrary manner." Despite Elliot's misgivings, he offered the services of his department, including an engineer to conduct a feasibility study.[4]

On paper, James O. Wright was the logical man for the job. By the time he arrived at the USDA in 1905, he had more than two decades of drainage engineering experience in Indiana, Illinois, and Louisiana. It was an exciting time to be a civil engineer in America. Coaxing water to wherever civilization desired not only represented an important contribution to the building of the nation but also could bring personal and professional fame. Los Angeles water commissioner William Mulholland was about to garner just that by diverting water to his city from a remarkable 250 miles away in Owens Valley. With men and mules, he built the longest aqueduct in the world. Congress endorsed such projects in 1902, when it passed the Reclamation Act for the purpose of developing the West. The prospect of converting the American desert into fruitful land by building dams and reservoirs and rerouting rivers attracted young minds from top engineering schools. Whether by choice or by default, others went into drainage reclamation, a somewhat less romantic career direction. The USDA's Division of Irrigation and Drainage Investigation never achieved the glamour and glory of the Reclamation Service, which was responsible for some of the world's most impressive engineering feats, and drainage engineers never created monuments as splendid as the dams of the West. But the drainage engineer's purpose was arguably no less noble than that of the dam builder.[5]

As the Disston experience had proven, large-scale reclamation projects usually required large capital outlays and technical and legal expertise as well as cooperation among independent landowners. To meet these challenges, legislatures mandated the creation of drainage districts that could draw on the technical resources of state agencies and levy taxes to fund projects. If the heyday for dam building began in the 1930s, that for drainage districts came in the preceding fifty years. By 1920, twenty-one states, including Florida, had authorized drainage districts with nearly sixty-six million acres of wetlands under their control. The USDA calculated that between 1906 and 1922, seven states had reclaimed nearly nine million acres. Most people acknowledged the benefits of drainage, such as increased crop yields, higher property values, and the abatement of mosquito-borne diseases. Typically, people wrote off the drawbacks, such as altered climate conditions, loss of wildlife habitat, and lower water tables and dry wells. Some of the most active drainage districts were in the Midwest, where Wright had gotten his experience and where, as Ann

Vileisis writes in her history of American wetlands, "glacially variegated wetlands . . . became a homogenized grid of square-edged farms."[6]

Broward envisioned precisely such a patchwork of civilization—ten-acre tracts "in square form"—for the Everglades. Wright obliged the governor by sending survey crews into the Everglades in late 1906, when Stoneman's differences with the governor reached their height. But the inauguration of a USDA study temporarily pacified Stoneman, even as the dredges continued to dig. Stoneman put his faith in professionals—scientists, engineers, managers, and bureaucrats generally—who brought non-political, Progressive Era reform to government. They would ultimately wreak their own havoc with the environment, but at the beginning of the twentieth century, they were regarded as paragons of efficiency and wise use. Stoneman trusted Wright's survey to be so "thorough and comprehensive that [it] will forever set to rest the mooted questions as to the feasibility and cost of reclaiming that vast region."[7]

Broward was confident that the question would be settled in his favor. In late August 1907, he, William Jennings, and an oversight commission of the Internal Improvement Fund traveled to South Florida to inspect the New River operations from the decks of the dredges *Everglades* and *Okeechobee*. The men observed water falling six feet over spillbanks into new sections of the canal and walked along a trail through sawgrass where days before Indians had traveled in canoes. Jennings filed a report concluding that the "work done has been something marvelous, and the achievements far beyond the most sanguine or hopeful expectations of those in charge." The New River channel was handling the volume of runoff with ease. Jennings had seen it with his own eyes, and it reaffirmed his fustian proclamation that drainage would eventually offer "flattering opportunities . . . for the accumulation of wealth."[8]

Wright showed himself to be a near equal to Jennings and Broward as an exultant voice of Everglades development. The drainage investigation office devoted one-sixth of its budget to his investigation, and in early 1909 he circulated an abstract of what could be expected in his final report. When the abstract reached Florida, the state legislature and fund trustees could not have asked for anything more splendid except dry land itself. Wright determined that eight canals would yield 1.85 million acres at an estimated cost of one dollar an acre. With the affirmative nod of Secretary Wilson, the legislature printed several thousand copies of the abstract for public distribution. The seeds of the great Florida land boom, normally associated with the 1920s, were planted.

Land companies and speculators latched on to Wright's abstract and later his full report. His assessments gave the voice of scientific authority to the pitch of the salesmen combing the country. Marketing brochures and newspaper advertisements reprinted excerpts from his report and speeches and declared Wright, a midlevel engineer, one of the world's leading drainage experts. Newspapers presented the information as if it were breaking news. Somehow the *Washington Post* got the notion that the Everglades would "afford an empire of some 7,000,000 acres," a figure that far exceeded even Wright's questionable claims. Stoneman's rival, the *Miami Metropolis,* incorrectly claimed that Wright was in charge of the Bureau of Reclamation. In a promotional pamphlet, *Where Nature Smiles,* the Everglade Land Sales Company quoted Wright proclaiming, "There are no engineering difficulties whatever in draining the Everglades." The June 1910 issue of the *Florida East Coast Homeseeker,* a magazine distributed by Flagler's Model Land Company, fabricated an unfettered endorsement from Wilson: "There is no large body of land lying within the boundary of the United States—in fact, not in any portion of the world—that will, when the drainage is completed, be of so great value as the once-despised Everglades of Florida."[9]

Wright turned out to be an artful self-promoter and manipulator, a schemer interested in ways to enrich himself and his reputation. Hitting the road, he traveled the state giving speeches promoting reclamation through drainage. At a 1910 meeting of the State Bankers' Association in Pensacola, far removed from the Everglades, he claimed to know of no comprehensive drainage project anywhere that had failed to give value to reclaimed land. He had made a similar appearance in Miami on January 30, 1908, when he was, for all intents and purposes, the second-most-important visitor in the city that day. The first was Governor Broward, who joined Wright after coming down from Fort Lauderdale, where the day before he had met with Miami businessmen and promised a dredge for their city. Wright's purpose in Miami was to explain how the project would work. In an address at the Iroquois Hotel, however, he failed to impress at least one person in the audience of about three hundred people— Frank Stoneman. Two days later, the editor warned readers, "It is to be feared that Mr. Wright has misled many of our citizens by an assumption of knowledge that he does not possess, and by leaving out of his address many things he ought to have said." Not long thereafter, Secretary Wilson received a letter from Florida senator James P. Taliaferro repeating Stoneman's accusations that Wright was going around stirring up false hope in Everglades drainage. Wilson then instructed Elliot to remove his engineer from the speaking circuit.[10]

None of Wright's bosses were aware of Wright's unethical land dealings. To supplement his USDA salary, he accepted stock deals and finder's fees totaling nearly twenty thousand dollars from land companies in exchange for U.S. government endorsements of a proposed reclamation project in North Carolina. At one point, he went before the state legislature to introduce and lobby for a statute that would secure the reclamation project. After lawmakers approved the legislation, Wright organized a land company, calculating that he and his coinvestors stood to net one million dollars from the venture.[11]

Stoneman, who had intended to wait for Wright's Everglades report before offering comment, could no longer restrain himself. In February, he noted that the optimistic voices that pointed to the agrarian success around the New River had failed to take into account that South Florida had experienced fifteen months straight of deficit rainfall. "To assume that under normal conditions a territory of hundreds of square miles in extent can be drained by a canal only a trifle over one hundred feet wide is to challenge the very first rules of arithmetic." Stoneman was predicting disaster when the rains returned.[12]

They came that October, and South Floridians were unprepared. Fifteen inches fell in the first five days, including more than seven inches in twenty-four hours, and the rain betrayed no sign of letting up. Roofs of homes and businesses started leaking, people walked knee-deep in

flooded streets, and cars were left stranded along roads. In parts of downtown Miami, the water rose above sidewalks and pushed its way through
storefront entrances like a demanding customer. Commerce and traffic
came to a standstill; small craft on the bay were swamped. The mouth
of the Miami River disappeared under a swelling sheet flow pushing out
of the Everglades. Nothing like it had been seen since a 1906 hurricane.
Fort Lauderdale reported that the New River was making little headway
toward the ocean and was instead overflowing for miles around. While
the prodrainage *Miami Metropolis* played down the flooding, a front-page
headline in Stoneman's *News-Record* reported, "State's Drainage Canals
Cannot Carry Off Water." In every direction, fields, groves, and even
canals were under water. The region had suffered a disaster, and it had
only rained.[13]

The disaster was mixed with human folly. Feckless land companies and
the state had encouraged farmers to settle in areas that had historically
been prone to flooding, areas where they would have never ventured if
not for the belief that the canals would keep them dry. At the same time,
the canals delivered water to areas that would normally have escaped inundation. Ironically, before Broward began digging in the Everglades, he
ignored a report by the chief engineer of the Disston project as well as the
preliminary findings of the Division of Drainage that Disston's dredging
had led to the inundation of previously dry areas. Another contributor
to the damage was Lake Okeechobee. The canals provided it with new
outlets into the greater Everglades and the neighboring cities. These potentially hazardous waterways initially went without much notice, even
though virtually every person living in South Florida knew that rain frequently came in torrents. To understand the local weather was to grasp
its vagaries. Among those who failed to do so were the men who set the
standards for drainage.

The person centrally positioned to influence those standards could not
exempt himself from the bunch. Wright issued his forty-page report the
next May, and it contained critical flaws. First, he calculated local saturation and runoff from rain based only on a daily average distribution,
which he deflated. He then underestimated the maximum amount of rain

that might fall on any given day. From these defective figures, he determined the carrying capacity of the canals. Built to his recommendations, they could not handle the many downpours, like the one in October, that commonly occurred in the region. Furthermore, he left the burden of keeping the region dry entirely to canals. Although he identified overspill from Lake Okeechobee as an important problem, he dismissed a containment dike as too expensive. Finally, he concluded that draining the Everglades would not alter the region's climate.[14]

The findings turned Elliot's stomach when he read them. He had scrutinized the abstract after the state and land companies adopted it as sales literature, so he was not completely surprised by the report. He nevertheless delayed its publication until he could make revisions. At the same time, people were writing the USDA seeking confirmation for plans to sink their life savings into Florida real estate. Elliot took the position that the prospects for the state's drainage plan for creating valuable and cultivatable land remained unclear. He put his caveat in a circular letter issued in January 1910, too late to save hundreds of investors from the fateful Everglades mirage.[15]

The circular provoked anger among the apostles of drainage. According to Elliot's later testimony, two agents from the Everglade Land Sales Company, E. C. Howe and Thomas E. Will, stormed into Elliot's USDA office. The two men demanded that Elliot withdraw his circular and send out a retraction. When Elliot demurred, they threatened him "with public exposure" and assured him that they were prepared to go over his head. Another officer with the company did just that, contacting Broward, who in turn wired Florida senator Duncan Fletcher with the claim that the USDA was "knocking" Everglades drainage. Fletcher went to see Secretary Wilson, who told Elliot to cease distribution of all Everglades-related information. Wilson then stopped the publication of Wright's report, peppered with Elliot's corrections and cautious qualifications.[16]

The suppression of these damaging materials did not fully satisfy developers, who wanted the imprimatur of the federal government to help promote Florida. Fletcher proposed a U.S. Senate resolution to that effect. During a congressional recess, the freshman senator met with Jennings and Wright in Jacksonville. Wright was by then a bona fide member of the state's prodrainage team. After Elliot revised the report, Wright resigned from the USDA to accept an offer to become Florida's chief drainage engineer. At the Jacksonville meeting, he and the others assembled official material related to the subject of Everglades reclamation dating back to statehood and the commissioning of Buckingham Smith's survey. Fletcher then had the collection printed as Senate Document 89. The Florida legislature printed and distributed to the public ten thousand copies. As a reaffirming final act, Florida lawmakers passed a joint resolution declaring that the "drainage of the Glades is absolutely feasible and practical."[17]

Inexplicably, Douglas never mentioned Wright in her work, though he was the kind of unscrupulous individual who made an ideal model for a fictional antagonist or warranted a nonfiction exposé. For that matter, she was not terribly harsh with any of the unsavory land merchants who show up in *River of Grass;* in contrast, as a newspaper columnist, she ridiculed a sitting president for his intellect and vocabulary, and as an environmental activist, she told a Florida governor that his predecessors had given away land like "drunken sailors." Sitting down in the state archives to read Senate Document 89, she found it as flawed as Smith's earlier report and equally unapologetic in its pro–real estate position. In *River of Grass,* however, she identified the report's chief architect as Thomas Will, whose reputation remained unblemished. Yet the bulk of the two-hundred-page document consisted of Wright's original report and two politically motivated appendages he composed.[18]

Wright turned the document into a peevish attempt to destroy Elliot. One of the appendages is a list of twenty-five "well authenticated" facts for "contract holders or prospective purchasers of Everglades land," describing drainage as a certainty, muck soil as undoubtedly fertile, and the Everglades as a healthy place for workers. The other appendage, "Why Was Wright's Report on the Everglades Suppressed?" describes Elliot as an opportunist and meddler who had revised Wright's work in an attempt to usurp the credit. Wright offered an emphatic postscript: "There is no other large body of land in the United States that can be drained or irrigated at so small a cost per acre as the Everglades of Florida."[19]

Wright's did not throw the final punch. At the behest of Florida congressman Frank Clark, who disliked the chummy relationships land companies had formed with the USDA, the House of Representatives scheduled hearings to look into the drainage issue and questions of fraud and maleficent influence. Elliot had by this time left government service, though not by choice. Prior to the hearings, he was fired for an alleged budgetary indiscretion, a charge that had originated with Wright, and indicted by a District of Columbia grand jury. Elliott and other USDA officials claimed that his firing and the suppression of his revisions of Wright's report had been instigated by politically connected land companies. Secretary Wilson had admitted as much two years earlier in a meeting with Clark.[20]

The USDA's Committee on Expenditures, less formally known as the Moss Committee, convened on February 3, 1912, conducted forty-three hearings over the next six months, and amassed 1,759 pages of testimony and exhibits. Stoneman was hardly surprised by the hearings. After they got under way, he wrote that the "revelations made to the Moss committee . . . are not new to those who reside in this section of Florida." But the hearings ultimately constituted less a battle over what to do with the swamp or how to do whatever was to be done with it than a battle over men's and the state's reputations. Wright remained Elliot's chief antagonist, offering testimony that followed the same line of acrimonious argument presented in his appendixes. But his testimony took a serious hit from that of Arthur E. Morgan, a former USDA employee who had established a reputation as one of the division's best and most respected field engineers. Morgan told the committee that he had been floored by the gross inaccuracies in the report. Wright's undersized canals would cause flooding downstream; his excavation costs were underestimated by half; and his calculation of the local evaporation rate was greater than precipitation: based on his figures, Lake Okeechobee and the Everglades would dry up on their own given enough time. To ensure that the committee understood what he was saying, Morgan added, "I regard Mr. Wright as absolutely and completely incompetent for any engineering work."[21]

Despite ample evidence of an Everglades land-sales scandal, the hearings produced no indictments. Even Wright escaped punishment, although the committee declared the insider dealings in North Carolina would have been grounds for dismissal if he had still worked for the federal government. Elliot's dismissal in turn had been a punishment too severe for any indiscretions on his part, said the committee. Wilson subsequently reinstated Elliot, and President William Howard Taft ordered the court case against him dropped. The outcome of the hearings was embarrassing enough to force Wright to resign from his post in Tallahassee. But he did not exactly distance himself from the state project. He took a position with a private construction company that had been contracted by the state to dig canals in the Everglades.[22]

Drainage remained more alive than ever, even though the engineering side of the Everglades project had begun to show signs of trouble long before the Moss hearings. In the absence of a viable blueprint for drainage, dredges had excavated only twelve miles of canals by 1909, very little land had surfaced, and, as Stoneman had predicted, the treasury had been drained. To keep the dredges running, the Internal Improvement Fund began selling off large tracts of its land—"the people's land," as Broward had called it—not to independent farmers but to big land companies. The trustees also conveyed 713,665 acres to railroad and land companies in a settlement after Jennings realized his morbidly bad odds of winning the legal dispute over more than 5,000,000 acres.[23]

Broward was determined not to leave office trailing a bankrupt drainage project and a string of broken promises. During his final week as governor, he closed on a sale of a lifetime. Richard J. Bolles, a western land developer, agreed to buy five hundred thousand acres of Everglades land for $1,000,000. A promotional pamphlet gloated, "With characteristic energy and decision of the Western man and his capacity to pick the grain from the chaff, [Bolles] readily saw and realized the value of the task Florida had undertaken." As part of the contract, the trustees agreed to spend $750,000 to "permanently" lower Lake Okeechobee by four feet and to finish digging at least five canals. Four of those canals were planned to run through land belonging to Bolles, who stood to be the prime beneficiary of drainage and real estate sales.[24]

Stoneman went on the attack. Broward's "drainage scheme" had failed, the homesteads promised by the populist governor remained under water, and no throngs of settlers had arrived to take possession of cheap land. "For the past two years, most strenuous endeavors have been made to dispose of the Everglades land, and the result has been, so far as can be ascertained, that less than two hundred acres have been sold to actual settlers, while land corporations have secured control of about two million acres." Stoneman estimated that the "common people" had paid an average of twenty dollars an acre for Everglades land, while corporations had paid one dollar. The Moss Committee, the *Miami Herald* pointed out, concluded that the Bolles firm had made a two-million-dollar profit from land sales. There was no one to blame but Broward. "The policy of the administration," Stoneman wrote, "is to answer no questions nor arguments, but to plunge ahead as fast and as far as time and funds will permit."[25]

By the time Broward's term as governor expired, Stoneman had scored at least one victory. The state conceded that the feat of Everglades drainage would require better planning. Nature had not readily submitted to Broward's willful claim that water ran downhill. In July 1910, the fund trustees contracted with Baltimore's Furst-Clark Construction Company to assume drainage operations. (As part of the deal, the firm purchased the state's four dredges for $984.06.) To pay the new contractor, the legislature authorized the Everglades Drainage District to float bonds secured by a new drainage tax. State officials also conferred with consultants hired by the Everglade Land Sales Company about how to facilitate drainage. At around the same time, Wright left his job as state engineer to go to work for Furst-Clark.[26]

As an added measure, the Everglades Drainage District commissioners and fund trustees—essentially the same people—hired three highly esteemed consulting engineers. Marshall O. Leighton had been the chief hydrographer for the U.S. Geological Survey (USGS); Edmund T. Perkins, a former USGS and U.S. Reclamation Service official, was now serving as president of the National Drainage Congress; and Isham Randolph had served on the Isthmus (Panama) Canal Commission and brought to "any enterprise . . . a guarantee of honesty, integrity, and technical efficiency." These extremely qualified men would have risked their reputations if they had not confirmed the abjectness of Wright's report, which they did. But

when the group submitted its own report in October 1913, it denied the
state nothing it wanted. The too-narrow canals could be salvaged with
proper excavation, and more canals could be added. "Gentlemen, our
conclusion . . . is that the drainage of the Florida Everglades is entirely
practicable and can be accomplished at a cost which the value of the reclaimed land will justify, the cost per acre being very small." The optimism had a familiar ring, and the state's response to it was the same as
before—it forged ahead.[27]

When Douglas arrived in Miami in 1915 and went to work for the *Miami
Herald,* South Florida was in the midst of a land boom that became famous worldwide. She soon learned who was chiefly responsible for the
hustle and bustle. There is little doubt that Broward was motivated primarily by a selfless belief that his drainage project was providing an important
and essential benefit to the people of his state. Put simply, in the argot of
the times, drainage was a good thing. Wresting control of nature was the
stuff of a civilized people. Men were trained to dam rivers, irrigate deserts,
excavate mountainsides, and drain swamps, and the public extolled such
successes, much like those of medical scientists battling an epidemic. Engineers were contributing to the improvement of human life, and their deeds
were constantly confirmed with honors, awards, and fine reputations.

Yet Broward ultimately surrendered to the temptations of personal
profit making. Immediately after leaving office in 1909, he went to work
for Bolles's Florida Fruit Lands Company at a salary equal to his income
as governor. Since he was still ostensibly bringing land to farmers, Broward could justify his move to the private sector with the belief that he
was continuing the honorable work he had begun as a populist governor. Many contemporaries would have honored any personal gains as
just reward for his public service. Others, such as Stoneman, would have
drawn a line between the public and the personal. Bolles was eventually
indicted on various counts of fraud after Broward died in 1910, and the
former governor might well have been implicated in these shady dealings.
Records give no indication of Stoneman's reaction to these events, and
Douglas made no mention of them in *River of Grass.*[28]

Stoneman never opposed the vaunted idea of drainage, just the Broward approach. By 1910, his editorials had adopted the refrain, "It is well to state that the so-called opposition to drainage in this state never has been directed against the development of the Everglades, but was made against the methods by which they have been exploited." Stoneman constructed a dichotomy between humans and nature, prioritizing the former over the latter. In that regard, his views did not differ from Broward's and were consistent with the prevailing philosophy of Progressive conservationists of his day. The meaning of the term *conservation* depended on the user. Broward and others freely spoke of reclamation as conservation, and humans always remained the defining center of this brand of conservation, with nature subjected to social constructions of good and bad, useful and not. The practice of conservation itself depended on humans controlling nature, albeit in an expertly managed, efficient, and provident way. As Stoneman advised, drainage "must and will proceed slowly as men learn how to drain, to irrigate, to plant, to fertilize, and to market." In conserving nature, conservationists were all too often conserving natural resources—timber, coal, water for crops, and reclaimed wetlands.[29]

Explaining the Everglades' part in this American saga ultimately evolved into the all-consuming passion of Thomas E. Will, the land agent who threatened Charles Elliot in his Washington office. Before going into land speculation, Will had held chairs in history and political economy at Kansas State Agricultural College. He eventually found his way to Fort Lauderdale, and from his home looking out toward the Everglades, he edited *Conservation,* the magazine of the American Forestry Association. Will worshiped at the feet of the country's first chief forester, Gifford Pinchot, the so-called father of Progressive conservation, and regarded himself as one of a "group of earnest men" who agitated for Pinchot's deified ideas. The Everglades were no forest, but they were suited to the Pinchot way. In an unpublished polemical tract, "Conservation in Earnest," Will said, "We are a nation of wastrels" who had "played bull-in-the-china-shop generally with the public weal"—timber, gas, soil, and water. It was important that the Everglades, a territory Will described as larger than Delaware and Rhode Island combined with soil as organically rich as "that of the Nile Valley—the ancient granary and life-saving service of the East," not be left to waste.[30]

Will's bald attempt to bully Elliot may have been prompted less by greed than by an attachment to an idea. Will was confident that Jennings, Broward, and other astute men of agriculture and business understood the Everglades dilemma, and it would be a sin against the cardinal precepts of conservation should their policies be impeded by prophets of doom such as Stoneman. Drainage was one of the Herculean challenges of conservation but one before which Floridians showed great fortitude: drainage was "not a theory, a provisional hypothesis or pipe dream" but rather a "fact in process of rapid realization." Will concluded his tract with a prideful declaration: "Let other states, in the language of Patrick Henry, 'Profit by' Florida's 'example.'"[31]

Other states would indeed have profited had they forsaken Florida as a bad example. History eventually bore out the validity of Stoneman's campaign. The man who could not keep a business solvent but who still knew a bad deal when he saw one was right. He was right about the rush to drainage without a proper acknowledgment of costs and complications, and he was right about the potential climate effects of drawing down such a large body of water. The Broward legacy is consequently a tarnished one. But the era is remembered for having fostered the deceit of selling "land by the gallon" (a phrase ironically given life by a real estate developer). This view represents the Broward-Jennings-Will-Pinchot way of looking at things—the legacy is measured by a utilitarian loss in property and economic opportunity. Another, less human-centered way to think of the Broward era is in its particulars as a rush to conquest. As Douglas concluded, the phrase "Empire of the Everglades" was born during the Broward era, which marked the closing of the Florida frontier.

Yet conquest, as Douglas knew and had witnessed, did not come to this last frontier only in the form of dredges and surveyors' 'stakes. It came first as it came to so many other American frontiers, in the form of the hunter's gun and a marketplace demand for indigenous wildlife.[32]

CHAPTER TWELVE

Marriage

Following her graduation and her mother's death soon thereafter, Marjory stood at a lonely crossroads. Wellesley had given
her a good education and had helped her develop the skills of
a writer, but she was unsure of her potential to be a published
professional author. Reflecting back years later, she wrote, "All
Senior year I had been aware of a growing dismay. I had been
writing steadily for four years and had produced nothing fit to
be submitted to the *Atlantic Monthly* or to be remembered." As
her college career was coming to a close, representatives from
private girls' schools visited campus to conduct interviews for
prospective teachers, offering "bed, board and prestige . . . to
compensate for the going wage of the inexperienced." Douglas remembered coming "to one great decision that June, 1912.
Nothing on earth could compel me to undertake a lifetime of
teaching." Through a process of elimination, ruling out first
one avenue in life and then another, she was determined to
find her way. For the want of something other than teaching, until she could find a way to become a published author,
she pursued something altogether unexpected. She borrowed
money from a college friend, Dorothy Applegate, rented a
modest apartment with her and another woman in Boston,

and enrolled in a course that prepared single women for employment in training department store salesgirls. With nothing to keep her in Taunton, she left the soulless house on Harrison Street for good.[1]

This new life soon became newsworthy. In February, *Boston American* feature writer Angela Morgan, later a nationally known poet and peace activist, was fascinated by the young roommates who had given up middle-class comforts for a frugal existence. Each of the three "splendid girls, charmingly bred, pretty, talented and dead earnest," was determinedly living on eight dollars a week. As part of their training as "efficiency experts," a favored classification in the parlance of the Progressive Era, they were discovering how to survive on the meager wages of department store salesgirls, precisely the individuals they would be mentoring. Morgan credited them with being "pioneers in the movement to train girls for salesmanship as college trains [others] for life." They shared two rooms and a bath for ten dollars a month each and kept their laundry and food bills to a minimum. They found a restaurant that served a ten-cent breakfast and others where they could have lunch and dinner for fifteen and twenty-five cents, respectively.

Morgan first sat down with the other roommates while Marjory was out on an errand. When she returned and joined the interview, she "captivated at once." Marjory had "clean-cut, regular features, happy eyes and a laugh that is tonic in itself and a personality brimming with charm"— that is, Marjory lacked the physical delightfulness Morgan saw in the roommates. The reporter apparently decided that comely women seeking economic independence even though they could easily find husbands made better copy. Marjory's forthrightness nevertheless gave the story punch. In words that would have given her grandmother and aunt vicarious pleasure, Marjory clarified that she and her roommates were not simply engaging in a onetime experiment. "We want economic independence and we are just learning how to obtain it." Morgan appreciated the candor. The roommates, she wrote, were "filled with the spirit of the new age, eager for womanly independence, and economic freedom."[2]

Behind Marjory's sunniness and determination lurked the gray clouds of depression and apprehension. A hovering numbness from the loss of her mother weighted her failure to find an exciting sequel to Wellesley. After she and her roommates completed their training, she left Boston and the East but managed to stay within the Wellesley family. Her long-time friend, Carolyn Percy, had accepted a teaching job at a private school in St. Louis and invited Marjory to join her there. Marjory secured a position with Nugent's Department Store, part of a local chain founded by an Irish immigrant. Nugent's had recently made national news when one of its buyers, Spencer Silverthorne, returned after surviving the sinking of the *Titanic* the previous spring. Marjory lived with Carolyn in a spare residence provided by the school, not far from work. Her job classified her as a social worker. Into the industrializing cities, wage work was attracting crowds of folk from the American countryside and immigrants from abroad. Some took jobs as salesgirls, and Marjory taught them basic skills from using correct English grammar to organizing their lives around the regimen of the new economy.[3]

The work, so far from her ambition, and St. Louis, so far from the familiarity of the Northeast, failed to gratify her. The splendor of the Grecian "palaces" built for the 1904 World's Fair, when St. Louis enjoyed its finest hour, was now hard to find in the nation's fourth-largest city. The riverfront was dirty and industrial, and the brown Mississippi was walled by levees, which seconded as cargo landings stacked high with shipping barrels by the thousands and with fresh-cut lumber from the forests of the Midwest, all coming and going on drab steamboats and train cars. Things turned bleaker when the school year ended. Carolyn returned home to New York to be close to her family, leaving Marjory to endure a sweaty St. Louis summer. She wrote a play during those few months alone, but it was never produced and subsequently lost. At loose ends herself, she moved back east after arranging for employment, again as an efficiency expert, for twenty dollars a week at the new L. Bamberger and Company department store in Newark, New Jersey.[4]

Department stores were an invention of the new economy. Architectural marvels towering over the proprietors' shops of the old economy, they brought consumers en masse face to face with products manufactured en masse. When Louis Bamberger opened his newest store in 1912, it occupied an entire city block, rose sixteen stories, with four more below ground, and connected its main merchandising areas with five "moving stairways." Its twenty-eight hundred employees included a tour guide to acquaint shoppers with the 1.2-million square feet of floor space. Palaces such as Bamberger's made consumption a culture, turning the chore of shopping into a pastime. Visually seductive and electrifying, they exerted a carnival atmosphere with their orgy of scintillating displays baiting shoppers. Department stores were full of the trappings of the good life— largely homogeneous. With the advent of easy-credit plans, they made Americans more like one another, dressing them in the same ready-made clothes and filling their homes with the same mass-produced furniture and accessories. With land no longer as easily acquirable as when the western frontier had been open, with most of that land having gone to corporations and speculators, and with urban spaces filling up with people, the consumption of mass-produced products became the new so-cial leveler, America's agent of democratization. To a reasonable degree, the working class could make purchases like the middle class, blacks like whites, Jews like gentiles, immigrants like the native-born.[5]

Despite Douglas's intimacy with this changing world, it never became a feature of her writing. She also left behind no letters, diary, or autobio-graphical fiction covering her time in Newark, her transitional moment. Other sources, nevertheless, enable a reconstruction of important parts of her life during these years. She rented a nice room on Lombardy Street, a short walk from the public library across an elm-shaded city park. Bam-berger's had its own lending library, and there was no shortage of books to fill her time. Her social life was less fulfilling, though. She was an out-going young woman who found herself alone much of the time, and the opposite sex still ignored her. Although she had shed the plumpness that stayed with her through college, she would have agreed with Angela Mor-gan's polite description of her looks, and she did not blame men for their lack of interest in her. Yet trapped inside this women of regular features was longing and desire and a curiosity about romance.[6]

One day, as she was leaving the store, she saw a coworker on the sidewalk outside, her arm hooked around that of a tall gentleman. Her

colleague introduced her to Kenneth Douglas, the church and social service editor at the *Newark Evening News,* the city's largest newspaper. He
exhibited an air of gentlemanly dignity, and Marjory's friend seemed to
be impressed with herself. Marjory gave Douglas little thought until she
ran into him days later at the public library circulation desk. After ex-
changing pleasantries, he gave her an inquisitive look and smile that suggested an interest beyond passing conversation. He soon began calling
on her, and at age twenty-four she for the first time became the object of
a man's desire, finding the attention strange and wonderful. Douglas was
about thirty years older than Marjory, around the age of Frank Stoneman.
The attention was strange and wonderful but also dangerously ensnaring.
He proposed marriage three months later, and some desperation compelled her to say yes.[7]

They married on April 18, 1914, with the Reverend George P. Dougherty performing the service at St. Paul's Methodist Episcopal Church,
around the corner from her room. One of her college classmates stood in
as a witness. A short honeymoon followed at the Hotel Belmont in New
York. Marjory waited until she returned to Newark to share the news of
her marriage with her family, and she did so by letter, sparing herself their
expected outrage in person. Her mother's brother, Charles Trefethen, immediately set out for Newark to meet Kenneth, and the newlyweds subsequently reciprocated with a visit to Marjory's family in Taunton. The Trefethens warmed somewhat to the well-mannered Douglas—as they never
did to Frank Stoneman—but never fully put their concerns to rest.[8]

Marjory by then had left her job at Bamberger's. Social convention
made the workplace a province of men and single women, so married
middle-class women were expected to stay at home, even when they had
no children to tend. While Kenneth continued working for the *Evening
News,* Marjory volunteered to read to the blind. She had taken her first
step backward into a dependent life, precisely the sort from which Fanny
and Florence and Wellesley had aggressively tried to keep her. Worse, she
had mortgaged her future to a man about whom she knew virtually nothing. Within two months of their marriage, his tainted past crept into their
lives, exposing him as an impostor and shiftless con artist. The real man

and his nefarious dealings thrust Marjory, hardly experienced in matters of love and deception, into a community scandal.[9]

The man she married had arrived in Newark in December 1913. Confident in bearing, he conjured an impression of vast knowledge and probity. He presented himself to people as Dr. Kenneth David Douglas, a specialist in community corruption, the holder of a doctoral degree, and the author of several books on sociology. None of this was apparently true. He took a position with the Bureau of Associated Charities, offering references from Toronto, where he had presumably worked on a newspaper, and then joined the staff of the *Newark Evening News*. Good with conversation, he ingratiated himself with important people in the community. One he befriended was the Reverend Dougherty, who rented the newcomer a room, and together they engaged in the Progressive talk of cleaning up society. At Dougherty's recommendation, the Men's Club of the Roosevelt Avenue Presbyterian Church, which sought to "remedy existing evils" inherent in urbanizing America, extended Kenneth a membership. He soon earned a reputation as a spirited moral crusader. The pungent obsession with moral laxity and the quest for new standards of decency, public and private, had maintained a seamless hold on American cities for decades. Taking up an assault against an abstract fiend—inevitably the immigrant alien—that threatened the purity of American middle-class society could win a man instant friends and community respect. In one of apparently many public speeches, before an audience of two hundred diners, Kenneth spoke of vice so clandestine and deeply embedded in Newark society and government that law enforcement officials could not root it out.[10]

Kenneth had lived in many cities—Toledo, Baltimore, Hartford, Elizabeth City, Oklahoma City. Through them all, ironically, the man who spoke in Newark so fervently against vice was shadowed by his own dissolute ways. He later said that he had wanted to clean up his life and start anew in Newark. But the old life turned out to be the new life. No more did he clean up himself than he did Newark. Soon after Marjory married him, his bosses at the newspaper received information from an undisclosed source that a man named David D. Douglas and fitting Kenneth's description had recently been sued for divorce in Toledo. When confronted, Kenneth confessed that he was indeed the same David D. Douglas. He claimed, however, that the divorce had been settled before he married Marjory and that she had known about it before they wed. He also alleged falsely that he had originally met Marjory in St. Louis. Clearing up the matter would be easy, Kenneth said. He would produce the necessary records without delay.[11]

He never did. Instead, he fled Newark the next day. Without disclosing the nature of his problems, he told Marjory that he was going to New York City for a medical exam. After getting off the train at Pennsylvania Station, he wired his resignation to the *Evening News,* maintaining that he had been ordered to a sanitarium.[12]

The newspaper launched an investigation, which revealed that Kenneth had committed perjury by describing himself as single rather than divorced when completing the application for marriage with Marjory. Reverend Dougherty had known about the divorce and agreed to go forward with the marriage only if Kenneth told Marjory. He said he did, but Marjory did not learn the truth until after they married. Even worse, the newspaper discovered that Kenneth had cashed three checks locally for a total of at least $310 drafted against a bogus account at a Toronto bank. Marjory wanted to believe, as her husband had told her, that a corrupt Newark official trying to silence his ranting against government vice had framed him. But a long history of misdeeds began to unravel. Kenneth had used aliases and concocted stories of woe to convince acquaintances in New York and Boston to cash checks for him, and an active warrant was out for his arrest in Toronto. By his own admission, he had also served prison terms in Baltimore and Hartford and had avoided another in Sing Sing with the sworn promise to leave the country.[13]

While Marjory later revealed some secrets about her former husband, she understandably remained quiet about the true extent of his swindling ways. Another secret she decided to keep to herself was her husband's charlatanism. Marjory was actually his third wife and potentially an unwitting party to bigamy. When he lived in Oklahoma, using the name John R. MacFarlane, he married in 1909 and divorced within a few months. After moving to Toledo, he entered a second marriage in 1911. In both cases, his wives sued for divorce on the grounds of neglect and desertion. As these lurid revelations came to light, Kenneth's former newspaper said his bewildering life represented "a sort of Dr. Jekyll and Mr. Hyde existence." A Bostonian acquaintance speculated that "there must be something wrong with his brain." Others said he "was addicted to the drug habit."[14]

In Newark, authorities drew up warrants for Kenneth's arrest for perjury and check forgery. Meanwhile, he left New York for Providence and then Boston. Police apprehended him, nervous and chain-smoking, at the apartment of two of Marjory's friends, where he had apparently gone to seek help before the women contacted the police. While in custody and awaiting extradition, Kenneth feigned a mental breakdown in hopes of being sent to the state hospital, but the authorities saw through his act. By the time he and his police escort returned to Newark, ten days had passed. Marjory had been staying at Dougherty's home during Kenneth's absence, despairingly trusting in his innocence. When he was arraigned, the judge set bail at three thousand dollars, disregarding Marjory's pleas for a reduction. Kenneth remained in jail for five months until his trial on November 10. He pled not guilty, but the judge sentenced him to the Essex County Penitentiary for six months, on top of the time he had already served. Reading the boxed headline in the *Newark Evening News* announcing Kenneth's conviction, Marjory must have felt the iron grip of cruel reality as she had when her parents separated and again when her mother died.[15]

Not surprisingly, everyone close to Marjory insisted that she leave Kenneth. Carolyn Percy took a job at a Newark school and moved in with Marjory, hoping to free her from the lies and betrayal. Many years later, Marjory wrote in her diary, "One feels so strongly the necessity of upholding the ideal structure of marriage, the almost imaginary creation of two people who must thereafter consciously work at it, in spite of everyone." She chose to stay with her husband. For his part, Kenneth knew all too well how to play the innocent victim, and his power over her remained undiminished. He begged for Marjory's understanding, convincing her that he deserved the loyalty of his wife and thus the benefit of her doubt. She got her old job back at Bamberger's so they could keep their apartment, and she visited him regularly in jail. When he was released in early 1915, he insisted that they move to New York City so he could start fresh and find work. They took a room in an inexpensive hotel on the Upper West Side. When Kenneth was out during the day, Marjory spent her time reading, mostly Conrad, and walking in Central Park. She harbored no animosity toward him; the marriage and their lives remained a vivid adventure.[16]

But Kenneth continued his old ways. He failed to find work, and he and his wife skipped out on their hotel bill (although she eventually paid it). They took accommodations wherever they could be had, while Kenneth continued to cast about, sometimes not returning at night. He became an even more mysterious character and apparently developed a drinking problem. At the point of desperation, he devised a plan to draft funds against an account of Frank Stoneman, the father whom Marjory had not seen since childhood, and obtained her signature to do so. She was completely unaware of the scheme, so submissive was she to every move and decision of Kenneth's male authority. She deceived herself into thinking the marriage made her whole, and she unwittingly sacrificed her autonomy—the same autonomy that had kept her from staying in Taunton when her mother was ill—to social convention. She squandered those precious faiths that Wellesley had instilled in her—the will and capacity to think for herself—on a man incapable of charting his own way in life.[17]

Then her father intervened. Frank Stoneman had read about the marriage on the news wires and even reprinted the announcement in the *Miami Herald.* He apparently learned of Kenneth's misadventures by the same manner, and after being alerted about the attempted bank drafts, Frank contacted his brother, Edward, a physician living in Springfield, Massachusetts, and asked him to locate Marjory. She had not seen Uncle Ned since childhood, but when they met again, he was a refreshing figure of composure and wholesome sensibility, passing no judgments on Kenneth's character while remaining utterly faithful in his familial duty to his brother and niece. He convinced the couple that for Marjory's welfare, they should separate and Marjory should join her father in Florida. Kenneth (if indeed that was his name) returned unceremoniously to New York and an uncertain future and disappeared into historical oblivion.[18]

A few days later, with money sent from her father, Marjory, filled with curiosity, boarded a train heading south to Florida and toward a hopeful future.

CHAPTER THIRTEEN

By Violence

By the laws of nature, the Everglades, like any wholesome wilderness area, were a violent place, as Henry, the young protagonist in Douglas's novel *Alligator Crossing,* recognizes soon after becoming acquainted with the region: "Everything that lived here—the alligator, the little fish and big fish, the turtles, the frogs, the dragonflies—lived on something else alive that was here, even the green plants in the clear brown water." Killing was the essence of a healthy ecosystem and of life itself. Yet when humans entered, the salubrious contest for survival assumed a new and dramatically different dynamic that disrupted mutually supporting relationships between predator and prey as well as the natural cycle of birth, death, and regeneration. "But Man was different. Man frightened Henry," says the narrator in *Alligator Crossing.* The measure of disruption depended on the culture of the entering group—its values, priorities, and dreams. When Western civilization appeared on the horizon in the square sails of Spanish galleons, major change in the elegant ecosystem was a matter of course. Europeans and their American offspring valued material things, prioritized a market economy, and dreamed of wealth and empire. Built around the cornerstones of science and reason, their society was supposed to have advanced, by the grace of God or by natural selection, well beyond the primitive cosmologies and mythologies of indigenous people, whose ecological footprint was comparatively light. But Western people unleashed an inorganic brand of violence against nature that culminated in ecological ruination of unprecedented measure.[1]

The unnatural violence came in many elemental forms and was enhanced by many technologies. Philadelphian Hamilton Disston, for example, employed surveys and dredges to impose civilization on wilderness. But sometime before his dredges first wolfed up muck, another, though older, market-driven technology was effacing the natural characteristics of the Everglades region. Men with guns took the lead over developers and farmers and bureaucrats in the conquest of the environment—a bloody conquest. Commercial hunters, sportsmen, naturalists, and Indians ransacked wildlife populations and brought the first human-induced ecological change to the Everglades. Florida and the Everglades had the fortune and misfortune of being endowed with remarkable specimens of exotic and highly extroverted wildlife. They formed part of the state's living aesthetic—the flora, fauna, and climate that brought animation and color to the landscape and gave a place its character apart from human creations. Florida banked its early tourist trade of the nineteenth century on the living aesthetic. In what Douglas referred to as a "concerted flood of genteel advertising," popular travel literature and magazines gave glimpses of a naturally beautiful Florida to a national reading audience. Each year, tens of thousands of warm-weather seekers flocked to the St. Johns River region, where they embarked on unhurried steamboat junkets to be awed by the wildlife and to bathe in crystal-clear springs. In their own nineteenth-century Victorian way, they were ecotourists, encountering real-life suggestions of the romanticized nature they discovered in the works of Virgil, Edmund Burke, James Fenimore Cooper, and Walt Whitman. During a visit to Jacksonville in 1905, Henry James said he had become "Byronically foolish about the St. Johns River."[2]

Yet the gratified visitors who had been beguiled by original Florida also assisted in its destruction. Florida's allure was harvested from nature and prepared for sale on local and global markets as fashion apparel and souvenirs. The trade in nature's novelties was a conspicuous public enterprise, nowhere more true than in Jacksonville, the hub city of nineteenth-century Florida tourism, and in the storefront display windows along its Bay Street, known as Curio Row. A travel guide written by tubercular lyricist Sidney Lanier said of Bay Street's inventory, "These curiosities are sea-beans, alligator's teeth, plumes of herons and curlew's feathers, crane's wings, mangrove and orange[wood] walking canes, coral branches, coquina figurines, and many others."[3]

The market for such items bred an army of commercial hunters. They penetrated the Everglades' Fakahatchee Strand for orchids, combed the beaches of Southwest Florida for seashells, waded through nearby swamps to cut cypress knees, plundered the shores for sea turtles and turtle eggs, ambushed mangrove islands for plume birds, and followed the nocturnal bellowing of reptiles for alligator hides. "There is no season of the year," remarked a former *Chicago Times* correspondent, when the hunter "need seek far for his prey." The state passed laws to protect wildlife, but market demand hardly slackened, and protective legislation often did little more than turn legal hunters into willful poachers.[4]

Favorite prey were alligators and wading birds. "One of the most distinguished figures of the Florida wilds," Frank M. Chapman of the American Museum of Natural History observed around the turn of the twentieth century, were the colorful plume birds. Alligators were "so thick" in the water, said a contemporary, that "you can walk across on their heads." The Everglades were a panoptic showcase of these two chief renderings of Florida's living aesthetic. Seduced by their easily had abundance, custodians of the marketplace—consumers, retailers, wholesalers, and hunters—turned the Everglades into what was arguably the world's most hostile place for wildlife. "'Eat or be et' is the law of the Glades," says Cottonmouth, a Burl Ives character in the 1958 B movie *Wind across the Everglades* who is a composite of every irascible wildlife poacher who followed a modified Darwinian code of violence.[5]

Charles Barney Cory followed the code. A Bostonian heir to a silk and wine fortune, he affected his era's kind of gentleman naturalist, seeking spoil and adventure. He spent the late decades of the nineteenth century traveling the world and sending correspondence to magazines and scientific journals with his observations of nature, typically made through the sight of his gun. One of his favorite places was South Florida, in part because he could combine his passions for the high society at Palm Beach's Royal Poinciana resort hotel with the primordial thrill of tracking wild game in the Everglades. These were hardly mutually exclusive indulgences among other male members of his class, who were usually sportsmen rather than naturalists. Cory was both. Suggestive of a Rudyard Kipling character, he invariably organized his hunts like safaris, wore an English field helmet that complemented his twisted and waxed handlebar mustache, and made a habit of having his photograph taken with his most prized quarry, panthers or black bears. He believed his sport benefited science and thus civilization. In 1895, he opened the Florida Museum of Natural History in Palm Beach, installing his mounted and stuffed trophies as the museum's exhibits.[6]

Around the time Cory made his first foray into the Florida wilds in the 1870s, sportsmen nationally were staking an advanced claim to organized conservation. They were the first to devote mass-circulated periodicals, such as *Field and Stream,* to outdoor sports and to use their publications, along with their unified strength, to lobby for wildlife refuges, hunting seasons, and game limits. In 1887, gentlemen hunters, who included Theodore Roosevelt and future National Audubon head George Bird Grinnell, founded the Boone and Crockett Club, the "first private organization to deal effectively with conservation issues of national scope." Members were not, however, so much crusading for nature as crusading for American manhood and against anyone who might impinge on favored hunting tracts. Their infatuation with the "strenuous life" and resolute sense of privilege incidentally benefited wildlife, though only select populations and typically only in places that suited these men's indulgences.[7]

Florida, a favorite hunting ground, generated oddly little conservationist sympathy. To his credit, Cory was less feckless than others. As Douglas pointed out, his 1870s protests against the hunting of Florida's plume birds constituted a virtual one-man outcry. Many in the silent crowd of sportsmen lacked any conservation ethic. A common scene orchestrated on riverboats, for example, was that of men standing at the gunwales with rifle or pistol freely taking potshots at wildlife. An early visitor to the Everglades remembered his misfortune of traveling on a Kissimmee River steamer with a dissolute hunter who from the bow "popped off his gun at everything that rose to fly . . . and that simply to exhibit his marksmanship." Steamers were the South's equivalent of trains traversing the western plains, where men pointed guns through open windows and shot down grazing bison. Making easy conquest of an alligator sunning on a bank or a turtle floating at the water's surface neither seriously tested the shooter's skill nor represented true sportsmanship. "Certainly this is an inherent savagery," wrote an enraged Harriet Beecher Stowe, who kept a winter residence on the St. Johns River and served as frequent witness to "those sons of Nimrod" engaged in such leisurely riverboat wildness.[8]

Cory's alter ego, the naturalist, also did not typically commune peacefully with nature. Naturalists—some of whom made a sideline of taxidermy—observed wild flora and fauna not only in undisturbed settings but also in laboratories. Killing was part of the calling—for some, the most stimulating part. A gun was as essential a tool as a pen for John James Audubon, who was appropriately captured in portrait with rifle on his shoulder, à la the sportsman. He shot hundreds of Florida birds to render them in ink. Other naturalists collected specimens for museums of natural history in Europe and the United Sates. One recalled approaching a rookery of pelicans and stopping to watch parents feeding their young, marveling at the adult's "wonderful" instinctive ability to "find its own nest among so many thousand." He then killed eighteen specimens in the name of science.[9]

Douglas personally knew several early South Florida naturalists and sportsmen. She idealized the former as druidic sages whose beneficent calling drew them to the front lines of wildlife conservation. As for the latter, their sport, in her oft-expressed opinion, was a self-indulgent amusement in killing. But she reserved her greatest reproach for the juggernaut that brought unparalleled unnatural violence to American landscapes everywhere. With neither repose nor remorse, it came in the form of the commercial game hunter.[10]

"Cain and the brothers of Cain" is the description Walt Murdock, the Audubon warden in *Wind across the Everglades,* gives to commercial hunters. Incentives of the marketplace led to the near extinction of beaver in colonial New England, the bison of the Great Plains, and the gray wolf in the Northwest. The same incentives had similar results with alligators and wading birds of the Everglades. In the absence of conservation measures, market hunters were all but free to extract handsome dividends from nature. Says the effusive Murdock, "Cain and the brothers of Cain raised their twelve-gauge shotguns and fired into the face of God."[11]

At the beginning of the second half of the nineteenth century, nature's storehouse, depleted elsewhere in the country by market hunters and their Indian partners, was comparatively overstocked in the Everglades. Seminoles emerged from their protective wilderness seclusion to become the area's principal commercial hunters before the 1890s, killing turtles, bears, wildcats, birds, alligators, deer, otters, and raccoons. By one estimate, hunting and trapping represented 66 percent of the cash income among Everglades Indians. Local and traveling white merchants connected Indians with national and international markets. One of these middlemen was Fort Lauderdale pioneer Frank Stranahan, who ran a store amid a grove of mature coconut trees, a tableau Douglas called a "tropical dream out of the South Seas." Indians and nature made him a rich man. He sometimes paid out more than a thousand dollars for commodities brought in by a Seminole party and could double his investment by reselling to dealers in Jacksonville, New York, and Havana.[12]

One of the most desirable of Florida's wild creatures and one of the most easily culled from nature was the American alligator. The giant reptile prowled freshwater swamps, streams, and lakes as far north as the Carolinas and as far west as Texas, but the identity of one of the country's most exotic states, Florida, was rightfully linked to one of the continent's most exotic creatures. The first known illustration of the American alligator by a westerner was that of Jacques LeMoyne, who accompanied French soldier-settlers to Florida in the sixteenth century. In a now-famous sketch, one of two alligators dominates the scene, which includes thirteen native hunters. The alligator evokes terror if not also evil. Although it breathes no fire, it is dragonlike and exaggerated in size, eclipsing its bare-bodied pursuers. In the background, seven natives with spears and clubs have overcome the second alligator as it struggles on its back, suggesting not only the fate of its counterpart but the general notion that nature itself, no matter how treacherous, can be subdued.[13]

In later centuries, the prehistoric reptiles symbolized both the human domination of nature and the darker side of the state's allure. They formed part of Florida lore, portrayed in magazines, books, and travel guides as "uncouth monsters." Authors of children's literature discovered Florida as a popular setting for stories, and human-eating alligators served as a favored "nemesis" for fictionalized young heroes. Yet the alligator aroused fascination alongside terror. No matter how abhorrent, it was an awe-inspiring wonder of nature. Before the end of the nineteenth century, after hunting had nearly eliminated alligators from the natural scenery, tourists began complaining that they could no longer be seen in their "native haunts."[14]

Enraptured visitors were partly responsible for the reptile's absence. Not only did they want to see one, many wanted to possess one or some part of one in one form or another. Few objects of nature seemed as versatile as a consumer product. Travel writer Julian Ralph came to that conclusion when he walked Jacksonville's Bay Street in the 1890s. It was, he said, "fit to be called Alligator Avenue, because of the myriad ways in which that animal is offered as a sacrifice to the curiosity and thoughtlessness of the crowds. . . . I saw them stuffed and skinned, turned into bags, or kept in tanks and boxes and cages; their babies made into ornaments or on sale as toys; their claws used as purses, their teeth as jewelry, their eggs as curios." *Forest and Stream* reported that in one year alone, Jacksonville shopkeepers had "disposed of" approximately eighty-four hundred alligators to tourists. Anticipating the commodity's decline, the main characters in a 1914 children's novel, *The Moving Picture Girls under*

the Palms; or, Lost in the Wilds of Florida, worried, "What would we do
for valises and satchels if we had no alligators?"[15]

Few people may have been more aware of the public's fascination
with the alligator than Kirk Munroe. Perpetually fit and trim, he was a
man given to worldwide wanderings when he and his wife, Mary Barr
Munroe, found a compelling votive offering in the natural bayside setting of Coconut Grove. Of all the places of marvel in the world they had
known, the couple chose to settle literally beneath the swaying fronds
of Biscayne's coconut palms in the 1880s. Writing books for boys provided Kirk with a living, and as South Florida's first notable writer, he
made alligators synonymous with spirited adventure of the frontier peninsula. He was also quite familiar with their extraction from the wild. In
an 1892 Cosmopolitan Magazine story, he told about a hunting expedition with Seminoles. As was typical, the pursuit occurred at night, when
the reptiles were decidedly more active. Hunters heard rather than saw
their prey: "Darkness had hardly well set in before muttered bellowings
began to sound from the stream." After a cormorant shot earlier that day
was strewn downstream of the hunters' boat, a torch was lit to illuminate
the alligators' eyes—in pairs "luridly red" against the black wall of night.
When an alligator advanced on the bait, a Seminole sent a shot "through
one of his glowing eyeballs." Another Seminole harpooned the sinking
body and dragged it to shore, where it was later skinned with the rest of
the catch. Munroe took aim at the sixth and last alligator shot that night:
"The report of the rifle was instantly followed by such a flurry of whirling,
thrashing and splashing, such showers of spray and bloody foam."[16]

The takings had to be substantial to be worth the evening's labor. Only
the skin of the belly and the clawed feet had market value. Before 1916,
when alligators were the only wild game that hunters could legally pursue
year-round, their hides usually fetched ten cents for twelve inches. One
could expect another twenty-five cents if the feet and claws remained attached. When Stranahan paid two dollars for an eight-foot hide in 1901,
he was offering top prices. Used for necklaces, the teeth brought five to
eight dollars a pound. Stranahan gave a nickel for each fresh alligator egg
and was known to buy them by the thousands from Seminoles. He would

then either resell the eggs in bulk to a dealer in Jacksonville or hatch them and sell the babies to tourists. A six-inch live alligator typically sold for a quarter.[17]

The reptiles paid heavily for white and Indian activity. Beginning in the 1880s, tens of thousands of alligator hides, rolled up and packed in wooden barrels, left Florida annually for leather companies in the Northeast and in Europe. Many were sent to Japan, where they were tanned, made into souvenirs, and exported back to Florida for sale to tourists. A total of 2.5 million alligator hides were amassed from the Florida wilds between 1880 and 1894. The state's ecosystem lost infinitely more in the eggs plundered from nests. Hunting restrictions instituted in 1916 sent hide prices skyrocketing and hardly initiated a trend against the slaughter. As late as the 1940s, a brokerage in Gainesville received eighty thousand hides annually.[18]

In the days before an animal's ecological contribution was understood, much less considered, wildlife protection required that an animal either satisfy as game or induce sympathy. The alligator met neither essential. "The alligator has no friends. . . . No Audubon Society espouses his cause," observed *Forest and Stream,* a magazine that juxtaposed "nature study" and "shooting" in its subtitle. The notion that the best alligator was a dead alligator was not the province of adulthood either, as *The Moving Picture Girls* and Kirk Munroe's stories suggested. Douglas's favorite magazine as a youth, *St. Nicholas,* published in the year of her birth a story glorifying the killing and sale of alligators, giving full details about their slaughter and the market value of their parts. Douglas offered a counternotion years later in *Alligator Crossing.* The morning after Henry's first night hunt, he privately questions whether he should follow his older companion's way of seeing life: "He'd got no business to go around killing alligators . . . , Henry thought, especially with lights and with guns that never gave them a chance. It wasn't fair."[19]

The state dragged its feet on protection until 1962, when it banned alligator hunting altogether. Lawmakers were generally devoted sportsmen who showed little interest in stopping the violence. There was also the problem of enforcement in a state that lacked wildlife wardens until the mid–twentieth century. In the Everglades, every season was open hunting season. This was even true for a sympathetic species, the plume birds, which had, in the statute books at least, legal protection not afforded the alligator.

Not knowing whether his real name was Alfred Lechevelier or Jean Chevelier, locals called him the Old Frenchman. He spoke a curious "sort of Pidgen English" and was apparently from Montreal, though he sometimes talked about life in Paris. People did know with certainty the Old Frenchman's mode of living. In 1881, he bought 120 acres on Pinellas Point near the mouth of the Tampa Bay estuary system, not to grow citrus or raise cattle, as others were doing, but to run a plume-hunting operation. He strategically located himself near the populous Maximo rookeries, on which he enforced a proprietary claim. One local called him the "worst scourge that ever came to Point Pinellas."[20]

Eccentric, hated, and ruthless, he was legendary, and not just around Tampa Bay. A stream on Pinellas Point acquired the name Frenchman's Creek, and in South Florida his name graced Chevelier Bay in the Ten Thousand Islands and later the company that built the state highway, Tamiami Trail, across the Everglades. After reducing Maximo to lifeless mangrove heaps, Chevelier and his adjuncts sailed south to a fresh supply of birds in the Everglades, where he accidentally shot a hole through his right hand. He adjusted, propping the gun barrel over his right elbow, aiming with his left eye, and pulling the trigger with his left index finger. It was not the quest for legendary status that drove him on; it was the incentive of the market and the lure of easy expropriation.[21]

Newcomers to Florida were startled to see snowy egrets, great egrets, little blue herons, great blue herons, roseate spoonbills, ibises, and wood storks stepping about on their stick legs in marshes and along pond and bay edges. Some birds stood to the height of a grown man's chest. Before hunters disturbed the wild, a flock in flight could form a "perfect cloud" against the sun. With warm temperatures, dry and wet seasons, mangrove islands and forests, and plentiful fish, the Everglades were perfectly suited as a habitat for the migrating birds. Most birds nested in integrated avian colonies in mangroves, called rookeries, where hundreds even thousands of a variety of gregarious species retired at dusk after a day of feeding and where in the spring and summer they nurtured their young. Douglas captured the evening retreat of birds making their way overhead from the coast back to the Everglades: "At sunset with full crops they would move in their white thousands and tens of thousands, with the sounds of great stiff silk banners, birds in flocks, birds in wedges, birds in wavering ribbons, blue and white crowds, rivers of birds pouring against the sunset back to the rookeries."[22]

For thousands of years, Florida's birds lived unmolested. Their bloodline dated to the Pleistocene, before the Everglades formed, when the birds' ancestors had lived with mammoths, bison, horses, camels, llamas, and sloths, indigenous fauna that failed to survive geologic and climatic changes and the crude weapons of early humans. The birds, more flexible and adaptable, did. But they could not endure the modern hunter's gun. As Munroe wrote early in the twentieth century, the Everglades were the "paradise of plume hunters and the purgatory of all birds."[23]

Damning them was, of all things, hats. The fashion industry at the time fixed feathers of all kinds and even whole birds (as well as other small animals, flowers, grasses, and sea moss) to women's hats as ornamental trimming. When volunteering in 1886 for the American Ornithologists' Union, an organization of professional scientists dedicated to the study and welfare of birds, Frank Chapman counted in two afternoons 160 birds on the hats of women walking about New York City's Uptown shopping district. Historian Jennifer Price writes, "In an era of rapid social and economic change and mobility, the use of Nature to set human standards was becoming a powerful hallmark of modern thinking." Birds had a feminine quality, so turning them into women's fashion made perfect sense. When middle- and upper-class women across the globe pinned on feather-adorned hats, they were, in Victorian vogue, transferring a bit of nature's beauty to themselves. The plumage of egrets and their long-beaked cousins—their feathers ample, dramatic, and frolicsome—were especially popular.[24]

Market hunters, Chevelier among them, began plundering rookeries in the early 1880s, when selling feathers to milliners in New York and Europe became a lucrative endeavor. Millinery was a seventeen-million-

dollar-a-year industry in New York, employing twenty thousand workers, most under sweatshop conditions. Plume hunters operated in a harsh
environment, but their work could enrich them. According to one young
white hunter, a "day's wages of plume-hunting" was equal to a month of
"'gator hunting." Seminoles could get tourists to part with several dollars per feather, although most feathers were sold to millinery agents,
who paid twelve to seventeen dollars per ounce, depending on the kind
and quality of feather. Hunters got the price of gold, thirty-two dollars an
ounce, for the snowy egret's fluffy mating feathers. One ounce of feathers
required killing four egrets.[25]

Not surprisingly, many locals supported themselves by trading in
plume birds. South Florida was not the sort of place where the average
individual who lived off the land or sea could hope to get rich—at least
not in the nineteenth century. Whites began settling on dry enclaves in
the vast wetland a few at a time just before the Civil War. Some of the
first settlers were veteran soldiers who stayed on or returned after the
last of the Indian fighting in Florida stopped. They carved out isolated
hamlets, which they gave names such as Flamingo, Everglades City, and
Chokoloskee Island, and they built unpainted board houses on stilts that
were surrounded by saw palmettos and slash pines. Life was in some ways
more difficult for South Florida pioneers than for those who settled on
the western plains. Indian raids had not been a threat since the Seminole
Wars ended in 1858, but before the days of dredges and drainage canals,
livestock had little rangeland. There was plenty of freshwater for staple
crops but comparatively less consistently dry terra firma in which to plant
them. Settlers thus shot birds for a source of protein for the family table.
"The pot-hunter has good reason for killing birds," wrote University of
Miami biologist John C. Gifford in 1925.[26]

After millinery agents began paying for feathers, locals obligingly
adapted their hunting habits to the demands of the market. Said Audubon warden Oscar Baynard, the money earned from pluming simply offered "terrible temptation to many real fine fellows." "Killing was just one
way of making a living, to Dillon," says Henry of his companion in *Alligator Crossing*. "The things were here for the taking. You'd be a fool not

to." John A. Johnson was so tempted not to be a fool that he quit his job as a federal warden charged with protecting Everglades birds. He was subsequently arrested by a former colleague while in the possession of five thousand dollars worth of feathers.[27]

Everglades hunters were part of a global market. Plumers were lodged throughout the world—Australia, Africa, the Middle and Far East, South America, and Southern Europe—and they shipped their feathers across regions, continents, and oceans. Few places in the world could match the size of the Everglades' avian population and their ensemble of species. One Florida hunter told a *New York Herald* reporter that in one season, he and a couple of "assistants" accumulated a total of 130,000 birds, mostly plume birds. In 1902, commercial salesrooms in London reported an inventory of 48,240 ounces of plumes, an amount that would have required the slaying of 192,000 birds and two to three times as many nestlings and eggs, all from the United States and most from Florida. Hunters cleaned out whole rookeries up and down Florida's coasts. Florida Audubon Society member Minnie Moore-Willson did not embellish when she wrote that the birds "are taking their last meals."[28]

She saw no worse devil than the market hunter, and the Everglades swarmed with them. After they exhausted bird supplies in one area, they penetrated deeper into the "bewildering labyrinths of the Everglades," leaving virtually no avian life behind. Feather agents papered the region with leaflets instructing readers how to skin birds properly and preserve the feathers and where to ship the bounty. Agents advertised in local newspapers to recruit native hunters with the promise of easy money, and they got responses. New York agent J. H. Batty advertised himself in *Forest and Stream* as a "Dealer in Objects of Natural History." He sometimes shot birds to collect them for museums but mainly did so for the market. His forty-five-foot sharpie schooner was a familiar sight on Florida's coasts, where he maintained a business relationship with three score commercial hunters. He supplied them with breech-loading shotguns designed with a twelve-gauge barrel and a less destructive and quieter twenty-two-caliber barrel, used for small birds and close-range shooting. Birds were hunted year-round, but the heaviest takings occurred in late spring, when

rookeries were considered "ripe." Nuptial feathers were still at their finest, hatchlings were fresh from their eggs, and adults were not likely to
abandon nests at the sound of gunfire. They instead rose up, defensively
hovering over their young, only to become easier targets for their predators. "The method is simple," observed Chapman; "any boy with a gun
can become a plume hunter."[29]

Not even sympathetic naturalists considered the consequences of losing so many vital inhabitants of a given ecosystem, of how imbalances
might afflict the local food chain. What unsettled naturalists was the cold-
blooded cruelty of the plume trade—the hundreds of distressed nestlings
left behind. Many writers of the day captured the perverse results of the
plume hunter's errand; none did so more poignantly than did Douglas in
River of Grass: "When the sun rose the ethereal whiteness of the plumed
parent birds shone like frost against the blue, blue sky. They were white in
the nights under the moon, or to the torches and firepans of the men with
clubs in canoes slipping along behind the lights. A few men with clubs or
shotguns rising suddenly by those low rookeries could kill and scalp hundreds of birds in a night. By morning the bloody bodies would be drawing the buzzards and alligators. The great black Florida crows that shed
the light like water from their feathers would clean out the dying young.
Ants in long lines as fine as pepper would carry off the rotting pieces of
their bones."[30]

A few hunters had difficulty stomaching such a gory sight. "I am done
with bird hunting forever!" said one. Another man who killed and skinned
alligators by the dozen without a tincture of misgiving believed that he
had not been "doing God's service" after he killed mother egrets and left
a feast for crows. The day after his first kill, a young hunter grieved for
the orphaned nestlings: "I couldn't stand it, hearing those hungry little
birds."[31]

Critics exhibited a perverse tendency to blame women for the mad
cruelty. A Miami judge threatened to enforce a state law outlawing the
possession of plume feathers by trying women who wore the ornaments
on their hats. The Audubon Society hosted public lectures portraying

fashion-oriented women as the enemy of birds. As one newspaper editorial put it, women "flit from shop to shop," select their attire, and make purchases that underwrite the millinery market. "We are willing to leave the irresponsible half of creation all their 'chiffons,'" one ornithologist wrote bitterly, "if they will only leave us our birds." But critics paid no mind to the fact that men owned the millinery factories and men shot the birds. Men were not by nature or nurture creatures of vanity, like women, as one *New York Times* writer clarified. But men who wanted to be seen with beautiful and fashionable women were in fact given to pride or public exhibition. Calculating the trade-offs, many men apparently deduced that "one woman in the house (if beautiful and good-tempered) is worth many birds in the bush—or in the Everglades." Those birds represented the price of both beauty and morality, categories defined largely by patriarchal society. Proper women concealed themselves from head to toe in heavy Victorian costumes. Their natural beauty was the province of the husband, not the public, which had to be satisfied with virtuous attire—artificial beauty, in other words. Women were neither totally passive about decisions in dress nor fully in control. Designers and retailers informed them about what was stylish and acceptable. Fashion was "Queen," one retailer reminded women. To enhance their comeliness, Victorian women relied on tasteful adornments—perhaps silk waists or French-cut jackets. No attire was complete without a charming hat from Paris, London, or New York, as one store advertised, made from only the "finest of velvets, the finest of plumes, birds, and feathers."[32]

Fashionable women and men, retailers, milliners, and hunters did not seek extermination but nevertheless very nearly got that outcome. The profligate killing of birds became a national epidemic. In 1898, the New York Zoological Society released a study that estimated an average 45 percent decline in the bird life in thirty states over the previous fifteen years. At 77 percent, Florida's decrease was the largest. Ornithologists reported that once-bustling rookeries, including Chevelier's Maximo rookery, had been turned into eerie ghost islands. By century's end, roseate spoonbills had all but disappeared, about two hundred great white herons remained, and only one pair of reddish egrets survived. As a consequence of the demand for the more expensive "snowy product," conservationists in 1911 could count only ten egret colonies in the Carolinas, Georgia, and Florida. The change was so remarkable that a *New York Times* correspondent reported that the Everglades, once "alive with the most gorgeous land and water birds in North America . . . are no longer made beautiful by their presence."[33]

By the twentieth century, a growing number of people recognized that vanishing wildlife was changing Florida's living aesthetic. In a 1908 *Harper's Magazine* article, A. W. Dimock was one of the few to lament the "passing" of Florida's largest reptile. In a rare observation for the time, he referred to the alligator's ecological value, noting the wildlife that thrived around the water holes alligators dug during the dry season and the rise in the number of water moccasins in response to their predator's decline. He was concerned mainly with the loss of an animal that "has always been the picturesque and popular feature of the peninsula." Daniel F. Tyler included both alligators and birds in the picturesque equation: "The Florida tourist," he wrote in 1880, "will be disappointed at not seeing more alligators and beautiful birds of plumage." Thirty-six years later, an Audubon official said something similar to *Miami Herald* staff writer Marjory Stoneman Douglas: "The one thing now that Miami lacks is birds." Her friend Charles Torrey Simpson, one of South Florida's most important naturalists, said, "It was birds that gave color and glory to the whole. . . . [T]hey are mostly a lovely memory." By that time, dredges were briskly ladling up bird habitats, lessening the possibility of a comeback even if the guns fell silent.[34]

Along with agricultural and forest products, hunted wildlife was one of Florida's top export commodities at the time. In the affairs of humans and nature, in the drama of wildlife destruction played out on the American frontier many times over, the Florida saga must be counted as one of the bloodiest. In the end, supplies could not last; the inventory was not being renewed. Land booms and drainage impeded renewal and provided important catalysts in the transformation of Florida's popular image, but the gutting of wildlife populations came first and diminished those things that gave Florida its original splendor. As Dimock fittingly put it, "The tourist has murdered the birds that beckoned him." Preserving the splendor ultimately became the cause of many good people early in the twentieth century, sometimes with tragic consequences.[35]

CHAPTER FOURTEEN

Killing Mr. Bradley

Douglas never met the ill-fated Guy Bradley. He was slain in 1905 near his Everglades home when she was still a schoolgirl in Taunton. But she eventually learned a lot about him. With his death, he became the lionized symbol of the slaughtered birds, his martyrdom desperately conceived by the National Association of Audubon Societies during the most despairing period in the enterprise of defending birds.

Twenty-five years later, Douglas revivified his martyrdom with a fictional account of the demise of an Everglades warden. The catalyst for the story was her most intimate contact ever with the Everglades. At the time, she was part of an official committee charged with selling to Congress and the public the idea of creating an Everglades national park. In January 1930, the committee led a delegation of federal lawmakers and bureaucrats and national conservationists on an exhaustive tour—by land, sea, and air—of the Everglades. Feather hats had long since passed from fashion, yet two days into the tour, members of the group confronted poachers preparing to shoot out a rookery. At the tour's conclusion, Douglas returned home a bit wiser about the Everglades. She gathered her writer's conscience with paper, pen, and lapboard, and went out on her back patio to compose a stand against the tenacious savagery. In June, the *Saturday Evening Post* published her most memorable short story, "Plumes." Its portrayal of humanity's capacity for morbid callousness "shook one reader to the core of her heart," as a Douglas fan wrote to the *Post*.[1]

Guy Bradley served as a rough model for the story's doomed hero, John Pinder. Both men possessed amiable reticence: Bradley preferred whistling a musical tune to conversation; Pinder preferred quiet solitude to frontier companions. Both were deputized as Audubon bird wardens: Bradley sought the job earnestly; Pinder accepted it reluctantly. Both lived, to use a description from "Plumes," "at that last end of Florida, where the low green land goes back to the green-running sea." And each was killed by a local man he knew—in Douglas's words, a "big man, burned yellow brown, calm, with calm eyes," who partnered with his sons in the illegal hunting and trading of plume birds. The most significant difference between Bradley and Pinder is in their backgrounds. Readers learn only that Pinder is an escaped convict from Pennsylvania who has found relative anonymity in the Everglades. His disreputable past, whatever his guilt or innocence, allowed Douglas to use redemption and conversion (achieved when he agreed to be deputized and thus take the side of the law) as a device to sharpen his ascension to hero.[2]

Bradley's background was comparatively common, at least among fellow Everglades dwellers. He grew up in the pioneering settlement of Lantana, a few miles south of West Palm Beach. The Bradleys had moved there from Chicago in 1876, when Guy was six, joining a handful of homesteaders who had put down stakes along the southern shore of Lake Worth, a placid body of blue water three miles from the Atlantic Ocean. Many of the local settlers hoped to convert their subsistence endeavors—farming, fishing, and hunting—into cash profit. Hunting gave Lake Worth an economic link to its adjoining backcountry, the Everglades, and an inlet dug to the Atlantic made the area more accessible to trade markets—and transformed the freshwater lake into a saltwater ecosystem. One hunter who sailed up the Lake Worth inlet with his family was Walter Smith, who killed Bradley twelve years later.[3]

Plume hunting was both a vocation and, particularly for boys, a pastime. Young Guy's family provided a living link between the two. The
Bradleys resided in a house vacated by the area's first commercial plume
hunter, and a year after arriving in Florida, seven-year-old Guy and his
nine-year-old brother, Louis, went on their first quest for feathers. They
trudged into nearby woods with the more experienced Charlie Pierce,
embarking on a short excursion in which the two older boys with guns
indulged the tagalong's presence. Seven years later, the Old Frenchman,
Jean Chevelier, chartered Pierce's twenty-eight-foot sloop for a lengthy
hunting expedition around the lower quadrant of the peninsula. Using
their own boat, Guy and Louis accompanied the Chevelier party through
the upper keys. Fifteen-year-old Guy shot ten birds, likely earning
between forty and fifty dollars.[4]

Bradley was ultimately no more destined to the career of a plume
hunter than is his literary surrogate. Pinder's decision to turn in the opposite direction comes after self-reflection, a moral awakening that puts
him in a dilemma. By quietly tending to his own business, he has found
refuge among people who dwell at the margins of civilization and "live
off the country," which in some cases includes poaching wildlife. So complete is his acceptance that he is taken into their confidence and told that
Two-Gun George Johnson has set his sights on shooting out a rookery
of snowy egrets. Pinder hesitates to betray those who have allowed him
sanctuary from the law. When he feels unexpected anger at the thought
of Two-Gun's deed, when his mind wanders to the impending horror and
he feels an "effete emotion," he tries to convince himself that the birds
mean nothing to him. Yet some deeper, unconscious will impels him to
tell what he knows to Audubon representatives, and he agrees to defend
the rookery.[5]

Somber reactions of this sort filled Bradley with a similar sense of mission. But his conversion evolved slowly and rode on the current of changing times, largely propelled by wildlife conservation. Even in the earliest
days of plume hunting, some level of public concern for the birds existed, enough to convince the state legislature to pass restrictive legislation in 1879. Though its actions represented a start, the legislature seemed

less motivated to protect birds than the vocation and avocation of some of its citizens since the law applied only to aliens operating in the state. And the measure did not impede anyone very much. The Old Frenchman, for example, went about his business cavalierly, in keeping with his name, and the peak years of plume hunting were still to come. In 1891, Florida legislators outlawed the commercial hunting of plume birds but failed to create adequate enforcement provisions.[6] One millinery agent subsequently delivered 130,000 Florida birds to the ever-voracious fashion industry. In 1910, New York banned interstate commerce in feathers, but many milliners simply fled to a friendlier state; others imported feathers from agents in Europe, who bought from middlemen in Havana, who bought from poachers in Florida. Congress's first protective measure came in the Lacey Act of 1900, which allowed the federal prosecution of anyone killing birds in violation of state laws. But the federal government, habituated to state sovereignty, hesitated to impose its authority over local wildlife. Then, responding to some two hundred thousand letters and to a barrage of Audubon lobbyists, including Laura Norcross Marrs of Florida Audubon, Congress added a ban on imported plume fashions to the Federal Tariff Act of 1913, at least a decade after most of Florida's plume birds were lost.[7]

Douglas wrote about these legislative developments in a nonfiction piece published in the *Post* in 1931, part of another spate of writing she undertook in the wake of the Everglades tour. To her, the disquieting discovery of plume hunters still at large suggested that the protective laws had "no teeth." If arrests did occur, the typical punishment amounted to a slap on the wrist, as when a judge fined a Florida couple twenty-five dollars and their accomplice one dollar for the possession of thousands of dollars worth of plumes. "After twenty-eight years it's still going on," exclaims the Audubon official who hires Pinder. "I tell you, the people don't care." The mortal version of this indifference was evident in the indignation Missouri senator James Reed expressed during floor debate over the Tariff Act: "I really honestly want to know why there should be any sympathy or sentiment about a long-legged, long-beaked, long-necked bird that lives in the swamps. . . . Let humanity utilize this bird for the only purpose that evidently the Lord made it for, namely so that we could get aigrettes for the bonnets of our beautiful ladies." *Aigrettes* was the industry's preferred alternative to the words *feathers* and *plumes* that, according to the *Miami Herald,* allowed the beau monde to separate fashion from the inherent slaughter. Popular denial gave Frank Chapman of the Museum of Natural History in New York reason to predict the extinction of several bird species in Florida. Another reason for the impending extinctions was Florida's continued failure to hire wildlife wardens. That responsibility was left to private interests.[8]

Chief among those interests were the American Ornithologists' Union (AOU) and Audubon. State Audubon societies established the national association in 1905. Marrs, Florida's representative at the organizing meeting, recalled, "I was one of a group of persons who met to consider if they should make a bold plunge into the stormy sea of opposition to Audubon measures and bird protection existing in Florida." Florida birds were not the sole motivation for the founding of the national association, but the plumage issue lent a sense of urgency to the proceedings. From its beginning, the national association piloted an aggressive lobbying and publicity campaign. In newspapers and magazines ranging from *Ladies' Home Journal* to *Popular Mechanics,* ornithologists and other experts wrote about empty rookeries and empty skies and the blood-soaked connection of these conditions to feather fashions. State groups pushed for the creation of bird sanctuaries and sponsored education programs.[9]

In Florida, sanctuaries were the specialty of Katherine Tippetts, the redoubtable thirty-three-year president of the St. Petersburg Audubon Society. With the tribal power of her organization behind her, she got the city commission to adopt a program to exterminate "tramp" cats, bird eaters that they were. Douglas knew of Tippetts and as a cat lover would have thought hers a daffy program. In Douglas's view, cats incidentally sustained the bird population by killing varmints that raided nests. In a 1926 story, "A River in Flood," she engaged in a bit of satire apparently directed at Tippetts by creating a feline hero, "Mrs. Tibbets," who brings bad luck to a pair of murderers. In other moves that Douglas could praise, Tippetts persuaded a major publisher to pull air-rifle advertisements from its juvenile magazines. She also oversaw the creation of eleven local bird sanctuaries, an achievement that secured her the state Audubon presidency, and she used her tenure to add thirty more sanctuaries to Florida's inventory.[10]

The mother of all bird sanctuaries was Pelican Island. A flat dash of sand and beach grass, three acres at most during low tide, it had long been a preferred nesting spot of royal terns, snowy egrets, brown pelicans, and others. It was also a favorite of plume hunters. On one occasion, a wealthy yachtsman had two hundred pelicans from the island shot and turned into a robe for his wife. Provoked, Paul Kroegel, a boat builder and son of a German-born homesteader, sailed out to the island to hold fort against further plundering. The birds came to trust the peaceable man, mustache curling over his mouth and eyes squinting in the shade of his slouch hat, sitting on the beach with a rifle resting across his lap. After hearing about Kroegel, William Dutcher, chairman of the AOU's bird-protection committee, went to Florida and hired Kroegel as an Audubon warden, agreeing to Kroegel's requested monthly salary of one dollar. With the help of National Audubon and the Florida group, the AOU convinced President Theodore Roosevelt to designate Pelican Island as a bird sanctuary. Warming to the idea of setting aside federal land as protected areas, he signed a March 1903 executive order making Pelican Island the first national wildlife refuge. Fifty-five other bird reservations and wildlife preserves followed before he left the White House.[11]

Because Florida had the most to lose in the war against birds, it had concerned citizens, and like the transgressors, they constituted part-time and full-time residents. In early March 1900 in Maitland, near Orlando, one such group gathered at the thirty-room winter home of New York silk merchant Louis Dommerich and his wife, Clara. The Dommerichs had turned their 210-acre estate, Hiawatha, which fronted Lake Minnehaha, into a private bird sanctuary. While Louis usually topped off the feeding boxes each morning, Clara called together their Florida friends to organize the state Audubon Society. The group of six men and nine women wasted no time in electing a board of officers from the ranks of the social elite: a clergyman, a college president, a judge, a former army general, and a writer. Laura Marrs, a café-society Bostonian and daughter of a former mayor of that city, chaired the executive committee until her death in 1926. The founders made Kirk Munroe, Governor William S. Jennings, and President Roosevelt honorary vice presidents. Dues were set at one dollar for regular members and twenty-five cents for junior members; the fee was waived for teachers, who were expected to be the conduit through which Audubon would pass its values to the younger generation. The Florida group's principal aim was to alert the public about the "wanton destruction of wild birds and their eggs," to discourage the purchase of feathers for ornamentation, and to emphasize the distinction between wild bird and game bird protection. Florida Audubon recorded its first lobbying success in 1901 when the legislature outlawed the killing of nongame birds and mandated bird study in public schools. Audubon characterized Florida's laws and similar laws at least five other states adopted as model legislation.[12]

Despite promising developments, including twenty new local bird sanctuaries and the Pelican Island sanctuary, the establishment of a badly needed corps of wildlife wardens eluded Audubon activists. Florida lawmakers were willing to restrict the activities of "negroes and crackers" but not legislators' personal pastimes. The responsibility of employing wardens consequently fell to the cash-poor National Audubon. The organization obtained an endowment from wildlife painter Abbott Thayer that permitted the hiring of four wardens in the spring of 1902. One was Kroegel; another was a Cape Sable resident named Guy Bradley.[13]

Bradley was thirty-two years old at the time and, unlike his fictional counterpart, married and the father of one son. His wife, Fronie, gave birth to a second boy a year later. The few existing photographs of Guy show a common walrus mustache hooding his upper lip. In one photograph, his hair is ruffled and he looks depleted from the subtropical heat and humidity. In another, he is wearing a suit and his hair is parted and slicked to the side. In both, his eyes are serene, and a badge is pinned to his chest. As a wildlife warden, he was deputized by the Monroe County sheriff's department in Key West. Some people said he seemed a little obsessed with his duties.[14]

The Bradley clan had moved four years earlier to Flamingo, a last-frontier settlement of fewer than fifty people at the "jumping-off place of the United States," as Douglas narrated in one of her stories. It was also in the heart of wading-bird country. Bradley variously worked as a hunting and fishing guide in the Cape Sable–Florida Bay region, conducted surveys for Flagler's Model Land Company, and ran the mail by boat to Key West. People knew him as an expert woodsman who, as one observer of the time said, "possessed a strong constitution, abundant energy, and indomitable courage." After learning about the warden job, he was eager for it and sought a letter of reference from Munroe. Tippetts also offered him one, and it was accompanied by another from the influential Marrs. In a letter to Dutcher, Bradley showed impressive candor: "I used to hunt plume birds," he wrote, "but since the game laws were passed, I have not killed a plume bird. For it is a cruel and hard calling not withstanding being unlawful. I make this statement upon honor." Douglas's Pinder similarly explains to the Audubon official who hires him, "Even if there wasn't any law, I'd hate to hear [the birds] were killed."[15]

Within two years after Dutcher hired Bradley at thirty-five dollars a month plus equipment, Audubon had thirty-four wardens keeping vigil in ten states. But no territory matched the prime difficulties and dangers of that put in Bradley's safekeeping. His jurisdiction extended to the entire county of Monroe, which included the keys and the southern portion of the Everglades, an area swelling with bird life and heavily armed poachers. The area also had long been a hotbed for smugglers, rum-runners, and moonshiners. Dwelling mainly in and around the Ten Thousand Islands, plumers as a bunch were unreconstructed lawbreakers. Many of those who were not Seminoles were former Confederate soldiers, Indian fighters, or both. Some were just simply reprobated outcasts who had fled the hassle of living by the social mores and rules of the "overgrown spider of civilization," to borrow a phrase from *Wind across the Everglades*. Plumers drifted into the swamp, where they could function more comfortably by whims of self-interest and, when necessary, violence. Pitched battles among plumers were not uncommon. At an egret colony on Alligator Bay, two groups squared off in a shootout before one fled. The victors ransacked the rookery and then burned it, permanently

destroying the habitat. The most ruthless among the local plumers was
Ed Watson of Chatham Bend, who was said to have killed as many as fifty
men and women and who decades later was fabled in Peter Matthiessen's
novel *Killing Mr. Watson*.[16]

In "By Violence," set in the Everglades and appearing in the *Post* in
1930, Douglas suggested the region's lawlessness. The story's central character is Martin, a fourteen-year-old boy who lives on Chokoloskee Island,
a small but settled piece in the conundrum of the Ten Thousand Islands.
Shaken by his father's recent death, Martin struggles to follow in the older
man's worthy footsteps as a skilled fisherman, guide, and family bread-
winner. By doing so, Martin is rebelling against two imperious uncles who
had previously "charmed" him with their loud talk and violent ways. Although Chokoloskee is a rough-and-tumble backwoods domain, Douglas
wanted to remind readers that cities also bred violence. Two of the other
main characters are Miami men who have sailed out to the islands and a
veil of mangroves, where they intend to kill another man from the city.
Martin witnesses the deed. He has previously seen much violence "in that
world island of his, surrounded and penetrated by the untouched, raw
wilderness and the naked, uncontrollable sea." He has seen "hurricanes
when the raving water almost closed over the island . . . a man just bitten
by a water moccasin . . . his father's face the time his baby sister had con-
vulsions. But this was different." Those incidents were not premeditated
violence perpetrated by humans but rather a natural violence that Martin
could not control or stop. Although unable to save the condemned man,
he can and does stop the killers from getting away with murder. Here in
the end is a law-abiding side to a legendary lawless backcountry, a compensating merit of the sort Douglas liked to bring out in stories.[17]

But such endings were usually unrealistic, unlike the ending of
"Plumes" and the Bradley saga. Poachers were not liable to be duped by
fourteen-year-old fresh-faced boys, at least not on the poachers' own turf.
Nor were they inclined to tolerate an official of the law, even an insider
or charitable neighbor like Guy Bradley. In spite of his badge worn so
proudly, Bradley was neither intimidating in size nor aggressive in spirit.
His main weapon was a single thirty-two-caliber pistol, a poor match for

the artillery of plume hunters. The Bradleys nonetheless had "the reputation of being the best rifle shots in the vicinity," and Guy, some locals
said, was "fearless." If nothing else, he was sternly committed to enforcing the law. Two of his father's uncles had been lawmen up north, and
his grandfather worked with the Underground Railroad. Herbert Job described Bradley to his Audubon bosses as being the right man for a difficult job and as "tough as a red mangrove."[18]

That was the expressed opinion of Frank Chapman, too. The New York
ornithologist traveled to Florida in 1904 to see the famous Cuthbert rookery, named ungraciously for the first hunter to shoot it out. Bradley impressed Chapman as a man with "pride in his office and an enmity for
lawbreakers." Systematic in his approach to protecting the plume birds,
Bradley educated citizens about plume hunting being a punishable offense, spoke to hunters directly about the law, and posted warning signs
made of painted muslin around his territory. He also established a network of informants to provide him with extra eyes and ears and solicited
the services of his brother, his brother-in-law, the mayor of Flamingo, and
the mayor's two sons to act as assistant wardens during the plume season. His father, who became postmaster, screened mail for illegal solicitations from millinery agents for feathers. Guy also monitored the meat
markets in Key West and in his motorized launch, *Audubon,* persistently
patrolled his rookeries. The most prized among them, Cuthbert was the
most difficult for poachers to reach and for Bradley to protect. He still
managed three trips there every nesting season, and in the respite from
the guns the once-devastated colony slowly climbed back to a population of four thousand. Yet just before Chapman arrived in 1904, poachers watching Bradley's movements again shot out the rookery. Chapman
predicted after returning to New York, "That man Bradley is going to be
killed some time. He has been shot at more than once, and some day they
are going to get him."[19]

The next year, Walter Smith set his own sights on the Cuthbert rookery, just as Two-Gun George sets his on the fictional Cocos rookery. Like
Pinder, Bradley knew about the impending assault. Smith and his family
had moved to Flamingo at the same time as the Bradleys and had done

so at the insistence of Guy's father. The elder Bradley thus "committed the greatest blunder of his life," claims Bradley's biographer. Originally from North Carolina, Smith was a Confederate veteran sharpshooter who had fought in all the major battles of the East, from Antietam to Gettysburg. He still carried the scars of a gunshot wound taken during his last skirmish in the Shenandoah Valley. In many ways, he was unlikely to have murdered Guy Bradley. The Bradleys and Smiths had initially remained friends in Flamingo, and the families had summer residences across the street from one another amid Key West's cooling trade winds. Guy's mother had helped to deliver the Smith children, and his wife was a close friend of Smith's wife. The two men had hunted together, which might have left Smith unclear about Bradley's fidelity to the law. Smith, however, had earned a reputation in Flamingo for being a quarrelsome neighbor, and in 1904 and again in early 1905, Bradley arrested Smith's teenage son, Tom, for poaching. The arrests enraged Smith, and he vowed to kill Bradley if he ever again tried to arrest one of the Smith boys.[20]

Smith fulfilled his promise on July 8, 1905. From his house in Flamingo, Bradley heard the report of rifle shots across the still water from the direction of the rookeries at Oyster Keys in Florida Bay. Smith was out there on his schooner with two men and two of his sons. Smith knew he was flouting the law in front of the enforcer, just as Two-Gun knows, after Pinder informs him, that the new Audubon warden will be watching over Cocos. Pinder was a lone law enforcer, as was Bradley that morning. All his assistant wardens were away when he set out in his launch, armed with only his pistol. As he approached the schooner, Smith fired a warning shot from his Winchester rifle. Bradley reportedly told Smith that he wanted Tom, who, along with his brother, Dan, had been on the island shooting birds. At least one more shot was fired. It penetrated downward near Bradley's left shoulder and exited at his right kidney. Smith and crew hastened back to Flamingo, where he retrieved his family and set sail for Key West. There he gave himself up to authorities. The next day, a friend searching for Bradley spotted the *Audubon* drifting in the current toward Sawfish Hole near Flamingo. Bradley's body was in the bottom of the launch, face down in a pool of blood.[21]

Pinder's fate is the same. He dies in the red-stained bowels of his boat after a daylong shootout with Two-Gun and three others. Two-Gun never turns himself over to the authorities. In fact, Pinder is killed by a shot fired by a law officer who has a warrant for the arrest of James D. Evans, a.k.a. John Pinder, a fugitive from a Pennsylvania prison. Two-Gun has been suspicious of Pinder's true identity for some time but has been obliged by the code of the backcountry to honor the man's anonymity until Pinder challenges Two-Gun's claim to the Cocos birds. The law officer accompanies Two-Gun to arrest Pinder—and to shoot birds.

"We have got to hang this man Smith," Chapman said after hearing the news of Bradley's death. "Otherwise we send notice to all our wardens that . . . there is no protection for them." But Smith's only punishment came while he was in jail when two of Bradley's brothers-in-law went up to Flamingo from Key West and set aflame the Smith house. Flamingo residents gathered to watch the sun-dried pine-board siding light up like a bonfire. National Audubon sent in one of Miami's top attorneys to assist in the prosecution, but the locals perceived the effort as meddling by outsiders, and Monroe County's eloquent, influential prosecutor changed sides to represent Smith before a grand jury inquest. The accused justified the killing to the grand jury by claiming that the warden had shot first. Although the jurors knew that Bradley's revolver had been found fully loaded and that Smith had previously threatened to kill Bradley, they decided that insufficient evidence existed to bring an indictment against the plume hunter.[22]

Despite this setback, conservationists hoped to make the best of the matter. With Bradley as the first casualty of the conservation movement, Dutcher, now head of National Audubon, hoped to gain the sympathy of the American public. "I believe this Bradley martyrdom will work for our good," an Audubon member wrote in a letter to Dutcher; "[I]t would distinguish our cause." As the murder and acquittal made national headlines, Dutcher played up Bradley's apotheosis at every opportunity, describing his widow and fatherless children as victims of greed and vanity. In a eulogy to Bradley, Dutcher wrote, "Heretofore the price has been the life of the birds, now is added human blood." At first, the hoped-for public outcry materialized. Even President Roosevelt and First Lady Edith Roosevelt affirmed their opposition to the "garniture of millinery."[23]

Milliners remained strategically silent on the Bradley slaying but vocally unapologetic about the slaughter of birds. Spokesmen had previously defended the industry by contending that its plumes originated as the molted feathers of adult birds retrieved from the ground by harmless collectors. In an article for a South Florida magazine, pioneer conservationist Mary Barr Munroe denounced the milliners' "dead feathers" subterfuge. In multiple public venues, Dutcher said that the claim was preposterous. By the turn of the century, the industry had begun spending heavily to defeat bird-protection laws. Importers and manufacturers of "fancy feathers" worried enough about their image that they proposed forming an umbrella organization to defend themselves against the "high-handed" tactics of the Audubon campaign. The National Millinery Association asserted that it represented an industry that displayed nothing less than "good-will." Signaling businesses' modern rhetorical defense against those who would protect nature, trade spokesmen argued that "unwarranted legislation" would hurt the multi-million-dollar millinery industry and consequently the economy. Hardworking people, they maintained, compelling the public to weigh the plight of humans against that of birds, would be forced out on the streets.[24]

The strategy worked. Dutcher was never able to capitalize financially on the Bradley murder. Donations to help continue the warden program simply failed to materialize. It was a huge disappointment. Wanting to avoid more bloodshed, Audubon officials all but surrendered the Florida battlegrounds to poachers. Cuthbert "will have to go," conceded Chapman, "no law or man to protect it." The legal system left the security of the remaining wardens in jeopardy as well. Marrs observed that "if the laws of the state of Florida cannot be enforced and criminals brought to justice, no man has a guarantee of his safety." Dutcher hesitated to place another warden in harm's way until the state established a game commission to enforce the laws. The Florida legislature authorized a commission in 1913, but it was abolished a mere two years later.[25]

Tragedy returned to the warden community long before that date, again striking the Bradley family. Guy's sister, Maggie Burton, and her husband, William, who had been Bradley's chief assistant, lost their son in an accident at the Dry Tortugas while William was trying to prevent tern eggs from being sold to markets in Key West and Havana. Then, in South Carolina, an Audubon warden was ambushed and killed by poachers, who were never arrested. In Port Charlotte, Florida, the patrol boat belonging to a missing warden, Columbus McLeod, was discovered submerged with sandbags. His shredded hat was still inside, with bits of hair, skull, and brain matter clinging to it. McLeod's body was never recovered.[26]

The plume hunters' trade at best slowly abated, as Douglas suggested by setting "Plumes" in 1930. Wading birds continued to face complete obliteration until women of the evening adopted plume-adorned hats as part of their professional accouterments. Feathers that once symbolized social status quickly fell out of favor with "respectable" women, who worried about mistaken identities. The introduction of enclosed automobile designs in the 1920s undoubtedly also contributed to the passing of bulky headgear. Another factor may have been World War I: the demands of supporting an army almost invariably lead to economized fashion designs. Finally, the economic crisis of the 1930s made expensive hats of any sort an anomaly. Dutcher's successor at Audubon, T. Gilbert Pearson, remained convinced that protective legislation, for which his organization and AOU were mostly responsible, had brought the plume war to a close. "American women quit buying feathers when they found they could not get them past our customs officials," he told Congress in 1931. "That almost entirely destroyed the egret plume trade." *Almost* is the key word here. A year earlier, Pearson was on the Everglades tour with Douglas when the delegation was warned about pluming activity in the area.[27]

More certainly, the protracted plume trade and the emergence shortly thereafter of the modern movement to save the Everglades kept alive the memory of Guy Bradley. His story was told briefly in two books published in the late 1940s, including Douglas's *River of Grass*, but plume hunting had all but stopped by that time and Bradley was fading from public memory. In early September 1960, however, Hurricane Donna crept up from the southeast and smashed into Cape Sable with 111-mile-per-hour winds, washing away part of the sun-baked shell ridge where Bradley's body lay in rest. A bronze plaque mounted on a block of poked limestone rock and placed by the Audubon Society disappeared, too. It was eventually recovered (though Bradley's remains were not), as if the memory of the warden who "gave his life for the cause," as the plaque reads, should not be lost. That memory was too important to the mar-shaling forces of the new movement.

In the decade that followed, the vitality of the Everglades ecosystem neared a point of collapse, as the once-great wetland reached its nadir. Drought was the only natural disturbance at the time, but humans had repeatedly drained, filled, dredged, diked, ditched, dammed, cultivated, subdivided, flooded, and polluted; they had introduced metastasiz-ing alien plants and hunted for marketable species. Custodians of Ever-glades protection needed a cultural hero around whom to rally, a sympa-thetic figure to whom they could attach positive myths. They found one in Bradley. Newspapers and magazines, museum exhibits, and park bro-chures reaffirmed his martyrdom; college students wrote research papers about his bravery. In 1988, the National Fish and Wildlife Foundation es-tablished the Guy M. Bradley Award, with a one-thousand-dollar prize going to an individual recognized for "achievements in wildlife enforce-ment." The Collier County Audubon Society presented a similar award to an outstanding local environmentalist, and National Audubon followed suit in 1997 with the Guy Bradley Lifetime Conservation Award. In 2004, a popular South Florida writer published a book about Bradley, calling him "America's first martyr to environmentalism."[28]

At the same time, despite Bradley's resurrection, an admiring public began holding up Douglas as Florida's original conservation activist and nature writer. No evidence existed to support the activist claim, but *River of Grass* proved that she was indeed a pioneering writer and by impli-cation supported the former contention. Added support came when a literary scholar rediscovered and reprinted "Plumes" during the 1980s.

Meanwhile, Florida's true original conservation activists, including Laura Marrs and Katherine Tippetts, tumbled into historical oblivion. Marjory Stoneman Douglas knew as well as anyone that these women and others deserved this designation, for soon after leaving Kenneth Douglas and moving to Miami in 1915, she watched from the sidelines as they took the activist playing field.

PART TWO

CHAPTER FIFTEEN

A New Life

In Jacksonville, Douglas changed trains from the New York and Florida Special and climbed aboard a sleeping car of the Florida East Coast Railway, owned by Henry Flagler. The lanky old man had died two years earlier, in 1913, at eighty-three, immortalized and tethered to history. He left a fortune to his forty-six-year-old third wife and a legacy of development and commerce to a state that embraced him as its baron of business enterprise. Riding on his train, Douglas would have been aware of Flagler's influence. The train stopped wherever he had built one of his elegant resort hotels, where wealthy Americans and Europeans cavorted: the Alcazar Hotel and the Ponce de Leon in St. Augustine, the Hotel Ormond near Daytona, the Breakers in West Palm Beach, the Royal Poinciana on Lake Worth, and the Royal Palm in Miami.[1]

By the time of Douglas's journey, Flagler's rail line reached all the way to Key West. The railroad was busiest during the winter, when tourists came south and Florida's winter vegetables and fruits went north. The tourist season had not yet begun and the crops had not yet been harvested when the train pulled out of Jacksonville. It was September and few passengers were aboard, which suited her. She had been traveling for days and was depleted, falling into nothing better than an unsatisfy-ing slumber. Wearing a blue worsted wool dress bought in New York, she opened the window after the train entered the South and, with her face turned mutely toward the fresh warm air, took in new scents and scenery.[2]

The North Florida landscape was obediently flat and lush, sometimes junglelike, although not tropical in an isothermal sense. Douglas had seen sabal palms (destined to become the state tree) since South Carolina, but in Florida, they, along with the low-lying saw palmettos waving skyward, seemed to stretch on forever. When John Muir traveled through the area in 1867, he called Florida's vast ranges of palms "dazzling sun-children." She saw, too, the heavy gray drapery of Spanish moss falling from live oaks. The trees' limbs were massive, reaching with capricious twists more outward than upward to form low umbrella-like canopies. They gave the South its best natural shade—and one of its preferred platforms for vigi-lante hangings. Most striking to her were the "matted walls of strange pine trees"—longleaf and loblolly—which for miles at a time blurred past her window like "marching armies . . . in retreat." Out of Jacksonville, the train crossed the famous St. Johns River, famous because Harriet Beecher Stowe had lived beside it and because it had made Henry James "Byroni-cally foolish." En route to St. Augustine, the track crossed over creeks and rivers and beside reedy coastal marshes and then turned slightly west-ward toward the St. Johns River again, through nameless, no-stop towns and beside dirt roads with mule-drawn wagons tottering past framed shacks. The next stop was Palatka, built on the site of a pre-Columbian Indian town and serving more recently as a port for "jungle cruises" on stern-mounted paddle wheelers that steamed down the Ocklawaha River to wondrous Silver Springs. Before the railroad, Palatka had dinned with river commerce, and the people who had controlled that commerce had built fine, colorful Victorian houses watching over the boats and barges slipping by.[3]

Douglas fell asleep before the train pulled into Titusville but then awakened briefly. Although less than 150 miles separated her from Jack-sonville, six hours had elapsed. Another six hours lay ahead before she would reach Miami. She read the sign identifying the station, but it meant nothing to her. Everything—her future and her sense of place in life—was hazy. The same railroad had taken her father and his first printing press to South Florida twelve years earlier, when Miami was the line's southern terminus. She was nervous about seeing him again and about meeting Frank Stoneman's new wife, whose name, Lillias, sounded eerily like the name of Marjory's mother, Lillian. She knew not what to expect of her father. Perhaps she would not like him, or he her. He had been an abstract familial component for eighteen years, nothing more than an image formed from a young child's memory and from family stories, good and bad. She hoped he would be kind and wise and understanding. As much as anything, she wanted to work on his newspaper. When she married Kenneth Douglas, she described herself in their wedding announcement as a writer, although she had not published anything since college or earned any money from her writing. She was now anticipating an opportunity to make good on her claim.[4]

At the very least, she would spend the two years in Florida that the state required for residency and a divorce, her only definite plan for the future. Her first major decision as an adult, marrying Kenneth, had resulted in a bout with lies, deception, and destitution. Although Kenneth left her emotionally spent, she never considered the heedlessness of her decision to marry him and never looked back on the experience with regret. It was "one of the best things that happened to me so long as I didn't stay married," she later said with a guarded chuckle. The experience had made her a bit wiser about herself. Marriage brought firsthand insight into male-female relationships, into the socially accepted dynamic of subjugation and submission. The marriage, or its failure, demonstrated the elusiveness and precariousness of a woman's aspirations, how they could so easily slip away even when circumstances seemed normal. Here was a real-life lesson for what Fanny and Florence had tried to teach Marjory in their indelicate ways; here was the living antithesis to "symmetrical womanhood." Florida perhaps would give her an opportunity to change all this.[5]

Sometime early in the morning, the train lumbered closer to her new life, passing through the recently formed Broward County, named in honor of the late governor, who had launched his Everglades drainage plan there on the New River. Growing up in Massachusetts, where American history had been "so full of Paul Revere," she realized, had deprived her of knowing anything about this new place with such a long and apparently interesting past. By the time the train finally eased into Miami at seven in the morning, she had fallen asleep again. The heat had broken during the night, and the air coming through the windows had been somnifacient. She awoke and looked out to see a small wood-frame depot painted a cheerful yellow and white. She was not expecting her father to arrive for another two hours, but she was too impatient to wait before surveying the place where he had found contentment.[6]

From the station, she walked east toward the uplifted sun, in the direction of the water, taking everything in. So much was different from the cities of the North. The streets were quiet. In the absence of the tourists, most of the local people were still asleep or were just beginning to rouse behind drawn window shades. The city looked a little bedraggled, bare and open to a soft blue sky, where solitary gulls and pelicans floated. The ground was thinly clad with grass, clumps of yellow-green and dusty from the sandy earth, and the stark-white streets were made of crushed shell and limestone marl. Most of the buildings were one or two stories, although a few had three or more, and were generally of wood construction. Although towering buildings of steel and concrete would soon rise as part of the imminent boom, they did not yet disrupt the low-slung skyline. A few royal palm trees reached as high as some of the architecture; their sleek, gray trunks and careful placement fooled her into thinking they were street-side cement columns. Later, after living in South Florida for decades, she came to mock visitors from the North who "don't know a tree from a lamp post."[7]

Walking on, she encountered the town's charm. She came upon an oak-shaded neighborhood of handsome houses and cottages with front porches and side porches, some screened, some open. The trees were old and heavy boughed and, she thought, looked like a forest someone had forgotten to cut. Then she saw Biscayne Bay, a "dazzling" blue-green and "diamond-edged," thirty miles long down to the upper keys and much more impressive than anything else around. Its magnificence awed her;

it made Miami truly beautiful. She did not know that motor sports pioneer Carl Fisher had already begun with skillful industriousness to dredge parts of the shallow bay and to uproot primitive mangroves to build Miami Beach or that Henry Flagler had done much the same less than two decades earlier at the mouth of the picturesque Miami River. There was little sense of other alterations that had preceded her—wildlife destruction and drainage and reclamation—and some time would pass before she paid attention to these things.[8]

Yet she was aware of the sun slanting down on the water. It cast the white light she had seen as a little girl on the family trip to Tampa and Havana, and it carried her back to twenty years earlier, when the family had seemed happy together. The sun still had the same transformative effect on her that she had experienced all those years earlier. It made her feel connected, emotionally and historically, to a strange place. It appealed to who she was ancestrally, a descendant of people who generation after generation tested new horizons. South Florida would be hers. The town struck her as "inadequate," for the moment at least, but living there indefinitely looked like a possibility.[9]

After reaching that conclusion, she felt better prepared to meet her father as she returned to the near-deserted train station. Back in the Pullman, she waited. She had become uncomfortable and hot in her wool dress, but she liked the heat. Before long, two men in the next car exchanged good mornings, one referring to the other as "Judge." A figure then appeared, tall and straight, in a gray suit, hat in hand, and moved down the aisle past the rows of seats. A lock of hair fell onto his forehead, and he brushed it back with two fingers. It was her father. She stood up to greet him. She later remembered a grave, hesitant look coming over his face.[10]

For the rest of her life, she believed he was taken aback because he was expecting to find in his daughter the beauty of her mother. Although Marjory thereafter claimed repeatedly not to be surprised by her father's manifest reaction, she seems to have been affected by it. "The Story of a Homely Woman," published in the *Saturday Evening Post* sixteen years later, evokes Douglas's abiding disappointment at not being the resplendent specimen she wanted to be for herself and her father. "It wasn't just that she had a huge, thin, twisted mouth, or that her eyes were dull pale, or that her nose was crooked, or that her features were put together wrong under her muddy skin," comments the story's narrator; "it was something in her, shut up and lost and twisted." The homely woman then confesses, "When he saw what I looked like, my father never spoke to me again."[11]

But Douglas was not shut up and twisted; she was entering an emotional revival by the time her father greeted her. Stoneman responded not with disdainful silence but with a "Hello, Sweetheart" and a reassuring smile and kiss. Perhaps he saw not homeliness but himself in his daughter. They had the same Roman nose and round hazel-brown eyes and the same elongated face. Whatever his thoughts, she quickly came to be at ease in his presence—and in Miami.[12]

In 1967, Douglas wrote an article for the *Miami Herald*, "When You and I Were Young, Miami." She was twenty-five when she moved to Florida; Miami was nineteen. In 1922, she wrote in her father's newspaper, "We are a frontier city, and we are the last frontier city. This is the heart of the last wilderness, the place to which the last Indians were driven, who fought for their liberty, the place last to be developed in the United States. When the lavish riches of our wilderness have been conquered there will never be any more frontier in the United States." She could make that statement because the Everglades, which the state was still trying to drain, loomed larger as the city spread westward and they remained unconquered.[13]

Douglas long perpetuated the idea that Miami had greeted her as a frontier town with only 5,000 people. Trusting her friend's observation, Helen Muir, attending a 1993 meeting of the Florida Federation of Garden Clubs, recited a seventy-year-old Douglas poem about Miami with a Willa Catherish title, "Pioneers, O, Pioneers!" One stanza reads, "New earth, new earth, beneath our feet / unmarked of ancient line." Miami may have been austere, notwithstanding its palatial resorts, when Douglas first saw it, but new earth it was not exactly. It was already dilating into a metropolis. Douglas's population figure of 5,000 was the approximate number from the 1910 U.S. Census, but the *Herald* had disputed the count, maintaining that it "was taken during the time of year when many Miamians were in various parts of the country spending the summer." More likely, the city had between 9,000 and 10,000 residents, the newspaper calculated. The Florida Census put the city's 1915 population at 15,437. Douglas was soon followed by thousands of other newcomers, who sustained the rapid pace of Miami's first growth spurt. In 1920, according to government head counters, 29,571 people lived in Miami.[14]

Douglas also discovered a city that, again according to the *Herald*'s estimate, was more than 50 percent black. Many in the nonwhite population were seasonal workers who came down from North Florida and other southern states and over from the Bahamas for jobs on farms and in resort hotels; the Census often overlooked such people. With Yankee transplants controlling the local government and economy, Miami was proof that a city did not have to be culturally southern to be segregated. Residential patterns were more rigidly defined in Miami than in many other southern cities, where whites were accustomed to having their help live close by—on the next block or even next door.[15] Miami blacks lived in the proverbial colored town across the railroad tracks from the white population, and to keep them there officials employed nationally common restrictive covenants. Following the 1915 release of D. W. Griffith's electrifying epic, *The Birth of a Nation,* and the sequential reincarnation of the Ku Klux Klan, hooded vigilantes on occasion marched into the streets to remind blacks and Jews of their proper and expected place. Douglas never liked this unchaste side of Miami.[16]

She did like its lack of an apparent industrial infrastructure. Miami may have had a sizable Yankee population, but it was no Chicago or even Taunton. Miami had a few cigar manufacturers (though not in numbers comparable with Tampa and Key West), artificial-stone manufacturing plants, and little else. To generate prosperity, Miamians of the 1910s were banking on agriculture and tourism—that is, climate. Miami had been born from climate, and nothing continued to advantage the city more. More than 125,000 tourists arrived in the Magic City each warm winter season, coming by train, steamship, and, with the completion of Dixie

Highway to Miami in 1915, increasingly by automobile. South Florida was prepared for them. Dade County, the youngest county in the state, had more miles of hard-surface roads than any other county. By the end of the 1920s, 20,000 rooms in 140 hotels made Miami fourth among American cities in hotel accommodations, and 1,606 apartment buildings averaging 10 units each made space available for multitudes more. From their wallets and pocketbooks, visitors dropped one hundred million dollars per year into the local economy.[17]

It was they who made construction another bankable industry. The thousands who joined Douglas in relocating to Miami had generally first visited the city as tourists. One was Carl Fisher, the man who turned speed into profit when he built the Indianapolis Motor Speedway. He arrived in the city two years before Douglas and soon thereafter embarked on what her father called a "great and noble improvement." He completed the construction of a bridge arcing across Biscayne Bay to the headland fronting the ocean. By deploying a steely entrepreneurial vision and sensational promotion schemes and by spending millions to cut miles of mangroves down to their stumps and then pumping bay bottom over them, he created Miami Beach. He planted palm trees, Australian pines, and oleanders between the streets that lay across the landscape like a fishing net. South Florida's most dynamic developer since Flagler, Fisher was more colorful and equal in his capacity to alter nature. Scores of other developers also plied their trade, though none like Fisher, and at every turn Douglas could spot new homes rising from clearings.[18]

Her father lived in one of the many new developments. After meeting her at the depot, he took her to his house in the Riverside Heights subdivision, the first west of the Miami River, where one could buy a six-room bungalow for fifty-five hundred dollars. Stoneman's house was an unpretentious two-story in the rectilinear style, which contrasted minimalist form with the florid designs of its Victorian predecessors. Its grandest feature was the wide front porch, and it resembled many of Miami's houses, more of them new than old. Inside, it was open and airy, and Douglas came to understand the reason for the simplicity. People spent much of their time on their porches; when inside, with the windows open, they lived with the outdoors. It was not to be wasted.

But outside the windows of the Stoneman house, the new Riverside Heights subdivision was barren except for the houses, which seemed to have been dropped from the sky on pillar foundations. The streets were unpaved, and empty lots were cleared, revealing only the charred remnants of the hardy wood of Caribbean pine trees that had been wasted in a refuse fire. After Douglas got to know Miami, she learned that most subdivisions had been developed with no effort to preserve the indigenous vegetation. A few hammocks south of town toward Coconut Grove, such as the "great dark jungle called 'the Miami hammock,'" had escaped bulldozers, though poachers had raided these oases for their orchids, bromeliads, ferns, royal palms, and tree snails. Live oaks and scruffy Caribbean pines with their unkempt understories were invariably quick to go, while developers typically planted palms and invasive Australian pines and created a monoculture landscape. "Look out your window," Douglas wrote for the *Herald* after becoming fully immersed in the way of things in Miami. "Can you see a pine tree? If you can, you're lucky. They are going fast. And everyday somebody cuts down a few more to make a new subdivision that, without them, will be as raw and ugly as plain dirt without trees can be." As young Miami grew older, Douglas developed a consciousness about the form of its growth. In "Pioneers, O, Pioneers!" she wrote,

We are the first to try the land
Coral, and marl and loam
To challenge with a careless hand
Acres that will be home.[19]

Douglas needed to get to know her father and his wife, who had married only the previous April. When Stoneman's rented car, with father and long-lost daughter, pulled up to the curb outside the Riverside house, Lillias came out and bounded down the steps to welcome Marjory with a smile and embrace. The affection deeply moved Marjory. Lillias was unpretentious and genuine while displaying the grace and warmth of a southern woman. Though she was devoutly religious, she was neither doctrinaire nor intolerant of the beliefs of others. She and Frank were members of the Trinity Episcopal Church and frequently entertained clergymen for breakfast. Lillias was a fine cook and always the proper hostess. "We didn't bother about being stepmothers or stepdaughters," Douglas recalled. "I was too old for that." They became fast friends and remained so until Lillias's death. If not for her insistence, Frank might not have intervened in his daughter's disastrous marriage and brought her to Miami.[20]

Frank was a kind man but stingy in expressing his affection. His Quaker upbringing and the contemporary culture of manhood equated silence with strength. As he explained to Marjory, he always believed that Lillian had abandoned him when she left with Marjory to live in Taunton, and he dealt with this perception by maintaining his distance. He resented the Trefethen family's role in the separation and seeming plot against him and therefore never sent money for Marjory's support. Money was always tight anyway. To support himself alone, he had to borrow, and he assumed that the Trefethens could adequately care for their granddaughter. By the time her troubles with Kenneth started, Frank had long been in the habit of removing himself from his first try at family life. Lillias forced a break in that habit.[21]

Marjory was a physical reminder of an unfortunate time, but Frank quickly learned to share life with his daughter. With her sense of humor and cheerful constitution, she added to Lillias's sunny energy. The three enjoyed attending concerts and plays, going to the movies—beneath a canvas top in the open air—and playing the only card game that Marjory knew, "I Doubt It." Lillias taught Marjory about old Florida, the families and proud southern heritage in the northern parts of the state; Frank taught her about local politics and the regional division in state politics. There was a disconnect in religious beliefs between devout father and the increasingly agnostic daughter and a palpable uneasiness between an envious parent who had failed to complete college and the offspring who possessed a diploma. But Frank and Marjory nevertheless discovered a great intellectual companionship. Everywhere she looked in the house, she saw long, full shelves of Frank's books. While so many of his race and class were investing in Miami's booming real-estate market, Frank gave his spare time to community service, working with civic organizations and the police court, and to reading. He preferred history and philosophy to her fiction, but they enjoyed deep discussions about politics, world events, great decision makers in human affairs, and Frank's experiences as a magistrate. She especially appreciated what she regarded as his Quaker sense of women as the intellectual equals of men.[22]

Frank also believed that a single woman such as his daughter should support herself. One day, he called home from the office to ask her to step in as a temporary replacement for the editor of the society page, Agnes Hallowes Floyd, who was taking a leave to care for her ailing mother. For her first piece, published on October 25, 1915, Douglas interviewed the sole woman who traveled the distance with the inaugural Dixie Highway motorcade, from Chicago to Miami in thirteen days. "She made me feel not only the fun and spirit of the adventure and fun that the whole project bubbles over with," Douglas wrote, "but also the deep underlying principle that has made the Dixie Highway not just a roadway but a final welding of the link of understanding and fraternal intercourse between the great north and the great south." Douglas in time gained a greater understanding of that link and of the idea and importance of regional distinctiveness, and she subsequently shared that understanding with *Herald* readers. Initially, she worked from home, using the phone and a typewriter, and sent in daily copy with a delivery boy. Through "sheer nepotism I got a job," she conceded to a young reporter years later. In reality, Frank knew that his daughter had the right qualifications: she was smart, interested in current events, and a skilled writer.[23]

Women had been working on American newspapers since the colonial era, when as journalists and readers they were still an uncommon commodity. In the early nineteenth century, a few more edged their way into the business, often entering through their activity with a social cause, such as abolitionism or temperance. After the Civil War, when improved educational opportunities expanded the population of women readers, when advertisers increasingly targeted female shoppers, and when

suffrage campaigns made women front-page news for the first time, publishers recognized the expediency of opening more positions to women.
In 1910, more than four thousand women were working as newspaper
editors and reporters. The society page for women was a common feature in newspapers across the country, and female editors often used it as
a springboard to more desirable positions or as an organ to promote political issues.[24]

Douglas soon replaced Floyd permanently and got a desk at the office.
The *Herald* was crowded into two stories of an east-side corner of a downtown building located within eyeshot of the wharf. It was a place of walls
painted an institutional green, smudged plate-glass windows, and bare
lightbulbs, of battered typewriters, paper dust, printer's ink, the relentless
clatter of linotypes, and the nocturnal rolling and shuttering of the press
below the wooden second floor of the city room. With only two or three
reporters and a few other employees—including future film star Joseph
Cotten working at the advertising desk—the *Herald* remained a small
local daily. But Douglas remembered her father making the editorial page
"far superior to the range of the paper," always thinking about the diverse
origins of the city's population and looking ahead to its growth.[25]

When Frank and Lillias took a one-month vacation in 1916 to travel
out west, he handed Marjory, less than a year in the trade, the editorial
page to manage in his absence. He apparently had more confidence in her
journalistic skills than she did. Some of the staff believed that she was too
green and ill informed about current events, and she hardly disagreed: "It
was if I were emerging from a comfortable fog to a world of events I could
only half understand, a war in Europe, trouble on the Mexican border,
trouble on the high seas and a state of which I was still ignorant." She had
an entire page to fill. When letters to the editor ran short, she sometimes
used obvious and humorous aliases and made up her own. Most challenging was writing copy for the section on short lighthearted commentary, and on many late afternoons she faced two empty editorial columns.
Following the sage advice of colleagues, she steered clear of local politics
and focused her commentary on uncontroversial subjects such as cleaning up the train depot and supporting the public library. On days that she

was feeling bold, though, she ventured out into state politics and international affairs. She was all too relieved when her father returned.[26]

The responsibilities of maintaining the society page subsequently seemed less demanding and fairly routine. She called on a few members of local women's clubs, attended their meetings and events, and gathered copy for her page. "There I was," she said years later, "writing about parties, weddings and notable winter visitors to the leading hotel in an insignificant city." On slow days, "when every event on the social calendar seems like Alice's wages, to be jam yesterday and jam tomorrow, but never by the wildest imagination, jam today," she would forgo a "stern adherence to hard facts" and exercise her imagination. On one such occasion, she conjured up a tea dance hosted by "Mrs. J. Augustus Snuphanpuh," with guests that included "Mrs. K. De Yellowplush," who wore a "lavender peau de soie, made quaintly on the lines of the kitchen apron for 1913." "A dainty refreshment course of baked beans and bread pudding was served on the back porch, decorated with brooms and mops, while in the centre of the table was placed a large bouquet of Dutch Cleaner."[27]

Mirth provided an outlet from work that did not always stimulate her. She preferred writing fiction, yet she was happy simply to be writing and making a living at it: "If what I wrote was hardly English Composition, I was entranced by my new life in a strange and new country."[28]

CHAPTER SIXTEEN

Conservationists

Women wearing plume feathers draped about their necks or atop broad, showy hats in Miami at the turn of the twentieth century were wise to avoid an encounter with Mary Barr Munroe. Fellow conservationists called her their "most militant power." To the tedious work of organizing, lobbying, and letter writing, she added tenacious street-level temerity. Out on sun-bright sidewalks, in hotel lobbies, and on church steps, she turned brilliant and intense eyes beneath a fashion-appropriate palmetto hat on unsuspecting women. Her approach was never threatening, and her voice was more didactic than hostile when she lectured women on the grisly origins of their vanity. But beneath a calm exterior lay rage. She was mystified that any literate woman could plead ignorance about the pandemic slaughter that had been going on for decades. She scoffed at the naïveté of those who tried to say that the bird of fashion had long been dead before sacrificing its feathers. Sometimes she got her message across, leaving a few contrite women in tears and winning concessions for more sensitive dress choices.[1]

Even if she did at times seem a bit fanatical, Munroe was no shrill sentimentalist. She and her husband, Kirk, a writer of adventure tales for boys, were able outdoors people of the rod-and-gun type. They moved to Coconut Grove in 1885, when South Florida was still rugged pioneer country where settlers sometimes had to track and kill their food. Yet this was also the time of the nationwide pogrom against avian species of every size, color, and feather, and she believed that no civilized society could live without the animated beauty and song of birds. When a state Audubon organized in 1900, she joined as a charter member and later sat on its executive committee. She authored one of the organization's "most valued leaflets," *Florida Birds Are Worth Their Weight in Gold.* She supported hiring Audubon wildlife wardens, including Guy Bradley, to provide security for the last of the great bird colonies living amid guano-stained mangroves. Around the time of Bradley's murder, she proposed setting aside a wooded tract in the Everglades as a wildlife protectorate. The next year, she started Bird Defenders, a club in which boys learned to esteem feathered friends rather than shoot them and loot their nests for eggs. In 1915, she founded the Coconut Grove Audubon Society, and she sat as its first president.[2] The group quickly earned a reputation as "one of the liveliest Audubon societies in the state." Three years later, she organized its complement, the Miami Audubon Society. The combined resolution of her organizations gave Dade County its first bird sanctuaries.[3]

Her activism was spurred by plain observable facts—the butchery of birds and their disappearance from land and water. Many authors of stories about Marjory Stoneman Douglas believe Florida conservation began sometime around the 1920s with this matriarch of the Everglades. But Munroe's insurgency was in full swing before Douglas arrived in Florida, and conservation in those earlier days was not about saving the Everglades. It was about preserving the living aesthetic, the beauty and distinctiveness birds and plants rendered to South Florida. The local struggle to preserve beauty spawned some of the country's earliest Audubon chapters and rallied support from organizations nationwide. It also aroused latent conservation ambitions in nonconservation groups, mostly women's groups.[4]

This was the era of the women's club movement, which was part of an international trend in the founding of organizations, from brawny labor unions to prim poetry clubs. Again, Munroe had an indisputable claim to events. She started the Dade County Federation of Women's Clubs as an extension of the Florida Federation of Women's Clubs (FFWC), of which she was a longtime member, committee director, and admired colleague. Federation members educated themselves on social and political issues and opened public discussion on those issues. In the kinetic age of progressivism, reform would have been less sweeping if not for the good industry of women who, though politically disfranchised, secured a spot at the center of the civil arena and jostled government and society toward new social and political responsibilities. From its beginning in 1895, for example, the FFWC brought forward an agenda every time the legislature went into session. The group focused on the Bourbonian lawmakers' perpetual back-burner issues, such as land for the Seminole Indians, a compulsory education bill, a bureau of statistics, a state board of charities, a state tuberculosis hospital, a girls' industrial school, road development, and the right of women to serve on school boards.[5]

Crowded club agendas almost always made room for conservation. Women such as Munroe made sure of that. Women's reading clubs commonly took up the issue of city beautification, and women generally organized for improved sanitary conditions and for industrial smoke- and noise-abatement ordinances in increasingly congested cities. The national General Federation of Women's Clubs maintained a conservation committee, and the group's lobbying accomplishments included state and national laws to protect forests, waters, and wildlife. Its first petition to Congress, given urgency by the carnage in Florida, supported a bill to outlaw trade in ornamental bird feathers. The FFWC's list of eighteen "departments" included conservation, bird protection, forestry, and waterways, which, along with others such as public health, civil service reform, and education, reflected women's vision of a better Florida. Some of them played active roles in National Audubon, which had mostly female members. In a rare moment of charitableness, the self-proclaimed sire of Progressive conservation, Gifford Pinchot, observed that "few people realize what women have already done for conservation." He was in part paying homage to his mother, Mary Eno Pinchot, who chaired the conservation committee of the Daughters of American Revolution.[6]

Guy Bradley may have been the nation's first martyr to conservation, but birds had no partisan as untiring as women. The chair of the conservation committee of the General Federation of Women's Clubs was making no casual observation when she said in 1916, "I know of no other state which is doing such good work in conservation along so many lines as the Florida Federation of Women's Clubs." Women, many from the FFWC, outnumbered men by nearly two to one among the founders of Florida Audubon. With a four-to-one female-male ratio, Munroe viewed her Coconut Grove Audubon as "predominantly feminine." The all-female Miami Audubon, her other seedling, joined the FFWC. Conservation and the federation were practically synonymous.[7]

In a 1911 guest commentary for the *Miami Herald,* Munroe wondered, "If suddenly every Woman's Club, and gathering which women, and women alone, conduct, should disband and stop working and talking, what would be the effect?" One answer is that birds would have lost their keenest allies. When Munroe died in 1922, mourners said that birds would struggle without an "especially kind friend." More to the point, women brought fundamental decencies to relationships with nature that were incongruous with Victorian manliness. Without the female protagonists, conservation in Florida would have languished at the level of resource conservation and game protection, so fatuously wedded were men to market values and sporting activities. As it happened, the insouciant plundering of nature agitated women, who founded organizations, lobbied for protective legislation, and left a legacy on which others, including Douglas, could build. Perhaps the most important tangible component of that legacy was Florida's first state park, a magnificent palm-tree colony and bird haven in the Everglades.[8]

Before it was a legacy and park, it had been a self-defined enclave of unaffected beauty in a vast amorphousness. In 1893, Indians told John and Marion Soar about a forest of royal palms and hardwoods sequestered in an isolated corner of wet prairie. Curious naturalists, the brothers asked to be taken there, and in a scene repeated many times in the history of New World exploration, indigenous people led white men to a hidden natural place. Located forty-six miles south of Miami and slightly north of Flamingo, the forest was actually a hammock, the largest of the Everglades' many splendid hammocks, their intense flora rising out of the prairie and sawgrass like tropical islands in the sea. This one had nearly a thousand native royal palms one hundred feet tall and standing like colonnades, with their distinctive glossy green crown shaft beneath a burst of fronds. Frank Chapman later called royal palms "arboreal monuments." The hammock was indeed memorable.[9]

Ten years went by, however, before another white person saw it. The Soars led John Kunkel Small of the New York Botanical Garden and Charles Torrey Simpson, recently retired from the U.S. National Museum, on separate expeditions to the palms. Simpson was awestruck. No "spot on earth" was "as beautiful as Paradise Key," as the hammock came to be named. Word of the sylvan jewel spread through the naturalist community, drawing others to the hammock, and eventually reached Washington, where the idea of turning Paradise Key into a national monument began to circulate before chief forester Gifford Pinchot took it to President Theodore Roosevelt. Observers commonly believed that Paradise Key was part of the property of Flagler's Model Land Company, and James Ingraham, head of the company, thought the monument idea a splendid one. But the plan was abandoned when clear title to the hammock turned out to be an impossibility until the Internal Improvement Fund had settled its legal disputes with the railroads. In the end, the vital section with the royal palms belonged to the state.[10]

The idea of the monument nevertheless continued to churn in Ingraham's mind, and he told the Munroes. Kirk remembered seeing such a place during an exploratory trip around South Florida in 1882. Mary, who chaired the FFWC's forestry department, suggested that the federation might use resources at its disposal to obtain protective status for Paradise Key. That was in 1905, a few months before the shooting of Guy Bradley and at the same moment Governor William Jennings was out west experiencing an epiphany about Florida reclamation. At the next FFWC convention, Munroe joined with Edith Gifford to present a motion to create a federal forest reservation at Paradise Key. Next to orchids, royal palms

were the favorite bounty of plant poachers, and the trees needed protection. The motion was adopted, but no immediate action followed.[11]

The years passed, birds and wardens continued to disappear, and people
began to refer to the proposed park as a bird sanctuary. Indeed, many of
the women, naturalists, and businessmen who were instrumental in the
eventual preservation of Paradise Key held membership in Florida Audubon. Munroe, who had known Bradley since he was a boy, would not let
old business go unfinished. When the federation elected May Mann Jennings its president in November 1914, Munroe reminded her, as she had
all the group's previous presidents, of the approved but latent motion. If
anyone could finally make the park a reality, Munroe believed Jennings
could.[12]

A smallish woman with short, light-brown hair, the forty-two-year-old
Jennings kept a fashionable wardrobe. If her values had been different,
she likely would have been the type of high-society woman who wore
feather hats. But Jennings was raised in rural Hernando County, where
nature's abounding presence gave her an appreciation for wild places and
wild things. During the same formative years, the nuns at St. Augustine's
St. Joseph's Academy, which she attended for seven years, imbued in her a
strong sense of social responsibility. Her father, Austin Mann, the charismatic leader of the state's Populist Party, passed on his gutsy political instincts, and she married William Jennings, whose governorship gave her
an expanded set of door-opening credentials. In public profile and duties, she was the perfect complement to her husband—if not his political
better. Her list of legislative lobbying achievements included twenty-six
items, from a compulsory education law to the establishment of the Florida State Library. Aided by supreme self-confidence, she was a terrific
organizer and leader and a gifted diplomat. The avatar of volunteerism,
she gave time to countless civic and social services and founded and
headed numerous public organizations, winning one service award after
another for her selfless devotion. No one was more involved in women's
political rights. She helped lead the state campaign for a federal suffrage
amendment, cofounded the Florida League of Women Voters, founded
the Jacksonville Democratic Women's Club, and, after the ratification of

the Nineteenth Amendment, managed Miamian Ruth Bryan Owen's successful campaign for Congress. Conservation kept Jennings equally busy.
She served on the executive committee of Florida Audubon, cofounded
the Florida Forestry Association, and oversaw the establishment and
management of Royal Palm Park.[13]

It may seem odd at first blush that the woman who championed Royal
Palm Park was married to the man who dusted off plans to drain the
Everglades. At the time, however, the irony would have been lost on park
proponents. There was little scientific sense of the systemic dynamics of
the Everglades environment—that the vitality of one part of the colossal wetland was connected to another. One proposal, for example, would
have surrounded Paradise Key with either a barbed-wire fence or a rock
wall. Scientific and conservationist minds at the time saw setting aside
one beautiful and tranquil space for birds and trees in exchange for exploiting the natural resources of another as a conceivable win-win proposition. With the establishment of Royal Palm Park, William Jennings,
Napoleon Broward, and all the farmers and land merchants could drain
their Everglades and have them, too. This was conservation—people-
first conservation—sensitive to market demands and anchored in human
definitions and manipulations of nature. Without this dominating spirit,
Pinchot could not get the maximum utility out of his forests, and Broward could reap nothing from the fertility of Everglades muck soil.

Conservation in this guise rested on the oft-stated principle of advancing the greatest economic and social good for the greatest number
of people. This was the big-gun defense the forces of conservation rolled
out against the forces of wasteful exploitation and the opposing forces of
preservation. The latter (nature-first conservation) argued that Pinchot's
approach constituted managing natural resources, not conserving nature.
Real nature was unbounded, and conservation amounted to the bound-
ing of nature according to the demands of civilization. As the sum of
human calculations, conservation was also subject to human miscalculations. The greatest good that conservation actually protected was not the
expansion of individual freedoms but domestic prosperity. Conservation
put government in the business of regulating nature—ensuring its conversion into natural resources—for the benefit of businesses that fueled

the economy that fueled the nation. Pinchot's forests and Broward's Ever-glades opened up spoils mainly to corporations, not to individuals. Lumber companies and industrial farms might have created opportunities for wage labor, but they lessened opportunities for land-based independence. Conservation, in short, was not democratic.[14]

Yet as far as anyone understood, the proposal to protect Paradise Key represented another good public deed by the FFWC. The park's location with regard to the rest of the wetland ecosystem did not seem to matter; nor did the fact that it would total only nineteen hundred acres, a mere postage stamp in the sixty-two-hundred-square-mile wetland, half of which Jennings and Broward had slated for agriculture. Establishing the park at all represented a significant accomplishment for the women, especially since the legislature's interest in a park was at best lackluster.

To prevent this lukewarm interest from devolving into legislative op-position, May Mann Jennings "set a terrific pace" in her campaign for the park. She was encouraged when the federation learned that the grove of royal palms was located on Internal Improvement Fund land rather than Flagler land. The FFWC then abandoned the idea of a federal establish-ment for a state park, allowing Jennings and the other club women to concentrate their efforts on home turf. Jennings first turned to Ingraham with a proposal that the Model Land Company donate a tract of approxi-mately 960 acres adjacent to the state land to be used as an endowment for the operation of the park. Since Flagler's widow, Mary K. Flagler, was a member of both the FFWC and Florida Audubon, the donation was a given. Jennings then arranged a December overnight stay at the home of Governor Park Trammell, where she had the ear of his wife, Beatrice. The next day, Jennings and a local federation member met with fund trustees and secured a provisional approval of the park.

Jennings had never seen Paradise Key, so Mary Munroe organized a trip to the site. Jennings was joined by other first-time visitors, including her husband, her son, and several FFWC officers. The group met up with Munroe in Miami and then embarked on a bone-shattering automobile drive out into the Everglades. Jouncing along, with the drivers keeping a two-fisted grip on flailing steering wheels, they followed the rock-and-sand corridor of the road, still under construction, that would soon run all the way to Flamingo. The fifty-mile trip took hours, but it was worth it. Amid the bromeliads, the featherlike maiden ferns, the aromatic scent of gumbo-limbo trees, and the more familiar royal palms, the group lingered in the future park, talking about where a lodge might be built and where walking trails might be cut. They would develop the park so that visitors would come. One thing was certain: the road out to Paradise Key would need to be a good one.[15]

Savoring her enthusiasm, Jennings returned to civilization and activated the women's network, which consisted of nearly nine thousand FFWC members, many of them related to state officials and skilled in the art of persuasion. The FFWC mobilized a statewide publicity campaign, William Jennings drafted legislation for the fund to cede the hammock to the federation, and in perhaps the most ironic juxtaposition of conservation with exploitation, Kathryn B. Wright, wife of beleaguered engineer James O. Wright, was charged with distributing copies of the bill and other relevant information to legislators. For her part, Jennings mounted an exhausting speaking tour.[16]

Outside the women's club community, she recruited a number of allies. Few were more faithful than a group of noted naturalists that included Charles Simpson, John Gifford, and David Fairchild, all of whom resided in South Florida. Others, such as Frank Chapman and John Kunkel Small, made Florida their home for research. The hirsute scientists (only Small lacked facial hair) were in their best element when descended into the most inaccessible quarters to gather specimens, while often incongruously cloaked in white shirts and ties. Few knew the tangled backcountry better than they, and few appreciated its riotous comeliness more. It was typically beauty, though, not habitat or biology, that came up in proposals to save a place such as Paradise Key, and enhancement of the living aesthetic was the usual prescription for preservation.[17]

Indeed, Gifford thought the Everglades were too wet. It was he "who taught" Douglas and her circle of nature-loving friends "the word 'ecology.'" What exactly Gifford taught is unknown, and whatever his understanding of the science, he used it to alter the landscape. The year after his wife, Edith, first proposed a Paradise Key reservation, he imported

Australian melaleuca trees to use as natural transpiration pumps (insatiable water drinkers) to reclaim land. The Everglades Land Sales Company published his book, *The Everglades and Other Essays Relating to Southern Florida,* which he dedicated to the "Memory of Napoleon Bonaparte Broward, 'Father of the Everglades Drainage Project.'" The cover showed a canal shooting out to the horizon, ferrying a fleet of pleasure craft and lined by picturesque coconut palms and South Seas plantation houses. It was an Everglades pastoral.[18]

Small maintained no connection to land merchants, and his ideas seem benign in comparison, though they too involved altering the landscape. Attached to the idea that nature needed to "be assisted," he recommended that the FFWC's "first concern" "should be to replace the forest" in the park "wherever man and nature have lately destroyed it." To that end, Jennings planned, with the assistance of the plant genius David Fairchild, to relocate flora from other hammocks, with the hope that the park would one day "equal the wonderful gardens of Java." Fairchild headed the U.S. Department of Agriculture's local Office of Foreign Seed and Plant Introduction, which over the years had turned into a gateway for exotic tropical specimens. His work conveyed the message that Florida should be tropical. And so too should the park.[19]

Simpson was to some account the sapient heretic among his naturalist brethren. In 1923, Douglas referred to him as a "second John Muir." It was a fair assessment. Simpson equated "improvement" with "mutilation." The "proper thing to do" with the park, he insisted, was to "LET IT ALONE." While the FFWC was wistfully pleased over a newly improved road leading out to the hammock, Simpson called it a "hideous eyesore." For one, the road builders had blazed through the center of the hammock, indiscriminately clearing away specimens of allure, and had blasted up limestone rock to be used as the roadbed to Flamingo. For another, the road opened a formerly secluded paradise to plant poaching. Simpson was nevertheless a cooperative collaborator in the campaign to create the park. He agreed to provide interpretive information to label the trees and rare plants along a planned nature path, and he compiled a list of fifty tree species in the hammock that was submitted with the park bill.[20]

Although the naturalists sometimes disagreed about what was best for nature, they equally lamented that drainage, development, and hunting were destroying those natural things that made Florida special. All of them published books or articles to raise consciousness and in some cases took direct action to end the violence against nature. Although Gifford reported enthusiastically that the Everglades could be drained for one dollar an acre, he simultaneously if counterintuitively advocated that the "whole of South Florida should be one big bird sanctuary." Too many men, especially white men, he wrote, "easily revert to a very primitive state" when they "'tote' guns" into the wilderness; they become "naturally vindictive toward anything that stands in their way." He feared that Florida's "majestic" trees were "destined like the flamingo, the parakeet and ibis and many other choice products of nature to pass on." Small worried, too, that the abortive security of Florida's birds would also befall its vegetation, summing up his sentiments in the title of his 1929 book, *From Eden to Sahara.*[21]

With the endorsements of naturalists and the promise of the Flagler tract secured, the FFWC's bill went before the legislature in June 1915. Jennings wrapped up her speaking tour and then made a final rush through Tallahassee to put last-minute touches on various pieces of legislation sponsored by the federation. She then boarded a train for the three-hour trip back home.

When the train rolled into the Jacksonville depot, hissing a final expulsion of steam from its wheel cylinders, Jennings was tired and worn. She disembarked, tipped the porter who retrieved her luggage, and looked forward to a healthful rest after her whirlwind first six months as federation president. It was wishful thinking. She had hardly settled at home when word came that she was needed back in Tallahassee. Some of the FFWC legislation, including the park bill, was in trouble. Overcome with fatigue, she dispatched her husband, William, and son, Bryan, to put out the fires and waited hopefully in Jacksonville.[22]

May Mann Jennings was up against not only an indifferent legislature but a fundamental difference between men and women. The sexes typically negotiated relationships with nature that were extensions of their respective roles in larger society. As mostly willing conservators of a salubrious home and righteous culture, women were expected to be moral guardians of the environment that uniformly sustained the physical, mental, and spiritual health of their families. Bird activists sometimes tried to appeal to a Victorian sense of womanhood and motherhood among those who wore the "white badge of cruelty." "No woman heart can stand up against such cruelty," said Mary Munroe of her street encounters with women. "I have many times been disliked for my trouble, and just as many times I have been thanked."[23]

On the flip side of the sex coin, men generally positioned themselves with Scripture and capitalist inclinations that constructed a society that placed humans over nature. Ecofeminists argue that a gendered consistency existed between the male's human/nature hierarchy and his man/woman hierarchy, maintaining that in behavior, attitude, and language, male domination of women was a virtual facsimile of male domination of nature. The latter was the substance of American civilization, carved as it was out of the "virgin" landscape. The North American environment engendered American individualism, a defining trait of American manhood, as men wrested from the rugged continental landscape opportunities for landownership and an independent means of support. Nature's wealth in resources contributed to the rise of a new entrepreneurial spirit and the infectious power of the capitalist economy—men's world.[24]

Douglas was keen to the different social sensibilities of the sexes. In 1923, she wrote, "Men are chiefly interested in the material improvement of their parts of the state . . . all related in some way to their earning capacities. Now the women voters are interested in these things also, but when they sponsor a bill in legislature . . . the thing that interests them is the welfare and advancement of people." Douglas might have invoked a real-life example in Mary Munroe, who sought to affirm the Everglades' native species and proclamations of beauty, and Thomas Will, who relished Everglades development, though he called himself a conservationist. Generations later, a growing number of women were on the same page as the young Douglas, arguing that women, acting as a community rather than as individual protagonists, democratized humans and nature and followed societal values that encouraged women to treat nature with the same nurturing that defined their domestic responsibilities. One can add that while nature exploitation empowered the individualistic male, nature protection empowered organized women. It makes sense that the histories of the Progressive conservation movement and the woman suffrage movement intersected and that women who wanted to vote also often wanted to protect the environment. Even before suffrage opened up new spaces in the public realm, a province of male mastery, conservation allowed women to shape the meaning of civilization and challenge the landscape, literally and figuratively, of male mastery.[25]

None of this is to suggest that female conservationists opposed men's entrepreneurial endeavors. May Jennings believed in what her husband proposed to do with Everglades drainage as much as she believed in the gestation of Royal Palm State Park. Yet with parks, wildlife sanctuaries, scenic drives, and public gardens, women sought to remove civilization's hard male edge. And since beauty and tranquillity of place superseded biology and ecology in conservation's purpose, women could in good conscience support the expansion of development projects. In her role as nature's steward, Munroe conceded that she could identify no "ecological" benefit in the big wading birds since they consumed no agricultural pests; nevertheless, these birds were worth saving as a consequence of the elegance they added to natural scenery. Munroe and the members of the Coconut Grove Audubon Society once drifted into a dilemma over the loggerhead shrike, which brought beauty and economic benefits into contention. In September 1916, she convened the Coconut Grove members, as one might convene a grand jury, to deliberate the crimes of the "butcher bird," as the shrike was unfortunately called. The question before them was whether to condemn the bird or let it live in peace. On the one hand, it was a "dangerous element," the conservationists said, because it preyed on young mockingbirds, a virtuoso among songbirds (and destined to become Florida's official state bird). On the other hand, the shrike had its "good qualities": its diet included insects and mice that damaged farm crops. In the end, the dilemma remained unresolved, suggesting the incompatibility of beauty and resource development as perpetual goals in Progressive conservation.[26]

There was nothing black-and-white about conservation any more than there was about the dialectic between women and nature. In other words, what impelled women to be advocates of bird life, wilderness preservation, and park development cannot be explained by catchall scholarly interpretations. Douglas further complicates the paradigm. She was a feminist, quite unlike most club women; she was single, disinclined to have a family, and no matron of domesticity; she never considered herself a nature writer even as nature remained a subject of her most important work; she looked back to her Quaker roots in search of model social and humanitarian values, which only sometimes illuminated connections to nature; and she was a lifelong learner, reading and studying social and biological sciences that equipped her with new ways to comprehend the ecological consequences of human behavior and values. To make her relationship with nature fit into the mold of that of either Jennings or Munroe, for example, would be to simplify the lives, values, and visions of all involved. Nor should their impact on Douglas's environmentalism be overstated, despite women's incredible skills at organizing for a cause and maneuvering through the land mines of a male-dominated world to advocate it. Save for Douglas reading bird poetry at a Coconut Grove Audubon Society meeting—as a member of the Booklovers rather than of Audubon—no evidence indicates that she participated actively in organized bird protection. Although she lent space on her society page to the avian cause, she never immortalized the work of club women in her fiction as she did a slain wildlife warden. Douglas's nonfiction mentions Mary Munroe only as the "dynamic, blue-eyed wife" of Kirk Munroe who got the *a* dropped from *Cocoanut Grove*. "Mrs. William S. Jennings . . . handsome and able," appeared in only one Douglas book, depicted as a stalwart suffragist.[27]

But Jennings appeared many times on the society page, which Douglas used to keep readers abreast of the uncertain progress of the FFWC's campaign to create the state park. Indeed, progress was hard to measure when Jennings, resting uneasily at home, received a telegram from Bryan on June 2, 1915, with the news that the park bill had passed the House, although it had halved the proposed one-thousand-dollar appropriation. The Senate had not yet acted on the measure. Then a few minutes after midnight on June 3, William wired that in the last hour before adjourning for a two-year recess, the Senate had approved the House bill, although it had removed the appropriation altogether. The bill ultimately gave the FFWC full responsibility for the park. The club women would have to develop and operate it without the benefit of state support, financial or moral. May Jennings nonetheless rejoiced.[28]

She gave little time to rest before implementing her ideas for the FFWC's latest acquisition. Much like the naturalists who were bound to more than the aesthetic of science, she believed that parks should be created not for "protective purposes" alone but "because of some choice natural beauty" and for "public recreation." As if there could never be too much beauty, she planned to have royal palms moved and replanted beside the two miles of roadway wending through the park, and she hoped one day to have royal palms standing all the way along the highway to Miami. Jennings's vision also required funds for the construction of a lodge, the most expensive item on the FFWC's wish list, to accommodate tourists and a visiting naturalist in residence. Other plantings should be undertaken, too, trails cut, and a bird sanctuary and game preserve established. Hiring a caretaker to keep out poachers and to oversee other tasks and daily operations was a first priority. To cover that person's proposed annual salary of twelve hundred dollars, the FFWC conceived a "mile-of-dimes" campaign, enlisting affiliate clubs to hold bake sales, bazaars, and other fund-raisers. Federation women sought donations from Audubon Societies to which they belonged. The Flagler tract, rented out to be farmed, was expected to generate some money, too. The effort received a windfall in the form of a onetime twelve-hundred-dollar appropriation by the Dade County commissioners.[29]

All was moving along nicely when the federation held its annual convention a week before Thanksgiving in Miami. The main event was the formal dedication of the park, which included a spectacle not seen since the Dixie Highway motorcade had raced into town. Early one lustrous morning, 168 automobiles rendezvoused at the Halcyon Hotel, a magnificent limestone structure with turrets at every corner. Shined up to show off, fine-looking touring cars, town cars, runabouts, open models, coupes—Model Ts, Cadillacs, Overlands, and Maxwells—lurched into gear to fall in line one behind the other, forming a mile-long caravan on the drive out to the park, more than eight score low-compression internal-combustion engines chortling in unison. The procession lasted hours, even though the road was now graded, oiled, and easy going. When the ceremony began at the park at nine o'clock, cars were still converging on the once-hermetic hammock. Appropriate to the motorcade if not the park, and in an era when easy transportation was being equated with personal freedom and the automobile was being hailed as a wholesome conduit between civilization and nature, the chair of the Dade County Commission, S. A. Belcher, extolled South Florida's road-building progress. No other state had constructed as many miles of the Dixie Highway, destined to become the principal artery connecting the Midwest to the South. Terminating in Dade County, where the road to the park began, now called Ingraham Highway at the suggestion of an appreciative federation, Dixie Highway "had paved the way for the . . . opening up and developing of all Florida."[30]

When the speeches finished, and after Jennings formally dedicated the park and the requisite clergyman gave the requisite closing prayer before bowed heads, several hundred visitors filtered down the nature trail the new superintendent had recently hacked through the hammock, feeling "fully the beauties of the tropical vegetation." It was a wonderful end to a glorious day for the federation, a crowning moment in its history and in the public careers of Jennings and Munroe. As the conservation chair from the General Federation of Women's Clubs noted, the FFWC had earned the distinction of being the only group of club women in the country to have secured and operated a state park. More remarkably, though unfathomed at the time, this park would later give birth to a rarified national park; it, in turn, would give birth to difficult ecological and moral questions about conservation and human miscalculations in controlling nature.[31]

CHAPTER SEVENTEEN

Rights

Although her *Miami Herald* predecessor limited the society page to unoffending prosaic items of the commons, Douglas quickly proved more adventurous. When she began covering club meetings, she was pleasantly surprised to meet so many educated, worldly women. They came from different parts of the country, many had lived abroad, and some spoke foreign languages. She found herself reporting on an unexpected range of club activities that included health and sanitation improvement, prison reform, conservation, Belgian war relief, Prohibition, and suffrage. She came to know the various men's organizations, too, such as the Masons, who were interested in business development and municipal operations. But she learned that women's organizations "in isolated places like this in many parts of the country . . . were a kind of self-produced university . . . a small, respectable pot, boiling away unnoticed, a stirring of minds, a spirit of inquiry, a new awareness of ideas." Here was her Wellesley indoctrination into the activist woman in living flesh, not the college-professor radical but the housewife and mother, middle class and privileged, who knew what she wanted for her community and state.[1]

Just as women had politicized their clubs, Douglas politicized the society page. On her third day on the job, she ran an article on woman suffrage. She was particularly interested in highlighting women in executive positions in higher education, including at industrial schools, to illustrate their leadership capabilities and thus their capacity for the ballot. She made such items a mainstay of the newspaper. When she took over as interim editor during her father's absence, suffrage pieces—the local and national movement and the club women behind it—moved from the second or third page to the front page and the editorial page. Suffrage work provided the real beginning to her activist life; her experience as a suffragist remained always personally important to her. Later in her long life, it gave her a historical foundation on which no other Florida activist in the late twentieth century could draw directly.[2]

By the time Douglas arrived at the *Herald,* the mantle of woman suffrage in Florida was passing on to a second generation. An earlier newspaper woman, Ella C. Chamberlain, had served as Florida's voting-rights trailblazer. In 1892, she attended a suffrage conference in Des Moines, Iowa, returned home to Tampa, and began barnstorming the state and writing fiery commentary for her column in the *Tampa Morning Tribune.* The following year, she organized the Florida Woman Suffrage Association in affiliation with Susan B. Anthony's National American Woman Suffrage Association. At the time, Wyoming and Colorado were the only states that allowed women to vote, although Idaho and other western states soon followed. The South was gelling into a one-party region, overturning Reconstruction to purge blacks and carpetbagger Republicans from the political process. In 1887 and in spite of the Fourteenth and Fifteenth Amendments, Florida Democrats mandated a poll tax and partisan poll watchers, thereby leading the other southern states in creating a white male political empire whose power brokers had little interest in opening the system to white women. The legislature never considered granting women the franchise during Chamberlain's time, and after she left the state in 1897, the movement for woman suffrage tumbled into decline.[3]

By the time it acquired renewed force, around 1912, expanded voting rights remained a long shot. Florida women were, nevertheless, more revved up than before. The national movement was generating noticeable excitement, and Florida now had more female residents to become excited. In 1913, local suffrage leagues sprang to life in Jacksonville, Orlando, and Lake Helen. A delegation of women then formed the Florida Equal Suffrage Association (FESA) to coordinate the effort statewide. Under May Mann Jennings's stewardship, the Florida Federation of Women's Clubs (FFWC) lent its considerable influence to the movement. By 1915, women were voting in a few municipal elections, but equal suffrage remained far away. Activists wanted the legislature to take one of three possible steps: allow primary voting for women, approve a constitutional amendment for woman suffrage in state elections, or—preferably—ratify the federal Susan B. Anthony Amendment (later the Nineteenth Amendment).[4]

With their numbers peaking at fewer than 800, Florida suffragists who organized rallies, wrote letters, gave speeches, and marched in the streets were never under the illusion that their job would be easy. Their movement represented a potential 139,000 female votes, enough to determine the outcome of elections and too many for illiberal legislators. Male chauvinists scoffed at members of the weaker sex for having deluded themselves into believing that they could handle a male responsibility. Dependency on the stronger sex was women's natural state. Psychologically and intellectually, they were ill equipped for the thorny world of politics, where tough, informed decisions had to be made about such matters as budgets, criminal justice, nation building, and war. Women's authoritative voices therefore should broadcast no farther than children and household help. To prove such claims, antisuffragists sometimes pointed to Montana's Jeannette Rankin, the first woman elected to Congress, who cast a "cowardly" and irresponsible vote opposing the U.S. declaration of war against Germany in 1917. Some suffrage opponents, men and women, went so far as to equate the female franchise with black voting. Sixty-three percent of Florida's potential female voters were black, a statistic that antisuffragists used to good effect. Insisted one, "We can club the nigger man away from the polls, but we couldn't do that with a black woman."[5]

Male chauvinism at times echoed when Douglas sat down to write her society page, and she stayed seated until she had written a satisfying response. "We had begun to think the question of intellectual equality no longer a timely topic," she wrote. Philosophers and scientists from each generation back to Plato had answered the question, and by this time, the "colleges and universities possessed sufficient data to satisfy" the doubters. Miami congressman Frank Clark was one of those doubters whose opposition masqueraded as chivalry: "Our women" should not be "plunged into the vortex of political life." Convinced that the "majority of good women" cared little about voting, he identified suffrage as a conspiracy of northerners and a "small coterie of women seldom at home." Douglas responded to this argument, too. While serving as interim managing editor, she printed a front-page photo of women suffragists with babies beneath a bold caption, "To Prove All Suffragists Are Not Spinsters."[6]

Despite the vitality of the opposition, Florida suffragists remained undiscouraged. They were well organized and had a lot of support. A national cast that featured Carrie Chapman Catt, Florence Kelly, Anna Howard Shaw, and Alice Paul swung through Florida for rallies. Florida had its own heavy hitters, too, including Annie Douglass Broward, May Mann Jennings, and Mary Bryan. Possessing verve and stamina similar to that of her friend Jennings, Broward was the widow of the late governor, the first president of the Jacksonville Women's Club, a cofounder of the Florida Parent-Teacher Association, and a vigorous supporter of children's welfare and Royal Palm State Park. Jennings brought the same limitless energy to woman suffrage as she exerted in her park activities. An officer of a regional suffrage conference wrote to her, "You are the one woman in Florida who can carry your state for suffrage." The estimation was excessive, but Jennings used her presidency to maneuver the FFWC into the suffrage camp, adding a formidable network of club women to the grand cause.[7]

For her part, Bryan was a newcomer to Florida, though not to politics. To ease the arthritis that wracked her joints, she and her husband, three-time presidential candidate William Jennings Bryan, moved to Miami in 1915 after he resigned as U.S. secretary of state. William was regarded as Miami's most illustrious resident during the ten years he lived there. Locals called him the Great Commoner, even though he built a home on Brickell Avenue, known as Millionaires' Row, and owned homes in two other states. He was famous for the Sunday Bible sermons he gave before overflow crowds in Miami's Royal Palm Park (a city park unrelated to the state park) and for entertaining guests by shooting ducks off the seawall from the backyard of his Villa Serena. Stoneman got to know him from his occasional visits to the *Herald* office, where he would "boom along about politics in that wonderful organ voice," Douglas recalled. The two Democrats rarely saw eye to eye, especially on religion. To Douglas, William, "tall and large domed," seemed bigger than life. She much preferred Mary, who was "gracious, composed, handsome, and perhaps the wiser." A law school graduate who had finished third in an otherwise all-male class, Mary was an early member of the Nebraska bar; she was a savvy political adviser to her husband and a sterling speaker. Douglas speculated that Mary would have had a brilliant career in public service had she not devoted herself to William's career.[8]

Douglas had thought little about becoming involved in suffrage since her college days, and the exact point of her entry into the movement is unclear. More than likely her work on the newspaper and her father's connections brought her into contact with activist women. She officially became one herself in February 1916, when she founded the Business Women's League in Miami. The league's stated goals were to help women, both single and married, find employment and prepare for the workplace. To raise money, the league operated a downtown lunch counter with a rare public accommodation, a women's restroom. Achieving the league's principal objectives, Douglas believed, depended on winning the ballot. In 1919, her organization joined the National Federation of Business and Professional Women's Clubs, founded that same year. Its agenda included ending sex discrimination in employment and pay and promoting a federal Equal Rights Amendment, which smacked of social sedition too extreme for many suffragists. In its first year of existence, the federation presented Douglas with an award of recognition for her work in Miami. When Mary Munroe's Dade County Federation of Women's Clubs held its organizing convention in December 1916, Douglas signed up the league, and she commended the "federation on the strong place of suffrage on its program."[9]

Douglas and other representatives of her organization also attended FESA's annual convention, held in Miami the next March. On the second day, she addressed a plenary session as the president of the Business Women's League. Pitching her voice across the auditorium as Malvina Bennett had taught the students at Wellesley, Douglas emphasized the colossal importance of the ballot in seeking "equal industrial opportunity and equal pay for equal work." Businesswomen wanted the vote not simply to make a better life for themselves outside the home. They believed it was "important as part of the great principle of democracy." Following warm applause, Douglas completed her public debut by impressing an audience that included the state's most redoubtable suffragists, Jennings and Bryan. In attendance, too, were the Reverend Dr. Mary Safford, outgoing president of the FESA and a national organizer, and elderly veteran suffragist Dr. Anna Shaw, former colleague of Susan B. Anthony and founder and past president of the National American Woman Suffrage Association.[10]

Shortly after the convention, Douglas's name began appearing on the FESA's letterhead as chair of the press committee and on the FFWC letterhead as state editor. Bryan, who had taken it upon herself to cultivate Douglas's involvement, then asked her to join four other women on a trip to Tallahassee to lobby the legislature for a bill giving women the right to vote in primary elections and for a constitutional amendment guaranteeing statewide suffrage. Consistent with Quaker tradition, Frank Stoneman too supported equal suffrage, and he thought she could also cover the event for the newspaper. In April 1917, she and Bryan boarded the train bound for Jacksonville and then Tallahassee, where they were to rendezvous with Jennings and Broward. When the train stopped in

Fort Lauderdale, Ivy Stranahan, the newly elected FESA president, joined them. Nine years older than Douglas, she was married to Frank Stranahan, the pioneer merchant who had traded with Indians and wildlife poachers, and she was a chief advocate of Seminole rights, including property rights, and one of the first members of Florida Audubon. According to legend, she convinced Frank to abstain from his profitable trade in plume feathers. Douglas was awed by the company of Bryan and Stranahan.[11]

Since her last train trip, the long passage through the pine forests of North Florida had changed little, but Douglas realized she had. She surveyed the rest of Florida clearly for the first time. She saw waterways, landscapes, and human habitations that she had seen before, yet Florida was now her home, the state where she was investing herself professionally and personally. She had been taking notice of its history, politics, and land. As the train approached Tallahassee, the pineland opened up to a rolling landscape of grand houses, enormous slumbering live oaks, and great magnolias. The city's famous azaleas were breaking out in pink and white, and the air was sweet with the scent of other spring blooms. A world apart from Miami and South Florida, Tallahassee was distinctly southern in appearance and spoken sounds, all "baked in prewar memories," she later said. It was very much a capital city with noisy political chatter and cigar-parlor deal making. All of its politicians and political hangers-on seemed to be doing their business at the Leon Hotel, where the women took rooms. Douglas could not help noticing the plentiful brass spittoons.[12]

The receptacles were equally bountiful in the Capitol building, and they came to represent to her the small-mindedness of the legislators. The next day, as each woman spoke forthrightly and eloquently before the House Committee on Amendments, the only life that seemed to emanate from their male audience was the metallic ping of tobacco-brown expectoration against brass. "We could have been talking to a bunch of dead mackerel, for all the response we got," Douglas recounted repeatedly over the rest of her life. That night, before a joint session of the legislature, with women packed quietly in the upper gallery, Bryan gave a ninety-minute speech. She talked about the history of equal suffrage; dismantled each objection to expanding the ballot; maintained that as the keeper of cultural and moral standards, a woman had the "right to have a voice in deciding the environment which should surround her children"; and finally appealed to her audience's regional identification by arguing that enlarging the South's voting constituency would similarly enlarge its proportional representation in Congress. She closed by promising that the "hand that rocks the cradle will never rock the boat." Douglas was mesmerized. She was also simultaneously irritated by the legislator in the seat beside her, she in her best dress sitting with a spittoon near her feet, and he with a juicy plug bulging in his cheek. Although the man was an expert shot, he, "from a one-town county," typified the sort of specimen who was determining her rights. She grew to have little regard for Tallahassee's "wool-hat boys," boorish counterparts to the city's equally chauvinistic "silk hats." She later concluded that Bryan was speaking "over the heads of the audience, to a future generation."[13]

The amendment committee reported favorably on the suffrage measure to the House. The Senate then approved the bill, but it failed on the House floor by two votes. The lawmakers were a tough crowd, especially the more reactionary bunch from North Florida, which Douglas called the "dim region," where the culture and politics, like the landscape, were an indiscernible extension of the bordering states of Alabama and Georgia. The five women left Tallahassee feeling dejected, but others returned each of the next three years, including for a special session in 1918. In the end, lawmakers passed on the opportunity to make Florida the first southern state to dismantle one of humanity's great oversights and instead made their state the last to do so—in 1969.[14]

If the results of the 1917 legislative session soured Douglas toward the way lawmakers ran the state, she saw in Florida's public women a little something of what she had come to believe in at Wellesley. Observing Jennings and Broward operate so deftly in the arena of brass-spittoon politics considerably raised Douglas's estimation of the two and reinforced her position on women's equality: "I thought, if the courage and resource and stamina of north Florida women among hard-dealing businessmen was typical it was a great waste of ability that more women were not serving officially in public office." She considered Bryan, Jennings, and the other suffragists "great women. . . . They were completely reasonable, wonderful women. . . . [Y]ou admired them."[15]

Yet although she and mainstream southern suffragists shared a belief that women should be enfranchised, Douglas's politics were much more radical. While others were willing to stop at the franchise, Douglas understood that the vote afforded women a single right, not genuine equality. Women's lives were still mere adjuncts to a male domain. Their customary place remained in the home, an arrangement not expected to change with the vote. Douglas's suffragist counterparts were not interested in altering the status quo to such a degree. Women such as Jennings and Bryan sought to use the vote to empower their work as public housekeepers, not to rearrange the sexual hierarchy, and they refrained from rhetoric that suggested feminist beliefs. Douglas endorsed the idea of the public housekeeper, but she also believed that women at times had to be willing to take their hand off the cradle and rock the boat; if women stood with men even when doing so further marginalized them, the right to vote was a fraud. After returning from war-torn Europe in 1920, for example, Douglas better understood the vote of Jeannette Rankin (and that of fifty-five male members of Congress) against entering the war. As the presidential election approached that year, Douglas implored *Miami Herald* readers, "Mr. Voter, will you please vote for the peaceable women who are peacemakers of the world, and were never known to make prisons nor to declare war, nor to fight battles. Just so long as the world votes for he peace they will have war, and as soon as they vote and elect she peace, they will have peace, then they can come rejoicing forever in the shes."[16]

Douglas jealously guarded her independence in a way that many of the women who impressed her did not. Although she followed convention by keeping her former husband's last name (something she later regretted), she did so because she thought a "Mrs." could more safely than a "Miss" negotiate the crowded avenues and risky alleys in male-dominated society. It "gave yourself protection in the world." At the same time, she refused to be identified by Kenneth's first name.[17] Women activists

commonly abandoned their own names in official documents and publications and referred to themselves by their husbands' names, as Mrs.
William Jennings Bryan and Mrs. Frank Stranahan did. On some occasions when their own names were used, they went out of their way to
offer parenthetical clarification with their husbands' names. In the collected biographies of the early FFWC women, written by their contemporary, Lucy Worthington Blackman (Mrs. William Fremont Blackman),
Blackman ignored the women's given names in favor of their husbands',
and she sometimes began biographies, including her own, by noting husbands' positions and relevant achievements. Melding one's identity in
such a way, Douglas believed, created a political handicap by restricting
public activities that might smear husbands' "good" names. In the wake of
her marriage, Douglas was unwilling to become a mere appendage of another, and she preferred to remain responsible only to and for herself.[18]

The subject of separate spheres left her doubtful if not altogether weary.
"It is getting a little bit late in the day for men to object that women are
getting outside their proper sphere," she asserted. "Nobody knows yet
what is either man's or woman's proper sphere, or how they are to find
it." She did not oppose the idea that women could opt for the traditional
domestic role but objected to strictures that confined women to the menacing social prescription of a specified place. A woman should have the
freedom to choose her path in life, whether that path led to motherhood
or a career or both. When the National Woman's Party first proposed
the Equal Rights Amendment in 1923, Douglas thought it was absolutely
necessary, and she volunteered her public assent. Doing so was consistent with her decision to be a professional woman and with the precepts
of "symmetrical womanhood." It was not consistent, however, with the
values of most of Florida's suffragists. In the *Southern Clubwoman* that
year, Jennings wrote, "I am unquestionably opposed to the Amendment
because it is a direct abridgement of states' rights and would repeal all of
the special protective legislation for women."[19]

Jennings's remarks epitomized the politically conservative vein that
pulsated within Florida's club woman community. She, Bryan, and the
FFWC, for example, vigorously supported Prohibition, an issue that was

dividing communities across the state. According to one early Miami historian, Bobo Dean of the *Miami Metropolis* suspended his attacks against
Henry Flagler to denounce drink and to praise Miami's Women's Christian Temperance Union, which one year invited to the city Carrie Nation, one of the country's most diminutive but physically aggressive dry
crusaders, famed for her proclivity to use a swinging ax to reduce pubs
and bars to kindling. Dean's counterpart at the *Herald*, Stoneman, neither publicly nor personally supported Prohibition. Douglas agreed with
her father. When she and the others left Tallahassee melancholic over
the suffrage setback, Bryan and Jennings at least could console themselves with the legislature's approval of a Prohibition amendment. Douglas could not.[20]

Even efforts to give women equal voting rights were limited by the decidedly elitist and conservative bent of those who led such efforts. Club
women in general and white southern Progressives in particular refused
to tamper with the social and political status quo with regard to blacks
and immigrants. One of Ella Chamberlain's principal motivations as a
suffragist back in the 1890s had been her repugnance for the upended
social structure of Reconstruction, which allowed, in her words, "intelligent, educated and deeply religious" southern white women to be "gov-
erned by the ex-slave . . . just emerging from centuries of barbarism and
servitude." Ivy Stranahan was less openly appalled two decades later, but
under her leadership, the *equal* in Florida Equal Suffrage Association
had a limited application. Hers was unconditionally a racially exclusive
organization working to enfranchise white women. In the run-up to the
1920 presidential election, the first national contest after the ratification of
the Nineteenth Amendment, Jennings helped organize the Duval County
League of Democratic Women in part so that white women could, in
the words of speakers at the league's organizing meeting, "protect their
homes . . . from negro domination." Jennings recruited Stranahan to form
a similar organization in Broward County.[21]

Douglas neither took an altogether liberal position on race nor supported the excesses of Jennings and Stranahan. Douglas was incredulous
that Miami had no school for black children, an oversight she blamed on
the city's northern-born leaders as much as its southerners. Landlords

who frequently came before her father's bench for failing to make basic improvements to the houses rented to blacks—"raw board, single-room Negro shacks," as she described them—received heavy fines, a penalty that pleased her. This was a time when countless "respectable" men across the country joined the Ku Klux Klan, as they might any civic organization. Membership nationally reached somewhere into the millions, with midwestern states boasting larger memberships than some southern states. A joiner of groups, but not this one, Frank Stoneman peered through the Klan's veil of civic good to see its anti-immigrant and anti-black obsession. Douglas felt enormously proud of her father's stand against the organization, editorially and literally. She talked often about the time she, Lillias, and Frank were out for a drive one pleasant evening when her father steered the car down Fifth Street "into a waiting hooded and sheeted Klan procession." A Klansman on horseback rode up and announced omnipotently that the street was closed, but Frank shouted the man out of the way, and the family sped through as the Klansman's horse reared back: "We were all yelling and screaming in defiance." On another occasion, a "polite Klansman, unhooded," called at the newspaper office to ask Douglas to start a Klanswomen's Auxiliary. She told him "what I thought of his organization." In general, she was horrified by the free-for-all racial violence common to that era—the lynchings, the beatings, the pseudo-enslavement of prisoners. She identified the viciousness as a holdover from the Old South, "adopted by most northerners." In reality, white-on-black violence was a product of the postbellum South, and northern whites, including those transplanted to Florida, at times adopted such techniques, as did those wool-hat boys she so despised in Tallahassee—the same ones who tried to keep her disfranchised.[22]

She never seemed to identify her oppression as a woman with that of blacks, however, at least not in the 1910s. Advocating better treatment of racial others was one thing, but accepting them as equals was another. Like most southern and northern whites in Miami, she believed that blacks had a separate place in society. In a scholarly article written for the sociological journal *Social Forces,* she referred to the "undeveloped negro." In the *Herald,* she once called for the creation of a special school "for the training of colored girls to be competent domestic servants," and she bought into the conventional belief that, as she put it, music and dance were "so much the province of the African mind." When *The Birth of a Nation* came to Miami, she sat through its twelve reels, even though she hated the cinema, and was captivated. She reviewed the movie on the society page, characterizing D. W. Griffith's masterpiece as "stupendous— magnificent—historically patriotic . . . the biggest constructive message that this city has ever seen." The audience of mostly northern natives who watched it with her had the same reaction, breaking into "uncontrollable applause" throughout the epic drama and "drowning the sound of the music." The movie had been touring the country for two years, and she would have been familiar with the controversy surrounding its "constructive message": that white supremacy was justified to protect the South, the nation, and white women from the half-witted, rapacious, brutish black man whose beneficial tenure in slavery had been truncated by the war before the cloak of African savagery could be completely divested.[23]

It is doubtful that her ancestors who sheltered runaway slaves would have been ready to accept political and social equality with blacks. Abolition was only one step toward equality, and many social reformers were not immediately ready to take such an ominous additional step. Douglas's views contrasted favorably with those of Jennings and Stranahan, but she nevertheless did not during the 1910s embrace civil rights with the same fervor she brought to other social issues. Like her environmental sensibilities, her racial beliefs evolved over the next eighty years.

Douglas was not at the time unwaveringly occupied with nature either as a writer or as an activist. She was a member of no Audubon society, though there were two in Miami, and she served on no women's club committee related to conservation, though there were many. As for the Everglades, she had not seen them. But nearly anyone who lived in Miami would have been affected by nature—the water, the birds, the tropical vegetation, the sun. She eventually reconnected with nature, but not until after she grew restless and left Miami for Europe in a labored search for romance and adventure.

CHAPTER EIGHTEEN

World War

Petty-officer first class Marjory Stoneman Douglas was miserable in her regimental duties. A midmorning riser by habit, she almost always arrived to work late and was reprimanded for it, although she still managed to receive decent monthly performance reports. She spent the day typing letters for surly naval officers, and when she corrected their grammar, which was often, they berated her for that, too. She had enlisted impulsively after the United States entered the terrible war in Europe in 1917. Her father had been predicting U.S. involvement for a long time, prompting some of his competitors to call his a jingoist newspaper. But Douglas herself had been writing some of the editorials "arousing for the war." "So in other words," she recalled years later, "I jingoed." She had just been reading the signs—one cargo ship after another being sunk by German U-boats—just as she was only gathering the news when her father sent her to cover the story of the first local woman to enlist. Everyone at the *Miami Herald* believed that the pioneer would be the wife of the plumber who owned the shop across the street. When a recruiting boat arrived in Miami, Douglas grabbed pen and pad and set off for the municipal docks to witness the woman's swearing in. But she never showed, and

Douglas became the subject of her assignment: "Those buzzards on the Key West enlisting boat brainwashed me."[1]

Before returning to the office, she telephoned her father. He was disappointed to lose his society page editor, but he admired her patriotism. At the moment, she was not feeling the antiwar influence of her former Wellesley professors or the pacifist streak in her Quaker heritage. She did feel the pull of her mother's side of the family, however, and she was "terribly concerned about France." Certain times called for war, and she wanted to do her part. Like the young men she knew who rushed off to combat with romantic notions in their heads, she hoped to find adventure. She might get to sail the high seas like her Trefethen ancestors and see the world.[2]

But the sea was not her fate, at least not yet. The navy assigned her to the reserve station down the street from the *Herald*. She continued to live at home and write occasional pieces for the *Herald*, usually about the war effort. This arrangement did not suit her other reason for joining the service, the one that suggested that she was not completely brainwashed by the recruiters. She had fallen for a man. She had seen him for the first time back when she covered the Dixie Highway finale. A reporter with the *Miami Metropolis*, he stood on the running board of the lead car as the motorcade rolled into Miami, a plume of white dust trailing behind. With his hair blowing back and eyes squinting against the wind, he cut a dashing figure. In her autobiography, she concealed his identity with a fictitious name, Andy.[3] His real name was Kenneth A. Rotharmel. He was from Bluffton, Indiana, and had attended Wabash College for three years before moving to Miami and taking a job with the *Metropolis*. He was two years younger than she, the captain of a tennis team called the Scrubs, and on a constant search for a new challenge. They became romantically involved (short of having sex, she claimed) in the summer of 1916 when they and friends rented a house on Miami Beach for a week of indolence. Carl Fisher's resort dreamland was still a flattened landscape with a web of streets, hundreds of freshly planted stick trees, and few structures. But the roseate sunsets, yellow moonlight, and ocean breeze were hypnotic enough for the friends to extend their stay for another week. Douglas realized then that she could never be an inland person living far from salt air. She also realized that she had fallen in love with a second Kenneth, and she suspected that he reciprocated.[4]

They considered an engagement but could not make it official. Marjory had to wait another year before filing for divorce from Kenneth Douglas, a complication that seemed to leave Rotharmel tentative. Then, as the war abroad escalated and American men were finding their way into the fighting by joining the Canadian and British military services, Rotharmel grew restive for action. In December, he joined the ambulance corps of the American Field Service with the expectation of going to France. Friends gave him a farewell dinner, and Marjory went to see him off on the midnight special to New York. The sound of the departing train's whistle carried her back to the imprisonment of the first Kenneth, when dread and worry filled the void created by her lover's absence. Once again left to wait for a man, she resented it. She hated the dark longing coloring her world and preoccupying her thoughts. An "intelligent woman in love with a man," she confided to her diary years later, "is less intelligent."[5]

As Marjory struggled with Rotharmel's departure, she understood his need to go abroad. A fighting spirit had begun to take hold across the country, and not merely of restless young men. During her time as the *Herald*'s interim managing editor in the summer of 1916, she published a news wire release about a unique military camp established at Chevy Chase, Maryland, for women, even though the national armed forces had not yet accepted them. Many women felt left out when, by the early days of 1917, Americans had begun sensing the need to commit to battle. Miami went about the usual business of catering to tourists. But more than before, the visiting and local populations verbalized the word *war,* and the newspaper headlines above the reported events in Europe and the ship sinkings in the Atlantic and Mediterranean grew bolder. Local men were rapidly signing up for service in the U.S. armed forces even before Congress approved a resolution of war on April 6 and instituted a military draft in June. The navy was the most popular branch among new enlistees in Southeast Florida. By April 10, more than two hundred men and three women had joined the navy.[6]

Those three women made history. They were among the first women ever officially to enlist in the American armed forces. In March, navy secretary Josephus Daniels outraged military purists when he announced the unprecedented step of authorizing women to enlist as yeomen in the reserve branch. Dubbed "yeogirls" and "yeomenettes" by the press, they were classified as yeomen (F) (for female) by the military bureaucracy. They were to be spared basic training but receive equal pay with men. On March 21, 1917, a twenty-two-year-old Philadelphia woman became the first enlistee.[7]

Six days later, with nothing more premeditated than journalistic duties, Douglas boarded the navy tug *Peoria,* which had steamed up from Key West a few days earlier on a recruiting mission. Before going back ashore, she was sworn in at the rating of chief yeoman, making her Florida's first female enlistee. The examining surgeon described her as being five feet, two and a half inches tall and weighing 115 pounds, with brown eyes and hair and a fair complexion. Another Miami woman followed her lead that day, and they became two of the country's initial crop of one hundred female navy recruits. Both joined the coast defense reserve, which obligated them to a minimum three-month term in their hometown districts. When a *Herald* reporter asked Douglas to comment on her enlistment, she took the opportunity to be droll. "I have nothing to say for publication," she responded, then added that "she would like to don a uniform with its wide collar and naval effect, and wear it around on all occasions to let the whole world know that she has enlisted."[8]

And she did wear a uniform, although only within the world of Miami and with her own effect. Complementing her dress whites, she put on a nonregulation dark-colored wide-brim hat, a trademark of her later years. A month expired before she wore any part of this uniform, though. She was still president of the Business Women's League and had not yet made her trip to Tallahassee with fellow suffragists. The league finally elected her replacement, and in April she reported for duty.[9]

According to one source, after Douglas expressed her concern about leaving the newspaper shorthanded, Frank Stoneman responded with uncharacteristic mirth: "What I'm wondering is what's going to happen to the Navy." Stoneman's was apparently more than a wry comment. "I was the most useless yeoman (F) the Navy ever had," Douglas later admitted, without apology. Three months after enlisting, her rating was downgraded from chief yeoman to yeoman first class. It was no surprise; she had no skills in shorthand or in taking dictation, and she was a poor typist, as were many other yeomen (F) who had no formal clerical training or experience. Douglas was utterly bored with the mindless routine of a clerk, and her demeanor repeatedly clashed with the military hierarchy. In March 1918, she requested a transfer to England or France, maintaining that she had the language skills to be a French interpreter. Her section commander and the district commandant endorsed her request, with the latter describing her as a "brilliant woman" who would serve her country patriotically overseas. She even obtained a letter from Senator Duncan Fletcher, who wrote directly to Secretary Daniels. But navy detailers were unmoved. Two months later, she requested her release from the navy. On May 21, 1918, her superiors obliged—"unanimously," she later quipped. "That day was probably as great a break for the Navy as the invention of the carrier."[10]

By that time, she had already arranged an overseas assignment with the Red Cross. She had been familiar with its work abroad for some time. Miami was awash in war-relief campaigns of all sorts even before the United States entered the fight, and Douglas had written about them for the society page. Readers learned about hungry Belgians, destitute Armenians, the Local Woman's Relief Association, the bandage-rolling activities of local Red Cross volunteers, and the Belgian Relief Committee of the Miami Women's Club and its production of stretcher pillows (sent to the ambulance corps via Rotharmel). For one story, she interviewed a visiting British Red Cross worker from the Women's Hospital in Serbia. Douglas confessed to readers, "My awe for a valiant and distinguished woman relief worker through contact with her gracious personality [and] that underlying intensity of strength and high seriousness that is characteristic of those who have looked the horrors of the war calmly and surely in the face, changed to a deep interest in the work for which she gave so much of herself."[11]

Self-interest also lay behind Douglas's desire to go abroad. Doing so would offer enriching experiences essential to a writer and would perhaps lead her back to Rotharmel. In the nearly two years he had been gone, they had maintained an irregular correspondence, and she occasionally published updates on his duties in France on the society page. The letters eventually trickled off, a circumstance that apparently intensified her eagerness to get to France: she later wrote a short story, "The Hummingbird Charm," that drew on what was likely a personal account of her desperation. The protagonist, Bostonian Miranda Gerard, has hungrily followed her infatuation, a naval officer named James Pinckney, to Port-au-Prince, Haiti. "When a girl is in love," Miranda rationalizes, "she is permitted to do something drastic."[12]

Douglas was going where approximately twenty-five thousand American women would ultimately go. They went as members of the U.S. Navy, Marines, and Army. Some were auxiliary workers for the YMCA and YWCA, assigned to entertain battle-weary troops and operate canteens. The Army Signal Corps employed women fluent in French as telephone operators, and the American Expeditionary Force hired female clerical workers. Twenty-five hundred women worked for the Red Cross, which had been in Europe since war broke out in 1914. Most of these volunteers served as hospital nurses, but many ran canteens and served as searchers, investigating the circumstances of men missing in action and acting as liaisons between wounded soldiers and worried families back home. By war's end, searchers had written more than two hundred thousand letters in fulfillment of their duties.[13]

Douglas was bound for different assignments when she took the train to New York en route to France in September. Before leaving for Europe, she succumbed to the great influenza pandemic and spent a month recuperating with her old friend, Carolyn Percy. They talked about their Wellesley days, New York and Miami, the possibility of Percy joining the effort in France, Marjory's potential engagement to Rotharmel, and her emancipation from Kenneth Douglas. Marjory's divorce, filed on formal grounds of "desertion and non-support," had been granted that spring.[14]

She finally set sail in October on a transport ship for a week's voyage to Bristol, England. After suffering a day or two curled up uneasily on the main deck next to seasick sailors, she gained her sea legs. She spent much of her time walking the outside decks with her hands plunged into the pockets of her gray Oxford topcoat, looking out at the rolling water blithely unmindful of lurking enemy submarines. Years later, she put the narrator of one of her stories on board a similar ship with twenty-five Red Cross women who were "new to the war that was going on there in Europe, had been going on for years, now real and vivid at last, because we were to have a part in it."[15]

She ultimately produced six *Saturday Evening Post* stories relating the experiences of female Red Cross workers in Europe during World War I. She was writing in the late 1930s, shifting away from her traditional Florida setting at a time when Europe was heading toward another large-scale war. Editors at the magazine may have suggested the contemporary relevance of her experiences of two decades earlier, or she may have been unilaterally moved to make a statement. Memories of a battle-scarred continent of crushed and starving people, the senseless terrors inflicted on the innocent, and an uneasy peace and conditions as dire and incendiary as war itself emerged in her stories with sufficient resonance, when the world was reeled against what she called the "backlash of history." Paragraphs seethed with her hatred of war, but she knew that the greatest relief effort in the history of the world had been flawed, had failed to stabilize Europe's masses, appease the disgruntled, and avert political vacuums filled by ruthless leaders. The autocratic ruler of a Balkan state in her 1938 "Athens to Marseilles" embodied the distressing truth of "the latest of the dictators, powerful even among the Hitlers and Stalins and Mussolinis"; "Let a man get his hand on one of these small middle-European countries, now, their borders brutally altered by the Versailles Conference, their people broken down by war and hunger and hurt pride and grief. Let him arouse their imaginations by fear and the hope of power. Let him promise them the fulfillment of their deepest racial cravings. Let him work directly on the young, starved, unfulfilled generations. There would be nothing he could not do with them."[16]

Douglas blamed the unchanging mess on the reckless male temperament. In "The Hand Is Quicker," which features two Red Cross workers
ministering to homeless, hungry refugees in a remote mountain village
in France, she opened with a feminine view of war that quickly succumbs
to machismo fantasies as women become players in those fantasies. "The
women who had shrilled for war were sobered as soon as the others. They
learned instantly that they were only women in a manmade world, excited, not by war itself but by the sight of men en masse, gaily, soberly,
doggedly, marching themselves into it." Like her story's wartime women,
Douglas had followed both Kenneths into difficult circumstances. But she
had saved herself by the time she wrote her war stories, and passages
within them portray feminist enlightenment, criticism, and renunciation.
For her predicaments with men, she blamed not heedless love but socially
accepted—indeed, expected—feminine weakness. To be a feminist was
to redefine the feminine apart from a gendered frailty, to be more than
the male-made world. She wrote that "the saluting and the heel-clicking
and the regulations, that went on endlessly in that confused time after
the Armistice when armies were changing back into men sick of fighting,
anxious only to go home, produced a kind of hatred in me, the least disciplined of women, dodging about the byways of Europe on my unimpor-
tant errands. I was happy and excited to be there, seeing it. But it was an
unholy joy to slip through that jungle of masculine pomp and restriction
with my tongue in my cheek."[17]

Douglas's protagonist in "The Hand Is Quicker" thought extensively
about her prospects for far-flung adventure and for humanitarian contributions in addition to her prospects for love. But, as Douglas wrote in
another story, awaiting her and other women was much "wretchedness
which the recent end of the war had not withdrawn from Europe."[18]

After the ship docked at Bristol, the members of Douglas's group boarded
the train to London. They were traveling on the Great Western Railway,
opened in 1838 and hailed as a singular achievement of the emerging
industrial age. The two-and-a-half-hour ride took them across an un-
scathed countryside through Reading and Bath and along the Thames

River. Stepping off the train beneath the wrought-iron arched span of London's Paddington Station, they encountered their first stark reminders of the great conflict. As many men as not were in military uniform, some of them having recently returned from the Western Front, some with missing appendages, all of them battered in some way physically if not psychologically. Even the business of travelers in civilian dress was driven by the exigencies of war. Most were strangers to one another, yet all were thrust into a common, unified mission to save Europe and the world from Teutonic imperialism. From Paddington, the women boarded another train for the English Channel and the crossing to France. They eventually arrived at Red Cross headquarters in Paris.[19]

Paris was the hub of the relief effort, and the place to find people. Douglas ran into a number she knew. She spotted one of her former instructors from Wellesley, Ethel Sullivan, walking across the lobby of the Red Cross headquarters, where Douglas too worked, and they exchanged felicitous greetings. On a separate occasion, a familiar man with an unfamiliar limp, a telltale sign of a bayonet or bullet wound of anyone in uniform, came by her office. Pete Robineau, an old friend from the *Metropolis,* had introduced Marjory to Kenneth Rotharmel in Miami and was now delivering good news. Rotharmel was assigned to an airfield in the countryside outside Paris, and Robineau promised to get in touch with him.[20]

Soon thereafter, Marjory was working at her desk at headquarters when she heard a voice from her past calling from across the room. She felt the warm tremors of pleasure as she looked up. Kenneth was standing there. That night, he took her to dinner and then for a stroll along city sidewalks. He had left the ambulance service eighteen months earlier, he told her, to join a French flying squadron, the Lafayette Escadrille. Although he had participated in seven major air battles, his face retained its youthful innocence, and he chattered on like an excited schoolboy. Yet he was a man surely enough, and in his French lieutenant's uniform with a chest full of medals, he looked the picture of confidence and matured strength. She was overjoyed by his company, even if there was some clumsiness and hesitancy. Their more familiar playful interactions would soon return, she was sure. When he confessed that he had been intimate with another woman, she was not bothered. He still wanted to marry her. And when he announced that he would be returning to the States as soon as possible, she could hardly begrudge him that. Three years at the center of action were enough for anyone. Still, the old feeling of abandonment crept over her. The day before he left in January, he was awarded the Croix de Guerre, and she was thrilled for him. Then he was gone, and she sat alone with the ugly pain of longing.[21]

But Paris would not allow her to wallow in loneliness. The city and the times harbored too many excitements. She rented a small second-floor dormitory apartment on Rue de Grand Chaumière with a window overlooking the back garden. She melded with a fun group of Red Cross workers, and they haunted a café called Queen of Hearts, where she heard stories about two young American writers, John Dos Passos and Ernest Hemingway, who were driving ambulances in Italy and advancing a new, spare writing style that reflected the war's lesson of the importance of the essential over the superfluous. Later in Italy, she introduced herself to Dos Passos, although she never saw Hemingway. Carolyn Percy arrived in France as a canteen worker for the Red Cross, and she and Marjory saw each other on the infrequent occasions when their schedules put them in Paris together. Douglas also became friends with a coworker whom in her autobiography she called only Frederick. He was from a newspaper family in Pennsylvania, which gave them an immediate rapport. He too had been married before, though he had a young daughter, and he began to think of Marjory as something more than a friend. Paris was the city of love, at least for Frederick.[22]

For Marjory and everyone else at the time, Paris was also the city of peace. On November 11, 1918, within two weeks of her arrival, the warring nations officially ended their conflict. That morning, the smallest of sounds broadcast up to her apartment from the strangely quiet streets below. The city was waiting in hushed anticipation of jubilation. Then at 11:20 A.M., the walls of her small apartment quaked as five cannon shots from across the River Seine sounded the signing of the armistice. The city erupted into riotous celebration, "too big for me or anybody," she

wrote at the time, "too big for words or emotion or even realization." She
went downstairs and outside into the street and was instantly swallowed
up by the "great cheering masses." For an hour, she joined in the fraternal singing and hugging and kissing. The festival of peace continued all
day, through the night, and into the next morning before finally exhausting itself. She "longed for a typewriter and deadline to race against," she
said, "and the need for running a few good words through my fingers
that would work off some of this emotion for me." Filing a dispatch for
the *Herald,* she told readers back home about the "sheer gorgeous luck"
of being in France during this unimaginable bedlam of celebration: "It's
the biggest thing I'll ever see."[23]

The transition to peace presented new difficulties, uncertainties, and
priorities. In "Athens to Marseilles," she wrote, "It is a queer time, just
after a war. It is not war, certainly. But it is not peace. The single tension,
the intolerable binding drama, is unloosed. Men, not armies, stumble
home to sickness, exhaustion, hunger, in the taint of thousands of filthy
deaths. Life itself seems to lag, drifting nowhere."[24]

Although war-tattered Europe needed the Red Cross as much as ever,
workers were being sent home. Douglas "hung around headquarters,
desperately catching at small jobs, anything, just to stay." Even with Rotharmel gone, she wanted to be in Paris. With the help of Ethel Sullivan,
she managed to obtain a transfer from a department that worked finding clothing for refugees to one that generated publicity for children's relief efforts. The undertaking to feed and house people in every corner
of the continent had no equal in modern times. The Red Cross established operating commissions in France, England, Italy, Russia, Serbia,
and Romania. Douglas traveled to all but two of these countries, generating valuable publicity for the financially strapped organization. The
year before her Paris assignment, the Red Cross had spent more than one
hundred million dollars and had depleted its funds, forcing administrators to choose among the hordes who needed aid. Red Cross membership
rose from five hundred thousand when the United States entered the war
to twenty million a year later, bringing in more money and supplies. Her

reports went across the news wires and into the *Red Cross Bulletin*. Beginning with the armistice celebration, her tour turned into a remarkable if also morbidly sobering adventure.[25]

As she moved across Europe, she primarily covered relief stories for the *Bulletin*, though on occasion she oversaw the relief work itself. The rubble of war and the dislocation afflicted on civilian men, women, and children left her with lasting images. So too did one natural occurrence — a June 29 earthquake that opened up gaping clefts in the Mugello Valley south of Florence. Tremors destroyed churches, schools, public buildings, and two hundred homes, leaving thousands of people homeless and more than one hundred dead. From Washington, the American Red Cross sent a cablegram assuring Italian authorities that help would arrive soon. Within hours of learning of the disaster, Paris had assembled a relief team and fifty-seven thousand dollars in supplies and aid money. The next day, the *Chicago Tribune* and the *New York Times* reported that "Mrs. M. S. Douglas" had been dispatched from Paris with nine carloads of steel barracks, tents, clothing, and food, with each car bearing a sign, "Rush for the Earthquake Sufferers in Tuscany." Somewhere en route, the barracks intended for the homeless disappeared, as did Douglas's wallet. She spent two weeks in the valley, where the "destruction looks exactly as it does on the French battle front," and experienced eighty smaller tremors during that time. Easing the crisis, the lost barracks reappeared just as rain was turning the olive tree hillsides into mud.[26]

After Douglas wrapped up work in the valley, she squeezed in R & R trips to Rome and Venice. Both cities reminded her of what was missing back home in Miami. In the indigenous beauty and sensible design of the Italian cities and of others, she found what she regarded as an exemplary and seductive side of Europe, lasting contributions to humankind. "Who knew," she later wrote about Florence, "that to build a bell tower, a church, a baptistry, to fill a public square with great statues, was to make Florence a real place . . . fit to stand out for four centuries, a place where people could go to learn what beauty is." Of Venice, she said, the "people who made" the city "had the sheer common sense . . . to realize that beauty pays." They "gave their own artists and architects and sculptors such a sense of intelligent support that the architects and sculptors not only did better, but the greatest in the world were glad and honored to be asked to work for the city of such people." Yet however much she was taken with Italy, she always looked forward to returning to Paris.[27]

She considered the great city the world's cultural and social epicenter. Transformed in the mid–nineteenth century from a dreary medieval relic to a modern metropolis by Baron Georges Eugene Haussmann, Napoleon III's handpicked planner, Paris charmed her, from its architecture to its landscaping and to its twelve grand avenues radiating out from the colossal Arc de Triomphe. She was paying tribute to the baron when she described his changes as "ruthless."[28]

France also gave her an opportunity to connect with her past. Wherever she went, she saw the volunteer services of British and American Quakers in action. An essential part of the relief effort by the Red Cross's assessment, they spread out across Europe to make agriculture productive again, to piece back together the infrastructure, and to rebuild houses. At Marne, in northeastern France, they established a children's hospital. Douglas went up to that region to look at the hospital and took the time to search for family roots. Gaining more confidence in interacting with locals as she developed a proficiency in the native language, her grandmother's language, she went to Rouen, a village of narrow winding streets on the Seine, where brass makers were plentiful and where she suspected distant relatives lived, though she found none.[29]

In April 1919, she and two other Red Cross workers were assigned to escort back to Belgium a trainload of refugee children who had spent the last years of the war within the secure mountain borders of neutral Switzerland. As relief assignments went, this was a sweet one. The children were animated and eager for reunion with their homeland, although Douglas was saddened to see that some had been maimed and some had lost one or both parents in the war. Her joy for the children's homecoming was similarly tempered by the slow pace of reconstruction in Belgium, which she blamed on the flabby incompetence of the monarchy. "I can't express to you," she wrote to her family, "the feeling of lifted spirits that came when we passed out of the desolation into the lovely unspoiled Normandy and the forest of Chantilly."[30]

Belgium was the poster child for American relief, but the miserable impact of war was nowhere else as complete as in the Balkan states, the site of Douglas's last major assignment. After initially traveling there by train and gunboat, she was told that with hardly a bridge or a railroad left intact, her travels henceforth would be completed by truck where the roads were open and by horseback, followed by pack donkeys, where not. The journey took her through the mountains of Serbia, where she noticed that Serbians had cut whole forests to "block the inexorable Austrian pursuit," and Albania, the "wildest and most picturesque country" she had ever seen, to ruined villages and makeshift settlements. A Serbian nationalist had sparked the war in 1914 when he shot Archduke Franz Ferdinand, heir to the Austro-Hungarian crown. In Sarajevo, she stood on the street corner where the event had occurred. From there, the main theater of fighting had shifted to the muddy trenches of northern France, but after the armistice the Balkan states were not in a position to rebuild themselves as quickly as were other parts of Europe. The Balkans' political future was sketchy. As had historically been the case, outside forces imposed new boundaries, this time in accordance with the Treaty of Versailles, and fascists, nationalists, communists, and Turks were struggling for territory and political control.[31]

These developments troubled Douglas, who found "puzzling" the "growing attitude at home against the League of Nations," which had the potential to put the Balkans back on a secure track. Having leapt directly from the Balkan wars of 1912 and 1913 to the Great War, the native people were exhausted from continuing conflict. The Red Cross reported that Serbia's needs were the "world's greatest."[32] No one had to convince Douglas of this. The banks, schools, and factories were shut down. The Red Cross ran all the hospitals, mere clinics; motor transportation was unavailable in most places; roads and railways were upended; the soil was depleted; and diseases related to malnutrition were reaching pandemic levels. A principal part of the Red Cross mission in Serbia was supplying people with seeds and agricultural implements. Douglas delivered many of her supplies—food and medicine—to Serbians living in caves. The relief effort averted famine, but the population was to a mournful degree homeless, and the country was flirting with demographic collapse. The war had extinguished 35 percent of the population, including twice as many civilians as soldiers, the highest toll among the allies. A staggering 53 percent of the male population had been killed, and another 9 percent had been turned into invalids. "On the women and children devolve the task of saving the country," wrote the *Washington Post*.[33]

Douglas would have doubted the logic of this statement if she had read it. Serbian women were unable to save many of their children from starvation and typhus, much less save their country. The Red Cross estimated that war had turned three hundred thousand Serbian children into orphans. At one point, Red Cross workers discovered twelve thousand children living on their own in a nomadic colony. Douglas would never forget their homeless wanderings or the sound of hungry babies crying for milk and mother. Years later, she shared her memories with *Herald* readers.

> I have seen tiny babies in the last stages of starvation, brought in perhaps to some American Red Cross station in the Balkans who were probably the most hideous things it is possible to look on. Because starvation does to a normally fat baby face just what old age does to a man. When the fat is gone the face is all withered and the bony structures of the temples and the cheeks stand out sharply, unnaturally in what should be a smooth baby face. Then the skin is often not so much white as that unpleasant, unhealthy yellow of old parchment, the skull is prominent and the whole look is a tiny, miserable ancient man. Then, again, you must know that a starving baby, a really starving baby does not cry. It is perfectly silent, because it has not enough strength to cry. The feeble flame of its life is very low, almost flickering.[34]

Several weeks in the Balkans were enough to deplete her, and she fled for the restorative milieu of Athens. There she relaxed, took in the sights, and dined at the foot of Mount Olympus, where the mythical gods of the early

Greeks had lived and held court. In her hotel room, she sat at a little table and wrote to her father and stepmother, sparing them her "memory of man's eternal, self-inflicted ugliness." Instead, she described what lay in view of her window, a "clean" and "modern" city and "across a little park and a huddle of roofs ... the Acropolis, warm and tawny in the sun against a sky soft and brilliant as Florida's."[35]

Florida was on her mind. A cable from her father arrived with an offer of a job as a *Herald* assistant editor and column writer. She cabled back her acceptance and then submitted her resignation to the Red Cross. In November, she caught a boat from Athens to Marseilles, where she would take passage to New York. Sailing from Athens took several days across tumultuous seas under cramped conditions on the "dirtiest, least sea worthy" of vessels. In addition to fifteen passengers, the boat's main cargo was olive oil, which filled the passageways with a gut-heaving stench. The trip was much improved by a group of passengers who, when not seasick, occupied their time by reading aloud from Robert Falcon Scott's *The Voyage of Discovery,* though it gave them little relief to learn that the crew of the *Discovery* had been reduced to eating blubber. The food on their own vessel was unbearable, often boiled potatoes and the "eternal tough mutton of the Balkans" flavored by "slightly rancid olive oil." When not reading, the Athens-to-Marseilles passengers "discussed everything discussable, from politics, religion, morals, face powder, and sub-chasing." Douglas was beginning to sense her return home.[36]

In a letter written at sea, she told Florence, Daniel, and Fanny that she was coming to Massachusetts for a visit in time for Christmas. She added, "Think of me kindly as one who did her best." A bit of the old Marjory had been left behind. Flush with maturing experiences, she had a worldly new perspective by which to evaluate life, herself, and South Florida.[37]

CHAPTER NINETEEN

Land Booms

Like Nick Carraway in *The Great Gatsby,* Douglas returned home from Europe wanting the "world to be . . . at a sort of moral attention." But Florida, especially Miami, was in the midst of the sordid affairs of a great real estate boom. She wrote about it in fiction and nonfiction with "unaffected scorn." In her "A Bird Dog in Hand," published in 1925, at the height of the boom, the protagonist, George Henry, sermonizes to his female companion, "Can't you see that all this buying and selling of land is wrong? Can't you see that it is . . . making people think of nothing but money?" The inspiration for her character was Henry George, the real-life social critic who linked land speculation to the unequal distribution of wealth. Inverting the name was an astute calculation. George Henry ultimately forsakes his "deepest principles" against owning land "when there are others who can't" and invests in real estate. Like speculating in the stock market, the prospect of getting rich quickly by buying Florida land dulled cautious instincts in spite of mounting publicity about too-good-to-be-true deals that indeed went bad. "Those were the days," her narrator intones in another story, "when people suddenly began to act with a kind of madness, as if Florida earth were semiprecious, more valuable than all the crops that could be raised on it." Florida had forty-two million acres of land and water, and agents seemed to be trying to sell and resell each and every acre. Transactions succeeded not with the aid of science, official dictum, or even pictures but with overplayed elations and bloated promises—lies, in other words. Douglas was particularly indignant at the land agents' wolfish and "dreadful" practices. "The realtors will get you," she wrote in a 1922 poem, "if you don't watch out."[1]

For her, the boom was an event of the 1920s, one that "spread from Miami" to the Everglades. Actually, the opposite is true. It raged in the hinterland first, in the 1910s, sullied and rapacious. Even after the exposed shamelessness of the Wright report, the state's distorted attempts at principled real estate promoting, Napoleon Bonaparte Broward's ugly coziness with an unscrupulous land merchant, the lies, the lawsuits, and the foreclosures, the public retained a messianic faith in the possibility that "great riches and marvelous development" could be had in the Everglades. Land agents staked out thousands of geometric farm-and-home lots in the Everglades at a time when Americans were drifting away from the country's agrarian roots. Florida's subtropics offered a last shot at living the old America, which was located right next door to the new, the urbanizing coastline. But there could be no new without a "good back country," insisted the *Florida Grower*, a not-altogether-impartial publication. By "good," the agricultural magazine meant developed, vast, productive, and profitable. And before anything else, the backcountry had to be settled. The "bird dogging" Douglas witnessed in the city was only an imitation of the strategies of land-company admen, mythmakers all, who knew how to close a deal, one after another and another.[2]

Few did so better than the people who followed the orders of Richard J. Bolles. A smallish New Yorker, he was partial to wearing a big Stetson hat, conceivably intended to symbolize the size of the previous ventures in Colorado gold mines and Oregon farmland that made him rich. After completing his purchase of half a million acres of submerged Everglades territory from the state—under Governor Broward—in 1909, Bolles launched the Florida Fruit Lands Company and hired the former governor to help him sell the land for twenty-four dollars an acre, a

twenty-two-dollar profit. Bolles's other salesmen crisscrossed the country, proclaiming the Everglades a paradise soon to be regained and offering a one-thousand-dollar-back guarantee if a buyer's land failed to meet
the company's promises that it was the "richest land not under cultivation to-day" and no longer under water. The idea was to sell contracts for
twelve thousand farm sites in various parcel sizes, most of them ten acres.
Each buyer would also get a lot in the town of Progreso, the commercial,
social, and cultural hub that Bolles planned. The farm sites would then be
distributed at an auction run by the contract holders, all done in Jeffersonian fashion. Bolles scheduled his "Progreso Land Lottery" for March
1911 in Fort Lauderdale.[3]

In the days leading up to the auction, investors packed the city's four
hotels (sleeping on cots in the hallway of one), rented rooms in people's
houses, and set up tents on scrubland. Tom Watson, a former Populist
vice presidential candidate who extolled the righteousness of the independent farmer, came down from Georgia to witness the event. He detected something unsavory: "I was there when these bargain seekers (or
I might say suckers) began coming to Fort Lauderdale," he later wrote.
"Fort Lauderdale two years ago had nearly 150 inhabitants counting men,
women, children and dogs. The town had 5,000 inhabitants on March
20." Although those thousands had arrived "jubilant," as the *Miami Metropolis* put it, their mood quickly soured. First Bolles reneged on his plan
to let contract holders conduct the lottery; then it became clear that the
real estate was still under water and that nothing had been surveyed. The
Washington Times called the affair "one of the biggest land swindles in
history."[4]

Grumbling in Fort Lauderdale evolved into lawsuits after would-be
Florida landholders had returned on solemn journeys back north. The
twelve thousand contract holders had paid Bolles $1.4 million, half the
total purchase price for 180,000 acres of land. The sure-footed land merchant brought in Florida governor Park Trammel, who testified that
Bolles had given no assurances that the state had not given him. The
court ordered him to accept no additional payments but allowed him to
keep the money he had already received. Bolles then twice evaded federal

criminal charges, first after a federal commission determined that his business practices had been those of an "honest man" and second after he died, likely from a brain hemorrhage, while traveling on the Florida East Coast Railway.[5]

Bolles's deal making epitomized the dark miasma of an agricultural empire that would not go dry, but he never believed that he had done anything wrong. Others in his line of work agreed; indeed, his competitors copied him. They employed agents around the country. Fifty real estate firms in Chicago alone touted the agrarian life on the most lavishly fecund soil in the most divine climate in the country. Readers could open newspapers in virtually any city on virtually any day and find advertisements for Everglades land. Agencies in the Midwest commonly quoted Illinois native and former Nebraska congressman William Jennings Bryan trumpeting Everglades reclamation as "one of the greatest enterprises on record." In Washington, D.C., land companies rented commercial space with large show windows where they grew plump vegetables planted in lustrous black Everglades muck soil.[6]

At the time of Bolles's death, few would-be farmers had actually settled in the Everglades. Wet nature still claimed most of the real estate. Some who gave farming a try at times lashed boats instead of the usual mules or horses to their front porches. The Everglades real estate market went bust. One land salesman who had seen thousands of acres sold over the previous few years said, "Now even a ten-acre sale is as rare as a cold day in June." Most mortgagees stopped making payments, and individuals and land companies defaulted on their tax payments. The majority of the land that had passed from the state to private interests during the Broward era reverted back to the state by the time of World War I.[7]

But such developments all formed part of a wild roller-coaster ride, and Florida soon climbed up the track again. War-ravaged Europe's demand for food stimulated a dramatic increase in new acreage put under the plow. This stimulus was most evident out west, but Florida invited comparisons since neither region was readily suited for cultivation in its natural state. Well-known geographer Frank G. Carpenter conducted a study to locate the best fresh arable land, commercial farming possibilities, and investment opportunities all in one place. The "richest earth," he said, referring to both fertility and profit making, typically lay submerged. He ultimately pointed not to the West but to the Everglades. The *New York Times* called Florida in 1920 the "last great unclaimed wilderness." The frenetic real estate sales and development, the excess, and the haste in South Florida constituted nothing more than a struggle to catch up with the rest of the country, a place negotiating its cultural center and settling in with the rhythm of robust American life. The West had experienced repeated booms and busts; as in Florida, they had been connected to massive railroad expansion, an "orgy of national advertising," and a topsy-turvy national economy. A boom in California had crested by the time of the war and by the time Florida was showing signs of new momentum. Each new boom offered an inspiriting sign that America was still on the move.[8]

The failure to expand drainage despite nature's continued stubbornness against the will of first Hamilton Disston and then Broward would be nothing short of un-American. After all, the West continued to be tackled by the "irrigation ditch," as Frank Stoneman's newspaper put it, and Florida should move ahead "with the drain." By 1916, with less than 150 miles of canals cut, settlement sparse, inundation still threatening, and land sales turning soft, various campaigns, including one led by the Back to Broward League, were launched to revamp the state's beleaguered and battered reclamation project. Bolles's disastrous Progreso Land Lottery taught not that drainage should be abandoned but that it should be done better. By the fall, a proposal had begun circulating to invite the incoming legislature for an excursion to developed, safely dry lands. "To us who know what the Everglades are capable of doing for the whole state," opined the *Herald*, "there is not the slightest doubt that . . . the veriest doubting Thomas among them will be converted to the practicability of draining the great Everglades." And they were. In March, a delegation constituting a legislative majority arrived for a four-day Everglades excursion. With William Jennings Bryan as celebratory ambassador, the tour inspired positive proclamations from legislators from counties far and near: "Seeing the Everglades takes away every possible argument against its speedy reclamation"; "The state must drain these lands if every foot of state land has to be mortgaged or sold"; "We can reclaim this great prairie as easily as we reclaimed arid regions of the west"; "The Everglades is going to be the garden spot of the world." After returning to Tallahassee, the legislators issued $3.5 million in new drainage bonds.[9]

Dredges soon went to work again so plows could get back in action. The state was building more canals, supplemented by pumping stations, secondary canals, and lateral ditches to facilitate runoff from cropland to the main canals. By 1925, 435 miles of canals had been constructed, including sixteen locks and dams, six major canals, and numerous minor waterways, at a total cost of seventeen million dollars. Land peddlers had long been hard at work again, too. When the state undertook the construction of a levee along Lake Okeechobee's southern shore in 1921, agents had a new sales pitch. Flaunting levee-side towns such as Belle Glade, Morehaven, and Okeelanta, boosters lauded newly built schools, churches, stores, and post offices. Farms were making money, they said, and they were not lying. Growers were producing plump vegetables like those in the display windows in Washington. Sugarcane grew sweetly under the sun, and boats laden with produce scurried up and down the artificial waterways. These were the "rich, easy years," says the narrator in Douglas's "Bees in the Mango Bloom," "when the citrus fruit colored golden on the rich trees, when the early tomatoes in one good year brought a man a stack of money, and the avocados and the new, great, rosy mangos were just finding the Northern markets."[10]

Yet the roller-coaster eventually had to tumble downward again. After a couple of deceptively idyllic growing seasons, heavy, unending rains fell on the region in late 1921, and water rose into the planted fields. People shut down operations and left for the coastal cities or the North. *Everglades land* had become a loaded term. Whereas it had once evoked rich muck and easy wealth, it again meant swamp and bankruptcy. But as the Miami Chamber of Commerce saw it, the problem was image. The chamber and the *Herald* contended that "the word 'Everglades,' as applied to the great section south of Lake Okeechobee, is a handicap to the state and to the section. The world believes that it means that that territory is all swamp, sawgrass and dense tropical growth, a place inhabited by Indians, rattlesnakes and alligators. . . . A change of name would assist in making that change in the minds of the people. What would you suggest?" The *Herald* and Chamber of Commerce offered one hundred dollars to the person who submitted the best new name for the Everglades. Five thousand suggestions poured in, ranging from the utilitarian Farm Glades, the expressive Floriglades, and the deceptively nostalgic Broward Lands. The grand prize went to Tropical Glades, an interesting choice given that in its announcement of the contest, the *Herald* had declared "tropical" to be a debilitating reference, potentially inviting but also potentially uninviting. Yet perhaps there was unwitting logic in the choice since the Everglades could be both.[11]

They never made things simple; that was certain. Property taxes rose nearly 400 percent during the 1910s to pay for the state's continued attempts to make land dry. But it remained wet whenever persistent rains fell. And where the land did stay dry for an extended period, biochemical oxidation posed a new frustration. In 1919, C. V. Piper, an "agrostologist" with the U.S. Department of Agriculture, broke the news to investors. The Everglades muck soil was actually a fibrous peat of mostly vegetable matter. Its much-vaunted richness or fertility resulted when the much-hated water prevented oxygen-starved bacteria from efficaciously decomposing the plant matter. Once exposed to air, the bacteria had a feast, and the soil disappeared before the eyes of covetous farmers. State officials had known about the problem since the Broward years but kept it under wraps. Then a 1927 Everglades Drainage District report disclosed that nearly five feet of soil had been lost during the previous fifteen years. Everglades soil also burned as quickly and easily as tinder, "right down to the shining white sand," said one befuddled farmer. Wet or dry, nature's wealth seemed bound to elude the agrarian entrepreneur.[12]

Even the implacable Thomas Will, the people-first conservationist who had stormed Charles Elliot's Agriculture Department office, left Okeelanta, the dike-protected farm town he founded and loved, heading for

Fort Lauderdale when the constant flooding and the oxidation became too much to bear. But he did not want to give up. The boom was revving up in the cities, and it seemed possible to catch "some of the golden spray from the coast cloud-burst [and] start real Glades development." He planned to go back and challenged others to come with him, supporting himself in the interim by selling urban real estate. He blamed the flooding not on the state's enfeebled engineering practices but on corner-cutting developers who refused to dig secondary canals. Douglas knew Will, and his stubbornness must have given partial inspiration for her George Henry. After George discovers that he has bought four hundred acres of "sawgrass and water," Pomona Brown, a reformed realtor who has fallen for him, is dismayed that a man of his intelligence turned out to be such an easy mark for the bird dogs. Chiding her for being the foolish one, he is not discouraged: "I'm going to fix it for you. Drainage and dikes—that's the trick." It will take "good engineers. . . . No boys— men," from "New York"—that is, no Browards. "The real wealth isn't in selling land," he instructs. "It's in keeping land, developing it" to "grow strange tropic things, rare crops."[13]

George's declarations convey not only the vision of Thomas Will but that of Douglas, who believed in the agricultural salvation of the Everglades through the production of tropic staples. At one point she apparently tried to act on her vision in some minor way, and she too became a participant in the boom. She lacked the farmer's gritty physical and mental toughness, with which she endowed the hero in "Bees in the Mango Bloom," Penny Heston, who perseveres against freezing weather, anxious creditors, head-shaking doubters, and a self-absorbed sister, proving all of them wrong and making a success of mango growing. Knowing her limits, Douglas and a friend, Marion Manley, who was the state's second licensed female architect and a busy one, employing several draftsmen, bought eight acres of agricultural land in the Big Cypress Swamp for $880. They planned to rent it out for cultivation, but farmers showed little interest. When the boom went bust in late 1925, Manley's business faltered, and she could no longer make payments. The mortgage was too much for Douglas to carry alone, and they ultimately defaulted on the loan. The land reverted to the seller.[14]

As for Thomas Will in Fort Lauderdale, during the interim in which he sought in vain to regroup the "Lost Tribes" to return to the Everglades heartland, he sold urban real estate.

Boom was the word on everyone's tongue by the time the real estate mania shifted to the cities in the 1920s. It was no illusion either. "Ten minutes to half an hour in any spot in the State," insisted the *New York Times*, "would convince the most skeptical eyes and ears that something is taking place in Florida to which the history of developments, booms, inrushes, speculation, investments yields no parallel." "The air was electric with talk of money," wrote Douglas. "'Hundreds' became 'thousands.' 'Millions' became a common word." The wild rush of investors originated from all over and included recognizable names—Harvey Firestone, Thomas Edison, James Cash Penney, Babe Ruth, Lou Gehrig, and Henry Ford. For four hundred years, white people had mostly stayed away from Florida, and now they were invading with a haste and fury that made the "Klondike rush seem tame." The state's permanent population expanded by 59 percent during the decade. The *Indianapolis Times* complained that "thousands of persons are leaving . . . in search of something for nothing in the land of oranges and speculators."[15]

Most were headed to Miami, accommodated by expanded rail and passenger-ship service and new highways. When the city celebrated its fifteenth anniversary in 1911, Henry Flagler wired his congratulations to city leaders, adding a few prophetic words: "I trust that your community will expand to far greater proportions." It did. The Chamber of Commerce calculated that three hundred thousand people visited Miami each year at the beginning of the 1920s. Some stayed permanently, distending the population by one hundred thousand by the end of the decade. The city received from fifty to seventy-five Pullman cars a day, bringing thousands of passengers from places where the war economy and the stock market had been good to their bank accounts. As they disembarked and crowded the little depot, they dispensed with their winter coats while continuing conversations begun onboard about realtors, subdivisions, locations, architectural plans, and profit potential.[16]

The city's best advertisement was excited chatter among the masses. Realtors, city boosters, and developers did their part to help it along. The 1920s were the heyday of headline-producing promotional schemes, ideally suited for the American Riviera, as Miami called itself. Carl Fisher used a circus elephant named Rosie to grab media attention for Miami Beach, and he had himself photographed in golf knickers and sweater standing on Rosie's back teeing off a ball cradled in her trunk. One winter, the Miami Chamber of Commerce hung a sign at the corner of Fifth Avenue and Forty-second Street in New York City with the words, "It is June in Miami." In one ten-day period after a brutal storm, the railroads reported ferrying eleven thousand passengers to America's Riviera. The best promoters of the day may well have worked in professional sports, but sports also made good booster devices. Realtor J. S. Blain paid for a two-page spread in the *Miami Daily News* inviting customers to come out to meet famous heavyweight boxer Jack Dempsey and shake his iron-grip hand. His occasional opponent, the beefy-shouldered Gene Tunney, was the sometime sales manager for Hollywood Pines Estates. Another broker employed members of Major League Baseball's World Series champion Pittsburgh Pirates to sell houses and land. A celebrity of another sort, William Jennings Bryan caught land-speculation fever and the promotion bug. "God's sunshine," the Christian evangelical claimed, was responsible for Miami's success; people wanted to share in the brilliance, and Bryan would let them—for the right price. He felt no betrayal of faith when he accepted one hundred thousand dollars, half of it in land, to use his ambrosian voice to spread the gospel of real estate investment. He need not worry about sinning, for Miami offered absolution. It was the only city, he said, where a lie in the morning would be truth by the afternoon.[17]

When Frank Stoneman looked down at the streets through his arched picture windows at the *Herald,* he saw a carnival of activity. In the wintertime, when the tourists were in town, the sidewalks were as crowded with people as those in New York. Miami had a special feature all its own, however. Pressed into the bedlam were small brass bands hired by real estate firms to play songs from the pop charts or original ditties. In 1925, Miami had some two thousand real estate agencies—more than barbershops, churches, and even law firms. Their doors typically stayed open until ten o'clock at night, and their twenty-five thousand salesmen, said a Toledo man mesmerized by the phenomenon, "seem never to sleep." Brokers papered advertisements on billboards along Dixie Highway, nailed them to pine trees in the soon-to-be-developed environs, painted them on downtown buildings, and pasted them on sidewalk garbage cans. Douglas saw no greater offense to the landscape aesthetic than these eyesores, especially billboards. She once waxed in poetic disgust.

> I went up to Ft. Lauderdale, and oh, the air was sweet.
> But oh, my heart—and oh, my eyes, on all roads, altogether
> Were billboards and acalypha on each side of the street.[18]

Her father was no fan of the uglified landscape of advertisements. He refused to play the real estate market and served as the model for Penny Heston's father in "Bees in the Mango Bloom," who "would not even discuss real estate. The tales of big profits bored him." Yet profits were big at the *Herald*. Newspapers across the country swelled from the advertising boondoggle, and none more so than his. The man who built Coral Gables, "Miami's Master Suburb," of Mediterranean Revival architecture, George Merrick, spent five million dollars on newspaper advertising. One- and two-page spreads for a single realtor or developer were common, and on some days the *Herald* staff had to turn away several pages of advertising. The newspaper's aging press operated around the clock as circulation increased from eighty-two hundred in 1920 to thirty-three thousand five years later. Stoneman and *Herald* publisher Frank B. Shutts bought another secondhand press, set it up in a garage across the street, and waited for a new plant to be built, a four-story affair with several new presses. In the meantime, 1925 came, the peak year of the boom. The *Herald*, previously a twenty-four-page daily at best, thickened into the largest and heaviest newspaper in the world, and it set an all-time record by devoting

twelve million lines that year to advertising. The January 1 edition was a
bulky 196 pages, more than 60 percent of which was given to real estate
advertising. The Sunday paper usually came in at 150 pages. One woman
told the circulation department that she would gladly subscribe to the
Sunday news but worried that its weight would crush her.[19]

The ballyhoo had its intended results. Records were set not only in advertising but in sales. In the course of sixty-three days, realtors turned
more than $7.1 million in property in Miami Shores, promoted as Amer-
ica's Mediterranean. In one eight-hour marathon, Edward "Doc" Dammers, whose firm employed one hundred agents, found buyers for 525 lots
in his new Central Miami development. To move high volumes of product in brief periods of time, realtors employed auctions. The standard ca-
cophony of bands, celebrity guests, entertainment spectacles, free food
and refreshments, giveaways, and courtesy shuttles resembled a county
fair on a sunny day, with a kind of wheeling and dealing any carny would
envy. When the lots of the four-hundred-acre Arch Creek subdivision
went on the block, they sold out in three hours for the grand sum of $33
million.[20]

The boom was more than the sound and fury of the sales pitch. A columnist for the *London Daily Telegraph* said after a visit to Miami that
"behind frenzied speculation, behind even those ludicrous charabancs
crowded with shirt sleeved 'realtors' selling lots on time-payment to the
music of the saxophone, there is something happening in Florida that is
very significant and real." Every year until 1925, local bank deposits set
new records. Eight months into 1924, the value of Miami's building permits had exceeded by 75 percent that for the entire year before, more than
twice that of any other Florida city. No American city could match Miami's
per capita housing construction and public improvements; in 1925, construction began on nearly five hundred hotels and apartment buildings.
George Merrick contracted with a builder to construct one thousand
homes at a cost of $75 million, probably the largest contract of its kind to
date. By his estimate, he invested $100 million for a return of $150 million
in sales. He was one of twenty local residents who donated $7 million to
break ground for the boom-financed University of Miami. Mortgaging

much of the whirlwind was the Miami Bank and Trust Company, which summoned a lot of attention when it built a new ten-story building. Not to be outdone, the realty board put up a fifteen-story structure, a monument to what the industry was doing for the city. Going one floor higher, the *Miami News and Metropolis* raised the News Tower, a spectacular Mediterranean Revival rendition of the Giralda Tower in Seville, complete with a beacon light trained across Biscayne Bay. The Dade County government eventually won the skyscraper race with a twenty-two-story courthouse. From a distance, the collection of steel skeletons looked like either a bombed-out city or one going skyward.[21]

Miami was actually going upward and outward. Stoneman wrote, "Streets were laid out and paved in territory then unoccupied. Curbs and sidewalks were constructed and lines of electric light poles were set out in anticipation of coming residents." Builders went farther and farther south and west of the city and in 1925 platted nearly one thousand suburban developments. To those who witnessed the growth, it must have seemed hardly a fish story when one local told the *Saturday Evening Post*, "The soil is so fertile that if a shingle is planted in it before sunup, it will grow into a fully equipped bungalow by nightfall."[22]

Many who hoped to get rich in Florida cared little about building houses. Stoneman could see those people outside his window, too, for what stood out most in the clamor below were the round tops of straw boaters. The popular warm-weather hats were not simply the style of the time; they were part of the unofficial uniform of the so-called binder boys, or bird dogs, who also typically dressed in shirtsleeves, knickers, and two-tone shoes. Their attire exemplified Florida's laid-back style at the same time that their activity represented the hard-charging hustle of American business. They were an invention of the boom and of the nation's lethargic interest in Florida turned apoplectic. Their system of buying and selling land—usually unseen by the buyer, for the land was the least important part of the transaction—resembled the process for buying stocks on call. Binder boys generally acquired the option to purchase a piece of land, often by invading auctions, with 10 percent down and the balance due at the time the title abstract was prepared, up to sixty days later. In the meantime, they went out on the sidewalks, to the train station, on the streetcars, to the crowds that attended the daily concerts at the band shell, working to sell these acquired options at a profit. Locals generally found the binder boys annoying and unsightly. Stoneman called them "veritable locusts of Egypt who had come to devour the land." They were dealing not in land or houses but in profits or dreams thereof. Ephemeral though the binder boys were, lasting only as long as optimism and confidence could be sustained, they were more than an ugly or colorful side of the boom. Their activities constituted one reason why property values in Miami in the first half of the decade increased 1,000 percent.[23]

Yet the binder boys did not dominate real estate sales. Most Miami land buyers intended to reside on their property in sturdy, well-built houses, and most did not make their investments sight unseen. It is a wonder, then, that any boom occurred at all. Subdivision lots were typically parceled out of soggy ground or mangy-looking pineland. The average newcomer, wrote Helen Muir, who moved to Florida in the 1930s and married Carl Fisher's attorney, dismissed as godforsaken the "land so lovingly translated by Charles Torrey Simpson down to the last gaudy grasshopper and land crab." But a dispossessed landscape was no worry for a developer of merit. Nature could be fixed—that is, bulldozed. In the tradition of Flagler and Fisher, booster optimism led to the removal of mangroves, the planting and transplanting of ornamental trees, the digging of drainage canals, the making of new land from the bay bottom (a wholly unregulated activity), and the conversion of thriving citrus groves into subdivisions. Prospective buyers were generally shown a rendering of a subdivision with sidewalks, carpet grass (grown in the Everglades), new trees—palms, citrus, and shade—and houses with ample porch space, the aggregate fronted by a beckoning gateway bearing a name affecting a pastoral illusion where scrappy earth or swamp once (or still) existed. In "A Bird Dog in Hand," Douglas mocked the developers' conjurings with her own: "Valencia Villas," "Tropical Townsites," "Seminole Prairie," "Palmyra Plaza," "Mulgoba Manors," and "Vallombrosa Gardens, the Suburb Astounding." Behind her waggishness was inflamed discontent with the artificiality. Douglas complained in the *Herald*, "We will continue to dispense hatred, wrath, superiority and scorn every time we pass a real estate subdivision that advertises in this very paper that it is 'landscaped' when the work has begun by clearing off every pine."[24]

This is to say nothing of the boom's reach to environments that supplied the extracted natural resources that built Miami. Hundreds of train carloads of building supplies—lumber, steel, and rock—arrived daily at the height of the construction frenzy. So much came on cargo ships that local businessmen organized to convince Congress to appropriate funds to deepen the ship channel in Biscayne Bay, as others had done in Flagler's day. Even together, the railroads and ships could not deliver enough supplies to meet the demand. The Florida East Coast Railway imposed a weeklong embargo in August 1925. In December, thirty-one ships were drifting at anchor while sixty in port were being unloaded. Lacking a wharf large enough for the transfer of natural resources from other parts of the country, the city set aside $1.5 million to create more docking space by "filling 1,000 feet of submerged land."[25]

Trains and ships hauling megatons of cargo perpetuated the metropolitan growth in South Florida, but the original catalyst had been the state's New River Canal and the land companies promoting the Everglades. An undeniable economic and development link existed between the urban coast and the Everglades. But commercial interests were only a single truss in the urban-backcountry nexus; the other was the living aesthetic. The breezes blowing off the Gulf Stream in the Atlantic assured Miami pleasant temperatures year round; the rains that cooled summer afternoons and watered gardens drifted in from offshore and from over the Everglades; the stilted wading birds that trimmed the city landscape and the sky above emanated from habitats elsewhere; and the mangroves that lowered waterfront property values spawned sea life that fed people and provided livelihoods or sport. When unyielding boosters turned up nature with a bulldozer, whether in the Everglades or in the metropolis, they wiped out Miami's natural wealth. Douglas relentlessly worried that Miamians put the organic qualities of their metropolis at risk when they took for granted the sustainability of its aesthetic bonds with the

Everglades. She reminded readers of this connection on multiple occasions, as she did in her poem "Out of the Everglades," "reprinted by request" in the *Herald* in 1922:

> Out of the Everglades glitters the river.
> Out of the Everglades, down to the sea,
> Bringing the breath of their vastness forever,
> Down in the city beginning to be.
> Built of the Everglades, rooted and worthy,
> Shining and valiant and singing and free.

Frank Stoneman was not the only observer of the city's activity from the *Herald*'s arched windows. After returning from Europe, Douglas watched, too, and in her new role as assistant editor and column writer, she had undisguised opinions about that activity and much more.[26]

CHAPTER TWENTY

The Galley Slave

After bidding Europe farewell, Douglas arrived back in Miami in January 1920. It was a different place from the city she had left fifteen months earlier, and she was a different woman. She was wiser in the ways of the world, had sharper instincts about people and the institutions and the events of their creation, and had stronger opinions about society and politics. She also soon began to find her writer's voice and finally to sort out her personal relationships with men.

She had recently ended her engagement to be married, not to Kenneth Rotharmel but to her Red Cross colleague, Frederick. In Paris, their friendship had taken the form of an amatory relationship. He fell in love and proposed a number of times before she unhappily gave in. They left Europe together and sailed back to the States, where she was expected to meet his mother and daughter. When she did, reality sank in. She told Frederick that she would not be content living in Pennsylvania, hoping that the revelation would end things. He instead offered a concession that complicated matters: he and his daughter would move to Florida. Marjory needed to find some distance to reflect. She left to visit Carolyn Percy, who was living and teaching in Greenwich Village.[1]

Escaping Frederick's orbit and spending time with Percy brought only temporary relief. Douglas was expected in Taunton for Christmas, an emotion-laded holiday in Massachusetts. The absence of her sweet mother weighed especially heavy, and her once vigorous grandparents seemed to have aged beyond reason. Daniel and Florence were in their nineties, and Daniel would live only three more years. Little had changed otherwise. Her high school with its grand tower and observatory, the public library of quarried limestone, and the Harrison Street house with Daniel's fruit trees were as she remembered them. The acrimony and backbiting were also the same. The visit left little emotional space in which to reconcile her predicament with Frederick. Florence and Fanny pulled Frank Stoneman to the center of Marjory's male problems. They wanted Marjory to stay in Taunton. But she was tired of others trying to direct her life, and she left Taunton behind for the time being and Frederick forever.[2]

Unlike five years earlier, when she had first taken the train to Florida, she was excited about going to Miami. She now felt rooted to the region; she was going home. Rotharmel was back in Miami, too, after having spent six months in the Midwest. Two months after her return, friends hosted a party in their honor. Marjory and Kenneth were again an item. But Rotharmel was struggling with the memory of the war, which had taken the lives of more than half the men in his squadron. Posttraumatic stress, then known as shell shock and usually left untreated, shadowed him, leaving the world in peacetime unsettling and unmanageable. He drifted from one job to another. Much of the time he was sullen and distant, and he and Marjory began to see less and less of each other. When a friend offered a job in Evanston, Illinois, he decided to take it. Marjory was still in love but had come to realize that the two would never be together.[3]

One of her World War I stories, written years later, offers what seems a wishful alternative outcome. In "The Message to Hassan Beg," Polly Andrews, a fine but fragile young Red Cross worker, goes to Europe in search of the young lieutenant whom she loves. She braves travel on horseback across physically dangerous Albanian terrain to reach him in Elbasan. With a tender promise, the lieutenant expresses his gratitude to those who had helped her on the journey: "I'll take care of her, the best possible care—from now on, myself."[4]

Marjory was convinced that ending her relationship with Kenneth was for the best. She did not again want to abandon herself, her independence and her profession, to a man's love, an unshakable distraction from everything else in life. From *Mobilizing the Mid-Brain: The Technique for Utilizing Its Latent Power,* published in 1924 by Frederick Erastus Pierce, she copied in her diary a line that had personal relevance: "Marriage as a goal is passive, unless coincidentally with the idea of marriage a woman has constructively developed her personality in such a fashion as to be a powerful directing force in the life of the man she marries." For a period in the 1920s, she clearly sought to reconcile female autonomy with spousal partnership or tried to find peace in her unsuitability for marriage and love. Another line in her diary read, "All women combine two mutually incompatible positions, the position of perfect strength and the position of perfect weakness."[5] The love of a man was Douglas's perfect weakness. Though she outwardly opposed male dominance, she remained susceptible to it. Loving from a distance was safer and allowed a kind of rapture that suppressed rancor and bitterness. Holding on to love also protected her from the entanglements of loving another.[6]

Her abiding feelings for Kenneth, whom she never saw again after his move to Illinois, were apparently not unrequited. Within two years of leaving Miami, he married and fathered a daughter. He named her Marjory.[7]

Douglas's passion for writing soon enough overcame that for a partner. Although newspaper journalism was Douglas's least favorite kind of composition, it kept her finger on the pulse of a thriving city and a nation. She put most of her productive energy at the *Herald* into her daily column, which debuted in March. More than anything else at the newspaper, it set her creative imagination free. Her bosses wanted a daily dose of original poetry, occasional book reviews, and reflections on city beautification and improvement; everything was to be light, humorous, and apolitical. Douglas was determined to maintain creative control, and there was no stopping her from using the column to express an opinion when the mood struck. She was not necessarily treading new terrain for female journalists, but most opinion writers were men. Her perspective and broad interests ultimately made hers the *Herald*'s most original and diverse column. So too did her sense of humor, as displayed in her inaugural column, published on March 7, 1920:

> **Preface.**
>
> We have spent two days and parts of two nights, when the neighbor's baby and dog howled and woke us up, thinking up a good snappy lead for this here colyum. . . . A colyum conductor's life is not a happy one. But we said we would do a colyum and do a colyum we will, even if the Original Editor [Frank Stoneman] cans all our brightest and pet ideas.[8]

Calling her column "The Galley Proof," which she later shortened to "The Galley," she signed off each day with her initials, "MSD," recognizable to former readers of her society page. Although she suspected that women would constitute her primary audience, it soon became evident that men were among her most loyal readers. George Merrick told her that he turned to "The Galley" every morning with "lively anticipation." A local attorney praised her "philosophic deductions," though he was particularly taken with her writing, which he ranked "with the very best from any pen." Her poetry was especially popular. Douglas called it doggerel, and while it rarely sounded like a jingle and revealed the proper elements of rhythm, symbol, irony, illusion, and meaning, her verse could be effusive and burlesque. Operating on the expectation that a poem would lead off every column, an expectation not always met, she resorted to a sort of production-line poetry. On occasion she hit on the right formula, and other newspapers would reprint her work. Even the discriminating *Scribner's Magazine* found one poem good enough for acceptance.[9]

Douglas let her column go off in many directions. Often witty and playful, she was equally capable of being serious, poignant, and critical. Her thoughts on child welfare, managed growth, education, improved sanitation, and free speech became standard fare. "What we can't understand," she wrote, "is how the people who decide what is or is not immoral in a book ever escaped the awful consequences of reading them." She made cases against the foreign trade tariff, convict leasing, and Prohibition. "Now that the Anti-Saloon League has gained prohibition, someone ought to prohibit the Anti-Saloon League." Her bosses never succeeded in stopping her from talking about politics: "There are two sound arguments against politics. The first is that they keep so many men running who were obviously built to walk and the second is that they are politics." Or foreign affairs: "One good reason why they haven't succeeded in getting everything they want from Germany is probably because they haven't yet threatened her with prohibition." Or social equality: "Labor and capital, all our political problems, our social problems, the question of proper education and proper government, are hindered because we have not yet set ourselves to know how to live with our fellow men."[10]

The issue closest to her heart was women's rights. With the Nineteenth Amendment becoming law in January 1920, women would have their first opportunity to vote at the national level, and the veteran suffragist wanted to ensure that they were confident and understood the duties of full citizenship. Ignore the usual guile and "horrid speeches" of the long-winded candidates, she advised, and let reason and national welfare serve as guides. After the primary vote, she wondered what had become of the familial cataclysm antisuffragists had vigorously prophesied: "We have failed to note the disintegration of the home and the defeminizing of the Lady of Our House." Douglas in fact encouraged voting women to embrace positive feminine traits. The outsiders to the cult of manhood had the potential to reform stale, attenuated electoral politics with a broadened flow of values and fresh ideas: "The spheres of men and women, the course and direction of their thoughts, in spite of all the conversation about modernity, are not the same." Traditional political leaders offered a catalog of Douglas's discontent with male authority—unimaginative, bellicose, clannish, and self-interested.[11]

An urban Progressive who put her faith in reform guided by an enlightened middle class, she espoused the opinion that the men who built and ran modern Miami ignored the needs of others. Tucked beneath a cover of resort-city pleasantries, concealed by the magic in the Magic City, was Miami's unmentionable impoverished ugliness. Poverty was officially justified as a natural part of any city's existence, a sort of countersign of success, yet one the leadership preferred to keep under wraps. *Herald* publisher Frank Shutts, with whom Douglas never got along, often objected when her column exposed abject conditions, as she did in one of her more trenchant poems, "Wayside Children and Cities." It questioned the values of "shining cities" when many children lived in "grey slabbed shacks in piney places." She would not go along with Shutts's "willful blindness." In a scintillating follow-up, she wrote, "You can have the most beautiful city in the world as appearance goes, the streets may be clean and shining, the avenues broad and tree lined, the public buildings dignified, adequate and well kept, and all the physical facilities for the richer life of the people, like schools and concert halls and libraries and churches, but if you have a weak or inadequate health department, or a public opinion lax on the subject, all the splendors of your city will have no value."[12]

Her father had been among the blind, too, until he heard a Rotary Club speaker give a talk that reinforced Marjory's jeremiad against a neglectful city leadership. Feeling his Quaker principles challenged, he thought of having the *Herald* create a baby milk fund and asked Marjory to oversee it with a local physician. She agreed. She knew from her time in the Balkans of the wonders that milk could work when "dropped into those withered bared gums."[13]

The milk fund, which served thousands of children before it was replaced by New Deal programs, provided a domestic extension of Douglas's Red Cross work. She later regretted that her selflessness had been limited to white children. Blacks, 52 percent of whom had traversed the Caribbean waters from the Bahamas and West Indies, represented 30 percent of Miami's population, a figure that did not include the uncounted domestic migrants who arrived during the tourist and harvest seasons. The city's alabaster leadership remained firm, sometimes with the aid of violence, in keeping black residents confined to their designated neighborhoods. Most blacks found work in the service industry, catering to the wants and wishes of white locals and tourists: cooking and serving their meals, clipping their lawns and trimming their hedges, suiting their fancy with music and dance, and cleaning up their dirt and clutter and removing their waste. Some good jobs that blacks could find elsewhere in the South were next-to-impossible to get in the subtropical city run by northerners. Blacks had a long history in the building trades, for example, but during Miami's boom, skilled labor bore an inexorable white cast.[14]

But milk alone would not have solved the problems that made blacks so vulnerable to white supremacy. Douglas wrote after leaving the *Herald,* "There were no agencies for welfare work of any kind, unemployment, family guidance. Housing, medical and legal aid were almost totally lacking." Dengue fever, malaria, and hookworm were a constant threat. "Colored Town," with its sand streets, unpainted "raw board" buildings, overcrowding, and sanitation problem, was a forsaken community. The "whole flow of public opinion was willfully indifferent" to it, she remembered. The one issue that the newspaper absolutely forbade her discussing was the state of local race relations, a rule followed by most southern newspapers. Likely originating with Shutts, the policy was enforced by Stoneman. As a police court magistrate, Douglas's father did not hesitate to fine landlords who allowed their slum properties to fall into disrepair. Yet as *Herald* editor, he would not allow the newspaper to print an exposé of the trouble he saw in court. There was no reason to suggest to tourists that anything but harmony existed between Miami's social groups. Elected officials and club women, all of whom wanted a cleaner, more livable, and more efficiently run city, generally thought in terms of white priorities. "My feeble peckings and scoldings only irritated people," Douglas reflected twenty-five years later, when she finally succeeded in getting improvements in neglected areas.[15]

If writings in "The Galley" are any indication, the decibel level of her complaints about the treatment of blacks was lower than she remembered. This was true even with her loud and clear cry against convict leasing. The system was largely a by-product of the Reconstruction South, when the region's penal population turned increasingly black. Despite the Thirteenth Amendment's abrogation of slavery, prisoners were leased out to employers at minimal cost to work in coal mines, dig canals and

ditches, and lay railroad tracks—in short, to engage in any kind of drudgery in which workers could be driven hard and for which they received
minimal shelter, food, and medical attention. The system was the southern states' professed answer to reducing penal costs yet remained an un-
abashed token of the measure of black life in the region. With the highest
incarceration rate in the Deep South, Florida kept timber and turpentine camps of the longleaf pine belt well supplied with convicts. Beatings,
disease, and a mortality rate several times higher than the state's already
high mortality rate made the convict work camps veritable death camps.
Under public pressure, the legislature outlawed convict leasing at the state
level in 1919, but the system continued to operate out of county jails.[16]

Two years later, the *Herald* received a news wire report of the death of
twenty-two-year-old Martin Tabert at a North Florida work camp. Douglas read the notice and sat down and composed perhaps the most important verse of her career, "Martin Tabert of North Dakota."

O children, hark to his footsteps coming, for he's walking soft and
slow.

Youthful wanderlust had led Tabert on an adventurous trek across the
country to the system that took his life. In December 1921, just outside
Tallahassee, a Leon County deputy sheriff arrested Tabert for riding a
train without a ticket. After he was unable to pay a twenty-five-dollar
fine, Judge B. F. Willis sentenced Tabert to ninety days for vagrancy, a
common charge that often translated into an individual's peonage. Tabert
was put in the custody of Leon County sheriff J. R. Jones, who had a side
deal under which the Putnam Lumber Company paid him an average of
twenty-three dollars for every prisoner he supplied to its shackled labor
force.

They took him out to the convict camp, and he's walking Florida now.

Tabert went to the charge of the company's "whipping boss," Walter Higginbotham, who had a reputation for using his fists, feet, and rawhide
strap to force work out of prisoners. Tabert, a slight fellow, fell ill with
malaria fever, a condition diagnosed by the camp doctor. When his work

pace slowed, Higginbotham resorted to his usual brutal methods—in Tabert's case, one hundred morbid lashes.

They nailed his coffin boards together and he's walking Florida now.[17]

Tabert's death outraged the nation. The *Washington Post* called on Florida to "carry its work of reform to the length that good government demands and humanity urges"—in other words, to abolish convict leasing. Other southern states closely monitored events as a Florida grand jury looked into Tabert's death and a legislative investigative committee evaluated the continued viability of convict leasing. Well beyond the realm of public remorse, the system had previously claimed the lives of hundreds of black convicts. Even reformers regarded labor camps as wastelands of humanity. But Tabert was white and from a well-connected family. His skin and class drew attention the system had long warranted.[18]

Douglas herself had never before taken a stand against the convict-leasing system. The *Herald* ran her ballad twice, the second time in response to reader requests, and it was reprinted in the *Macon (Georgia) Telegraph* and the *Literary Digest* and read before the Florida Legislature. Although the state's star witness, a jailer, died en route to testify after being poisoned, the grand jury indicted Higginbotham for murder. At trial, the jury found him guilty, but the state supreme court overturned the conviction and ordered a new trial. It never occurred. In legislative debate over a proposal to abolish convict leasing, Senator N. J. Wicker of Sumter County, who six years earlier had supported mortgaging the state to drain the Everglades, said that abolishing convict leasing would "make it an honor to be a convict." If his colleagues agreed, they nonetheless outlawed the system, effective January 1, 1924. Other southern states soon followed.[19]

Martin Tabert. You can rest from your walking now.

Douglas meanwhile made a successful adjustment to single life. She failed to understand people who, as she said, were "so afraid of being alone." Solitude was the necessity of the writer, but apart from professional need,

Douglas derived personal comfort and security from it. Moments of "quiet calm"—sitting outside in the sun and a soft breeze, amid luminous colors, or inside in front of "an open fire with a book and a kitten purring"—brought into focus her place in the mortal crowd. She savored these moments, "very sure that children know them often, and wise people and the kind who never grow old, because there is no passing, exactly, of this great stream of being, but only a deeper and deeper gusto for it, and with it, and because of it. One is never alone, then, but only a cell in the tremendous [adventure] of life going somewhere, being something, being itself."[20]

Despite its personal comforts, being alone must have at times left her feeling self-conscious about her status as a single woman. She refused to allow herself or anyone else to see her as a spinster, as she saw Aunt Fanny. The spinster had died with the advent of the modern age. "Well, where is she today?" Douglas asked in "The Galley." "The ones who might have been old maids are out writing columns in newspapers or running farms or being lawyers or painting pictures or doing—well, frankly, doing a lot of awfully interesting things and having a great time at it."[21]

Despite putting a premium on time alone, she had a plethora of friends. Miami, as she said, was a "crossroads for much of the world." There were always new people to meet, different people with whom to socialize. Miami Beach had Carl Fisher's Roney Plaza, which featured the Roman Pool and a dance floor outside in the sea breeze and under the moonlight. Natalie Newell's bookstore provided a haven for people of an intellectual bent. A coterie of Douglas's friends often met on the beach to swim or at the river or a canal to fish. Douglas frequently ate dinners out, often with male companions to whom she made her platonic preferences clear. The elderly "Uncle" Barbour Lathrop was a wealthy Californian with aristocratic grace, eccentric charm, and a volcanic temper, who socialized with David Fairchild and his wife, Marian, the daughter of Alexander Graham Bell, and they too became Douglas's good friends. She also spent time with members of the Deering family, heirs to the International Harvester Company fortune, who had a remarkable collection of art and books as well as an Indian mound on their property. In particular, she enjoyed French Club outings with Marian Deering. Alice Harris founded the University of Miami's French department and spoke the language with Douglas; her husband, Franklin, a pianist, helped to establish the university and toured with musical comedy shows. And Mary Bryan always remained a friend.[22]

Another of Douglas's friends and mentors was Jessica Waterman Seymour. With a cultured intellect and a passel of civic-organization memberships, she was a keen prophet of regionalism, an ideology that was evolving into a full-fledged movement. In St. Paul, Minnesota, her primary residence, she was an active patron of the visual and dramatic arts, serving on several local and state boards. In college at the University of Arkansas and Harvard, she had studied art. Her interests began to center on the vernacular when she shifted into regional planning and worked with Scottish biologist and pioneer ecologist Patrick Geddes, whose disciples included Lewis Mumford. Soon after retiring with her husband, Robert, to their Everglades investment property, Jessica Seymour began moving adroitly across the state in the circles of women's clubs and men's luncheons, talking about regionalism.[23]

She was a regular reader of "The Galley" before meeting Douglas. Seymour may well have seen in the columnist a regionalist in spirit if not name and decided to recruit her into the movement and probably introduced Douglas to the *Journal of Social Forces,* a sociology publication founded by the maharishi of regionalism, Howard Odum of the University of North Carolina. After proclaiming his journal a "splendid organ of modern social thought," Douglas defined regionalism for readers: "It concerns itself with making the people of a locality more conscious of the unique possibilities of that locality. . . . It is developing local poets and painters and writers. It is teaching people, all over again, to enjoy the richness of their own boundaries . . . beginning with their own roots and their own soil." Geography, not fixed political lines, fostered a region's cultural and physical aesthetic in place of the demarcated "utilitarian drabness" of the usual urban setting. Just as it valued a localized culture, regionalism valued natural elements. Working with rather than against nature, however, did not necessarily translate into preservation. Pursuing harmony between culture and nature and the exceptional in both lay at the heart of regionalism. If that meant replacing a sweet gum with a tropical palm, then so be it, as long as the regional ideal was met. Douglas approved.[24]

Soon after they met, she and Seymour formed a mutually supporting partnership. The midwesterner made the rounds of club and association meetings and the New Englander proselytized through her column. Douglas usually kept her sights on home, trying time and again to cultivate Miami, a blossom sprouting in a scrubby patch on the edge of the rarified Everglades, into something beautiful and special. Miami had little sense of itself in a subtropical setting, she complained. It should be known worldwide "by the beauty of [the] out-of-doors" and a collection of showcase parks with tropical plantings found nowhere else in the country. In "Builders," composed for "The Galley" in 1920, she offered a poetic lament for Miami's slapdash approach to growth and its desultory future. After receiving enthusiastic responses, she ran the piece again when the city was poised to adopt a new charter. The poem opens with a rendition of Miami's birth—and a revealing assessment of male and female values:

> Mothered by beauty such as earth makes known
> Fathered by all the greed of men, hot, gritty
> Eager to mark this also his own.

It closes with a wish:

> Gardens and gracious lanes and new set trees
> Swept streets and shiny, careful subdivisions . . .
> A city rising to a mighty future
> Greater than all men's dreams that gave it rapture.

The great urban models she suggested for Miami were European cities— Rome, Florence, Athens, and her beloved Paris—whose beauty, emanating from the local culture and physical surroundings, she had admired while serving with the Red Cross.[25]

When local movers and shakers announced plans to establish a university, it was an exciting moment for Douglas. She not only was present at its founding but over the years befriended its presidents, helped develop its library, taught there from time to time, and ran its university press. In an article written for the third issue of Odum's journal, she apparently wanted the university's founders to know her thoughts. Miami's should be a "university of the future," she argued, a regional university. It "must be the product of its own place, and an interpreter of it." It should also enhance a national community. Here was a key idea in the regionalist ethos: diversity strengthened the national fabric. With a "welter" of people and regions, the United States had the opportunity to contribute not just one outstanding place of a single kind to greater civilization but many outstanding places of many kinds. If Miami's university sustained architects, developers, engineers, and landscape designers who incorporated the regionally unique and natural into their work, Miami, she reasoned, could grow into one of the grand cities of the world. New York was the country's only recognized world-class city at the time. As the arbiter of subtropical living, Miami should strive for that ranking, too.[26]

A city's real potential could be found in the "new geography," she told Miamians sometime before plans for a university were announced. Not altogether novel, "new" geography emerged in Europe in the late nineteenth century and found a small audience in American universities during Douglas's Wellesley days. As she explained, it deals "with what is called 'regional geography' as opposed to 'political geography.'"

> You cannot begin with economics or industries, you cannot begin with people, you cannot begin with groups or societies or systems of government or anything else, until you have first considered the earth on which the whole rests and which conditions everything. "The new geography" holds that geography and botany . . . is the fundamental study. . . . That is why we have harped so much upon our botany, upon our trees and shrubs and flowers, because they are the inevitable background from which we get, not just pleasure, but food, clothing and shelter. The geography and the botany of south Florida are the two most important studies for any development of south Florida.

The new geography framed her thoughts when she looked out the window of her father's boom-development house, rode her bicycle out to the city's environs, or took a sunset drive with a friend and saw regionally defining Caribbean pines wrenched and broken and heaped into excavation pyres. At first she did as others did and dismissed the trees as "dreary," "monotonous," "unstimulating," and "uninteresting." Then, around the time she met Seymour, she began defending their rightful place in the subtropical geography and apologizing for "our blindness, oh great pine." Many years later, after she formed her allegiance to Everglades protection, she added water and the ecological relationships of humans to the new geography equation and renamed it environmental geography.[27]

Regionalism and the new geography had turned her into a regional snob. She was forever at pains to counter the never-ending complaints, emanating from visitors and transplanted locals, about Florida's flat landscape and seasonless climate. Florida had mountains, went her stock response. One need only "wake up any morning and be able to look out as far as the eye will, across the lacy pinelands with their bigness, their fine open sweep, and then . . . ascend with a leap of genuine emotion to a range of shouting cloud mountains, whiter than whiteness." And off to the east was a vision of the "sea, lime green and jade and jasper and foaming, cool and roaring away from the horizon." Then there was the "weather, this inimitable, sparkling, snappy golden and peacock weather." Northerners "who say there is no difference in the seasons are simply talking through their hats. A tropic winter, the whole feeling of it, is as different from tropic summer, at its coolest, as chalk is from cheese."[28]

To preserve a regional distinction based on climate, land, water, and fauna, Douglas and Seymour faced a tremendous challenge in establishing a unity of attitudes among a wide assortment of people originating from other regions. Douglas hoped for cultural common ground: "I believe also, because we are not cramped here within walls, because we don't have to worry about cold and heat and coal and heavy clothing, about all the restrictions of northern life, but can live with the sun and the winds, that, if we choose to have it so, thought can be freer here than in many other places. We should develop into freer communities, freer personalities, living here."[29]

Achieving this free expression depended on having others manifest a regionalist ethos. An important place to begin was in architecture, the most overt expression of a region's values and a visual reminder of those values and how they were organized around the natural setting. Design that closed out South Florida's inviting climate especially irked Douglas. "We are so wedded to our northern ideas of roofs and walls and ceiling," she wrote. "All we need is a floor, a roof and some wire screening and we can forget about storm doors and sodding the cellar. All we need, really, is a change from a near frigid to a tropical attitude of mind."[30]

By the time "The Galley" columnist finished composing thoughts on such matters as regionalism, evening would have arrived. Douglas would proofread her draft, pass it by another editor, make changes, and then send it to the composing room, where the day's copy was converted into galleys. Colleagues at the *Herald* rarely saw her at the office before 9:30 in the morning, which she thought was an early hour. More than once she scoffed at the "yokel who first circulated the rumor that the efficient person gets up early." Many writers felt the muse in the morning, but she preferred to sleep late and dally before sitting down to serious work. As she eased into her workday, she checked news wires and read the *Herald* and other morning newspapers. These sources generated much of her column material—a quip, a poem, a comment. Other ideas came from conversations with friends, community events, or outside reading. She was a devotee of *The Freeman*, a superbly written modernist literary review with radical political ideas whose contributors included Lewis Mumford, Lincoln Steffens, Bertrand Russell, and Thorstein Veblen, who had been a classmate of her father at Carleton College. *The Freeman* was one of many recommendations she made to readers. She also discussed books she had recently read. One of her first columns highlighted *Plunderers,* by Henry Doyen, an adequately written novel jammed with corrupt politicians, New York tough guys, beautiful and intrepid women, all gathered around a fair depiction of Everglades land fraud.[31]

Filling up a page-long column never came easily to Douglas. Sometimes she sat at her office desk with her chair turned toward the window, staring out at the geometric shapes of rooftops or watching cloud mountains

and the occasional approaching airplane glide past. She worried that the
growing enthusiasm for real estate would send a building rising up to
block her view. The images in her sight came back to her a few years later
when she wrote "A Bird Dog in Hand." From the window of his Flagler
Street hotel, George Henry "gazed over tiled roofs, corrugated-iron aw-
nings, traffic bells, blaze of billboards upon roofs, Spanish stucco facades;
out to the sheer rectangular lift of occasional fourteen-story office buildings, gleaming blocks of white frosting or skeletons of black structural
armor a-whir with riveting; out to a tower in honey color and ivory, like
the fine blossom of an unruly garden; out to the superimposed perfect
bubble of the sky."[32]

Regionalists believed that cities should move outward, not upward, a
growth strategy that hinged on adopting inspired city planning and the
"scientific attitudes of mind," as the Herald columnist put it. What made
urban space appealing in the scrutinizing gaze of Seymour and Douglas
was suggestive of the national City Beautiful movement and the principles of the era's leading urban reformers and designers (including Jane
Addams, Alice Hamilton, and Lewis Mumford) and landscape architects
(Frederick Law Olmsted, John Nolen, and Beatrix Farrand, all of whom
Douglas mentioned in "The Galley" at one time or another). Club women
took the movement to the grassroots, calling for zoning ordinances,
public parks, tree planting, landscaped boulevards, waste recycling, and
managed growth. Add an open view of the bay, beaches, and ocean, and
these were among the most frequent topics of discussion in "The Galley":
"Man must have beauty. It is as much a necessity with him as food, shelter and clothing."[33]

Although city planning had been around since the previous century,
Florida municipalities had failed miserably to embrace it. Planning was
a necessity of the industrial city, opponents facilely insisted, not of a city
spared smokestacks in the already beautiful subtropics. But seeing beauty
so casually trampled, Douglas and Seymour thought that any city growing
as hastily as Miami and as crowded with diverse interests demanded an
orderly system. Everything in the urban machinery was interconnected,
like the great web of life itself, and only scientifically managed coordination between constituent parts could ensure a decent quality of life. Even

child welfare, Douglas maintained, "ought really to cover all sorts of topics, such as better water and sanitation and good roads, and clean streets
and public parks and playgrounds."[34]

Miami's city manager, F. H. Wharton, thought that the club women
were on to some good ideas. He evidently read "The Galley," too. Douglas
received an invitation to join seven other women to serve as his advisory
board for the "making of Miami a greater city," and at least temporarily,
things were looking up for urban Progressives. But whatever felicitous
hope they initially harbored for urban reform was expeditiously dashed
by gray-suited development interests that challenged nearly every reform-
ist recommendation as an impediment to growth and free enterprise—in
short, to the boom. Miami disappointed Douglas: "I could argue that land
should be set aside for parks, while land was cheap, I could talk about this
new thing, zoning, and the newer and hazier thing, city planning. . . . I
could write and write. No one paid attention."[35]

Douglas did not limit her attention to the urban environment. Around
this time, in the early 1920s, she began gathering with friends out beyond
the edge of town, where they would build a fire to make breakfast and
coffee, lounge about and talk, and fish in a canal. And she saw the Everglades for the first time. She drank in the sheer silence in the "immense
and illimitable" bigness of the land and sky, including the wading birds
of all shapes, sizes, and colors, feeding and in flight and in dazzling numbers. On one outing, she estimated that she saw forty thousand of them:
"There were rivers, streams, festoons of wings. It's a sight you'll never see
again." That bigness—the "immense and illimitable"—was also a logical
defining element in the regional geography. Increasingly artificial Miami
had thus far failed to find a way to make itself special, but the Everglades
were unique in the world. After one weekend outing, Douglas was moved
to celebrate them in a "Galley" poem that closed,

> I have seen as in a vision this thing about the Everglades,
> Meaning and grandeur,
> Beauty and terror and hugeness,
> But most the ultimate life thing,

Earth-thing,
Sea-thing,
Thing of eternal male and female,
True always to a law and a road
which is ours to follow.
True for Florida.
True for you and me who shall know Florida through them.
True for the ends of the earth to which these Everglades
Eternally shall send new and immense meanings of the minds and
    the living of you and me.[36]

Yet what she envisioned in all the immensity was the same thing that the cosmopolitan boosters envisioned. "The wealth of south Florida, but even more important, the meaning and significance of south Florida," she wrote in 1923, "lies in the black muck of the Everglades and the inevitable development of this country to be the great tropic agricultural center of the world." The Everglades were the rural component in what Odum's Chapel Hill colleague, Rupert Vance, called the "region of the organic complex."

Out of the Everglades, city undaunted,
Forum of river and trade winds and sea.
Go forth in sight of the earth that unvaunted,
Waits for your challenge to quicken and be.

Douglas saw the vaunted "lavish" tropical growths on cultivated fields in the Everglades as the ideal commercial complement to Miami's subtropical sunshine tourist industry. Short of advocating drainage, her vision of a productive hinterland was consistent with that of inveterate Everglades promoter Thomas Will. If, after her own thwarted eight-acre venture in agriculture with Marion Manley, Douglas could only relish the agrarian life vicariously though fictional characters such as Penny Heston in "Bees in the Mango Bloom," her enthusiasm for the commercial "improvement" of the Everglades remained vital. If she loathed the marketing practices of greedy land companies such as Will's, she appreciated the agrarian pastoral they painted: a wonderland of pineapples, mangoes, citrus, and other fruits not grown elsewhere in the United States.[37]

This was her version of ecology, the "proper fitting of plant to environment," even if humans needed to procure that plant from somewhere distant. She learned this approach from her friend, David Fairchild, who through his U.S. Department of Agriculture Office of Foreign Seed and Plant Introduction imported from across the globe bounties of commercially promising tropical plants—thirty-one thousand alone at the Kampong, the Coconut Grove residence he called a "home on the edge of the tropics." He ultimately found himself at odds with a "nativist" impulse (one that supported the exclusion of foreign plants) in his profession and in 1918 retired early. Douglas nevertheless talked glowingly in her column about his success in intensifying the region's tropical appearance: "We are discovering a thousand marvelous things, plants that are indigenous to India and China and Africa, fruits and vegetables, medicinal herbs and condiments now being imported to America at great expense, take to a life here in tropic south Florida as if they had never known anything else. We simply must begin with our geography, our regional geography." Her brand of regionalism in the end meant transforming geography and even disregarding the native at times as much as deferring to it.[38]

And at the moment she was lauding tropical growth, she was paying tribute to a regional improvement of the built environment type: the cross-Everglades construction of Tamiami Trail. This marvelous highway was to connect Tampa to Miami—the edge of the subtropics to the heart. The trail slowly began to take shape in the 1910s, when whites still approached crossing the Everglades with palpable trepidation. For more than a decade, road gangs dynamited through the Everglades' rock underbelly, followed by strange, mantis-like dredges that literally walked above the canal from which they dug blasted limestone spoil for the chalky white roadbed that paralleled the waterway. Here was the Ninth Wonder of the World, said Trail Blazers (boosters), who included Thomas Edison, Henry Ford, and the ubiquitous William Jennings Bryan.[39]

The trail was the regionalist's answer to a "sever[ed]" region. Douglas composed two odes that extolled the "vision" behind its construction

292]PART TWO

and the "greatness" that would result from it. By way of their physical obstruction, the Everglades had "spoken": they were "calling for the trail," and when that call was answered, East Florida would meet West and they would together become "one, hence, forever." Few at the time seemed to realize or care that the ribbon of limestone and asphalt would lie across the state like a dam across a river. After it was completed in 1928, the thirty-foot-wide causeway and its spoil canal caused an ecological disruption that was more precise than the state's haphazard reclamation project. The trail lowered the region's water level; exposed muck to the eroding open air; opened the area to logging, oil exploration, and plant poaching; and diminished natural habits. Charles Torrey Simpson, a farsighted and often lone thinker, said, "I feel that no more complete botch has been made of any project within the lifetime of any of my readers." As late as 1931, Douglas remained convinced of the blacktop's benefits to civilization and of the invincibility of the Everglades.

> Tourists roar across from Miami to Tampa in four hours and never once get their feet wet. The Everglades stretch out infinitely at each hand and many people never really see them. Yet there they are, the unconquerable, the inviolate, with only this tiny thread, like a faint rift in their silences and their strangeness.... [T]he Trail is there. But the Everglades, even as they were in the beginning, remain.[40]

By the time the 273-mile highway opened with a Miami–to–Everglades City motorcade snaking beneath a medieval arch of limestone rock and mortar, Douglas had quit the *Herald*. She wrote her last column on July 31, 1923, offering no suggestion that she would write no more. In the context of her life far ahead, the last passage was a fitting one, a hint of her evolving understanding of things: "Out beyond, out where the vast wideness of the Everglades opens on each side, you can find roads where the air is almost chilly at night, wet and chilly, with a tang in it and the fresh clean smell of acres of green growing things silent under the stars. Is it because the waters of the bay are shallow and so retain the warmth more, and that farther west they get the sea winds from higher up, or what? We have always been curious."[41]

Douglas's maternal grandmother,
Florence Trefethen, who raised
Douglas. Courtesy Florida State
Archives

Douglas's paternal grandparents, Mark Davis
Stoneman and Aletha White Stoneman.
Courtesy Florida State Archives

Douglas's mother,
Lillian Trefethen Stoneman.
Courtesy Florida State Archives

Marjory Stoneman at about eighteen months and 24.5 pounds. Courtesy Florida State Archives

Trefethen and Stoneman families, at the Trefethen house in Taunton, Massachusetts, 1893.
Front row, left to right: Aletha Stoneman; cousins Forrest Rundell Jr., Mabel Hopson, and Pauline Hopson; Aunt Fanny Trefethen (sitting behind cousins); Florence Trefethen; and Lillian Trefethen Stoneman (on porch rail). Back row: Uncle Forrest Rundell; Aunt Katie Stoneman Rundell; Aunt Alice Hopson; Uncle George Hopson; Daniel Trefethen; Frank Stoneman; and Marjory Stoneman. Courtesy Florida State Archives

Governor Napoleon Bonaparte Broward.
Courtesy Florida State Archives

Marjory Stoneman,
Wellesley College, 1912.

Legenda Board

MARJORY STONEMAN, 1912	*Editor-in-Chief*
MADELEINE H. LANE, 1912	*Associate Editor*
FRANCES EGAN, 1912	*Business Manager*
MARGARET THOM, 1913	*Assistant Business Manager*
MILDRED B. WASHBURN, 1912	
GRACE M. BOYNTON, 1912	*Literary Editors*
NORAH V. FOOTE, 1912	
LYDIA C. BROWN, 1912	
GRACE F. SLACK, 1912	*Art Editor-in-Chief*
MARGERY MACKILLOP, 1912	*Assistant Art Editor*

Marjory Stoneman and the board of the Wellesley College senior yearbook, Legenda, *1912.*
Courtesy Florida State Archives

Miami Herald *staff, 1914. Managing Editor Frank Stoneman is standing to the right of the left column. Publisher Frank B. Shutts appears to be standing in the middle with his arms crossed. Courtesy Florida State Archives*

Frank Stoneman.
Courtesy Florida State Archives

East Florida Street, Miami, 1912, much as Douglas would have seen it when she arrived in Miami for the first time. Courtesy Florida State Archives

Seminoles in Miami Palm Festival Parade on Flagler Street, 1921. Courtesy Florida State Archives

William Bryan Jennings, Bryan Jennings, and May Mann Jennings
at Niagara Falls, 1901. Courtesy Florida State Archives

Marjory Stoneman
Douglas, ca. 1920.
Courtesy University of
Miami Libraries

Kenneth Rotharmel in his
French lieutenant's uniform,
ca. 1918. Courtesy University of
Miami Libraries

Marjory Stoneman Douglas outside her Coconut Grove house, late 1920s.
Courtesy Florida State Archives

The front of Douglas's house, built in 1926, early 1950s. To the right is the corner of Franklin and Alice Harris's house, later the home of Carolyn Cole. Courtesy University of Miami Library

The back of Douglas's house. The French doors open into her living room/workshop. Her bedroom is on the far left. Courtesy University of Miami Library

National Park delegation touring the Everglades, 1930. Ernest Coe, the "Papa" of Everglades National Park, is the man in the bowtie. Courtesy Florida State Archives

The Goodyear blimp that carried the national park delegation above the Everglades, 1930. Courtesy University of Miami Libraries

The Shark River in the Everglades. Courtesy Florida State Archives

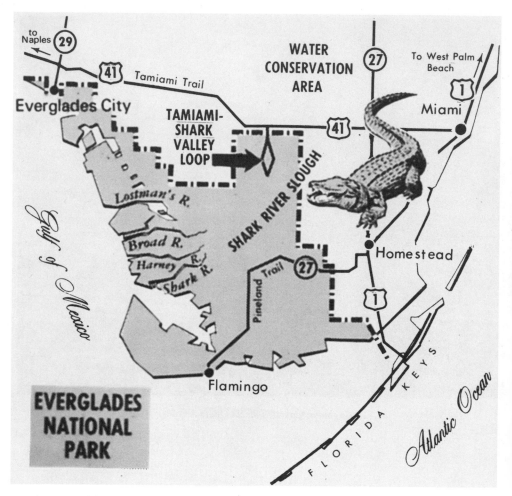

A map of the original Everglades National Park, dedicated in 1947.
Courtesy Florida State Archives

Commemorative Everglades National Park Stamp issued in 1947 and used on mailings to promote Marjory Stoneman Douglas's The Everglades: River of Grass. *Courtesy Florida State Archives*

Seminole Indians presenting President Harry S. Truman with a traditional handwoven shirt at the 1947 dedication of the national park. Courtesy Florida State Archives

Marjory Stoneman Douglas at a signing of The Everglades: River of Grass *at Burdine's department store in Miami, 1947. Courtesy Florida State Archives*

Marjory Stoneman Douglas standing in front of a book wagon, 1940s. Courtesy Florida State Archives

South Florida friends, 1955. Left to right: Henry Field, a respected anthropologist who published one of Marjory Stoneman Douglas's books and who opened his house to secret meetings between government scientists and activists during the Everglades jetport struggle; Philip Wylie, a writer and activist who in the 1950s exposed to the nation that Miami was dumping its raw sewage into Biscayne Bay; Douglas; Helen Muir, writer and longtime friend of Douglas; and Charles Baker, cookbook author. Copyright Ray Fisher

Back patio of Marjory Stoneman Douglas's house, late 1950s. Left to right: Marion Manley, one of Florida's first licensed female architects; Douglas's uncle, Charles Trefethen; and Douglas. Courtesy Florida State Archives

Douglas at her desk at home with one of her cats, probably Jimmy, 1975.
Copyright Ray Fisher

Joe Browder, Audubon's southeastern representative, in the Everglades, 1968.
Photo by Patricia Caulfield, courtesy Joe Browder

Young activists who worked with Joe Browder to stop the jetport in the
Everglades, 1973. Left to right: December Duke, Lili Krech, and Mary Beth
Norton. Courtesy Lili Krech Neale

Left to right: Marjorie Carr, who led the fight against the Cross-Florida Barge Canal; Art Marshall, a scientist who worked with Marjory Stoneman Douglas on many projects; and Douglas, early 1970s. Courtesy Florida State Archives

Marjory Stoneman Douglas in Clewiston, Florida, trying to help farm workers, with Annie Mitchell, head of the local Harlem Tenants Association, 1970. Courtesy University of Miami Libraries

Marjory Stoneman Douglas in Argentina at the childhood estancia of
William Henry Hudson, 1970. Courtesy University of Miami Libraries

Marjory Stoneman Douglas at the dedication of the state Department of
Natural Resources' Marjory Stoneman Douglas Building, 1981. Governor Bob Graham
is directly behind her. Courtesy Florida State Archives

Governor Bob Graham presenting Marjory Stoneman Douglas with the
Florida cabinet's resolution honoring her, 1985. Courtesy Florida State Archives

Marjory Stoneman Douglas, late 1970s.
Courtesy Florida State Archives

Marjory Stoneman Douglas at the Pahayokee Trail, her favorite place in Everglades National Park, 1983. Copyright Ray Fisher

Marjory Stoneman Douglas, 1987. Photo by John Gillan, courtesy University of Miami Libraries

Left to right: Diana Chapman Walsh, president of Wellesley College; Marjory Stoneman Douglas; and fellow Wellesley alumna and First Lady Hillary Rodham Clinton at the White House during the ceremony at which Douglas received the Presidential Medal of Freedom, 1993. Courtesy Kathy Gaubatz

President Bill Clinton saying good-bye to Marjory Stoneman Douglas after her stay at the White House, 1993. Official White House photograph, courtesy Kathy Gaubatz

Courtesy Tribune Media Services

Hurricanes

Douglas liked intense weather, the whirring and buffeting of a New England snow squall, the reverberation and darkened heaviness of a subtropical thunderstorm. These poetic natural dramas had an aesthetic in their motion, sound, and color that could move the senses in much the same way as a great work of art. Douglas found a spiritual quality in great natural forces that withered the cosmic relevance of human action. They reminded one that nature remained in control. Writing a book about the history of hurricanes, then, as she did in 1958, appealed to her on multiple levels. Living in the heart of hurricane country also lent a certain logic to such a project. She knew people who had experienced the worst of the great storms. She had been in some of them herself, and she knew and wrote about the man, Fred W. Gray, who made his living studying them and trying to help others deal with them. During their shared time in South Florida in the 1920s, the region was hit by two hurricanes pivotal in U.S. history.

Chief of the Miami office of the U.S. Weather Bureau, Gray was a reserved man who approached his work like a pensive scholar. His slight constitution was appropriate to the small operation he ran, with a single assistant, at the Federal Building downtown. A bureau career man, he had been in Miami since the establishment of the weather station in 1911, sometime before his neatly trimmed beard turned gray. As the city boomed, he watched buildings rise up to tower over his modest station and distort the accuracy of his rooftop anemometers. They were among his few forecasting tools, which included maps, charts, barometers, and telegraphs. He also followed professional hunches, but they could be devastatingly wrong.[1]

Correct hunches and accurate science were most important during the July to November hurricane season; September had historically been the most dangerous month for Florida. Years after his tenure there ended, Gray completed a study showing that Miami had a one-in-twenty chance in a given year of being the target of hurricane-force winds; only Key West and Pensacola were at higher risk.[2]

Florida's number came up in 1926. On the morning of September 14, the Weather Bureau in Washington, D.C., received a radio transmission from a ship reporting a major storm trolling through the Atlantic two hundred miles north of St. Kitts in the British West Indies. Like most Atlantic storms at that time of year, this one had gathered its winds around the Cape Verde Islands, northwest of Senegal. It then moved westward at a speedy nineteen miles per hour. By the time it crossed the ocean and reached the Turks Islands, it had ratcheted its course to the northwest, with winds reportedly blowing up to 150 miles per hour. On Friday, September 17, it bore down on the Bahamas.[3]

Gray was tracking the storm through telegraphs he picked up from the Western Union depot a few blocks' walk from his office. After receiving the messages, he scrupulously posted weather advisories with the local press. Still, Friday's *Miami Herald* ran a front-page story that said Florida was safe from the storm's path. Indeed, a soft breeze lingered beneath azure skies outside Gray's office. That morning, Miamians had been treated to a spectacular sunrise projecting a bloodred and orange metallic light, a display of beauty that, unknown to most observers, almost certainly signaled a hurricane's approach.[4]

Later on Friday, the thinking in Washington about danger to the mainland had begun to change. The Weather Bureau directed its stations in Southeast Florida to hoist storm-warning flags and to take precautions for the arrival of "destructive winds" by Saturday morning. The word *hurricane* was not mentioned. Gray alerted local officials and the newspapers and then raised above his office and the municipal dock a single square flag with a black square center on a red background, the bureau's silent tocsin. That afternoon, the *Miami Daily News* passed along the bureau's information to its readers, also without using the word *hurricane*.[5]

Hurricanes were precisely the reason for Gray's presence in Miami. His was one of scores of reporting stations the bureau planted in the Caribbean and on the continent, with more than fifty in Florida alone. The personnel in those stations were the bureau's eyes for foul weather. Gray's reports and warnings to the Miami community were only as good as his communication with Washington and its communication with its reporting network. On September 17, both Washington and Gray waited for any scrap of information transmitted from Nassau. A 1:00 P.M. report noted that the barometric pressure in Nassau was continuing to fall and that winds had rushed up to a steady fifty miles per hour. That was the last transmission from the Bahamas for days. Tracking the hurricane was now left mostly to guesswork; there was little else Gray or anyone else could do.[6]

When Miami's setting sun slipped below the horizon, conditions remained clear and calm. By 8:00 P.M., a quilt of clouds had eclipsed the night's stars, and the wind picked up and rain drummed hard against the windows. Gray, his assistant, and a reporter on hand from the *Daily News* fielded between two and three telephone calls a minute and answered questions with what little was known about the hurricane's course. The *Herald*, anxious to send its Saturday morning edition to press, asked Gray for a conclusive determination of the hurricane's direction, but he had learned nothing new since the early afternoon. *Herald* editors decided to be optimistic.[7]

That was before 10:00 P.M., when the needle of Gray's barograph flicked downward. Negotiating buffeting winds to reach the Western Union office, Gray wired his barometric findings to Washington. It was becoming increasingly evident that during Nassau's nine hours of silence, the storm had tacked toward Miami. At 11:00, Washington issued hurricane

warnings for Southeast Florida. Sixteen minutes later, Gray received instructions to hoist the second red and black flag. Hurricane. Outside, as
he worked the lanyards and the rain beat hard against his face, the wind
lifted him off his feet and dropped him on his backside.[8]

Once inside, he recorded the deteriorating conditions in his log. By
2:30 A.M., the hurricane's forward winds were squarely on the city and
reaching 60 miles per hour. But the storm had hardly begun to blow.
A half hour later, phone service went dead. At 3:42, the top of the rain
gauge blew off, and the wind velocity accelerated to 115 miles per hour,
bringing the rain in driving sheets and tearing at everything standing. At
4:00, electric power was lost. The building went dark. Gray borrowed a
flashlight from the *Daily News* reporter to make readings and record his
entries. At 6:15, the wind slowed and the howling stopped. The eye of the
storm was passing over Miami. Gray's next observation reflected a city
of transplanted northerners who had no awareness of the peculiarities of
hurricanes.[9]

People began to stream outside to examine the wreckage, and automobiles threaded through the gathering crowd. Gray was horrified. Unlike
most others, he knew that the lull would last only a few minutes and that
stronger winds would follow with the back side of the hurricane. Running
through the streets, he pleaded with people to return to shelter. The worst
was yet to come, he shouted. He was like a madman trying to coax the
condemned back from purgatory, but they thought that they had escaped
to paradise and that he was talking about going on to hell. People fell to
their knees and kissed the ground in thanks for their lives.[10]

Not even Gray realized just how bad the storm would become. At 6:45,
two minutes before the wind shifted from the south and returned to gale-
force speeds, Gray's mercurial barometer plummeted to 27.61 inches,
and the needle of the barograph fell below the recording sheet to 27.54.
The final corrected reading reduced to sea level was 27.61 inches, one of
the lowest ever recorded in the United States. At 7:30, an anemometer
on the roof of the hospital clocked the winds at 128 miles per hour; at 8:12,
the wind snapped the instrument loose. Later estimates had gusts reaching a blistering 175 miles an hour.[11]

Except for buildings, all that stood vertical leaned in different directions—light posts, power poles, street signs, trees. Buildings either stood fast as wet, hulking monuments to rigid construction or surrendered themselves to the pounding elements. Palm fronds, tree branches, trash cans, shingles, boards, bricks, and debris of all shapes and sizes sailed in the gray, rain-washed rush of air. For those who were stranded outside after the lull, death was as likely to come as a result of hurtling projectiles as by drowning in the rain or sea.

The wind was not the worst of it. The back of the hurricane lifted the gray ocean out of its natural recess. Miami Beach disappeared under water. If Gray had looked out from the top of his building to the east, he would have seen the Atlantic Ocean rather than Biscayne Bay. A surge of nearly twelve feet pushed water three blocks into the city. Some three hundred vessels ultimately washed ashore or sank. A tidal wave, or bore, fifteen feet high charged up the Miami River, where fifty craft had sought safe harbor, turning them into a "mass of wreckage," as Gray later noted. Water washed houses off their foundations and rose three to five feet in the first floors of secure structures. The Roman Pool at Carl Fisher's Roney Plaza on Miami Beach burst open and poured half a million gallons of water into the rising ocean. Many people who had tried to drive across the causeway to the mainland during the lull were washed away or drowned inside their cars. In Coconut Grove, the storm surge rising fourteen to fifteen feet was, Gray estimated, the "greatest ever caused by a storm on the coast of the United States." Douglas was having a house built there at the time, a half mile from the bay.[12]

At half past noon, the wind finally slackened and settled. After being surprised by the back side of the storm, some people were unsure of what the weather would do next. No one could imagine the cold mass of wreckage awaiting outside. Exhausted, they left their shelters, passing from one nightmare to another. Some wondered if they should be happy to be alive.

Frank Stoneman had some sense of what to expect. He had ridden out the 1906 hurricane, previously Miami's worst, to which his newspaper had attributed more than four hundred dead. But that was then. Miami had much more to lose now. He, Lillias, and Marjory had fortuitously been out of town during the storm, he and Lillias in Jacksonville and Marjory in Taunton. After reading about the hurricane in newspapers, Marjory was left somewhat incredulous. She telephoned her father's house, and he answered. His house had escaped damage, he said. That was encouraging news, and she asked if he would check on her house. The *Herald*'s Saturday edition that reported Miami would avoid a major brush with the hurricane had been put to bed in his absence. Going to press before gathering all your facts, as Frank had always told Marjory, can come back to bite you. Stoneman's drive out to Coconut Grove brought into sharp relief how big the bite could be. Anything remaining upright seemed an oddity on an obliterated landscape. Denuded palm trees looked like giant flamed-out matchsticks; oaks and pines were cleanly picked skeletons. Roofs had been torn off buildings; some buildings had been torn off their foundations and deposited in the middle of the road; other buildings had been crushed and splintered into great piles of wood or concrete. Stoneman maneuvered around downed trees and power lines, high-and-dry boats keeled over on their sides, automobiles collapsed from the weight of the storm's water and washing sand. In clothes dried stiff and wrinkled, bewildered people combed through the wreckage along the roadside looking for salvageable belongings, lost pets, and missing loved ones. Most were without electricity, telephone service, food, and potable water.[13]

Driving through downtown Miami, Stoneman encountered devastation in a concentrated mass. The waterfront could have been mistaken for a landfill of discarded construction material. Watercraft were everywhere. A five-thousand-ton freighter and three yachts lay motionless in Royal Palm Park. Its band shell remained in one piece, but not much else in the city did. Sides had been shaved off of some of the taller buildings, which looked like giant cutaways for an architectural convention. Sand was everywhere, inside everything and across roads. So much, so daunting were the heaps of sand and rubble and the tangled wires and crumpled metal that reconstruction seemed an impossibility. Some of the country's newspapers doubted that the Magic City could ever rebuild itself.[14]

The scene was very much the same in Coconut Grove. The main road through town, a boulevard that the late president Warren G. Harding had pronounced the most beautiful in the country, was unrecognizable. A six-ton barge had washed ashore and leveled five bungalows. When Stoneman turned onto Stewart Avenue and drove up to his daughter's house, however, he could breathe easy. With missing roof shingles and broken windowpanes, it looked like nothing worse than a vandalized building. It was standing. Watermarks stained the exterior walls, and seaweed and other debris had seeped inside. But Douglas's contractor had laid only the subfloor, and she had not yet moved in furniture.[15]

She was fortunate. From Fort Lauderdale to Miami, 9,100 houses had been damaged and 4,725 others destroyed. Miami, which had enjoyed sixty million dollars in new construction that year, absorbed the brunt of the storm and suffered approximately seventy-six million dollars in private property damage—64 percent of the city's assessed real estate value. Dade County reported 150 dead and 6,000 people in need of medical attention. Twenty-five thousand in the Miami area were left homeless.[16]

But the damage spread further afield. The hurricane hurled its force west into the Everglades. The preceding July, a storm had swept into the region, swelling the waters of Lake Okeechobee and breaching the dike— completed the previous year and measuring eighteen feet high and forty feet wide—at the town of Belle Glade and leaving the dozen settlements ringing the big lake vulnerable to floodwaters. Despite that danger, when the September storm came through, people were asleep in their beds and caught "like rats in a trap," as one local put it. The area was already saturated from heavy summer rains, and the dike again failed to hold. It had been built to protect crops and not human lives, Florida congressman Herbert Drane later admitted. Although the canals had brought the level of the lake down five feet, oxidation had at the same time lowered the reclaimed land, and, in accordance with Governor Napoleon Bonaparte Broward's familiar mantra, water ran downhill. As it spilled across fields and streets and towns, official totals recorded 150 people killed. But the region had a sizable migrant-worker population, which meant the real number was probably two or three times higher.[17]

In the hurricane's immediate aftermath, the nation's newspapers turned their attention on Florida. Readers gawked at the stories of "Florida horrors"—climbing death and injury counts and the danger of a typhus epidemic from the commingling of storm water and wastewater. A special relief train rushed in record time from Chicago to Miami, and the Red Cross issued appeals with an urgency resembling that of wartime; ultimately, in monetary terms, the damages exceeded those of the deadly storm that had hit Galveston, Texas, in 1900. A resort city loathed such stories. After two subsequent blows, South Florida's congressman, J. Mark Wilcox, conceded that a hurricane "is not a good thing to talk about . . . because it is not good advertising." After San Francisco's 1906 earthquake and fire, local officials had downplayed the event for fear of scaring off potential new residents and investors. For the same reason, state boosters in the wake of a 1925 Santa Barbara earthquake turned away disaster relief funds originating outside California. The September storm that struck the other side of the continent a year later came to be known as the Great Miami Hurricane, an unfair designation in the eyes of local businessmen. Miami was only one point of contact, the victim among many hapless others along the storm's two-thousand-mile journey.[18]

Miami officials tried to counter press reports of a crippled, ailing, and perhaps terminal city. While Governor John Martin declined aid offered by other states, Miami mayor Edward Romf claimed a month after the storm that his city was whole again, even though parts of the trolley line remained a mass of twisted steel and the Miami Beach causeway resembled a string of archipelagoes rather than a roadway. The winter vegetable crop had been wiped out, and citrus growers were prepared for an equally barren season. Even the *Herald* purposely adjusted damage estimates downward. The tourist season began in November, and, wanting to preserve the economy's mainstay, boosters said that Miami would be ready.[19]

Miamians had more than the tourist season on their mind, however. There was also the boom to think about. The market had begun softening earlier in the year. Bank deposits fell off in Georgia and Florida, and mortgage-lending concerns collapsed. By summer, a genuine banking crisis had befallen Florida. Three Miami banks closed, and in July delinquent tax sales were scheduled for fifteen thousand parcels of land. Also in July, at the annual meeting of the Florida Association of Real Estate Boards, industry personnel engaged in a rare bit of self-scrutiny by criticizing their own overindulgence. Unwilling to let the boom go, they embraced their "Decalogue of Florida," which counseled, "Thou shalt prepare thyself for the happy habitation of man; thou shalt drain thy swamps, bridge thy rivers and build thee highways to the uttermost parts of thy hinterland." Then came the hurricanes.[20]

The September storm took on the popular aura of the tempest that unraveled the boom. Apocalyptic nature conveniently let humans and their excesses—high-stakes real estate speculation, rapid development, inflated property values, creative financing, and overeager lending institutions—off the hook in explaining the bust. The *New York Times* quoted one observer who said that the storm was "independent of human conduct." Some homeowners and a few local officials attributed the wreckage to shoddiness in hurried boom-time construction, but the financial and the physical ruin otherwise was perceived as having Nature's fingerprints all over it. The more prosperous Americans grew and the more their built environment flourished, the more people were willing to think of themselves as innocent victims of that goddess, Nature, and her wicked temper. There was nothing coincidental in the Weather Bureau's eventual practice, begun in 1949, of giving female names to hurricanes, furious and unpredictable phenomena that they were. It was all part of the myth. Even as scientific knowledge expanded and even after the bureau adopted a gender-neutral policy in hurricane naming, the myth of natural disasters remained potent, even into the twenty-first century: wrote *Miami Herald* journalist Edna Buchanan in 2004, "No more deadly force exists than the wrath of wind and water; no killer as merciless as Mother Nature on a homicidal spree."[21]

The more providential-minded saw Nature's wrath as the Lord's wrath. Rending the air at his Calvary Baptist Church in New York City, the

Reverend John Roach Straton told his congregation two Sundays after the 1926 hurricane, "Beautiful Miami did depart from God's way! She turned after the worship of Mammon. . . . The Sunday sermons were forgotten in the mad rush for Gold. But God did not forget." Austin Peay, Tennessee's Bible-quoting governor, publicly proclaimed the hurricane divine reckoning for Miami's sins. The comment annoyed Stoneman, and when the governor's private residence was washed away in a flood a few weeks later, the editor enjoyed the irony, writing that Peay now "had nothing to say about punishment for sin."[22]

Douglas the agnostic did not buy into the religious argument, but she also was not one to blame Miami's wreckage solely on Mother Nature. Long before Flagler drove his railroad on to Fort Dallas, people had known that hurricanes periodically swept through South Florida and that hundred-mile-an-hour winds could wreak enormous destruction. Like earthquakes and floods, hurricanes made convenient scapegoats for calamities of human making. People consistently put themselves in harm's way. But even as they cast blame, people seemed so distracted by the promises of modern society—that civilization had the technological capacity to satisfy virtually every desire—they were serenely oblivious to the impact that even well-behaved nature could have on their lives. Many years after the 1926 storm, when Douglas's publisher, Stan Rinehart, mentioned in passing the idea of writing about hurricanes, she saw an opportunity to reverse this disconnect. "It is time to realize," she wrote in the introduction to *Hurricane,* "what part these astonishing storms have played in all our history, by their presence, or even by their absence, in discoveries, in settlements, in war and peace, in the thoughts and habits and fortunes of all the people whose lives, in five centuries, have made records of them."[23]

She had previously published two fictional pieces on big blows. One, written for a Florida magazine, is a story based on a first-person rendering of the 1906 hurricane and the loss of 124 laborers building Flagler's railroad across the keys. The other is a *Saturday Evening Post* piece suggested by the 1935 Labor Day hurricane, which washed away between four hundred and five hundred souls, the majority of them military veterans fighting off depression-era destitution by working on the Overseas Highway in the keys. That same year, the U.S. Weather Bureau reorganized, attempting to improve its forecasting by opening regional offices in New Orleans and Jacksonville. Yet hours before one of the most powerful hurricanes in recorded history made landfall, bureau forecasters were still calling it a tropical disturbance.[24]

With her nonfiction work, Douglas sought to flesh out the human drama missing from previously published academic books on hurricanes, though not without sacrificing important science. She corresponded with scores of scientists and weather experts and consulted nearly four hundred publications. Research trips took her all over Florida and up and down the Atlantic seaboard as well as to Jamaica and Martinique. In Cuba, she interviewed Jesuits at the Belén School, whose nineteenth-century predecessors had pioneered hurricane tracking.[25]

The hard work earned her favorable reviews. One said that the 400-page *Hurricane* "may well be one of the most fascinating books of the year, fiction and non-fiction." Yet for whatever reason, critical praise failed to generate much of a reading audience. Nearly a dozen magazines, including the *Saturday Evening Post,* declined first serial rights, sales fell flat, and the book never received wider recognition. Four years after publication, royalties had not yet offset Douglas's advance of twenty-five hundred dollars. Mockingbird Books reissued an abridged 119-page version in 1976, a poorly conceived monograph that languishes in scientific tedium without the original's driving narrative.[26]

In its original form, Douglas's book is a study in nature's sovereignty from the precolonial period to the 1950s. Spanish Florida was the appropriate place to begin. From writing *River of Grass,* she already knew how hurricanes had shaped the conquest period. The flotsam of storm-wrecked ships, including bodies of men in strange dress with hair growing from their faces, washing ashore suggested to aborigines that another sort of world existed somewhere beyond the ocean's horizon. The Spanish in turn received their first detailed accounting of Glades Indians from Hernando d'Escalante Fontaneda, who lived for twenty years in South Florida after his ship was overtaken by a hurricane. For every mile of Florida coast, Douglas calculated in *Hurricane,* a galleon reposes beneath the sea.[27]

If Spain could measure New World experiences in the tonnage of lost ships, Britain could make a similar measurement in lost colonies. The weather in North America's rebelling thirteen, Douglas wrote, "lay behind all the facts of their histories, and worked an electric charge in the varied lives of Englishmen and Europeans who settled here. It made them American." Throughout the revolutionary conflict, hurricanes frustrated British attempts to land military forces and to bring fresh provisions up from the Caribbean. During the war's turning point at Yorktown, Lord Cornwallis was left without sea power to match the enemy's because hurricane season had made the Royal Navy too squeamish to sail.[28]

Given weather's assist in victory, it seems apropos that two Founding Fathers, Thomas Jefferson and Benjamin Franklin, passionately observed the weather. In fact, extreme weather forced the U.S. government to expand its bureaucracy by getting into the business of forecasting. In 1870, the Army Signal Service launched a national weather-forecasting operation that depended largely on communication with reporting stations around the Caribbean. Public dissatisfaction with the system's unreliable forecasting prompted Congress to create the U.S. Weather Bureau within the Department of Agriculture in 1891. Still, the *Old Farmer's Almanac* and arthritic joints seemed to be better predictors of weather. Hurricanes were the bureau's greatest foil. The first to go undetected pounced on Cedar Key, Florida, in September 1896. It left 114 dead on the gulf island before battering its way up to Pennsylvania.[29]

The worst moment in bureau history came with the 1900 Galveston hurricane, which killed more than eight thousand people. Although Galveston had a national weather station and although Cuban climatologists had precisely tracked the hurricane across the gulf toward Texas, Washington never issued a hurricane warning. In a show of American and institutional chauvinism, it dismissed the competence of Cuban weather forecasters and gave full credence to the official U.S. observer in Havana, who said that the storm stirring up the Cubans was insignificant. The bureau nevertheless avoided public and official censure by creating diversions, accusing the Cubans of a plot to discredit the bureau and making its meteorologist in Galveston, Isaac Cline, who lost his pregnant wife in the storm and kept his cool throughout, into a national hero.[30]

Florida, however, would not allow the bureau to thrive on its own incompetence. The state lay in the path of nearly 40 percent of all hurricanes that struck the United States. A staggering fifty-seven hurricanes stormed into Florida between 1900 and Douglas's death in 1998. After she settled in Miami in 1915, nine hurricanes turned on Florida before the September 1926 storm became the first to hit her adopted city. At the local level, she observed, the hurricane demanded that the city adopt building codes for more durable construction. On the national level, "there was a concerted demand for better hurricane warning service, and better plans for hurricane relief." In reality, Douglas concluded, the public was asking the government to save people from themselves.[31]

With or without federal help, Miamians were not ready to cede their boom to nature. With millions of dollars pouring into the city from insurance settlements in the wake of the disaster, Miami got a shot in the economic arm that boosted a lethargic construction industry. "Destruction," the New York Times wrote, "meant reconstruction." The tourists returned, and the real estate business perked up again in 1927, a hurricane-free year for Florida.[32]

The next year opened with a stable economy, and then the summer came. The rains were heavier than usual through July. Farmers welcomed the precipitation as long as flooding did not carry seeds away or rot planted crops. For the workers in the fields, most of them black people who had come from the Bahamas, other southern states, and off the East Coast migrant circuit, dark clouds mobilizing above often meant relief. The rain felt cool on the skin; it washed the sweat off faces and out of clothes, and the air breathed full. July passed like this. Then, on August 7, a hurricane blew in just north of West Palm Beach, slashing across the state with hundred-mile-an-hour winds, causing $250,000 in damage, and killing two people. It also left people nervous about a repeat of 1926.

September was the month to worry about. On the tenth, the S.S. *Commack* was six hundred miles due east of Barbados when it reported encountering winds of thirty-eight miles per hour. The next morning, the

Weather Bureau issued an advisory for a tropical disturbance sixteen hundred miles southeast of Florida. Subsequent reports logged increasing winds. When they reached gale force, the hurricane headed toward land, hitting Guadeloupe, St. Kitts, Montserrat, the Virgin Islands, Puerto Rico, the Turks, and the Bahamas. With winds raging between ninety and one hundred miles per hour, the storm itself killed three hundred people; many others later died from exposure and starvation.[33]

The storm's island-hopping course made it easy to track, and given the events of 1926, weather officials might have been wise to err on the side of caution. Yet Gray predicted that the storm would arc away from Florida after careening through the Bahamas. Gray had plenty of doubters this time. The *Palm Beach Post* ignored him and warned that the "present course will bring hurricane winds to the lower coast." Then, in the early hours of Sunday, September 16, Gray changed his prediction and said that the storm would hit Florida, but with nothing more than fifty-four mile-per-hour winds. Finally, at 10:30 A.M., he issued a hurricane warning, too late to spread the word. Only approximately one in forty residents had radios, and fewer had telephones. Anyone who did not happen to see the red and black flags, hear the news from someone else, or doubt the Weather Bureau's effectiveness was in for a terrible and sudden surprise.[34]

By 2:00 P.M., 150-mile-per-hour winds were wracking West Palm Beach, and they brought eighteen inches of rain. The storm's center passed somewhere near the city, accompanied by a forty-minute lull. Gray estimated that the hurricane's winds rotated out thirty-five or more miles, forming the center of a system that spanned a monstrous five hundred miles. After the back half of the storm departed, West Palm Beach looked much as Miami had two years earlier, and twenty-six people were dead. Miamians were spared the worst this time.[35]

The people living out in the Everglades around Lake Okeechobee were not, however. The hurricane plied its way to the northwest, across the pinelands and out into the sawgrass region. No place in Florida and few in the South were as remote as the farming communities in the Everglades. They were hard places to live even in the best of weather. Travel to the outside world took place along drainage canals or narrow, rutted roads that were prone to flooding. Communication to other areas was equally haphazard. Farmworkers, who typically lived without electricity, telephones, or newspapers, got their news mainly by word of mouth. A class and racial gap existed in access to communication, just as in access to credit, property ownership, and education. The privileged (always white people) at times gained information that others did not, and if they chose not to send it along, the underprivileged (mostly blacks) remained ignorant. Such was the case in 1928. In light of the Weather Bureau's equivocation, only sketchy information about the hurricane was available, and although some whites spread the word about a storm striding across the Atlantic, others sent their workers out on a seemingly routine day into fields planted with beans, celery, carrots, and sugarcane and ripe for harvest.[36]

The result was a senseless tragedy, as Zora Neale Hurston illuminated in *Their Eyes Were Watching God*. One of the protagonists, Janie, working in a Belle Glade bean field on a bright and peaceful day, notices bands of Seminoles streaming past en route to an unknown place. When she asks where they are going, the answer is, "Going to high ground. Saw-grass bloom. Hurricane coming." She is amused: "You couldn't have a hurricane when you're making seven and eight dollars a day picking beans." Some people believed that Florida's Indians had otherworldly senses or the innate ability to read signs in nature, including those pointing to a coming hurricane—a red sky at dawn, the feel of the air and the way it carried sound, or peculiar behavior by birds or other animals. Whatever the reason, many nonfiction accounts confirm that the Seminoles were not fooled by the placid weather preceding the hurricane.[37]

There was also the critical matter of Lake Okeechobee. Under normal conditions, engineers kept it at a level slightly above the muck and people on the other side of the dike. But in the three weeks leading up to the hurricane, the lake rose three feet. Levees or dikes are earthen dams that hold back water with nothing more than the mass of their composition. As the 1927 Mississippi flood and the 1926 hurricane had shown, calculating the right mass to contain a body of water is tricky science. The volume and

weight of water constantly change, depending on temperature, evaporation, and recharge from rain and rivers. Containment is not a natural
condition for water, which always looks for a way to run or flow. Lake
Okeechobee—730 miles square and fifteen feet deep, "uh whole heap uh
water," as Janie's companion, Tea Cake, says—did just that in 1928.[38]

The September 1928 hurricane lost none of its power when it hit land,
clamoring down on the Everglades late Sunday afternoon with the same
intensity it had exerted against the coast and pushing the lake's water to
the southeast, toward the towns of Belle Glade and South Bay. The water
rose from four to six feet—eight, by some estimates—and as its weight
against the levee increased, the mass of one could no longer contain the
mass of the other. The levee broke and the water flowed. The wind and
the rain were doing their own incredible damage. The lake turned into a
wild, deadly river that swept away virtually everything in its broad path,
including livestock, wagons, cars, tractors, trees, houses, and people.

Countless interviews, memoirs, and letters tell the story of the desperate struggle for survival. People huddled alone and with others in dark
closets, in bathrooms, in hallways, and in attics above the rising water. Inspired by real-life experiences, Hurston had Janie and Tea Cake ride out
the storm in a house. Crouching low on the floor and wondering what
the Almighty has planned for them, they "seemed to be staring at the
dark, but their eyes were watching God." Houses lost their roofs, rolled
over, spun on their piers, and floated away, often without the huddled oc-
cupants inside knowing. People who had been washed into the raging
current clung to downed trees, furniture, dead livestock, anything that
buoyed them, and they floated for miles. One boy was swept from Torry
Island over the levee to the Agricultural Experiment Station eight miles
away in Belle Glade. He survived. Many others did not.[39]

With an official toll of 1,836 dead in Florida, the 1928 hurricane was one
of the worst in U.S. history. The search for bodies stopped after six weeks,
and for many years thereafter, farmers clearing fields came across skeletal
human remains.[40] Most of the dead drowned, and most were black. Blacks
were less likely to have been warned of the impending storm, given access
to means of evacuation, offered shelter in a structure sturdier than a shack

or shanty, and counted when they went missing. After the storm, "when the time of dying was over," in Hurston's words, blacks were conscripted to clean up the mess and recover bodies, tasks that exposed them to diseases associated with decaying corpses. White bodies were prioritized for caskets, built from salvaged wood. Black corpses were typically heaved into mass graves—as many as 674 bodies at a time—or stacked for cremation on an open pyre. For the living, relief agencies prioritized property owners over others. Says Hurston's character Tea Cake, whom gun-toting whites force to spend the day after the storm recovering bloated corpses, "Dis town is full uh trouble and compellment."[41]

The Red Cross, the area's principal relief agency, endured sharp criticism for its handling of the disaster, though not for the way it treated blacks. By early October, agency officials determined that their work was complete, only to be blasted for not doing enough. The organization then shifted its efforts from refugee relief to rebuilding communities, including the construction of new homes. It supplied beleaguered farmers with seed, fertilizer, and fuel to restore the agricultural economy. In other words, the lesson about the human role in natural disasters, the lesson Douglas conveyed in *Hurricane*, had yet to be learned. What Everglades residents and Florida officials believed would be best for all was improved forecasting—even though the Weather Bureau boasted of its expert and precise tracking of the 1928 hurricane—and a more massive dike. The federal government finally listened, marking a major shift in its relationship with the Everglades.[42]

Stories

In spring 1923, Douglas suffered something of an emotional breakdown. Over the years, she had experienced moments when consciousness evaporated into a trance of nothingness. Similar episodes haunted a character in one of her stories: "She would be talking to someone quite reasonably, her words coming clear and measured. . . . Then for a moment . . . the air across her face would stop, the motion of the waters alongside, the light on the wall, the hurrying hand of the clock, the blood in her body." Perhaps the same psychological glitch that incapacitated her mother had been passed along. Douglas guessed that she was experiencing a delayed reaction to the strain of her childhood, marriage, and roller-coaster relationship with Kenneth Rotharmel. She also believed that the experiences of fellow relief personnel Ernest Hemingway and John Dos Passos had been psychologically troubling, incidentally impelling their bare-bones writing styles. Beneath her nimble composure may have lurked war-related unease, even if it did not strip her prose to unadorned essentials.[1]

Douglas was living at the time with her father and his second wife, Lillias, at their new Spring Hill home. Her upstairs bedroom had a sedative view of the Miami River, where bird song emanated from the canopy of the shade trees. The ambiance, with a wooden desk eased into a corner, lent itself to productive activity. Yet despite the ideal setting, she confessed to herself occasional grave displeasure in living there. Even eight years after their reunion, her father never wanted to talk about her Taunton childhood and never felt at ease with her college education. They clashed over her suggestion to expand the baby milk charity to include other family services, such as counseling, job training, and low-interest loans. Molded by the frontier tradition, Frank had a bootstraps attitude about life. Charity for innocent babies was one thing; handouts for adults were another. He had confronted hardships and had climbed unaided out of more than one hole. Although he was more open-minded than most of his generation on the question of social equality, when it came to personal fortitude, he exhibited a conventional blindness to the advantages accorded his race and sex.[2]

Douglas also felt a certain disquietude about her future at the *Miami Herald*. She had never adjusted to the pressure of daily deadlines and the relentless demand for news material, and she spent her workdays in a permanent state of unease. When writing about the city's failings, she sensed the rancor of publisher Frank Shutts and occasionally of her father, proud men who had helped build Miami from the ground up. Frank Stoneman nevertheless expected her to follow him as editor of the *Herald*, but after expending the last of her emotional reserve on Martin Tabert and convict leasing, she felt the full measure of her depletion and knew her days at the newspaper were numbered. She was only thirty-three and exhausted, yet she was already thirty-three and professionally unfulfilled.

Soon thereafter, her father discovered her bed empty. Wearing only a sleeping gown, she spent much of the night ambling through the neighborhood in a semiconscious fog. The doctor was called in, and he diagnosed her condition as "nerve fatigue." He advised a professional change. It was just as well. "I never was a good reporter," she once told a young journalist. "Father used to send me out on a story and I'd come back with three sunsets and an editorial."[3]

She wanted to write fiction. She already had a literary agent, Robert Thomas Hardy of New York. He had been selling her one-line quips and epigrams to magazines since her Red Cross days, when she needed to raise one hundred dollars to cover her transatlantic passage. After she left the newspaper, he sold her first story in 1924 to *Black Mask,* a pulp magazine founded by H. L. Mencken and George Jean Nathan as a moneymaking venture to endow their literary serial *Smart Set.* The latter, sophisticated and avant-garde, published modernist writers such as Eugene O'Neill, Dorothy Parker, Ezra Pound, and D. H. Lawrence. The hardboiled *Black Mask* specialized in detective stories, romance, and mystery. Douglas chimerically envisioned that "White Midnight," an unremarkable buccaneer tale, would be picked up for screen adoption. It never was. But *Black Mask* paid her a considerable six hundred dollars for the story, and *Ainslee's* bought two others. Her career as a fiction writer was launched.[4]

During the summer of her breakdown, Douglas decided to spend time in Taunton with Fanny and Florence. En route to New England, she stopped off in New York to meet with Hardy. Her talent was too good for pulp serials, he told her, and he wanted her to submit a story to the *Saturday Evening Post.* In the heyday of magazine writing, serials such as *Collier's, Scribner's,* and the *Post* were principal venues of many noted writers, including Ernest Hemingway, F. Scott Fitzgerald, and Willa Cather. Before the Great Depression, magazines paid good money for short fiction by these authors. In 1929, Fitzgerald got four thousand dollars from the *Post* for one of his stories. Although sometimes accused of prostituting their talent, he and others viewed magazine writing as a pardonable means of support for the literary seriousness and toil they put into larger, more meaningful opuses. For Douglas, writing for the *Post* was a goal, not a rationalization.[5]

She took Hardy's advice and spent much of her time in Taunton developing a story for the *Post.* Under the twenty-five-year editorship of George Horace Lorimer, the magazine evolved into the most popular publication of its kind, distributed weekly to nearly three million subscribers. From its cover art by Norman Rockwell and his imitators to its fiction stories, nonfiction articles, and advertising, the *Post* was a glossy banner of Americanism. Critics complained that Lorimer substituted the myth of national greatness for the reality of patriotic chauvinism and cultural smugness by avoiding or whitewashing highly charged issues such as race and immigration. The stern-jawed editor was unapologetic about his preference for molding a national consciousness around an admixture of "nineteenth-century values and twentieth-century opportunities." He wanted wholesome stories that took readers to interesting places and displayed a bit of conflict, dilemma, irony, romance, and success, something neither as trite as pulp nor too highbrow or political for a general readership. Douglas decided that contemporary Miami would make a good setting, an exotic, tropical world that glistened in the popular imagination.[6]

For her first submission, she settled on the title, "At Home on the Marcel Waves." She created a female protagonist, Augusta McCann, who speaks with nautical idioms betraying a salty, seafaring sturdiness and the confidence of a world traveler. McCann has retired from the sea and gone to Miami, where she rescues a failing beauty shop that belongs to a delicate and shrinking New England spinster, Julia Trimble. With exercise, massage, and beauty treatments, complemented by her marcel iron, McCann whips Trimble into shape, and together they do the same for the flabby, sallow women wintering in Miami's hotels. McCann is the model of robustness until she falls for an unemployed piccolo player who is secretly after her money and the distraction jeopardizes the beauty shop's success. She eventually regains her wit and exposes his artifice. The beauty shop's future is restored. Before publishing the story in 1924, Lorimer had Douglas rewrite the ending twice to create a properly joyful outcome.[7]

Douglas had obviously borrowed liberally from her past—the connection to the sea, the old maid from New England, and the woman possessed by love and fooled by a man's con game. All of her stories were set in South Florida, the Caribbean, or war-torn Europe. The Everglades, sea islands, volcanoes, and tropical storms frequented them as well, and to enhance the readers' experience with a setting, she gave detailed descriptions of the local environment and weather. She studied the *Post* closely to glean some hint of Lorimer's preferences, yet her stories likely resonated with him in ways her studious readings would not have suggested. He was a great lover of nature and an active member of conservation groups and the national park movement (sans roads and automobiles), and his wife, Alma, devoted herself to humanitarian aid in postwar Europe.[8]

Outrages against humankind are frequent themes in Douglas's stories. Much in the way of her contemporaries, such as Eudora Welty and Flannery O'Connor, and the greats who inspired her, particularly Charles Dickens, she wove social criticism into her fiction. Her messages were usually subtle, as would be acceptable to the *Post,* but her voice was vital. Some of her stories center on young people, whom she generally portrayed as underdogs struggling against personal weaknesses, doubting and indifferent relatives, or various shady figures. Perhaps the best example, "By Violence" (1930), tells the story of an Everglades boy who outwits two murderers and traps them for the authorities. Probably not coincidentally, Douglas gave her young hero the first name of Martin Tabert. Having previously sought to make the real-life Martin a martyr to an unjust system, Douglas created in the fictitious Martin a hero who overcomes both the fear and the willful independence—his own destructive system—that had originally brought him into association with the story's antagonists.[9]

Douglas usually brought love stories to a felicitous ending, too. Modern writers, she complained, were "going in for grim and very unpleasant reality, now that the loves celebrated by the moderns are unrequited affections, repressions, shattered illusions and all sorts of anatomical whatnots." Although she had suffered her own shattered illusions and had engaged with war's tragedies, she never gave in to the cynicism that infected Hemingway and Dos Passos. Happy endings also satisfied Lorimer's expectations. As much as she admired his magazine, she knew it was formulaic, including, as she said, voicing the "cult of the romantic young man in business." She followed this convention in "A Bird Dog in Hand" with George Henry's turnaround from principled social critic to land developer, even while she cast a dark cloud over land-boom real estate practices. She also surrendered the autonomy and dignity of her female character. After George chides Pomona Brown for doubting his investment decision, she feels herself regressing. "I guess I don't know—anything," she confesses. "But if you think you can teach me, so that I'll be some good to you—oh, George, please."[10]

Douglas's preferred female protagonist rarely surrenders. With its untamed landscape, observes historian Susan A. Eacker, Florida offered nineteenth-century women writers—including Harriet Beecher Stowe and Ellen Call Long—a "gendered freedom" that they exhibited in their lives and work. Douglas followed that tradition, developing autobiographical protagonists who are intelligent, sensible, and resolute women, often of New England origins. They are moderns with independent minds and ambitions whose existences do not depend on men, though these women might still fall in love. Many are trying to emancipate themselves and their families from the clutches of insufferable men who leech off the hard labors of their women. Douglas never deployed a suffragist as a main character or integrated the movement into a plot, perhaps because her fellow activists were too conventional. Minor characters are of this sort, and Douglas often takes them to extremes—inattentive mothers, overattentive grandmothers, and high-strung aunts. Her female heroes stand up against these other women, as Penny Heston in "Bees in the Mango Bloom" does to validate her hunch about the success of growing mangoes in South Florida.[11]

Not all of Douglas's female protagonists are physically strong like Penny, but they are at least emotionally strong in ways that only men of the day were supposed to be. Margaret Rhodes in "From the Terror by Night" is such a woman. She is a wealthy widow caring for two older stepchildren and her own son, six-year-old Andrew Rhodes III, who is under constant threat of abduction. When the inevitable happens, she insists on being involved in the negotiations and refuses to give in to the kidnappers' demands: "I shall do nothing that they say do. I shall not offer a single cent." After the news of the kidnapping breaks in the press and Margaret publicly takes her stand against the "terror," bundles of letters arrive accusing her of "caring more for money than . . . for the life of her own child." Friends and family intervene, but she refuses their advice to pay the ransom.[12]

Douglas's story was inspired by the historic kidnapping of twenty-one-month-old Charles Lindbergh III, who, like Andrew, would have been six at the time of her story's publication in 1936.[13] Margaret's courage is not simply for personal benefit, she tells a close associate: "This thing has gone on long enough in this country. Somebody's got to stop it if it kills us—my son and me, I mean. It's what we can do for other children. It's what I must do for other mothers." Margaret eventually prevails, and her son returns safely. In the Lindbergh case, the ransom was paid, but the baby was found dead. Charles Lindbergh had assumed control of the kidnapping's investigation, which critics say he botched. Douglas may have believed that if Anne Morrow Lindbergh had taken charge, the outcome would have been different. At the very least Douglas believed that Anne—a Smith College graduate, accomplished aviator, and prolific writer—was as capable of dealing with grave matters as her husband. Here lies an important difference between the two women. Margaret, conveniently a widow, has no husband whose sovereignty she must challenge. Douglas's female protagonist played against bad guys but not against social convention, thereby satisfying the *Post* formula.[14]

Lorimer rarely rejected Douglas's work. By the time "From the Terror by Night" appeared, she had published fifty-seven stories in sixteen years. When the *Post* did pass on a story, Hardy usually sold it to *Cosmopolitan, McCall's,* or *Woman's Home Companion.* In 1929, *Smart Set* published one of her pieces. Lorimer started her at five hundred dollars a story and gradually increased her compensation until it reached twelve hundred dollars. In 1925, on the strength of her success in the freelance world, she concluded she was ready for a house of her own.[15]

She knew exactly where she wanted to live. While she was living with Frank and Lillias, she and friends would ride bikes out the dusty-white limestone road southeast from Miami to the hammock-shaded village of Coconut Grove. It was the area's oldest established community, where people lived on the bay's edge beneath coconut palms leaning into the trade winds. The Grove had shunned the trend of "going after progress," Douglas wrote, and retained "a bit of old south Florida, as lovely, as remote, as anything in the South Sea Isles." Before moving there, she felt a kinship with its residents—intellectuals, artists, and naturalists peacefully ensconced in a green Bohemia. Palms, banyans, and hardwoods gave the Grove a jungle canopy, and shower-of-gold trees with long racemes of yellow flowers, her favorite, and the "lavender-blue clouds of the jacaranda trees" gave the rest complementary color. She loved the Grove for the "delightful smells of blooming things, the honey-and-arnica of sapodillas, the sweet of lime and grapefruit, the spice of the long pink lilies of the coral bells." She loved it for the "magnolia warblers, red-starts and black-throated blues. The painted and indigo buntings . . . dashing blue jays and three different woodpeckers, and . . . the yellow-and-black orioles."[16]

Henry and Bertha Schulz, a couple she met through her erstwhile fiancé, Frederick, owned a piece of land in Coconut Grove they called the Patch. In 1925, they offered to sell her a section fronting 50 feet of Stewart Avenue and dropping back 160 feet and to hold the mortgage. Douglas's friends, Franklin and Alice Harris, bought an adjoining lot; Natalie Newell, who operated a bookstore, bought another; and the Schulzes built a house on the remainder.[17]

Douglas commissioned a commercial architect, George Hyde, to design a "sensible house open to the breezes." It was silly, she had written in her column, to "build a house down here without taking the Florida conditions into account." Hers was to be quaint but practical, to withstand the extreme weather and to function primarily as a place to work. "All I needed was one big room with living quarters tacked on," she once said. Working from that idea, Hyde provided a single ten-by-ten-foot bedroom with a seven-foot ceiling; a kitchen that could accommodate a breakfast table only if she opted for a hot plate rather than a stove and oven; and a tiny bathroom she painted flamingo pink. The principal room, entered via the front door and with French doors opening out to a modest back patio, was for work and entertaining visitors. Hyde gave it a fireplace and ample space, including a fourteen-foot vaulted ceiling with exposed wooden beams and casement windows that admitted plenty of sunlight and fresh air. The walls were painted the color of "old parchment" and were as thick and sturdy as those of a factory. And, indeed, they withstood the 1926 hurricane. The $250 insurance settlement she received was enough to cover repairs and pay for wide-planked pine floors that ran through the house. Pecky-cypress exterior wood trim, likely from Everglades trees, lay against cream-colored stucco walls. The sloping roof had scalloped-edged asphalt shingles and rounded fascias. All of these features gave the house the distinct look of an English country cottage, though hers was nestled in a tropical garden.[18]

The house went up slowly. The first contractor absconded with her down payment, and his replacement worked on the house as she sold stories. Money was tight at times. She wrote in her diary in February 1926, "Still in financial difficulties, but so far more able to take them lightly, although tomorrow or next day the shell of protection may crash in." She had been writing "furiously," sometimes working on two or three stories at a time with as many more "in mind." By late winter, she found she needed to scale back to a more sensible pace. Doing so had an unexpected literary payoff: "At least I have more of a chance to succeed because as far as I can tell there is no fever and somehow the stuff is coming deeper and more human."[19]

In part to give her a writer's privacy, the house was set far back from the road. This location also gave her a view of her neighbors' backyards, while their houses overlooked her front yard. From Douglas's main doorway, located in the northwest corner on the side away from the street, the view took in the garden behind the Harrises' two-story Mediterranean Revival house, and theirs had a side bay window that overlooked the grassy area in front of Douglas's, where she might have put a driveway if she had driven a car. When she moved into the house in 1926, she stocked it with used furniture, a few antiques, family pieces, and books, including the set of Dickens from Taunton. She had a drop-leaf mahogany table that had belonged to writer Malcolm Ross; her old friend, Carolyn Percy Cole, found a yellow marble-top coffee table in a New York shop and shipped it to Douglas. An Italian walnut table, called a dueling desk because of its hidden drawer that would hold a sword, became a catchall for papers, books, letters, and stories in progress. During a trip to Key West, she bought a bellpull from Java for the front door, "à la Jane Austen," she said. She composed a poem, "A Simple Solution," touting her preference for austerity:

The trouble with the U.S.A.,
It's very plain to me,
Is wanting more than it should need,
All unlike me.
My wants are modest, plain, and few,
Of fine simplicity.[20]

Friends said that the house suited her. She quickly adapted to it with her daily freelance writing schedule. She rose late, sometimes after ten, and brewed a cup of tea while she filled her bird feeders and fed the cats, usually strays that adopted her. Three mornings a week, she joined friends for a swim at the beach. The rest of the day, she wrote. In the evenings, when she was not dining out and dancing at the Romey Plaza Hotel, she fixed a light dinner and read late into the night.[21]

Out on the back patio, red brick in a crosshatch pattern and facing the southeast, she found her favorite place to write about heroes and heroines and tropical settings. She sat in a canvas chair, pen in hand and a paper pad and wooden lapboard across her legs. She never had the patio covered or screened; she preferred it open, the better to appreciate the fragrance of the native frangipani, the song and activity of birds, and Cuban brown anoles darting about. Around a corner, bees built a hive in the house's eaves and their honey ran down and inside the exterior wall. She told her handyman to leave the bees alone. As a late sleeper, she usually missed the sunrise, but in the evenings, she caught the luminous yellow backlight of the sunset silhouetting the green and brown of the trees. She watched the drama of warmer afternoons, when steel-gray clouds piled up over the bay less than a mile away, edged onshore, and unburdened their loads in a quick thundershower. Afterward, she loved the fresh-scrubbed look of the earth, the revitalized colors in the wet grass, sand, and tree trunks. On calmer afternoons, the breezes coming off the bay would die late in the day, regather themselves after an hour or so, shift, and blow out from land, signaling big shorebirds to make the twilight return to their rookeries. Their low-flying commutes always uplifted her, even on melancholic days.[22]

In the first year she lived in the house, the *Post* published twenty serialized novels and 437 short stories. Her stories were never lost in the crowd. Two were selected for publication in O. Henry Memorial Award collections. In 1928, the memorial committee awarded "The Peculiar Treasure of Kings" the $250 second-place prize. Set in the Caribbean when steam-powered vessels were beginning to replace sailing ships, to the consternation of old salts, the tale represented one of her many forays into a male-centered coming-of-age theme. "Kings" is written from the point of view of a father, a veteran first mate who "had never once had a smell at a command" but who watches as his estranged son moves up from second mate directly to captain of a three-masted schooner. Despite a few missteps, the son succeeds as captain, just as Douglas, the descendant of sea captains, succeeded with a convincing portrayal of life aboard a sailing ship, showing great nautical familiarity.[23]

A few years after "Kings," she again won recognition, this time for a play. Loosely based on her father's viewing of a Miami hanging, *The Gallows Gate* unfolds through the eyes of a condemned young man's mother, offering a perspective on capital punishment rarely considered by the courts and the public. The plot revolves around a backcountry Florida family and two brothers who stray into criminal behavior. One is killed in a shootout with a sheriff, and the other is sentenced to hang for murder. The forlorn mother awaiting her son's body at the gallows gate is not the play's only sympathetic character. Her sons' destinies are the tragic creation of their father's malicious and brutal ways. In this work, Douglas embraced her Quaker ancestors' rejection of the Old Testament teaching of an eye for an eye. The play shies from an explicit challenge to the death penalty, which most Americans of the time supported. Instead, it offers a conscience-prodding illumination of the complex and potentially mitigating circumstances behind murder, showing the act as the result not of a single spontaneous or calculated event but of cumulative events drawn out over time, unrelated to the victim, and beyond the conscious control of the perpetrator. One newspaper called it a play of "moral philosophy." The Miami Chamber of Commerce chose it to represent the city's Civic Theater at the state tournament for little theaters. The "class of the tournament," *The Gallows Gate* was unanimously awarded first prize, allowing it to compete in the 1933 national playwriting contest in St. Louis, where it again took top honors.[24]

The awards, a steady demand for her work, and a "workshop," as she called her house, gave Douglas relative security in self-employment. "I love being a free-lance writer," she said in 1953. "With no dependents, a well-oiled typewriter and decent health, you can live indefinitely, so to speak, on your own fat." She was the first woman on both the Stoneman and Trefethen sides to achieve a truly independent life, and much to her grandmother's relief, she was not destined to die in a rented attic. Florence lived long enough to read Marjory's first magazine stories and may have even seen in the female characters particulars she and Fanny coveted but never obtained. Douglas's unsavory female antagonists may have similarly emerged from her notion of the debilitating consequences suffered by women like those in her family, including her mother, when society forced them into unwanted roles. And yet even for the successful author, as with the affirming female protagonists, independence was rarely acquired without a struggle.[25]

To show a woman's native strength, Douglas occasionally turned to nature. In scrubland or swamp and during fair weather or foul, her female protagonists tended to move with confident, graceful ease. If they were not outwitting men, they pragmatically countered male blunders, excesses, and uselessness. Douglas's heroines possessed the energy and fortitude of the other sex, and though equally tough and gutsy, they were never masculine.

Cousin Agnes Page in "Goodness Gracious, Agnes" embodies this redoubtable but feminine female. Freshly relocated to South Florida from Boston, she is the admirable opposite of the two cousins with whom she lives, a codependent brother and sister who are vainglorious but emotionally fragile gold diggers. They see themselves as "ultramoderns," however, and Agnes as regressively eccentric. They are horrified when Agnes, tall and sleek and square shouldered, shuns white linens for khaki trousers. Her high boots are similarly ghastly, as is her habit of tromping around the backcountry possessed by a sense of mission to save mules, cows, and other common animals from callous acts. Agnes is tough but not macho, sensitive but not weak. Men are fools for her. The story reaches its climax one night in the deep of the Everglades where a crowd is warming up for a dog-and-wildcat fight. Having gone out alone, Agnes confronts her antagonists, who are eager for "deliberate cruelty," by show-ing cold-steel nerves and a revolver that is "shining and steady and pur-poseful." Her courage tested, she succeeds in her singular effort.[26]

Characters came to Douglas in the faces and actions of people she saw on the street, on the bus, at the library, in a restaurant. Agnes Page's ori-gins are unclear. The exemplar of female rugged individualism, she is per-haps a composite modeled after unpretentious women such as Douglas's Wellesley professors and South Florida pioneers such as Mary Barr Mun-roe. Unlike the American male, who proved his self-reliance on the fron-tier or in the wilderness by dominating and destroying it, Agnes stands guard over nature, manifesting a courage and independent spirit that any man can respect. Her most macho aspect is the revolver, which she uses to tame the animal man. In a case of life imitating art, Douglas in her later years came to resemble Agnes: sans revolver, Douglas took a stand to safeguard Everglades wildlife against hunters, government bureaucrats, and habitat destroyers.[27]

The place of nature in her stories suggests a telling prelude to the even-tual direction of her life. She rarely painted a setting without including activity in the landscape and sky: high winds and seas in "Wind before Morning"; a hurricane in "September—Remember"; the cutting sawgrass and sinking muck in "The Road to the Horizon"; the island mountain and tropical vegetation in "A Mountain in the Sea"; the active volcano in "Vol-cano"; the mangroves in "Charcoal"; the "wide dreaming country, flat as a painted floor" in "The Mayor of Flamingo"; the "gilt and rose" sunset af-terglow and the "beloved tree" with the "strange smooth trunk" in "Solid

Mahogany"; and the Caribbean pines, "endlessly alike, endlessly monotonous, and yet with an endless charm and variety," in "Pineland."[28]

Descriptive and certainly heartfelt, passages describing natural places and things earned her the classification "nature writer." She never agreed with it. When Wellesley College officials presented her with an alumnae award in 1977 for nature writing, she politely protested. "I am not a nature writer," she wrote to the awards committee. "I am a similar breed, but not quite the same." She explained that her work had "been written from the point of view of nature, or the environment, in relation to people, and people in their relation to the environment." "Plumes," her 1930 story based on the Guy Bradley killing, to some degree bears out her argument. The sustaining elements linking her story's human and nonhuman worlds are acquisitiveness and the attendant violence, buttressed by the story's sympathetic elements—not only helpless birds but also an ex-con engaged in a selfless act. She returned to slaughtered birds five years later in "A Flight of Ibis" with a different kind of hero, an altruistic photographer who uses camera flash and film to save a colony of ibis from would-be poachers. Yet again, the plot line strings together elements of a human story—in this case, the blossoming love between a man and a woman.[29]

Douglas may have held herself to her personal standards rather than to those of nature writing, but her body of work as a whole shows that the argument she presented to the awards committee is not terribly convincing. First, Douglas conceded that she wrote from the "point of view of nature." Her characters' behavior explores the dialectic between humans and nature, thereby suggesting at the very least an inferential philosophical reflection on nature. Her ex-con's burgeoning animal-rights ethic, for example, symbolizes what she advocated for society. Second, civilization, the residence of her characters, is often ugly, ribald, and devitalizing, whereas natural places, lacking in human encumbrances and interferences, are just the opposite—compelling, palliative, and inspirational—and therefore superior. Her preferences were always clear, as in "Pineland": "Sometimes the pine woods came so near the road he could smell their sunny resinous breath. . . . He felt the comprehension of them growing upon him—the silence of their trunks, the loveliness of their tossed branches, the virginity of their hushed places, in retreat before the surfaced roads and filling stations, the barbecue stands and signboards of the new Florida." Third, many of her stories evoke an ecogendered perspective (which some observers might call ecofeminist) as they unfold to subvert a patriarchal culture that dominates both women and nature. Fourth, she made nature a central character with a will of its own, as suggested in titles such as "Volcano," "Wind before Morning," and "Solid Mahogany." Such stories commonly climax not with humans triumphing over nature but with humans learning to recognize and sometimes to defer to the power of nature in the drama of life. And fifth, a writer must sometimes surrender to the fate of labels attached to her work.[30]

Yet after all is interpreted and argued, one should respect Douglas's own felicity. One label she accepted was that of a "regionalist." While she was still composing "The Galley," she wrote, "We need . . . regional interpreters in the United States. We must have a deepening sense of the immediate beauty and romance of our surroundings. . . . Carl Sandburg has done it for Chicago, Edgar Lee Masters for the middle west, Robert Frost for New England, among others." Douglas installed herself as that writer for South Florida: "The most important thing, the one factor which colors and shapes our lives and has always colored and shaped the lives of man, is this wrinkled old earth under our feet." She effortlessly translated this idea into her fiction—not always regional fiction—sometimes with obvious clarity. In "Far Up the Black Mountain," one of her World War I stories set in the Balkans, she opened, "There are places in this world that by the sheer force of their geography overwhelm one with their sense of impending drama."[31]

Regionalism explains her writing as well as anything else. Her New England female characters transplanted to South Florida, for example, were not simply autobiographical renderings; they were regional ones. She, like thousands of others, came to Miami from the Northeast or Midwest with an established set of attitudes and habits that sometimes clashed not only with the many other cultures filling the region but also with the local geography. Adapting to the physical surroundings was essential to life in South Florida, and adapting was an essential element in her stories.

South Florida, she believed, not only provided material for her work but inspired people to be creative. It was "like the Mediterranean," she said, "in climate and general outlook, and you know what the Côte d'Azur does to writers and artists. Turns them out in droves."[32]

South Florida turned out Douglas. Embracing her region's geography in all its colors and animations led her to write her little-known first book, a sixty-four-page gardening guide, *The Book of Twelve for South Florida Gardens* (1928). The title referred to a dozen flowering trees, shrubs, and vines that formed the basis of successful South Florida gardening. She co-authored the book with Mabel White Dorn, founder of the South Florida Garden Club and a "woman with great latent force," in Douglas's words. The common "handicap" of any would-be gardener, the authors warned, was importing improper habits from other parts of the country. The authors were speaking from experience. Dorn had relocated from Chicago to South Miami, where she found the floral landscape "hot and bleak and shadeless," unable to support her northern plants. Success in fostering a tropical African tulip tree eventually changed her impression. According to Douglas, Dorn then began "to look around her and see with new eyes the high pineland, the mucklands, the hammocks and sands of South Florida about the Everglades." Dorn had met Jessica Seymour around the same time as did Douglas and soon became a patron of regionalism. Echoing regionalist philosophy, Dorn and Douglas wrote that South Florida "should be made as unique as its possibilities."[33]

The unique in Douglas's form of regionalism was not necessarily nativist in its botanical priorities. The standards she and Dorn laid out in their book did not prohibit botanically suitable transplants from far-off places. The African tulip came from tropical West and Central Africa, the banyan and shower-of-gold trees originated in India, and the jacaranda migrated from South America. All contributed elementally, in Douglas's mind, to the essence and hue of the natural setting around her new home in Coconut Grove.

She eventually realized the harm caused by certain invasive exotics, some of which her trusted advisers in the botanical world had introduced to her region. And she might be forgiven for wanting to make her place in the subtropics more vividly real, artistically stimulating, and provocatively alfresco. Yet she was not one among the crowd who called for the subversion of the native scrubland, and the hapless Caribbean pine had no more vociferous advocate than she. Finally, if her aesthetic prejudices had not run toward the original and if she had not looked to her immediate surroundings for literary subjects and settings, she would never have been asked to write her best-known and most important book, *The Everglades: River of Grass,* an exaltation of the regional and the native.

The Proposal

Coming in from the Everglades light, Ernest Coe adjusted his gray eyes to the dim interior of the old store. His clothes were sweat stained and wrinkled from the fifty-mile drive out Tamiami Trail to Chokoloskee, an island fishing village that slumbered near the mouth of Turner River. Except for a dark tie and tan complexion, he was a walking swatch of alabaster. He wore linen pants, a white cotton shirt, and white canvas shoes, and his eyebrows and fuss of hair were as snowy as the nuptial plumage of egrets. Someone who knew a thing or two about plumes was the store's walrus-mustached proprietor, Ted Smallwood. When he built the gray-board store as a lean, taut man back in 1906, he put on a hide room for preparing the bird and alligator carcasses brought in by white and Indian hunters. He raised the store on stilts and capped it with a low-pitched roof to minimize the ripping impact of hurricanes. The whole town was on stilts. Just in front of the hide room was the main sales counter, which Smallwood made from heavy slabs of Dade County pine, the hardy cousin of the Caribbean pine that Marjory Stoneman Douglas venerated.[1]

When the white-clad Coe mimicked the locals and languorously leaned on his elbow against the counter, he still looked and sounded like a city slicker. And as city slickers often did, he had come to talk about a proposition, one that promised more customers for Small-wood and a bigger (and legal) economy for the town. Smallwood was in-trigued but mindful of the locals and outlanders, who tended to be sus-picious of change and downright hostile when strangers wandered into their midst. The recently opened Tamiami Trail had already brought the clamor of civilization closer, and now Coe, a New Englander by origin and accent, was proposing a national park. Its gateway would be a skip across the water on the mainland.[2]

People who knew Coe marveled at and sometimes recoiled from the volumes of energy he expended trying to sell the park. His quest began soon after he moved to Miami in 1925. Sixty years old at the time, he and his wife, Anna, had come down from Connecticut. He held a degree in fine arts from Yale College and had been trained in landscape architec-ture in Europe and Japan. After nearly forty years of designing gardens and estates in New England, he was drawn to the possibility of transplant-ing his skills to a region that would stimulate him with new kinds of flora. He turned his gaze to booming Florida. He and Anna bought a house in lush Coconut Grove, and he opened an office in Coral Gables. Neigh-bors liked him because he gave them gardening and landscaping tips. He in turn sought tips in real estate investment, but like so many others, he speculated and lost money.[3]

He was enriched, though, by the intellectual life he discovered in his new surroundings. Before long, he joined a group of learned natural-ists—David Fairchild, Charles Torrey Simpson, and John Gifford among them—who met every few weeks to discuss scientific papers on the area's natural wonders. Acting on the initiative of Harold H. Bailey, the group called itself the Florida Society of Natural History. Bailey, an ornitholo-gist with the Bureau of Biological Survey and son of one of the found-ers of the American Ornithologists' Union, sometimes took Douglas on bird-watching outings and taught her about local wildlife. He served as a partial model, along with T. Gilbert Pearson, for a wizened ornitholo-gist character in her unpublished story "Birds and Women." At a soci-ety meeting in 1923, Bailey said that he would like to see a national park in the Everglades to protect avian life. He made the suggestion again in a published book on Florida birds that contained Douglas's poem "To a Buzzard Swinging in Silence."[4]

The society meetings often dwelled on the unremitting exploitation of natural Everglades endowments. The region was like an unlocked store-house; whatever had an immediate commercial value was being taken, and whatever remained was at risk of commodification. The feather trade was still decimating the few remaining bird colonies; canneries were ex-cavating clam beds; charcoal factories were stripping mangrove brakes; timber concerns were cutting ancient cypress strands; poachers were prospecting for any merchantable animal and plant; and oil companies were exploring for crude. One firm had even developed a process for making paper and wallboard from the peat of muck. Bailey's father, H. B. Bailey, started talking about a national park somewhere at the peninsula's end, and Harold Bailey proposed such a park just south of Lake Okeecho-bee, in the area most affected by drainage and land sales. Much of its custard apple swamp was still intact, though, and unpaid tax bills were sending private submerged land back to the state. In Washington, D.C., at around the same time, National Park Service director Stephen Mather met with the interior secretary to discuss a national park to preserve "an untouched example of the Everglades." The discussion was only one of many that took place as the idea gestated.[5]

The concept had been around for some time. Mary Barr Munroe and Edith Gifford had proposed a federal reserve for birds and plant life back in 1905, and their proposal eventually produced Royal Palm State Park. In various books, John Kunkel Small, Charles Torrey Simpson, Minnie Moore-Willson, and Ales Hrdlicka, an anthropologist of native cultures, had all spoken of some kind of national sanctuary in the Everglades. As sympathetic as the natural history society's members were to the park idea, they never acted on it.[6]

Meanwhile, Bailey took Coe out and introduced him to the much-talked-about wetland. Coe was instantly hooked. He began studying the Everglades in books, documents, maps, and scientific papers, all of which soon cluttered his Coral Gables office. He returned to the wetland time and again, driving out as far as the uncompleted Tamiami Trail would take him, cruising down Ingraham Highway to Paradise Key, and jouncing along the unpaved road to Flamingo, a road Douglas described as in the "condition of a third-day's battlefield." He hiked out beyond his parked car, always carrying a walking stick as defense against snakes. At night, he settled on a soft spot in the sand or grass, rolled up in a blanket, and pulled a pillowcase over his head as defense against mosquitoes. He was enchanted by the plant and animal life; the hidden bays and rivers, so many of them ungraciously named after plume hunters; the sparkling water and light; and the broad vistas. He preferred the scenic variety of the lower Glades. A neighbor's invitation to take a truck down to Cape Sable to gather a load of wild orchids pushed him into the mode of an activist. He found the suggestion revolting and mentioned it to Anna at breakfast one morning; she wondered, as others had, if the area might be right for a national park.[7]

Neither the Coes nor anyone else at the time, save for a scientist or two, understood that the environmental conditions of the lower Glades depended on what was happening in the upper. Under natural conditions, water spilled over from Lake Okeechobee into the custard apple swamp and wended its way through the sloughs down to the lower region. This was the wetland's cardiovascular system, and any blockage, such as artificially dry land or excessive hemorrhaging, as through a diversion canal, affected the organism at the natural end of the flow. What Coe did comprehend was the need for a bulwark against spreading development. After the 1926 and 1928 hurricanes, the federal government promised to help the state with upgraded flood-control measures around Lake Okeechobee, which would surely stimulate agricultural expansion in the area. The scheme also suggested that property values would rise and make the cost of a park in the upper Glades prohibitive.

Coe then started talking to people about the possibility of a park in the lower Glades. Bringing along lantern slides, he lectured at rotary club, garden club, neighborhood, and civic meetings. He went into the backcountry to talk to Indians and white squatters. Some whites, driven to their seclusion by an unease with authority and social conventions, threatened him with bodily harm. Under safer conditions, he cornered people on the streets in Miami. Typically a "serene, unhurried" man, he showed a dogged tenacity bordering on obsession when discussing the park idea, incessantly and without thinking of others. People made excuses and pried themselves away. He was a fanatic, they complained. Douglas said he was a "prophet."[8]

Before the Great Depression, the federal government was no more intrusive in the daily lives of individuals than the mailbox in front of their houses. The average citizen, not just hermits dwelling in wilderness interiors, preferred to keep Washington at a measured distance. In truth, Americans' relationship with the environment had long shaped their relationship with Washington. The federal government was generally welcomed to assume oversight of waterway navigation, irrigation projects, bridge construction, and flood control. Catastrophic occurrences, such as the Mississippi River flood of 1927, which displaced seven hundred thousand people, heightened that reception. The flood was bracketed by the 1926 and 1928 hurricanes, and the three events combined, argues historian Raymond Arsenault, to propel a "revolution in American attitudes toward disaster relief and federal responsibility."[9]

When the still-fresh memory of the first hurricane collided with the experiences of the second, Floridians grew eager for outside reinforcements in life-threatening struggles with nature. The state had not proven itself equal to the task: someone in the Lake Okeechobee region was even rumored to be plotting to assassinate the Internal Improvement Fund's chief drainage engineer. In the wake of the 1926 blow, Congress bowed to public pressure and ordered the U.S. Army Corps of Engineers to survey Lake Okeechobee and its tributaries. The corps had just finished digging a drainage canal connecting the lake to the St. Lucie River (overloading the brackish St. Lucie Estuary and Indian River Lagoon narrows with freshwater and killing sea grasses, oyster beds, and other marine life). But after looking around and determining that it could do more, the corps recommended to a U.S. House of Representatives hearing on "flood control in Florida and elsewhere" the construction of a levee ten feet above the lake's maximum water level. Congress remembered the people who had perished when the waters of Lake Okeechobee breached the levee during the 1928 hurricane and authorized approximately ten million dollars as part of the 1930 River and Harbor Act to build a new dike and enlarge the St. Lucie and Caloosahatchee Rivers/Canals. In 1937, the same year that Zora Neale Hurston published *Their Eyes Were Watching God*, the corps completed the first phase of the project. When all was said and done, Florida got two refitted rivers and an eighty-five-mile limestone and earthen levee cupping the lake's southern shore. The Hoover Dike, as much as 215 feet wide and 38 feet high, substantially beyond the original 10-foot cushion, not only performed its retention duties with ease but hid one of the country's largest lakes from the view of anyone standing on the dry side of the dike.[10]

Coe was confident that a national park could coexist with flood control. In the immediate aftermath of the 1928 hurricane, he formed the Tropic Everglades Park Association to make his park idea official. Coe served as executive secretary, with David Fairchild, retired from the plant introductory center, as president. A few members of the natural history society joined them, as did Coe's brother-in-law, Gilbert Grosvenor, president of the National Geographic Society and one of the organizers of the National Park Service. Coe and Fairchild moved their operations into a small office in the county courthouse and went to work full time. People started calling Coe "Papa of the Everglades."[11]

Coe and Fairchild's first task was to convince the state of the value of their proposal. National parks were located on sites conveyed to the Department of the Interior by individual states at no cost to the federal government. Coe proposed that Florida take acreage acquired under the Swamp Land Act and give it back to the federal government. Parks traditionally occupied land deemed economically worthless, an important selling point in the creation of Yosemite and Yellowstone out west. Drainage in the Everglades had hardly been financially successful, but promised federal assistance for the Lake Okeechobee region might improve the agricultural dynamic in the northern Glades, Bailey's original choice.

Coe's association wisely focused on the generally unwanted parts of the south and the Cape Sable region. Coe also took advantage of the notion that a national park was a prestigious distinction for a state, and one that generated tourists and capital.[12]

Lawmakers in Tallahassee listened. In May 1929, they created the Tropic Everglades National Park Commission, intended as a complement to Coe's private organization, and authorized the new commission to acquire lands for transfer to the Department of the Interior. The commission's executive council then elected Coe director.[13]

The state's support, as well as a modest traveling budget, gave Coe a fresh burst of enthusiasm as he set out for Washington to sell his park idea. *National Geographic* scheduled an article for its January 1930 issue, and Coe wrote a full-page article for the *Washington Post,* asking rhetorically, "Why Not a Tropical National Park?" Why indeed? Coe's use of *tropic* and *tropical* showed a deft shrewdness. In addition to a geographic actuality, *tropic* was a concept and aesthetic, a centuries-old European construction imposed on an exotic New World environment. As an idea, *the tropics* represented one or both of two extremes. At one, they were a hot, buggy pestilential purgatory, evoking images of invisible fevers and fluxes and visible creatures and elements that could do horrid things to the body and mind. At the other, they were a salubrious paradise, enthralling and luxuriant, a green Valhalla where, as German naturalist Alexander von Humboldt put it, nature was "more forcibly" manifested. From the first contact, Western culture had maligned the Everglades as the purgatory tropics. The Miami Chamber of Commerce had attempted to counter that persistent image with its 1922 name-change contest, choosing the fruitful Tropical Everglades. It was a matter of swinging minds to the other extreme. Six years later, Coe trusted in the positive power of the tropic descriptive (though it later came to haunt him). He was unwavering about its inclusion in the park's name, which he believed would serve as northerners' only needed reminder of the Everglades warmth beckoning in the dead of winter, when other national parks were closed. More importantly, South Florida had the only subtropics within the continental United States, and for that reason alone a park belonged in the Everglades. America's protected natural heritage should not be left incomplete.[14]

Coe had his work cut out for him in Washington. Florida senator Duncan Fletcher fostered legislation requesting that the Department of the Interior prepare a report on the practicality and benefits of locating a park in South Florida. Since the establishment of Yellowstone in 1872, the department had reviewed more than five hundred proposals and through 1931 had created only twenty-five national parks. Coe could easily sell plans for a garden or estate grounds, but now he was trying to sell plans for a parcel of earth that, at twenty-five hundred square miles, was twice the size of Rhode Island. Everglades would be second in size only to Yellowstone among national parks and would showcase a variegated geography. Coe envisioned the Everglades park ranging from the Big Cypress above Tamiami Trail down across the Cape Sable pinelands and sawgrass region and to the coral reefs of the upper keys. It was more than he would ultimately get.

What he did get was Royal Palm Park, which with the passage of state legislation in 1921 totaled four thousand acres. Soon after the inception of his association, the Florida Federation of Women's Clubs voted to donate Royal Palm after Congress authorized the national park. Former federation president May Mann Jennings still oversaw Royal Palm's operations. Its existence had depended largely on her energy, and she was as enthusiastic as anyone about the donation.[15]

More promising news arrived in January 1930. The Park Service announced that it would send a delegation to tour the Everglades. Coe had done his homework, impressing Washington officials with a concise proposal accompanied by detailed maps. Horace Albright, the Park Service director; Arno Cammerer, the associate director; Roger Toll, Yellowstone National Park superintendent; Caspar W. Hodgson of the National Park Association; and Herman Bumpus, Park Service education director, agreed that a Florida trip would be worthwhile. They were joined by Audubon head T. Gilbert Pearson and Florida congresswoman Ruth Bryan Owen. Coe and Fairchild scrambled to make arrangements in

Florida. The visitors would devote one day to an automobile tour and another to a boating excursion. Someone suggested commissioning one of the Goodyear blimps docked in Miami to thrill the party with an aerial view of the Everglades' spherical canvass. Fairchild wrote to Owen that he hoped the visitors could "adjust their senses to such a radical change as that involved in the shift from a foot of snow to mangos in bloom." He need not have worried.[16]

Awaiting the group's arrival in Florida were David and Marian Fairchild, Anna Coe, and Marjory Stoneman Douglas. Inviting Douglas to serve on the association board made sense. Coe had taken her on many Everglades field trips. Since returning from Europe, she had turned into an adamant bird watcher and a regular companion of wintertime ornithologists, including Frank Chapman and Arthur Cleveland Bent, a Taunton native and one of the country's leading chroniclers of bird lore. Beyond this avocation, she was a writer with access to the *Saturday Evening Post* and the *Miami Herald,* an active editorial promoter of the park. Although she had not yet written her most environmentally evocative short stories, her old newspaper column revealed a militant love of the region and its distinct biological communities. She had called for a new ethic in the way South Floridians interacted with their physical surroundings, and she had embraced the work and ideas of Fairchild, Simpson, and other naturalists. "Dr. Fairchild," she wrote, "says that Miami can teach the whole world how to live in the tropics. . . . That means that south Florida will be a place where new ideas will be created." She had of course also praised the construction of Tamiami Trail and endorsed the advance of tropical agriculture in the Everglades. But Coe too accepted the development around Lake Okeechobee, and he saw the trail as useful for getting visitors out into the Everglades. "You and I have ample reasons to be friends," Coe told her; "we both have a common interest in the Everglades National Park." The organized excursion would provide her first real exposure to the Everglades beyond the terminus of an improved road.[17]

When the delegation arrived in South Florida, the weather was picture-perfect and cool enough to keep the bugs down. The sightseeing began with an overhead cruise in the dirigible. Douglas sat next to an airsick Coe, who was quietly retching into a bucket. The faint, distant horizon was an astonishing sight, as was a vast drift of white birds—egrets or ibis—passing below and indifferent to the important sightseers above. The scene could not have been more idyllic if Coe had staged it. Albright later related the moment to interior secretary Ray Lyman Wilbur: "I believe that the old idea of an Everglades with dense swamps and lagoons festooned with lianas, and miasmatic swamps full of alligators and crocodiles and venomous snakes was entirely shattered." As Coe had hoped, the visitors had made the shift on the tropicality spectrum.[18]

The next day, the party went down to the keys and boarded a yacht for a tour around Florida Bay and Cape Sable and up Shark River, walled on each side by sprawling mangroves. Several party members arrived in heavy outdoors garb and leather boots but quickly shed all in favor of cotton shirts and pants and canvas shoes, à la Coe. Compliments of the hosts, everyone had received a palmetto-thatch sun hat handwoven by Seminoles. Approaching sunset, the party anchored in Tarpon Bay, rowed skiffs out to nearby rookeries, and watched for the evening return of birds. Pearson identified each kind for his companions. Again, Coe might have choreographed the entire experience. Douglas later remembered that the sightseers "sat spellbound, looking up. The free leap and flight of the great, free birds brought to them the same curious lift and surge of delight. . . . They said, 'Oh!' and 'By George, did you ever see anything like it?' and 'Look, look, there come more of them. More of them.'"[19]

Back on the yacht, the visitors dined beneath an "enormous white moon." Late-retreating birds occasionally passed overhead, their audible wings beating in the dark accompanied by an occasional, invisible "rawk, rawk." By Douglas's recollection, the group talked blissfully and only about birds. Then the tone of the conversation changed when a man rowed out of the night and angled his boat up to the yacht. He knew people of influence were on board, and he came to tell them of men in the area who were planning to shoot out one of the last of the great colonies. The group learned that Cuban fishermen commonly came up to Florida to cast their nets for mackerel and to venture into the Shark River to shoot egrets. Back in Havana, they could sell the feathers to agents for between ten and twenty-five dollars a bird. The agents then shipped their product to Paris, where milliners were trying to revive passé feather fashions.[20]

Douglas converted the evening's interruption into a scene in "Plumes," which she wrote soon after the Everglades excursion. Her story's protagonist, John Pinder, is the man who approaches the yacht, on which a group of northerners are dining in a perfect moonlit setting. On board is the head of Audubon, and Pinder tells him that Two-Gun George, a rough-hewn local character, plans to raid a rookery. The Audubon man is leaving the next morning for New York but persuades Pinder to be deputized to protect the rookery. In a nonfiction piece, "Wings," published in the Post a year later, Douglas gave the details of the actual Tarpon Bay event. Bumpus went off to talk to the mackerel fishermen, who returned polite, noncommittal nods when he pled the birds' case. Pearson then hired two local men to watch over the rookery. He returned in May and raised five thousand dollars to employ a total of eight wardens, all federally deputized, for four months during the mating season. Over the years, Audubon had spent forty thousand dollars to protect Florida birds. Organization officials had thought the plumage trade was dead, but a local market for meat and eggs and a small foreign market in feathers generated enough demand to frustrate perpetual attempts at protection. The struggle, in Pearson's words, ultimately represented a "love's labor lost."[21]

Douglas admired Pearson for his quick action in the Tarpon Bay matter and for his Quaker principles. He had acquired his love of birds while rambling the woods around his boyhood home in Archer, Florida. He took degrees at Guilford College and the University of North Carolina and then returned to Guilford to teach. In 1902, he founded the Audubon Society of North Carolina and pushed for the passage of a state law protecting songbirds. Ten years later, he was in New York serving as director of National Audubon. During his twenty-year tenure, he grew into a large, heavy-footed man, quite a contrast to the sprightly birds that defined his life. He also earned a reputation for being a secretive and imperious but effective leader. To Douglas, he was among that special breed of fighting Quakers. She wrote "Wings" largely as a celebration of his work.[22]

Despite his and others' fighting spirit on Tarpon Bay that night, the mackerel fishermen took the birds. It was a tragic denouement, but one that worked in Coe's favor by helping to demonstrate the need for a park. In May, Douglas published a full-page article in the *Herald* that included fifty-seven testimonials that Coe had secured from local and university scientists and naturalists. Gifford Pinchot weighed in with his considerable influence. Others cited Everglades as the only potential year-round member of the national system. The Department of the Interior endorsed the creation of an Everglades park, doing so at the time it was accepting the transfer of state land to create the Great Smoky Mountain National Park, the second east of the Mississippi River. Hoping to complete what Grosvenor described as a "magnificent string of Eastern seaboard national parks," interior secretary Wilbur forwarded a special nine-page recommendation to Congress and President Herbert Hoover.[23]

Coe's chief ally on Capitol Hill was Representative Ruth Bryan Owen, the first woman from Florida to serve in Congress. Owen had joined seven other female representatives when she was elected by a sizable majority in 1928. A regal woman, she spent nearly ten years on the Chautauqua circuit and taught public speaking at the University of Miami. Not surprisingly, people frequently compared her with her father, William Jennings Bryan, and she used her inherited oratorical skills to promote the Everglades. She also impressed the Washington crowd with her stamina, efficiency, and cool nerves around wild things. The *Washington Post* called her the "Junoesque lady from the Everglades." Coe was ecstatic.[24]

In late fall 1930, Owen cosponsored a national park bill, which was referred to the House Committee on Public Lands. She paraded in a dozen supporters to testify during hearings. Coe spoke, of course, as did Pearson, Bumpus, and John Kunkel Small. Recounting the South Florida trip, Albright said he had "never seen any place where there were so many interesting things at every turn." From the opposition came the assertion that the Everglades were good for nothing more than slimy vermin. But Owen had prepared for this old windbag argument. One of her witnesses, Howard Kelly, a Johns Hopkins University gynecological surgeon and part-time Everglades resident who touted himself as having been "born with the taste of a naturalist," insisted that "there are snakes of south Florida which ought to be kept." From a duffle, he produced a king snake, a denizen of his library. He kept his testimony short, but his eloquent descriptions of mollusks, "fleshy fungy," and birds—"beautiful intelligent citizens of the wilds"—mesmerized the committee. Then at some point, Owen, who was known to climb trees to collect snails, picked up the snake and allowed it to dangle across her shoulders.[25]

Soon after the House hearings concluded, the Senate's Public Lands Committee decided to send a group to see the Everglades firsthand. Departing the day after Christmas, the delegation, including six senators and five of their wives, arrived in Miami by train on the morning of December 28. Once again, Coe had fired off telegram after telegram to Fairchild with instructions for the visit. The senatorial group followed a similar itinerary to that of the national park group the year before, ending another "perfect week," as Coe wrote to a friend, on January 2.[26]

The Senate committee wasted little time in approving the park bill, leaving Coe cautiously hopeful about winning over the full Congress. But then he lost his most important inside ally. During Owen's 1931 reelection bid, when an economically bedeviled nation reasoned that lifting Prohibition would translate into jobs, she lost after remaining allied with her parents' everlasting harangue against liquor. Although her successor, J. Mark Wilcox of West Palm Beach, advanced the park agenda, the worsening economy changed congressional priorities. The Senate passed the park bill, but the House decided that it could not justify spending for the initial improvements required of a new park. Coe wrote to Governor Doyle Carlton, "It was found as anticipated that opposition was largely due to misunderstanding. That the Everglades National Park was just 'another' Florida promotion scheme had been a knotty argument to explain away although wholly untrue." Coe felt the sting of the Broward era and the 1920s land swindles, though he acknowledged the "untimely" nature of the park proposal, writing to Frank Stoneman, "That the Park bill did not pass the House was due wholly to the stress of present economic conditions." Coe nevertheless remained irrepressibly confident that the park idea had too much "intrinsic merit" to fail.[27]

Returning to basics, he ramped up the publicity campaign. Douglas wrote another magazine article and a Florida Department of Agriculture bulletin. The article linked the proposed national park to a system of Florida state parks then under development. The twenty-nine-page bulletin, *Parks and Playgrounds of Florida,* was written in collaboration with a Department of Agriculture scientist, Ralph Stoutamire, who published on subjects ranging from land drainage to bullfrog farming. His coauthor's regionalist sensibilities are evident in the bulletin's emphasis on the rarified beauty and natural denizens of the Everglades. And the prose is pure Douglas: "Prairie-like reaches of saw grass and swamp, lion-colored under the sun, dotted with queer jungle islands of cypress or palmetto or buttonwood or holly and tangling, green silence, and the incredible, impressible country of the mangroves." Her most in-depth study to date on the Everglades, the bulletin, which expanded in size in each of two subsequent reprints, served as useful preparation for writing her most important publication and for cultivating relationships with knowledgeable scientists.[28]

Meanwhile, Coe was back on Capitol Hill. Although he had only the fiscally conscious House to convince, he risked nothing to lassitude. He emphasized at every turn that the "acquisition of the land will impose no expense upon the Federal Government." The state would bear the fiscal burden of private property buyouts, and the process would take years. Only then would the federal government incur a burden in setting up the park, he said, adding a depression-era carrot by maintaining that the new park would provide jobs for "several hundred men." To keep the Everglades on Washington minds, he had coconuts shipped to House members, the president, and the secretary of the interior. To all, he made available signed copies of John Kunkel Small's *From Eden to Sahara.* He also revived an idea inaugurated by Owen, who framed copies of Douglas's poem "I Am the Mangrove" and sent them to Washington colleagues. He and Owen saw the poem, as did a fan who had read it in "The Galley" in 1923, "as a manifesto!" The last stanzas suggest the strength of progress and national pride embodied in a park-worthy natural place.

Behind me grows a barrier, woven of my roots,

Behind me advances the armies of the conquering grass,

    Dry footed.

    I shout my challenge,

    Silently, silently.

    I stride, triumphant.

Buffeted, victorious, out across shallows, out to the sea ways,

I am the pioneer, I am the forerunner, I am the adventurer.

    After me comes earth.

    I am the mangrove.

    Look.

    I build.[29]

After the original bill failed, the House asked the Department of the Interior to appoint a special committee to study the Everglades proposal. Interior turned to the National Park Service, which then turned to Frederick Law Olmsted Jr. and William P. Wharton. Wharton served on the boards of directors of the American Forestry Association and the National Park Association, and for a time he held the National Park Association presidency as well. Olmsted carried the name of his father, the most influential founding practitioner of American landscape architecture, but was no mere maladjusted son trading on his famous parent's good reputation. Although he had cut his teeth on two of his father's most celebrated projects, the Biltmore Estate and the 1893 World's Columbian Exposition in Chicago, his own talents had subsequently carried him to the top of the landscape architecture profession. The younger Olmsted had also helped frame the language in the legislation that established the National Park Service in 1916. Fifteen years later, he and Wharton spent two weeks exploring the Everglades. Fellow tradesman Coe was their escort, dressed much of the time in his usual white with a dark bow tie, bringing to mind an ice cream vendor. Olmsted and Wharton reported back their unqualified support for the new park, and the Park Service conveyed this information to the House of Representatives in January 1932.[30]

The House bill nevertheless failed again. In early fall, Coe met with Albright and Cammerer in Virginia's Blue Ridge Mountains, where the Shenandoah National Park was soon to be established. Coe was starting to feel a sense of urgency, worrying incessantly that if the bill were not approved soon, the continued exploitation of the region would ruin it for national park status. But Albright and Cammerer assured Coe that the Everglades was "all important in the rounding out of the Eastern Group." Then in January, Wilbur toured the Everglades in the company of Fairchild. The interior secretary followed up the trip with a recommendation for "prompt action by Congress."[31]

Finally, through parliamentary maneuvering, the bill passed the House in May 1934. Fiscal watchdogs in the Senate had previously added a provision prohibiting appropriations for the park until 1939, a restriction to which Coe and other park proponents had already agreed in principle. President Franklin D. Roosevelt, who believed that "there is nothing so American as our national parks," promptly signed the legislation and issued an executive order removing all federal land within the proposed park area from settlement and sale.[32]

The responsibility of parceling together the remaining parklands now lay with Coe. As head of the state's Tropic Everglades National Park Commission, he had to acquire private land through state purchases and condemnation and transfer state land to the Interior Department. This latter task seemed like a pro forma matter. The Internal Improvement Fund controlled that land, however, and the composition of its membership represented northern Florida's political power brokers, many of whom grumbled at the prospect of giving up 60 percent of the state's real estate portfolio to a national park that would bring tourist dollars to southern Florida. The dyed-in-the-wool southerners in Tallahassee had even less of an appetite for a loquacious Yankee from Connecticut. In 1937, in one of his first actions after taking office, the newly elected governor, Fred Cone, an attorney from longleaf country on the Georgia border, dismantled the park commission's executive council. He then appointed a new director, even though law mandated that the council elect the director, and left the rest of the seats on the council vacant. He also withheld funding, casting the commission into indefinite limbo. After eight years of dedicated work, Coe was fired. The state owed him twenty-five thousand dollars in back salary.[33]

Douglas had known the sting of the wool-hat boys and hoped that Coe's dismissal would not prove fatal for the park. The prophet soldiered on the best he could, trying to maintain the thrust of earlier years, while Douglas turned back to the business of writing short fiction. She published an average of three stories a year over the last half of the 1930s. Magazine writing had not permitted her an extravagant life but kept her fed, clothed, and sheltered. She was content with her professional life, though she remained interested in new possibilities. Events began falling into place that would lead her to such possibilities and to an even more intimate engagement with the park.

The Book Idea

The doctors at first said eighty-three-year-old Frank Stoneman was too old to survive major surgery. Then, when complications related to a kidney stone worsened, they decided an operation was his only hope. His wife, Lillias, could not be with him on the morning of his surgery, February 1, 1941. She was ill and confined to bed at home under the care of her younger cousin, Mildred Shine. Marjory was at the hospital, and she and her father last spoke as the orderlies wheeled him away to the operating room. When the doctor later came out to share the worst, she pulled her grief-stricken self together and prepared a page-long biography, which included several reminiscences of friends and colleagues, for the *Miami Herald*. Douglas wanted readers to be aware of the unknown parts to the familiar public man, his beliefs, personal integrity, and habits of life—the sensible way he treated blacks and whites the same when they came before his municipal court, the time he fined himself for driving through a red light, the unselfish energy he gave to civic life through the work of the Masonic Lodge, the long hours he put in at the newspaper, the abstemious life he led manifested in the plain clothes he wore, and the egalitarian ideas he held about women.[1]

The biography paid tribute to Stoneman as the model citizen of the world. Testimonies of the loving husband and the good father were only implied. Stoneman had orchestrated his life primarily around community, directing its rhythm and progression when and where he believed he could. Douglas never seemed to begrudge him this arrangement in priorities, and father and daughter remained close in their own way. After moving to Coconut Grove, she continued to spend two or three evenings a week at the Spring Garden house playing checkers or reading books with him. Their relationship had achieved a level of shared comfort, with a salutary intellectual companionship and a mutual avoidance of touchy family subjects.[2]

It was typical that he never retired from the editor-in-chief post at the *Herald*. It was also typical that he did not leave a written record of his family. Instead, in the year leading up to his death, he began writing a column about his city's past. Titled "Miami Memories," it bequeathed to readers beloved renderings of the city's history, its growing pains, and its adjustment to national and world events. Appropriately, funeral services were held at Trinity Episcopal Church, which he had helped found, and standing as his honor guard were the Knights Templar, proud gray-haired men in dress regalia from the James Canell Masonic Lodge, which he had also founded. When the pallbearers passed beneath the gabled row of drawn swords, lying atop the casket were Stoneman's scabbarded sword and naval-style chapeau, festooned with snowy egret plumes.[3]

Lillias remained bedridden, so Marjory was the only family among the mourners, who included the mayor and Frank Shutts. Retired for four years after selling the *Herald* to the Knight family of Akron for $2.25 million, Shutts gave the eulogy, remembering Stoneman as a civic gentleman. "The people of Miami owe more to Frank Stoneman, much more, than they realize. His love for this city was a continually demonstrated fervor." Shutts closed with a reference to the philosophical Stoneman, who had not feared death because he had enjoyed life. "No one has ever been able, yet, to look beyond the veil," Shutts remembered Stoneman saying. "But whatever lies over there, whatever it is, no matter what, it is all right."[4]

Aunt Fanny had died three years earlier, and the two deaths brought an end to the rancor and grudges within Marjory's family. Fanny left the Taunton house and fourteen thousand dollars she had relentlessly squirreled away over the years. In the midst of the national depression, the house sold for a miserable one thousand dollars, but Marjory's portion of the estate, divided with her uncle, Charles Trefethen, and her cousins, enabled her to pay off the mortgage on her house. For all his efforts to do well, Frank's estate was smaller. Marjory and Lillias shared $11,331 in cash, a car valued at $150, and books worth $50. Douglas convinced the *Herald* to buy the house and hold it in trust until Lillias's death. Douglas's part of the inheritance then allowed her, as she said, to get out of the magazine business. She was fifty-one years old, and she was ready to write books.[5]

She had given nearly twenty years to magazine writing. It led her to teach a course at the University of Miami from 1924 to 1927 on short fiction. One student remembered her as an "unendingly patient" instructor who "did her best to bring out anything of value that was latent in me." During the Great Depression, the demand for stories remained strong, and she fared better than some of her friends, including Marion Manley. Manley had been Douglas's original choice to design her house, but the state's first licensed female architect had been too busy with work on the new University of Miami and estates of the wealthy. When things were booming, the two women had made their ill-fated investment in Everglades real estate. But then came the bust. Manley fell onto hard times, and Douglas took her in. Manley built a small room off the kitchen and resided there for some three years.[6]

Around this time, friends and admirers of David Fairchild conceived the idea of doing something to honor his work in botany and his importation of tropical plants. During her long friendship with David and his wife, Marian, Douglas spent countless hours at their eight-acre bayside Coconut Grove residence, the Kampong (Malay for "village"), and she and others first hammered out the plans for the national park there. Over the years, the Fairchilds had hosted numerous celebrated individuals, including Henry Firestone, Thomas Edison, and Marian's father, Alexander

Graham Bell. National Geographic's Gilbert Grosvenor and his wife, Elsie, Marian's sister, lived next door. David had used the Kampong as an introduction garden for many of the eighty thousand varieties of plants he imported, some of which he shared with friends and neighbors. In some ways, the Kampong was the intellectual soul of and aesthetic standard for the tropical Grove. Friends envisioned a botanical garden of a similar order, but larger and open to the public. Robert H. Montgomery, a wealthy New York businessman and part-time Miami resident inclined to the role of benefactor, purchased an eighty-three-acre site for the garden in the Grove and on the bay, and he donated funds for plant development. He also hired Douglas to write what ultimately became a twenty-three-page promotional pamphlet and funded her research trip to the New York Botanical Garden. Douglas gave the dedication speech at the 1938 opening of the Fairchild Tropical Botanical Garden, and she served as the first secretary of its board of trustees and remained a longtime member and officer.[7]

Although the pamphlet was relatively short, it was a much longer form than the short stories she had been writing, and it may have prompted her to make a change she had been considering for some time. Three years later, two weeks after her father's death, her last *Saturday Evening Post* piece appeared, a fictional story about a boy and a man who steal across all of the accursed elements of the Everglades. She felt ready to set aside the short story and write a novel. But, once again, her crossing between literary genres was bedeviled by a nervous breakdown. One moonlit night, her neighbors, Franklin and Alice Harris, were awakened by shouting and moonlight baying. They discovered Douglas had abandoned herself to aimless wandering outside in a nightgown and bare feet and took her to a doctor. Unlike her mother, she always recovered from these disturbing lapses and returned to life's normal routine.[8]

If stressful, the transition was liberating and long awaited. Douglas's writing diary indicates that a novel had taken embryonic form in the mid-1920s. It also reveals a creative confinement she had felt in familial scrutiny and censor. "Working on idea of *South of the Sun*. See it quite clearly as a novel. Would hope to do it frankly and beautifully, with the theme that life is a web of so many and intricate threads, beauties, interests, with sex not always of supreme importance. Perhaps an underlying cause but in actuality only a highlight. Question is not only can it be done but also, would it disgrace the family too much? Not that I care much about that. It could be written under another name." At the time, she and publisher John Farrar were discussing a book, and after she won the O. Henry Memorial Prize for "The Peculiar Treasure of Kings," an editor from Doubleday, which sponsored the prize, asked that she consider publishing with his house. Financial rather than familial concerns likely forced her to set aside the book. Eventually, Fanny's and Frank's deaths and the small inheritances freed her at a time when the growing popularity of movies, followed by the emergence of television, began taking a toll on story magazines. Working without a book contract or advance, she resurrected her old novel from a drawer and began writing *Road to the Sun*. To give herself a little income, she accepted a part-time position as book-review editor for the *Herald*. Then the Japanese bombed Pearl Harbor.[9]

Miami was quickly swept up in the war. Florida's ample sunshine, cheap land, and junglelike terrain attracted the military as readily as tourists and real estate speculators. The Department of War invested heavily in the state, establishing 172 installations there before the end of the conflict. Beach resorts took on the guise of training camps and hospitals. Grousing Miami Beach hotel owners were forced to give up seventy thousand rooms to Army Air Force personnel in 1942, when resort operators had expected a record number of tourists. The money flowed in anyway. Floridians earned two billion dollars in 1943, up from less than half a billion ten years earlier. Commissary demands pushed the citrus industry to perfect the concentrate process, which revolutionized citriculture and sent Florida's sales past California's for the first time. New wealth and hundreds of thousands of uniformed men did not, however, translate into security. German submarines prowled shipping lanes a few miles out in the Atlantic Ocean and sank twenty-four vessels. Reminiscent of the Spanish era, dead sailors and other flotsam washed onto Florida beaches.[10]

Douglas never wrote about this new war or incorporated it into any of her fiction. The previous conflict had been the war of her generation and was enough for her lifetime. She was fully absorbed in her novel, not to be distracted as before. What did catch her attention was a contract offer to write a nonfiction book. Her friend, Hervey Allen, dropped the offer into her lap. An admirer of his poetry before ever meeting him, she described him as the "interpreter of a region," the Deep South. They apparently met in 1934, when both spoke at the third annual Winter Institute of Literature (which in the early 1940s Douglas began directing). Allen was a year older than she, a towering fourteen inches taller, and originally from Pittsburgh. A shell-shocked World War I veteran, he first made a name for himself by writing poetry about the bloody waste of war. The year before the symposium in Miami, Farrar and Rinehart released his most successful work, *Anthony Adverse,* a historical novel. Though a hefty twelve hundred pages, it was one of the most widely read books of the 1930s, selling two thousand copies a day during the first weeks after its publication. In 1936, Warner Brothers and David O. Selznick brought it to the screen, where, starring Fredric March and Olivia de Havilland, it won four Oscars.[11]

Two years earlier, Allen had begun spending winters in Miami. South of town at the edge of the Everglades, he built a modest limestone bungalow that was nearly as much screen porch as house. He called it the Glades and beside it put in a garden of tropical plants. Though he also owned houses in Bermuda and Maryland, he fell in love with the Everglades and did most of his writing at the Glades. He also began editing Farrar and Rinehart's popular Rivers of America series. Canadian-born author Constance Lindsay Skinner had launched the series in 1935. It emanated from her belief that rivers drove the course of history in the settlement period of North America. She envisioned producing twenty-four books illustrated with artist sketches and incorporating the literary talents of novelists and poets. She died in 1939 with the galleys of Carl Carmer's *The Hudson* in her lap.[12] Allen and Carmer assumed coeditorship of the series in 1943. Skinner had seen the completion of six titles, including one about Florida's Suwannee River, and had initiated plans for a book on the St. Johns.[13]

Allen thought of Douglas and the Miami River and dropped in on her one day to talk about the idea. Writing for her friend had great appeal, but she was skeptical. The Miami was an unremarkable waterway. As she turned the idea over in her mind, she thought of perhaps pairing it with the Everglades. True, they were not a river, at least as far as anyone, including Douglas, had yet conceptualized them, but they were much more impressive and vivid than the Miami, integrated more definitively with humans in the region's history. And she was already acquainted with their literary potential. Incorporating them as an illuminating backdrop might give a book about the Miami a greater chance. They would certainly make the project more interesting. Although he domiciled at their doorstep, Allen had not considered the Everglades for the series, probably because he, like everyone else, saw them as a swell of unbroken swamp. She held roughly the same image, but for a long time and particularly in light of recent talk of a national park, they had haunted the American imagination. Allen's love for them ultimately made Douglas's idea an easy sell. In November, she signed an agreement with Farrar and Rinehart that provided her a fifteen-hundred-dollar advance for a book on the "Miami River, South, and the Everglades."[14]

A slow evolution in the sciences formed the backdrop for Douglas's literary transformation. For some years, ecologists had struggled to claim a respectfully visible place for their discipline in American sciences. Ecology did not significantly shape the idea of her book, but in later years, after emerging from its arcane existence, ecology influenced perspectives on *River of Grass* and its value to the environmental (some called it ecological) movement. The German academy had been familiar with the word *ecology* since 1866, when physician turned Darwin interpreter Ernst Haeckel used it in a two-volume work on the great naturalist, and by the 1880s European scientists had accepted ecology as a serious field of study. On the other side of the Atlantic, however, ecology remained seriously obscure.[15]

Its American beginnings are typically traced to Stephen Forbes, a Civil War veteran with muttonchop whiskers who taught at the University of Illinois. Primarily an entomologist, he spread his talents in botany, aquatic biology, ornithology, and zoology over a sixty-year career that produced more than four hundred professional papers. As a forty-two-year-old

professor of entomology and zoology, director of the Illinois State Laboratory of Natural History, and state entomologist, the inexhaustible Forbes
exhibited his genius in a pathbreaking paper, "The Lake as a Microcosm."
Read to a small gathering of regional scientists in the Illinois River town
of Peoria in February 1887, the paper marked an extraordinary moment
in the history of American science. His audience that night heard for the
first time the essential concepts and language that would later define ecology. Arguing that a lake constituted a "little world within itself," he laid
out the fundamental idea of a holistic aquatic community. His was a violent community of feeding and predation, where insects, fish, and birds
scrambled along a chain of survival. This was the "dynamic equilibrium
of organic life and activity" in which the disturbance of any one species
"must speedily have its influence of some sort upon the whole assem-
blage." Forbes laid the foundation for a new field of study, which people
began calling the new natural history.[16]

The edifice rose slowly. The first course of bricks was set in 1898 when
Henry C. Cowles at the University of Chicago and Frederic E. Clements
and Roscoe Pound at the University of Nebraska submitted their disser-
tations. All three went on to brilliant careers. Pound produced a slew of
publications on botany before leaving the field for law, where he established himself as a leading theorist on sociological jurisprudence. The
"tirelessly diligent" Clements moved on to the University of Minnesota
and eventually the Carnegie Institution of Washington, and the "solitary
and self-reliant" Cowles continued at Chicago. Surrounded by supportive colleagues, admiring students, and living wetland and grassland laboratories, they followed separate but similar lights in plant science, establishing the Midwest as the academic center of ecology and leading the
discipline into the first decades of the new century. In 1915, a handful of
scientists, including Cowles and a gray-whiskered, seventy-one-year-old
Forbes, organized the Ecological Society of America. Five years later, it
launched the journal *Ecology*.[17]

The word itself nevertheless remained despairingly absent from American college dictionaries. Editors of science journals decided the field
was too obscure to be mentioned without a defining footnote. Stuffier

universities of the East refused to give ecology academic standing and chafed at the mention of the "barbarian institutions of the middle West" as the birthplace of a new science. Practitioners did not help matters. In 1903, W. F. Ganong, a straight-from-the-shoulder Smith College ecologist, told a group of botanists in Philadelphia that "ecological publications in America are too often characterized . . . by a pretentiousness of statement and terminology unjustified by their real merits." Cowles, who complained his discipline was adrift in chaos, could not disagree. Ecology fielded a smorgasbord of practitioners who arrived from botany, zoology, aquatic biology, entomology, and animal science with the biased approaches of their disciplines. Striking for intellectual focus, Cowles believed that ecologists should converge on questions of evolutionary adaptation, while others thought of genetics as the proper pursuit. The discipline's analytic center eventually settled on the physical properties of a biological community and the mutual associations between species and their environment.[18]

Still, ecology continued its search for a clear identity and an autonomous place in the sciences. As late as 1936, one scientist saw ecology as "extraordinarily polymorphic." Plant ecology remained persistently separate from animal ecology, and in spite of Forbes's cross-territorial research, aquatic communities and terrestrial communities stood as disconnected objects of study. British scientist Arthur G. Tansley began to pull things together somewhat when in 1935 he advanced the concept of the ecosystem, a less balkanized formulation of the interdependent biological community. Four years later, Clements and University of Illinois zoologist Victor Shelford, a pioneer in animal ecology, published *Bio-Ecology*, a book that braided together animal, plant, and aquatic sciences and suggested the "synthetic ideal" toward which the discipline was ambling. But one of the book's keenest critics was G. Evelyn Hutchinson, a Yale University limnologist. Sporting an unwieldy bush of hair that offered something of a vivid testimonial to countless windblown days outdoors, Hutchinson championed the study of energy flow through ecosystems. By his assessment, one of the shortcomings of *Bio-Ecology* and of the ecology discipline itself was the failure to make connections between human culture and the environment—in particular, the human impact on the environment.[19]

The practical application of ecology, beyond the starchy world of field laboratories and classrooms, helped to sharpen the scientific understanding of those connections. Around the turn of the century, conservation-oriented bureaucrats of the Progressive Era began turning to ecology to facilitate the sustainable management of forests, ranges, wildlife, and other extractable natural resources, mainly in the public domain. Gifford Pinchot, for example, believed that foresters needed to understand trees "as members of plant communities" and advised forester trainees to study ecology. At the same time, scientists felt a distressing urgency to study disappearing environments as axes felled woodlands and plows turned up indigenous grasslands with accelerated dispatch. The Great Depression and the birth of the New Deal ushered in a whole new round of opportunities for applied ecology and simultaneously elevated the science's academic credentials. Various government agencies, including the U.S. Soil Conservation Service and the Tennessee Valley Authority, drew on new scientific expertise to deal with the lingering consequences of robust wartime and postwar economies and heightened environmental aggressions as Americans tried to hold onto the waning good times. Problems were most acutely visible in the airborne topsoil in the Dust Bowl states of the Great Plains and in the eroded hillsides, gully-washed flatlands, and newly formed miniature Grand Canyons in the Southeast, some of which became tourist attractions. These particulars demonstrated the toll of intensive agriculture in a capitalist economy, suggesting Progressive conservation's narrow field of influence outside public properties. Progressivism's failures, however, were water under the bridge. A liberal flow of ideas from ecologists rose during the New Deal and helped to restore lost landscapes, advance land-use planning, and prevent repeated environmental mishaps.[20]

Enlightenment, as is often the case, had its limits. Science offered new ways of understanding nature, but bureaucrats are proficient at distorting knowledge and expertise to serve agendas. New Deal programs prioritized economic restoration and resource management over and sometimes at the expense of nature protection. Without dulling old economic aspirations, the government put farmers back in business with the help of ecological science, whose insights bureaucrats tapped to curtail the chances of future agricultural disasters but not necessary environmental ones, such as silted waterways or downstream water shortages. For their part, ecologists typically were too engrossed in scientific inquiry (which is a kind way of saying they were out of touch) to minister to the politics of conservation. Some scientists peered out from their laboratories long enough to reject the notion of using ecology to institute social doctrine. As a whole, ecologists before the 1960s were anything but horn-rimmed proponents of organized subversion or activism.[21]

Paul B. Sears, a Henry Cowles student who headed the conservation program at Yale University, said as much. Clements and Shelford numbered among the few exceptions to the rule of political neutrality. Another was Sears. In 1935, when wind-lifted dirt from the Plains states was dusting the East Coast, he published an eloquently written scientific exposé, *Deserts on the March*. Echoing John Kunkel Small's message for Florida in *From Eden to Sahara*, Sears linked agricultural land policy with a sacred cow that had not suffocated in the dust storms—an aggressive marketplace economy. Because of that aggressiveness, the American West was turning into a desolated environment. Sears, who wore a fedora in the field to block both the sun and the dust and advocated planting weeds to reduce the latter, wanted to motivate politically lethargic ecologists to help the public see the error of civilization's excesses. Doing so would naturally require more rapidly elevating his discipline's status in the American academy. In a paper delivered at the 1955 meeting of the American Association for the Advancement of Science, he observed, "The average [European] biologist knows more ecology than his colleagues in this country." At the optimum moment in the 1930s, concludes one latter-day ecologist, *Deserts on the March*'s fretful red flags drew little attention.[22]

When Douglas signed her contract with Rinehart, scientists had only begun to decipher the ecological complexities of the Everglades. For a writer setting out on a new book project, this situation had its advantages.

Years hence, Douglas often said that she was "fortunate in finding a subject no one knew too much about."[23]

Science, however handicapped by its procrastinating acceptance of ecology, was essential to getting to know her subject. Though she was not formally trained beyond the requisite college introductory courses, she associated scientific knowledge with social progress, and she regarded those who did not as having an "ostrich attitude of mind." For her, modern science began with "that astonishing man," Darwin. Even before the famous Scopes monkey trial, she was aware of the advancing culture war, and she made her loyalty to science boldly clear when, in "The Galley," she expressed dismay at anti-Darwinists: "A thing must not be true, they think, because they do not like to think it is true. And that . . . is the state of mind which persecuted the first man to believe that the earth was round and it is the state of mind which would willingly put a blight on all progress, for the sake of maintaining its own opinion."[24]

Douglas had known the most celebrated anti-Darwinist, William Jennings Bryan, and he was long gone by the 1940s. Not many of the old-school naturalists were around either. Small and Charles Torrey Simpson had died in the late 1930s, and Frank Chapman and T. Gilbert Pearson passed away while she was in the middle of her research. Fairchild survived his colleagues and was eager to help his friend, although he had not kept up with the changes in his field. He did put her in touch with John H. Davis of the Florida Geological Survey, who gave her still more referrals. She also made an appointment with John Pennekamp, who had succeeded her father as editor at the *Herald*. Both he and Douglas knew enough about the Everglades to know how much they did not know. Beyond birds, sawgrass, hammocks, and a handful of plants, the Everglades remained geologically, biologically, and certainly ecologically a mystery. Pennekamp encouraged her to visit the U.S. Geological Survey (USGS) office in the courthouse to talk to Garald Parker.[25]

Parker had been in Florida only since 1940. Born in an Oregon sawmill town, he grew up in the Northwest and worked as a schoolteacher and principal for several years before pursuing graduate training in geology and biology at the University of Washington. Soon after he completed his degree, the Geological Survey offered the thirty-five-year-old Parker a twenty-six-hundred-dollar-a-year job at its new Water Resources Division office in Miami. That fall, he, his wife, and their two children drove across the country in a new Dodge sedan, pulling a home-built trailer packed eight feet high with all their possessions. They arrived in Miami coming across Tamiami Trail, giving Parker his first glimpse of the place where he would do much of his fieldwork. Not long after he settled into the new job, the Japanese raided Pearl Harbor, and all of the division's Miami staff except Parker left for the military. He witnessed the war from the window of his seventeenth-floor office looking out toward the Atlantic—the exploding ships, the depth charges dropped from PT boats, and the shoreline horribly littered with debris and bodies.[26]

The Water Resources Division office, of which he was now in charge, had been located in Miami for a specific reason. Since the early years of the twentieth century, the city's potable water source, shallow artesian wells drilled through the limestone, had suffered from saltwater intrusion, forcing water engineers to move the municipal well fields farther in from the coast. In 1938, a thousand city wells, located nine miles inland by that time, along with private wells in Coconut Grove and Coral Gables, went salty. The city was desperate to find a way to keep its precious water pure. Parker was charged with responsibility for mapping out the hidden underground and discerning the saltwater's encroachment pattern. He and his staff drilled hundreds of exploratory wells along the coastal ridge and as far out into the Everglades as the Big Cypress Swamp, sometimes hauling their equipment into remote wet areas on airboats. They often traveled like the explorers of the previous century, encountering on foot, on horseback, or in canoe the natural elements and the same bedeviling hardships. "The Everglades were practically impenetrable," he later remembered. They were also treacherous. One night, his team set up camp near Clewiston and woke the next morning to find their horses dead; "mosquitoes had stung them so much their nostrils closed."[27]

This was the price of scientific discovery. Parker determined that Southeast Florida, from Boca Raton to Florida Bay, sat on a self-contained aquifer with an undulating depth of between 90 and 180 feet. Underlying it was an impenetrable layer of green clay, now known as the Hawthorne

Formation, that sealed off the shallower aquifer from the Floridan Aquifer. The former's only source for recharge was rain and the Everglades, and it was the sole supplier of drinking water for South Florida's population. Parker named this formation the Biscayne Aquifer.[28]

He made another discovery, too. Drainage and usage had lowered the fresh groundwater level and thus brought denser saltwater up to the depth of the artesian wells. Deep wells reaching below the saltwater were not an option. Parker had dug 862 feet through the clay and into the Floridan Aquifer only to find the water too heavily mineralized for use by homes or farms. By cutting Everglades canals down to the Atlantic and by dynamiting the Miami River rapids, reclamation engineers had also destroyed natural barriers between the fresh surface water and saltwater, allowing the latter to wash up the canals and create problems from above. Parker calculated that the freshwater table would have to be maintained at a minimum of 2.5 feet above sea level to keep the saltwater below the draw of wells. To do so would require the construction of what he called saltwater control dams at the lowest possible reach of the canals and rivers. This meant a soggier South Florida environment, more like the original. His proposals generated strong resistance from reclamation advocates, but women's clubs and civic organizations began inviting him to speak at their meetings. By 1953, the dams were in place, marking the beginning of the constant monitoring of the Everglades environment.[29]

Although technically no ecologist, Parker established himself as the foremost authority on the systemic character of the Everglades. The proof of that claim was backed by a professional bibliography that exceeded forty reports and papers dealing with not only groundwater conditions but also "soil-water-plant relationships" and the ecological impact of development, agriculture, and drainage. He had delved into the reports of early explorers, drainage and land companies, the Internal Improvement Fund, the Everglades Drainage District, and the Lake Okeechobee Drainage District. He consulted with experts at the state's universities, Fairchild's old Tropical Plant Introduction Station, the U.S. Weather Bureau, the National Audubon Society, and the National Park Service.[30]

For Douglas, Parker's presence in Miami was a stroke of good fortune. Whenever she met with him at the courthouse, his chart-littered office became a classroom. His approach to geology was like that of her Wellesley professor, Elizabeth Fisher, who brought several disciplines together in her lessons. Parker described himself as a "geologist-biologist-hydrologist." By his recollection, Douglas came to see him twenty or thirty times and made several trips out into the Everglades and the Big Cypress with him. She was eager to learn, and he to teach. He was in the early stages of his research when they first met, so she witnessed his research in progress. And when he learned something new, so did she.[31]

In the end, his invaluable work guided the development of the natural history part of her book. No individual received the same level of recognition in her acknowledgments. She opened the book with a lengthy chapter on "The Nature of the Everglades." She consulted field scientists and engineers at the Florida Geological Survey, the U.S. Soil Conservation Service, and the University of Florida Everglades Experiment Station. But the major sections of the chapter—"The Grass," "The Water," "The Rock," and "Life on the Rock"—reflect Parker's tutelage.[32]

His expertise carried her to her most important discovery. In a 1985 letter to Parker's second wife, Bernadette, Douglas noted her "profound indebtedness to him":

I will never forget how kind Jerry was to a wild woman who had to write a book on a subject about which she knew nothing. I said, "What are the Everglades anyway?" and he said, "That's easy; wherever you find a flow of fresh water south of Lake Okeechobee with a lot of sawgrass growing up in it out of the rock, you can be sure that that is the Everglades." He gave me a horticultural map of south Florida which showed the course of the Everglades, and it was his insistence that they were not swamp but that they were a sheet flow of water that made me wonder if they were not a river, so I went back to him and asked him what a river was anyway, and he said that a river is a body of fresh water moving more in one direction than the other. So I thought about that and then I said to him, "Do you think I could safely call it a river of grass?" and he thought about it for a minute and said, "I think you could."

After completing his principal study of the region's groundwater, he gave her a copy. "That was really the basis for a great deal of knowledge," Douglas told Bernadette Parker. His research confirmed Douglas's original decision to write about the Everglades rather than the Miami River.[33]

Then came the book's perceptive subtitle, *River of Grass*. Although the concept represented a biological oversimplification, as the book itself reveals, Parker liked this shorthand. No one before had conceived of the Everglades as a river. In the published account of his 1897 Everglades expedition, Hugh Willoughby perhaps came closest when he spoke of water "moving in one principal direction or the other." Willoughby somehow escaped Douglas's list of consulted works, but she did have the Indian name *Pahayokee*, meaning grassy water, in mind when her book gave the Everglades the imprimatur of a "river of grass."[34]

Here was something more felicitous than the Miami Chamber of Commerce's hundred-dollar *Tropical Glades*, which smacked of a papered blazonry feebly pasted over the old to announce the new. *River of Grass* had a glue that would stick. The term's origins in a book suggested thoughtful reflection or scientific investigation rather than the rush to monetary bounty. And what on earth are tropical glades anyway? Were they enticing or repulsive? The name *Everglades* was similarly problematic, as the Chamber of Commerce noted. But *River of Grass* evoked a picture one could see clearly and behold affirmatively and even wistfully: a sauntering flow through green nature. *River of Grass* also redefined, even subverted. It was a poetic subversion at first, merely dismissing the swamp for the river. Eventually, though, it would undermine the principle of those who churlishly treated the Everglades as a wasteland, who thought to discard, ruin, or remain indifferent to them. The full impact of revision—imagery and meaning—built gradually over the ensuing decades. No one, including Douglas, foresaw the changing context of the environmental century and the evolving importance of her book.

Douglas's reconstituted understanding of the country's greatest wetland came alongside her book's seminal contribution to the Rivers of America series. Hers was the thirty-fourth of the sixty-five books in the collection, with the last published in 1974. Volumes in the series typically open with the most elemental geographic description of the river in question before expeditiously shifting to the book's principal subject, people. Indians are dealt with first, expeditiously again, before too much space is taken from a rousing narrative on the development of American civilization, often interpreted melodramatically as the sum of murder, mayhem, and transcontinental adventure. The narratives run to the highly anecdotal and often border on tall tales. In a slight departure, Carl Carmer devoted the first chapter of *The Hudson* solely to natural history. This chapter is a mere five pages, however, whereas the opener of Douglas's volume runs fifty-one pages, all of them about nature, wild and freewheeling and lacking in a single human footprint. They illuminate the dynamic interactions among biotic elements, the life cycle of the wet and dry seasons, and the "subtlety and diversity, a crowd of changing forms, of thrusting teeming life" enclosed within the deceptive simplicity of the sawgrass river.[35]

None of this is to say that she strayed from form. The series editors wanted storytellers, and she was a virtuoso. The rest of the 390-page book, with the exception of parts of the last chapter, describe the human experience, and plenty of it resembles folklore and legend. Yet throughout her storytelling is nature, an ever-present variable in the course of human activity. Michael Branch, a scholar of literature and the environment who has spent ample time exploring the Everglades, argues that *River of Grass* shows that Douglas "was ahead of her time in comprehending the vital importance of nature-culture interactions to a full understanding of place." Some earlier writers exhibited the same comprehension, including James Fenimore Cooper, William Henry Hudson, Willa Cather, and many others, but Branch is right on the mark in writing, "Douglas's brand of historical anthropology anticipates the work of current environmental historians in its recognition that stories about landscapes are ultimately inextricable from stories about human dwellers in the land—the exigencies of place mold and shape patterns of human culture, and the ambitions and technologies of human communities cause them to alter the landscapes they occupy." Hence, she wrote about Hamilton Disston, Napoleon Bonaparte Broward, Guy Bradley, and Ernest Coe, although she ignored May Mann Jennings and Mary Barr Munroe and the other club women activists.[36]

Yet hers is anything but stock great-white-man history. Of fifteen total chapters, she gave seven and part of another to the history of Florida's first peoples and the Seminoles who came later. She thought of Indians in the tradition of her Quaker ancestors, as human beings with a viable culture, people with a history. While avoiding sentimentality, her portrayal of them rejects the traditional historical perspective left by the victor. She allowed her subjects to speak for themselves, if not through written documents then through their actions and their artifacts. She regarded them as defeated by their invaders, though not exactly conquered. Vestigial numbers survived, and while the Spanish and Anglo empires proved themselves supreme, their cultures were not superior, as their relationships with others demonstrated. In revisionist if not heretical language, uncomfortably close to the 450th anniversary of the discovery of the Americas, she wrote, "After Columbus had opened up a New World, island after island of Indian people, by slavery, torture, hard work, homesickness and disease, thousands after thousands of men, women, chiefs, children, priests, fishermen, warriors, had been blotted out."[37]

Her interpretation was the academic if not moral superior of professional historians, a particular that may account for the fact that *River of Grass* received no contemporary acclaim for its contribution to the study of Florida Indians. It was produced at a time when policymakers were on the verge of substituting New Deal initiatives respecting Indian autonomy with renewed emphasis on assimilation. Seeking to duplicate this retrenchment, those who stubbornly controlled the production of knowledge scrambled to write the bronze savage into the margins of history textbooks and then egregiously into oblivion. There was no need to alert schoolchildren to past sins. *River of Grass* ultimately and remarkably anticipated a new generation of scholars of the 1960s that delivered the historical record from the self-interested elite and offered traditionally dispossessed subjects—blacks, women, ethnic groups—their rightful pages.[38]

Douglas was writing history but was not following the lead of the discipline's practitioners. She corresponded with Melville Herskovits, a

Northwestern University anthropologist who had recently published a groundbreaking ethnographic study, *Myth of the Negro Past,* for referrals on experts on Florida Indians. One, a young, relatively unknown anthropologist named John Goggin, gave her a detailed and fresh vision of the Indian past in Florida—another academic, like Parker, in the throes of major research. Goggin and Parker placed Douglas's work on the cutting edge in 1947. But she learned from others, too. Herskovits's work informed her about slave life. Lydia Parrish, married to artist Maxfield Parrish, shared information on maroons and black Seminoles. Douglas also benefited from assistance from a fussy but generous collector of Spanish documents and maps, David O. True of the Florida Historical Society. Her research at government agencies, libraries, and archives took her all over the state and the country, across to the Bahamas, and into the Everglades. She spent many nights on the western apron of the wetland in Estero with the welcoming people at the Koreshan Unity, founded in 1894 as a new Jerusalem. She found immense pleasure in traveling to new places and revisiting old sites and rekindling friendships. She also got pleasure in the process of gathering and passing along new information.[39]

Writers often hope that they are creating something worthwhile for posterity. Douglas hoped she might at the very least expand the knowledge of her contemporary readers, offering a corrective interpretation of a physical place and the cultures associated with it; she never spoke of the goal of stimulating political consciousness. And what future generations might gain from her labors was anyone's guess. She also did not know that her book would have the fruitful coincidence of appearing in print simultaneously with the dedication of Everglades National Park. These events proved a boon not only to the book, the park, and the Everglades but also to posterity.

The Park Idea

The Civilian Conservation Corps (CCC) was one of the most popular of Franklin Roosevelt's many New Deal agencies. It was so in part because its projects produced something tangible, unlike those of the ditch-and-fill variety, and something beyond the wages of relief work. The CCC tidied up the American wilderness, making it more presentable and accessible to sightseers and vacationers. Another attractive quality was the disciplined battalions of clean-scrubbed, uniformed young men who personified all-American principles that were supposed to rescue the country from economic distress: hard work, cooperation, and loyalty to family. The CCC was also the progeny and personal favorite of FDR. Within days of moving into the White House, he sketched out plans for the new organization. Set to work in the vernal season of 1933, it was his administration's main apparatus of conservation—his tree army, as some called it—working in concert with the Forestry Service and the National Park Service.[1]

Down in Florida, May Mann Jennings, the matriarch of Royal Palm State Park, took notice. Seventeen years after Royal Palm's dedication, Florida still had no other state parks. The dereliction was unacceptable. After the CCC was set in motion, she wasted no time in getting to Tallahassee with an idea for the governor and the state forestry service board, headed by her son. She wanted to use the CCC to develop a system of parks. It seemed a savvy solution for a tourist state strapped for funds and in need of places of bucolic escape for its urbanized citizens. When she had knocked on legislators' doors six years earlier to lobby for state parks, she was politely rebuffed. But now she was bringing the promise of New Deal money. And it was that very money that at long last funded a state park service, with the CCC building the parks—seven new ones by the time it left Florida in the early 1940s.[2]

Built is the operative word here. The way any park is selected from and demarcated in a chosen territory presupposes something artificial. As historian Dave Nelson puts it, desired physical appearances for Florida parks were shaped less by the naked wilderness than by CCC and park officials' images of "visitation, aesthetics, and . . . personal likes/dislikes." "Improvements," "beautification," and "natural clean up"—imperatives in identifying nature with cultural preferences—heightened the "level of outright 'creation/construction.'" More went on than the construction of access roads and picnic shelters, the grooming of beaches, the prevention of fire, and even the introduction of exotic plants. "Nature required action," writes Nelson, a former Florida park ranger.[3]

That was Jennings's thinking. For Royal Palm, she secured Florida's first state park CCC battalion, which worked under the direction of the National Park Service. Two hundred men set up camp in nearby Homestead. The head of the Florida Conservation Commission talked of a "New Deal for the bird life of America"; Jennings called the park "God's own Garden." "Our main thought," she wrote, "was to conserve and guard the natural beauty of the tropical jungle and make it accessible to the public." The CCC revamped the lodge, damaged by a hurricane four years earlier, and built a garage behind it for visitors' cars. Workers leveraged up limestone rock to build a "power house" for electric and water systems, a feed house for deer, and a lily pond. They ran a telephone line to Homestead, cut new roads, and rocked the park's hiking trails, which they doubled in length. Planting five hundred palm, mahogany, and other hardwood trees to restore the hurricane-damaged terrain was the most ambitious project, requiring the blasting of holes into the limestone. The fatigue-clad battalion put in seven and a half months of work before being shipped out to build Highlands Hammock State Park in Sebring, the first addition to the new statewide system.[4]

CCC energies then shifted from restoring nature to recrafting it. When all was done, the superintendent at Highlands Hammock described his park as the "work of creative artisans." Each new park began as did his, with a master plan formulated on the premise that raw nature was unsuitable to the public's taste. It was hence redeemed to match blueprint renderings, drawings, and on-the-spot decision making. When visitors came to the parks, rounded a bend on a trail or road, and gazed across the way, they were unaware of how different their harmonious vista was from what had previously existed, when the landscape was still littered with avowed chaos. Dead trees, stumps, and living trees with burn scars were tagged for removal. When the graceful lines of an ancient sand dune obstructed the public's ocean view from the beach casino at Fort Clinch State Park, officials ordered the dune leveled. As a rule, shovels and sweat removed saw palmettos, a native heat- and drought-resistant verdant cover for Florida's sandy earth. When a former CCC worker was asked why the plant had to go, his response was instructive: "We were building a park."[5]

Certain animals could not stay either. Snakes were the most obvious targets of elimination, hacked with hoes and shovels with adrenalin-charged abandon. Killing contests and recreational hunts were held, and camp newsletters kept a running death count. Bobcats and panthers were shot so that deer were sure to throng sylvan settings that visitors might see. Fish for sport fishing were other valued species; at Myakka River State Park, they were propagated by clearing out predaceous garfish and snapping turtles.[6]

National parks were transformed in much the same way. By rule, they were to be preserved and appreciated in a state of "pristine" wilderness, and the first directors of the National Park Service pooh-poohed state parks for going too far in redesigning nature to accommodate visitors. In reality, though, a bit of human engineering went on in the national counterparts, too. The most obvious example was predator control—the removal of mountain lions, wolves, and others for the protection of preferred wildlife and to ensure beautiful scenery free of nature's violence. Wilderness purists objected. They also challenged railroads, roads, and highways built to deliver hordes of sightseers. Territories that were candidates for a park could not pass the general public's scrutiny without offering something awe inspiring, odd, or oddly beautiful—a waterfall, a painted cliff, or a geyser. Recreational possibilities—camping, hiking, swimming—were an equal expectation. In 1903, recreation's priority was literally carved into the clinker stone lintel of Yellowstone's (Theodore) Roosevelt Arch at the Gardiner entrance: "For the Benefit and Enjoyment of the People." When CCC crews began assembling thirty years later, pleasure was fated for expansion. FDR believed that parks were "indeed a 'pleasuring ground' for millions of Americans."[7]

In lobbying for his South Florida national park, Ernest Coe highlighted standard recreational possibilities—fishing, boating, bird watching. He still, however, had to live with the physical facts of the Everglades. Congress, the National Park Service, wilderness advocates, and the public insisted that parks possess something of monumental quality that would distinguish the nation's natural heritage—a towering rock or mountain, a cascading waterfall, or a deep echoing canyon. The cookie-sheet-flat Everglades, their highest elevation eight feet above sea level, had nothing that resembled the up- or down-shooting graces or raging motion that suited American visual tastes. Writing in defense of the Everglades, Douglas questioned people who narrowed their sights to the point of thinking that a "national park must have mountains sticking up rockily in it, or canyons gashing dizzily through it, or geysers sizzling or any other sight that assaults the astonishment." She and Coe insisted that Americans adjust their panoramic expectations of wilderness. Adding Everglades to the existing national inventory of parks would require upending cultural and institutional convention.[8]

On these grounds, wilderness advocates initially minimized the value of an Everglades park and in the process made Coe's job more difficult. He would have preferred to do without, for example, the stridence of Robert

Sterling Yard, a founder of the Wilderness Society and a onetime head of the National Park Association (NPA). The Wilderness Society had been organized in 1934 partly in response to the damaging work of the CCC, while the NPA had been created in 1919 as a watchdog for the National Park Service. A former newspaper and magazine editor and best friend of Stephen Mather (the first director of the National Park Service), Yard had rigid opinions about setting aside only primitive places as parks of the nation, and he insisted on keeping them primitive. He cast a reproachful gaze on CCC projects. Facilities and roads should be kept to a bare minimum, even if that meant limiting public access; national parks were not intended for windshield tourists. He did not completely dismiss human indulgences, however. For those few who would venture from road into wilderness, he insisted that parks betray spectacular scenic qualities.[9]

On both the primitive and the scenic accounts, Yard believed the Everglades an unlikely specimen. Much talk in Florida about how a national park would bring in additional tourist dollars only deepened his suspicion that the wrong values were pushing its proposal, that the whole idea was part of another Florida land scheme. By the end of the 1930s, the national parks hosted twenty million visitors annually, and people in Florida estimated that one million would visit Everglades, one of the few parks to be open year-round. Seeing existing national parks turned into tools for local commercial development disturbed Yard. He knew enough science to recognize that what went on outside a park affected the inside, and the commercial activity—farming, drainage, wildlife poaching, road construction—around and within the proposed boundaries of Everglades had begun to dismantle original conditions.[10]

Yard's holistic understanding came from ecologists—primarily University of Illinois zoologist Victor Shelford. A first-generation student of Henry Cowles, Shelford was a premier figure in animal ecology. He was also a cofounder of the Ecological Society of America and the principal force behind the Committee on the Preservation of Natural Conditions, which functioned as an advocacy group for, as he put it, the "preservation of natural places with all their native animals." A scholar with an activist edge, Shelford, like another younger Cowles student, Paul B.

Sears, at times criticized colleagues who confined their science behind ivy-covered walls. "The biologists of our country have been very derelict in their duties toward the preservation of plants and animals," he said in a 1938 message to the NPA. As a trustee of the group, he had been excited by the recent publication of a comprehensive study conducted by three National Park Service field biologists. Their two-volume *Fauna in the National Parks of the United States* made recommendations that echoed those of Shelford's committee. Both said in essence that national parks should be natural parks, not aesthetic or biological specimens of human preferences. *Fauna,* for example, discouraged predator control. Shelford proclaimed, "Wolves and other predators and herbivores in numbers have lived together for thousands of years . . . with far better maintenance of natural conditions than in areas where control has prevailed." Dead trees were another bane of the park service, which regarded them as "unsightly." The authors of *Fauna* affirmed the value of dead trees as habitat for small wildlife. Shelford hoped that the Park Service would adopt *Fauna's* "guiding principles" as policy. It did so in 1934 but rarely followed them. When parks began looking to get their ecological act together in the 1960s, Lowell Sumner, who thirty years earlier had proposed that biologists monitor CCC projects, urged the service to pull the forgotten *Fauna* down from dusty shelves. All that service personnel sought had been "figured out years ago."[11]

Mindful of the distance the Park Service kept between itself and ecology, Shelford, like Yard, was ambivalent about the proposal for an Everglades national park. He was apparently the first scientist to note that the Everglades were a boundless interconnected ecosystem and to warn that tampering with one section sent a rippling effect across the whole. In a letter to a fellow preservationist, Yard repeated Shelford's observations that "drainage operations north and east have affected all the Everglades so that primitive conditions everywhere are passing." Instead of a park, Shelford suggested the Everglades might be better preserved as a wildlife reservation or national monument. Yard too considered those alternatives.[12]

He nevertheless remained skeptical about the Everglades' scenic offerings, and he was not alone. William T. Hornaday, the bold, bewhiskered,
retired director of the New York Zoological Park, was the wildlife conservationist with the oldest living relationship with the Everglades, dating back to 1875. In a 1932 letter to John Kunkel Small, Hornaday recalled
the ever-bewildering wetland: "I found mighty little that was of special
interest, and absolutely nothing that was picturesque or beautiful." Although the "Everglades Swamp is not as ugly and repulsive as some other
swamps . . . it is yet a *long ways* from being fit to elevate into a national
park."[13]

Yard's and Hornaday's opinions were in the minority among those that
bore weight. Reflecting on the 1930 delegation trip, Caspar W. Hodgson
of the NPA said, "I am a mountain man and so were most of the others of
the party, but the mountain men fell first." Herman Bumpus said, "There
is no place on our entire Atlantic coast line that compares in beauty with
the tract that runs to the east and west from Cape Sable"; Henry Cowles
said that the Everglades would make a "wonderful park"; Henry Fairchild Osborn of the American Museum of Natural History said they were
"teeming with great scenic interest"; Gifford Pinchot said they were "full
of the most vivid and most interesting life on land, in air and in water";
and Douglas said, "There will be no park in the world so unique, so different, so rarely and queerly beautiful."[14]

Here in these rallied subscriptions was a crucial argument. If the Everglades revealed a primitive beauty and realized recreational opportunities, they also bore value in their distinctiveness. With their inclusion,
the national park system would more completely represent the grand and
diverse canvas of natural America. Support in the press and in congressional testimony was almost always accompanied by the word *unique*.
Coe and Fairchild threw it around with great zeal, usually attaching to
it *tropic* or *tropical*. No other park lay in the same southern latitudes or
had plume birds, mangrove forests, sawgrass savannahs, bromeliads, orchids, palm trees, commingling bodies of fresh- and saltwater, and alligators and crocodiles. FDR's first interior secretary, Harold Ickes, declared

the Everglades a "wonderland—America's only continental tropics." His predecessor, Ray Wilbur, however, recommended that Congress drop *tropic* from the park's authorized name, calling the descriptive "unnecessary and undesirable" and suggesting its potential to stir up dark images in tourists' minds. Coe was predictably livid if not also personally aggrieved, since he had argued the word's merits from the beginning: "The word 'tropic' marks this Park project as distinct as compared with other national park projects," an exasperated Coe explained once again in a letter to the director of the Park Service, Arno Cammerer. If necessary, Coe implied, he would seek special legislation to settle the matter. Congress did just that when it eliminated *tropic* from the authorization bill.[15]

In the end, the word made no difference. But science did. Coe and Fairchild had the near-universal support of the scientific community. Its members drove home the point that Everglades would provide sanctuary for "biological features not rivaled in the world" and "largely as nature designs them." Ensconced in the Everglades' physical uniqueness were rare opportunities for scientific study. The arguments hinted at changing standards: biology might supersede scenic monumentalism. The debate over the park also signaled shifting values in the scientific community. The turning point came late on the first day of the December 1930 House committee hearings, when Bumpus, the Park Service's education director, was testifying. A marine biologist by training, he told the committee that there was "no single park where you can study the marine life of to-day." Representative Phil Swing of California interrupted, "But, Doctor, you are developing a very interesting thought. I have been laboring under the impression heretofore that the yardstick for the committee to use in selecting the national park was that of a showman; that it was the spectacular that we were to consider. Now you are giving us a thought, and a very interesting one, that a piece of ground which has educational value, scientific value, rises to the height of national-park value." Bumpus replied succinctly, "I think you have it all right."[16]

The argument for biology and science was the key that eventually unlocked Yard's thinking. After returning from the delegation trip, Hodgson offered two important observations: traditional impressions such as

Yard's were dated, and landscapes need to be viewed on their own terms. The Everglades environment, Hodgson said, was "very elemental and primitive and certainly more biological than anything I have yet struck anywhere." Despite his ambivalence about the Everglades, Shelford had a similar notion: a place that may seem "below park standards" could actually exhibit "high standard qualities from a biological point of view." What ultimately changed Yard's mind was apparently the findings of Frederick Law Olmsted Jr. and William P. Wharton's survey, which the NPA had commissioned in 1932. Olmsted and Wharton conceded that the "scenery is to the casual observer under most conditions somewhat confused and monotonous," but the native flora and fauna possessed the "great force of novelty," adding up to a great "climax region"—that is, through a process of ecological succession, a given place reached a state of perpetual equilibrium between plant and animal communities. The consultants were tapping into the science of Frederic Clements, who had fathered the climax thesis and who made the same observation about the Everglades in an article published four years later. Olmsted and Wharton were particularly moved by the unbounded swaths of mangrove forests along the coast and sloughs and the great flocks of plume birds that bred and fed in and around them. Too much looting of magnificent Everglades life had occurred for the remainder not to be protected and cultivated back to abundance. The most compelling reason for the park, they concluded, was "to bring a large area in this region under public control for the conservation of its notable biological features and of the environment on which they depend."[17]

Coe had arrived at a similar conclusion, though he was apt to deploy any argument that might advance the spirit of his cause. In a *Washington Post* article calling for a park in the tropics, he shamelessly equated the Everglades with the "life-giving virtues" of Juan Ponce de Leon's mythical Fountain of Youth. More legitimately, he educated himself in the biological matters of the Everglades. He recommended that Secretary Ickes read pages 135–38 in the much-ignored *Fauna*, lying at his fingertips. One of the study's distinct qualities was its tendency, like Shelford, to conceive parks as part of a larger interconnected biological place. Policymakers by habit and preference thought only within boundaries, but map lines de-marcating a park were no fortification against activity going on outside. Treating a continuous environment differently on either side of a park's boundaries, ignoring the ecosystem that transcended bureaucratically drawn boundaries, often endangered biological connections vital to the act of preservation. Bureaucrats could sometimes be responsive to that idea. Congress in 1950 enlarged the boundaries of the Grand Teton Na-tional Park, for example, and over the years, additional territory around Everglades National Park was put into protective custody. But as the his-tory of the nation's so-called biological park would show, patchwork ecol-ogy did not always piece together an adequate solution.[18]

Coe also likely consulted with a suntanned, prophesying wildlife techni-cian with the Department of the Interior, Daniel B. Beard, who was doing research in and publishing articles on the Everglades. Writing in 1938, Beard allowed that the sights in the Everglades will not always "make Mr. Jonnie Q. Public suck in his breath." But Beard, who was headed toward a career with the park service, was not forwarding an "indictment against the Everglades as a national park, because 'breath sucking' is still not the thing we are striving for in preserving wilderness areas." Showing insight that placed him with Shelford and the authors of *Fauna,* he worried that the park's intended boundaries were potentially problematic. "With water as the basis for all life in the proposed park," he admonished, "any deflec-tion of flow north of the [Tamiami] Trail would cause profound ecologi-cal changes throughout much of the park area. A drainage canal along the Tamiami Trail does this to some extent at present, but it may be cor-rected. With water at a premium since drainage operations were under-taken at Lake Okeechobee, control of the cypress and Everglades coun-try north of the Trail is essential." These observations were borne out in the 1960s, and Beard learned firsthand how prophetic he had been. Nine years after recording his findings, he became Everglades National Park's first superintendent.[19]

In the end, biology won. Congress gave it statutory valuation when it authorized the park on May 30, 1934. Much celebration broke out in Flor-ida. Everglades defied tradition, establishing a historic first in the national park idea. It met the usual standard for recreational opportunities with ease but came into the system without the benefit of an edifying scenic monument. Central Florida's *Zephyrhills News* declared that Everglades "completely reverses the usual conception of a park." Congress dedicated priority to a "treasury of biological wealth." Section 4 of the legislation, articulating the park's principal function, mandated that its designated area "shall be permanently reserved for wilderness." Giving clarity to the matter, the measure added that enhancements for public access shall not disrupt the "unique flora and fauna and the essential conditions." In the once unvaunted, still occasionally maligned Everglades, nature protected trumped monumentalism and recreation.[20]

Much work of the bureaucratic kind was required for the park to move from *Congressional Record* to physical fact. There was the sticky matter of transferring state land to federal ownership, and the stickier one of acquiring private land. The latter (accompanied by the firing of Coe as head of the state's national park commission) could not happen until appropriations were forthcoming, and they would not be for some time—and never would there be enough. There was also the matter of Indians living in the Everglades, some within the boundaries of the proposed park. With numbers totaling more than five hundred, they were descendants of the hundred or so who, during the Third Seminole War, had escaped to the natural defenses of the Everglades. Since then, overhunting commercial game—to which Indians contributed—agricultural and land-boom encroachment, and even the limited success of drainage had begun pushing a self-sustaining people toward dependence, if not to the edge of extinction. The promised park portended yet another challenge to peaceful survival.

In March 1935, Bureau of Indian Affairs (BIA) commissioner John Collier and his boss, Ickes, arranged to confer with Seminole leaders about these problems. The national press called their planned meeting a "Pow Wow," one in which Seminoles would offer the "Great White Father" the "pipe of peace" and sign a treaty ending the "100-year" "Redskin 'War.'" The press's clumsy attempt at whimsy was no less insipid than its facts

were wrong. Congress had ended the practice of signing peace treaties
with Indians in 1871, and land, not war or peace, was the issue currently
at stake with the Seminoles. The meeting nevertheless was historic (the
press got that much right). Neither a BIA commissioner nor an interior
secretary had ever before met with Seminoles.[21]

The Washington entourage arriving in West Palm Beach included
Ickes's wife and grown son. There was also a sizable press corps snapping photographs as the visitors squinted in the Florida sun. After spending the night at the Royal Worth Hotel, the group embarked on a wide
looping tour of the Everglades, caravanning west into agricultural lands,
where Ickes surveyed the U.S. Army Corps of Engineers' dike expansion at Lake Okeechobee. From there, they headed southwest to Deep
Lake and the "lost" camp of Seminole Johnny Buster. Pulling to the road's
edge, the cars let out their passengers, who hiked a half mile into the
brush and encountered the kind of dusty privation and near starvation
that had brought them to Florida. Next on their route was Everglades
City, where they overnighted before seeing the Glade Cross Mission. Run
by sixty-two-year-old Deaconess Harriet M. Bedell, whom Douglas described as "like a small steam engine in dark-blue petticoats," the mission put less effort into religious conversion than into helping Indians develop a crafts cooperative. Finally, the entourage followed Tamiami Trail
into Miami and then returned to the upholstered comfort of West Palm.
In two days, they covered the kind of territory that twenty years earlier
would have taken white men a week to cover.[22]

Collier and Ickes now felt ready to meet formally with Seminoles.
Indians had a better understanding than whites did of the Everglades as a
living system and had witnessed unnatural change in that system from the
inside out. Etched into the land were the stories of the nonnatives' entry
into Pahayokee, stories of a tragically unfolding drama. "The Indians,"
wrote Douglas in *River of Grass*, "before anyone else, knew that the Everglades were being destroyed." Approximately 160 Seminoles came to the
meeting to plead for a buffer against advancing white civilization. Along
with a per capita stipend of fifteen dollars a month, they asked for three
million acres of protected land. Neither Ickes nor Collier flinched at the

request. Both were Indian rights advocates—Collier talked about "this Red Atlantis"—who favored the reversal of traditional policy to assimilate Indians and annihilate their cultures, as the 1887 Dawes Act mandated. Fifty years later, 63 percent of Indian country had disappeared. One of the purposes of the Florida trip was to encourage Seminoles to adopt the principles of the New Deal's Indian Reorganization Act, which was intended to facilitate political and social self-determination by shoring up reservation governments and tribal economic independence. In Florida as elsewhere, success of self-determination meant ensuring that Indians had enough land to sustain them. Ickes knew that acquiring three million acres was beyond the grasp of Congress, which would never agree to the monthly stipend either, but he was able to tell the Seminoles the federal government was at that moment negotiating for three smaller tracts of land. He went as far as saying that he thought Indians might be able to retain hunting, fishing, and ceremonial privileges within the park's boundaries. In fact, the 1934 legislation authorizing the park included language that protected "existing rights."[23]

If Indians were allowed to retain their territorial run, Everglades promised to redefine the national park ideal yet again. Just as biological considerations had lain beyond preconceived qualifications for a national park, resident Indians challenged preconceptions of suitable decor for park landscape. The National Park Service considered Indians too wild for the controlled, semiwild aesthetic deemed proper for white visitors. Historically, the service had relocated settled groups when necessary and had prohibited Indian use of parklands altogether. This policy was easiest to enforce when interlopers were squatting in disputed territory, but in the Everglades, Seminoles had legal ownership of ninety-nine thousand acres that lay in the belly of the future park.[24]

Seminole landownership and land use had always been confounded by uncertainty and ephemeral government commitments. When Douglas moved to Miami, South Florida's Indians were scattered across nine hundred square miles in twenty-nine camps, and 90 percent of them lived on white-owned land. Complicating the situation, the Everglades dwellers were descendants not just of warring Seminoles but of numerous territory-wide clans, representing two language groups and numerous factions within those groups. Some Indians complained that those who met with Ickes and Collier did not represent all those subgroups. To coordinate Florida Indian relations, the BIA in 1913 assigned an agent, Lucien A. Spencer. Douglas knew Spencer through her father: the two men had become friends after Spencer set up the agency headquarters in Miami. A former Episcopal clergyman, Spencer groped for policies that represented a practical middle ground between autonomy and assimilation. Some Seminoles accepted Christ, to Spencer's great satisfaction but to the displeasure of other Seminoles, most of whom embraced their own cosmology. Christian or not, Seminoles struck most Miami residents and tourists as mere exotic strangers who quietly canoed downriver to town each morning. Clad in traditional dress of bright-colored calico, they came to trade their wares and trinkets. Then around sunset, they slipped quietly back into the swamp beyond.[25]

Douglas felt a Quaker's sympathy for the Seminoles but until *River of Grass* had done no more for them than occasionally reprint the viewpoints of Indian advocates on the society page. In later years, people remembered Ivy Stranahan, one of Douglas's suffragist colleagues, as the Seminoles' best white friend. Born on the west bank of the Suwannee River, Ivy Julia Cromartie spent her adolescent years on her family's South Florida homestead before taking a teaching job in the New River settlement, where five years later Governor Broward began digging his first Everglades canal. In quick succession, Ivy met, fell in love with, and married the settlement's postmaster and trading post proprietor, Frank Stranahan. Beginning in 1900, she spent much of the next six decades addressing the needs of Seminoles, whose years of trading with Frank contributed significantly to the Stranahans' wealth. Next to the trading post, she set up an outdoor school for Seminole children, and for a number of years she chaired the Seminole Indian committee of the Florida Federation of Women's Clubs (FFWC) and served as director of Indian affairs for the National Association of Women's Clubs. Through these organizations and in letters to and meetings with Florida senator Duncan Fletcher, Spencer, and subsequent agents, she labored tirelessly for conditions that would facilitate Indian self-sufficiency.[26]

An equally energetic light, but in many ways Stranahan's opposite, was Minnie Moore-Willson. Although physically sparrowlike, Moore-Willson had the comportment of a bird of prey. Hers was an aggressiveness usually accorded exclusively to the other sex, and she consequently alienated many potential allies. She viewed men as no greater than her equal, choosing, for example, to hyphenate her maiden name with her husband's when she married James Mallory Willson in 1890. They had met in Kissimmee, where he worked in real estate and she wintered to escape the cold of her native Pennsylvania. No couple possessed a greater affection for original Florida. They were charter members of the Florida Audubon Society, and in publications and speeches, Moore-Willson raged against senseless bird slaughter. Indians were part of the Florida they wanted to preserve. Both Moore-Willson and Stranahan saw the Seminoles as wild and in need of cultural uplift, but Moore-Willson thought Indian culture superior to Western in one regard. A steady opponent of drainage and commercial hunting, she maintained that Indians lived more wisely with the natural world, with Seminoles standing as the only true "custodians" of the Everglades. In 1896, she published *The Seminoles of Florida,* the first full-length account of postremoval Florida Indians, which one latter-day expert describes as "poorly written, undocumented . . . and almost totally unreliable for its ethnohistoric content—yet perfectly attuned to the national sentiment for reform of federal Indian policies." Its brisk sales nationwide indeed indicated the Progressive compassion for the defeated following the Plains Wars. The book also magnified Moore-Willson's reputation as an activist. Three years later, she, her husband, and others organized Friends of the Florida Seminoles, and through it they convinced the legislature in 1917 to set aside ninety-nine thousand acres in the lower Everglades as a reservation. After the ceremonial signing of the legislation, the governor presented Moore-Willson with his gold pen.[27]

The lower Everglades reservation was plagued by controversy from the beginning. Stranahan and the FFWC characterized this particular parcel of land as woefully unsuitable for farming and grazing. Although the present generation of Seminoles subsisted primarily by hunting and trading, expecting them to engage in a life of husbandry was not, in this case, a matter of white cultural imposition. Their prewar ancestors had been successful planters and ranchers. Moore-Willson knew this, but she regarded the acquisition of any land as a victory for Seminole welfare and the start of establishing additional holdings. A member of the FFWC's Seminole Committee, she criticized her fellow club women for not seeing things her way and more than once invited the censure of Stranahan and federation president May Mann Jennings.[28]

When plans for the national park were announced a decade later, Moore-Willson rallied from a hip injury to mount a one-woman publicity crusade. She gave speeches in Florida and New York; published articles, editorials, and pamphlets; and sent out an endless stream of correspondence. On at least two occasions, she wrote to Douglas asking for assistance with publicity, referring in heated fervor to her correspondent in one letter as Marjorie Stillman and in another as Margaret Stoneman. Such was her attention to detail beyond the big picture. She had envisioned and called for a national park or reserve at least ten years before Coe did so. When his efforts produced results, she saw an opportunity to force the government's hand on the Seminole issue. She appealed for an additional hundred-thousand-acre reservation on arable land adjacent to the park and insisted that the Seminoles receive unfettered access to parklands. Policymakers tended to side with her. Governor David Sholtz and members of his cabinet, who visited Seminole country a year after the Collier/Ickes trip, favored new reservation land and the open territorial run for the Seminoles. In a letter to Moore-Willson, Coe said that habitable land for Seminoles should be carved out along with the park.[29]

But on one major point, Moore-Willson disagreed with the others, including the FFWC, which she believed was trying to silence her. She wanted the existing reservation preserved; all the others wanted its empty lands conveyed to the national park in exchange for territory outside park boundaries. Coe even opposed Seminole access to the park beyond privileges as vendors and employment as tour guides. Recognizing the mournful deficiencies in the swampy lower Everglades reservation, many Seminoles remained indifferent to its fate as long as they received fruitful land in its place. But one Seminole group, exploiting the legend of unconquered people who sustained a war without official end that had claimed the lives of 2,000 U.S. soldiers, refused to make concessions. Representing perhaps 360 Indians, its leaders threatened to take up arms if forced to surrender land or move onto reservations.[30]

True to history, the white majority got its way. State legislation transferred the ninety-nine-thousand-acre reservation to the federal government. In return, the state created one new reservation and the federal government three, encompassing less but more suitable land than that in the lower Everglades. The Department of the Interior and the National Park Service took a position against extending Indian rights within the park to include hunting and fishing. No war broke out, but the Everglades Indians also were not systematically forced onto the new reservations. Most began drifting onto them over the years, and others continued to squat and hunt wherever they pleased, fostering disputes that continue to the present day.[31]

Coe was pleased that the Interior Department passed on the opportunity to turn Everglades into a precedent for Indian rights. The animals and plants within a park should be free of all human interference, he said. Yet before the park's dedication thirteen years later, Coe experienced something of the sentiments of the cheated Seminoles when he learned that politics undermined the sanctity of designated parkland no less than Indian land.

Dedications

Douglas finished reading the page proofs of *River of Grass* in early June 1947. After sending them off to Rinehart, she dashed next door to share the consummation with her friends, Franklin and Alice Harris. Franklin went to his piano and improvised a celebratory melody dedicated to her literary milestone. Her own dedication, in *River of Grass,* went to the memory of her father, "Who Gave Me Florida." Frank Stoneman had actually given her much more. He had stepped in at a timely moment and offered her escape from a devitalizing marriage. Her chance at a new professional career was his gift, too, inching her closer to her dream of writing and publishing a book, which came true thirty-two years later, when she was fifty-seven. She had coauthored the work on South Florida gardening in 1928, but at only 64 pages it was really a booklet. At 390 pages, *River of Grass* was unquestionably a book, with a sole author and the imprint of a major New York publishing house. She always considered this one her first.[1]

She had written the entire book in longhand and then hired a typist. When she worked at the newspaper, the typewriter had ruined her for graceful composition. To the mechanical conveyance of thoughts to paper, she preferred the intimate

touch of fountain pen to pad beneath hand. The original manuscript submitted ran twenty thousand words over the publisher's expressed limit.
Rinehart asked her to pare it down. She cut nineteen thousand words,
and her editor was pleased. For the book's artwork, Douglas suggested
Robert Fink, a successful New York illustrator she had known twenty
years earlier when he lived in Florida and illustrated advertisement copy,
some of which she wrote, for George Merrick's Coral Gables Corporation.
Fink had also done occasional work for the *Miami Herald*. Over the years,
she had admired his drawings in magazines and he her stories. When
Rinehart offered him six hundred dollars to work on *River of Grass,* he
knew expenses would run much more. But the book had special meaning
for him, and he spent a few thousand dollars of his own money traveling from New York to South Florida. Reminiscing about the old days, he
and Douglas ventured into the Everglades to "scour" the region for native scenes to photograph for his drawings—a stand of mature Caribbean
pines, an alligator sunning on the bank of a slough, a cracker house in the
scrub, a dredge hollowing out a canal. For the cover, he produced a full-
color illustration of American egrets lifting off from a mangrove island.
Showing action in brilliant hues, it was one of the most striking covers in
the series. Douglas was thrilled.[2]

A run of seventy-five hundred copies of the book, which included a
thousand signed Florida editions, was printed in September. Rinehart delayed the release until November 6, exactly one month before the dedication of Everglades National Park.[3]

The timing of the release was both fortuitous and strategic. As late as
summer 1947, no one knew when the park would become a reality. Governor Fred Cone, the man who fired Ernest Coe, was succeeded in 1940
by Spessard Holland, a park enthusiast, though for reasons that would
have repelled someone like Robert Yard. The park was "just about the
biggest single business proposition pending," declared Holland. A Bartow
native whose flop of hair parted precisely down the middle resembled a
bird in flight, Holland thought the park's location in South Florida was
especially desirable, since, as he argued, motor tourists would travel the

length of the state—including Bartow—to get there, buying gas, staying in motels, and eating in restaurants along the way. Holland turned out to be a wartime governor, though, and had to table park plans while he dealt with home front issues. Just before leaving office, when victory abroad lay in sight, he met with his successor, Millard Caldwell. Both men knew that their state would soon be off the military gravy train, and they decided that Caldwell should push ahead with the park.[4]

A small-town lawyer from Milton, near the Alabama line above Pensacola, Caldwell was immersed in the incestuous world of Panhandle politics. Although surrounded by his region's many naysayers, he reactivated the park commission by appointing twenty-five members and an executive director, August Burghard, a Fort Lauderdale advertising executive and avid yachtsman. Caldwell asked May Mann Jennings to join the commission, though not Douglas or Coe. Coe had not shrunk from his ambition, though. Even as his wife, Anna, lay on her deathbed in the summer of 1940, he wrote to each gubernatorial candidate urging him to remember the park. When Holland won the election, he and Coe met in person to discuss matters.[5]

Coe was not the only person lobbying the governor-elect. As citizen and *Herald* editor, John Pennekamp worked nearly as hard, if not as long, as Coe to make the park a reality. Some people began calling Pennekamp the new father of the Everglades. Pennekamp, who had previously worked at the *Cincinnati Post,* had moved from his native Ohio to Miami at the peak of the real estate boom in 1925. He joined the *Herald* as city editor and eventually rose to the post of associate editor. Freedom of the press and conservation were his pet issues. He was a chain-smoking, coffee-drinking workaholic who collapsed from a heart attack in 1940, when he was thirty-nine. He took a month off, stopped smoking, and then returned to his earlier hectic pace. When Caldwell was elected, Pennekamp hastened to educate the new governor on the merits of the park. Caldwell in turn appointed the editor to the park commission, on which he served as chair of the legislative committee.[6]

A new and increasing urgency fell over the second meeting of the commission's executive committee in Jacksonville in October 1946. Olympic

National Park had been dedicated in June, though it had been authorized four years after Everglades. More importantly, members were concerned about the unbroken routine of plundering and prosaic lawlessness in the region. Two weeks earlier, several commissioners had joined Audubon representative Charlie Brookfield on a tour of the Everglades, and while driving along Tamiami Trail and Loop Road they passed two cars "just loaded down with orchids" and four others with men and shotguns. Dan Beard attended the meeting on behalf of the U.S. Fish and Wildlife Service. His agency had assumed oversight of the would-be park, and he constantly found himself on the front lines of an aged conflict. The committee members regarded him as they might a field commander coming in from battle to make an operations report. Beard's army was small and ineffective, and it lacked orders to pursue the enemy. Five men were in his charge, he said, but none had the state's authority to enforce protective laws. His men were outgunned and outraced by resourceful poachers; many were using airboats and airplanes. "The place is being gutted," he said. After the meeting, Pennekamp contacted Caldwell and urged him to deputize the federal men.[7]

Some people, even those operating within the law, still regarded exploitation as the most suitable purpose for the Everglades. The academic journal *Economic Geography* held fast to old beliefs, declaring in 1944, "The Everglades, once the synonym for inhospitable and repulsive wilderness, shelter of sullen aborigines reluctant to come under the yoke of civilization, refuge of renegades who would escape the mandates of law and the tenets of order and justice, have now become the symbol for success in reclaiming waste places of the earth for man's welfare and comfort, and making them a place for cultivation of fruit and flowers, or staple foods and specialized luxuries." The journal had been crowing about the renewed agrarian spirit flourishing since the upgrading of Hoover Dike began. Sugar and vegetable growers were amassing landholdings around Lake Okeechobee; the state made it easy for them. Ninety-five percent of the land in the Everglades Drainage District (EDD) was in arrears on taxes. To put it back in production, the legislature passed the Murphy Act, which required county clerks to advertise the sale of the land to the

highest bidder. In some cases, buyers walked away with deeds after paying pennies an acre. At the same time, the bankrupt EDD remained accountable to bondholders. Holland negotiated a payoff at fifty-six cents
on the dollar, which allowed the EDD to secure a $5.6 million loan from
the Reconstruction Finance Corporation. For landholders, this development meant that the drainage tax would be kept in check and that the
EDD would continue to expand the drainage system.[8]

Help came from scientists, too—primarily agronomists who analyzed
the Everglades muck soil, which was both a godsend and a curse. Farmers
discovered to their dismay that when the soil was freshly drained, it contained toxic properties that infected their crops with what they were calling "muck sickness" or "reclamation disease." Allowing the soil to weather
for a few years purged the impurities, though it also delayed profit making. The Everglades Experiment Station at Belle Glade devised a chemical solution, essentially copper sulfate, that allowed new land to be put
into immediate production. Subsequent crop yield bore out the truth in
the hoopla about muck's potential. In the winter, the black soil produced
green snap beans, lettuce, cabbage, celery, and lima beans.[9]

Yet one problem solved was replaced by another. The exposed peaty
soil not only oxidized, as agricultural stalwart Thomas Will had learned
in the 1910s, but also inconceivably caught fire. Sometimes it did so like
an inferno, set ablaze by hunters burning sawgrass to expose their quarry,
farmers burning out weeds or incinerating trash, smokers mindlessly
tossing away butts, or lightning finding its mark in the dry ground. In
early 1943, flames consumed 250,000 acres, and in the summer of 1945,
the smoke drifting out from the Everglades was thick enough during the
day to force Miamians to turn on interior lights and drive with head-
lights on.[10]

Muck fires or no, most people believed that agriculture could coexist
with a park limited to the lower Everglades. The experiment station had
long since concluded that the soil in the southern region was mostly unsuitable for profitable farming, sparing the park committee from the improbable task of putting its spawn in the middle of a blooming agricultural district. The vast majority of the land in the proposed park district,

however, was in private hands, and virtually all lay above Tamiami Trail. Further complicating matters, landholders believed that encased in the bedrock below the rich, black muck was even richer, blacker oil. Florida was no Texas or even Pennsylvania when it came to oil. Exploration began in 1901 but was soon abandoned when two wells near Pensacola, drilled beyond a thousand feet, turned up dry. Numerous test wells were sunk around the state in the 1930s. All failed. When World War II heightened the demand for crude, Florida, like many other states, sought to induce oil exploration, offering a free lease to forty thousand acres and fifty thousand dollars to the first company to strike a viable oil field. Humble Oil (now ExxonMobil) won the prize in 1943 when it established a 11,626-foot producing well in a place it called Sunniland in Collier County.[11] Sunniland was a gusher by no one's calculation and barely profitable. But oil was like gold—or like Florida real estate in the 1920s: speculation alone could make people feverish with the idea of realizing riches overnight. Collier County's namesake and largest landowner, the already-rich Barron Collier, claimed he could smell oil in the ground, and he and other landowners imagined Texas-like opportunities in the Everglades.[12]

The prospective fortune in the ground was a prospective roadblock above it. By law, the Interior Department could accept only unencumbered land for parks. Florida U.S. representative J. Hardin Peterson eliminated that obstacle in late 1944 by introducing a bill allowing the establishment of a park after the "major portion" of land was conveyed and on the condition that the Interior Department obtain "exclusive jurisdiction" to the remainder within ten years. Florida's landholdings amounted to 454,000 acres, less than a quarter of the park area, which had already been shrunken from Coe's original 2,500 square miles to the 2,000 authorized by the 1934 legislation. At the Jacksonville meeting, Holland made a strategic move on behalf of landholders by recommending limiting land acquisition to south of Tamiami Trail, where the state's holdings concentrated. The largest private parcel below the trail, 1.25 million acres at Cape Sable, belonged to the Model Land Company, which signaled that it might cooperate. It did, but not without conditions. The most important was a ten-year retention of its mineral rights. Coe's park was growing

smaller by the proverbial minute, and now it was to be sequestered behind the dam-like trail, a development that later proved disastrous.[13]

With the Model Land Company deal looking promising, Caldwell did
his own negotiating. Early in 1947, he went to interior secretary Julius
Krug with the request to proceed straightaway with the establishment of
the national park. A sympathetic Krug offered an exception to the "major
portion" rule by agreeing to a "new minimum" as long as the remaining
land was forthcoming. In April, the legislature voted to hand over state
land, keeping mineral rights to 45 percent of it, and to appropriate two
million dollars and grant condemnation powers to the Interior Department for the acquisition of the outstanding acreage. In early June, just as
Douglas was returning her page proofs to Rinehart, Caldwell delivered
the deed to the state land—previously federal land—to Krug.[14]

The remaining private parcels did not come easily. Property owners
organized the Everglades National Park Landowners Association, led by
Ivar and Mary McDougal Axelson of Coconut Grove, and put up a determined resistance. The group claimed to favor the national park but maintained that its size should be limited and that mineral rights should be retained for twenty-five years. The Axelsons contended that oil exploration
and production was a protracted endeavor that required the extra time.[15]

Pennekamp had heard from too many angry landowners to believe
that an organized group of them had sincere intentions. He wrote several
editorials accusing the landholders of delaying the condemnation proceedings to ensure maximum profits for themselves. By his calculations,
there had originally been 157 private landowners in the designated park
area, and after the park commission was reactivated, that number suddenly jumped to 217, most of whom, he figured, resided in other states.
Florida's attorney general, J. Tom Watson, joined the opposition when he
filed a suit to enjoin the state treasurer from facilitating land condemnation with the two-million-dollar appropriation, arguing that condemnation would wrongfully deny citizens their rights to mineral deposits. He
claimed to be safeguarding the public good. Pennekamp accused Watson, who was running for governor, of headline grabbing. The court ultimately embraced the public-good argument, too, but in favor of a park

for the people rather than mineral rights for the individual. The legal dust did not settle for more than a decade. Well into the 1950s, landowners continued to squabble with the state and federal governments over property rights.[16]

While Pennekamp was fighting his battles, a storm of a different sort began brewing. Two hurricanes blasted South Florida that fall: as Douglas wrote in *Hurricane,* "1947 was a terrible hurricane year." Nine storms visited the United States. The first to hit Florida was a slow-moving September monster that expanded to nearly five hundred miles across and stretched out to a long fifteen-day life. Heading northward in the Atlantic after originating in Cape Verde, the storm abruptly peeled off to the west across the Bahamas, Fort Lauderdale, and the Lake Okeechobee agricultural district. Worse than the sustained 155-mile-per-hour winds was the rain. Seven to ten inches fell, inundating all the coastal cities. The *Herald* said Homestead "resembled Venice, Italy." The water level in Okeechobee reached a stunning twenty-one feet, and the people living around it wondered whether the federal government's sprawling dike would hold. It did, but not without floodwaters building up in Moore Haven and Clewiston and the surrounding fields. Agriculture accounted for one-third of the estimated fifty-nine million dollars in damage.[17]

South Florida had hardly dried out when the second hurricane struck in early October. With eighty-mile-per-hour sustained winds, it was much weaker. Yet similar to its predecessor, it dropped six inches of rain in seventy-five minutes at one point near Miami. The chief of Red Cross rescue said, "We have never had a water situation like this before." In the end, the storm washed away 178 homes and took the lives of 4,298 domestic animals and 23 humans.[18]

If left waterlogged, the public had this time been mercifully warned about the hurricanes. The Weather Bureau finally demonstrated its worthiness with timely and accurate forecasting. Whatever new credibility it earned, however, it jeopardized when it joined with the army, navy, and General Electric Corporation to launch a cloud-seeding experiment that failed miserably. When the second hurricane was heading out from the coast of Jacksonville, government "hurricane hunters" in a modified B-17 flew into the eye and broadcast eighty pounds of dry ice in the hope of "softening its muscles." The hurricane then took a sharp turn toward Savannah and Charleston, where it inflicted strong winds, flooding, and death.[19]

The twenty-five-million-dollar, eighty-four-mile Hoover Dike had withstood the most intense winds since 1928, and, despite evidence of seepage, the Army Corps of Engineers pronounced its masterwork "invulnerable." Still, no one could claim that the locals had remained dry. The rains had arrived earlier than usual that year, and by March the government's pumping stations reached full capacity and stayed there. Before, between, and after the hurricanes, the rain seemed never to stop, delivering a biblical-style deluge of one hundred inches for the year. Between muck fires and hurricane floods, events were indeed beginning to read like a story from the Old Testament. The EDD took advantage. It issued what became known as the "Weeping Cow" booklet, its illustrated cover featuring a bovine despairingly neck deep in water, which propagated the idea that coastal cities would be secure only if the Everglades were kept dry. The outcry for flood relief quickly reached decibel levels nearing those that had arisen from the human tragedy of the 1928 hurricane. County commissions across the state drafted resolutions demanding adequate flood control in the Everglades. In Washington, the staffs of Senators Spessard Holland and Claude Pepper wrestled with stacks of constituent letters filled with the same pleas. If anyone doubted the need for relief, the *Herald* reminded them that the "Everglades remain untamed."[20]

Relief had become a concept congruent with government action only since the New Deal years. Once too defiantly proud to ask for or accept assistance, the public now expected it; once hesitant to consider providing it, federal agencies were now territorial about dispensing it; and when it came to water projects, the Army Corps of Engineers was an insistent specialist. It preyed on wetlands, destroying more than any other individual or entity in the nation's history since the corps' beginnings in 1775. It was conceived in time of war, when engineers were assigned to build breastworks for the Continental Army. In time of peace, it perpetuated its existence by demonstrating its usefulness in civil-works projects. It built the Washington Monument and Library of Congress, though its true ambition was to wrest civilization from the yoke of nature. Scattered across the country, its projects came to represent a sort of institutional iconography of civilized society's power over environmental forces—in particular, water. In the 1930s, it assisted and competed against the Bureau of Reclamation on projects that launched the great dam-building era in the West. It also partnered with the Works Progress Administration to construct seven thousand miles of levees along the Mississippi River and its tributaries after the original levees built by the corps failed to hold back the venerable river during the fatal flood of 1927. Whatever its failed projects, the corps retained a rock-solid belief in its capacity to make water behave in ways beneficial to society. And it always managed to get more money for more work from Congress, whose members were eager to bring corps projects home to the voters. So in 1947, when rumblings emerged for improved flood control in the Everglades, Colonel Willis E. Teale of the Jacksonville District dutifully announced just before Thanksgiving that his office would have a plan ready by January.[21]

The chief of engineers, Major General Raymond A. Wheeler, submitted the report to Congress in February. He called it a "comprehensive plan of improvement for flood protection, water control, and allied purposes." The flood-control region would reach from the upper St. Johns River to Florida Bay, constituting a system of "canals, dikes, pumps, and reservoirs" for the purposes of water conservation, soil improvement, temperature "amelioration," and saltwater abatement. Developed in stages and over a period of many years, the system would take hundreds of millions of dollars to construct and several million annually to maintain. The EDD, which in 1949 was replaced by the Central and Southern Florida Flood Control District (FCD), was most enthusiastic about the corps' so-called conservation areas, maintaining that they would be "operated for the greatest good for the most people." Spread over thousands of acres of Everglades territory—but only lands deemed unsuitable for farming—the conservation areas would produce invaluable benefits, including soil conservation by retarding oxidation, a freshwater supply for agriculture and municipal waterworks, and flood control. The *New York Times* referred to the project as a "Little TVA." Governor Caldwell called it "conservation."[22]

According to Wheeler, no "group" opposed the plan. After more than sixty years of false starts, debacles, and depleted budgets, all the elements of a realistic strategy for managing the Everglades were finally coming together. Local and state officials and Florida's congressional delegation backed it. The Interior Department endorsed it as well, based on the corps' claim that it would prevent both flooding and drought in the national park, a claim that army engineers, it later became apparent, felt little obligation to back up. The plan even had the support of the Audubon Society, which assumed that water management would mean more water for wildlife.[23]

But trying to dictate nature's behavior had caused the problem in the first place, argued Ernest Lyons, a solo public voice decrying the plan as folly. Lyons was the editor of the *Stuart News* in Martin County on the east coast, where the St. Lucie—half river, half canal—released its silty wash from Lake Okeechobee and upstream farmlands. Over the years, various vaunted Everglades enterprises had instilled in the people of Stuart the value of doubting and defiance, the sometime sum of uproar, with the cigar-chomping newspaper editor leading whatever charge was to be led. "South Florida started out with a marvelous flood control plan," Lyons wrote in 1949. "Nature designed it. It consisted of vast, perpetually inundated marshes and lakes interconnected by sloughs." Lyons's argument suggests the growing influence of ecology, but exactly one century earlier, a few lone members of Congress made a similar unheeded argument when debating the Swamp Land Act. In a real sense, Lyons was coming from the same place as his late colleague in the trade, Frank Stoneman. His chief concern was safeguarding the public interest by bringing common sense to government. "Buying swamps and keeping them for natural flood control would be a far better plan than to mortgage ourselves forever to drain them and keep them 'under control' for landowners who picked them up for nothing."[24]

Some of the stoutest opposition to the project had nothing to do with preserving natural systems. Large landowners, such as the Collier family, Ernest Graham (father of future Florida governor Bob Graham), and Joseph Lykes, were sure that they would be saddled with a heavier tax burden once the corps was set loose. Still, nothing could trump flood control, and not even these heavyweights got much of a hearing. When Senator Holland trotted the authorizing legislation—and its $208 million price tag—through Congress, he simply ignored the opposition and listened to the cheering from the gallery and colleagues. The new flood-control district distributed a pamphlet celebrating the project as "conservation in action," mirroring the Progressive perspective of Governor Broward and Thomas Will—the idea that natural resources were being harnessed for the better use of humans. The difference between the early "conservationists" and the later was in the shift from drainage to management, but with the common absence of preservation.[25]

Six years later, the Florida Department of State joined the conservation and propaganda bandwagon when it produced, with the cooperation of the corps and the FCD, *Waters of Destiny*. The department's venture into documentary filmmaking took the stylistic standard established by Pare Lorenz's melodramatic 1936 *The Plow That Broke the Plains*. If Great Plains wind and drought were the great enemy during the depression era, then in South and Central Florida, water was the "vicious scourge of mankind," asserted the narrator in *Waters of Destiny*—"Too much of it on one hand; not enough of it on another." Raising the specter of the disastrous 1947 season and the "crazed antics of the elements," the film reminded viewers that when the rains came, the financial loss was great—"Millions of dollars . . . floated away." When the rains left, the land was "leached and sucked dry." Both the script and the narrator's voice oozed with a patriotic reverence that seemed borrowed from a contemporary Cold War reel on communist subversives. As with the Reds, so with nature: "Something had to be done, and something was." Technology, the product of American fortitude and genius, in the hands of the Army Corps of Engineers, would render civilization the victor over its greatest domestic enemy.[26]

Dry weather obliged the day of the park's December 6 dedication ceremony at Everglades City, a town of fewer than one thousand residents and the location of the park's western entrance. Cirrus clouds high above raked a blue sky, and a silky breeze blew off Chokoloskee Bay, leaving the usual humidity for another time. Nature, though, was not the sole provider of the idyllic conditions. The day before, state workers prepared for the ceremony by spraying five hundred acres of the surrounding wetlands with DDT. No one was swatting mosquitoes at the gala fish fry held along the tarmac of the local airfield, where ninety gallons of beans, seventy-five gallons of coleslaw, and fifty-six gallons of pickles were served, along with a ton of locally caught mullet. President Harry Truman came over from the nearby private Rod and Gun Club, where he had attended a luncheon with sixty-four invited guests. His motorcade had arrived that morning from Naples after he flew up from the Little White House at Key West, to which he would return that evening. His staff had him following a precisely planned itinerary. It allowed a few minutes with a delegation of four Everglades Indians. Press photographers converged when William McKinley Osceola presented a traditional handwoven shirt to the president. Apparently no one mentioned the Seminole reservation the federal government seized for the park a decade earlier. The dedication of Everglades was not supposed to be about humans possessing nature. But the uniqueness of the twenty-eighth national park seemed to go unnoticed as people focused more on traditions.[27] Said the *Washington Post*, after thirteen years of waiting, the public was eager for the national enshrinement of the "vast Everglades of romantic and mysterious legend."[28]

Douglas's diary entry for that day, conversely, was understated. "Dedication Everglades," she wrote, elaborating no further. National Audubon president John Baker had come to Miami and offered her a ride out to Everglades City. Some 4,500 people, including 150 Seminoles, attended the ceremony. Douglas had a reserved first-row seat in front of the speakers' platform. May Jennings was among the seventy-two "platform guests." Coe, not to be forgotten, sat near Jennings. The invitation list designated him the "Everglades Park originator." He had at first declined to participate in the event, giving his regrets, a friend said, "with all good humor, at least outwardly." The park that had been his life's work did not exist. The president was dedicating 706 square miles, which excluded the upper keys, the Big Cypress, and any land north of Tamiami Trail—a parcel small enough to fit within Lake Okeechobee. Over the years, Coe had felt the effrontery when Washington bureaucrats, despite his thunderous resistance, removed the word *tropic* from the park's name and then whittled down its size. After Secretary Krug accepted the state's deed to the smaller parcel, the spirit of the snowy-haired retiree withered. He sent off a letter to Park Service director Newton Drury offering to close down his volunteer park association. Drury convinced Coe that useful work remained to be done. When Coe subsequently declined the invitation to the dedication, Pennekamp contacted Coe and told him that he was the real father of the park. Friends finally convinced him to attend the ceremony.[29]

The event must have left him with mixed emotions. The Fort Myers High School band opened with "Hail to the Chief." An invocation followed, asking the Lord to bless the park. The band then played a rendition of the state song, "Swanee River." Pennekamp served as master of ceremonies, and August Burghard gave introductory remarks. The first person he introduced was Coe, calling him the "'grand old man of the Everglades National Park'—the Honorable Ernest F. Coe." Pepper, Holland, Caldwell, and Krug then spoke. Caldwell thanked Coe and his association for their hard work over the years, and Holland, turning toward Jennings, recognized the efforts of "thousands of Florida club women." Douglas remembered that as the president approached the dais, she reflected on days past, on the breathless sights of birds, the plume hunters, and the inevitable campaign of Ernest Coe, sitting now in front of her.[30]

Truman's speech focused on conservation—a "vital necessity," he said. "Different from all other parks," Everglades represented "another great conservation victory." As a primitive, tropical land, it stood as a new kind of commitment to safeguarding nature that was manifested not, he said, "in a haphazard or piecemeal manner." Coe, looking out at his badly shrunken piecemeal park, might have cringed at that moment. Furthermore, the president was not talking about conservation in the context of safeguarding wildlife determined as preservation worthy; he was speaking of conservation as a utility of free enterprise, and he linked parks with the sustained "harvest" of natural commodities vital to the national economy. Conservation was a mere antidote to excesses associated with consumption. "If we waste our minerals by careless mining and processing," Coe heard the president say, "we shall not be able to build machinery to till the land. If we waste the forests by careless lumbering we shall lack housing and construction materials for factory, farm, and mine. If we waste water through failure to build hydroelectric plants, we shall burn our reserves of coal and oil needlessly. If we waste our soil through erosion and failure to replenish our fields, we shall destroy the source of our people's food." These agricultural references alluded to the purpose of the comprehensive flood-control plan being expeditiously drawn up that moment by U.S. Army engineers. Wasting water in the Everglades meant allowing it to flow to the ocean without first watering crops; wasting the soil meant allowing it to burn up after drainage, before it nourished vegetables and sugarcane.[31]

The park's authorization had demonstrated how attitudes were changing; its dedication demonstrated the limits of change. Protected nature could not compete with domestic economic interests. A railroad company brochure from the time suggests the extent to which minds were inured to adapted habits: "The River of Grass . . . is retreating before the onslaughts of modern pioneers and yielding its miraculous 'PAY DIRT' for the production of vegetables and other important crops."[32] The future would bear out the statement's truth and add an ironic twist. Commercial forces and their Army Corps of Engineers allies would engineer the Everglades' retreat into an attenuated core of a once expansive wetland and the surrender of their natural hydrology to bureaucratic management. And while the Everglades retained their economic importance, that of the relic iron horse would soon lapse.

Rain fell on November 6, the day *The Everglades: River of Grass* debuted in bookstores. Its appearance preceded by a few months the one hundredth anniversary of the release of the first focused study of the Everglades,

Buckingham Smith's report. Jacketed in Fink's artwork, Douglas's was a handsome book, with a weight and dimension that had the feel of substance and quality. Inside were history, science, and stories never before strung together and told in a storyteller's voice that articulated the insights of a vibrant and ponderous mind. Scant record exists of Douglas's reaction to seeing her book in print. She must have felt the past four years of work and emotion rushing up into a climax of accomplishment, when all attention turns to the author and her literary offspring. The fifty-seven-year-old Douglas wrote to her Florida friend and fellow writer Marjorie Kinnan Rawlings, "It is such a strange thing, at my age, to be doing my first book, that I have found myself overcome by something like shyness. For the first time in my life."[33]

The book's reception undoubtedly pleased her. To promote its release, Rinehart arranged to have one of the Indian stories from the book, "An Early Pocahontas," published in the November issue of *Reader's Digest* and sent three hundred booksellers special envelopes with black-and-white imprints celebrating the national park and the publication of *River of Grass,* posted with a recently issued Everglades National Park commemorative stamp. The day after the park dedication, the book made the *New York Herald Tribune*'s "What America Is Reading" nonfiction list (behind seven World War II memoirs). At $3.50 a copy, its first printing of seventy-five hundred sold out before Christmas; Rinehart promptly ordered another five thousand copies. John Selby, a Rinehart editor, told Douglas that *River of Grass* "is my favorite of all the Rivers books." The Sunday *Chicago Tribune* featured it on the front page of its book section, one hundred newspapers in Florida announced its release, and Douglas was an invited speaker at women's and civic clubs around the state. Reviews in the national press were enthusiastic. The *New York Times* described her depiction of the Everglades past and present as "fascinating and intricate." Writing in the *Atlanta Journal,* regionalist author Harnett T. Kane declared, "Few Americans have ever written so sensitively, so skillfully, so magnificently of any part of their land." John Hersey, who won the Pulitzer Prize in fiction for *A Bell for Adano,* said that Douglas's volume would "undoubtedly remain unique among the Rivers of America series, unique, in fact, in any company." It had a "compactness of natural imagery that is dazzling and, above all, an organization and discipline that approach poetic form."[34]

Perhaps the most critical review was offered by Junius E. Dovell, a history professor at the University of Florida. In the year of *River of Grass*'s publication, Dovell earned a doctorate at the University of North Carolina at Chapel Hill, completing a massive study of the history of the Everglades as his dissertation. As a work of environmental history, it was unprecedented and remarkable. Dovell covered as much territory as Douglas, sometimes with greater detail and with a keen understanding of the human engagement with the natural environment. No one was better qualified to assess her work. Dovell identified numerous errors—mostly misspelled names and incorrect figures—and discussed overlooked source material. He must have been struck with the sinking feeling that the publication of *River of Grass* had ruined his chances for publishing his dissertation, which it did, and he might have been unfairly harsh. But he remained professional and displayed no hint of bitterness. He closed with a compliment: Douglas "has captured and glowingly depicted romance and history of the whole of Southern Florida and has preserved for posterity a highly readable record of fact and folklore." In a *Herald* article anticipating her book's release, the embarrassed author noted the mistakes and promised to ink corrections into any book she autographed.[35]

Fan mail began to arrive at her house and at Rinehart's New York offices. Rawlings, who in a jacket endorsement declared *River of Grass* a "beautiful and bitter, sweet and savage book . . . recommended . . . to all readers concerned with American life and the great relations of man and nature," wrote to reaffirm her affection for Douglas's opus. Lawrence E. Will, son of Okeelanta founder Thomas Will, congratulated Douglas for presenting the Everglades story "in so compelling and enjoyable a manner." Coe complimented his friend for a "thrilling . . . most important addition to the literature of our state and nation." Washington bureaucrats took notice, too. National Park Service director Newton B. Drury sent a sportive message: any reader, he said, who "fails to get the 'feel' of the Everglades . . . is a dull clod, with no poetry in his soul, and I want none of his company."[36]

Both her mellifluous prose and her impressively bold interpretations enthralled readers. She opened the first chapter with an emphatic statement about the Everglades' singularity and the last with an emphatic four words about their fate. Readers went from "There are no other Everglades in the World" to "The Everglades were dying." Bearing the elegiac title "The Eleventh Hour," the final chapter spoke of the "school boy's logic" of drainage and other fool's errands in Everglades exploitation. But in spite of her alarm—or in disbelief of her own prophecy—the chapter is not all doom and gloom. She believed that in the hands of scientists, engineers, and the federal government, technology could preserve the great wetland. She did not, in other words, place herself fully in the let-nature-alone camp of Ernest Lyons. Like Coe, she thought the Everglades could make room for both a park and farming, though what was good for farming would also be good for wildlife. She subscribed to water management for the protection of the domestic water supply against saltwater intrusion and for this gem of a new park, incentive enough alone to ensure wise water policy. Believing that park boundaries would balloon out to Coe's original vision when the state reconciled the land disputes, she wrote that when the federal government "can control additional acres north of the Tamiami Trail," it will "impound surface freshwater on which the whole life of the lower Glades depends. It will be the only national park in which the wild-life, the crocodiles, the trees, the orchids, will be more important than the sheer geology of the country."[37]

Her trust in federal water management as a beneficent panacea came back to haunt her. In later years, observers closely reading her book raised the issue of her fatal belief in the government's hopeful project. Looking more deeply into the record, they also pointed confirming fingers at an unpublished article, circa 1948, in which Douglas granted savior status to the Army Corps of Engineers, the project's architect and builder. In the grand sum, here was a shocking truth about the woman public opinion hailed a prophet. But circa 1947, when she heard policymakers say "flood control," she thought "water management." When they envisioned the commercial benefits of flood control, she envisioned the broader social and environmental benefits of water management. She had no way of knowing at the time that in truth the corps put little importance in the park. She was not alone. Research by the scientist who guided her think-ing as much as anyone did in this area, Garald Parker, led him to con-clude that past policies had reflected the wrong priorities, and for the present he hoped for the best. Decades would pass before he too became a "concerned scientist," a quiet critic of using science to subdue nature: "We can't farm or otherwise exploit the Everglades and keep it too."[38]

But if Douglas stumbled before reaching the mountaintop, such stum-bling, even falling back down, is natural. Who for that matter, ecolo-gists among them, did not think the human touch added a bit of civi-lized magic to nature? Even as she might have failed to transcend certain faulty ideas, she did in other ways write ahead of her time, and not solely about Indians but about the Everglades' providence. Her understanding of the natural working system of the Everglades was quite remarkable, and she seemed to prophesy what others would need to know scientifi-cally about the Everglades to make a convincing case in later decades—her case as an activist—to change minds and defective policy. Central to that commanding knowledge was a discussion about evaporation and transpiration, an "unending usage of all that water that has fallen and that flows." The "green growing things," she recognized in her seminal first chapter, "draw up the water within their cells and use it and breathe it out again, invisibly" in an "unending usage of all the water that has fallen and that flows." "It is the subtle ratio between rainfall and evaporation that is the final secret of water in the Glades. We must know a great deal more about that ratio . . . to understand its influence on the weather, on frosts and winds and storms." She went on to talk about the Kissimmee River–Lake Okeechobee–Everglades system, which "maintained the persistent fine balance" of the "long heart of this long land." "If Lake Okeechobee and the lakes and marshes north that contribute to [them], if rivers and swamps and ponds had not existed to hoard all that excess water in a great series of [natural] reservoirs by which the flow was constantly checked and regulated, there would have been no Everglades. The whole system was like a set of scales on which the forces of the seasons, of the sun and the rains, the winds, the hurricanes, and the dewfalls, were balanced so that the life of the vast grass and all its encompassed and neighbor forms were kept secure." In "The Eleventh Hour," she nicely summed up the historic relationship between humans and the Everglades in the environmental century, to date and to her death and beyond: "To the intricate and subtle relation of soil, of fresh water and evaporation, and of runoff and saltwater intrusion, and all the consequences of disturbing the fine balance nature had set up in the past four thousand years—no one knew enough to look." In later years, she came to speak of this "fine balance" as ecology.[39]

What counts in the end is not whether Douglas was a "prophetess in prose," as one journalist anointed her in 1952, but whether she and her book were remembered and how that memory served society. Whatever its shortcomings, the strengths of *River of Grass* stood out. In 1948, the *Quarterly Review of Biology* expressed "hope" that the book would "provide the needed stimulus for the establishment of an intelligent conservation program for the entire Everglades." Audubon's Baker too saw the "delightful" book's potential to stir an environmental consciousness, predicting its adoption as a primer for future political action. Indeed, hers was the only book in the Rivers of America series that went on to such a valued future. By then, too, the "river of grass" metaphor had entered fully into general parlance. Senator Pepper used it in his speech at the park dedication, giving it its first public pronouncement apart from the book. From there, the metaphor and metaphoric land began taking root in minds, literature, popular culture, and law, quietly growing into an expression of endearment and a new reality for a place—a providence—worth protecting.[40]

The year 1947 was a notable moment in the environmental century. It saw the opening of a new chapter in Everglades history, the arrival of a favorable new descriptive, a national park, and a book of literary, historical, and scientific merit. All, and more, would be needed to help right the eventual wrongs of the Army Corps of Engineers' water-control project just over the horizon. Three decades later, Douglas, by then a full-fledged activist, observed of the park's dedication, "That is the beginning, really, of the environmental movement in Florida.[41]

PART THREE

An Unnecessary Drought

Wallace Stegner was the kind of writer Douglas admired. He produced well-researched, authoritative history in the style of a novelist, which he was, and nature frequently figured integrally into his work. He also deployed the voice of an activist, whenever he felt the environment was imperiled. In the 1950s, in response to the Bureau of Reclamation's announced plans to construct two massive water reclamation dams on the Colorado River, with the reservoir of one reaching into the Dinosaur National Monument, he edited *This Is Dinosaur.* It was the first of the "battle books" produced to defend an environmental cause. The federal government, he believed, should use its power not to destroy but to protect precious wild places. By birth, temperament, and professional preference, the bushy-haired, sometimes aloof Stegner was a westerner, a lover of broad horizons and semi-arid grasslands. This noble environment fired both his imagination and his activist streak. But he had a warm spot for the East, too, and he loved all nature. So when Everglades National Park was endangered by what ultimately rolled into a five-year drought, he left for Florida to write about its broad horizon and grassy wetland.[1]

The park was more than twice its size at the 1947 dedication. By 1950, the Interior Department had surmounted court challenges and mineral-rights disputes to cobble together additional parcels of land to enlarge Everglades from 706 square miles to just under 2,000, coming closer to Ernest Coe's original vision. Still, the park accounted for less than 7 percent of the vast Everglades area, and still no vital watershed above Tamiami Trail fell within the park boundaries. Senator Spessard Holland, though a park champion, was beholden to the business and agricultural interests that eyed that upper territory, and he continued to head off proposals to extend the park in that direction. When in the late 1950s another move in Congress for expansion came forward, Holland and President Dwight D. Eisenhower's administration ensured that private property remained secure, including that leased to growers, ranchers, and oil companies. Between 1950 and 1960, hard-fought battles in Congress yielded the park a mere 269 more square miles.[2]

The drought settled in the next year. Florida was prone to long dry spells, and the indigenous flora and fauna had learned to survive them. But this one lingered from 1961 to 1966, longer than most. Groundwater levels in some areas, including the park area, dropped to as much as a foot and a half below mean sea level. And where there was drought, there was fire. In the summer of 1962, more than half a million acres of woodlands, prairie, and exposed muck soil went up in smoke; people in Fort Myers were washing Everglades ashes off their cars. In the winter of 1965, 1,650 pairs of wood storks, a smaller number than usual, arrived for nesting season. But sloughs and solution holes were drying up, and fish died by the millions. Within a month, natural instinct told the birds that available food sources could not nourish their broods, and they abandoned their stick nests, leaving behind eggs and hatchlings for crows and buzzards.[3]

Back in 1938, Daniel Beard had predicted that with "protection" and "wise administration" Everglades could become an "outstanding park." But something had gone terribly wrong. His successor in the superintendent's post, Stanley C. Joseph, was taking desperate measures to save the park. His rangers, in coordination with the U.S. Air Force, dynamited holes in the limestone to create ponds. They blasted twenty and then launched Operation Alligator Rescue. The gator population had already dropped by 95 percent since 1930, mainly because of poaching. To save the remnants, rangers lugged around portable generators to stun alligators with 220 volts of electricity before moving them from overcrowded holes to new ones. The rangers also planned to dig a pit more than a mile long and twenty feet deep from which they could pump some seventy-three thousand acre feet of water, less than one-quarter of the park's annual requirements. The park was approaching its twentieth anniversary, and it was dying.[4]

Stegner arrived in the Everglades in late November 1966 and gathered some startling information. The water level on the south side of Tamiami Trail, the park side, was eighteen inches lower than that in the conservation areas in the north. The government's thirty-eight-foot Hoover Dike around Lake Okeechobee, which after more than forty years of construction and reconstruction would finally be completed the next year, sent overflow water toward the east, preventing it from surging southward as it once had. The much-vaunted conservation areas, fed by canals and the Big Cypress Swamp, were supposed to compensate for the diversion. When Stegner investigated, however, he discovered that the floodgates that allowed water to run underneath Tamiami Trail and into the park were shut tight. The Army Corps of Engineers and the state's Central and Southern Florida Flood Control District—with an assembly of farmers, real estate investors, and businessmen sitting on its governing board—were refusing to share water with the park. Language in the 1948 water-management plan included the promise that the project "would not damage or interfere with this great national park," and at the dedication ceremony, President Truman had pointed out that Everglades served "not as a source of water but as the last receiver of it." This made no difference to the water czars, who pretended that something else had been said and agreed upon. In 1965, they directed 186,000 acre feet down the Caloosahatchee and St. Lucie Canals into the Gulf of Mexico and the Atlantic Ocean, enough water to spread a two-inch revitalizing sheet across 2,700 square miles. Army engineers explained that the precipitous lowering of the lake's water level was a necessary precaution during hurricane season; releasing water gradually to the park posed a risk to people and croplands. All the while, though, the 1,130-square-mile agricultural district south of Lake Okeechobee never wanted for water. And while saltwater intrusion was disrupting the delicate marine ecosystem around the southern Everglades' mangrove belt, municipal wells remained clear and replenished.[5]

Resource maldistribution was not a new revelation. In water-supply priorities, the park had always stood third in line behind agriculture and the municipalities, where 2.1 million people now dwelled. Park friends had begun complaining about the shortage in 1961. National Audubon generated enough publicity in the national press to excite bitter reproval from the flood-control district. The *New York Times* called the drought "man-made," the *Christian Science Monitor* took army engineers to task for co-opting the word *conservation* to describe their practices, and the *St. Petersburg Times* demanded a congressional investigation. Superintendent Joseph complained about the water released to the ocean while his park remained desperately parched. National Park Service director Conrad Wirth complained, too, to his boss, Interior secretary Stuart Udall, to whom Stegner served as a special assistant. Udall wrote to army secretary Elvis J. Stahr Jr. asking for relief. Stahr responded seven dry weeks later. The army was unwilling to accept responsibility for the park's water problems, he said, and it would not dispel the park's misery by quenching its thirst. The "available water " was to be allocated to "potential water users," which did not include "birds." Stegner soberly observed, "The flood control project had become a reclamation project sympathetic to the needs of agricultural interests."[6]

Udall responded by calling for army engineers to undertake a water study to find a solution. The corps first balked and then budged after the Senate Committee on Public Works adopted resolutions in 1962 and 1963 and the House requested a study in 1965—actions demanded by South Florida environmentalists. Although the corps put the 1948 comprehensive flood-control plan together in a matter of months, the engineers took three years to complete the new study. Construction of the flood-control project had gotten under way in 1950 and eventually extended into eighteen counties and more than 15,200 square miles of territory, nearly equivalent to the irrigated territory of the big-dam projects in the West. By the mid-1960s, the corps had completed a dizzying 1,300-mile network of canals and levees. With seventy-five dams and spillways and eleven pumping stations ensuring that water went where managers wanted it to go, project costs had escalated to $381 million. But the project was only 45 percent complete; final costs were estimated at $500 million, 150 percent more than the corps' original price tag. Moreover, army engineers never bothered to determine the water needs of the park. As far as they were concerned, according to Colonel Robert P. Tabb, who was in charge of the new $400,000 study, water supply to the park had not been "included and recognized as a project purpose."[7]

While Congress waited for the report, public pressure forced the Corps of Engineers and the flood-control district to make concessions. Sacks of mail from sportsmen, civic organizations, and others arrived at the Washington offices of Florida's congressmen with pleadings for park water. "Surely Man, who is capable of sending men and rockets into space," wrote students from Sabal Palm Elementary School in Naples, "can devise a method of saving and providing water and food for animals who need so little for survival." In 1966, the Interior Department finally secured an interim arrangement with water managers to open one of the Tamiami floodgates. It was hardly enough—"bottlefuls," said one observer. Then, a week later, the sky opened up into a downpour. The engineers shut the gate, and thousands of deer drowned in the flooding conservation areas. That year, sixty-seven inches of rain ultimately fell.[8]

By the time the dilatory corps sent Tabb's report to Congress in July 1968, the drought had long passed. To his credit, the colonel produced an eloquently written document, unlike the typical government study that can second as a cure for insomnia. His interpretation of particulars, however, was as fanciful as his prose was graceful—and defensive in tone. Never inclined to self-criticism, the corps was utterly incapable of considering its own fallibility, and Tabb, a World War II combat veteran, was a loyal soldier who toed this intractable line. He refused to look much beyond natural conditions for the cause of the park's woes. Not surprisingly, he turned the drought into the principal scapegoat. The problem was "incidentally" exacerbated by canals that diverted the southward flow. But these were state canals, Tabb clarified, dug "years before there was a Federal water-control project in the area." Tamiami Trail was another contributor to impeded flow, and while the roadway had not been a corps project, Tabb failed to mention that army engineers had kept its floodgates closed. He clearly believed that by general mandate, the park's problems should not be the business of the corps, but if called upon, the engineers could fix things. By the corps' calculations, the park required three hundred thousand acre feet of water per year. To meet that demand, Tabb recommended steering more water to the conservation areas and less to the ocean, improving and enlarging the canal system, and raising the maximum level of Lake Okeechobee by four feet. The corps' estimate for the corrective modifications was a cool seventy million dollars.[9]

Many who had praised the 1948 plan were now skeptical about allowing the corps, as Audubon put it, to "evaluate its own project and report on its own errors." Agencies such as the Army Corps of Engineers had done much to abuse the public's trust. As early as 1951, former interior secretary Harold Ickes called army engineers "spoilsmen in spirit," a "self-serving clique" that "wantonly wasted money on worthless projects." Never one to hold his tongue, Supreme Court Justice William O. Douglas, a fiery environmentalist, echoed Ickes in a 1969 *Playboy* magazine article, "The Public Be Damned." He recounted the corps' history as a budget killer that stoically engaged in "rampant vandalism." He placed responsibility for the Everglades drought squarely on the army engineers, working "with the connivance of real-estate developers and prospective tomato farmers." More than just Douglas's impassioned nature made him so strident and defiant in this case. He was all too familiar with his culture's dismaying habit of excess and despoliation.[10]

Across the land, Americans were taking countless liberties with the environment. The watershed moment in excesses came with victory in World War II. Victory translated into justifiable economic might, economic might further translated into military power and diplomatic authority, and all translated into domestic and worldwide security. Whatever success in war might prompt, cold war with the Soviet Union reinforced. But victory was also tainted by a patriotic ethos that valued self-indulgent behavior and a self-deserving attitude. The mightiest and wealthiest nation should adopt a living standard to show off its greatness, and to the victor should go the spoils. Indeed they did. By the mid-1950s, U.S. consumption of nonrenewable resources equaled that of the rest of the world combined. Consumption and its connection to national security and identity were not new to the age. But prewar America differed from postwar America in the new, sharper emphasis on consumption and in the new technologies that fueled the race to material prosperity. With unprecedented growth came unprecedented environmental decline.[11]

Postwar expansion and insecurities also generated new policies of environmental indifference. The New Deal's ethic of sustainable conservation, whatever its flaws, received little play during the Eisenhower years. The Republican president exhibited scant awareness of his party's fabled conservationists, Theodore Roosevelt and Gifford Pinchot. Conservation instead was a pesky drag on business activity. Interior secretary Douglas McKay, an Oregon car dealer, believed in partnering government with private business interests, and to carry out his agenda, he replaced competent government professionals with market-oriented appointees. One of his first dismissals was Albert M. Day, head of the Fish and Wildlife Service and former boss of Rachel Carson. Beginning to establish a national audience for her nature writing, she went public to protest, declaring, "The action against Mr. Day is an ominous threat to the cause of conservation and strongly suggests that our national resources are to become political plums." Her fears were confirmed. "Giveaway" McKay, as his critics called him, made virtually the entire system of national wildlife refuges available for oil and gas leases. And his department revived the Truman administration's latent proposal for the reclamation dam that would affect Dinosaur National Monument. The department then fought furiously on behalf of the idea, only to lose out to Stegner and other environmentalists.[12]

Heightened natural resource consumption and wilderness encroachment were not the most conspicuous postwar environmental problems. New technologies sped up the production of manufactured goods and substituted synthetic materials, typically petroleum based, for natural ones, with little concern given to waste by-products. Whatever net advances Americans had made against water and air pollution in the Progressive years rapidly receded into morbid losses. In October 1948, for example, citizens of Donora, Pennsylvania, literally choked on a toxic fog largely composed of fluoride emissions from U.S. Steel and other factories. When the city experienced a temperature inversion, the air killed twenty people. The U.S. Public Health Service and the steel giant cited the temperature inversion as the lone culprit. By the 1950s, the automobile had surpassed factories as the usual suspect in air pollution. An American infatuation that was driving the postwar economy and the preferred suburban lifestyle, automobiles were responsible for what people began calling smog and for as much as 70 percent of the lead settling in the environment. In 1955, Congress authorized a three-year study on air pollution, but it was only a study. The administration wrote off pollution as the province of individual states, even as it connected them with a new federal interstate highway system that encouraged increased automobile use.[13]

Eisenhower gave the same listless concern to water pollution. When Congress failed to renew the 1948 Water Pollution Control Act, the White House issued not a squeak of protest. In the law's eight-year life, Congress appropriated only eleven million dollars to clean up municipal sewage and industrial waste, even though twenty-seven million dollars annually had been budgeted. One study revealed that 1,247 factories were dumping waste into the Ohio River and its tributaries. In McKay's home state of Oregon, residents could no longer swim in the Willamette River because of the pollution from pulp mills. In Massachusetts, factory discharge and fecal bacteria from the Brockton sewage-treatment facility sapped the oxygen from the Taunton River, and native shortnose sturgeons, herring, and oysters were disappearing. In Douglas's other hometown, something similar was happening to Biscayne Bay. A conservation coalition calling itself the Natural Resources Council of America determined that two billion dollars would be needed to pay for proper municipal water-treatment plants around the country. But the money was not there.[14]

People usually associated pollution with the industrial Northeast and Midwest or car-crazy California. But it had begun creeping into the South, which since the depression had started to rethink its dependence on agriculture and to go after manufacturing. Florida was supposed to be different, though. It was supposed to have a sunshine economy. It was supposed to lure visitors, not factories. In reality, it had smokestacks and the like and was as friendly to industry as to tourists. William Bartram's Elysium had set aside designated waterways as industrial rivers, which companies could pollute at will. Harriet Beecher Stowe's enchanting Ocklawaha River was being excavated into a cross-state shipping waterway on the order of the Panama Canal. Henry James's Jacksonville qua Genoa was shrouded in a haze of sulfuric acid so potent it dissolved nylon stockings. Across the Panhandle, the stench of rotten eggs wafted perpetually from the St. Joe Paper Company mill. In Central Florida, the phosphate industry was fouling both air and water. Every Florida municipality was dumping untreated effluent into some body of water, sometimes ominously close to where the tourists leisured.[15]

Pollution slowly dragged national conservation organizations out of their virtual wilderness seclusion and into peopled environments. One of the best-organized national groups addressing the contaminated environment was the Natural Resources Council of America. Its 1946 founding membership included the Wilderness Society, the National Parks Association, and the Izaak Walton League. To be effective, council members learned that they would have to go after bureaucrats and politicians on pollution issues just as aggressively as on reclamation and wilderness encroachment. Environmental groups employed a relatively new tactic: lawsuits. A pro bono attorney became a prized asset, and some larger and wealthier groups, such as the council and the Sierra Club, created legal defense funds.[16]

Picking their way through the courts would have been more hazardous than not without scientific expertise. Science had advanced the manipulation and destruction of the environment to its postwar levels and had in fact been the reason for many lawsuits. In opposition, the environmental community immersed itself in the exactitude of science for its own purposes, ultimately setting scientists against scientists. While atomic experts, for example, saw in nuclear fission utopian miracles—from health cures to agricultural advances to eternal peace—ecologists and others warned about radiation fallout. Joining that chorus in the early 1960s was Douglas, who cited the failure of the power industry and the Atomic Energy Commission to devise a viable plan for disposing of spent fuel.

By this time, the science of ecology was coming of age. An increasing number of colleges and universities began to offer courses, concentrations, majors, and advanced degrees in the field, and the scholarly approach to ecology was shifting from single-species studies to ecosystem studies. The most important figures driving the academic shift were Eugene P. Odum and Howard T. Odum, the ecologist sons of Howard W. Odum, the University of North Carolina sociologist who had been one of the main influences in Douglas's regionalist thinking. The senior Odum's sociological insights also influenced the way his sons saw the natural world. At the heart of regionalism pulsed the idea that diverse parts and their interconnected harmony formed the sum of the whole. The idea meshed with the Odum brothers' observations made while exploring the woods, streams, and fields around their boyhood home in Chapel Hill. By the time they entered graduate school in the 1940s, holistic ecology was already a working principle, but the Odums made it authoritative. The older, beak-nosed Eugene studied with the celebrated Victor Shelford at the University of Illinois, while the mentor of the taller, equally beak-nosed Howard, known as H. T., was Yale's G. Evelyn Hutchinson, a limnologist who emphasized links between ecology and human culture. In 1953, Eugene published *Fundamentals of Ecology*, written in collaboration with his brother. A revolutionary textbook, it fixed the ecosystem at the center of ecological study and interpreted energy flow as the connecting silk in the web of constituent parts.[17]

There is no evidence that Douglas read the Odums' text, but the scientists with whom she eventually began working to restore the Everglades ecosystem certainly did. For generations, it remained the field's standard classroom textbook, and the Odums' concept of ecosystem ecology formed the scientific foundation of modern environmentalism. Beyond the Odums, a growing battery of ecologists were following Shelford's and Paul B. Sears's idea that scientists had an important public role to play in assessing environmental conditions in a changing world. Outside the usual endeavors in land and forest management, ecologists began lending their expertise on questions dealing with toxic chemical use, waste disposal, pollution controls, and ecosystem destruction and restoration. Some served as scientific advisers to activist campaigns; others led those campaigns. The Ecological Society of America was a founding organization of the Natural Resources Council, an affiliation that pleased Shelford. That same year, he shut down the society's advocacy committee and launched the Ecologists' Union's Friends of the Land, which was also a charter council organization; in 1950, Friends of the Land changed its name to the Nature Conservancy. Ecologists remained of a mixed mind about getting involved with pressure groups such as the Sierra Club and the Wilderness Society, wondering whether theirs should be a subversive science, as Sears called it in 1964. But as a whole, they agreed that policy decisions affecting the environment—such as building a power plant next to a bay, as happened in Miami—should derive from an intellectual foundation of science rather than pork-barrel politics.[18]

Some scientists who had the talent conducted their advocacy via the printed word. One who did and whose values signaled evolutionary moments in the ecological community was Aldo Leopold. Leopold was a dyed-in-the-wool midwesterner, born and raised in Iowa in the late nineteenth century. He began a professional career with the U.S. Forest Service, obedient to the Pinchot model of utilitarian conservation. A hunter and fisherman and a specialist in wildlife management, he thought that federal lands should remain open to sportsmen and supported the practice of predator control. But then he witnessed the fatal consequences of deer overpopulation in the Gila Wilderness, which he had helped establish, and began to question his participation in wolf eradication. What right did humans have to the wilderness that wolves did not? When no other species killed to change an environment, how could humans justify doing so? Had reason become mixed up with arrogance? Recognizing that ecologists possessed the ability to diagnose environmental damage "invisible to laymen," he began to insist on the ethical responsibility to arouse public opinion. With other discerning and scientific minds, he cofounded the Wilderness Society in 1935, seven years after leaving the Forest Service, and involved himself with a half dozen other similar organizations.[19]

But he is best remembered for his *A Sand County Almanac,* published in 1949, the year after his death. The context in which he crafted the book bore similarities to that in which Douglas crafted *River of Grass.* Just as she wrote with an edifying long view of change in her region, he wrote of his own corner of Wisconsin. She approached her subject as a writer with an understanding of science, and he approached his as a scientist with literary skills. If she was the heretical revisionist historian who exposed past mistakes, he was the first-person philosopher preaching a salutary corrective for the hereafter. His book's leitmotif was the proposition for a land ethic, by which he meant the enlargement of the individual's ethical relationship with the social community, which emphasizes cooperation over competition, to include "soils, waters, plants, and animals, or collectively: the land." Reviewers praised Leopold as "both a better writer and a better naturalist than Thoreau," and his book's appeal spread. Those who came to call themselves environmentalists tucked it under their arm and carried it as the holy writ of a true prophet. It contained a thousand and one quotable insights. Collectively, they provided the catechism for a budding new movement.[20]

Rachel Carson's *Silent Spring,* published thirteen years after *A Sand County Almanac,* achieved even greater eminence. Its existence, coupled with previously published books with related messages, indicated the rapidly changing environmental conditions and the popular disquiet stirring outside the traditional conservation groups and a few activist scientists.[21] Indeed, the publication of *Silent Spring* constituted a momentous event in the environmental century and, in the words of Carson's editor, Paul Brooks, "may have changed the course of history." Though a scientist whose environmental sensibilities had formed along similar ethical and ecological lines as Leopold, "she was not at heart a crusader." Before *Silent Spring,* she had wanted to write popular but intelligent books that reflected nothing more political than her love of the English language and the natural world of the sea and shore. Her day job as publications editor with the U.S. Fish and Wildlife Service had allowed her to moonlight as an author, although ten years elapsed between the publication of her first book in 1941 and her second. While she felt stifled, she conceded that the service gave her the resources and time to travel and explore new places.[22]

One place service duties took her was the Florida Keys, in 1950, which afforded a side excursion to the Everglades. No evidence indicates that she read *River of Grass* before her trip (indeed, if missing the proper metaphor is any indication of a gap in her reading list, she referred to the Everglades as a "sea of grass"). Carson and her friend and colleague, Shirley Briggs, spent nine hours one day bouncing and sloshing around on a three-axle, twelve-wheel swamp buggy with a boiling-over radiator. The vehicle had been developed and was driven by a gladesman, Don Poppenhager. Everglades dwellers had become entrepreneurial adapters to changes effected by the national park and advancing development and business ventures. Poppenhager used his swamp buggy to transport sightseers and birdwatchers into the sawgrass and wet prairies and oil-company personnel out to exploration sites. The ride delighted Carson and Briggs, his first-ever female passengers, and the buggy's elevated open-air bench seat treated them to an affecting vista. "The feeling here is of immense space," Carson wrote in her field notes, "from the utter flatness of the land and the great expanse of the sky. The cloud effects were beautiful and always changing, dark and ominous in the west and north—white and fleecy with rainbow lights in them."[23]

A year later, Carson published *The Sea around Us.* An eighty-six-week bestseller that Douglas devoured and later quoted, Carson's second book generated the resources that allowed her to leave the service and write full time. Within a few years, the foreboding escalation of chemical pesticide and herbicide use prompted her to begin cataloging personal and scientific testimonials of the environmental consequences. By the end of the decade, she was intellectually and emotionally ready to put her findings in a book, and she built her story around a world that had gone mad for chemicals, especially the overnight sensation DDT. When DDT was applied during World War II, the military acclaimed the chemical a lifesaver for having stanched the killing spread of louse-borne typhus among troops. After the war, manufacturers took DDT into the agricultural market, where farmers acclaimed it for saving crops. Working in tandem, the chemical industry and Department of Agriculture crafted a public-information campaign that elevated insects to the status of the country's number 2 enemy, trailing only communists. Touting wondrous synthetic agents such as DDT, Dieldrin, and others, chemical companies promised to "eradicate" bugs in the air, the trees, the grass, and the home, all with no threat to human health. Carson sought to impeach that claim. She was careful to condemn not technology (though industry defenders insisted she did) but the reckless application of it. Like Leopold and others, she placed humans in nature and at the top of the food chain, in line to receive toxins that pass surreptitiously along trophic levels. Then came her supreme affront to technocrats and their government and corporate benefactors who set themselves above the rest of the living world, a similar charge to the one Douglas eventually leveled against army engineers. The arrogance supporting the belief in scientific omnipotence and its beneficent purposes in reengineering nature, Carson concluded, endangered the future existence of human life.[24]

Serialized in the *New Yorker* before its release, *Silent Spring* put the chemical industry on the hot seat. It spent $250,000 to silence the hysterical spinster and expose her bad science, as its hired experts characterized the situation, only to have such authoritarian ravings generate greater interest in the book. The commotion caught the attention of Washington bureaucrats and climbed the chain of command to Udall and then to President John F. Kennedy. Carson testified at a congressional hearing on the dangers of chemical pesticides, and the administration launched its own study. In the cruelest of ironies, a year and a half after *Silent Spring*'s debut, at age fifty-six, Carson succumbed to breast cancer, still the scourge of chemical apologists. So much had been set in motion, she said, and so much was left to do.[25]

Today's scholars and environmentalists typically identify *Silent Spring*'s publication as the mobilizing force of a new environmental movement. This crusade brought the polluted landscape into focus with wilderness preservation and wildlife protection and led to the professionalization of the staffs of national groups, while the volunteer corps shifted to the local level. A national stir arose, greater than that created by the Sierra Club and Audubon; the movement formed from a constellation of localized citizen-based groups that sprang up to tackle immediate problems, sometimes in coordination with national groups. Equally important to this new movement was an advanced ecological understanding, informed by *Silent Spring*, that helped identify problems and challenge the conditions that spawned them.[26]

Ecology's entry into Florida affairs and citizens' groups actually started before Carson's decisive work. As early as 1946, Florida Audubon was concerned about the commercial rush to use DDT, identifying the pesticide as a killer of birds and marine animals. The year before, local officials broadcast DDT over Miami to arrest a possible polio outbreak, though science had never connected the crippling disease with insects. Both the Florida Anti-Mosquito Association and the state board of health recognized that DDT's danger to the noninsect world "dwarfs on a grandiose scale the mere elimination of mosquitoes," and, still, state workers fogged the wetlands for the Everglades National Park dedication ceremony. Florida's fresh air was turning toxic, too. The 1957 legislature created the Florida Air Pollution Control Commission to monitor the levels of atmospheric sulfur oxides and fluorides produced by the phosphate industry. The commission resulted from the cage rattling of ranchers, citrus growers, and concerned residents in Polk and Hillsborough Counties, where industrial emissions corroded television antennae and automobile roofs and killed ornamental plants. The concerned citizens employed science to link the corroding environment to the phosphate industry and then agitated for state relief.[27]

Caught up in another battle—on the green, wet side—Governor LeRoy Collins made civic use of science. In St. Petersburg, Leonard Ratner, a

Chicago developer, proposed a major dredge-and-fill project in Boca Ciega Bay, a vital estuarine environment plundered sixty years earlier when the plume-hunting Old Frenchman Chevelier shot out the great Maximo rookery. The army engineers too had left their trademark imprint, digging a fifteen-foot-deep ship channel through the bay, turning the bottom up into spoil islands and destroying several hundred acres of fecund marine habitat. When Ratner acquired rights from the Internal Improvement Fund to fill 504 acres of bay bottom to create waterfront real estate, locals rallied and formed the Alliance for the Conservation of Natural Resources.[28]

Collins crucified the developer's proposal as a "monstrous desecration." *St. Petersburg Times* publisher Nelson Poynter took a similar position in print. Poynter had gotten to know Rachel Carson when she came to St. Petersburg to work at the Marine Research Lab, and he gained a new perspective on the ecological consequences of waterside development. Additional backing came from a scientific study that Collins commissioned at the urging of the U.S. Fish and Wildlife Service. Completed in 1956 by Robert Hutton, a marine biologist formerly of the University of Miami, the study was a first among environmental-impact statements that came to be a common feature of the new environmental movement. It failed to deter the prodevelopment St. Petersburg County Commission, however, from voting unanimously to permit the project. The alliance sued, only to face dispiriting losses all the way up to the state supreme court.[29]

But more important than the outcome was the action putting growth merchants on notice that others were scrutinizing their behavior. Developers would have been unwise to interpret victory in the Boca Ciega case as a confirmation of a future open to footloose development. By the next decade, opposition awaited virtually every new proposal to change wet and waterside landscapes. No place was better for new environmental awareness than South Florida. The unnecessary drought was just one instance in which opposition redefined previously acceptable environmental consequences as unacceptable and held culpable parties accountable. People such as Wallace Stegner knew that the drought was not the problem but the symptom. In witnessing the determined inaction of the powers responsible for exacerbating the drought, Stegner wondered whether the Army Corps of Engineers would come "to be known as the agency that killed the Everglades." But he had also seen stirrings of a new movement that might transform the Everglades' fate should the corps retain its sanctimonious ways. Douglas saw the stirrings, too, though she initially watched them from a distance as she stayed busy writing books, editing and publishing the writings of others, and dancing herself into the hospital.[30]

Perishing and Publishing

In the years following the publication of *River of Grass,* Douglas reached the age in which more people in her life began dying. One was her father's second wife. Lillias Stoneman and Marjory had remained close after Frank's death. Marjory would find a ride over to the Spring Garden house to have dinner with Lillias, read to her, and talk about the rustic Florida of Lillias's ancestors. Lillias passed away on March 6, 1956, at age eighty-nine. She had lived long enough to see three of Marjory's books in print and to be moved by the dedication to Frank in *River of Grass* and by the appearance of her name in the acknowledgments. A decade after her death, Lillias's stories of old Florida helped inspire Marjory to write a history of the state.[1]

Uncle Charlie Trefethen, the last of Douglas's Taunton family, was the next to go. Sometime in the 1940s, after losing his wife of many years, he started riding the bus from Worcester, Massachusetts, to Coconut Grove to stay with his niece for the winter. He eventually gave up the North altogether and moved in with her, taking the little room off the kitchen as his own. Since Marion Manley had tacked on that room in the 1930s, the house had remained virtually unchanged. It was more

hidden, though, by grown-up vegetation. Much of it was mature plantings that Mabel Dorn had brought to Douglas years earlier: a bucida,
or black olive tree, a mahogany tree, and an oleander bush. At the front
door was a "snowy mass" of Christmas star jasmine, another gift from
Dorn, and the bellpull from Java. Douglas spent hours outside, puttering in the subtropical garden, her mind sometimes wandering and other
times working on how to plot out a story or precisely phrase a sentence.
Her "dear little uncle" followed a quiet routine that respected her writing
time. He was easy to live with, tending to himself, jolly with her friends,
and full of witticisms. "Start walking and you get someplace," he used to
say. Whatever broke or leaked around the house, the mechanic, engineer,
and inventor fixed. She dedicated her third book to him, "who always
said that if you want to get a thing done, you'd better do it yourself." In
June 1957, he died in bed.[2]

Friends were dying, too. Among them was the irrepressible Ernest Coe.
He went out in 1951, having lived long enough to see new land tacked
onto his park. He was eighty-four, alone, and virtually broke. Although
his *Miami Herald* obituary called him the "Park Father," younger people
and newcomers to the area typically thought of the paper's editor, John
Pennekamp, as the sire of Everglades. In 1963, Florida named a state park
after Pennekamp, not Coe. To his credit, Pennekamp reminded others
about Coe, although not without claiming his own patriarchal role. Those
who had campaigned with the true father saw injustice in faulty memory.
Douglas tried to correct it with a tribute she wrote for *Audubon* magazine, "The Forgotten Man Who Saved the Everglades." She preferred to
think of Pennekamp, whom she admired, as the park's "midwife."[3]

Douglas was losing other friends, too. There were the Harrises next
door, steady companions until the end. Her childhood friend and college
housemate, Carolyn Percy Cole, bought the Harrises' house, a towering
two-story edifice compared with Douglas's little cottage, with an orange
barrel-tile roof and smart Mediterranean features. Just before Uncle Charlie's death, Cole completed renovations and began wintering in Coconut
Grove. It was a nice arrangement. Through the years, Cole and Douglas
had remained the closest of friends, known by others as the "Wellesley

girls." Soon after their time in France during the war, Carolyn Percy had married a wealthy and much older opera singer named Kelly Cole. From New York, they moved to Bennington, Vermont, where Kelly died within a few years of the wedding. Douglas was writing for magazines during this time, and she stayed with Cole for a year after her husband's death. Almost every summer thereafter, Douglas returned to spend a few weeks. She always brought work along and devoted regular hours each day to writing. Cole's niece, Jean Areson, lived with Cole and looked forward to those visits. Preferring Cole's diminutive "Marney" for Marjory, Areson came to think of her as a "pseudo-aunt." "She was fun. She was fun to talk with. She told stories about her youth."[4]

Writing fictional stories for magazines had paid better than writing books. Sales for *River of Grass* peaked in 1947 and 1948, when the book went into its third printing. In the latter year, royalties for approximately eighty-eight hundred books paid $5,300. The next year, the sale of around nineteen hundred books earned her $1,126. During the depression, she had made as much for each of her *Saturday Evening Post* stories, and she could write three or four in a year. Although the book remained with Rinehart into its seventh printing, royalty payments settled at between one and two hundred dollars a year. When the book went to paperback, she got ten cents a copy. To make extra money, she wrote book reviews for several newspapers and composed an occasional "Topic of the Times" column for the *New York Times*.[5]

She also continued to write books. She followed up *River of Grass* with the novel started many years earlier. Rinehart gave her a fifteen-hundred-dollar advance in 1949 for a book she was calling *Dark Companion*. When it came out in January 1952, the title had changed to *Road to the Sun*. She dedicated it to her mother, "who knew the beauty and the terror." Embodied in the inscription was the elemental theme of the novel, the fortunes and misfortunes of the human experience choreographed with serene and tempestuous events of nature. The 340-page book was released in Miami in early December 1951 and then on the national market after Christmas. More than eighty-five hundred copies sold the first year, and critics liked it for being "intensely poetic," "mature, thoughtful," and a "beautifully written tale of expiation." Marjorie Kinnan Rawlings, who was finishing up *The Sojourner,* her first book in ten years, wrote to Douglas, "You have done it! . . . [W]hile the ordinary reader will be conscious only of the smooth narrative, the fascinating inter-play of characters, the marvelous feeling of the Everglades, the beauty, the style, I know what has gone into it." Douglas had called up old themes from her short-fiction days— murder and hucksterism, love and despair, renewal from ruin, empowerment after submissiveness, human assertiveness in the land, and nature's assertiveness in human events. South Florida, as before, gave her a setting, and her regionalist leanings shaped the contours of the book's plot. She was South Florida's regionalist of record. Six months after the book's publication, the University of Miami awarded her an honorary doctorate of letters for her creative contributions to the "Florida scene." She had inserted the region into the national narrative, revealing a cultural and physical distinctiveness owing not simply to an indigenous uniqueness but to the absorption of influences of external or universal origins. Sometimes she saw resistance. The culture in and around the Everglades contained elements imported from elsewhere that set it at war with the native environment.[6]

In the successes and disappointments of her novel's protagonists, Ellen and Jason Horne, are American culture and all its messy confluence with the subtropics writ small. The book opens with Ellen standing on the young couple's property, their hope for prosperity, taking in a panoramic view of an Everglades pastoral, "from one rim of the sky to the other." They have come to this part of the world from elsewhere, she from New England and he from "far places" (à la Kenneth Douglas). It is the hour after the Broward years, during the muckland rush preceding World War I. The couple has invested not only savings but hard work in precariously dry farmland. Beside it runs a canal that Jason helped dig before they married, when he worked on the dredges. Along the canal's straight edge, he and his hands have built a dike so that the Hornes can grow vegetables and rice. Their next-door neighbors are the Yandells, originally North Florida people who follow backcountry traditions and seemingly set their ambitions not much above mere survival. Hemp Yandell is the type, his wife tells Ellen, who is disquieted when a place grows too crowded with people. Such was the omen of drainage. The day after Jason's dikes are dynamited in a regionwide effort by earlier settlers to destroy the canals, he shoots and kills Yandell. Ellen stays with Jason through his various trials and incarceration. Though he is acquitted, his conscience gets the better of him, and he leaves for the war in Europe. Ellen goes on to sell real estate and is caught up in the warping influence of high-fever deal making of the 1920s. Jason returns from Europe little better for his agony and takes up a hermitlike residency on an island in the Everglades, where men are adrift in murder and lawlessness. It is a land of contrasts, and Jason's immersion in it gradually brings spiritual regeneration. Man's wildness—regressive and destructive—differs from nature's wildness, which manages at a level of harmony and continuation. But before he can fully restore his life, he is injured in a confrontation with bootleggers, and he feebly calls for Ellen. She comes to him as a hurricane, the 1926 storm, begins to blow. Jason is apparently dying, Ellen is ruined from the real-estate bust, and the story closes as the hurricane's eye passes through. It is not simply the end, though, for Douglas knew that rejuvenation came after storms.[7]

Road to the Sun was the last fiction she wrote explicitly for adult readers. After a promising debut, sales stalled. In the second half of 1952, she received a seventy-six-dollar check for 146 copies sold; in the first half of 1953, the check was twenty-nine dollars for 56 copies. She submitted chapters for a proposed "Wrecks and Treasures book," but Rinehart passed on it. She had another book project in the works, however, and a contract. Powerhouse publisher Charles Scribner's Sons had contacted her a year earlier with a proposal to write a book for its new series of junior novels. The Strength of the Union series was intended to highlight historical themes "of importance to each State of the Union." Scribner's was looking for a "southern touch" to add to its list and thought Douglas might have research material from her Everglades project that could form the basis of such a book. The contract, signed in April, included a five-hundred-dollar advance.[8]

Freedom River came out in fall 1953. She opted not to write down to her audience and instead chose to develop a story, set in early-nineteenth-century Florida, that dealt with moral dilemma, social judgments, and, as the *New York Times* put it, the "ever-with-us question of race." Just a few months after the book came out, the U.S. Supreme Court handed down what was arguably the most cataclysmic legal decision of the twentieth century, ruling in *Brown v. Board of Education* that segregated public schools were inherently unconstitutional. Young minds, therefore, were confronting precisely the questions that *Freedom River* raised. Douglas's bald moralizing was risky for a young-adult book that parents would potentially screen; the other titles in the series tended to read like patriotic screeds. But hers was the only one to make the "New York List," and the *Library Journal* awarded it two stars. The *New York Times* called it "historical fiction at its best."[9]

With the possible exception of *River of Grass*, *Freedom River* represents Douglas's most overt and powerful work of social commentary in book form. She began the story in 1845, the year Florida entered the Union as a slave state. Very quickly, the twin issues of racial and social justice come to haunt the relationships among her main characters, three boys— one white, one black slave, and one Miccosukee Indian. They live in an Everglades world where greed and exploitation too often take the upper hand over fairness and moral integrity. The reckonings among these opposing forces comes in the final chapter, which suggests that a future of separateness and estrangement for the companions threatens if convention holds sway. Richard and Eben, the white boy and his slave, witness the coming-of-age ceremony of their Indian friend, Billy. Ceremony will not define Richard's own passage into manhood; becoming a man true to the white South will require him to honor the slave system and ignore the paradox in his culture's sworn ideals and its iniquitous treatment of Eben's and Billy's peoples. But Richard's mother is an abolitionist, and her moral teachings creep into his conscience. All peoples share some natural rights, though some deny those rights to others. With the Everglades looming as the story's backdrop, the book allows ecological history to serve as a metaphor for human history—or vice versa. Freedom is a river that flows to everyone unless humans redirect or impede its natural course.[10]

Regionalists were avid social critics. Loving and promoting a place usually meant having high expectations for a region to be better than its best attribute. Willa Cather's wine-stained prairie and desert land of the West was succumbing to the fences, cattle, and staple crops of a migrating American culture. William Faulkner's white southern brethren, who vilified their region's literary emissary, were manically obsessed with the black man. Douglas in 1952 clarified her specific views as a critic of her region: "I have always argued that South Florida is a unique and little understood place, which should be developed in line with its singular potentialities. That's the basis of everything I've written about South Florida—culminating in *The Everglades: River of Grass*, which is a study of this region, its true possibilities, and the mistakes that have been made about it. *Road to the Sun* really has the same theme."[11]

After writing *River of Grass*, Douglas briefly took her vision and criticism off the printed page and into the streets. In 1948, she teamed up with her neighbor and friend, Elizabeth Virrick, to address social and environmental problems in Coconut Grove. Underneath the heavy vegetation that sheltered the Grove's white citizens lay a sad enclave, black and officially ignored, festering in Third World squalor. Miami's half million residents were racially segregated, and its artsy, intellectual enclave had a slum. Add a backdrop of steel mills, and it could have been Birmingham; a muddy river, and it would have been indistinguishable from New Orleans; antebellum mansions, and Miami would have looked the same as Charleston—except that segregation was more acute in the Florida city. When two sociologists used the 1940 U.S. Census to measure racial separation in 187 American cities, based on an index of 100, Miami posted the highest score, 97. In the black areas, the iniquities against which Judge Frank Stoneman had railed from his bench in the 1910s endured thirty years later. In Coconut Grove, more than four thousand descendants of early Bahamian immigrants and black migrants from southern cotton

and tobacco fields were crowded into a few city blocks. Where the boundaries of Colored Town began, city services and code enforcement pretty
much stopped. Irregular garbage collection left heaping piles of refuse
rotting at curbside. Children played in the streets and vacant lots for want
of recreational areas and parks. Houses were like oversized wooden crates
or concrete pillboxes, unpainted and in disrepair, owned by landlords,
white and black, who invested as little as possible to profit as much as
possible. Indoor plumbing and electricity were luxuries. People retrieved
water from outdoor spigots and relieved themselves in the nearly four
hundred backyard privies. Police protection was as scant as any other
municipal service.[12]

Ghettos were as old as American cities. They were as common in any
region of the country as in Lexington, Kentucky, and Erie, Pennsylvania,
the cities in which Elizabeth Virrick had been born and raised. In Coconut Grove, she and her husband, Vladimir, owned a modest apartment
building—white tenants only—uncomfortably close to the blight. They
had been living in Miami since their honeymoon there in 1925, and Elizabeth eventually joined the Coconut Grove Civic Club. At one meeting,
the guest speaker, Theodore Gibson, the ably charismatic pastor of the
black Christ Episcopal Church, pressed the members of the all-white audience to recognize their role in the black Grove's wretchedness. In addition to being a "diminutive, chain-smoking, orchid-loving, garage cera-
mist," Virrick was a good listener, and she wanted to help. She and Gibson
organized the Coconut Grove Citizens' Committee for Slum Clearance.[13]

Slum clearance was a subjective term in postwar America. It customar-
ily resulted in the clearance of poor people, those with few means of political power, and the replacement of slums with businesses or middle-class
white dwellings; alternatively, it meant the development of high-density
public housing. Though intended to improve the living conditions of the
poor, the Housing Act of 1949, for example, was perverted into something of a statutory bulldozer leading to less desirable ends for the poor
while directing millions of federal dollars to private developers and real
estate interests. Fifteen years earlier, Frank Stoneman had been among
the civic elite who led the effort to build Liberty Square, the nation's third

public-housing project, which became home to 243 black families. The effort was not totally altruistically driven. At that same moment, the *Herald* said of Miami's black citizens, "The advance of the Negro population is like a plague and carries devastation with it to all surrounding property." The idea was to quarantine the plague and to rid the resort city of an eyesore of dilapidated shacks. But by subsequently building additional public housing in what became known as Liberty City and concentrating the poor and black population there, Miami was creating a cauldron of dispossessed and increasingly disenchanted people (one that exploded into riots in 1980). The Reverend Gibson knew better than to pack humanity in tightly. "My people are living seven deep," he said. He and Virrick, later joined by Douglas, were thinking in terms of bringing public improvements to a low-density residential community and thus stabilizing it, not uprooting or hemming in its residents.[14]

Minimal exertion was required to recruit Douglas's active support. Virrick and Gibson's goals were consistent with her still-unfulfilled vision of Miami, first articulated in "The Galley," and joining the Citizens' Committee honored the values of her Quaker ancestors. Change was quick to come. Virrick convinced the city to institute regular garbage pickup and persuaded the water department to extend service to all blocks within the black Grove. The city then passed an ordinance requiring a flush toilet, sink, and septic tank for every residence. Following Douglas's suggestion, the Citizens' Committee organized a fund to help homeowners comply with the upgrade requirements. Two years of intense lobbying against city planners, a favored developer, and real estate interests, requiring aggressive strategies and counterstrategies and a public referendum, finally produced zoning reform that prioritized low-density development.[15]

Douglas was the Citizens' Committee's official mouthpiece. She wrote an article for the *Ladies' Home Journal* about the citizen-initiated improvements in Coconut Grove. She also secured a five-hundred-dollar grant from the University of Miami's Department of Government to fund research on a book, authored by her and Virrick, about slum-clearance initiatives in nine American cities, including Miami. Neither author was prepared to blame slum dwellers for their misery. The "present menacing dimensions" of slums, they wrote, were the sum of "undemocratic injustice, lack of opportunity, maladjustment, bitterness, loss of energy and earning power." Rinehart declined Douglas's pitch for the book, which was just as well. She and Virrick could never coordinate their schedules to complete more than twenty pages of a rough manuscript.[16]

Poverty was nothing less than a form of enslavement, and escaping was a matter interconnected with political freedom. This was how the poor generally saw it, and this was how Douglas saw it—in the hungry children she encountered in Europe after the war and later in the black children in Miami's derelict neighborhoods. Suffrage had obviously been an issue involving the freedom of women, but it also was a tool that could be used to combat poverty. Many of the nation's suffragists had worked to free the poor from their plight. Reformers had hoped that the great congress of female voters would reduce poverty significantly. Freedom of expression formed the basis for such hopes. It was the instrument of open protest, essential to any socially conscious journalist or writer. With characteristic wit, Douglas summed up her views on free speech in a November 1922 "Galley": "A free discussion of ideas seems to be about the hardest thing there is to get in this country. The minute you say something someone else does not agree with, his cry is that you ought not to be allowed to talk at all. I like best the old motto of Voltaire . . . who said, 'I disagree with every word you say, but I will defend to the death your right to say it.' It seems to me that is the only possible atmosphere in which men can learn to use what gray matter they have been given."[17]

Her fealty to constitutional freedoms never waned. In 1955, the founders of the Florida Civil Liberties Union asked her to join their new board of directors. The Greater Miami Chapter, as it was known, the first chapter of the American Civil Liberties Union (ACLU) organized below the Mason-Dixon Line, came into being in the midst of a communist witch hunt led by a brazen, politically ambitious state attorney named George Brautigam. Based in Miami, Brautigam launched a June 1954 grand jury investigation to ferret out communist activity. He had the backing of two state laws, one passed in 1941—essentially a facsimile of the federal Smith Act passed the preceding year—that prohibited verbal or written advocacy of communist doctrine, and the other passed in 1953 that out-lawed membership in any subversive organization. The catalyst in his investigation was a series of articles written for the *Miami Daily News* by Damon Runyon Jr., son of the well-known sportswriter of the same name. In McCarthyite fashion, Runyon claimed to have uncovered local communist activity and printed the names of several alleged Reds. As he saw it, the local Jewish cultural center operated as a Communist Party front, and nearly all the names he listed were those of members. In the 1948 presidential election, many had backed the Progressive Party candidate, liberal politician Henry Wallace. The people whom Runyon alleged to be communist also tended to agree with the recent *Brown* decision, as evidenced by the cultural center kindergarten's open policy toward black children. Playing to the media, Brautigam subpoenaed the people identified in Runyon's articles and conducted his grand jury investigation like a local version of the better-known House Committee on Un-American Activities (HUAC). Several witnesses invoked the Fifth Amendment and refused to answer questions. Charged with contempt, they were brought before circuit court judge George E. Holt, who found them guilty.[18]

Thirty-one "unfriendly witnesses" ultimately went to jail. In November, the state supreme court overruled Holt's actions, but Illinois Republican representative Harold Velde brought HUAC to Miami to reinforce Brautigam's efforts. Hearings conducted by Florida's Legislative Investigative Committee then followed, part of a highly orchestrated statewide campaign of harassment against alleged communists, civil rights activists, and homosexuals. The Florida committee characterized the Florida ACLU as being "dedicated to race-mixing, destruction of American way of life . . . ingrates of southern hospitality . . . willing pawns of a foreign ideology."[19]

Miami was a three-ring circus of repression that destroyed the livelihoods of scores of citizens. Robert Thorner, the owner of a local roller rink, saw the wave of oppression building early on and wrote to the ACLU's New York office in June asking for help. He and his wife, Cindy, had been Wallace supporters, and they were members of the First Unitarian Church, another quarry of Red hunters. With New York's help, they and several concerned citizens organized the Greater Miami Chapter of the ACLU. It is unclear who approached Douglas to join the founding board, but her civil liberties sympathies were well known, and organizers hoped that her name and connection to the *Herald* would offer the group a beneficial profile. The Legislative Investigative Committee falsely identified her as the organization's director. She was never more than a board member, and that more in name than in action. No record of her attending meetings exists, her name disappeared from the board of directors after two years, she never noted her membership on her résumé, and she left nothing in her papers to indicate her involvement. Her autobiography is similarly silent, and few friends of later years knew of her relationship with the organization.[20]

Douglas took an interest in at least one item on the Florida Civil Liberties Union's agenda, aggressive opposition to the practice of reading the Bible in Dade County schools. At the time, the Coconut Grove Playhouse hosted the new play *Inherit the Wind,* which re-created the 1925 Scopes monkey trial with special emphasis on former Miami resident William Jennings Bryan. Douglas loved the play and wrote a review for the *Coconut Grove Village Post.* She praised the ACLU for involving itself in the trial, which represented a struggle for "freedom of thought and speech." Without going into specifics, she offered her gratitude for the local chapter's efforts: "The play is an excellent reminder [that] our freedoms are always on trial. And I am glad . . . Miami has the first chapter in the South of that old and much tried but still necessary organization."[21]

On a personal level, Douglas needed to write and publish books to make a living, but doing so nonetheless represented a labor of love that consumed the bulk of her time and energy. Between 1958 and 1960, she published three volumes. One was *Hurricane,* which she researched during the start-up years of the Miami ACLU and dedicated to Carolyn Cole. Another was a departure from anything she had written before. Research for it ultimately stirred latent memories and long-retired feelings. When J. B. Lippincott asked her to write a twenty-thousand-word travel book about Paris, she had not been to her beloved city in forty years. It was now the world's fourth-largest, with seven million inhabitants, and it had been overtaken by modern desires and tastes. The "tremendous rushing" of automobile traffic rattled her, as did the removal of trees from the Champs Élysées, which was "shabby with salesrooms and neon signs." The grand old city was still "utterly familiar," though, and as nearly delightful as before. It remained in her mind worthy of Miami's emulation. Released in 1961, *The Key to Paris* earned royalties that averaged under $350 for each of the first six years after its publication, just enough to pay for her trip to Europe.[22]

Sales records for the third book, published two years earlier, have disappeared. There is no indication that it enjoyed exceptional success, though a nonprofit environmental publisher, Milkweed Editions, reissued it in 2003. Douglas had been an obvious choice to contribute to a young readers series published by John Day of New York. Each book in the series was set in a national park. Writing *Alligator Crossing* shepherded her along through familiar historical, social, and geographic territory. The book is a coming-of-age story, and like her earlier short fiction, it casts the human relationship with nature into a moral lesson. The main character, Henry Albert Bunks, is a knobby-kneed, "sunburned, sun bleached" boy who flees despairing family circumstances, including an alcoholic stepfather, and the vile city streets of 1950s South Florida. Early in the book, the disaffected Henry trades the mean urban jungle for another kind of jungle, the Everglades. There he befriends a wildlife poacher, Arlie Dillon, who demonstrates a visceral connection with the same nature he plunders. Survival for Henry comes easier in the wilderness than on the streets. He is enchanted by what Dillon teaches him about the dynamic community of flora and fauna, the way nature looks and works, but he is also disturbed by Dillon's violent ways toward nature. Yes, Henry thinks, Dillon is right, many things in the wild can cause harm, such as the moccasin Henry just allowed to slither away, and "you had to watch out and be careful. But he did not see why he should kill." Douglas was clearly sending readers a message about animal rights, suggesting that by 1959, the year the book was published, her beliefs were turning more radical. She called up a stock historical backdrop that includes hurricanes, Henry Flagler's railroad, Guy Bradley's murder, and the drawn-out development of the national park. She treated the park as the culminating point in a progression toward greater social and environmental stability in a ravaged region. Literary scholar Melissa Walker observes that *Alligator Crossing* is a "book about the discovery of paradise rather than its loss."[23]

In Douglas's personal paradise, friends were an essential quality. People, in turn, took pleasure in her. One friend described her as "full of energy, sparkling, into literature, wonderful. . . . She also enjoyed French food, traveling, dancing and romance." Another friend said, "She is full of fun and her conversation crackles with humor." Men especially liked her, remembered Jean Areson, but she kept up her guard lest one drag her helpless self away from happy independence. She liked old bachelors uninterested in romance or marriage "because they weren't a threat to her" and enjoyed gay men and younger men for the same reason. She looked for the latter as dance partners, and well into her seventies, she frequently spent the evening in their company. In 1963, after one particularly long night of dancing with a man fifty years younger than her seventy-three, she approached death's door. She awoke the next morning feeling strange, experiencing stabbing pains in her abdomen and trembling with fever. Her condition worsened during the day. Cole was in town and insisted that Douglas call a doctor. He diagnosed peritonitis, caused by a ruptured appendix, and admitted her to the hospital, where she was also diagnosed with a hiatal hernia and treated for gallstones. Her medical bill ran up to fifteen hundred dollars, and at the time her only sources of income were a "few small royalties" and sixty-eight dollars a month from Social Security. She applied for a relief grant from the Carnegie Fund for Authors, which had previously helped her with expenses for her uncle Charlie, and received three hundred dollars.[24]

It was a rare moment in a long life whenever Douglas felt financially secure. "She never had enough money to live well," said Areson. When Cole died in 1972, she left her dearest friend a life estate in her house next door so Douglas would have a steady source of rental income. But the house turned out to be a relentless money trap, requiring endless repairs and improvements that cost more than the income from rent. She was perpetually reduced to applying for grants intended for starving artists to help her live and pay for research trips.[25]

To make ends meet, she sought work outside of writing. In 1960, she became director of the University of Miami Press. It was a part-time position that allowed other pursuits yet exposed her to the latest scholarly work in a variety of disciplines, particularly biology, anthropology, and history. At the time, she founded Friends of the University Library and sat as its president for six years. Fifteen years earlier, she had joined the fundraising group for the Coconut Grove Library, convincing the group to call itself Friends of the Coconut Grove Library Association. "She was the first person to use the word 'friends' in connection with anything in this area," said Helen Muir. Age limits forced her to retire from the university press after only three years, just as she received the fifteen-hundred-dollar hospital bill.[26]

She decided to start her own press. Naming herself president and "editorial staff" and running it from her home, she called the imprint Hurricane House Publishing. In its approximately ten-year life, the press published perhaps two dozen books, ranging in topics from local history to gardening to poetry. In some cases, she was dealing with first-time authors and took delight in playing the role of writing mentor. The first books appeared in 1965, among them *River of Grass*. Rinehart's seventh and final printing occurred in 1959. Rinehart sold her the plates, and she reissued the book and thus kept it from going out of print. Not long thereafter, she wrote *The Joys of Bird Watching in Florida* as a guide for beginners, and Hurricane House published the volume in 1969. She organized book signings for her authors and herself. "This publishing business is great fun," she told a friend, "but it takes time also."[27]

Even with time given to Hurricane House, writing remained her principal business. With a private local press in 1973, she published *Adventures in a Green World: The Story of David Fairchild and Barbour Lathrop*, about the plant work of her two late Coconut Grove friends. Before that, Harper and Row published *Florida: The Long Frontier* in 1967. A history of the state from the precolonial period to the mid–twentieth century,

The Long Frontier bears the stamp of the Annales school of historians, which originated in France. In a keynote address to the Florida Historical Society a few years later, she said, "I am very much of the opinion that a great deal of history is not so much the individual people. . . . I am very much more interested in what is the more or less modern French school of historical writing, which is a study of the great forces . . . that produce the movement of people and economics, the beliefs, the way people live, the way they think." Her interpretation of Florida's frontier as temporally long (*la longue durée*) and physically long (geography's causal role in history) alone suggests the French influence.[28]

The Long Frontier was her first book published by a major press in several years. Carl Carmer, who had coedited the Rivers of America series with Hervey Allen, thought no one was better qualified than she to write a Florida history for Harper's Regions of America series, which he was now editing. She came on board in 1960, but first the bout of appendicitis and then cataract surgery delayed the project. When the book finally appeared, she characterized it as the "first history of Florida written not as a textbook." Florida was due for such a book. World War II, which had introduced hundreds of thousands of military personnel to the state; residential air-conditioning, which was making the South a more tolerable place to live year-round; and Social Security, which relieved retirees from dependency on their families, were collective combustibles in Florida's population explosion. The state had more than six million residents by the mid-1960s, with most of the increase coming from new arrivals, who by the 1970s were outnumbering the state's natural increase by more than ten times. Douglas and her publisher hoped that the newcomers would have an interest in learning about their adopted state's past. Florida newspapers universally welcomed the book. One reviewer said that the "gifted author . . . finally gave a thriving young state, bulging with newcomers, the brilliantly written history that it had been lacking." More than six thousand copies sold in the first six months after its release.[29]

The sales were a welcome boon, as was an unexpected inheritance. Around the time of *The Long Frontier*'s release, her old bachelor friend David True, a fellow lover of Florida history with whom she dined nearly every week for several years, died and left her ten thousand dollars. The money made her life easier for a time and helped to fund a new book project, which she would come to call a "definitive" biography of William Henry Hudson. Frank Chapman, the ornithologist who had devoted many years to studying bird life in the Everglades and who had contributed an article on the Argentine naturalist to *Audubon* magazine, first suggested the idea of a Hudson biography to Douglas in the 1940s. Hudson's best-known novel, *Green Mansions,* published in 1904, had made her an instant devotee. As soon as her Florida history went to press, she applied for a research fellowship from Wellesley College. She was "startled and delighted," as she told friends, when at her late age she won it. A year later, she received a similar grant from the American Philosophical Society. She used the first fellowship check to visit Hudson's birthplace near Buenos Aires. Eight more research trips to Argentina and England, where he spent his professional life, followed over the next two decades.[30]

The more Douglas learned about Hudson, the closer she drew to him. Not long after his death in 1922, his legacy was shunted out to the borderlands of the literary and scientific worlds, and Douglas believed that he deserved better. His work, notably that set in his native South America, was fertile with timeless environmental insights. She felt a "common thread" connecting her to his loner personality, his love of birds (he was a founder of the Royal Society for the Protection of Birds), his attraction to an older partner, and his doubts about an afterlife. "It is useless," he wrote, "their telling us when we die we are instantly judged and packed straight off to some region where we are destined to spend an eternity. We know better. Nature, our own hearts, have taught us differently." There was an activist call in his writing, too, a lament for the loss and "disfigurement" of wild things and places in South America, that resonated with her. "I have a very great feeling for Hudson, and great feeling for what he did," she told a reporter. "He found a thing that he could do in his work for the protection of birds, and he proceeded to do it for the rest of his life."[31]

By the end of the 1960s, she had an opportunity to pursue a similar eventful course. With one environmental crisis following another in South Florida, other people came to recognize that she had done something in her own work that might help protect the Everglades—her equivalent to Hudson's South American jungles and pampas. She did not, however, enter the early battles of the newly proclaimed war against environmental ruin, which were waged by others, people she knew, respected, and appreciated.

Grassroots

In the 1960s, Douglas still refused to get behind the wheel of a car. The prospect that she would ever do so had passed, though not because she was in her seventies. Miami's roads had become treacherous. They had always been in some way or the other. She remembered when they were sand and limestone, dusty uncertain byways that gave little traction to cars that rolled over easily. The roads were eventually paved, and more land was bulldozed for new, more stable cars. But now there were too many cars, impatient surging rivers of them. Back in the 1920s, she "shudder[ed] to think" what Miami would be like with a rush hour and gridlock. Forty years later, Miami had permanent gridlock. The local governments were unable to build new roads or improve old ones fast enough. Construction was everywhere; it was a relentless roadway drama that slowed traffic to a hopeless crawl. To help ease conditions, the city created a bikeway system, one of the first in the country, but it hardly made a difference. The automobile traffic became so heavy that people feared riding bikes. The unfurling numbers of vehicles were a consequence of the mindless pursuit of growth, about which Douglas had warned in the 1920s. South Florida's population was growing faster than anyplace else in the state, and Florida was growing faster than any state in the country. Although Dade County had approximately the same land mass as Delaware, Dade had nearly one million residents in 1960, twice as many as Delaware. Close to half of them had arrived since 1950, coming from all over and bringing cars and different driving habits with them.[1]

And the cars created more than traffic problems. When Douglas looked out over the city's skyline, growing taller, broader, and glassier with modern architecture, she saw a haze on wind-calm days. The local dumps burned bloated mounds of refuse. Industry supporting new construction, in particular asphalt and cement manufacturing, filled the air and the waterways with pollutants. The airports, accommodating more flights each year, did the same. But the trail to the main pollutant source led to Americans' latest shining chrome and paint infatuation. "The automobile," wrote Douglas friend and resident activist Juanita Greene in 1971, "eats up space, uglifies the scene, pollutes the air, picks the pocketbook with heavy hand, and terrifies and kills at a routine, predictable pace." Enabling these bad qualities, local government spent from five to ten times more on roads than on public transportation. By 1960, Miami had half a million cars, and photochemical smog. People began comparing the city with Los Angeles.[2]

At the time, Douglas was not standing in front of planning boards shaking a reproachful fist. She was aware, though, of the harmful imbalance developing between nature and expansive, technology-happy civilization. Florida's east coast cities "sprang up like coral growths between sky and sea," she wrote with derision. Her regionalist dream of an inspiriting Miami blending refreshing subtropical nature with a reciprocating culture had perished, dashed by ugly unplanned growth. Her disenchantment extended out beyond the city limits, too. The arcadia of tropical plenty she had wished for the Everglades had been plundered by corporate agriculture and servile government bureaucrats. In a 1959 article for *The Rotarian,* she turned against the Army Corps of Engineers for the first time. The paternal hand of flood control was beginning to show itself in all its worst manipulative ways. She had been convinced that the corps' water-conservation areas would prevent development and agriculture from consuming the entire upper Everglades around Lake Okeechobee. But she saw just the opposite happening now that the "great agricultural interests" were protected from flooding. There were reports of "too much fresh water" being sent down canals and "silting up the bays and destroying saltwater fishing," just as Ernest Lyons had predicted, and fifteen years after Garald Parker identified the source of the trouble, saltwater was still seeping into Miami's drinking wells. The national park too was "endangered by the loss of fresh water . . . being squandered," Douglas said, two years before the unnecessary drought.[3]

Yet during the drought, ears did not ring with the noise of her protests. Wallace Stegner, an outsider, sounded the kind of discouraging voice she did not. *The Rotarian* article advanced a worthy corrective to *River of Grass*'s sanguine view of federal water management. But the article amounted to a momentary outburst unsustained by subsequent years of relative silence. The modern movement in Florida, she later observed, had been launched in the pivotal year of 1947. But she made the transition to emeritus status rather quickly after that year and before actually earning tenure as an activist. Instead of throwing herself into campaign organizing in the early 1960s, she watched from the sidelines while others, people she knew, lined up for a decade of struggles.

The movement debuted in organized form, months before the climactic release of *Silent Spring*, at a meeting of the Metro commissioners (a consolidated representation of county and municipal governments) in January 1962. It emerged from a union of environmental concerns—wildlife preservation and pollution—and was prompted into action by Ludwig Enterprises' announced plans to construct the Seadade oil refinery and deepwater port at South Bay, the lower end of Biscayne Bay.

At the helm of Ludwig Enterprises was founder Daniel K. Ludwig, one of the world's few billionaires. The general public hardly knew the man, but his rags-to-riches storybook life, his rise from humble Michigan beginnings and an eighth-grade education, beguiled aspiring entrepreneurs. He was the "American Onassis." He pioneered the supertanker; developed the Princess chain of resort hotels in Mexico, Bermuda, and the Bahamas; and blazed the venture trail to the South American rain-forest, where he sought but failed to turn profitable resources out of his three-million-acre Brazilian domain. He succeeded elsewhere with in-vestments in commodities of nature—oil, salt, timber, iron ore. In Dade County, he was proposing the development of a petrochemical complex on a twenty-two-hundred-acre site squeezed between Everglades Na-tional Park and the John Pennekamp Coral Reef Preserve. The latter was America's first underwater state park, intended to protect sensitive coral reefs from poachers who used hammers, chisels, and sometimes dyna-mite to harvest specimens for the tourist market. Ludwig planned to do his own chiseling to cut a forty-foot-deep shipping canal straight through reefs and across Biscayne Bay. His proposed fifty-thousand-barrel-a-day refinery was touted as a "logical center for commerce" between the United States and four continents. It promised a $130 million annual payroll for 18,540 employees.[4]

Tourists spent six hundred million dollars in Dade County, however. This was one of several arguments presented at a Metro commission-ers' meeting by a newly formed citizens' group, the Safe Progress Asso-ciation (SPA). Commissioners listened cordially to its arguments for an hour, after which Ludwig's representative, James A. Bush, made a ten-minute appeal for their support. Ten minutes was enough. The commis-sioners voted unanimously to rezone the Seadade site "industrial unlim-ited." The *Miami Herald* endorsed the refinery, and the *Miami News* said Seadade would create one of the county's "most valuable assets" out of a "marshy, mosquito-infested wasteland." City officials across the way in tourism-dependent Miami Beach were less anxious to trade sunshine, clear jade-colored water, and white beaches for the belching waste of heavy industry. The refinery would discharge oil, phenol, caustics, and compounds with a high biochemical oxygen demand into the bay and sulfur oxides and particulate matter into the air.[5]

The SPA's main objective was to feed this kind of information to the public and elected officials. Its founder, Lloyd Miller, an employee of Pan American Airways at Miami International Airport, was the restless son of a Reading, Pennsylvania, labor leader and the godson of socialist and former presidential candidate Norman Thomas. Miller was also the president of the Mangrove chapter of the Izaak Walton League, which he and some fishing buddies had started years earlier. He organized the SPA with some of those same friends. Its membership was small—a dozen or so "nondescript people," as Miller described them—and the proposed refinery was not their only concern. One member was the somewhat dour but highly creative Philip Wylie, whose 1930 novel, *Gladiator,* had inspired the Superman comic-book character. Early on, Wylie led a one-man public-health crusade, writing at one point in a 1951 *Look* magazine article, "Florida: Polluted Paradise," about the raw sewage spilling into Biscayne Bay. With its dirty secret now exposed to tourists, the city built its first wastewater treatment plant on Virginia Key in 1956. Dade County, however, continued to pump thirty-five million gallons of inadequately treated waste a day into canals and one hundred million gallons into the Atlantic. Another SPA member, W. T. Lain Guthrie, an airline pilot, exposed the county when he used dye to show health inspectors that the toilets at the Florida Power and Light (FP&L) plant flushed directly into the bay. A coliform study conducted by the Hoover Environmental Legal Defense Fund described the Miami River and the bay as open sewers. Yet as late as 1969, the Dade County pollution-control department had never monitored coliform counts; in fact, it did not own a boat to do so.[6]

Irresponsible government of this sort stuck in the craw of others who joined the SPA. One was Juanita Greene, a twenty-year veteran reporter with the *Herald.* She generated numerous articles taking SPA's side even as the editors of her newspaper endorsed the refinery. One of her *Herald* colleagues was Belle Scheffel, the treasurer of the local Nature Conservancy and a founder and past president of three area garden clubs. She hit the women's club circuit after the SPA lost the commission vote, giving speeches wherever she could and collecting a stack of antirefinery resolutions along the way.[7]

The "intellectual center for environmental thinking in south Florida," in the assessment of one activist, was Polly Redford, yet another writer. Her husband, James, was one of SPA's founders, and both Redfords were Audubon Society members and had helped organize the Izaak Walton

League. In 1963, Polly published her first book, *Raccoons and Eagles,* for which National Audubon president Carl Buchheister wrote the foreword and Stewart Udall provided a jacket endorsement. Redford assessed the state of American progress by examining its relationship with her two subject animals. The survivalist raccoon had flourished by rushing in to fill the void when the "march of progress" trampled out larger, mightier animals, but the eagle, lacking the same verve around humans, had fared poorly, declining to 417 nesting pairs nationwide, including 88 in Florida. "If [the eagle] dies," Redford warned, "we will be remembered as a nation that loved liberty, conquered a continent, sent rockets to the moon, covered the earth with radioactivity and beer cans, but was too poor to save the national bird." What distressed her as much as the eagle's prospects was the apathy public officials exhibited regarding the possibility of turning one of the country's most aesthetically inspiring and ecologically productive places, Biscayne Bay, into a sterile wasteland. The SPA did not oppose industry itself, she clarified in a 1964 *Harper's Magazine* article, but merely dirty industry.[8]

Precisely. Pollution was industry's litter, or private property misplaced, the SPA reminded others. Though small in size, the organization constituted something more than a cluster of alarmists getting their dander up over an isolated issue. Too much was happening around the country for their concerns to be dismissed. Two years earlier, the 608-foot tanker *P. W. Thirtle,* owned by Sinclair Refining Company, steamed into a soupy fog near Rhode Island and ground onto the rocks fifty yards off the coast, opening a gap that let oil float into Narragansett Bay, where a young Marjory had sailed with her uncle and grandfather. To keep the tanker afloat, 331,000 gallons of crude were discharged. Oyster beds and other marine life were decimated. Of some two thousand ducks coated in coagulated oil, three hundred were washed and relocated to Florida. Beyond Narragansett Bay, the number of oil spills increased as demand for the commodity increased, and the stakes grew higher as oil tankers—including Daniel Ludwig's oil tankers—grew in size.[9]

Ludwig Enterprises declared that it ran only clean operations. The declaration, an industry standard, made SPA members gag. They issued their own: "There is no such thing as a pollution free refinery." Furthermore, the group added, the auxiliary industries that cropped up around refineries, about which Ludwig representatives remained strategically silent, were notorious polluters. Lest they appear indifferent to clean air and water, the Metro commissioners hurriedly adopted a pollution-control ordinance in 1963, claiming that it was the toughest such measure in the country.[10]

The new law failed to put the activists at ease. They initiated a bumper-sticker drive to raise money and awareness. Read one, "Promises Now . . . Flagrant Pollution Later!" But the group needed more than self-adhesive proclamations. James Redford knew the importance of "lin[ing] up your scientists." The SPA's original dozen included a petrochemical engineer, a civil engineer, and three University of Miami biologists. No comprehensive scientific survey of Biscayne Bay had ever been done, so the SPA collected data from studies on oil refineries and pollution published by federal agencies and private institutions, including the American Petroleum Institute, and obtained a "warning report" from Miami's city manager. It then published an ominously titled pamphlet, *The Creeping Peril! Industrial Pollution and You—Fact Book,* which warned that a major tourist center was at risk of turning into the "Smogville of the south." Redford and Scheffel concluded that gathering scientific information was no less important than an old reliable strategy: giving talks at women's clubs, whose network reached, by Redford's calculations, four hundred thousand people in Dade and Monroe Counties alone.[11]

The SPA was clearly becoming a threat to business interests, some of which turned nasty. Miller's dog was poisoned and his car vandalized, and opponents spearheaded a campaign to have Pan Am fire him. James Redford was accused of fostering a sinister "Master Plan," and the University of Miami's executive vice president instructed its biologists to refrain from political activity, although the directive never stuck.[12]

Despite the steep odds, this David of resident citizens' groups, with a minuscule budget, no staff, and a handful of volunteers, toppled the giant. Metro commissioners held off on issuing a building permit. They were no more forthcoming in allowing the dredging of the shipping channel, which would also require the approval of the Florida cabinet and the Army Corps of Engineers. Incidentally aiding the SPA was opposition to Seadade deployed by the developers of Islandia, a string of thirty mostly unpopulated keys in South Bay. The developers intended to construct estate homes, a tropical vacation resort, and a six-million-dollar marina with two hundred boat slips, plans that would surely be ruined if a highway of oil tankers ran across the waterscape.[13]

Then, unfortunately for the developers of both Seadade and Islandia, Miller hit on a spectacular idea: turn South Bay and Islandia into a national park or preserve that would be the aquatic equivalent of John Pennekamp State Park. The idea caught on. Even the Metro commission was intrigued, asking Udall to consider the possibility. The interior secretary ordered a scientific study of the bay, and in late 1963, he flew to Miami, took a charter flight over the area, and returned to Washington convinced that he had seen a notable prospect for the national park system. Proponents were thinking in terms of a national monument that would enlarge the already expanded vision of federal preserves ushered in with the founding of Everglades National Park. Of the eventual 100,500 acres set aside for Biscayne National Monument, 96,500 would be underwater. Targeting Congress, the National Park Service distributed a slim printed proposal for the monument jammed with underwater color photographs of the "fantastic marine nursery." This environment, the service declared in a separate master plan, supported the "richest and most varied tropical marine biota in the entire Caribbean area." Nearly as compelling, the keys of Islandia, once the territory of Tekesta people and a gold mine for wreckers, were sated with tropical hardwoods and migratory birds. Polly Redford wrote that when the people of Dade County learned exactly what lay within the proposed boundaries, they "reacted like someone who just discovered a dusty Rembrandt or Stradivarius in the attic."[14]

Yet not everyone had the same appreciation for Nature's canvas. Fearing the certainty of restrictions on power-plant development on the bay, FP&L encouraged Governor Claude Kirk to stand against what the company portrayed as an aggressive federal takeover of state property and an egregious insult to John Pennekamp State Park. Florida's and the South's first Republican governor since Reconstruction (along with Winthrop Rockefeller of Arkansas), Kirk was brassy and defiant and did essentially as he pleased, even if that meant offending party bosses and big business. He did just that when he supported a protected bay. At the same time, the Islandia developers tried to use their considerable influence with Metro commissioners. But on the environmentalist side was Hardy Matheson, whose family had given the city Matheson Hammock Park, an untrampled remnant of the Miami hammock that had lured the Munroes, Fairchilds, and Douglas to Coconut Grove. Matheson was elected to the Metro Commission on virtually a single platform, to save the bay. Using family property, he arranged to make Tropical Audubon, the descendant of Mary Munroe's defunct Coconut Grove Audubon, a landowner on Elliot Key to ensure the organization's legal standing against Islandia.[15]

With local opponents held somewhat in check, Miami representative Dante Fascell, who emerged as one of the Florida environment's best friends in Congress, introduced the bill to create the monument. The opposition invoked the powerful trope of economic development. South Florida real estate investor Charles "Bebe" Rebozo, future president Richard Nixon's main "leisure-time crony and confidant" and Biscayne Bay neighbor, asked Fascell to withdraw the bill. It was a polite request from an old acquaintance, but Fascell politely declined, instead asking National Audubon's southeastern representative, Joe Browder, to come up from Miami and work with his staff on the campaign for the bill. Fascell also met with John Saylor, the key Republican member of the House Interior Committee. The Pennsylvanian was staunchly conservative politically but proudly green. He was the lead Republican sponsor of the 1964 Wilderness Act and a dam hater from Johnstown (which retained a long memory of a devastating 1889 dam break and flood) who introduced the Wild and Scenic Rivers Act in 1968. Saylor accepted Fascell's invitation to join James Redford on a fishing trip around Biscayne Bay and Elliot Key. Browder went along, too, and took a photograph of the prized sailfish Saylor landed. His support, along with a promised one-hundred-thousand-dollar grant for the monument from Herbert Hoover Jr. and his family's foundation, added enough momentum for Fascell to push the bill through in 1968. In October, President Lyndon Johnson signed into law the bill establishing Biscayne National Monument.[16]

Among the rationales for setting aside protected territory, ecological preservation finally outranked recreation. Congress was placing a premium on coral reefs, turtle grass, sponges, and sea horses. "All management programs and objectives," declared the biologists who composed the Biscayne National Monument proposal, will ensure the "perpetuation of the complex ecological *processes.*" Still, the monument's priorities did not dismantle old interests. In April 1974, Dade County commissioners declared all of Biscayne Bay an "aquatic park and conservation area." Their decision came after bacteria levels and fish kills rose above state and local standards, conditions that interfered, they said, with recreational activities.[17]

The Seadade affair signaled the beginning of something more epic than a national monument. A new generation of activists and organizations heeded the call to environmental protection. In 1971, University of Miami Press published a "battle" book, *The Environmental Destruction of South Florida,* with essays written by these activists, most of whom Douglas knew. She and Greene eventually worked together to protect the Everglades; she had suggested the idea for Polly Redford's *Raccoons and Eagles;* and she and Fascell eventually developed a close professional and personal relationship centered on the Everglades. Another contributor to the book and on the front lines of the Biscayne Bay battle, a man who would bring epic change to Douglas's life, was Joe Browder, a local television news reporter who worked with Audubon, first as a volunteer and then as a paid regional representative.[18]

There was also Alice Wainwright. A woman of New England stock and compulsive decency, she was resourceful and smart. After being widowed during pregnancy, she moved to Miami, worked her way through law school, hung out her shingle, and raised her son. Coconut Grove contented her most as a place to live. She and Douglas became friends, vacationing at least once together at the Wainwright summer home in Maine, and she joined Douglas and Virrick on the slum-clearance committee.

Offended by the disadvantages unfairly imposed on selected social groups, Wainwright sought elected office. When she won a seat on the city commission in 1961, she beat a candidate who said that "no woman of dignity" would get into politics. She brought dignity to the city commission, however, in the form of a badly needed environmental consciousness. "The environment of the city is as important as the preservation of the environment of the countryside," she said; a place's ecological health was essential to civic betterment. During her four years on the commission, she shepherded the passage of ordinances that required the landscaping of new parking lots and restricted the use of chemical pesticides, and she convinced the city to purchase Sewell Park on the Miami River. When she left the commission, she shifted her energies to work as a board member and then president of Tropical Audubon, helping to stop the Seadade and Islandia projects. But there was no respite in this environmental business.[19]

On the heels of the Seadade struggle, FP&L's new power-plant facility at Turkey Point set alight a new controversy. The chair of the power company's board, McGregor Smith, had a clear vision that seemed unlikely to draw critics. Turkey Point, he said, "was conceived as a happy partnership between man and nature." After losing a battle, with the opposition led by Greene and members of the Izaak Walton League, to expand its existing plant at Cutler Ridge, FP&L sought to stay out of the path of spreading residential areas. It located the semiremote Turkey Point property, a thirty-two-hundred-acre undisturbed mangrove-trimmed scrub and wetland expanse on Biscayne Bay near Card Sound, twenty-four miles south of the city. To keep the industrial impact at a minimum, Smith hired a conservation supervisor. The utility planted coconut palms and mahogany trees and left the indigenous mangroves and buttonwood trees virtually untouched. To create beaches for separate Girl Scout and Boy Scout camps, it used spoil sand from the 3.5-mile canal dug to barge fuel oil to the plant. It milled trees downed during Hurricane Betsy in 1965 to construct shelters and picnic areas for the scouts and blazed hiking trails through the scrubland. As a benefit to the University of Miami's Institute of Marine and Atmospheric Sciences, FP&L set aside a tract with saltwater ponds for a shrimp-breeding laboratory. Finally, Smith leased fifteen hundred acres to Tropical Audubon for one dollar a year to be used as a wildlife sanctuary. National newspapers congratulated FP&L for creating a beacon of industry and nature coexisting for the good of all. One especially exuberant journalist concluded that since FP&L had improved Turkey Point, forty new bird species had joined the original sixty living there. It was hard to take issue with the utility's Good Samaritan behavior. But one question nagged some environmentalists: Was FP&L attempting to direct the public's attention away from some hidden infamy? The answer was probably no. But Smith believed "that ecology can be improved. . . . If our ecology had not been changed, we would not be here today talking about large power plants."[20]

Tropical Audubon and scientists at the University of Miami began publicly talking and complaining about precisely that fact. The scientists included biologist Taylor Alexander; ornithologist Oscar Owre, a future president of Tropical Audubon; and Gilbert L. Voss of the Marine Institute, an oceanographer and veteran activist. His impassioned presentation at a 1957 conference at Everglades National Park had helped to bring about the establishment of John Pennekamp State Park. Voss was also the principal investigator, accompanied by four University of Miami scientists, on the first comprehensive scientific study of Biscayne Bay, ordered by Secretary Udall. Douglas knew Voss and wrote the foreword to one of his books on Florida's coral reefs, his scientific love and specialty, noting, "He demonstrates the importance of the efforts of a single individual who determines that there is a problem, and who dedicates his time and energy to solve the problem."[21]

The problem at Turkey Point was hot water and the plant's proposed expansion. The utility was operating two oil-fired generating plants, but the population in its service area had increased by a factor of 2.5 since 1950, while consumption of electricity had increased twelvefold, mainly because of a new household amenity—air-conditioning. Anticipating continued growth, FP&L obtained permission from the state and the Atomic Energy Commission to construct two nuclear plants. Government regulators failed to consider the possible environmental consequences.

The Atomic Energy Commission portrayed nuclear power as the space-age answer for safe, efficient energy, and many environmentalists supported it over coal and hydroelectric plants. A decade before the accidental release of radiation at the Three Mile Island power station near Harrisburg, Pennsylvania, widespread protests against nuclear power had not yet materialized. Turkey Point's opponents did not campaign against nuclear power itself. Rather, they objected to the prospect of adding water, heated as a result of its use to cool nuclear generators, to the 1.8 gallons per minute that FP&L was already pumping into the bay from the existing plants and to a new discharge canal the utility was excavating. Scientists believed that discharge at a temperature of ninety-five degrees or higher would harm marine life—in particular, shrimp, crabs, and turtle grass. To test their hypothesis, they initiated studies funded with grant support from one of the bay environment's most reliable patrons, Herbert Hoover Jr., and his Hoover Foundation.[22]

The "real test" for the young environmental movement in South Florida, by Browder's reckoning, was Turkey Point. Seadade's Ludwig had been an outsider, an interloper whose ties to the local community were tenuous, and his business enterprises were not the kind that yielded much sympathy from locals. Things were different with FP&L's Smith. Everyone living in the region had a stake in his utility's services, as he did not hesitate to remind people. And Smith, who was fond of wearing a white Bahama hat sporting an emblem, which he had created, adorned with the image of an anhinga and reading "Turkey Point Wildlife Refuge," was community as well as business oriented. With that one unsolicited gift alone, the utility could well have been considered to have gone beyond the call of duty to give benefit to community life and to protect nature. Fifty years earlier, an age ago, people would certainly have thought so. But by the 1960s, the new movement turned on the insights of ecological science, which focused on systemic biological relationships and thus discounted as fallacy the idea of setting aside a cordoned-off parcel of land as smart conservation. As Owre and others pointed out, if FP&L killed the marine life around Turkey Point, the aquatic birds among the hundred species counted by the national press would abandon the refuge. Whatever his loyalties to the community and to nature, Smith remained in staunch denial about his power plant's burdens on the bay. Thermal pollution did not exist, he said; a "fairer term would be thermal effect." Natural cold spells, not his power plant, harmed life in the bay. The warm discharge water stimulated marine life. This he knew, he told a water-pollution-control advisory board, from fishing on a cold day off Turkey Point when in a "matter of three hours" he reeled in between one and two hundred live ones.[23]

Environmentalists quickly grew tired of Smith's fish stories. Tropical Audubon occupied an awkward position as the recipient of Smith's gift of the refuge. But Wainwright decided she was not prepared to sacrifice principle as thanks for the utility's generosity. By 1970, a year before the first nuclear plant was to begin operations, the echo of her group's objections, magnified by scientific research, had reached Tallahassee. Governor Kirk, who turned out to be a quick study on the environment, entered the conflict. His environmental adviser, Nathaniel Reed, maintained a dialogue with Tropical. On Reed's recommendation, Kirk asked the federal government to intervene, and from that request the Water Pollution Control Administration (WPCA) of the Interior Department organized a state-federal water-pollution conference to be held in Miami in February. A month earlier, in Pensacola, the WPCA held a similar conference that culminated in orders to several polluters to clean up their discharge into the Perdido River and Escambia Bay. For nearly a year preceding the Miami conference, scientists and local, state, and federal officials had been gathering on their own each month at the University of Miami in what they called the Marine Decisions Seminar to brainstorm proposals for pollution-control policy and cleanup measures. Surprising none of the participants, John E. Hagan III, who directed a study for the WPCA, asserted on the eve of the February conference, "We've got to clean up the Miami River, the Coral Gables Canal, Snapper Creek and other badly polluted streams" that released dirty water into the bay. He emphasized that the system could not afford the added stress of a massive hot-water discharge. The statement was a bad omen for FP&L.[24]

For the first time, a federal agency was taking up the problem of thermal pollution, another bad omen. Generating its own tepidity was the exchange between the two sides—scientists, environmentalists, and the Interior Department on one and FP&L alone on the other. Two hundred people filled the chandeliered conference hall at Miami's Sheraton Four Ambassadors Hotel. Browder came down from Washington, where he was now working with Friends of the Earth. His old Tropical Audubon colleagues were there, too. A passel of University of Miami scientists came out, scrambling to and from the Sheraton between classes. Many had been urged on by Owre, who had also convinced the National Oceanic and Atmospheric Administration to do flyover infrared images to show the bay's hot-water zones.[25]

Jeanne Bellamy, who covered the event for the *Miami Herald,* described it in mixed metaphors as a "verbal ballet, enlivened by linguistic karate chops among the performers," some of whom were "heroes" and some "villains." FP&L's point man, Vice President A. M. Davis, said that the utility had always been careful about bringing the temperature of its discharge from the oil-fired plants down to or below Dade County's mandated ninety-five-degree maximum. Environmentalists argued that FP&L was misinformed about the cooling capacity of its system and cited Hagan's study showing that damage from the discharge had spread to a 670-acre area in the bay. Gilbert Voss pointed out that the fatalities of microorganisms measured a devastating 100 percent, and Owre presented dramatic visual evidence with his color-coded aerial photos. The University of Miami scientists angered Davis, who believed that they were testifying as advocates, and he accused them of submitting reports that were "devoid of scientific objectivity." Following Smith's line of argument, Davis contended that there were "benefits of warmth" to the marine life. He brought in his own scientists, who contradicted those from the university. As added proof of his claims, he produced nine photographs of schools of fish swimming through healthy beds of turtle grass: How could his camera's lens lie?[26]

The conference moderator, Murray Stein, an assistant commissioner with WPCA, was having none of it. He chided Davis for repeated misstatements and exaggerated claims. Davis had no fallback strategy; FP&L had been backed into a corner like a lone animal surrounded by multiple pursuers. Interior was clearly one of them. Despite Stein's attempt to run the conference with a show of fairness, he could not hide the department's predilections. The threat to the new Biscayne National Monument, which FP&L had opposed, was too great for comfort, and during the opening session, assistant secretary of the interior Carl Klein read a statement from his boss, Walter Hickel, describing Card Sound and Biscayne Bay as "two of the cleanest bodies of water in the world." To keep them healthy, Hickel asked FP&L to stop digging its canal or risk facing legal action. Furiously jotting down notes, Bellamy later speculated that the conference was "plainly just a curtain-raiser for a showdown in court," and she was right. When FP&L rebuffed the request, Hickel asked the Justice Department to act.[27]

Turkey Point became a test case. The Department of the Interior's suit was the first against thermal pollution. Industry insiders and environmentalists from all over the United States closely followed the case. All of those involved knew that they were looking toward a changed future. The stakes would be different for polluters if citizens remained circumspect, and pollution was now defined more broadly than visible dirty emissions. The parties in Florida reached a settlement that seemed to satisfy both sides. The good citizen once again, FP&L agreed to build, along with its nuclear plants, a seven-thousand-acre closed-cycle cooling system, thereby eliminating discharge into the bay.[28]

Activists could claim another important victory in a swelling confluence of issues. They had protected the bay from raw sewage, stopped an oil refinery and major development, and won a national monument. They had also helped bring an end to unnecessary droughts—they hoped— by pressing for a federal water-release guarantee for Everglades National Park.

The victories had not been easily won. In a Public Works Subcommittee hearing, dubbed "People vs. Wildlife," to appropriate funds for the expansion of the Army Corps of Engineers' already mammoth flood-control project, Wisconsin senator Gaylord Nelson and Maine senator Edmund Muskie faced off against Florida senators Spessard Holland and Edward J.

Gurney. Giving preference to the thirst of the region's expanding population, Holland proclaimed the supremacy of state's rights in the control of watersheds within state borders, even while he was asking for more federal money to fund the federally engineered system that controlled the water. He and Gurney, who would compile one of the worst environmental voting records in Congress and against whom Douglas voted in his bid for the Senate, opposed a guaranteed water supply for the national park. Florida newspapers tended to back their senators. A guest columnist for the *Gainesville Sun* said that the "popular 'River of Grass' description of the hydrology tends to be misleading." Rain, not flow, was the principal water source for the Everglades. But the writer may not have read beyond the subtitle of Douglas's book. Based on Garald Parker's research, Douglas made a sound argument about evaporation, transpiration, surface-water accumulation, and flow.[29]

She also would have taken issue with another of the guest columnist's claims: that canals and other water-control devices had increased the inflow of water to the park "during the period 1965–1969 over that which would have been expected to occur under natural conditions." Holland too made that claim. But at this point in the life of the reconstructed Everglades, it was impossible to say what was "natural." Nelson echoed this point, arguing, perhaps idealistically, for a Malthusian measure in response to Holland's and Gurney's expansionist priorities: growth should be determined by the limits of the region's natural resources beyond those of the park. He and Muskie got the water-release guarantee incorporated into the Flood Control Act of 1970, the seventh since 1948, which required the Central and Southern Florida Flood Control District to husband enough water in its conservation areas to provide the park with no less than 315,000 acre feet of water annually and to do so according to a schedule determined by the park service. Everglades would be quenched.[30]

Yet water in the Everglades involved more than the wet life of the park. With each new stirring and grassroots campaign, seamless connections between the urban and extraurban environments became clearer. The Everglades were no longer an unknown landscape on a distant horizon that city dwellers tucked away in their subconscious. The Everglades were there at people's water taps and in the sugar and vegetables they put on their tables. They flanked the houses people built farther and farther west of Miami, where Douglas had long ago sat with friends on the fenders of automobiles in the stark stillness watching the sunset and feeling the cool air, "with a tang in it," washing up the Miami River from Biscayne Bay, reaching out into the "wideness of the Everglades." The Everglades were also in the environmental initiatives that generated national media attention, none more so than one to keep the uncommon vastness free from urban bigness in the form of a big-city airport.[31]

CHAPTER THIRTY

The Jetport

It "looked as if just about all the important natural values in South Florida were under serious attack," observed Joe Browder of the 1960s. For environmentalists, campaign followed and overlapped exhausting campaign, with no lag time to rest or regroup. The small community of activists somehow always managed to mount defenses and keep straight the copious ecological, political, and strategic details of numerous issues—unnecessary drought, Seadade, Islandia, Florida Power & Light (FP&L). Their task was made easier by the realization that all the campaigns were interrelated, like parts of an ecosystem. The opposition took that approach. From multiple directions, the forces of development advanced across the region, from the Everglades to Biscayne Bay and back to the Everglades again, leaving in their wake one ecological insult after another.[1]

One person who fastidiously kept each campaign sorted in his head, as a cartographer might a landscape, was Browder. He was in his twenties when the cause gripped him. Based on his appearance—precisely groomed hair, black horn-rimmed glasses, and slightly shorter-than-average height—Hollywood would have pegged Browder for the role of an egghead banker rather than a tough-guy savior of reptilian swamps. But everything Christopher Plummer brought to his role as a bird warden in *Wind across the Everglades*—nobility of purpose, dogged determination, selfless motives—Browder brought to his real-life activist role (except soppy dialogue). And he was never happier than when schlepping through chest-deep water of a solution hole occupied by alligators. He had been intimate with nature since his childhood in Miami during World War II. The Browders lived at the Everglades Hotel, billeted with Army Air Corps officers and their families, across the street from Bayfront Park. Unruffled by the activity of war, the park's birds partook in their own bustle. They were Browder's world of wonder. When a neighbor gave him a book about birds, curiosity was transformed into a "more disciplined" interest, which was reinforced when his first-grade teacher taught the junior Audubon course mandated by the state. The family subsequently left Miami for Havana and Mexico, eventually settling in Amarillo, Texas. His love of the outdoors was nourished in each new setting. He won a scholarship to study ornithology at Cornell University but dropped out when the scholarship proved to be inadequate. He returned to Amarillo, married his longtime sweetheart, Joan Arrington, and worked as a policeman and a news reporter. During a visit with his father, who had retired to Miami, he fell in love with South Florida all over again. The local NBC television affiliate offered him a job, and in 1961 he and Joan moved to Florida.[2]

Miami was receiving its first wave of Cuban exiles at the time, and because he spoke Spanish, Browder was a logical hire. Along with Latin and Cuban issues, his beat included general political and municipal affairs. On one occasion, he looked on with trepidation when he covered the ceremony celebrating the completion of the last water-control structure erected by the Central and Southern Florida Flood Control District (FCD) along Tamiami Trail. It was another triumph over the broadest river's natural flow, and except when a fickle bureaucracy ordered floodgates open, it was a consummation of the perfect hydrologic segregation of the upper and lower Everglades. Because he hung around city hall much of the time and because they shared similar views, he formed a relationship with the vice mayor, Alice Wainwright. At her behest, he

was voted onto Tropical Audubon's board of directors. There he began
to spend time with another board member, Polly Redford. She encouraged him to focus his news work on the Everglades and Biscayne Bay
and to use his sources to keep environmental groups abreast of the latest
developments.[3]

Not long thereafter, National Audubon's Tropical Florida representative, Charles Brookfield, announced his plans to retire. An old friend of
Douglas, Brookfield had begun as an Everglades "refuge manager," hired
by Audubon in 1946. When the national park was still an entity only on
paper, he led tourists on Everglades outings, almost always filled to capacity. It was an effective way to promote the park. He also worked hard
to raise money for Audubon's establishment in 1954 of the six-thousand-
acre Corkscrew Swamp Sanctuary, an old-growth relic of the Big Cypress
Swamp saved in the last hour from the lumber yard. He was a good and
able veteran for whom Audubon needed to find the right replacement.
Brookfield, who had originally recruited Browder into Audubon and
who called on his assistance for making annual Christmas bird counts,
talked to the young reporter about taking the position, as did Redford
and Wainwright. As the volunteer vice president of Tropical Audubon,
Browder was already being tagged as a "zealot," a "tenacious bulldog,"
and a "brash militant," references sometimes bestowed out of admiration
and sometimes not. Brookfield, Redford, and Wainwright simply thought
that Browder was dedicated. They liked his energy, leadership qualities,
command of the facts, and ability to argue a point. They encouraged him
to consider a full-time position with National Audubon. Doing so would
mean trading the adequate salary of a news reporter for the mediocre one
of an employee of a nonprofit organization. But Browder valued nature
more than material life. Neither he nor Joan (who later became a biologist for the National Oceanic and Atmospheric Administration), though
the parents of two young boys, hesitated in the decision. As a going-away
gift, Channel 7 allowed him to produce a one-hour documentary on any
subject. He chose the Everglades drought, and the news director titled the
special *Come Hell or High Water*. In 1968, Browder went to work as the first
in National Audubon's new network of regional representatives. He chose
a small office on Mary Street in Coconut Grove as his headquarters.[4]

Around the same time, he went to Washington with Lloyd Miller, Hardy Matheson, and Dante Fascell and stood proudly by as President Lyndon Baines Johnson signed the bill authorizing Biscayne National Monument. The Seadade and Islandia disputes had been put to rest, but the FP&L controversy was kicking up. This matter alone would have filled his plate. But Browder learned that Dade County was planning to build a behemoth airport in the middle of the Everglades. All the ecological insults provoking all the recent activist campaigns would not have done as much damage to the organic regional image and ecosystem as this one incursion.[5]

The issue dominated his tenure as Audubon's regional representative. It was first brought to his attention in early 1967 by Dan Paul, a public-spirited, Harvard-educated attorney and an ideological cousin of Douglas who defended the twin causes of honest government and citizens' rights, not to mention municipal parks and a public waterfront. Paul told Browder that the Dade County Port Authority was secretly buying up land in the Everglades, and he was suspicious about its intentions. Browder still had his day job with the television station and was preoccupied by Biscayne Bay matters. Then he received a telephone call from Robert Padrick, chair of the FCD. Padrick said that the Port Authority was about to announce its plans to build an Everglades airport. When selecting the site, neither the Port Authority nor the Federal Aviation Administration had consulted with the FCD or the national park, though the airport was to be located six miles from the park at the western edge of the FCD's Conservation Area 3. When park superintendent Roger Allin received the news, he shot off a letter to the Port Authority expressing concern about the noise and physical proximity of jet airplanes taking off and landing, which would cause "wildlife dislocations, abandonment of habitat, and consequent alterations of the park for visitor use."[6]

At first, the airport was intended for training flights only. But within two months, the Port Authority's deputy director, Richard Judy, began talking about passenger service and aircraft manufacturing. Boosters called the facility a jetport rather than an airport. Jet travel was beginning to edge out propeller planes in the commercial airline industry, and the word *jet* placed Miami squarely within this novel age. But not only would

Miami be ultramodern. The planned facility would be the largest in the world, larger than Miami itself and larger than the four largest airports in the country combined. "No matter how big they build the monsters of the airlines," crowed Port Authority director Alan C. Stewart, "we'll have space for them." Padrick had called Browder because the plans included a transit corridor accommodating an air-cushioned shuttle traveling at 150 to 200 miles per hour between Miami and the airport, straight across the middle of the conservation area, from urban environment through controlled wilderness to developing environment.[7]

In the wake of the Seadade escapade, activists knew that local government officials lacked a higher appreciation for protecting South Florida's precious nature. But the persons in charge seemed to have no memory of the public's demand for environmental civility. Located on the north side of Tamiami Trail within the Big Cypress Swamp, the airport was a twisting knife in the ecological heart of the already ailing Everglades. Birds, alligators, panthers, plant life, and water flow would feel the pain. The Port Authority was unmoved, at first claiming that Miami's existing airport would reach capacity by 1973 (an estimate later lengthened by ten years). Dade County saw in the jetport not economic sustenance but economic expansion. Miami had considered itself a center for commercial flight since the 1920s, when its aviation director declared that "future developments by airways companies will be of untold benefit to this vicinity." Working on that precept, the authority was expecting its facility to service not just Miami but the whole lower peninsula, including the eagerly anticipated Walt Disney World, scheduled to open in 1971. The jetport would have six-mile runways, long enough for simultaneous takeoffs and landings, and would eventually accommodate fifty million passengers and one million flights a year. It was bold, it was big, and, from the environmentalists' perspective, it was pure hubris.[8]

The Port Authority quickly moved ahead with its plans. It completed eminent-domain proceedings in August 1968. The groundbreaking ceremony, with Governor Claude Kirk turning dirt out with a shovel, was held on a fine, sunny mid-September day, which the Port Authority proclaimed "Supersonic Jet Day." In December, while bulldozers were working in the

Everglades, Padrick convened a meeting in Coral Gables of representatives from several interested parties, including the National Park Service and the Army Corps of Engineers, as well as Browder and the Sierra Club's Gary Soucie. They were hardly a group of natural bedfellows. Only Browder and Soucie openly insisted that the airport be moved completely out of the Everglades.[9]

They seemed to have an ally in Nathaniel Reed, the governor's special assistant on the environment. Tall, with an Ichabod Crane–like lankiness, the thirty-five-year-old Reed came from a wealthy Republican family that had developed Jupiter Island, a barrier island between the Atlantic Ocean and Indian River, east of the upper Everglades. While many parts of South Florida had been leveled into moonscapes by developers of the slash-and-burn type, the Reeds worked to retain Jupiter Island's dense natural character. This green world was young Reed's playground, where he explored and fished streams and estuaries and cypress swamps. After college and military service, he returned to Jupiter to run the family's real estate and hotel business. An active and loyal member of the Republican Party, he went to work for Governor Kirk in 1967 for one dollar a year. The "Great God of Growth" was ruling his state into ruin, and it needed to be stopped, Reed thought. He looked to Theodore Roosevelt as the "standard-bearer for the enlightened management of natural resources." Reed was eager to reassert his party's forgotten conservation tradition, though enhanced by the ecological principles of the new movement. He was constantly weighing the costs and benefits of conventional forms of development against environmental preservation, and in the long term the latter came out on top. Reed had deftly persuaded the governor to endorse the Biscayne National Monument. After the monument was secured, Reed turned his attention to the Cross-Florida Barge Canal and the Everglades jetport, each of which, he concluded, amounted to an environmental atrocity. At the Coral Gables meeting, he emerged as a unifying figure, getting the various parties to agree that the Port Authority should be required to defend its chosen site.[10]

Other meetings followed, with some of the original participants dropping out and new ones joining in. In April 1969, twenty-one national groups and one state group, the Florida Audubon Society, formed the Everglades Coalition, which immediately appealed to the U.S. Department of Transportation to rethink its position on the matter. Transportation, however, was funneling grants, which ultimately added up to seven hundred thousand dollars, to the construction of the jetport, abetting the Port Authority's strategy of building as quickly as possible. It was harder to stop a project that was already a reality than one still on the drawing board. Once again, the Department of the Interior would find itself rescuing its Florida park from the actions of another federal agency.[11]

Alligators and their declining population helped rally the rescue effort. Poaching in the 1960s stretched back in an unbroken historical strand to the days when bird feathers and alligator hides had been harvested at will. The birds were relatively safe from hunters now. But with alligator shoes, handbags, and suitcases back in style and hides selling out of the wild for between six and seven dollars a foot, the ancient reptile was in grave danger after two hundred million years of existence. A population of millions had fallen to an estimated twenty thousand. Routinely shipping between ten and fifteen thousand hides to market a year, poachers were coming close to doing in both their quarry and their illicit trade. The penalty for poaching could be stiff—up to ten thousand dollars in fines and ten years in prison. But Florida had never overcome the problem of enforcement, even with National Park Service rangers and state game wardens patrolling the Everglades.[12]

Then, as it happened, an "on-the-spot investigation" into poaching was the first order of business for President Nixon's new interior secretary, Walter Hickel. Critics complained that his March 1969 trip to the Everglades was mere show. During a controversial confirmation hearing, Hickel, an Alaskan car dealer, had stated that he opposed "conservation for conservation's sake"—that is, the protection of nature was desirable only when linked to some knowable human purpose. Yet the "tough-talking, nature-conquering pioneer," as Browder called him, turned out to be a sheep in wolf's clothing. His South Florida itinerary included a day of paddling and repartee with Governor Kirk, who had invited himself along. The next day followed with a "summit meeting" at a hunting trailer, suitably stocked with beer, at Lostman's River. Drinking into the night led to a 2:00 A.M. lesson in alligator hollering, given by Kirk. "They scared every damn alligator" out there, recalled Reed. At some point between swigs, Hickel promised to reassign rangers to give Everglades additional manpower and to earmark one hundred thousand dollars from Interior's budget for alligator protection. For its part, the state would help Everglades Indians start up alligator farms for the purpose of restocking the wetland. In the midst of this deal making, Hickel and Kirk talked about water appropriations for the park and the environmental implications of the jetport.[13]

Jetport defenders denied that any real controversy existed beyond the objections of a handful of shrill nature lovers. Activists were also accused of misleading the good people of Florida. A consulting engineer for the Southwest Dade Farmers and Landowners Association claimed that the jetport would affect Cape Sable no more than it would Gainesville, a six-hour drive to the north. The Lake Okeechobee dikes and Tamiami Trail "had nothing to do with" conditions in the park. There had not been a natural connection between the water of the lower and upper Everglades for twenty-five thousand years, he concluded, apparently not knowing that the Everglades were only five thousand years old. The idea of a disrupted river of grass was pure myth, one the public bought into because an "author selected this name for the title of a book."[14]

One prodevelopment strategy involved reducing the jetport issue to a simple matter of prioritizing the needs of humans over beasts, an old but still sharp saw. The press portrayed Hickel's Everglades trip as a mission to "save the alligator"; jetport supporters claimed that their mission was to save humans. Governor Kirk had recently told a group of friends that if he had to "choose between the deer of the Everglades and man, I would have to choose man." His transportation secretary, Michael O'Neil, said, "I call the Everglades a swamp. My children can't play in it. . . . I think people come first." When making claims about saving humans over birds and alligators, however, O'Neil and others were not talking about preserving basic needs for humans, such as ensuring adequate recharge for the Biscayne Aquifer and thus drinking water for the human population;

they were fixated on fostering economic development. The Port Authority's Judy sought to plant these goals in high moral ground, casting the inevitable destruction of the Everglades in a larger divine plan. In a letter to the Dade County Commission, he made a not-so-oblique reference to the Book of Genesis, chapter 1, verse 28, pledging the Port Authority to fulfill the "responsibilities of all men to exercise dominion over the land, sea, and air above us as the Higher Order of Man intends."[15]

While Judy sought confirmation in the Good Book, Browder looked for it among local citizens. He hoped first to tap into the human resources and experience of Tropical Audubon and the Mangrove chapter of Izaak Walton. The latter, under the leadership of Lloyd Miller and James Redford, refused to "actively oppose a passenger jetport" in the Everglades, arguing that the installation would facilitate improved regional planning that "can only come from a sincere effort toward environmental control." Given what Browder, Miller, and Redford had done together to save Biscayne, Browder was beside himself. But two other sporting organizations came on board without his coaxing. One was the Broward County Airboat, Halftrack and Conservation Club. Around since 1952, it had been organized to ensure that recreational interests were retained as both the national park and flood-control projects expanded. The other was the Florida Wildlife Federation (FWF), an affiliate of the National Wildlife Federation, a signatory of the Everglades Coalition. Both groups pulled their membership primarily from hunters. The Big Cypress was favored hunting ground, and as the sportsmen saw it, the jetport promised to spoil game habitat. Even alligator poachers sided with Browder. Astute in ways other environmentalists were not, he recognized that environmental concerns were not the sole province of the middle class or the social elite, such as the members of Tropical Audubon and all its predecessors back to the beginning of the environmental century. The working class and poor, who were disproportionately afflicted by impaired environments in their living and working places, appreciated clean water and air and healthy conditions as much as anyone. Browder also knew that hunters formed a well-formed, well-connected constituency practiced at getting behind an issue and delivering the vote in Tallahassee.[16]

This was especially true of the fifty thousand members of the FWF and their organization's leader, a former plumber named John C. Jones. Jones believed that hunters played an integral role in wildlife management— nearly as important to a healthy ecosystem as air or water. So when something came along to disturb things he got his feathers up. Someone once called him a "redneck with a sense of moral outrage." Jones thought that was about right. A Florida native born in 1932, he married his sweetheart from junior high, Mariana Beebe. Both grew up at the edge of wilderness in Palm Beach County. They did everything together—hunted and fished, built their house (from locally grown trees), joined the FWF, and loved the Everglades. Before going to work for the FWF full time, Johnny operated a plumbing contractor's business and did a lot of lobbying in Tallahassee for the Master Plumbers Association. Making the move over to direct the federation was easy, except that his annual income dropped from fifty thousand dollars to twenty thousand dollars. Mariana went to work at the federation, overseeing daily operations, at the same salary. That helped to make up the difference. But she would have worked for nothing. "I am with him all the way," Mariana confided to Douglas in a letter, calling her husband a "fireball" who "eats, lives and breathes conservation."[17]

Johnny Jones was now lobbying for hunters, who, just like plumbers, were his kind of people. He had a knack for talking to legislators and cabinet members. Most were hunters, too, and he knew how to speak to them, as if they were sitting in a gun club chewing the fat, telling stories about killing a deer or spending time with the wife and kids. When the talk came around to serious business, he always got straight to the point, and he never lied to anyone. He never lied, for example, about his thoughts on the Army Corps of Engineers' flood-control project: it was nothing more than a reclamation plan. He said that the fat cats and bureaucrats had sold the fine citizens of Florida a "bill of goods." He was something like a bulldog, both in manner and in his stocky, short-legged build. But he was never surly, and he had a folksy way of using expletives like *damn* and *hell* and *son of a bitch*, but he was never offensive. He also knew that the best way to get a law passed was to leave lawmakers with as little work as possible. In his twenty-odd years with the plumbers and the hunters, he wrote more than sixty pieces of legislation. Browder remembered him as "one of the real unsung heroes" of the jetport fight.[18]

There were younger heroes, too. One was Charles Lee, already a movement veteran at age nineteen. His was a self-motivated indoctrination into activism that grew from seeds sown in his deep love for the outdoors, and he could identify the germinating stimulus. One day, when he was just fifteen, he had been steering his aluminum motorboat, pushed along by a puttering five-horsepower outboard, through a mangrove creek off Dumbfounding Bay. He had followed this course countless times, but on this occasion he came upon a dragline dredge at one of his favorite fishing spots. Developers in those days were still "pretty much" having their way with the bay, and Lee started writing letters to the editor of the *Miami News*. Jim Redford read them and invited the young fisherman to join the Izaak Walton League. Some of the Izaak Walton folks were also members of Tropical Audubon, so Lee joined that organization, too, and became a junior director. He found himself surrounded by an inspiring group of adults—Lloyd Miller, Jim and Polly Redford, Alice Wainwright, and Joe Browder—who by their example helped him plot his course in life. During the campaign to win approval for the Biscayne National Monument, he went along with scientists to take water-temperature readings at the Turkey Point power-plant site and joined in a protest against thermal pollution at the FP&L building in Coral Gables. At Browder's Audubon office in Coconut Grove, Lee met a small congress of young people like himself.[19]

One was Juliana Field, a student at the nearby Everglades School for Girls. Her parents were independent scholars whose research assistant, Judy Wilson, was also Browder's chief assistant at Audubon. The Fields were good friends with Marjory Stoneman Douglas, someone Juliana had known most of her life, and they supported Juliana's volunteer work with Audubon. During the jetport campaign, she and Lee drove out to the Everglades to meet with landowners in isolated shacks and trailers parked down limestone gravel roads, far removed from telephone lines and postal service, and to meet with hunters, poachers, and otherwise unsociable types out on Loop Road at the rowdy Gator Hook Lodge, a patched-up roadhouse raised on wood pilings above the thornbushes and occasional inundation. The two young people hoped to get a read on ways to "stir up trouble to stop the jetport." One proposal sought to turn the Gum Slough area into a drainage district so that it could be developed, and some landowners were excited about the possibilities of riches in appreciated real estate values. Other Everglades dwellers were more xenophobic than money hungry, and Field later remembered meeting a few who packed pistols and resented the prospect of an airport.[20]

She was not the only girl from the Everglades School who cared about the wetland. Another, tan with sun-streaked wavy brown hair reaching just below her shoulders, appeared in Browder's office one day unannounced. Introducing herself as December Duke, she said that her neighbor, Marjory Stoneman Douglas, had suggested that she see Browder about doing volunteer work. Duke's family lived around the corner from Douglas, and when December was only of bike-riding age, she would pedal by the cottage on Stewart Avenue hoping to catch a glimpse of the famous writer. Douglas sometimes quietly busied herself in the front garden, looking wise beneath a splendid sun hat. Duke and her friends "worshiped" Douglas and hated anyone who destroyed the living landscape. Duke eventually met Douglas on one of those bike-riding occasions. The author of *Freedom River* and *Alligator Crossing* liked young people, and the sociable girl's ancestry would have interested Douglas. December's great-grandfather, Benjamin Duke, a tobacco and textile heir turned philanthropist, and his brother, James, helped pay for the college costs of T. Gilbert Pearson, the future National Audubon president whom Douglas knew and about whom she wrote. December Duke had her own passion for bird life and natural beauty. She often spent weekend and summer days sailing on Biscayne Bay, and her father frequently led the family on Everglades outings, hiking into a cypress dome or boating up Shark River Slough and exploring Indian mounds.[21]

Around the time Duke went to see Browder, in 1969, she also met Virginia Hine. A cultural anthropologist, Hine had been among a group of people whom the Everglades School invited to participate on a panel of professional role models. She was coauthoring a book at the time with University of Minnesota professor Luther Gerlach on contemporary "movements of social change." Gerlach and Hine originally had been interested in the more familiar forms of organized activism of the 1960s, such as that of the civil rights movement, when Hine, who lived in Miami, took notice of the Biscayne Bay events. They got Gerlach's attention, too, and he came to Florida with notebook, pencil, and movie camera. He spent several days shadowing Browder, even through the reedy marshes and cypress swamps of the Everglades, although Gerlach kept his distance from solution holes inhabited by alligators. He and Hine were consequently among the first scholars to study the modern environmental movement, predicting that it would lift the "rising tide of public opinion" on deteriorating environmental conditions identified through scientific investigation. They called this new impulse the "ecology movement."[22]

Duke and her friend and classmate, Lili Krech, saw a role model in Hine and asked her to serve as their outside mentor for an independent project required for seniors. Hine agreed and recommended they study the cooling-water discharge from FP&L's Turkey Point power plant, which at the time was under the scrutiny of state and federal agencies and environmentalists. Duke and Krech got a sobering lesson on how progress often translates into new or exacerbated environmental damage. Tutored by their mentor's husband, Alden Hine, a University of Miami marine scientist, they investigated the area around the discharge zone. They took water-temperature readings, which in places exceeded the prescribed limit, and donned masks and snorkels to get a firsthand look at dying turtle grass. They interviewed fifty people, including environmentalists, scientists, Interior Department personnel, and FP&L employees. A guided tour of the plant completed the research. In May, they presented their senior paper, "Thermal Pollution: Man's Blindness toward the Consequences of His Actions." Their findings concurred with those of scientists who presented at the Interior Department's conference on thermal pollution the next year. Duke and Krech closed with a question: "How many bays and rivers will be polluted before man realizes the consequences of his actions?"[23]

Duke could not stop thinking about the consequences. After graduation, she began noticing algae blooms and fish kills in the bays, no doubt
provoked by unusually hot summer 1969 temperatures. Some people saw
raw sewage at the core of the problem, suspecting that despite public
complaints dating back to Philip Wylie's 1951 *Look* magazine exposé, the
city was unable or unwilling to accommodate the population growth it
eagerly sought and continued to send untreated sewage into the bay. To
prove it, Duke went down to city hall with a sack of peanuts, flushed
them down a restroom toilet, and directed city officials to the waterside
to watch the peanuts come washing out. The tactic had achieved useful
results before, and it did so again. Four years later, the city and county
formed the Miami-Dade Water and Sewer Authority, and by 1975, the
Virginia Key wastewater-treatment facility, built after Wylie blew the
whistle, had been expanded by 50 percent.[24]

Duke and Krech also worked with Browder on the jetport campaign.
When they first came aboard, Browder drove them and some of their
classmates out Tamiami Trail to give them a thorough introduction to
the rare beauty and ecosystem dynamics of the cypress swamp and Everglades. Usually dressed in a straw cowboy hat, its brim curled up on the
sides, and a short-sleeved denim shirt with an Audubon patch on the left
sleeve, Browder was known for his leave-no-stone-unturned guided tours,
sometimes lasting into the wee hours of the morning, long after some
participants had grown irritable and tired. Before returning to Coconut
Grove, Browder took the party by the jetport site. The contrast between
the original and the excavated environments was startling. Filled with a
sense of mission, Duke and Krech, along with their classmate, Mary Beth
Norton, began leading groups out into the Everglades on the weekends,
with Krech driving her father's Jeep and Norton driving a Volkswagen
minibus full of people. The fenced-off construction site was off-limits to
the general public, so on one occasion, Duke telephoned the Port Authority and said she was with a group of anthropologists who would like to
see the ceremonial site of the Miccosukees' ritual Green Corn dance, located on the jetport tract. Sacred ground where boys were inducted into

manhood in a new-year ceremony, it was now a horrible and disturbing sight, scraped clean by earth-moving equipment.[25]

No one was more disturbed by this desecration than the Miccosukees. Hoping to form an informal partnership with them, Browder met with Buffalo Tiger, leader of the Miccosukee Tribe of Florida, which seven years earlier had gained official recognition as a separate group from Florida Seminoles. Miccosukees were the dominant tribe in the Everglades, the people most affected by government policies in the region. Known as Heenehatche, Tiger had grown up in a chickee. As a youth, he crafted rawhide drums that he sold to tourists traveling along the newly constructed Tamiami Trail. After the Miccosukees gained federal status, he was elected chair. He was operating an airboat service when Browder met with him. The Port Authority had told Tiger that the jetport development would not pollute the environment or disrupt the Indians' way of life and that the new facility would create jobs for Indians. But these assurances were nothing more than additions to a string of broken promises. Tiger and his people had already lost much of their ancestral land to development and the flood-control project, and they had seen wildlife populations begin to perish with the unnecessary drought. "It happens to Indians year after year: progress wasting the hunting grounds," Tiger told a *New York Times* reporter among the legions of national media that began covering the jetport controversy. L. G. Hardin of the Association of Red Men sent a letter to the *Christian Science Monitor* that concurred with Tiger's sentiments: "Is there to be no end to the genocide in the name of progress?" Nothing was more revealing of cultural annihilation than the Port Authority's leveling of the Green Corn Hammock. Both Hardin and Tiger complained that whites had already severed their essential ties to the earth and remained insistent on destroying those of Indians. "You can't make it," Tiger said of nature in general and the Everglades in particular. "You can't buy it. And when it's gone, it's gone forever."[26]

To stir congregants beyond the choir, Browder needed a respected individual with a high public profile, someone who embodied the wisdom of an elder. That person would be Marjory Stoneman Douglas. She attentively observed what he was doing, watching the environmentalists as they juggled their many campaigns. During this period, she published *Florida: The Long Frontier.* She wrote the book as a historian, but she allowed herself a moment to look ahead. In the epilogue, she observed, "In Florida, especially, the people are being called on to choose between blind obedience to the sheer increasing pressure of population and the vital necessity for building finer cities in a balanced and preserved natural background which alone can give them meaning and value. The future lies in them and in the strength with which man himself can set his powers of creation against his impulses for destruction. Perhaps this is the unending frontier." She was writing about others—Browder, Soucie, Wainwright, Lee, Field, Duke, Krech, the Redfords—but she too was the future.[27]

The Conversion

The story has become legendary, a part of the irreducible public persona that came to be the woman of the Everglades, told countless times in newspapers, magazines, speeches, and interviews. No one remembers the exact date of the event other than that it occurred sometime in 1969, but the other essential facts are clear. One evening around eleven o'clock, Marjory Stoneman Douglas was shopping at a Coconut Grove convenience mart, the Quick & Easy Food Store, when someone called her name. It was Joe Browder's assistant and office manager, Judy Wilson. Amid the night-owl customers straggling in to buy cigarettes, milk, and other piecemeal shopping items, both women were there for cat food. They paused for a quick chat.

Douglas was connected well enough through the daily news and civic-minded friends to be fully aware of Audubon's decisive role in the recent environmental campaigns. The refinery and jetport impressed her as tragically stupid and grotesque. If someone had been challenged to propose the best way to destroy a place's rootstock of beauty and unique character, these two projects would have taken top prize. To some degree, she liked how Miami had grown from the "small, inadequate old" city it had been to now offer "quiet communities in the midst of all the living, turbulent, growing place." Miami had good hospitals, as she saw it, good schools, museums, and libraries, which she had helped promote at the University of Miami and in Coconut Grove. Of course, Miami's development had been a mixed blessing, illuminated most vividly by the transformed natural setting, but she found comfort in the labors of others to instill in small-minded government and industry leaders the value of environmental civility. She most admired the stamina of activists, especially Joe Browder, the good soldier of nature who stood on the front lines of each successive battle. When she saw Wilson in the grocery store, she offered an elder's approval. "What a good job you are doing," she said.[1]

Wilson had known Douglas for many years and admired her tremendously. They had met at the Cambridge, Massachusetts, home of Julie and Henry Field. A member of the wealthy Marshall Field retail family, Henry was an Oxford University–trained anthropologist who in the late 1930s had served as head curator of the Field Museum of Natural History, endowed by his great-uncle, Marshall Field. At the time Douglas met him, Henry Field was a research fellow at Harvard. Julie was a scholar of the Amazon and an outspoken advocate of its protection. The Fields spent part of their year at the Coconut Grove estate of Henry's mother, an old friend of Douglas, and were members of the local crowd whose intellectualism was the boiling cauldron of enlightening political thought, sometimes turned to action. When in Massachusetts, Douglas occasionally visited Henry and Julie. Wilson had worked as their assistant, and after being introduced to the writer from Florida, whom she found smart and irresistibly mirthful, Wilson borrowed the Fields' copy of *River of Grass*. She saw Douglas again in 1966 at the annual meeting of the Florida Audubon Society, which was presenting her with its Special Award of Merit. The Fields moved to Coconut Grove permanently the same year, and Wilson came along with them. Under the imprint of the Field Research Projects, Henry published *Adventures in a Green World*, Douglas's book about David Fairchild and Barbour Lathrop, Field's great-uncle. She was a regular dinner guest, too, sometimes with Carolyn Cole in tow, and Douglas's infectious humor and keen intellect made an impression on everyone, including the Fields' daughter, Juliana, who volunteered in Audubon activities that Wilson often supervised.[2]

On that night in the convenience store, Wilson asked Douglas what she was doing to contribute. "But dear," Wilson remembered Douglas saying with the mien of a torchbearer, "I did. I wrote the book." Wilson pressed: "But what have you done lately?" Douglas was nonplussed. She was past her seventy-ninth birthday, part of a retiring generation that should be stepping back and passing the flame to a new generation. There, with cat food in hand and a friend waiting in the parking lot to drive her home, Douglas took her leave with a polite "Call me if I can do anything."[3]

Wilson accepted the response as an invitation to press on. When she told Browder about the encounter, they agreed that Douglas possessed practical assets that could benefit the campaign against the jetport. Her ties to the area were long-standing and extensive, and she seemed to know people everywhere. There was a "clarity of vision" in her public speaking that would help others understand the full depth of the crisis. Equally important, Wilson remembered, "she carried the authority" to urge on the public the necessity for taking action. Hers would be an appeal to people's emotional and intellectual sides: "She knew with her heart and knew with her head."[4]

The day after Wilson's chance encounter, the phone rang on high volume at Douglas's house. Browder was calling from his office to ask if he could come over to talk. They had previously met at literary and social events when he was still flagging down the news for WCKT. He liked her from the start. She was no-nonsense but witty, a font of local and state history who spoke with energy and grace and wisdom. And he saw how others reacted to her. Charles Lee had first met her at a Tropical Audubon meeting in 1967, when she was the evening's guest speaker, talking about William Henry Hudson. She was an "extremely immense person," he recalled, immersed in a "broad spectrum of ideas. She was a renaissance woman . . . an intellectual force of tremendous breadth. You got that feeling when you were around her." Juanita Greene believed the same: "It was exhilarating to be around Marjory. A very unusual person. I never met anyone like her. She had that talent of enchanting people." Public events were made for her. She enjoyed speaking and making new acquaintances, and she was good at both. But along with the public side, Browder knew was a private one that many writers guarded closely.[5]

He got a glimpse of hers when he drove over to Stewart Avenue. He pulled Audubon's lumbering 1968 Chevrolet station wagon to the edge of her lawn. Next door was Carolyn Cole's house, regionally conventional with its Mediterranean architecture and pastel colors. He walked across the grassy way to the curious little house that better befit the village setting in Jonathan Swift's Lilliput. At the door, he was met by a crisp cultured greeting, backed by a bantam, white-haired woman. Invited inside, he stood in the big workroom, where yellow light entered through casement windows and beamed from a floor lamp's hundred-watt bulb. The room seemed decorated mainly with books. Weighing down handmade shoulder-high book cases were well-worn copies of writings by Henry James, Willa Cather, Anthony Trollope, William Shakespeare, Joseph Conrad, and Rudyard Kipling—plus all twenty volumes of Charles Dickens, each of which Douglas read once a year. Stacked on a settee immediately inside the door, on side tables and chairs, on her dueling desk, and tumbling to the floor were other books, borrowed from friends and the library, books from which she was working. Some project was clearly in the making.[6]

She offered Browder a cup of tea as he brought her up to date on his own project. Construction had gotten under way on the jetport's first runway, and training flights were scheduled to begin sometime before year's end. He was concerned that the Big Cypress would be incorporated into the artificial hydrology that regulated the eastern Everglades and the national park. The "airport," he told her, "was just an indicator of other pressures to come." The campaign to confront it was accruing national support, but it needed a resident voice of authority and experience to target Floridians "who cared about civic virtue and community values." Many adversaries saw him as little more than a shrill "butterfly chaser"; Dade County Port Authority director Alan Stewart had in fact said exactly that about Browder and the others. Douglas, by contrast, would be held in higher regard. She was part of a pre–World War II (even

World War I in her case) coterie, which also included her friends Helen Muir and Alice Wainwright, that valued Miami not as a slice of real estate but as a place in which to sink roots and enjoy life. Her more than fifty-year relationship with the community, combined with her breadth of knowledge and elocution skills and the imprimatur of her book, gave her a gravitas with area civic and women's clubs that few people could equal. Straddled between the wild and urban worlds, her consciousness might benefit the campaign by demonstrating to others, people who paid little attention to things beyond the urban realm, the gravity of their connection to the Everglades. Indeed, as she simply put it, "Every time it rains, we know the Everglades are there."[7]

Douglas listened attentively to Browder's proposal. Although sympathetic, she had two concerns, neither of which was age. First, she was entrenched in her work on the Hudson biography and in fact had only recently returned from a research trip to Argentina. Having obtained grants to pay for such trips, she wanted to follow through with her project. Second, she questioned the effectiveness of one person. Browder's answer to both concerns was for her to start an organization that would assist her and "legitimize her voice." This organization would be free from the entanglements of a national organization and would concentrate its energies on the jetport, allowing her to manage her time between political and intellectual endeavors. She liked Browder, feeling an instant rapport with the well-spoken young man of apparent integrity, the veteran of other campaigns whom her friends Polly Redford, Charlie Brookfield, and Alice Wainwright praised. Outrage over environmental abuse moved him to action, but he never let outrage control his action. For the scrupulous Browder, the issue of any campaign was not about taking down the big guy, as it was for some other activists, for the swaggering show of doing so. It was a matter of the big guy and everyone else doing what is right. It was a matter of social and environmental ethics. Douglas had always felt that same way and promised to get back to him.[8]

A few weeks later, she called and asked to be driven out to the jetport construction site. It was a hopeful sign, and Browder obliged. They drove nearly an hour through Miami traffic and out along Tamiami Trail. On the way, she spotted an otter slipping into the dark water from the spill-bank of the canal that skirted the north side of the trail, precisely the roadway and canal Douglas had praised decades earlier. Browder pointed across the distance toward what was known as Conservation Area 3, where the high-speed corridor was to connect the jetport to the city. Approximately thirty miles to the north was a seventy-eight-mile drag-strip-straight stretch of the state's Route 84 that connected Naples on the west coast to Fort Lauderdale on the east, another highway traversing the Everglades. The road had been recently constructed under a cloud of bitter controversy. Critics said the two-lane tollway would never pay for itself and, even worse, would become a motorists' slaughtering ground. The American Automobile Association dubbed the new highway Alligator Alley in an attempt to mock its viability, but the state liked the reference so much it put up big green highway signs displaying the name. And the critics were wrong: by the end of its first year in operation, it was well on its way to paying for the seventeen million dollars in bonds floated for its construction, and only two automobile fatalities had occurred. Officials, however, were not counting other types of roadkill. Conveying more than twenty-eight hundred cars a day across the Everglades, the highway was in fact a slaughter ground for deer, raccoons, snakes, otters, bobcats, and panthers. No one had figured in environmental costs. Alligator Alley was an ecological nightmare of the Tamiami Trail sort, slicing through pineland, sawgrass, and cypress swamp and not incidentally obstructing the flow of water. Douglas never liked Route 84.[9]

And here now threatening to do more of the same was the jetport situated between the alley and the trail. When Browder and Douglas arrived at the construction site, it was surrounded by an eight-foot chain-link fence crowned with barbed wire. Next to the entrance gate, a sign with oversized aviation wings read, "Ground was broken Sept. 18, 1968 for the world's first all-new jetport for the supersonic age." The bulldozed landscape created a scar the likes of a clear-cut mountaintop except that the runway and auxiliary roads taking shape revealed the clean-edged architectural straightness of a planned environment. As Browder and Douglas got out of the car, she quietly studied the scene. The jetport—the motives behind it, its physical placement in the Everglades, and its implications for future growth in the area—ran contrary to her regionalist perspective. One might just as well plant a tasteless enclosed shopping mall with a barren asphalt parking lot in the middle of Coconut Grove. The jetport, however, was larger than a neighborhood affliction. On the drive back, Browder and Douglas discussed the type of organization she might create. Her leadership skills, dating back to 1916 and the Miami's Business Women's League, were rusty, but Browder again assured her that plenty of competent people would help run the organization, and the Hudson book would not have to be neglected. The impending environmentalist was moving closer to giving herself over to the movement.[10]

She did so at Fairchild Tropical Botanic Garden, a personally appropriate place. She had served on the garden's board since its founding in 1938, later joined by Alice Wainwright. Not long after Browder showed Douglas the jetport, she attended the Ramble, Fairchild's fall garden festival, to sign copies of her books. She sat at a table in the shade of a ficus tree. One interested browser was a young man with a military haircut and glasses. They struck up a conversation. His name was Michael Chenoweth, and he was freshly discharged from active service in the Army Corps of Engineers and was now a reservist. As a corps insider, he took a sympathetic view of the agency, "knowing the political realities that they have to live with," yet his environmental sensibilities ran strong. He thought the jetport was ill conceived and had written letters to the Port Authority saying so. Douglas asked him how the jetport might be stopped. It was a "big problem," he recalled telling her, and he had no answer. "Well," she said, "Joe Browder says I should start an organization." The name Friends of the Everglades had come to mind, and she asked Chenoweth what she should charge for membership dues. He thought fifteen or twenty dollars. She thought not. "I want schoolchildren to be able to join. We'll make it a dollar." Chenoweth took a bill from his wallet and handed it across the table. "You're my first one," she said to her new member.[11]

At that moment in November 1969, Friends of the Everglades was born. The next spring, Wainwright wrote the organization's charter. Douglas served as president; Florence Coey, a 1936 Wellesley alumna and a professor in international studies at the University of Miami, became vice president; and John P. Pritchett, a banker friend, took the post of treasurer. Douglas's efficient house soon began performing double duty as a workshop for the Hudson biography and as headquarters for Friends. She described the new group as a "grassroots organization . . . to insure a better future for the Everglades which is the heart of the region of South Florida." Her initial task was to speak to the public directly about the utter necessity of protecting the Everglades from the airport and similar affronts. "What I'm most worried about," she said repeatedly over the next decade, "is man's ignorance of the importance of the Everglades." Elevated by the rightness of her commission, she traveled the long state giving talks at women's club meetings and civic organization luncheons, always the willing emissary no matter how small the turnout, and at college campuses, where she tapped into the youthful energy of the era's activist core. Michael Blaine, a former student who chauffeured her to and from the classes she occasionally taught at Miami-Dade Community College, volunteered to drive her to engagements. Another friend, Everett Skinner, provided a converted camper van that allowed a small group of Friends to accompany her.[12]

Whenever she spoke in public, she was aware of how lessons from Malvina Bennett's elocution classes took over. Sixty years later, she could throw her voice with ease; it was flawless, strong, and out of sync with her age. News reporters loved to write about that impressive voice. She spoke both well and informatively and with sound moral authority. Her talk, "South Florida and the Future of the Everglades," identified what the "Everglades region really is," the troubles the region faced, and how those troubles were related to Floridians' relationship to the Everglades. Over her lifetime, she asserted to attentive listeners, the Everglades and the upsurging human capacity to subdue nature had collided in an apocalyptic struggle that left the grandest of wetlands and the people of South Florida with an uncertain future.[13]

She asked for the public's ear, and she got it. She also got new members. At each engagement, she placed her purse on a chair or table with its mouth gaping. She would tell the assembly that membership in Friends was a simple matter of writing one's name and address on a piece of paper and dropping it into her purse with a dollar. At each gathering, ten or twenty people would follow these instructions. "She never let anybody out of her sight that didn't have a membership," said Joe Podgor, who drove her to many talks. "She was very cute about it." Back in Coconut Grove, more dollars arrived through the mail. Membership rose briskly to several hundred with representation in sixteen counties; within the next couple of years, more than three thousand people from thirty-eight states were paying dues, with some making larger donations. The annual fee remained at one dollar to ensure a broad membership base, both demographically and geographically. Recruiting school-age children was important to Douglas, who believed in fostering a social consciousness that would carry into adult life. She had witnessed that process firsthand. Douglas had sent the teenaged December Duke to Browder as a volunteer: Duke graduated from high school and went off to college in New York, founded a group called Environment!, and organized against Eastern Airlines' exploitation of the Everglades. College led Lili Krech to Colorado, where she set up chapters of Ecology Action on several college campuses. In 1972, Charles Lee went to work full time for Florida Audubon. All three also joined or worked in partnership with Friends of the Everglades.[14]

Douglas was strategic too in the way she organized her fledgling group. She adopted a loose management style, seeking to avoid becoming bogged down in the quagmire of a multilayered organization and time-wasting meetings. She scheduled one board meeting each spring, convening in the first years at the Riviera Country Club in Coral Gables and then at Fairchild Garden. The paid staff consisted of a part-time secretary who often put in full-time hours. Douglas invited one volunteer to serve as chair in each Everglades county, a point person who would be her local eyes and ears and would summon her when an important public meeting required her presence. After the organization's agenda was set, she relied on these chairs, her various drivers, the part-time secretary, and other volunteers to help implement the plan. For the first time in her life, she was a full-time activist.[15]

No one was more impressed with her transition to a committed activist than Douglas. She was not the kind to grow idle in old age, but before Browder came along, she had been content with the semiprivate life of a writer, maintaining an unmitigated fidelity to "Mr. Hudson," as she called him. Yet she continued to subscribe to her Quaker ancestors' belief that those who walked the earth were burdened with the moral and social responsibility of setting humans straight when their behavior threatened the welfare of others, human and nonhuman alike. Long ago in "The Galley," she had consistently praised the worth of wild creatures, from the low-slung sand crab to the vertical wading bird. In a poem about earthworms, oysters, and jellyfish, she made a "Plea for Wider Justice" and argued for the extension of "democracy" beyond the human population: "We're not darned superior / We only like to think we are." Her beliefs anticipated Aldo Leopold's land ethic, though hers emanated as much from an inherited fervor as from empirical experience. "I can't help myself," her Collier County chair, Franklin Adams, recalled her telling him on more than one occasion. "It's my Quaker background."[16]

She was not the one who turned the Everglades into a cause, and she did not seek to join that cause. It had come to her, as she openly acknowledged. Before Browder arrived at her doorstep, the Everglades had been little more than a topic in her writing, at most the focal point, along with the sun's tropical white light, of the geographic region with which she was enamored. This sustained love affair with a region combined with her sense of social obligation that prepared her to move an environmental project to the center of her orbit, doing so at the beginning of her ninth decade. Age had never been a discouraging voice; it had instead provided the time to allow everything to fall into place, like pieces in a complex jigsaw puzzle.

Key pieces came from a half-century literary relationship with the Everglades. It began with her newspaper column and was followed by her short fiction and then by her first major book. All were integral to her developing intimacy with the rarefied wetland and to the placement of guideposts in the long uphill and by no means charted path to full-fledged environmental activism. Her columns had virtually been forgotten by the 1960s, rolled up in the celluloid obscurity of microfilm reels, and the relevance of her short and long fiction had not yet been discovered. To the environmental community, the essential contribution in her literary relationship with the Everglades was *River of Grass*. Although it began as a book for general readers, it eventually joined others that served as the intellectual foundation of a specific environmental issue and for the new age of environmentalism: Aldo Leopold's *A Sand County Almanac* on the midwestern and southwestern countrysides, Wallace Stegner's *This Is Dinosaur* on Echo Park, and Rachel Carson's *Silent Spring* on chemical pesticides. Yet unlike those books, *River of Grass* offers no prescription and makes no demand for a new land ethic; though her voice was reproving, Douglas restricted her criticisms to past abuses. She did not, as did the other authors, write her book as a call to arms. But the lack of an activist intent makes *River of Grass* that much more remarkable. "The book," as Douglas called it, immediately became the cultural and natural historical record for the Everglades, what they had been, what they had meant to various people whose lives were linked to them, and what they were becoming. The volume trained a probing light on the iniquities in the stratification of culture over nature. It served as the constitution for Everglades protection, retaining the tenets of the national park's founding agenda before it had been obfuscated, impeded, and all but forgotten. And lest any maker of policy, law, or business enterprise forget, *River of Grass* spelled out the benefits of a healthy Everglades to life, including human life.[17]

The book won Douglas awards and praise from environmental groups even before she started Friends. In 1963, Fairchild Garden awarded her the Thomas Barbour Medal for Conservation for *River of Grass* and for her participation in Ernest Coe's park association. Three years later, on the other side of the peninsula, in Lehigh Acres, where Judy Wilson had seen Douglas speak, Florida Audubon presented her with a Special Award of Merit at its annual convention, noting that her book and her stature "may yet rally the forces to save the Everglades." "She has given us the Everglades," asserted Audubon's magazine, *Florida Naturalist*.[18]

The book's power was also plainly evident in the worth public-minded individuals found in it. One point person in the Everglades campaign,

Nathaniel Reed, was affected not long after its publication. When Reed was a freshman at Connecticut's Trinity College in the early 1950s, a literature professor assigned *River of Grass,* describing its prose as "one of the best examples of the English language." For Reed, who had spent much of his teenage years tramping about the Everglades, sometimes with botanist Frank Craighead, the book brought the diverse human and nonhuman elements together into an interconnected, poetic landscape.[19]

Its influence might have stopped with Reed had Douglas allowed it to go out of print rather than rescuing it with Hurricane House. By 1970, the book had begun to enjoy a revival as a new generation of concerned Floridians adopted *River of Grass* as a ledger of environmental mistakes and warnings and as a testament for activism. Mockingbird Press put it out in paperback in 1974, a pivotal time in South Florida environmental politics. Adams believed that *River of Grass* galvanized the Everglades movement and propelled it forward. Wilson found the book nothing short of inspiring. It "told you the things you needed to understand to protect the place," she said, showing "how complex and wonderful things were." It "gave you ammunition." Victoria Tschinkel of the state Department of Environmental Regulation said that the book's erudition and literary force "made everyone feel they were stewards of the Everglades."[20]

One of the book's greatest gifts was its author and her many assets—in particular, the knowledge she had gained from writing the volume. The book gave her the Everglades and then led her to Joe Browder's invitation to become involved. Browder appreciated *River of Grass* for its sobering history, "literary power," and "ethical voice," all of which he wanted to regenerate into activist influence and power. "Her outspoken ethical leadership," he said, "defined the goals in a public way and . . . made it much easier for those people who were working the more overtly political side of the campaign to succeed."[21]

Fifty years earlier, her voice would have been propped up by the organizational structure of a women's club. Douglas's Friends epitomized the micro in the macro postwar transformation in institutional outlets for female environmental activists. Issue-oriented, gender-integrated groups were the new organizations on the block, doing the good work many women early in the environmental century found most satisfying among the many issues on their clubs' agendas. The new movement was built on an activist heritage (as well as the energy of the modern women's movement, which paralleled the new environmental movement) sustained by the memory of Mary Barr Munroe and May Mann Jennings. Succeeding the founding generation of activists were Polly Redford, Juanita Greene, Jeanne Bellamy, and Alice Wainwright. Like their predecessors, some of this later generation were club women, all enjoyed middle-class status in white society, and all embraced broad concerns of social betterment. Unlike the earlier activists, at least three of the heirs accepted the label *feminist,* all were professional women, and all devoted their energies to organizations with mixed memberships.[22]

The environmentalism chapter in the history of women's clubs had not closed altogether. Club women remained eager to lend logistical support by getting out the vote or by inundating public officials with letters. "I am always very happy that the garden clubs have taken up the cause of the environment," Douglas wrote to one group. Soon after accepting the first membership dollar from Chenoweth, she gave a luncheon address to the Garden Group of Ocean Reef in Key Largo. She talked about her desire to get an environmental organization off the ground, and the group promptly voted to give her four hundred dollars. A few days later, a woman who had sat next to Douglas at the luncheon sent a hundred-dollar check. Douglas described that five hundred dollars as the start-up capital for Friends and considered the Garden Group, which sent a donation every spring, as Friends' "parent organization." She continued to beat the anti-jetport and environmental drum before women's groups and to chase down new members. As a club speaker, she was in great demand, to the point that she eventually began declining invitations and substituting a single talk at the annual fall flower show for individual talks. "If I started speaking to [individual] garden clubs," she later said in a note to one assistant, "I'd never see the end of it."[23]

The eighty-year-old Douglas had known the first activists, had sometimes joined with them, and was the vivifying continuity in the women's tradition between the old and the new eras of activism. And *River of Grass* reminded people of the seamless saga of restive human forces ever in re-volt against nature and of the organized toil countering that revolt and unfolding out of the past and into the present.

As eventful as was Douglas's entry into environmental activism, Browder for now remained the most important ground-level force. Saving the Everglades from jet planes, a mass transit system, and urban sprawl also required reinforcements from the top, in the Department of the Interior, Congress, and the White House. Interior secretary Walter Hickel and his undersecretaries were determined not to lose a park to the roughshod behavior of another agency or department, local or federal, and they had powerful allies in Congress. In spring 1969, Henry Jackson of Washing-ton announced plans for the Senate Committee on Interior and Insular Affairs, which he chaired, to hold hearings to reconcile the conflict. At the same time, Congress was looking to resolve differences between Inte-rior and the Army Corps of Engineers over the past unnecessary drought. Attacked from multiple sides, the park was an underdog desperate for protection, and it was coming. As Jackson prepared to launch his hear-ings, the Interior and Transportation Departments agreed to commission a study of the jetport's ecological compatibility with the park. Jackson's committee was also working to formulate what ultimately became the National Environmental Policy Act, which required that environmental-impact studies be undertaken and made available to the public before the federal government underwrote or permitted a major project.[24]

The idea of the Everglades study originated with undersecretary of the interior Russell E. Train. No stranger to warm winters in South Florida, Train was friends with Reed, and with the help of Reed and Governor Claude Kirk, who was now convinced the jetport was a bad idea, they persuaded Hickel to authorize the study. Train then tracked down Luna B. Leopold, a senior scientist with the U.S. Geological Survey, who was in the midst of field research in Wyoming, and asked him to head the study. The second son of the late Aldo Leopold, the author of several books, and a member of the prestigious National Academy of Sciences, Luna Leopold had built a national reputation as a leading expert on river hydrology.

Browder and the other environmentalists welcomed Leopold's appointment, believing that a scientist with his background would see the question as they did. Leopold also depended on scientists based in Florida—
in particular, Arthur R. Marshall with the U.S. Fish and Wildlife Service
and the Geological Survey's James Hartwell and Milton Kolipinski—to
do the primary research and in fact write the report.[25]

Marshall, who acted as Leopold's South Florida coordinator, had established a relationship with environmentalists during the Seadade
controversy. Consorting with them violated an order from Interior, yet
no restrictions were put on scientists' contact with jetport supporters.
Hartwell, Marshall, and Kolipinski therefore ignored the directive and
routinely but surreptitiously met with Browder, Charles Lee, the Sierra
Club's Gary Soucie, and others at Henry Field's seven-acre bayfront estate, where Field, the quintessential host, served tea and pastries. Not
even the trusted Reed knew about the gatherings, held before Douglas
started Friends. She knew about them but never attended.[26]

Dade County commissioners grew increasingly nervous. The governor
and cabinet were beginning to express ideas about moving the jetport
to a new location outside the Everglades. But before going against the
Port Authority, the commissioners decided to authorize an independent
study, spending seventy-five thousand dollars to hire former interior secretary Stewart Udall and his consulting firm, the Overview Corporation.
A third, independent study was also launched. The National Academy of
Sciences (NAS) funded a grant to have sixty scientists examine regional
planning and water needs in South Florida, with special emphasis on the
implications of a jetport planted in the Everglades.[27]

With all the administrative attention given to Miami's airport quan-
dary came the expected national media scrutiny. Writing as a special correspondent to the *New York Times,* Brooks Atkinson took the evolving
popular image of the Everglades to a new level, flipping an old notion
on its head when he asked, "Will man turn a refuge into a wasteland?"
Time magazine, *Smithsonian, Business Week, Look, Life,* and *Playboy* all
carried stories. Taking a lesson from Douglas, *Family Weekly* said that
to understand the extent of the controversy, "it is necessary to grasp the
most important fact about the Everglades: namely, that it is not a great

swamp, as it appears, but actually a free-flowing river." On the *CBS Evening News,* Walter Cronkite reported on the jetport affair, which also was the subject of a ten-minute piece on NBC's *Today* show. Those two networks and ABC aired specials on the Everglades. In virtually every case, journalists revealed an unmistakable sympathy for the ecosystem and the park. The Port Authority was painted as the bad guy, and the majority of the twenty-four thousand letters that burdened the staffs at the offices of Governor Kirk and Secretary Hickel agreed with that dark hue.[28]

The Port Authority was winning no popularity contests. It remained irreverently defiant, arrogant, and uncaring. No one better personified its attitude than its director, Alan Stewart, who did so unabashedly. He held fast to his vision of an industrial center congealing around the jetport and the city of Miami expanding toward it, and he was perversely determined to make this happen. "A new city is going to rise up in the middle of Florida," he declared publicly, "whether you like it or not." One Port Authority official, Ben Shepard, claimed that the Dutch had "completely destroyed the ecology of their land and yet it's supporting human life satisfactorily."[29] Deputy director Richard Judy clarified that regardless of what the studies reported, "We're going to build the jetport." He was equally blunt about who the Port Authority saw as the enemy. "The forces that will come into play will destroy the conservationists," he eagerly prophesied. He and Stewart spewed rhetoric indicating that they saw natural places as little more than the obsession of butterfly chasers—a quaint obsession when it did not interfere with their designs, malignant when it did. "Don't worry, Joe," Stewart patronizingly told Browder. "We'll keep a few trees up and hire an Indian guide to take the tourists on jungle cruises—we'll protect your environment." Stewart also promised to provide earmuffs to alligators so the planes would not disturb them. When Jackson's hearings convened in Washington, Stewart refused to go, seeming to view the affair as unworthy of his consideration. Science and the park, his spokesman said, were "trying to put the federal government in control of everything in south Florida."[30]

The June 1969 hearings on Capitol Hill may not have gone that far, but they ultimately ensured alligators a future without earmuffs. Sitting on the Interior Committee along with Jackson were Edmund Muskie and

Gaylord Nelson, the Senate's staunchest environmentalists. Nelson said at one point, "Either we stop the jetport at the present site, or we publicly admit that we are going to destroy the park." As many observers had predicted, the committee members came out against the jetport, with scientific backing for their stance. The Leopold report was officially released on September 17, 1969, and environmentalists smelled sweet victory. The principals of the clandestine meetings at Field's house decided that the report should open with a death-knell statement against the jetport: "Development of the proposed jetport and its attendant facilities will lead to land drainage and development for agriculture, transportation, and services in the Big Cypress Swamp which will inexorably destroy the south Florida ecosystem and thus the Everglades National Park." The NAS report appeared the next day and essentially confirmed the Leopold study. Udall's report followed in December, giving the go-ahead to the jetport as long as it was built as a "clean enclave"—that is, as long as it would include nothing more than runways. By this time, however, Udall's findings were moot.[31]

The Nixon administration had already made its first major environmental decision. Transportation secretary John A. Volpe had pledged to abide by the conclusions of the Leopold study and agreed to cooperate with Hickel. Relying heavily on Reed's advice, Kirk made his opposition official in September by recommending an alternative site in Palm Beach County. With nowhere to turn, the Port Authority relented to negotiations with the Departments of the Interior and Transportation and the governor's office. Finally, in the "Jetport Pact" signed the next year, it agreed to seek a new airport location, in exchange for which the federal government would reimburse the twelve million dollars the Port Authority had already spent and would permit training flights to continue until the new facility was completed. "Against all odds, the birds have won," announced Philip Wylie in the New York Times.[32]

The Port Authority lost in part because of its vociferous willingness to destroy the Everglades. That kind of attitude no longer held currency in the public arena. It had begun to go out of style when Coe set out on his long journey to national park creation, a journey to protect the remaining wildlife from the sanguinary habits of poachers. It began to go out when Douglas introduced the public to the notion of an uncommon river running through an uncommon region, a river of geological and biological wonder. The Corps of Engineers nevertheless continued dismantling the Everglades ecosystem but did so while propagating the notion that its activities were good for the people and the park. For a while, a trusting public had deferred to the army engineers' professed good intentions, but when the corps revealed a lordly indifference during the drought, the public forced the engineers to mend their ways. Much like the corps, the Port Authority thought it could live in the Broward-era past while the rest of the world marched ahead.

The late 1960s and early 1970s were a turning point in the environmental history of the Everglades and of the entire nation. Interior secretary Hickel told Hugh Downs during NBC News's Everglades documentary, which won an Emmy Award, "I think there's been a new set of values, and it isn't just the young who are talking about ecology—it's America as a whole." The Senate's ecotriumvirate—Jackson, Muskie, and Nelson—and a presidential administration that detected political capital in responding to the public's *Silent Spring* concern steered the federal government into the new age of environmentalism. By the time Richard Nixon entered the White House in 1969, the Sierra Club, the National Audubon Society, and the Wilderness Society had doubled or more than doubled their memberships since the beginning of the decade. In early December, he inaugurated the federal government's formal recognition of the new age with the signing of an updated Endangered Species Conservation Act, which considerably expanded the list of compromised flora and fauna. On January 1, 1970, at the broad presidential desk in his Western White House in San Clemente, California, he put his pen to the National Environmental Policy Act. The ongoing debate over the Alaskan oil pipeline illuminated the need for impact studies, while the Miami jetport controversy demonstrated their utility, with the Leopold and NAS studies described as models for the federal requirement. On April 22, Gaylord Nelson kicked off the national celebration he conceived as Earth Day. Three months

later, Nixon created the Environmental Protection Agency (EPA) to coordinate federal environmental policy that had been previously diffused
across more than eighty agencies and departments. One of the EPA's first
orders of business was to enforce the new Clean Air Act, which tough-
ened the national air-quality standards and compliance deadlines of the
1967 Air Quality Act. The next year, Congress passed the Clean Water
Act, intended in part to protect wetlands, and the EPA banned domestic
use of DDT.[33]

A few years earlier, high levels of the pesticide had been discovered
in the eggs of bald eagles nesting in the Everglades, as DDT insinuated
its way through the Everglades and Lake Okeechobee fish the eagles ate.
Both bodies of water accumulated pesticide runoff from agricultural
areas. The offending water, dirty and diverted, became Douglas's and
Friends of the Everglades' next preoccupation. The new era of environmentalism belonged to her as much as any other era that intersected her
life—woman suffrage, magazine writing, the national park movement.
By the time of the jetport struggle, she had gained an educated sense of
what had gone awry in the Everglades, which people, rightly or wrongly,
started to call hers.

Regionalism and Environmentalism

"Your predecessors gave away Florida land like drunken sailors," Douglas reminded Governor Reubin O'D. Askew. She knew he wouldn't do the same, though. He was arguably Florida's most liberal chief executive ever. A World War II combat veteran, a chaste nonsmoker and nondrinker, and a Bible-reading Presbyterian, Askew fit in well with folks back home in Pensacola. Panhandle whites were as socially and politically conservative as those across the border in Alabama and Georgia. Their elected state representatives, collectively known as pork choppers for their penchant for appropriating taxpayer-funded projects for themselves and supporters, had controlled state government since Reconstruction. Douglas referred to them as the wool-hat boys—those men who had gracelessly rejected the suffragists in 1917. Despite Askew's liberal views, he represented his district in the legislature for twelve years and got himself elected to the governor's office twice. The minute he entered the latter in 1971, he was hell-bent on carrying out reforms. He called for a corporate income tax, a moratorium on the death penalty, racially integrated schools, more blacks and women in government, full public disclosure of state business, and a prioritization of environmental protection. "Ecological destruction," he later emphasized in an appeal to conventional values, is equivalent to "economic suicide."[1]

Proposed environmental policy soon enough put him at odds with the Florida cabinet, a popularly elected body. Askew proposed that the cabinet members and their individual departments surrender environmental decision making to what the press dubbed a new superagency, the state's equivalent to the federal Environmental Protection Agency. The agency would be accountable to the governor alone. Most of the cabinet members opposed the proposal, which twice failed in the legislature. After the second defeat, Askew locked horns with the cabinet again, this time over a successor for the retiring head of the Department of Natural Resources. The cabinet was leaning toward Harmon Shields, the department's director of marine resources, whom Askew might have accepted had the bureaucrat not lobbied against the superagency. To delay Shields's confirmation, Askew resorted to parliamentary maneuvering in hopes that the public would step forward and convince cabinet members to change their minds. Such was unlikely—cabinet members were known to relish their authority. Two of them, including the well-girded agricultural commissioner, Doyle Conner, accused Askew of "just playing politics." Secretary of State Richard Stone elevated the Shields confirmation to the "Cabinet's last stand."[2]

In the middle of this fracas, Douglas wrote to Stone, just as Askew had encouraged citizens to do. As a public servant, Stone had established a record that environmentalists could neither praise nor discredit. He usually supported Askew, but not in the case of the superagency or Shields. Douglas lectured Stone on the long history of abuse in the Everglades, which she said Askew was trying to reverse with the development of sensible water- and growth-management policy. Stone therefore should take the governor's side. The press called Douglas's letter "scathing." One of Stone's detractors ran off five hundred copies and, in an apparent attempt to undermine Stone's expected run for the U.S. Senate, sent them to his political backers. Stone told the press that while he knew he "had to respect the flag," he was not of the impression that he "had to respect Marjory Stoneman Douglas."[3]

The dismissive remark was perhaps not well considered. Douglas generated attention; the press's interest in her letter and in Stone's quoted retort was manifest proof of that. She was more than a quaint media story; people quickly learned the octogenarian with trifocal harlequin glasses and ceramic pearls matching her silky white curls was a smart, able activist whose open-hearted eloquence could repel antagonism with the full force of its truth. And she was organized. Referring to Friends of the Everglades, *American Forests* magazine observed that as the jetport conflict was coming to a close, "another group is now forming to be ready for the next campaign." The speaking schedule Douglas maintained would have exhausted a thirty-year-old. She was constantly appearing before civic organizations, city and county governing bodies, and environmental conferences as well as the legislature and the cabinet. At the Florida Wildlife Federation's annual banquet in 1975, state attorney general Robert Shevin presented her with the governor's Conservationist of the Year award. Douglas's role remained the same as it had been from the start—to remind policymakers of a new environmental ethic, to project the movement's vitality, and to act as a liaison between it and the public.[4]

It was easy for her to go to bat for Askew. His ideas were remarkably consistent with the regionalist agenda she had embraced for fifty years. One of his priorities was to craft the state's first legitimate growth-management policy. For most of the state's history, Florida's land and natural resources—in particular, water—had overwhelmed a small population. Then, over the course of a generation—Askew's generation—the balance had abruptly shifted. Two of his more sober predecessors, LeRoy Collins and Claude Kirk, had realized that prioritizing growth had run its course beyond the limit of benefits. Nowhere had the scales tilted so deeply toward growth than in South Florida. During the 1960s, the urbanized area of Dade County sprawled outward by more than 60 percent and threatened the East Everglades. Schools were overcrowded, roadways were overtaxed, sewage treatment plants were inadequate, yet development interests continued to rule Metro government. The Environmental Protection Agency reported that in tests for chloroform—a probable human carcinogen—in the drinking water of eighty cities, Miami recorded the highest levels. The report came out around the time the Metro commission adopted new environmental-protection and development guidelines. Unconsciously echoing Douglas's long-ago call for wise growth, *Science* magazine wrote that the people of Miami must now decide whether "to create a well-planned semitropical garden spot or . . . to adjust to life in another sprawl-city."[5]

The compelling factor behind Metro's guidelines was not invisible, tasteless chloroform but another unnecessary drought. In spring 1970, dry land was turned to flooded land, drowning wildlife populations, when the Central and Southern Florida Flood Control District (FCD) worked hard to avoid wetting the ankles of farmers. A year later, those former killing fields were hard-baked terra firma, and the park was once again at the back of the line holding an empty water cup. Filling it would have required the FCD and the Army Corps of Engineers to send a sheet flow across cropland that lay between Lake Okeechobee and the park. But there was no atonement for the disaster of the 1960s, and they did not. Unlike before, desperation hit close to home. Fire raged across 750,000 acres, dusting the cities and their suburban offspring with ashes. East of the Everglades, the combined urban/suburban population was pushing three million, and the profligate thirst for green lawns was unchanged if not more severe. Saltwater contamination forced Miami to shut down eight municipal wells and impose unwelcome conservation measures. At the drought's peak, Robert Rackleff, a future speechwriter for Edmund Muskie, was putting the final touches on another Florida "battle" book, *Close to Crisis: Florida's Environmental Problems.* He found it noteworthy that although Florida had an average of nearly 1.5 billion gallons of freshwater per day falling from the skies, the state, especially the wettest part, was gulping for more.[6]

Uncertainty had long lingered about how best to manage South Florida's demographic changes and its most tirelessly debated resource. The year before the drought, before accusations of its truckling to agriculture had reached their height, the FCD joined with the University of Miami's Center for Urban Studies to host an Everglades Conference, in the same month and place as the Interior Department's thermal-pollution conference. Attending were 135 scientists, engineers, bureaucrats, elected officials, and environmentalists, plus 42 students. One had only to walk through the convention hall and read name tags to learn the who's who of Everglades politics, including veterans Joe Browder, Gary Soucie, Robert Padrick, Arthur Marshall, James Hartwell, Frank Craighead, and Marjory Stoneman Douglas. Craighead and Douglas had the longest histories with the Everglades. A forest entomologist, Craighead had been benignly scrutinizing the wetland since 1915 and had retired to South Florida in 1956. At the time of the conference he was finishing up a brilliant book on South Florida's trees and ecology.[7] Douglas used the meeting to learn about new scientific findings from Craighead and others, and from government scientists she wanted to learn the best means for effecting policy change. She herself had been invited to add historical dimension, and her chief contribution preceded her attendance. One of the panelists' primary tasks was refining the definition of the Everglades, starting with that laid out in the conference program: "Contrary to some popular beliefs, the Everglades are not a jungle of great trees and dark lagoons of water. The original Everglades were aptly described by the Seminole Indians as 'Pa-hay-o-kee,' meaning 'River of Grass.'"[8] The conference provided participants with the opportunity to make introductions, exchange business cards, learn about the work of others, and voice the need to save the Everglades from an untimely extinction. Whatever else it accomplished is unclear. But that was enough of a beginning.

Tangible fruits came from the next conference, held a year later. Askew convened this gathering at the urging of Florida Audubon Society president Hal Scott. As before, the attendees included 150 experts from across the scholarly, bureaucratic, and activist spectrum. They met at Miami Beach's Balmoral Hotel for what turned out to be the milestone Governor's Conference on Water Management in South Florida. The *Miami Herald* judged the assembly "one of the most important conferences held in Florida." Askew wanted his state to acknowledge its past sins and find "solutions to recurring crises brought on by either too much or too little water." Here was Florida's environmental history in a nutshell. In making his opening remarks, the deaconlike Askew might have been standing before a church pulpit. He spoke with feeling, apocalyptic honesty, and more than a whisper of admonishment. South Florida was at grave risk of becoming the "world's first and only desert which gets 60 inches of rainfall a year." He addressed the water wars among agriculture, the cities, and the national park; the industrial pollution and effluent in inland waterways; the excessive number of leeching septic tanks in urban areas; the saltwater intrusion in coastal regions; and the subsidence of exposed muck soil. Then came the admonition: humans, unlike other animals, are "guilty of years of thoughtlessness and neglect. But also unlike animals, we have the ability to protect and restore—as well as the ability to spoil and destroy."[9]

Douglas witnessed this electrifying performance. Her residency in the state spanned seventeen governors, and never had she heard one whose words resonated so closely and passionately with her beliefs. Askew was the presbyter of those who would make new water policy for the state. She wanted to do more for him than write a reproving letter to the secretary of state about an appointment to the Department of Natural Resources (a battle Askew lost), though that was important, too. After the conference, "three days of very hard work chewing the rag about what should be done about Florida water," in Douglas's words, she went on the road as she had during the jetport campaign. The number of solicitations to speak before civic and environmental groups was more than she could accept. Local newspapers often announced her pending engagement and then interviewed her to write about it afterward. The talks and interviews gave her the opportunity to preach the "regionalism gospel," as one newspaper put it, and to "analyze the changes which are transforming Florida."[10]

Whenever her speaking circuit shifted to Florida's west coast, she took the opportunity to spend congenial time with Jean Areson. The niece of Carolyn Cole, Areson was the closest thing Douglas had to living family outside distant cousins scattered about in mostly unknown places. Cole had died in 1972, not long before Areson and her husband moved to Sarasota from Hoosick Falls, New York. Douglas had known Areson for forty years, and whenever they got together in Sarasota they talked about Carolyn, New England, and the multiple challenges facing Florida. Areson had always known "Marney" to be disciplined about her work. After retiring no earlier than midnight, she would rise relatively late, work for hours in her room, and appear at dinnertime to repose with a cocktail before a light meal. If there was no engagement scheduled that evening, they would play word games—competing to see who could make the most words out of a larger word, such as *Listerine*—and withdraw to the Aresons' pool for a leisurely swim, an old and undiminished pastime of Douglas. She had taken to wearing hats by now, even while swimming after sunset. They were wide-brimmed straw hats with cloth bands tied on the sides or backs. She acquired versions in black, red, and natural and chose which color to wear based on season, occasion, and mood. They became her recognized style, very much a part of the memorable public figure she was becoming as an activist.[11]

Areson got her first look at that public figure in late January 1974, when she drove Douglas to give a talk to the Manatee chapter of the Izaak Walton League. Sarasota was located outside the Everglades system, but Douglas believed that what she had to say about the Everglades applied to the entire state. Bad water management and overcrowded spaces were like locusts in the West; they would show themselves eventually. Citizens should get involved, she encouraged her listeners, urging them to learn about the projects and philosophies of government agencies, monitor them, and prod them toward environmental responsibility. She lauded grassroots organizations as effective conveyances of local voices, though she could not endorse the Izaak Walton League's standing motto, "Study to be quiet," which she believed silenced voices and put too much faith in government leaders. "They won't worry about you in Tallahassee," she said. "Know the extent of your natural resources, where your water is going. . . . You have the right, the privilege and the democratic process . . . and a chance [to save] a perfectly beautiful, unique region."[12]

Douglas routinely offered a flesh-and-blood example of how she had been a victim of undiscerning trust in government bureaucrats. Audiences heard an apologetic speaker say that when she wrote *River of Grass,* she had been beguiled by the miracle of equitable water distribution promised by the Army Corps of Engineers. "I thought then . . . that the engineers were going to fix everything. . . . I can see how wrong it was when they called it a flood control board." Describing her book's praise for the corps as "perfectly ghastly," she confessed that the engineers had made her a "terrible liar."[13]

Although she had begun to express doubts about her fealty to the corps as early as 1959, the new movement offered her an opportunity to make amends for her misguided beliefs and to reassert her regionalist beliefs. "I am becoming more and more a regionalist," she said at the Sarasota talk as well as at Stuart, Clewiston, and wherever else she spoke. There was of course no "becoming" a regionalist; she had been among the first hom-ilists. At the Governor's Conference on Water Management, she crossed paths with H. T. Odum, the son of one of regionalism's chief architects, Howard Odum, whose work she had cited in her newspaper column fifty years earlier. The son was a professor at the University of Florida, and his innovative work on natural systems was the progeny of the auspicious union of his father's sociological concepts and ecological science. One of the major proposals in the seven-page report resulting from the con-ference, which Douglas wholeheartedly endorsed, recommended the re-placement of the FCD with a regional water-management district. The former had been conceived during a season of hurricanes and heavy rains and habituated toward creating dry land, whereas the latter was proposed to ensure "water quality for the long term benefit of the environment of the region and the State." Odum regarded watersheds as ecosystems, ben-efiting society and wildlife most when kept intact. Florida had created its water problems by injudiciously following political considerations to carve up resources. The new South Florida district's area of responsibil-ity would include the Kissimmee River, the Lake Okeechobee basin, the Everglades, and the Big Cypress watershed—in other words, the entire Everglades hydrological and ecological reach.[14]

The official recognition of the full ensemble, however belated, must have been a confirming moment for Douglas. It was all right there on pages 24 and 25 of "the book." "The whole system was like a set of scales," without which "there would have been no Everglades." Twenty-four years after she wrote these important words, a conference of scientists, engineers, and activists convinced the governor and the legislature of the ecological truth about the Everglades, for what was a river of grass if not a watershed and an ecosystem? The next year, Askew signed into law the Florida Water Resources Act, which authorized the creation of five state water-management districts. Their geographic demarcation would conform to watersheds—if necessary, running through the middle of counties rather than deferentially tracing their political boundaries. The FCD was eventually replaced by the South Florida Water Management District, which indeed included the entire Everglades system.[15]

"County lines have nothing to do with the water picture," Douglas told a gathering at the Marie Selby Botanical Garden in Sarasota. "The geography and geology of each region is so different there are different sets of problems." In the tradition of her former geography professor, Elizabeth Fisher, she always spoke beside a map she brought to each engagement. It was a cartographic rendering of the Everglades watershed, water flow, and various geographic components, and when unrolled it was bigger than she. Although she called the new legislation the "epoch-making result" of the conference, she did not agree completely with the district divisions, and she sometimes told her audiences so. She believed that Florida had not five but three actual watersheds: the Everglades, the St. Johns River, and the Suwannee River—all, incidentally, representing Florida's contributions to the Rivers of America series. The Northwest Florida Water Management District in the Panhandle, she argued, needed to be a part of an interstate district, since the Panhandle's rivers originated in other states. Big-bellied Atlanta, for example, sent wastewater down the Apalachicola, already saturated with DDT, to the oyster fisheries of the Apalachicola Bay and the Gulf Coast.[16]

Yet even enlightened management could never make the Everglades whole again. That she understood. A study released after she began touring the state confirmed the changes she had witnessed over the decades: the Everglades hosted only a 10 percent remnant of the wading-bird population that had frequented the region before the peak of the plume-hunting era. She remembered traveling the Everglades with Ernest Coe and the national park delegation in 1930, watching with the others the "skeins of birds, layers of birds, flying in waves, covering the whole sky from long before sunset to moonrise hours later. . . . An ornithologist friend estimated we'd seen 40,000 birds." Now the region's estimated total avian population numbered fewer than 250,000.[17]

Foiling a return to original numbers after the plume-hunting years was the bulwark of mechanical devices that had superseded the ecosystem. Twenty-three years and five hundred million dollars after the corps began construction of its grand Romanesque waterworks, army engineers had corseted the Everglades to 52 percent of their original swelling size. On a map, the canals splaying out from Lake Okeechobee seemed to imitate the lines in a kaleidoscope. Four highways ran through the once end-less vastness, two on a north-south axis and two—Alligator Alley and Tamiami Trail—on an east-west. A one-hundred-mile levee separated the Everglades from the east coast cities, though not before suburban devel-opment advanced unimpeded into the so-called East Everglades. Noth-ing stopped the cattle ranches, orange groves, and vegetable farms from creeping in from the west. Above Lake Okeechobee, agriculture acquired some forty-five thousand dry acres when the snaky Kissimmee River was straightened into a drainage canal. Below the big lake, the Everglades Agricultural Area mushroomed out to between five hundred thousand and seven hundred thousand acres, depending on who was measuring, and developers were attacking on every flank. Five water-conservation areas rose and fell to levels ordained by the engineers and bureaucrats. The River of Grass no longer flowed—not by its own accord.

Douglas compared the changes in twentieth-century Florida to "going over Niagara Falls in a barrel." They were often precipitous and furious, allowing little time for preparation and no opportunity to turn back; people would have to face the consequences, good or bad, and uncertain until the end; what was done was done.[18]

Change in South Florida magnified change in the rest of the state, but not by much. Two national economic recessions and a statewide building slump were not enough to stop hordes from moving to the state of sun-shine, warmth, and easy living in the 1970s. During that decade, Flor-ida's population grew 43 percent, remaining just shy of the ten million mark. With the opening of the much frothed-over Walt Disney World in 1971, which was expected to bring in eight million additional tourists each year, Central Florida, at the head of the Everglades watershed, stood at the threshold of rapid transformation. For the first time, a landlocked part of the state was being swept up in the spreading "fires of density," to use Douglas's words. As the multitudes arrived, the water supply shrank. By 1970, Florida had lost approximately 49 percent of its fresh surface water since statehood, and much of that remaining was too impaired with pollutants for safe swimming and fishing. Just northeast of Orlando lay Lake Apopka, formerly Florida's second-largest freshwater body and an "angler's paradise"; drainage and levees had now shrunk it down to the state's fourth-largest lake, pea green and putrid with recurrent fish kills from algae blooms touched off by agricultural runoff. Noonan's Lake near Gainesville, the Fenholloway River running through Taylor County, Tampa Bay on the west coast, and Escambia Bay in the Panhandle simi-larly faced biological death from waste discharge issuing from agricul-tural runoff or pulp, phosphate, and chemical industrial pollution. Fresh-water springs in Polk and Hillsborough Counties had stopped flowing because the water demands of the unquenchable phosphate industry had lowered the level of the aquifer by forty to sixty feet, while the industry's discharge turned the downstream Peace River yellow, suggesting the vari-ant Piss River. Developers were making land from water in virtually every coastal bay, river, and sound, as if Governor LeRoy Collins had illumi-nated a green light in the 1950s when he fought the fill project in Boca Ciega Bay. In the waterways where the Corps of Engineers dredged chan-nels, marine grasses died, clear water turned murky, and life disappeared, consequences that had come in utter violation of the Clean Water Act of 1972. The Cross-Florida Barge Canal, another corps ecological debacle, rivaled the Everglades in the number of debates and hearings it stirred up in Tallahassee and Washington, the level of national press it attracted, and the seeds of discontent it sowed.[19]

From these seeds and others came the collective harvest of the new movement, gathered from popular initiatives at the community or regional level across the state. They were joined together by no central organizing structure but rather by the shared language, politics, and emotive force of citizen activism and the informative prescriptions of ecological science. The 1970s were a momentous decade in Florida. Only the cumulative West and perhaps California alone produced movements that could compare with the robustness of Florida's. A profusion of new local chapters of the Audubon Society and Sierra Club arose, with exploding memberships to match. Marjorie Carr and her Florida Defenders of the Environment, formed in 1969 and drawing on the expertise of ecologists, worked undauntedly to stop the barge canal. Her husband, Archie, attended the South Florida conferences and then wrote a lyrical book on the Everglades. Sarasota citizens mobilized against the plans of the Arvida Corporation, the self-proclaimed pioneer in building condominium towers, to excavate seven hundred thousand cubic yards of bay bottom to make land for one of its developments. The episode inspired the 1977 novel *Condominium,* by best-selling author John D. MacDonald, which followed his *A Flash of Green,* published in 1962 and declared the first ecological novel, a proclamation of resident campaigns to stop bay-fill projects in 1950s Sarasota. MacDonald also condemned the proposed Everglades jetport in a *Life* magazine article, for which he consulted Douglas and Browder. Florida attorney general Robert Shevin, a devoted supporter of Askew's policies, launched a special investigation into illegal dredging projects, a particular problem in the ecologically critical keys. Prompted by public outcry over overstuffed landfills, he also pursued a special tax on nonreusable containers.[20]

On the national scene, the new decade opened with the first annual Earth Day celebration on April 22, 1970. Engendered by Senator Gaylord Nelson, the event was consecrated by Americans across the land— twenty million, according to Nelson's estimate. Each participating community laid out plans for celebration. Some were buffeted by protests and others visited by nothing more than peaceful teach-ins, parades, concerts, cleanup rallies, and tree-planting campaigns. The major television networks aired Earth Day specials. Some state legislatures took advantage of the heightened spirit to enact environmental legislation. Congress went into recess so members could participate in events with constituents.[21]

The day in Miami was tinged radical. Groups that had been hardly visible before, including Survive! and Environment!, suddenly surfaced. Their memberships were generally formed by high school and university students, striking a discreet urgency that others typically interpreted as insolent impatience. These groups infuriated officials and businesses in the leisure trade when they posted signs on beaches warning tourists to stay out of the "Dangerously Polluted Waters!" Engaging in an old, familiar deed, a faction calling itself the Eco-Commandos poured yellow dye into toilets, whence it found its way into the bay. They held a protest rally at city hall and joined in the Dead Orange Parade, a procession of two dozen "pollution floats" tracing the route of the Orange Bowl Parade and led by mothers with strollers and placards declaring the pollution of adults to be the debt of children. Sympathetic employees of the public library wore gas masks and displayed a black-draped coffin holding a globe of the earth. Perhaps the most moderate events were schoolchildren's cleanup and tree-planting activities and daylong teach-ins on college campuses, where students and faculty wore green armbands. Philip Wylie, his face wizened nearly twenty years since writing his damning and be-damned *Look* magazine exposé, urged students at Miami-Dade Junior College to prepare for a "lot of fights." Buffalo Tiger spoke, too, having recently won the fight against the jetport, and declared pollution and overpopulation the making of white cultural values. Students at Palm Beach Junior College gave a Polluter of the Week award to the county for dumping partially treated sewage into Lake Worth, long ago the shimmering backdrop for the Guy Bradley family. Ross McCluney, a doctoral student in physics, organized events at the University of Miami and followed up with his "battle" book, *The Environmental Destruction of South Florida*. His fellow students buried time capsules of unpolluted water and air with a written account of the jetport victory. Bud Owre, Milton Kolopinski, and other scientist activists took to the podium in support of the earth. Joe Browder and Virginia Hine spoke, too. The day's activities, she said, ominously signaled that ecology might come to be a "subversive science" leading to "unconventional techniques—even revolution." Some veteran activists were put off by the youth "insurgency," yet at least one told Hine and Luther Gerlach that "all the rap sessions, speeches, eco-tactics workshops, demonstrations, and the general hoopla of the events" had decisively radicalized her.[22]

Lawmakers in Tallahassee sent mixed messages as they observed the occasion. The House opened the day's session "by resolving in favor of Earth Day." It then passed legislation restricting the use of DDT, outlawing the sale of products made of alligator hides, and limiting the sale of state-owned submerged land. But it was too much to expect the legislature to be a fully reformed body. Over in the Senate, the Natural Resources and Conservation Committee killed a proposed phosphate severance tax that would have helped control the industry's pollution.[23]

Still, Earth Day captured the momentum of the new decade. A year later, the Governor's Conference on Water Management in South Florida converted that momentum into new statewide environmental policy. James Hartwell, who attended the conference, said, "I am optimistic enough to say that Florida is developing a new environmental ethic." It was, and few other states would match it. Along with adopting the Florida Water Resources Act, the state created a preserve in the Fakahatchee Strand, the principal slough in the Big Cypress, hidden beneath a primeval jungle of rare orchids and bromeliads that plant hunters and timbermen had plundered for a century. In the spirit of the Fakahatchee initiative, for which Douglas had called in her speeches, the legislature passed the 1972 Land Conservation Act, model legislation—duplicated only in Washington, California, and New York—that allowed the state to issue $240 million in bonds to purchase environmentally endangered land. In decades to come, the law made Florida the leader in conservation land acquisitions.[24]

The state's shift to land purchaser from land seller, as in the Internal Improvement Fund's early days, unsettled property-rights advocates. Some had acquired their land from the state at below-rock-bottom prices and were uncomfortable with the idea that the state would be buying back land, even at above-market prices. Members of this camp suspected that the Fakahatchee Strand acquisition was a prelude to a much larger acquisition. They were right.

The raging jetport battle had confirmed the logic of turning the Big Cypress Swamp into a preserve. Joe Browder, whom the National Park Service eventually named Citizen Father of the Big Cypress Preserve, had for a long time thought that carving the Big Cypress out of the original plat for the national park was an insult to Ernest Coe's and Daniel Beard's spot-on vision. That was to say nothing about the insult to the ecological wholeness of the Everglades. The Big Cypress occupied twenty-five hundred square miles of the western Everglades. Although its namesake trees—bald cypress and pond, or hat-rack, cypress—were the region's dominant species, the sylvan landscape was interspersed with wiregrass and pine flatlands, tropical hardwoods, ficus, and royal palms. Floridians had been fighting over or in the Big Cypress since the Seminole Wars and had been exploiting its natural endowments for just as long. Early in the twentieth century, sawmills began cropping up on land leased from Barron Collier, who owned most of the swamp, and before all was done timber workers extracted 400 million board feet of pine and 360 million board feet of cypress, some of the country's oldest. The timber was milled and fashioned into coffins, pickle barrels, stadium bleachers, wall paneling, house siding, and shingles. The trees proved resilient, nevertheless, and by the 1950s, a second-growth forest of "enduring cypress," as Douglas called them, had established itself.[25]

The idea of a Big Cypress preserve was not new. An amateur herpetologist named Ernest Taylor had thought of it in the 1950s when he was trolling around the state trying to hook the public and state officials on a proposal to establish Corkscrew Swamp Sanctuary in the eastern part of the Big Cypress. After National Audubon brought in the resources to make the 6,080-acre sanctuary a reality in 1954, protecting the world's largest stand of old-growth cypress, Taylor wanted to do the same for the rest of the Big Cypress but lacked the wherewithal.[26]

Sixteen years later, the participants at the governor's conference in Miami urged Askew to seek, à la Taylor, federal protection for the Big Cypress. Browder, who had moved on to Friends of the Earth, again led the charge from the trenches and made use of his contacts in Washington.

Dante Fascell came on board and drafted House legislation for the preserve. He, Browder, Askew, and other participants in the governor's conference testified at a subcommittee hearing of the House Committee on Interior and Insular Affairs, held in Fort Myers. Hartwell read a statement drafted by four ecologists and one hydrologist, including Marshall and Craighead, emphasizing that "about 55% of the average annual overland flow into Everglades National Park since 1940 has been from the Big Cypress watershed."[27]

Predictably, the idea of a preserve produced strident opposition from developers and property owners. Brushing aside science, the East Collier Land Owners Improvement Committee maintained that the water of the Big Cypress naturally flowed away from the park and into the Gulf of Mexico. And more important to preserving ecosystems was preserving the constitutional right of property ownership. No one could determine the exact number of people who held legal claim to land in the 570,000 acres blueprinted for the preserve. Figures ranged between thirty and fifty thousand. A busy and vociferous minority wrote to newspapers and lawmakers and attended public hearings, often lugging along placards that read, "I would rather give my land to the Russians," or "Join the Audubon Society and help make people extinct."[28]

These were mild responses. One property-rights advocate, identifying himself as the "research director" of the East Collier group, distributed leaflets around South Florida like a Seventh Day Adventist secretly leaving scriptural texts on park benches. One leaflet declared Joe Browder guilty of a "crime" that "equals any ever committed against mankind." Others on the list of criminals included State Senator Bob Graham, Nat Reed, Henry Jackson, and Reubin Askew. Another leaflet simply went too far: "I believe any citizen killing these people trying to take our land would receive all the blessings God and the House of Heaven are able to bestow on any great hero." Reed and Graham "were sufficiently concerned" by this lack of subtlety to report it to the Federal Bureau of Investigation, which failed to dissuade the perpetrator. Browder, however, had managed to carry over to the Big Cypress campaign the variegated coalition formed against the jetport, including wildlife poachers. One was Bill Shoelerman, better known as Gator Bill. Despite his illicit hunting activities, Browder and Reed befriended the affable Shoelerman and enlisted his services as lead guide and protector against alligators and water moccasins when Henry Jackson and Julie Nixon Eisenhower, standing in for her father, toured the Big Cypress. Shoelerman was in his element when out in the swamp but no less so when he paid a visit to the property-rights crusader and told him that if any harm came to Browder, Reed, or the others, an earthly wrath would come down. The threats stopped.[29]

Stumping around the state, Douglas was sympathetic to the landowners, but only to a point. Trade-offs had to be made, she said, for the "clean air we breathe, and water we drink." She sent postcards to the members of Friends of the Everglades, urging them to write to the interior secretary requesting the purchase of the "Big Cypress watershed." Soon thereafter, the country became rattled by the OPEC oil embargo, and she warned audiences that oil companies had turned their sights on the Big Cypress. She was most concerned with the low priority the Department of the Interior appeared to be giving the matter. The department was now headed by Rogers B. Morton, a beef-cattle rancher who had succeeded Hickel after he was fired for environmental views that evolved as those of the administration devolved. Douglas's concerns were confirmed when she, Johnny Jones, and others were scheduled to meet locally with an assistant secretary, who sent a deputy in his stead. The meeting went poorly. Douglas insisted on a five-year moratorium on drilling. Not only did the deputy "hedge," so too did Florida Audubon, she wrote to Browder after the hearing. *Audubon* magazine regularly accepted oil-company advertisements, she complained, and Exxon bought the space on the back cover of Florida Audubon's *Florida Naturalist*. She knew oil would win, and she blamed Florida Audubon director Hal Scott for his friendly demeanor toward the industry.[30]

Oil was not the only threat. The Gulf American Land Corporation, started in the 1950s by brothers Leonard and Jack Rosen, spawned the 173-square-mile Golden Gate Estates on the western apron of the Big Cypress just south of Corkscrew Swamp. The ambitious development included more than 800 miles of roads and countless vacant soggy lots, despite 183 miles of drainage canals and twenty-four water spillways. Gulf American was known to have a cozy relationship with the Collier County board of commissioners, who irritated Craighead to the point that he called them a "perverse group of politicians." The name-calling got the attention of Askew, who wanted to keep development and all other intrusions to the watershed out of the Big Cypress. This time, a majority of the cabinet supported him.[31]

But the congressional bill to authorize the preserve, written by Browder and cosponsored by Lawton Chiles in the Senate and Dante Fascell in the House, was stuck in committee. Jones flew up to Washington and went over to Capitol Hill to pry it out. Florida, he learned, would have to put up part of the appropriations for the land purchase. Jones took off for Tallahassee to meet with Askew and Graham, who decided to use money from the 1972 Land Conservation Act. Jones, Graham, and Askew's staff director, Al Galbraith, wrote the law. At Jones's request, Douglas went to Tallahassee to lobby for the bill. In a stunning vote, the legislature agreed to appropriate forty million dollars.[32]

His homework done, Jones returned to Washington. He and Senator Jackson managed to get the bill out of committee. Additional help came from a thirty-thousand-acre July fire in the Big Cypress, which preserve supporters blamed on excessive drainage. Congress ultimately appropriated $116.9 million to add to Florida's $40 million, laying the groundwork for the largest private land purchase in National Park Service history. In 1974, President Gerald Ford signed legislation creating the Big Cypress National Preserve, which included part of the Ten Thousand Islands. Once again, federal land that in the nineteenth century had become state land for the purpose of economic development became federal land for the purpose of environmental protection.[33]

All the same, details of the establishment of the preserve could not escape controversy. For the first time, the expansion of National Park Service holdings in the area did not require Everglades Indians to move. They obtained perpetual rights to their territory in the Big Cypress and safeguards that would permit them to engage in traditional activities, which now included giving tourists airboat rides. Some environmentalists complained, but most were more disturbed by another improbable concession. Oil companies were allowed to explore for crude, owners of improved property—no less a tar-papered hunting shack—could retain ownership of their land for twenty-five years, and sportsmen were allowed to hunt indefinitely with the aid of their airboats and swamp buggies. In congressional testimony, Reed warned, "The area will be used and used hard." But Browder believed that because hunters, especially Jones, "had fought hardest to save" the Big Cypress, it would have been "unethical to drive them away."[34]

Next to Browder, Jones was the man of the hour. Douglas had first met him in 1970. He and his wife, Mariana, were in Naples attending the second annual conference of the Environmental Confederation of Southwest Florida, a five-county coalition headed by Friends of the Everglades county chair Franklin Adams and formed to protect the western portion of the Everglades. The Joneses knew of Douglas but had never seen or met her. "Everyone was aflutter that Marjory Stoneman Douglas was going to speak that night," remembered Mariana. "She was absolutely fascinating," said Johnny. She was making a pitch for regional policies and planning. She launched into a soon-to-be-familiar attack against the FCD and Corps of Engineers, arguing that the puny objectives of the former had outlived their usefulness and the big promises of the latter had gone astray.[35]

When Douglas and the Joneses were introduced, they congratulated each other on the recent jetport victory. Still, Douglas had a bone to pick and went straight to the point. "You represent hunting," she said to Johnny. "I want to talk to you about that. I do not like that." Jones remained the practiced diplomat. He pointed out that the two of them agreed on "99 percent of the issues" and suggested that they could accomplish much together if they set aside the one difference. A short time later, as if to test his compatibility claim, she telephoned for a favor. She wanted to have the purple gallinule removed from the state's game-bird list. He was not familiar with the small wetland dweller of dramatic purplish-blue, green, and red coloring. Jones said that he would do what he could and phoned a few Florida Wildlife Federation members. No one hunted the gallinule, but some federation members wanted to keep the list intact to avoid giving in to "antihunters." Jones failed to see the point and as a favor to Douglas successfully lobbied for the bird's removal from the list.[36]

Douglas and Jones's future partnership was strengthened by the person who had introduced them, Art Marshall. Douglas and Marshall had participated in the 1970 conference organized by the FCD and University of Miami and another the next year organized by Douglas and Friends of the Everglades. Marshall was an early member of Friends who had long been involved in South Florida environmental causes; like Jones, his relationship with the Everglades dated back to his Palm Beach County childhood. His family had moved there from his native Charleston, South Carolina, in 1925, when he was six; seven years later, the Marshalls moved to Miami. In 1944, he stormed the beach at Normandy during the D-Day invasion, and he subsequently participated in the liberation of Paris and the release of one thousand Jews at the Ohrdruff death camp. He returned home not only with posttraumatic stress but also with his mind on important things, including Florida's environment. He completed a bachelor's degree at the University of Florida and then a master's in marine biology at the University of Miami. That brought him a job with the U.S. Fish and Wildlife Service.[37]

Marshall's activist years began with his professional career, and Douglas believed he was one of the most important contributors to the environmental cause in 1960s and 1970s South Florida. The Seadade threat to the Everglades and Biscayne Bay first attracted him. He provided scientific data to environmentalists pushing for the national monument, and he took federal and state officials on ecotours of the bay, sometimes combined with a little fishing on the side. He was one of the contributors to Ross McCluney's *The Environmental Destruction of South Florida*, writing an essay on the natural life around and in Lake Okeechobee and the Kissimmee River. "It is time—well past time," he wrote, to "abandon the centuries-old belief that man's dominion over the earth includes its willful destruction." He was the principal investigator and writer for Luna B. Leopold's report. No one knew life's precisely choreographed dependence on Everglades water better than Marshall. Just before leaving office, Governor Kirk fittingly placed him in the first group of Floridians—

along with Nathaniel Reed, James Redford, Robert Padrick, and Marjorie Carr—to receive the Governor's Conservation Award.[38]

By that time, Marshall had left the Wildlife Service for the position of director of the Division of Applied Ecology at the University of Miami. Askew soon tapped Marshall to serve as the governor's scientific point man on the Everglades. Marshall and four other scientists formed a "special study team" to report on the state of South Florida's water resources. "The Everglades is not just stressed—it is distressed," Marshall told the governor and cabinet, "a condition brought about to a major degree by past works of the flood control project." The report convinced Askew of the need for the 1971 conference on water, and to organize it he turned to Marshall and John DeGrove, a Florida Atlantic University political scientist emerging as the state's leading growth-management expert. The two were also part of a fifteen-member task force that drew up the environmental agenda for the phenomenal 1972 legislative session. A year later, both men attended Askew's Conference on Growth and the Environment in Orlando. "South Florida's industry is growth. Growth adored, sacrosanct, revered," Marshall wrote to his friend, Reed. In an environmental planning study for south Dade, he argued, the "environmental problems" of the Everglades "wilderness" were "inseparable" from the "environmental problems" of South Florida's "urban area."[39]

This sort of perceptive observation grabbed Douglas's attention. She was equally blunt about growth, calling it an "ominous cloud over the Everglades." "We're fighting the Federal Government, the U.S. Army Corps of Engineers, water management, realtors and demographics." Not "everything has to grow," she said. "The end of growth is death—not life: a plant grows and then dies; all societies grow and die. There is no such thing as unlimited growth. . . . The more people there are, the more artificially we have to live to sustain life." She liked to hear Marshall say the things he said, and she in turn said things that he liked to hear.[40]

The "quiet, courteous," sometimes vulnerable, scientist with a Roman nose bore a slight resemblance to Frank Stoneman. Douglas thought of Marshall as a visionary, like her father; others, prompted by the predictive models he created to determine the fates of ecosystems, called him a prophet. In her autobiography, she said that while her phrase *river of grass* had changed people's thinking about the Everglades, Marshall later filled in the science that explained why they were worth saving. She credited Garald Parker's expertise as the basis of her book and Marshall's as the basis of her activism. But Douglas was being modest. Whether or not Marshall knew it, his science was an extension of that which she first tendered to the public in 1947. Browder, who admired Marshall immensely, believed that Douglas's knowledge had "informed and motivated" her younger colleague "rather than the other way around." Whatever the case, the articulations of the writer and the science of the ecologist fell into correspondence with each other when Douglas and Marshall met and formed the intellectual foundation of her activist life, which carried on for nearly three decades.[41]

The Kissimmee

In 1982, Douglas declared, "Conservation is now a dead word." When she made that statement, she was speaking before the Sarasota Wellesley Club and college alumnae, all of whom were generally much younger than she. By this time in her life, macular degeneration had begun to cloud her eyesight, and she had traded in her harlequin-framed trifocals for large, owl-shaped frames with thick lenses. Wide-brimmed hats and faux pearls were still compulsory complements to her public image, though, and her voice was still stentorian, her diction perfect, and her posture finishing-school straight. Her thinking remained clear, too. Conservation alone—that is, protecting natural endowments—no longer offered practical solutions to Florida's environmental problems. Too much had been lost. "You can't conserve what you haven't got. That's why we are for restoration."[1]

She was referring to undoing the damage done by the Army Corps of Engineers and the Central and Southern Florida Flood Control District's (FCD's) colossal Everglades replumbing scheme begun in 1948. The natural ecosystem needed to be pieced backed together again, she believed, starting with its Kissimmee River watershed, plundered in the last phase of the long project. "Probably the worst" undertaking of all, Douglas told audiences, was this phase, nine years in the making. Completion came in 1971 with the final impoundment of the oxbows of the Kissimmee. Engineers superimposed a 30-foot-deep, 56-mile canal atop the length of the natural S-shape of the 103-mile waterway. It was a hash mark through a continuous dollar sign carved in the land; the one on paper added up to thirty-five million. Before the canal and during extreme weather episodes, the river overflowed into the ill-located town of Kissimmee. Channelization was justified primarily with an inflated cost-benefit ratio. As with the south side of the lake, flood control in the river basin meant land reclamation for farmers and ranchers but at the cost of the loss of vital feeding grounds and habitat for animals in a place once described as a wild kingdom. To siphon dry the flood plain, the canal sprinted through several locks and pools and dropped twenty feet by the time it reached Lake Okeechobee. As if the ecological infliction were not enough, the corps changed the Kissimmee's name to the bureaucratically sterile C-38, for Canal 38.[2]

C-38, or the Kissimmee Ditch, as some people ungraciously called it, brought Douglas invitations to speak in Lake Okeechobee towns, such as Clewiston. This was agricultural country, guarded and self-preserving, though it existed by the will of the corps. On every canal, levee, and bridge there was a familiar brown and bronze sign with the turreted-castle insignia of the corps, there to remind locals of their benefactor. But tampering with the elements had gone too far for the comfort of some locals. C-38 sent more water into the lake than had the alluvial Kissimmee River. To keep water at mandated levels during wet season, Okeechobee frequently had to be pumped lower. Whenever engineers spirited lake water through the massive steel gates down the St. Lucie spillway in anticipation of a storm, people downstream amplified old complaints about the impaired St. Lucie, officially labeled C-44 and one of the nation's most DDT-contaminated rivers. There were other problems, too. By directing the flow of the uncoiled Kissimmee past the hushed oxbows, the corps relieved the river of its natural capacity to filter dirty water, which originated in crop- and rangeland saturated with manure and inorganic fertilizer. Farmers deposited a half million tons of fertilizer on Florida soil each year, most of it in the south. When it rained or when farmers irrigated or flushed out their barns, the lake received runoff with elevated nutrient levels from c-38 and, in particular, from Taylor Creek and Nubbin Slough, which spoked out from the lake's northeast bank. "That ditch," Johnny Jones growled, "is of no use for controlling big floods. . . . It just means more cows to crap in the water." This was Douglas's thought, too, if not her sort of eloquence.[3]

In the aquatic world, the slightest unnatural stimuli can set off a biological free-for-all that can devastate a prosperous ecosystem. Fertilizer and livestock waste washing down c-38 translated into flowering algae blooms in Lake Okeechobee, which translated into hypoxia, or depleted oxygen levels in the water, all of which translated into eutrophic conditions and aquatic catastrophe. What environmentalists and sportsmen hated to see most in the big lake was thousands of dead fish bobbing on the surface. Whenever they did, they knew who and what were responsible. Both the corps and agriculture downplayed the problem and their complicity in it. The corps, forever tinkering with its work, went a step further. It started talking about increasing the height of its Okeechobee dike to store more water for farmers. Some of that extra sustenance it planned to acquire by back pumping nutrient-rich water from the drainage canals into the lake again. Douglas's old friend and mentor, Garald Parker, now a senior scientist with the Southwest Florida Water Management District, had issued a report two years earlier warning against the eutrophic consequences of "reverse-pumping." But the bureaucrats ignored the alarm. The back-pumping proposal horrified people who swam and fished in the lake and the businesses that catered to such recreational pursuits.[4]

Environmentalists saw such a plan, which contradicted the logic not only of wise policy but also of clean water and a healthy ecosystem, as par for the course—that is, as high-handed and arbitrary. No sooner had the corps completed c-38 and eliminated the surrounding wetland than the FCD announced yet another plan: it and the corps intended to reflood fifty thousand acres of the same land they had spent millions to drain. "We are going to try to put back as much of the natural cycle as we can," said the

FCD's director of planning. In effect, observed a *St. Petersburg Independent* editorial, the corps would be "shoving its machinery into reverse."[5]

By first intruding on the Everglades environment and then reducing its ecosystem to dependence on that intrusion, the Army Corps of Engineers sought to justify its continued usefulness in South Florida. Corps officials believed that they were acting in unison with the sentiments of Congress and that they could adapt to new times and attitudes despite their behemoth organization. With the passage of the National Environmental Policy Act, the corps saw a new role for itself in environmental problem solving, and it responded with military snap-to to President Nixon's directive that federal agencies should bring themselves into compliance with the new law. Even earlier, corps leaders claimed, their agency had begun incorporating "aesthetic and environmental values in project planning and construction." During the 1960s, the corps considerably expanded its staff of landscape architects, biologists, foresters, and sanitation engineers, referring to them as "specialists in environmental sciences." In the same year that William O. Douglas issued his *Playboy* denunciation, army engineers referred 355 water-pollution cases to the Justice Department. Not surprisingly, the engineers thought that Justice Douglas had been capricious with his opinion.[6]

The corps was also involved in a pivotal legal conflict with Florida developers that was reminiscent of Governor LeRoy Collins's St. Petersburg showdown, except that this time, the developers lost. Alfred Zabel and David Russell filed suit when the corps violated the norm and denied a permit for another dredge-and-fill project in Boca Ciega Bay. Their lawyers argued that the corps' authority extended only to development proposals that interfered with navigation, which had not been an issue in this case. The corps had instead, and for the first time ever, based its decision on protecting the marine environment. In the landmark *Zabel v. Tabb*, the U.S. Court of Appeals for the Fifth Circuit unnerved developers when it found that the 1968 National Estuary Protection Act mandated the corps' decision. The country, "including Congress," wrote Chief Judge John R. Brown, had become "aware of civilization's potential destruction from breathing its own polluted air and drinking its own infected water."[7]

The corps' chief of engineers, Lieutenant General Frederick J. Clarke, might have said that Judge Brown was also talking about corps leaders' awareness. His engineers, he said, had recognized that "if the people of the country were changing what they wanted, we'd better get in step and find a way to do it." Accordingly, in 1972 he formed the Environmental Advisory Board with the idea that the board would facilitate understanding among the corps, the public, and the environmental community. Among the board's first members, specifically invited by corps officials, were Roland Clement, vice president of National Audubon, and Lynton Caldwell, a political science professor and drafter of the National Environmental Policy Act. Perhaps it was survivor's instinct, but Clarke believed the corps' military discipline uniquely positioned it to march to the drum of a new environmental ethos.[8]

To environmentalists, corps discipline constituted the source of many of the country's environmental problems. Leaving the protection of nature's landscape, much less the restoration of it, to those who had gouged and shoveled it into ruin evoked expected comparisons to the wolf's charge of the henhouse. The corps was simply too seasoned to growth and development to give it credibility as an environmental decision maker. Boca Ciega Bay, after all, was Florida's most polluted bay in part because army engineers had been so chummy with developers. After the FCD announced the reflooding plan for the Kissimmee River basin, a first among environmental restoration plans for the corps, Florida Audubon issued a public statement demanding that the Department of the Interior and the Environmental Protection Agency (EPA) take over the project. The corps had already done enough damage. Browder's Friends of the Earth and the Sierra Club could hardly agree more. Together, they analyzed the corps' required environmental impact statement regarding its existing projects in the flood-control district and declared the document "grossly vague and generalized." It was a poorly disguised "attempt to justify a decision previously made to construct the proposed works, rather than an evaluation to determine which of many alternatives is in the public interest."[9]

Douglas, who for years continued to fret about the lake and the Kissimmee River, had little patience for the corps and the FCD. She doubted their ability to lumber into the new age, to see nature as something other than an object to control and develop, or to admit error in their ways. As for the engineers themselves, she pitied them. Though she thought they were well-meaning and decent people—"They don't beat their wives"—she came to refer to them in Freudian terms, as emotionally arrested men acting out childhood frustrations from when their mothers forbade them to play in the mud. She once told a Miami audience, "When you fly over Florida you see the curving lines of our coast, the old meanders, the waterways and lakes, but wherever you see a straight line, whoosh from horizon to horizon, the Corps of Engineers has been there."[10]

Still, like her friend, Joe Browder, she thought that the vices of army engineers were too easily exaggerated. The corps was only doing what it was supposed to do; its public-works projects were dictated by powerful political interests served by groveling politicians. Said Nathaniel Reed of the engineers, "They were not evil. They were extraordinarily ignorant," though they were also "extraordinarily trained" in a field devoid of ecological realities. Reed was charitable in his public statements, but in a private exchange with Browder, he sent a copy of the satirical *Harvard Lampoon*, which had mocked up an issue of *ACE Comics* featuring Sergeant Silt in "Ordeal at Okeechobee." Atop heavily armored earth-moving equipment and equipped with military-issue, alligator-ripping chainsaws, he and his corps platoon were duty bound to "keepin' our country straight and flat and free!" The *Lampoon*'s satire was in keeping with the less charitable interpretations of Harold Ickes and William O. Douglas, who said that the corps ran its projects through Congress like it ran bulldozers across the countryside. The state of the environment in 1970s Florida suggested that none of these interpretations was wrong.[11]

When speaking about the Everglades, Douglas preferred the word *repair* to *restoration*. The term came from Art Marshall, and with it she turned her speeches into minicourses in ecology. The new federal requirement for environmental impact statements created a heightened demand for ecologists in the public arena. Consulting firms, businesses, and utility companies indeed lured a growing number of ecologists with handsome salaries and grants. Environmental organizations quickly learned the value of appointing them to their staffs or boards. Many were simply public-interest minded individuals, caught in the infectious swell of social activism of the 1960s and 1970s. In 1976, Notre Dame biologist Robert P. McIntosh observed, "The essence of the modern environmental movement is that it is now clear at all levels of human concern—scientific, sociopolitical, and religious—that man's fate, on earth at least, is intimately and ultimately integrated with the natural and managed ecosystems of the earth, their biogeochemical processes, nutrient cycling, transformation of energy, and productive capacity."[12]

Marshall was a member of a vigorous community of politically minded Florida scientists who reached this conclusion sometime earlier. Douglas's circle of activist colleagues included many people, but on the subject of the wet South Florida environment, she went to him most. "Art," said Browder, "was just a miracle." Others might do the organizing, but Marshall educated the activists and the policymakers. During the jetport affair, when he was still with the U.S. Wildlife Service, he showed environmentalists how to "use the federal process to force greater exposure and more deliberation about federally funded projects." "He was to the environment what Einstein was to mathematics," said Jones. Marshall was annoyed by the "bureaucratization of science," the commissioning of useful empirical data that is never put to use. The government had been generous in funding studies to assess the ecological plight of the Everglades, he wrote to Reed, but all the research in the world was worthless if it was not incorporated into policy. Marshall wanted the studies to stop and the repairs to begin.[13]

Douglas fully agreed that Florida needed to point itself down the road historically less traveled. "She admired Art enormously," said Marshall's assistant at the University of Miami, Susan Wilson. "She was always searching, trying to get answers to her questions. . . . The man was a giant, as Marjory recognized, and, of course, the admiration was mutual." At a West Palm Beach meeting with several environmental organizations in the fall of 1975, when Douglas was eighty-five and still running Friends, the two founded WATER! A Coalition of Citizens Concerned with Florida's Water Resources. Douglas conceived the name, its capital letters and exclamation point a symbol of the modern, post–Earth Day movement. Fifteen groups formed the WATER! coalition, including the Florida Wildlife Federation; the Airboat, Halftrack and Conservation Club; Florida Defenders of the Environment; chapters of the Audubon Society and Izaak Walton League; and the West Palm Beach Garden Club. Marshall took the position of program chair, and Douglas headed the organization, disseminated educational information, and generated publicity, which usually required nothing more than a public appearance.[14]

The coalition quickly generated attention. State attorney general Robert Shevin attended as a special guest at WATER!'s second general meeting, held in February 1976 at the old Everglades Experiment Station in Belle Glade, within striking distance of various corps flood-control projects, a roadside alligator farm and attraction, and sugarcane fields, which the group toured. Two quick and important victories followed. At the top of the group's agenda was planning strategy for pushing for the implementation of the 1972 law authorizing the state's five water-management districts. Implementation had languished under the weight of confusing bureaucracy and the lack of revenue. Despite its many critics, the imperious FCD had preserved its reign. But before the end of 1975, it was replaced by the South Florida Water Management District. Not surprisingly, Douglas ultimately had run-ins with the new district, but for the time being, progress seemed to be in the offing. In 1979, the EPA used a provision in the Safe Drinking Water Act to designate the Biscayne Aquifer as a sole-source aquifer, meaning one that supplied at least 50 percent of the drinking water to the region's human population. Friends of the Everglades communication director Joe Podgor spearheaded the campaign for the designation, which gave the EPA the authority to determine whether federally funded projects for the Everglades area would damage the aquifer. What had previously been considered a useless wasteland, announced the *New York Times,* was now a "prime resource." These events were essential to the development of South Florida's first sensible water-management policy, which would enable the repair of the Everglades ecosystem—precisely the new coalition's goal.[15]

Douglas knew as well as anyone that WATER! would have been nothing without science. Embodied in the organization's name was the formula for the Everglades' restored health, which was articulated in Marshall's "rain-machine" thesis. Marshall was a big-systems scientist, a "Gaia
theorist," as Browder remembered, who conceived the earth as a single
living organism. Marshall wrote to Reed that the "first dictum of ecology
[is] that we cannot do merely one thing." He referred to both destruction
and repair, for every one thing was tethered to every other thing that constituted the organism, whether that organism was the globe or the Everglades. Water connected the Everglades to the rest of the world, connected
the usually conceptually disconnected urban and rural environments. The
unrelenting city landscape had plainly stressed the Everglades, but few
people considered the full reality of how the altered hinterland affected
urban life. Marshall attributed South Florida's extraordinary droughts
and microclimatic changes to decreased evaporation resulting from the
50 percent loss in wetlands. Rain was needed to restock the groundwater,
which recharged the Biscayne Aquifer, which filled the water glasses in
the city and sprinkled sodded lawns. This was only half the cycle. The
persistence of bloated gray clouds shedding an adequate measure of rain
every year depended on evapotranspiration from the surface water—the
Everglades' gentle sheet flow.[16]

Scientists debated the legitimacy of the second part of Marshall's equation, although the long drought of the 1960s and the other in 1970–71
seemed to sustain his rain-machine thesis. So too did the National Oceanic and Atmospheric Administration. At the time, it was in the middle
of a five-year experiment with weather modification in South Florida,
trying to draw rain on demand by seeding clouds with particles of silver iodide. The experiment suggested that scientists could develop technology to fix a problem that, from Marshall's and Douglas's perspective,
flood-control technology had created. In a Friends publication, Douglas and Marshall reduced the problem to basics and pulled the rug from
under the presumptive superiority of technology: "Management of water
in the Everglades . . . has converted it from the solar-driven system it was
to a highly intensive fossil-fuel system. This exchange drastically displaces

the solar-driven processes which produce wetland vegetation, peat and muck, potable water, fish, and wildlife. The prime means through which solar energy activated the system to produce those essential resources was sheet flow—an essential function which has largely been lost." Recapturing the sheet flow, they believed, would require removing the intensive fossil-fuel system.[17]

Douglas was a slavish devotee of the rain-machine thesis. She worked it into her speeches and press interviews, proclaiming, "Whether you're a developer or environmentalist, the message is the same: if the Everglades go, then South Florida becomes a desert." Wordsmith and former publisher that she was, she knew how print communicated authority to a concept, particularly when that concept carried the imprimatur of experts. At her direction, Friends published a sixty-three-page booklet, *Who Knows the Rain? Nature and Origin of Rainfall in South Florida,* in 1982. It was another "battle" book for the region, the first in Friends' new South Florida Regional Studies Series. The lead author, Leonard Pardue, was a retired U.S. Weather Service meteorologist who had served as the main scientific adviser for Douglas's hurricane book. He and his coauthors neatly concluded that replacing wetland with dry land and concrete would bring "lowered water levels in coastal aquifers, salt water intrusion, increased heat island size, and tendency toward desert formation."[18]

Their scientific prophecy was not entirely new. In *River of Grass,* Douglas had observed that the local climate was a "question of the ratio between the temperature and the rainfall and the evaporation." And she apparently unwittingly recalled the foretelling, if lonely, claim advanced by her father and an engineer acquaintance in 1906: draining the Everglades would render climate changes that South Florida would ultimately regret.[19]

The rain-machine thesis lay at the heart of what environmentalists were calling the Marshall Plan. Twenty years of watching the breakdown of the healthy ecology of the Everglades went into Marshall's eighteen-point blueprint for the repair of the Everglades. First, he argued, bureaucrats needed to recognize the "physical and functional limits to the resources of the Everglades." He wanted several canals closed off, most of the spill water diverted away from the Gulf of Mexico and Atlantic Ocean, and hydrology restored to certain drained lands, steps that would regenerate muck, indigenous vegetation, and wildlife habitat. He highlighted the need to clean up the lakes of the Kissimmee River basin and to restore the original sheet flow down to the big lake, on to the sloughs and sawgrass marshes, across and back from the Big Cypress, beneath Alligator Alley and Tamiami Trail, through the park, and out to brackish mangrove country—unimpeded, free, and natural. The key element to repairing the Everglades, to make them natural again, was the restoration of the Kissimmee River. "The river is still there," Marshall wrote to Douglas after flying over the embargoed oxbows. "It's the water that's been taken away."[20]

The debate over the river originated at the outset of the channelization project. Before the Army Corps of Engineers ladled up the last of the channel muck in 1971, Marshall was sitting in front of the Florida cabinet demanding restoration. He convinced Askew that as long as a "ditch we didn't want" existed, so would South Florida's water problems, in all their manifold forms. The legislature responded to four years of public debates, as well as to the weighty lobbying of Johnny Jones, by passing the Kissimmee River Restoration Act in 1976. Here, at last, said Marshall, whose fingerprints were all over the legislation, "was man's chance to unshackle Mother Nature from human bondage." The act created the Kissimmee River Coordinating Council, a group of scientists charged with creating the blueprints for a workable restoration plan, which would include redeeming the river and buying back land in the old floodplain. The often depressive Marshall was feeling optimistic for a change. "We're on the road, Marjory," he wrote to his friend. "Not only for the Kissimmee, but for Lake Okeechobee and restoring the River of Grass."[21]

Douglas was on that road with Marshall all the way, a soul mate on a shared philosophical and political journey. In Marshall she saw what she had seen in the "indefatigable" Ernest Coe. "It takes someone like him who can stand all kinds of misfortune," she said, "because the idea he's got is such a truly great one." That idea resonated with Douglas's observations in *River of Grass,* and it emerged in the mission statement of the Friends of the Everglades: "To protect, restore, and preserve the Greater Kissimmee-Okeechobee-Everglades Ecosystem, and the water that is the lifeblood of the world's only Everglades." "You've given us a great job to do," Douglas wrote to Marshall when he first began articulating his plan. The credence she gave his ideas received confirmation from a trusted friend and adviser, Garald Parker, who fully endorsed the Marshall Plan.[22]

No one should have been surprised that the road to restoration proved more tortuous than the original river itself. The 1976 legislation translated into little more than additional scientific study and years of delay. Both Marshall and Douglas grew impatient for the movement of dirt and the shifting back of water. "We've been working hard for Kissimmee River restoration," Douglas updated Browder in Washington in a 1977 letter, "foiled somewhat by agriculture, cattle & sugar but going on from what I believe is a good position."[23]

She might have added the South Florida Water Management District (SFWMD) to the list of obstacles. The new agency adopted as a motto "Preserving the Everglades since 1949," but over that time, water managers had permitted the loss of nearly half the Everglades. Douglas and Marshall repeatedly appeared before nature's self-proclaimed protector asking for a commitment to action. Nathaniel Reed became a member of the district's governing board in 1978, and Douglas appreciated the environmental sympathies he brought to the body. But she saw him, as she did Marshall when he was a member of the flood-control board, as "helpless." It was obvious to her that the new agency retained an old flood-control mentality that stifled any gestures toward reform. The district's executive director, John R. "Jack" Maloy, talked reform but seemed to practice tradition. He had begun with the district in 1965 and came under the influence of its chief engineer, William V. Storch, the man responsible for piecing together the complex replumbing system. Storch eventually realized that his project had some unintended negative consequences. He began to fret over the masses of new arrivals inundating coastal cities and invited by his project. In 1968, he wrote a book on the environmental effects of drainage on the region, and by the 1970s he had begun arguing that water availability should be perceived as a measure for limiting rather than promoting growth. This was Marshall's kind of logic, and at times he quoted the engineer in statements to the district's governing board. Maloy echoed his mentor—for example, when criticizing the "chamber-of-commerce mentality" "that bigger is better, regardless of the consequence." Yet Maloy sent anything but a discouraging message to growth merchants when he made such observations as "People are number one—the public water supplies safety from floods." He was a "true believer" in his water-management system and in resource management generally. That mistakes had been made with the Kissimmee were apparent, but he was not willing to let the river go free again. He resolved to "modify the way we operate: raise the water level to flood more marsh and fluctuate the levels to approximate natural conditions."[24]

Whenever he made such a remark, whenever he seemed to be talking as if he were Mother Nature herself in command of the elements, Maloy's detractors shook their heads. Some observers believed that an imprudent disconnect remained between the district and ecological science despite Maloy's occasional use of the word *ecology.* Jones certainly thought so. At one point he publicly censured the district's "damn" board of governors as "devils" and "whores for the sugar daddies"—the corporate sugar growers around Lake Okeechobee. Douglas's commentary was cruel if less aggressive: "You'd think a child of 8 could do better planning." She found Maloy to be disapproving, unreasonable, and hopelessly loyal to relic policies. In the foreword to *Who Knows the Rain?* she claimed the transition from the FCD to the water management district yielded the "same complete power over water control and no improvement in the policy of water conservation." Although a loyal Askew supporter, she hoped a new governor would replace Maloy and the recalcitrant board members with acceptable appointees. "Meanwhile," she wrote Marshall, Maloy and gang were "up to more mischief."[25]

That mischief included, among other things, back pumping dirty water into Lake Okeechobee. The Army Corps of Engineers had gone ahead with that disquieting plan even as it was talking about Kissimmee River's restoration. Environmentalists insisted that the corps stop back pumping. The SFWMD would need to direct the corps to end the practice, but the district refused to do so despite repeated requests from

Douglas and others. Douglas traveled to Tallahassee to meet with the head of the Department of Environmental Regulation (DER), to whom the water-management district answered, but got nowhere. Douglas and others were already fighting DER chief Jay Landers over the state's proposal to open up the Big Cypress to additional oil exploration. In the fall of 1977, after securing the pro bono services of a high-powered Miami law firm, Friends joined with the Florida Wildlife Federation in a suit against the DER, the SFWMD, and the Florida Sugar Cane League in which the plaintiffs asked for an "immediate halt" to the back pumping.[26]

Naming the Sugar Cane League in the suit made legal sense; it also had a strategic benefit. Environmentalists argued that sugar growers, ensconced in their vast property holdings wrapping the northern and western sides of the lake, used Okeechobee water to irrigate their fields and the lake for dumping their nutrient-enriched excess water. Identifying the Sugar Cane League with the DER and SFWMD also lumped the three entities on the defensive, painting the not-so-unrealistic picture of the state and agriculture as happy consorts. The defendants denied the existence of any special relationship, but the plaintiffs were sure that when it came to water use, the state turned on agriculture's every move. Such also seemed to be the case when hearings began in late spring 1979. The sugar industry resented being singled out as a polluter, and the water-management district and the DER took sugar's side. All three maintained that the scientific data were insufficient to show any harmful effects of back pumping. Jones and Douglas would have found that claim laughable were it not so egregious. The environmental groups' lawyers accused the opposition of stonewalling and presented reams of conclusive data from numerous scientific studies, some of which had been conducted by the district itself. But to no avail.[27]

The case came before the state Division of Administrative Hearings. One month into the proceedings, the hearing officer, Michael R. N. McDonnell, disclosed that he was a close friend of Landers and the chair of SFWMD board, Robert Clark. It was a jaw-dropping revelation. The environmentalists' petition requesting that McDonnell step down brought no relief, and defeat was beginning to take on the same perceptible smell of the water they wanted cleaned up. After McDonnell issued the Final Order, one of the plaintiff's attorneys wrote to Douglas acknowledging their loss, though in good lawyerly fashion he mitigated the extent of it. The DER and SFWMD won their request for a thirty-month study free of any mandate to stop the back pumping. Yet the judge's final order contained some favorable points for the plaintiffs. The hearing officer conceded that the lake was in a "eutrophic state," that it was getting worse, and that the situation was the product of "man's activities." The forces of temporizing could no longer deny the ecological trauma of back pumping.[28]

Throughout the conflict, Douglas, Jones, and Marshall never diverted their attention from the other source of trouble, c-38. They all continued meeting with the water-management board and making long trips to Tallahassee to talk to law- and policymakers, submitting one resolution after another, all signed by virtually every Florida environmental organization and every South Florida sporting group. Much like Marshall, Douglas had at one point been optimistic about positive change. "I've seen the ruin," she told a *Miami Herald* reporter, "but now I see hope for restoration." Yet hope was ebbing. Since the passage of the 1976 Restoration Act, the calendar had shifted to a new decade and no real action had been taken toward dechannelizing the Kissimmee. The SFWMD estimated the costs for reopening the oxbows, backfilling the canal, and buying back the private land on the floodplain at more than thirty-two million dollars. A *Herald* reporter was apparently unprepared for Douglas's sharp retort when that expense was raised as a reason to retain c-38: "Cost? Oh, my dear girl, the costs wouldn't be so great as the expense of allowing an increase of pollution in our fresh water. The costs of not doing it are monumental." Giving up on Tallahassee, Friends and several partner organizations petitioned Congress and the president. But still no one was willing to confront the monetary burden.[29]

By the spring of 1982, when Douglas had the occasion to visit Marshall at his woodsy family home in Interlachen, the two were running out of options. Marshall had long since left his position at the University of Miami. Not much of a fund-raiser, he had not been able to keep the Division of Applied Ecology going. He began teaching as an adjunct professor at the University of Florida, commuting to Gainesville with a single bumper sticker on his car: "Repair the Everglades." He also served on the St. Johns River Water Management District's board of governors in Jacksonville, sitting as president for a year. Money was tight, and Marshall could not afford the expense of frequent trips to South Florida, so he and Douglas communicated via the mail or in person whenever she could visit him. Interlachen was a 350-mile drive from Miami, in the heart of Putnam County, logging country not far from where Martin Tabert had been killed six decades earlier. Douglas walked into Marshall's house that spring and joined a gathering of like-minded folks. To virtually everyone there, according to Al Burt, a friend who lived not far away on a beloved slice of scrubland, she exuded the "style of a grand woman." She took a seat in an armchair with a glass of scotch in her hand and sparred genteelly with a man who sat on a stool in front of her. Marshall had an idea for a new strategy. He was half serious but tempted, and Douglas turned to him to play along. They thought Kissimmee restoration might get a new level of attention if she were to put on her red hat, which people called her fighting hat, go out to the edge of c-38, and start shoveling dirt into the canal. Someone thought she might be breaking a law—civil disobedience, all the better. "I love it," she exclaimed, coming up out of her chair. "I love it."[30]

Grande Dame

For fellow concerned citizens, Douglas developed an efficient six-point strategy on "how you can protect the environment." A few points were standard fare: "Join a local environmental society"; "Call a few neighbors and friends to form a group to study the legislation of city, country, state and federal laws"; and "Do what you would do best to help your group." Others were classic Douglas: "Know your region. . . . Whether a native or a newcomer, you will be fascinated to learn about your unique region, its rivers, lakes, coasts, roads, cities; its climate, soil, plants and animals"; "Speak up. Learn to talk clearly and forcefully in public. Speak simply and not too long at a time . . . always from sound preparation and knowledge. Be a nuisance where it counts, but don't be a bore at any time"; and "Be depressed, discouraged, and disappointed at failures and disheartening effects of ignorance, greed, corruption and bad politics—but never give up."[1]

By the 1980s, Douglas had taken on an activist persona that for the most part complied with her recommendations. It remained with her for the rest of her life and even outlived her. The media, her followers, her opponents, and political opportunists had helped to create that persona, as did Douglas. "She

deals in very tangible action," Governor Bob Graham said, "whether environmental, scientific or political, but she also understands that there
has to be a sense of magic, that people have to be inspired to what is bigger than themselves, longer than their lifetime." The magic began with
the inspiring unwearied vitality—manifested in her voice, posture, and
enlightened mind—of one who lived the longest life. "Of course I don't
get tired of it," she said at age ninety-five of her full-time effort. "I don't
get tired of breathing either." The public looked to her as the scion of a
family of Everglades experts and as Florida history itself, and she in turn
presented herself as less the demure grandmotherly type who dispenses
ancient folk wisdom than as the unreserved grande dame who took her
energy and sophisticated knowledge into the streets. The hat, pearls, and
thick glasses were all part of the persona. They were a reminder of who
she was, what she was capable of, and what she was representing.[2]

They also helped her willfully exploit whatever special status society
granted to a woman well into her senior years. She thought it ridicu-
lous that age alone could bestow authority. On April 7, 1985, both the
state legislature and the cabinet opened their sessions by recognizing
Marjory Stoneman Douglas's birthday. In response, the *Miami Herald*,
which editorially had grown less supportive of environmental initiatives,
said she "deserved it," clarifying that she "wasn't honored for her longevity." Instead "this diminutive woman" was honored for defending Florida's natural landscapes, thinking toward the future, and for the "iron will
she evinced in her battles." If she were going to be honored, that is exactly
what she wanted.[3]

But as long as age did serve as an asset, she would take advantage
of it. Her seniority, status as a woman, and even frailties became tools
with which to accomplish her ends. In ways that a younger person could
not, she could be cantankerous, opinionated, and critical and still be effective. "They can't be rude to me," she told *Time* magazine during the
back-pumping struggle. "I have all this white hair. I take advantage of
everything I can—age, hair, disability—because my cause is just." In her
personal life, too, she was clever about such things. "I've caught on to
this thing about a wheelchair in airports," she confessed to friends. "They

put you through ahead of everybody, get you a taxi and you're off to the hotel with no trouble at all." When lobbying in Tallahassee, a wheelchair also enabled her, with the help of a companion, to dart easily from place to place and person to person, making her case for cleaning up Lake Okeechobee and restoring the Kissimmee River. Her hearing had started deteriorating at about the same time as her sight, but she let neither interfere with her work. "No matter how poor my eyes are I can still talk," she once clarified. "I'll talk about the Everglades at the drop of a hat. Whoever wants me to talk, I'll come over and tell them about the necessity of preserving the Everglades. Sometimes I tell them more than they wanted to know." She learned when speaking before various boards and assemblies that her hearing aids, combined with all the other courtesies accorded her geriatric status, assured a gentlemanly decorum that allowed her to extend her comments beyond the specified time limit (in violation of her dictum about being concise). Even when she was politely asked to stop, she simply feigned deafness and continued. "Marjory never ever really cared about time," said Joe Podgor. "She knew that she had things to say, and when she got them all said, then she was done." Once done, she usually had impact. "Marjory has stage presence," said James Hartwell. "I look at the expression on the faces of decision makers. She grabs them." In a rare moment of self-criticism, Jack Maloy said, "Mrs. Douglas has had a great effect on people like me. We've closed the gap between how far out in front she is and how far behind I am."[4]

Douglas would have disagreed with the water-management director over how far that gap had been closed. The stubborn decision makers, the fixed bureaucracies, and the defeats never immobilized her, though. Shuffled off into the past were those things that had set her back—the complicated and enervating family and love relationships, the publication deadlines, and the "nerve fatigue." Old age liberated her, and environmental work energized her. "I'm doing what I want to do," she said. "I'm having a marvelous time." When she began stumping around the Lake Okeechobee region at ninety-four to drum up support against a proposed new coal-fired power plant in the Kissimmee River basin southeast of Orlando, a campaign she ultimately lost, she said, "I got a new lease on life just learning about the damn thing. One way to stay alive is to get good and mad now and then." An admirer at the time thought of her as the "soul of youth." Flattered, she might have thought about how she was unlike women activists from her early days, those who accepted social conformity and their husbands' hegemony as rules, and how she was more like those of the new era: "I think that, primarily, I'm an individual. . . . I think I'm something of my own, but I couldn't characterize it. I'm not a conformist. . . . Frankly, I'm a pretty modern woman. My thinking is up to date. In fact, in some ways, I'm ahead of some people."[5]

She had recently showed her provident thinking and senior prowess at a county commission meeting. Out in western Dade County were the East Everglades, promoted as part of South Florida's "expanding frontier of industry," as the "path of progress" in terms of roads, housing developments, shopping centers, and the Aerojet Corporation. A hopeful but ultimately rejected National Air and Space Administration subcontractor, Aerojet bought twenty-five thousand acres from the state in the early 1960s for an average of $125 an acre. The company had long ago shut down its operations, but it was proposing to start up again to manufacture rocket boosters. Not far away, vegetable farmers tilled thousands of drained acres at the edge of the Shark River, a principal coronary artery of the Everglades, and claimed that their muck-grown tomatoes had no equal. Home builders had invaded the area, too, and ten thousand people now lived not far from Miami's main drinking-water wells. Developers even built houses on the west side—the *wet* side—of the Army Corps of Engineers' flood-control levee and wanted to expand further. The environmental-protection and development guidelines adopted by the Metro commission in 1975 and championed by James Redford's Committee for Sane Growth were supposed to prevent this kind of sprawl. Yet from one end of Douglas's life to the other, land was still being sold by the gallon. Another holdover from the earlier era was her attitude toward developers. She complained, "The way they come around and tell lies and blackguard people, you'd think they were dying of starvation and that their only hope of getting a square meal was doing that." If there was no logic in people living and laboring where flooding was so common, no logic was needed; the government often met cries for relief with a solicitous response. Douglas and others arranged meetings with the South Florida Water Management District (SFWMD) and with the governor and cabinet, and she registered "loud" and "violent" protests about East Everglades development and government policy.[6]

She was in this feisty mood when she entered a high school auditorium commandeered to accommodate the crowd at a county commission meeting. To the several hundred landowners, gathered from an East Everglades community that owed its existence to levees and drainage canals, Douglas was the "anti-Christ," a sentimental environmentalist who was willing to trade people's livelihoods and homes for the protection of reptiles and birds. "Go back to Russia, granny," someone shouted when her time came to speak, late in the evening, after everyone else had spoken. Thronged by boos and jeers, she made her way undiminished down the center aisle. She was seeking to persuade the commissioners to limit construction on 155,000 acres of privately held land "of critical environmental concern." After pulling the microphone down to her level, she waited for a break in the escalating noise. "You damn butterfly chaser," came a voice from above the din. Finally, she said, "Look. I'm an old lady. I've been here since eight o'clock. It's now eleven. I've got all night, and I'm used to the heat." In the end, the commissioners voted with the environmentalists, though the struggle over the East Everglades was not over.[7]

One newspaper reporter called Douglas "one of Florida's natural resources" for her willingness to take on such rough-and-tumble fights, some of which took her outside the Everglades cause. Whenever the opportunity arose, she spoke out against nuclear power plants: "I say forget fission when you can get fusion." Alarmed local residents asked her to assist when a developer petitioned to rezone Fort George Island, between Jacksonville and Fernandina, to build condominium towers. She convinced the governor to help protect the "island of great historic and environmental value," and then she caught a plane up the long coast of the peninsula to attend a hearing on the issue, which was settled in favor of preservation. Not long thereafter, when Juanita Greene procured a booklet, published by the Sea Grant College at the University of Florida, on salt-tolerant landscape plants that recommended the melaleuca tree and the Australian pine, whose root mass disrupted sea turtle nesting habits, she immediately showed it to Douglas. "Someone like you needs to give [the publisher] a good dressing down," Greene said. Douglas soon extracted a promise from the college to remove the offending plants from future editions of the booklet. She also stepped forward to assist her friends Marjorie and Archie Carr in Florida Defenders of the Environment's successful effort to gain state regulation requiring turtle-excluding devices on fishing trawlers, whose nets were drowning hundreds of green, loggerhead, and Ridley turtles, all recognized as either endangered or threatened species. Closer to home, she lobbied Broward County and Fort Lauderdale officials to establish a gopher tortoise preserve, which they did. She also put the forces of Friends of the Everglades behind a campaign for a stronger tree ordinance in Dade County, where development, having for so long run roughshod over the landscape, had left only 10 percent of the area covered by green shade.[8]

Douglas remained committed to her environmentalist's dictum to "study" and "act intelligently when the appropriate opportunity arises" rather than to "act too quickly." When challenged, she always had the facts to support her argument. She had a ready repository of experts at her disposal, but she realized that not all public-minded citizens had that advantage. Believing that it was important to keep the general public abreast of various environmental issues and initiatives, such as the back-pumping controversy, she did so in part with the *Everglades Reporter,* which contained copy written by her, Art Marshall, Johnny Jones, and other members of Friends. At her request, a group of retired schoolteachers living in a Miami condominium complex volunteered to address, fold, and mail the quarterly publication. Friends also distributed environmental literature to thirty college and public libraries. To coordinate all of these activities, the Environmental Information Service was established as an appendage of Friends. Launched by Podgor in 1978, the service was also intended to show citizens and citizen groups how to "'wade' through the bureaucratic maze" of local government to access public information about zoning, planning, and environmental problems. The task could be daunting, but it was necessary when going up against an opposition with a team of experienced, well-paid experts and lawyers.[9]

One way to stop or slow them down, Douglas learned, was to invoke the legal requirement of an environmental impact statement. She believed that science was invariably on her side, and an environmental impact statement marshaled the data with which the other side had to contend. The statements also bought time while activists gathered force. She was blatant about this strategy. In a letter to the editor of the *Florida Times-Union* written during the Fort George Island controversy, she told readers "to insist that an environmental impact study should be made. That would give us time to see that Fort George Island is put on the National Register of Historic Places." To limit development and groundwater contamination around a new regional airport in Fort Myers and to save hammock area from a parking lot in the John D. MacArthur Beach State Park in Palm Beach County, she pestered the governor and his staff for ecological studies. She followed the earlier scrutinizing gaze of Philip Wylie, Polly Redford, and many others to Biscayne Bay when she argued that a poorly located landfill was leeching toxic substances, including hospital surgical waste, that caused fish kills. Friends and the Izaak Walton League obtained a ten-thousand-dollar grant from the ever-generous Herbert Hoover Jr. to conduct a series of toxic-substance studies, which the Environmental Information Service published. Biscayne Bay, Douglas said at the time, was the "coast of the Everglades."[10]

Wherever else she ventured in the larger movement, nothing distracted her from the besieged River of Grass. Not long after President Nixon pulled the funding from the jetport, the SFWMD deemed the favored alternative location, Site 14, as too environmentally sensitive for development. Growth merchants and the Dade County Port Authority, having rejected the alternative sites, began making serious noise about reopening the Everglades site, doing so with such frequency that Joe Browder and Douglas felt like they were being forced to watch a terrible movie that kept coming back to the theaters. With each exasperating return, they had to write another review, he from Washington and she from Coconut Grove, explaining once again why the plot was so bad. During the nation's oil crisis in the 1970s, drilling in the Big Cypress was another vexing issue. Although the enterprise was protected in the legislation establishing the preserve, she and Marshall repeatedly attempted in vain to stop it. In 1976, she told the Florida cabinet, "More and more we feel we are losing so much of our original Florida to the Big Interests. . . . The oil they find in Florida will not solve any of the country's fuel problems. The state's million barrels of oil is only a spit in the ocean." She insisted that airboats, swamp buggies, and hunting also were unsuitable for a protected wilderness. But she never moved policymakers to break a promise to those who had put political muscle behind the preserve.[11]

While a tortoise pace exceeded that of the state's restoration initiative, other signs indicated increasing global recognition of the Everglades. On April 6, 1982, the day before her ninety-second birthday, the National Park Service hosted a ceremony celebrating Everglades National Park and its rarified environs as a World Heritage Site and an International Biosphere Reserve, an exceptional combination of designations given by the United Nations Education, Scientific, and Cultural Organization (UNESCO). Invited to speak, Douglas was the "star" of the event according to a National Park Service publication. Park superintendent John Morehead presented her with a bouquet of birthday flowers. The authors of the Department of the Interior's World Heritage nomination report, submitted to UNESCO in 1979, had consulted several scientific books on the Everglades but had clearly relied most heavily on factual information in *River of Grass* and borrowed only Douglas's "poetic utterances." "They are, they have always been, one of the unique regions of the earth," the report repeated from the book's opening and best-known section, ending the quoted passage a page later with, "It is a 'River of Grass.'" She told the sun-drenched audience about what the Everglades had been, what they had come to be, and what they should be. Her words were the model of "eloquence," though they were also "stinging." She concluded with a hopeful observation about the science of ecological restoration: "It would be the first time, perhaps, in the United States of America that a region that has almost gone to complete ruin has been brought back by the understanding and technical wisdom of its citizens."[12]

Except for Douglas and Buffalo Tiger, only government officials sat on the speakers' platform. None of the officials could claim to have exerted themselves to turn the tide back for the Everglades. Douglas's active involvement hardly exceeded that of some who had not been invited—Marshall, Browder, Jones, and Nat Reed. And still the public eye trained on her more often than on anyone else. It seemed that minds could not separate Everglades history and nature and their unfolding vista and ecological challenges from the elderly "crusader." Combined with her almost incomprehensibly long life and undiminished vigor, that crusader image suggested something messianic about her connection to the Everglades, a walk-on-water affirmation for everything she said or did in connection to them. Perhaps not coincidentally, newspaper photographers often squatted low before the small woman to take their shots, looking upward, preferably with the sunlight illuminating her hat's broad brim for a halo effect. Here was the apotheosis of Marjory Stoneman Douglas. If not divine, she had become in the public eye one among the select whom she had once identified as possessing a mortal wisdom that prevailed from the earth—"farmers and naturalists and shrewd old women who have borne many children." The national and local press contrived an endless list of pithy Everglades appellations for her: "Our Lady of the Glades," "Guardian of the Glades' Spirit," "First Lady of the Everglades," "Empress of the Everglades," "Everglades Evangelist," "Grande Dame of the Everglades."

Now and then, the press would try to make the citified nature lover more like those who appreciated the Everglades from the buggy inside out. When that happened, protective friends worried that she was being turned into a caricature. On one such occasion, when she was ninety-three, she was invited out to the Everglades for a ride in a hand-hewn canoe with a Miccosukee Indian. Douglas, conceivably thinking of the valuable exposure for her cause, was excited enough to wear a pair of blue alpaca slacks she had often worn when researching her book. "This is reinforcing old relations with the Everglades," she said after the canoe ride. "It was wonderful getting out into the open with the wind coming all the way from one horizon to another." But the candor of Juanita Greene, who covered the event for the *Herald*, revealed the lengths to which the event had been staged. As people gathered for the launch, someone spotted a pygmy rattler and, wrote Greene, "quickly bashed and tossed [it] into the Glades." The canoe ride took place in shin-deep water behind the gift shop of the Miccosukee Cultural Center on Tamiami Trail, and the canoe was not hand carved by Miccosukees, who preferred airboats and swamp buggies, but imported from Panama. The ride lasted no longer than it took her escort, Eefalahatchee, to use a hardware-store pole to push the canoe out fifty feet and back; the craft itself was twenty feet long. According to Podgor, who drove Douglas to the photo shoot, the canoe mostly remained lodged in the muck so the nonagenarian could be easily lifted in and out.[13]

Another boat ride eight years earlier had brought Douglas together with Podgor, who became her faithful companion, escort, and intellectual confrere. Podgor had grown up in Miami Springs with a love for fishing in and around the Miami River. After graduating from the University of Pennsylvania, where he majored in English literature, and returning home in 1970, he discovered polluted water at an old fishing spot on one of the river's intermediary canals, an early rib of the Broward drainage system. There was also the "smell of rancid barbecue on a wrong-way wind that produced a noxious experience for the people on the west side of town." Podgor began investigating. The polluter was remarkably like the one Frank Stoneman had discovered fouling the Miami River in the 1910s, a plant rendering animal by-products. Complaints to city hall got Podgor nowhere. So to bring attention to the problem, he organized the Miami River Regatta, which became an annual, three-day affair that included canoe races, a fishing contest, ecoclinics, and food booths to raise money for charity. The main event on opening day was a nighttime river parade with a grand marshal and beauty queen. In 1975, Podgor decided to scrap beauty for something or someone of more substance. He knew Michael Chenoweth, the first member of Friends, and asked to be introduced to Douglas. Podgor was a little awed, "as if I was talking to Queen Elizabeth," when they met. He explained that he was looking for a parade dignitary who personified the cause for clean and plentiful water. "Can I paddle my own canoe?" Douglas responded.[14]

It was the beginning of a fruitful relationship. Podgor joined Friends and took part-time jobs so he could throw himself into the organization's work. He was instrumental in getting the Environmental Protection Agency to designate the Biscayne Aquifer a sole drinking-water source and the Everglades its watershed. He also set up the Environmental Information Service, and he spent hours talking to his new best friend about literature, ecology, and politics. Whatever his accomplishments and however close he and Douglas became, he never got over the feeling of being "starstruck" in her presence. "She had an extremely healthy, maybe even an overactive, distrust of authority," Podgor remembered. "She wanted to tell the truth straight in a person's face and be done with it because that's the best policy. She didn't pull her punches, publicly or otherwise. . . . That was Marjory's way. She endorsed and encouraged it, and you felt good at the end of the day when you went out yelling the truth at the tree-tops and had this living legend backing you up, holding you on her shoulders. You couldn't lose even if you did lose. . . . With Marjory, you didn't care because it wasn't so much whether you got there. It was whether you got there right."[15]

Another person with whom on occasion she got there was someone she met at the regatta. Sitting on the boat with her as grand marshal was State Senator Bob Graham. After the river parade, both made speeches about water and pollution, his strained and inelegant, hers just the opposite. Afterward, gay festival music backdropped a riverside stroll as they chatted about Florida and the area's early settlers, including his parents, whom Douglas knew. Graham was a nine-year veteran of the state legislature who had earned his environmentalist stripes when the property-rights evangelical put a bounty on his head along with those of Browder, Reed, and Henry Jackson during the Big Cypress campaign. When Douglas met Graham, he was still referring to himself rather stiltedly as D. Robert Graham. He was naturally reserved and formal but still friendly, even engaging, and smart. He was the kind of man with whom she might become dangerously enamored, to the point of putting feelings before proper political reflection. Friends later suspected that at times she might have been more the schoolmarm with him than the admirer.[16]

Daniel Robert Graham's upbringing had offered little to encourage a future environmental reformer. He grew up twenty miles northwest of Miami in a two-story, coral-rock house on seven thousand acres. His early aural universe included lowing dairy cows. His father had moved to Florida during the boom days to grow sugar in East Everglades muck. When that venture failed, he converted to dairy farming and cattle ranching, ultimately accumulating wealth and power. Ernest "Cap" Graham remained persistently mindful of Everglades development, something he, a stern teetotaler who snarled barroom expletives, mostly supported but sometimes cursed. When engineers were building Tamiami Trail, he complained that without culverts running beneath the roadway, Everglades water would back up and flood land to the north—his land. Worried about rising drainage taxes, he was among a coterie of large landholders who challenged the Army Corps of Engineers' flood-control project. Stopping it was a virtual impossibility, but the group managed to have a greater share of the tax burden shifted to the cities. By the time his youngest son joined the legislature, agriculture in three South Florida counties was using 58 percent of South Florida's water and paying 12 percent of the taxes levied to support the Central and Southern Florida Flood Control District.[17]

The younger Graham had known the great source of that water as early as he had known any other. "What the Mississippi River was to Tom Sawyer," he always said, "the Everglades were to my childhood." From his bedroom window, the view opened out to boundless sawgrass, and from that vantage point he witnessed the environment's extremes. In times of drought, he saw black smoke trailing up into the sky from the burning vegetation and muck. In the wet season, the River of Grass was like the Mississippi before levees: it tended to flood. The Grahams lived on elevated ground. Approaching hurricanes turned their rock-sturdy house into a shelter for friends and workers, as happened during the hurricanes of 1947, when Robert was eleven. He remembered surveying the scene from the second floor after the fall storm: to the south and east as far as one could see, "it was just a sheet of water."[18]

Graham also saw the Everglades from the fiscal vantage point of the family's sugarcane, dairy, and cattle business (which included a ranch in Moore Haven on the southeast bank of Lake Okeechobee) and its interests in real estate development. After graduating from Harvard Law School in 1962, he returned to work in the family enterprises. But he was drawn to politics, predicting that he would ultimately become governor. He was elected to the State House in 1966 and then won a seat in the State Senate in 1970. He remained virtually unknown outside of South Florida when he decided to make a bid to succeed Governor Reubin Askew in 1977. To raise the candidate's profile, Graham and his chief strategist borrowed an idea from Iowa congressman Tom Harkin: one day each week, Graham spent a full shift in a different job. He taught grade school, bused tables, sailed with a shrimp trawler, repaired roofs, sold shoes, hauled garbage, picked tomatoes and oranges, and worked his way into the governor's mansion. But the expertly choreographed campaign did not assure a seamless transition into the office. His tenure as chief executive began with a thud. Detractors and disappointed supporters alike called him Governor Jell-O for his seeming inability to stand firm on an issue. He eventually shored up his leadership with initiatives in education reform and environmental protection.[19]

Despite Askew's efforts, Florida's environment was ailing. Graham inherited a state that received one thousand new residents a day. It also had turbid and shrunken bodies of water in every direction. The Environmental Protection Agency soon identified as many hazardous-waste sites in Florida as in virtually any industrial state of the North. Graham took notice. Although he came from agriculture and development, which along with population growth were the main perpetrators in the state's degradation, his environmental programs represented creative firsts, winning him a Conservationist of the Year award from the National Parks and Conservation Association.[20]

Douglas served on the association's honorary committee and was thrilled to have the award go to Graham and thrilled to have him as her governor. "He's a hot boy," she said when introducing him at an Everglades Coalition meeting and after working with him for several years. "I think he's the first governor ever to really understand the problems of the Everglades." Developments on the federal level had begun to distress her, as they did other activists. She had been optimistic about the environment staying high on the Washington agenda under President Jimmy Carter. As a presidential candidate, he publicly endorsed the Kissimmee's restoration and appointed Joe Browder as his campaign's energy and environmental coordinator, a position Browder held as adviser to the Department of the Interior after Carter's election. A scientist by training, Carter tried to educate the nation on the ecological importance of wetlands, 53 percent of which had been consumed by the spread of civilization. But by that time, wetlands, preserves, and endangered species were losing their appeal in Congress, and Carter lacked enough appeal to restore them.[21]

Progress on the environmental front slammed to a halt when his Republican successor took office. Ronald Reagan could not conceive of partnering sound environmental policy with his probusiness agenda. He eliminated Carter's tax credit for alternative energy and even removed the new solar-power system on the White House roof. His "snap judgments" about economic and environmental concerns, Douglas said, "set us back 50 years." "I don't think he gives a damn about the environment. I don't think he gives a damn about national parks. In other words, I don't appreciate Mr. Reagan." His first interior secretary, James Watt, parceled out the country's natural heritage to the barons of oil and gas, timber, and mining. He was a bold-faced born-again Christian who openly endorsed the scriptural instruction to subdue the earth, an imperative to be met to its fullest before Jesus' return. Days after the crusading secretary took office, Nat Reed blasted his fellow Republican for a full hour in an address before the Sierra Club's annual meeting. A week later, the Associated Press quoted Douglas as saying, "I don't like Watt. He has no idea of conservation." She clarified that like the secretary, she supported private interests, "but not at the expense of the public interest."[22]

Reagan and Watt confirmed her growing disapproval of Republican Party values. "If Democrats don't use what Reagan has done to the environment," she said, thinking ahead to the 1984 presidential election, "they're more stupid than I think." When former vice president Walter

Mondale was in Florida campaigning for the Democratic presidential nomination, he grabbed a photo-op, next to a once-polluted lake, with Carter's former interior secretary, Cecil Andrus, and the country's best-known elderly environmentalist. Feigned or real, his sympathies for a scrubbed-up environment were hardly enough to keep Reagan from winning a second term.[23]

Given the retrenchment in Washington, someone such as Graham in Tallahassee sustaining the momentum of Askew and Claude Kirk seemed an undisguised blessing. On two occasions in the summer of 1983, Douglas spoke in front of Graham's cabinet in Tallahassee (receiving a standing ovation during one speech) and walked away victorious. The cabinet agreed to a consolidation of the Rotenberg and Holey Land tracts, which were situated between Water Conservation Area 3 and the Everglades Agricultural Area, south of Lake Okeechobee. The idea was to use the two tracts as a retention area for agricultural water that would otherwise be back pumped into the lake. The cabinet also voted to acquire fifty thousand acres in the East Everglades and to "uphold the South Florida Water Management District's emergency order to alleviate flooding in" Everglades National Park. Recalling the 1850 Swamp Land Act, Douglas told the cabinet, "Here it is over 130 odd years afterwards and we have this marvelous opportunity to correct probably one of the first mistakes that was made in the state of Florida on land ownership, and that is the acquisition of this 50,000 acres." Graham also turned a discerning eye to the SFWMD—a growing irritant to Douglas, Marshall, and Jones—and appointed Reed to its board of governors.[24]

Despite the star of progress that Graham represented, Douglas did not always toe the expected line. On one occasion, the nonagenarian was in Tallahassee, staying as a guest at the governor's mansion and seeking to stop industrial development around Dade County's northwest well field. The county commission had approved the planned development, but John DeGrove's Department of Community Affairs appealed, requiring a decision from the cabinet. Graham had recruited DeGrove, Askew's growth-management adviser, to head the state's growth-management agency, and over the years De Grove wrote to Douglas to express his appreciation for her wise counsel and for the fact that she had allowed him "to be a student in [her] classroom." The cabinet and governor nevertheless voted unanimously to confirm the county's decision. Friends of the Everglades also became involved in a running dispute with the governor and state and federal agencies because they sidestepped restrictions on development in north Key Largo, allegedly doing so behind closed doors in violation of Florida's government-in-the-sunshine law. Four endangered species, including the American crocodile, lived in the area. Mike Chenoweth did, too. Since joining as its first member, he had become active in Friends, and he and his wife, Pam Pierce, whom he met after Douglas purposely rearranged seating cards at a Friends banquet, were watching whenever developers came snooping around.[25]

Graham did not take a hard line against farmers or developers any more than he did against environmentalists. A reasonable balance, he thought, could offset both extremes. As governor, he would do more for environmental protection than any of the state's other chief executives, yet he still had something of a growth streak, even as highways, overpasses, housing developments, and the din of population saturation were consolidating around the family's old coral-rock house in a formerly rural corner of Dade County. He and Douglas in fact stood apart on a roadway that would affect precisely that part of the county: the upgrade of Alligator Alley into an extension of Interstate 75. Early on, he had written to her asking for "help to ensure a transportation system that will protect and enhance the environmental and economic health of our state." Graham believed that the new interstate would accommodate South Florida's certain growth. Douglas wrote back and said she opposed the plan. She, Marshall, Browder, Jones, and many others questioned South Florida's continued expansion, and they failed to see how running a four- or six-lane motorway, bringing more cars and people across the pathways of wildlife and the already impeded river, could benefit the state's environmental health. But the Federal Highway Administration approved the project in 1973, and environmentalists knew that the highway was a done deal. In large part because of Marshall's efforts, opponents managed to divert the highway away from the Tamiami Trail corridor, a route that, as Browder put it, "would have been a disaster for Everglades National Park and Big Cypress." They continued to press for more modifications, easing off only after receiving assurances that the interstate would be accompanied by the expansion of Big Cypress National Preserve by more than one hundred thousand acres, that interchanges and lateral roadways would be kept to a minimum and built with protective designs, that water flow beneath the new highway would approach natural conditions, and that wildlife corridors would steer animals away from the pathway of cars. Douglas continued to pester the Environmental Protection Agency about possible contamination of Biscayne Aquifer from automobile runoff, and she politely sparred with Jones about access roads for hunters. In the end, she agreed that the new highway represented a significant improvement over the old road.[26]

The Big Cypress expansion was part of the third of three programs that formed the marrow of Graham's environmental agenda. He funded them with an increase in the tax on real-estate transactions. In 1981, he introduced Save Our Rivers, a three-hundred-million-dollar program that allowed the state to purchase environmentally important watersheds to protect freshwater sources. The next year, he unveiled Save Our Coasts, which targeted sensitive sand-dune shores to be turned into state parks. The last of the pedigree was Save Our Everglades.

Inaugurated in the third year, it had peculiar origins. Johnny Jones had long been frustrated in his efforts to get Everglades restoration on the governor's agenda when he was unexpectedly aided by a 1981 article in *Sports Illustrated*'s best-selling swimsuit edition. The article railed against the environmental abuse in Florida. Although the piece said nothing that the *New York Times, Washington Post,* and *Christian Science Monitor* had not already said, *Sports Illustrated* quoted Jones describing Graham as a do-nothing governor. The criticism won Jones an audience with Graham and the opportunity to push for the restoration of the Kissimmee River. Jones took along a well-primed Art Marshall, who delivered a twenty-minute lecture on Everglades ecology. Before leaving, they gave Graham a copy of

For the Future of Florida, Repair the Everglades, a pamphlet published by Friends and outlining the Marshall Plan. The governor reciprocated with a promise that he would "do it"—fix the Kissimmee.[27]

Graham met soon thereafter with his environmental adviser, Estus Whitfield, retained from the Askew administration. They initiated a series of planning meetings with scientists, state agencies, environmental and sporting groups, farmers, ranchers, and cane growers. Jones and Marshall too were consulted. After drafting a plan to be called Save Our Everglades, Whitfield and Graham huddled in the governor's conference room with three experts who were reviewing the proposal: Earl Starnes, a University of Florida professor of urban and regional planning; Nelson Blake, a Syracuse University professor who had written a compelling history of Florida water management, *Land into Water—Water into Land;* and Marjory Stoneman Douglas. The meeting "was mostly a reality check," Whitfield said, "to get the blessing of heavyweights." Graham subsequently wrote to Douglas, "You have set a standard of commitment that we will all strive to emulate."[28]

Graham announced the program at a press conference in early August. The ungainly reading of the mostly bulleted statement obscured the true passion he felt for the land beyond his boyhood backyard. "We will attempt in the next 17 years," he said, "to heal the damage inflicted over the past century." He set a goal for the troubled wetland to "look more like the Everglades of the year 1900 than the Everglades of today." Although he overlooked the ravages that had been inflicted on wildlife populations by the turn of the century, Graham was thinking mainly in terms of the ecological function of the Kissimmee-Okeechobee-Everglades system. His program had the look and feel of the Marshall Plan. He wanted to "reestablish the values of the Kissimmee River"; restore the natural water conditions in the Rotenberger and Holey Land tracts and Everglades National Park; make hydrological improvements to Alligator Alley and Tamiami Trail; and purchase the fifty-thousand-acre Aerojet property using bond money from the Conservation and Recreation Land Fund, established by the legislature in 1979. Nature, not humans, he suggested, had been right all along about the kind of environment that would best stimulate life in South Florida.[29]

Although a handful of critics said that Graham was simply gathering into a single package scattered initiatives already in the works, the environmental community offered a ratifying response. Speaking for Friends, Podgor said that Graham's program constituted an acknowledgment that "we ignored [the Everglades], we butchered it, we hacked at it, and it still hung in there, and now we're realizing that we really can't improve on it." To help bring the new program to life, Friends joined with Florida Audubon, the National Wildlife Federation, and several other organizations to form the Everglades Coalition, a revived version of the original founded during Askew's governorship. Although the federal government had proven to be a good environmental ally in the recent past, Douglas preferred that the state take the lead in Everglades restoration. As long as Reagan occupied the White House, she did not trust Washington to act responsibly.[30]

As if to prove her right, the Corps of Engineers threw up a roadblock in the path of Save Our Everglades. Engineers had stalled restoration since 1976, when the state first mandated the river's redemption. When Graham tried to set the belated effort finally into motion, the corps said it could not allow the state to put dirt back into its canal without congressional consent. Some critics charged that the corps was simply unwilling to admit that one of its projects had been anything less than a scrupulous contribution to the public good. Still, the corps was supposed to be reinventing itself, and it allowed a somewhat hollow concession by permitting the SFWMD to build, at its own expense, temporary steel dams that would divert water into a few designated oxbows.[31]

A year after announcing Save Our Everglades, Graham invited Douglas to join him in planting a seven-foot cypress tree at the inauguration of the Kissimmee River Demonstration Project. Douglas bought a new pantsuit for the occasion. The governor and some sixty others—including Johnny and Mariana Jones, Charles Lee, and Nathaniel Reed—convened at river's edge in Martin County. There the young governor and elderly environmentalist, in a perfect pose for photojournalists, planted a tree. As an impromptu final touch, Douglas, perhaps thinking back to the spirited gathering at Marshall's Interlachen home, persuaded Graham to toss a shovelful of dirt into C-38 as a gesture toward restoration of the un-redeemed river. "It was a truly historic moment for me," she wrote to the governor after the event. A year later, Graham invited her to accompany him for a boat tour of a restored oxbow. She wrote to a group of Wellesley alumnae, whom she called the Robinettes, in anticipation of the event. "I think it will be great fun," she said. "Governor Graham is the most inter-esting and highly educated and capable man, whom for some years I have enjoyed as a friend."[32]

One friend who should have been there was Art Marshall. Douglas had always credited him with the scientific argument that had helped inform so many minds. But Marshall was making no more scientific arguments. He had passed away in February 1985, killed by lung cancer and a life of heavy smoking. Graham, who visited him in the hospital a few days before he died, described the sixty-five-year-old scientist as a "prophet" and a "major influence" in the creation of Save Our Everglades. Doug-las traveled to Gainesville to attend his funeral. The two had been more than partners engaged in a cause; they had been friends and confidants, he often opening up about the personal struggles he encountered on the way to his unfulfilled dream of a healthy Everglades. After his death, she wrote to the Robinettes, "No one can ever do for the state what he did." Three years later, an appreciative U.S. Fish and Wildlife Service renamed the 221-square-mile Loxahatchee National Wildlife Refuge after him.[33]

Justice and Equality

Every hour, an electronic clock spoke to Douglas at home. "The voice of the man I live with," she sometimes joked to visitors who heard the time of day intoned. The clock symbolized how she conformed to a life without sight. In good light, she could make out cloudy shapes and contrasts, but the eight-power magnifying glass she once wired to her glasses to read numbers in the phone book was now useless. She no longer had the eyes for writing, either, not even in the big looping scrawl slanting upward across the page that had for a short time become her script. An ophthalmologist at the University of Miami said surgery might restore some of her vision, but Douglas said she was comfortable with her eyes. She dictated everything, and her assistants read documents, letters, and drafts of Hudson chapters to her. Friends dropped by and did the same with choice items from the newspaper or a book, waiting for the inevitable moment when she corrected their pronunciation of a word or their rhythm in the recitation of a poem. With "cautious confidence" she moved around the house "along memory-paths," noted George Rosner, one of her most caring friends, who took control of her checkbook and scrupulously watched over her minuscule finances. On bright days, she oriented herself through a combination of memory and the sunshine streaming through windows and doors. It was a poetic denouement to a life so long attached to natural light.[1]

More than light and generous friends helped her maneuver through each day. In a dictated letter to the group of Wellesley alumnae she called the Robinettes, she said, "The joy of my life is that I have a constant supply of wonderful records and tapes from the Talking Book Office of the public library. It is a marvelous service [that] makes all the difference in the world to my pleasure in life." Twenty-two members of the Class of 1912 were still alive, but Douglas was probably the only Robinette who had three secretaries; they handled Friends of the Everglades business, personal affairs, and writing projects.[2]

Keeping track of her daily schedule alone was a task that required an assistant. Hardly a day in her calendars from 1987 to 1989—from her ninety-seventh year to her ninety-ninth—lacked some scheduled activity. There were dinner, birthday, and wine-and-cheese parties; board meetings of Friends of the Everglades and the Biscayne Nature Center over which she presided; luncheons with the Native Plant Society, *Miami Herald,* Friends of the University of Miami Library, and the Wellesley Club; interviews with newspaper, magazine, and local broadcast journalists (National Public Radio, CNN, CBS, NBC, PBS, a German television station, and a high-school newspaper reporter) and with documentary film crews, including crews from Greenpeace and the National Geographic Society; trips to Tallahassee, Orlando, New York City, Washington, D.C., Princeton, and Sarasota; lunches with Nat Reed, Lawton Chiles, and Marjorie Carr; dinners with Alice Wainwright, Kitty Dukakis, and beach-bum balladeer Jimmy Buffett, who was leading a campaign to protect Florida's endangered manatees; speeches before the Save the Panther group, the Committee on the Future of Florida, the Episcopal Churchwomen of St. Thomas, and the Federal Women's Program; and award banquets honoring friends, colleagues, and, most frequently, her.[3]

Douglas's schedule also included book signings. In 1987, she published her autobiography, *Voice of the River.* The title was appropriate for someone whom Florida governor Bob Graham called the "poet, the sledgehammer advocate, the constant conscience of the Everglades." With jacket endorsements from Graham, James Michener, and Peter Matthiessen, the 272-page book was the product of two hundred hours of interviews conducted by John Rothchild over a two-year period. Rothchild was a Floridian who wrote for *Time, Rolling Stone, Harper's,* and other magazines, and when he and Douglas first sat down with a tape recorder, he had just published *Up for Grabs: A Trip through Time and Space in the Sunshine State,* a slapstick account of the bungling yet rapacious fortune seekers and visionaries from the Spanish to the present who had deflowered a paradise land.[4]

As was true for so many people who eventually gravitated to Douglas, Rothchild's first encounter with her came at a protest rally. In 1973, he and other locals in Everglades City, where President Truman had dedicated the national park twenty-six years earlier, were challenging a developer who sought a bridge permit for a planned housing project. Douglas spoke at a public hearing sponsored by the Army Corps of Engineers. Rothchild was reminded of "Scarlett O'Hara as played by Igor Stravinsky" when he saw the environmental defender in her wide-brim hat and "huge dark glasses." The locals defeated the developer. As far as Rothchild was concerned, Douglas's apostolic presence had won the day. At the time, he knew little about this antique of a woman beyond the public image of her stopping bulldozers and bureaucrats in their tracks. Only by accident did he learn about the real Douglas when he conducted an exhaustive search for an architect who would design an open-air house without air-conditioning. He ended up hiring Douglas's old friend, Marion Manley, now in her eighties. Manley gave Rothchild a storied rendition of Douglas's life from New England to Florida to Europe and back to Florida, inspiring Rothchild to read *River of Grass.* After he relocated to Miami in 1980, he made acquainting himself with the author-activist a priority.[5]

He eventually met a small woman who sat in a small house and made a big argument for the personal value of spending time alone. She was similarly vocal about the virtues of pigheadedness. He spent little time in her presence before learning her hardened opinions on matters of politics, foreign policy, social justice, and the environment. She was quick to correct but equally quick with a wit that softened the edges. Her long view of life and vivid recall were astounding. She could guide him to a particular passage in a book resting in a particular place on a particular shelf and then recite the passage from memory. Conversation was truly her domain, and when conversation whipsawed from, say, a discussion of the recent war in the Falkland Islands to William Jennings Bryan evangelizing in Royal Palm Park, her clarity never faltered. In her cavernous workroom, Rothchild found the manifestations of her life, her priorities, and her values—indeed, he said, her "mind turned inside out." Like him and his family, she lived without air-conditioning. Nor did she have a television, and though "old enough to be prehistoric by Florida standards," she was remarkably self-sustaining (at least for the present). When not dining out with friends, she cooked on a two-burner hotplate in the narrow kitchen sans oven. At cocktail hour, she poured a scotch and soda for herself—from the assorted bottles of liquor and tonic water lined up on the counter to the left of the kitchen sink—and the drink of preference of any present guest. She served from a small round tray with a dish of unsalted peanuts. Books towered in hazardous stacks and cascaded from side tables and chairs. Her desktop, covered with a white embroidered tablecloth, stored the manuscript pages of the Hudson biography, a work still very much in progress. The furnishings had not changed since Joe Browder's first visit eleven years earlier, and cats still drifted in and out with typical feline ease. Chair cushions sank a little lower, though, and mixed in with the clothbound stacks were books on records and on tapes. Near the desk were boxes of envelopes and letterhead for Friends of the Everglades. Hers was an unpretentious and utilitarian setting.[6]

Lying about also, beneath papers and books and on tables and chairs, were awards. They were everywhere except on the walls for obvious display, though a few discreet statuette knickknacks sat on the upper shelf of a bookcase. Awards were not new to her, but the growing number of them by the 1980s made updating her résumé a constant chore. She accumulated honorary degrees from nine universities and colleges. Literary and journalism honors numbered nearly as many, but most of the recognition came for her environmental work. In 1990, Broward County opened the Marjory Stoneman Douglas High School; not to be outdone, Dade

County named an elementary school, a park, a street, and a day after her, marking the occasion with a ceremony that included four hundred guests. Even the Miami Ballet Society honored her with a luncheon and a lifetime-achievement award, though she had no particular connection to the art. In 1989, she flew to New York for a dinner banquet at the Waldorf Astoria to accept *Ms.* magazine's Woman of the Year award; she returned to the Waldorf a year later for a tribute from the Garden Clubs of America. She was Person of the Week on Peter Jennings's *ABC News,* and *Rolling Stone* magazine welcomed her into its hall of fame, along with Greenpeace, the Nature Conservancy, David Brower, Worldwatch Institute founder Lester Brown, and unleaded gasoline. After the National Parks Conservation Association gave her its first Award for Citizen Conservation, which brought with it five thousand dollars, it created the Marjory Stoneman Douglas Award, given annually to an individual or organization that contributed outstanding work to benefit national parks. When she was ninety-nine, she flew out to San Francisco to be named an honorary vice president of the national Sierra Club. She subsequently wrote to a friend that she regretted that blindness kept her from enjoying the full splendor of the marvelous city by the bay.[7]

One of her most conspicuous honors, something she could not lose beneath a pile of books, came when the Department of Natural Resources dedicated its new headquarters in Tallahassee in her name. Completed in 1980, the building was situated outside downtown, away from the other state installations, on a three-hundred-acre campus of longleaf and loblolly pines. Though minimalist in design, the structure was remarkable for its 2,772 panels of gold-tinted glass that gave the building's ten stories a seamless mirror finish.[8]

To her friend, park ranger Sandy Dayhoff, Douglas confided that she was somewhat annoyed by the honor. The best evidence for her life's work, she insisted, would not be her name on a building but the Everglades made healthy again. She accepted the honor anyway, flying up for the dedication in 1981, escorted by a Major Little of the Florida Marine Patrol. When her time came to speak, with whirring cameras following her to the lectern, she took the microphone in hand and addressed the three hundred in attendance. She was humble and polite but also firm, raising her left fist into the air and complaining about the environmental malevolence of James Watt and Ronald Reagan. The May sun reflecting off her oversized sunglasses in tandem with the building behind sharpened her message. At her back were the governor and cabinet, sitting in folding metal chairs, and she let them know that she would still hold them to the highest environmental standards, building or no building. After the ceremony, the press flocked to her. She saw an opportunity to express her disappointment in Graham's support of the Alligator Alley/I-75 extension. She also shared her thoughts on the importance of activism. "Protecting the environment has never been done before. We're pioneers," she said, echoing anthropologist Luther Gerlach's observation years earlier. "What I'm fighting for is the environment. Towns and villages and buildings come and go, but when you're fighting for air and land and water, you're fighting for fundamentals."[9]

A few years later, in another gesture of recognition, she was inducted into the Florida Women's Hall of Fame. Once again, she was thrown into consternation. When Rothchild met her in 1980, Douglas was still an outspoken feminist who thought that separate, state-sponsored forms of recognition for women's achievements reinforced false differences between the sexes. Susan Wilson, a fellow activist who was studying for a master's degree under Art Marshall, got an unexpected lesson in gender politics when she told Douglas that "women, if they're going to expect to get ahead and compete with men, had better get themselves ready and educated." Douglas retorted, "Nonsense! Men don't have to prove themselves. Why should women?" At the time, the states were again considering the Equal Rights Amendment (ERA). Douglas reiterated her lifelong support for the ERA in numerous speeches and media interviews. In 1975, she entered familiar disquieting territory when she testified before the state legislature on behalf of the amendment, reminding lawmakers that she had been there nearly sixty years earlier when their wool-hat-boy predecessors had rejected woman suffrage. The reigning coterie in Tallahassee had its own ideas, however, and as in 1917, the State Senate killed the ERA with four votes in 1975 and two more in 1977. A few years later, when

Douglas first heard talk of putting her in the Florida Women's Hall of Fame, she told Rothchild that she would prefer a Citizens' Hall of Fame. She was nevertheless admitted not only to the Florida hall but also post-humously to the National Women's Hall of Fame.[10]

Never having been one to brood over bad fortune, she believed that women still could build on gains made since before her sex could vote. Her intimacy with the past yielded a featured appearance in a 1981 doc-umentary that the National Organization for Women commissioned on the ERA. Organization leaders believed that an interview with an early suffragist would make a nice touch for the documentary. The filmmaker, Carl Kesser, knew Douglas, who at age ninety-one was still bearing the torch. The Emmy Award–winning director transported his film equip-ment only a few blocks from his Coconut Grove studio to interview his subject at her home. Days later, he presented the film at the organiza-tion's annual convention in Washington, D.C., before an audience of one thousand activists. The documentary opened with an uninterrupted three-minute monologue by the forthright Douglas sitting at her desk. She summed up her thoughts precisely: "I have one or two very decided opinions about the necessity of the ERA amendment. It has a parallel al-most with the three great amendments that clarified the Emancipation Proclamation. The equality that we talk about is not an equality of so-cial relations or individual relations or certainly not of individual brains or ability. It is a simple equality in the face of the law." Others, including Betty Ford at the Lincoln Memorial, quoted parts of Douglas's mono-logue in speeches that weekend. The convention kicked off the National Organization for Women's Countdown to Equality campaign before the film went on a countrywide tour.[11]

At the other end of the decade, Douglas made her national debut as a women's rights activist. Newspapers and magazines had started mention-ing her feminist views when describing the full political dimension of her life. So too did the country's smallest if not best-known feminist, Lisa Simpson. In a 1989 episode of the animated television series *The Simp-sons,* she shows her baby sister, Maggie, the centerpiece she has made for the family's Thanksgiving dinner, which displays three female figures.

"It's a tribute to the trailblazing women who made our country great," Lisa pridefully explains. "See, there's Georgia O'Keeffe, Susan B. Anthony, and," she says, pointing to the last papier-mâché statuette, "this is Marjory Stoneman Douglas." Lisa presents Douglas not just as an Everglades environmentalist but as part of a historical confluence that had in various ways expanded the scope and meaning of American democracy not merely to include new participants but also to bring their concerns and priorities into the democratic fold of justice and equality. Reconciling the women's issue in favor of equal rights meant Americans could, as Douglas said in Kesser's film, "get on with the work of being responsible citizens."[12]

Two months earlier, Douglas was at Princeton University expressing ideas not only about natural rights but about natural selection. Her celebrity, views, and long-ago experiences brought an invitation to speak in a lecture series commemorating the university's twenty years of coeducation. Her sponsors promoted her as a "longtime feminist." Although she was ninety-nine at the time, her voice was as orotund as ever. Chronicling the social and political ascent of women during the past century—her lifetime—she invoked the authority of science. Darwin "made clear the nature of man upon Earth and, in consequence, the nature of women was also discovered." Descent with modification in effect demonstrated that "there is no difference between the brains of men and women."[13]

Douglas was never so radical that she favored a complete erasure of accepted distinctions between the sexes. Women still needed their own sanctuaries. She believed that the Ivy League universities' admission of female students was beneficial, but she hated to see women's schools similarly opening their enrollment to men. Accepting an honorary degree from Queens College in North Carolina, a holdout among women's schools, she indicated that some things had not changed since her college days: "Men are dominating. Women need the time to find out who they [are]." Traditional women's colleges such as Skidmore, Vassar, and Sarah Lawrence had gone coeducational; she was pleased that her alma mater had not.[14]

Douglas remained loyal to Wellesley, and the college returned the favor. A decade after winning the alumnae research grant to pursue her study of Hudson, she and two other environmentalists and writers received an Alumnae Achievement Award. She flew up for the ceremony, which included a panel discussion on environmentalism and the opportunity to give a class lecture. She spoke on expository writing to what she described as a "keen group of girls." She then returned in 1985 for the first Marjory Stoneman Douglas Lecture, an annual series the college created after the Miami Wellesley Club raised fifteen thousand dollars to endow a lecture by a distinguished speaker on the subject of what Douglas called "environmental geography." "I have long attributed my interest in geography and the environment," she wrote to the Robinettes, "to dear Miss [Elizabeth] Fisher's course in geography." Wellesley brought her back again when she was 104 for the twenty-fifth anniversary of the Alumnae Achievement Award, putting her on a discussion panel about public service. When Wellesley's president, Diana Chapman Walsh, paid Douglas a visit in Coconut Grove a year later, Douglas gave Walsh her Presidential Medal of Freedom, awarded the year before, for the college. "I have no living relatives," Douglas told the *New York Times*, "so Wellesley is like my family and it will be there long after I am gone." Walsh in turn described Douglas as "everything we hope a Wellesley alumna can be, someone who goes out in the world and makes a difference through the force of her intellect, determination and personality."[15]

Even in the modern world of her senior years, Douglas believed that women continued to offer a valuable perspective on life, different from that offered by men. In particular, she believed that women had a unique view of the human relationship with the nonhuman world. In many of her speeches, Douglas talked about a clean environment as "women's business." She told *Time* magazine, "it's an extended form of housekeeping." More personally familiar with old age than with the duties of home and family, she once explained to a St. Lucie audience, "A great many women after menopause—if I may be so bold—have excess energies and need to find outlets for those energies. The environmental field needs these people." Just as she surprised audiences with unexpected physiological observations of this nature, the avowed feminist must have surprised listeners with her comments about men's and women's gendered responsibilities. But such comments put her in line with many modern ecofeminists who believed that women were either socially or biologically programmed to look at nature with more sympathetic eyes than those of men. Douglas agreed with Bella Abzug, founder of the Women's Environment and Development Organization, who said that women "have the social values of caring and responsibility. These must be fused into what are now predominantly male priorities and policies."[16]

Douglas had a chance to meet Abzug when the former New York congresswoman made that comment at the World Women's Congress for a Healthy Planet, held in Miami in 1991. The *Herald* reported that the "most poignant event" during the opening-day session, upstaging a rousing speech by Abzug, was the "brief appearance by feminist, environmentalist and centenarian Marjory Stoneman Douglas." Introduced as a "child of the 1890s and a role model for the 1990s," Douglas, sitting in a wheelchair, let her smile linger after the audience rose for an ovation.[17]

The central theme of the conference, attended by nearly one thousand people, was population growth and its consequences, all too familiar to the South Florida centenarian. The United Nations had recently issued a report linking the world's spiraling human numbers with the loss of critical tropical forests, groundwater depletion and surface water pollution, species extinction, and exhausted farmland. As the conference participants knew, controlling reproduction rates meant becoming entangled in complicated issues, including changing the attitudes of men who saw a high number of offspring as proof of their virility. There was also the combustible issue of family planning and abortion rights. Douglas advocated both. To a receptive audience at Princeton, she said in reference to abortion, "It's not [murder]; it's birth control. We don't have enough food." On a previous occasion, she was more blunt, calling overpopulation the world's "greatest menace." "There are just too many damn people. . . . The more people there are, the more artificially we have to live to sustain life."[18]

Her feelings for humanity inspired her environmental activism. "My opponents accuse me of caring more about birds and fish than people," she said after the dedication of the Department of Natural Resources building, "but they can't prove that." Douglas had begun her public life as a social activist, and in her late age, during her environmental heyday, she still maintained that her proudest accomplishment was writing the Martin Tabert ballad. It made complete sense when the Dade County Women's Coalition for a Healthy Planet, pledged to the belief that protecting the nonhuman world was a basic human right, made Douglas its honorary chair. When Amnesty International approached her for assistance in 1985, she eagerly signed a petition, during a photo shoot at her house, for the release of Yugoslavian intellectual and political prisoner Miodrag Markovic. As much as anything else, her fellow environmentalists admired her contributions to humanity—her years as a suffragist, Red Cross worker, and slum-clearance reformer. She wanted to talk about social issues more than environmental ones, said Browder of the occasions when he would come in town and take her to dinner at a cheap lobster shack on Dixie Highway. "She was a much deeper person" than the Everglades grandmother of myth.[19]

Female colleagues felt a special attachment to the veteran social activist. She had defied the odds of first her sex and marital status and then her age and had passed along this defiance to activist women of younger generations. They possessed admirable credentials, but they believed that Douglas had helped to make their accomplishments possible. "Marjory was an inspiration to women," said Juanita Greene. "She was a living symbol that women could make it on their own. . . . That was before women's lib, before Betty Friedan." The young December Duke had hoped to see the torchbearer, not the environmentalist, while riding a bike down Stewart Avenue. And Judy Wilson had no reason to think that the elderly Douglas she encountered that night in the Quick & Easy Food Store might refuse when prodded to take up another cause.[20]

Although Douglas had reached the point in life when she had to rely on technology or the goodness of friends to maintain a relationship with books, she refused to allow blindness, any more than old age, to keep her from work in the public interest. Getting into the environmental business proved an extension of her lifelong interest in social justice, and no regional venue better than the Everglades illuminated the commingling abuse of nature and humans. In *River of Grass,* she had written with passion about the tempestuous history of Everglades Indians, and she had learned by simply observing life in early Miami about the black Bahamians who crossed warm Gulf Stream water every year beginning in the 1910s to find seasonal work at resort hotels and in agriculture. Locals knew them as conchs, a reference to a staple in their island diets, and for their singsong, island voices. Beside them in the fields, stooped over ripe tomatoes or hacking at burned sugarcane, were native-born workers. Harvest work was often a stepping stone to nowhere. Only convict labor was worse, although many seasonal and migrant workers slipped into the living hell of peonage, a condition that the Federal Bureau of Investigation acknowledged in the 1940s and that continued into the 1980s and later. At an average of three dollars a day for sunup to sundown labor, pay could hardly support the definition of wage work. The rented living quarters provided by farmers were nothing short of hovels with minimal, if any, sanitation facilities. The abjectness at these camps gave great drama to Zora Neale Hurston's *Their Eyes Were Watching God.* Ernie Pyle, soon to become famous as a war correspondent, visited the region in 1940 and said, "I'm glad I'm not a sociologist for I wouldn't know what to make of the Everglades." Nineteen years later, nothing had changed for harvest workers except that their numbers had grown when Howard Van Smith of the *Miami News* won a Pulitzer Prize for bringing national attention to the inhuman plight of four thousand workers in a migrant camp in Immokalee. Following Smith's lead, Edward R. Murrow and his producer, David Lowe, arrived in Belle Glade with a CBS film crew a year later. The creator of exposé-style television journalism, Murrow used *Harvest of Shame* to pique the conscience of television viewers the day after Thanksgiving, implying that their stuffed selves were the ultimate beneficiaries of haggard farmworkers. He also did not let growers off the hook, quoting one straight-faced employer who said, "We used to own our slaves; now we just rent them."[21]

The documentary outraged Spessard Holland, who called it a "malicious distortion." To justify his words, he claimed that a woman who told Murrow she had fourteen children and earned one dollar a day was in actuality supporting only seven of her offspring; the others, he explained, had died. Voicing the accepted argument of the day, he asserted that the woman's meager earnings were her reward for indolence.[22]

This was a pivotal time in South Florida history. Two years earlier, revolutionary Fidel Castro had taken control of Cuba, and a rush of nearly two hundred thousand émigrés had fled the island country for the United States. Most ended up in South Florida, where the flavor of the existing population was northern and Jewish. The exiles, who became permanent residents and produced first- and second-generation Cuban Americans, buttressed by two subsequent waves of Cuban émigrés, changed the overall demographics. Douglas appreciated the makeover, having always believed that Miami was regionally appropriate as a Latin city. "Marjory had a keen appreciation for diversity of all kinds," remembered Browder. "She wasn't at all socially judgmental." She loved to think about the new Miami as a "tropical place filled with tropical people."[23]

What she didn't like was the boost the Cuban Revolution gave to American sugarcane production. Before Castro, sugar had taken a backseat to truck farming in the Everglades, although the sweet crop continued to entice. Peter Henry Rolfs, a University of Florida agronomist who in the early 1900s helped bring attention to Paradise Key, called sugarcane the "ideal crop for Florida." One of his contemporaries claimed that the "cost of producing a ton of cane in the Everglades of Florida will be less than in any portion of the cane growing sections of the world"; another said that sugar culture would "reach beyond the limits of prophesy"; and yet another, on the eve of the 1926 hurricane, predicted that the Everglades would become "our newest national sugar bowl." Even Cuban competitors admitted that reclaimed Everglades land had great potential for cane growing. But for years, Florida growers, led by Clarence R. Bitting of the

U.S. Sugar Corporation, a "big, aggressive, and forceful man," complained to Congress about the federal quotas for foreign and domestic sugar that restricted the acreage for production in Florida.[24]

Then in 1960, President Dwight D. Eisenhower imposed a Cold War embargo on sugar from Castro's Cuba. Eisenhower's successors retained the embargo and put quotas on other imported sugar. They also supported federally subsidized guaranteed minimum sales prices. This meant that in the mid-1980s, American consumers were paying twenty-one cents a pound for sugar when sugar sold elsewhere in the world for three cents a pound, and U.S. taxpayers were funding the federal government's price supports. It was one of the greatest boondoggles in agriculture. When sugar's market price dropped below the established minimum in 1985, taxpayers shelled out seventy-eight million dollars to beet and cane growers. Taxpayers also subsidized Florida sugar's access to impounded water, dry land, and cheap offshore labor and paid to clean up its pollution. Castro was the best thing that ever happened to U.S. domestic sugar production. The region around Lake Okeechobee, labeled the Everglades Agricultural Area by the government agencies that created it, quickly validated earlier predictions by becoming the nation's sugar bowl. Some 49,000 acres devoted to sugar morphed into 321,000 in ten years and then to more than 400,000. Plainly ignoring the windfall in subsidies and import restrictions, the sugar industry officially credited its phenomenal growth to the U.S. Department of Agriculture's decision to lift acreage controls in 1960. Two decades later, the Everglades Agricultural Area was shipping seven hundred million dollars in farm products annually, six hundred million dollars of which came from sugar alone—40 percent of all domestically grown cane. The country's largest sugar grower, U.S. Sugar, was headquartered in Clewiston, to the north of Lake Okeechobee. Connecting Clewiston to the sugar towns of Moore Haven, Belle Glade, and South Bay, U.S. Highway 27 acquired the name Sugarland Highway. The hapless ghost of Hamilton Disston, it seemed, had finally been exorcised from the region.[25]

Yet despite the agricultural and corporate success, the specter of abused farm labor survived. Murrow had made a point about American-born farmworkers, but soon after his documentary aired, masses of the natives began fleeing the migrant circuit and the cane fields, replaced each fall by masses of temporary offshore workers. They numbered ten thousand in 1988—95 percent of all South Florida sugar workers—and were unceremoniously known as H-2 workers, a designation taken from the 1952 federal law that authorized domestic employers to seek temporary foreign labor. Under the law, foreign laborers were not supposed to compete with domestic workers. Yet as hundreds of resident workers in the Lake Okeechobee region searched for employment, the Immigration and Naturalization Service office in West Palm Beach rubber-stamped employer applications for H-2 workers.[26]

Offshore workers who found jobs on the sugar plantations were not always prepared for what their American employers offered. If Hurston's bean cutters had endured bad conditions, the black wall of smoke rising above the horizon indicated that others were even worse off. Cane cutters entered freshly burned fields looking something like gladiators. On top of two layers of clothing to protect themselves against the razor-edged leaves of the cane, they wore aluminum guards on their shins, knees, and hands to protect themselves from swinging machetes. Their steely appearance proclaimed anything but a position of power. The law belonged to their employers. Local officials and the justice system had a history of countenancing employer action, even criminal action, against dark-skinned foreigners. Sugar growers typically amassed their power by sending labor recruiters to the islands to assemble a worker pool exceeding needs by 30 or 40 percent. The surplus workers stood at the ready to replace any noncompliant workers, who were then blacklisted. Here was Florida's own *On the Waterfront* in dark flesh and desperate sweat.[27]

More so than the stevedore's wharf, cane fields were a netherworld of hard labor and broken promises. Recruits were told, for example, that transportation to the United States would cost them nothing but learned soon enough that these costs would be deducted from their pay and placed in an escrow account. Those who failed to complete 50 percent of their contracts would lose that money. Others would get it back only after they paid their home country a tax that helped cover the costs of the program. Twenty-three percent of each employee's pay went into a forced savings account, to which employers had access when there was a dispute over worker debt. Every year, the Florida Sugar Cane League printed a glossy booklet that highlighted the industry's beneficent contributions to the economy, society, and labor force. Among its claims was that it provided some of the "finest farm housing in the country." But this was just another of so many insidious fictions. Echoing Murrow, a 1970 Senate subcommittee report on worker "powerlessness" exposed the enduring shame: "A migrant camp is a microcosm of nearly every social ill, every injustice, and everything shameful in our society: poverty almost beyond belief, rampant disease and malnutrition, racism, filth and squalor, pitiful children drained of pride and hope, exploitation and powerlessness, and the inability or unwillingness of public and private institutions, at all levels, to erase this terrible blight on our country."[28]

In South Florida, one institution, Florida Rural Legal Services (FRLS), was willing to take on the challenge. Conceived in 1966 during Lyndon Johnson's War on Poverty with an eight-hundred-thousand-dollar grant from the U.S. Office of Economic Opportunity, FRLS was part of the proliferation of nonprofit community-action programs and public-interest groups that brought new energy to two largely unsuccessful areas in the civil rights struggle, economic betterment and legal justice. FRLS was committed to empowering dispossessed groups, mainly agricultural workers, by giving them access to quality legal assistance. Achieving early policy and legal victories, FRLS quickly became a controversial entity in South Florida, in part because it achieved early victories. It won a Department of Labor ruling against Jamaica's worker payroll deduction that paid for the recruitment program; a federal court decision against a local vagrancy ordinance; another federal judgment against "retaliatory evictions" when workers and employers were involved in labor disputes; and an agreement from Lee County to stop diverting welfare checks from their rightful recipients to creditors. FRLS also helped rural workers form a number of community-improvement organizations, including day-care centers and housing and transportation cooperatives. Adding to the organization's controversial image was the way it was driven by contentiousness. "It is in the nature of the adversary system," wrote a staff attorney, "to cause controversy and it is its glory that out of controversy comes justice."[29]

Douglas appreciated the FRLS, valuing it as the modern-day equivalent of her Quaker ancestors' stand against slavery. Before he died in 1982, Tobias Simon, who had cofounded the Miami chapter of the American Civil Liberties Union and who had been the organization's busiest trial attorney, served on the FRLS board. The public-interest group's focus on Everglades agriculture also intersected with her environmental work. In 1970, she went to Clewiston to meet with the Harlem Tenants Association, a group dedicated to acquiring decent and affordable housing for local workers. When on speaking tours for Friends of the Everglades, she subsequently connected the conditions of the Everglades environment with the living conditions of Everglades workers. Even decades earlier, with *River of Grass,* she had written of a malignant culture of greed that exploited humans as eagerly as it did nature. So she was well aware of the breadth of agriculture's infamy in 1985, when Juanita Greene, who had written stories on migrant labor for the *Miami Herald,* suggested taking Douglas out to Immokalee to become acquainted with the work of the FRLS.[30]

The drive over to the western edge of the Everglades to rural Collier County took more than an hour, but to Greene, Douglas "was always good company." She was also always clear about where she stood on issues. Even before becoming aware of the ecological fallout, she argued that the government had no business encouraging the development of a sugar industry in the Everglades. She had seen its impact on the island countries of the Caribbean during her magazine-writing days, when she had traveled the region to write about tourism, active volcanoes, earthquakes, and revolution. But she came away with an understanding of the complex relationships among sugar, nations, people, and the land, especially in Jamaica and Haiti, the latter forever in political turmoil. Sugar had for centuries stood at the center of Caribbean life, the main impetus behind European colonization of the area, the main staple in the colonial economy, and the main reason slaves were taken from Africa. By the late nineteenth century, Americans had developed the sweetest tooth in the world next to Britons, and the United States had become the chief export market for Caribbean sugar growers. Federal price supports that had been good for U.S. domestic sugar had been bad for the Caribbean. Douglas, who visited Haiti on more than one occasion, including during the U.S. occupation in the 1930s, knew from firsthand observation that a destabilized economy could mean an unstable government. When she began stumping for the environment, she talked again and again about how U.S. sugar policy drove Caribbean workers into the H-2 program and political refugees onto leaky boats trying to reach Florida, setting both groups up for mistreatment in the Everglades. "Sugar should be raised in Puerto Rico, Haiti and other West Indian Islands," she wrote to a friend, thereby giving people work and allowing them to stay at home.[31]

Despite her blindness, Douglas came to see through Greene's eyes how Immokalee made a poor specimen of a home away from home for foreign workers. An off-the-beaten-path place located at a forty-five-degree bend in State Road 29, the little town claimed Florida's largest migrant-labor community, people who lived in overcrowded aluminum mobile homes and concrete housing units that resembled prison cell blocks, people who boarded decommissioned school, military, and Greyhound buses six mornings a week to ride out to tomato fields and citrus groves that, even in the fall, turned into scorching ovens by afternoon. Some of the workers picked for A. Duda and Sons, one of the country's largest vegetable grow-ers, exposed a decade earlier by a series of *Washington Post* articles and an FRLS lawsuit as having subjected workers to some of the worst housing in the country. At one point, FRLS convinced Duda to put space heaters in the houses; the company then deducted the price of the heaters from the workers' paychecks.[32]

Douglas and Greene met with the attorney who had worked the Duda suit, Rob Williams, who had joined FRLS soon after graduating from Har-vard Law School. Greene had interviewed Williams for her stories, and he happily obliged when she mentioned wanting to bring her friend out for a tour of Immokalee. Williams knew Douglas by reputation and after meeting her was impressed by the ninety-five-year-old's nimble mind. His guided excursion around the dusty streets of Immokalee was reminiscent of Emily Greene Balch's tours of Boston's ghettos. Juanita Greene described every detail for the blind Douglas. She wanted to help, to say more about the subjugated in her speeches, to write haranguing letters to important people. She had recently written to Governor Graham asking him to take "some official action against" the problem of AIDS in Belle Glade. With its enlarging permanent population of Haitian refugees—unwelcome newcomers and domestic workers left mostly unemployed by the H-2 program—Belle Glade had become morbidly afflicted by rampant intravenous drug use and unhappily defamed as the AIDS capital of the United States. After leaving Immokalee, Greene and Douglas drove over to investigate conditions in Belle Glade, which resembled those Douglas had seen fifteen years earlier when she met with the Harlem Tenants Association in neighboring Clewiston.[33]

Advocating for better migrant conditions was frustrating work. Poor housing and exploitation remained the industry standard, and pernicious incidences of peonage continued to surface. One of Douglas's secretaries photocopied a 1986 article in *Common Cause Magazine* on the political power of sugar growers and, apparently after reading it to Douglas, tucked it away in a folder with other such publications. The article discussed President Reagan's plan to roll back the subsidies for domestic growers so he could help the economies of the Caribbean basin. Secretary of State George Shultz called the subsidies a "crime." On this one improbable issue, Douglas found herself on the same page as the man who had led the conservative revolution that offended her core values. But sugar outmaneuvered Reagan in Congress. Even Douglas's favorite governor, Graham, repeatedly backed sugar price supports after he was elected to the U.S. Senate.[34]

Despite their advocates and despite Department of Labor wage guarantees, cane cutters did not see real change until the next century. By the 1990s, the hourly wage guarantee had climbed to $5.30 an hour, but under a complex piece-rate system employed by the industry, the hourly earnings averaged less than $4.00, prompting class-action law suits. The industry then began converting to mechanical harvesting, relieving itself of the burden of field labor. Sugar could not be beaten in the social-justice arena, and victory in the environmental arena, Douglas learned, was equally improbable.[35]

The Gathering Twilight

Hundreds of well-wishers—friends, strangers, young, old—came out on April 7, 1990, a beautiful Saturday afternoon, to sing happy birthday to Marjory Stoneman Douglas. Her centennial celebration took the form of a public picnic held at the north end of Crandon Park. Its eight hundred acres had originally been a coconut plantation, and its owner, the Matheson family, friends of Douglas, had donated the land to the county on the condition that a causeway be built from the Miami mainland across the bay to Virginia Key and to Key Biscayne, where a park was to be located. The causeway was built and the park was dedicated in the same month that *River of Grass* debuted, and development quickly followed. In 1990, the park gave temporary sanctuary not only to people overwhelmed by the concrete artificiality of urban life but also to fertile sea turtles, some of which had journeyed across the Caribbean, depositing their eggs in the white-sand beach. Within sight and audible range were Key Biscayne's condominium and hotel towers, cinder-block houses, and retail centers, all epitomizing South Florida's stuccoed and palm-tree-planted built environment. "This fragile shoreline," Douglas said of the park, "with its mangroves, coastal hammock and ancient reef, is a

precious part of very little that still survives of our unique environment."
Keeping the nesting grounds secure from poachers and shore lights that
would disorient the turtles' return to sea formed part of the mission of the
Marjory Stoneman Douglas Biscayne Nature Center, which was hosting
the birthday event at Crandon.[1]

The center was the brainchild of Douglas and Mabel Miller, a public-
school science teacher. In 1982, Douglas organized a task force of educa-
tors and environmentalists to explore the possibility of creating a facility
to enhance the environmental education programs of the county schools,
support laboratory and field research, and promote "environmental
awareness in our multi-ethnic community." Three years later, the task
force formed a nonprofit corporation under the name Biscayne Nature
Center and organized a board of trustees with Douglas as president. After
obtaining the school board's endorsement, the trustees secured a location
in Crandon Park. They then added Douglas's name to the center. The state
Department of Education came through with a $1.8 million matching
grant in 1991 for the construction of a permanent facility. A groundbreaking ceremony for a sleek, state-of-the-art research and education complex
was held on Douglas's 108th birthday. She was too infirm to attend.[2]

That was not true eight years earlier. Part of a winding motorcade, a
1958 Dodge convertible delivered her to the center, housed temporarily in
a portable classroom, and into the full rhapsody of the waiting crowd. She
was led to a fan-backed wicker chair and, with cameras snapping, raised
clasped hands over her head to acknowledge onlookers. The three-hour
event included speeches, live music, birthday singing, cake cutting, and
remarks by Douglas. "It's just a birthday," she said, not ungratefully. A
more important use of well-wishers' festive energy, she added, was fighting to save the environment. When a reporter asked whether the Everglades could be saved, she replied, "I'm neither an optimist nor a pessi-
mist. I say it's got to be done."[3]

Her centennial unfolded into a string of festivities and bestowals. On
March 30, the Friends of the University of Miami Library kicked off the
celebrations with a banquet with its founder as honored guest and speaker.
On April 8, the ever-loyal Miami Wellesley Club hosted a private dinner

party with 218 guests. The city hung a "Happy Birthday" banner across the Northwest First Street bridge, the airport ran an announcement on its electronic message boards, and the county commissioners ordered her portrait hung in the government office building next to that of U.S. representative Claude Pepper. Senator Bob Graham entered a statement in the *Congressional Record* acknowledging her birthday: "It is our responsibility to instill in America's youth the same vision, commitment, and limitless energy which Mrs. Douglas has dedicated to protecting our environment." Before the month was out, she visited Everglades National Park for the ceremonial unveiling of a bronze statue of the endangered Florida panther dedicated to her and Ernest Coe. She had prodded each new superintendent at the park to give formal recognition to the forgotten Coe. The sculpture was nice, she told Sandy Dayhoff, who over the years had invited Douglas to teach in the ranger-training program, but the "papa" of the park deserved more. Next came a trip to Tallahassee. The cabinet had previously named her a Great Floridian, so the legislature adopted a resolution declaring her the "Lady of the Everglades." In return, she offered wise counsel in legislative chambers: "Public opinion is the strongest force in the world and through which alone [activists] can succeed." Lawmakers gave her a standing ovation.[4]

Her next birthday seemed a continuation of the previous, except it included a most welcome gift. The Internal Improvement Fund voted unanimously to declare Douglas's house worthy of state purchase by virtue of its occupancy by "one of Florida's most distinguished citizens." In the hope of bringing her financial relief, friends had persistently lobbied for such an action. History was now taking a marvelous ironic turn: the agency that had begun the fateful process of transforming the Everglades, the same process that had turned Douglas into a forthright activist, was according her the means to carry on. Douglas received $140,000 and a life interest in her home. The Land Trust of Dade County, which assumed management of her property in 1994, procured an additional $6,000 in state money to pay for structural repairs and the installation of a central air-conditioning system. Douglas had been using a single window unit that admiring appliance-store owners had donated in 1988, replacing a clattering old used one purchased a few years earlier. She had come to depend on the generosity of others to get by. Income from Social Security and royalties from *River of Grass,* which was generating annual sales of between two and three thousand copies, and other books was barely enough to support her modest needs. She had been receiving $425 in rent for the Cole house until a squabble erupted between her and the tenant. After Hurricane Andrew severely damaged the house in 1992, the city initiated condemnation proceedings. The Land Trust, which had bought the house from the Cole heirs, failed to act in time, and the house was razed.[5]

In the meantime, the 101-year-old was distracted by more pleasant developments. For one, she was received by Britain's Queen Elizabeth and Prince Philip, who were on their first visit to Florida and touring Viscaya, built during the land boom by Charles Deering of International Harvester Company fortune. At the queen's request, the host country's senior environmentalist visited the 108-acre Venetian estate and presented the royal couple with a signed copy of *River of Grass.* The Nature Center also won its $1.8 million grant that year. In lieu of the ceremonial hoopla of her previous birthday celebration, Douglas asked people to plant trees for her. Governor Lawton Chiles obliged with "Plant a Tree for Marjory," a statewide event in which 100,000 trees were planted between Douglas's birthday and Earth Day. The first to go in the ground was a silver palm planted at the Nature Center. Chiles followed by planting a bald cypress in the lawn of the governor's mansion.[6]

On her next birthday, the South Florida Water Management District (SFWMD) set in motion not a tree-planting but a tree- and plant-removal campaign, Operation Clean Sweep. In the early days, many exotic plants joined humans in the invasion of the Everglades. But conservationists were concerned with trying to stop not an inflow but an outflow of pilfered plants. The concern eventually shifted in the other direction. Invasives had come to be another tale of humans adding something foreign to the environment, another type of pollution that became a healthy ecosystem's burden. More than one hundred exotic species, along with new insects and pernicious organisms, had come into the Everglades by some means—in the gunnysack of an explorer or hunter, in a visitor's automobile or boat, in the bowels of a bird that fed on ornamentals in nearby residential gardens. Not all exotics were pests, but the small number of troublemakers was disproportionate to the problems they caused. Three were notably menacing—the melaleuca tree, the Brazilian pepper tree, and the Australian pine.

The Brazilian pepper and Australian pine had been around the Everglades longer than Douglas had. Locals liked the cooling shade of the Australian pine and the artistry in its twisted trunk, even as the tree aggressively supplanted native vegetation with a comparatively sterile ecology. In 1922, Douglas advanced an aesthetic argument against the tree, writing in her column, "We, for one, are a little tired of Australian pines everywhere, and think, meekly and modestly, that it wouldn't be any harm to try a few mahoganies in a few places." The drought- and flood-resistant Brazilian pepper was advertised in New York nursery catalogs in the 1830s but did not reach South Florida until the 1890s, when Douglas's friend John Gifford had propagated it. Representing her bridge between eras, another friend, Frank Craighead, in 1971 made one of the first official notations of the Brazilian pepper's presence in the park, worrying about the possibility of a disastrous spread. By the 1990s, the state had begun spending millions of dollars annually on eradication, and the National Park Service was kicking in several hundred thousand more.[7]

The melaleuca, another Australian native, had also grown into an expensive invader, and Gifford again was the guilty party. Douglas and her secretaries gathered historical materials on the tree, including testimonials by Gifford and David Fairchild stating that Gifford had received in 1906 what was apparently the first melaleuca seeds shipped to the United States. The two plantsmen cultivated the species from seedlings at Davie, north of Miami, and the melaleuca then fanned out and formed tree forests in the Everglades, too dense to provide habitat for animals while soaking up tons of water. Gifford had indeed intended to have the tree dry up the Everglades. Over the years, the naturalists' opinions of their horticultural deed diverged. Gifford, who boldly identified his work as the "conquest of nature," noted in the 1940s, "No one can predict what he will do when he drops a seed from foreign parts in a new environment. If it happens to be a weed, he may regret it, but if it is an ornamental and useful tree, he has done well for himself and posterity." Fairchild, reflecting at around the same time, questioned the appropriateness of the two men's gift to future generations. "I thought," he wrote after inspecting a series of photographs chronicling the progress of the melaleuca, "that they threatened to sweep over the Everglades and transform their broad prairies into an Australian landscape." The idea did not seem to bother the Army Corps of Engineers, which planted melaleuca to secure the ground around the base of the Lake Okeechobee dike. The trees soon invaded the lake bed, and by the 1980s, the diffusion had infested half a million Everglades acres; pure stands occupied forty thousand acres. Some people called the melaleuca the fire tree: each new Everglades blaze—and the fires grew increasingly common—triggered the trees to release seeds into the ashy, up-for-grabs environment. Scientists estimated that during a 1989 fire that charred three hundred thousand acres, melaleucas discharged billions of seeds.[8]

In 1959, Nixon Smiley of the *Miami Herald* succeeded Fairchild in questioning the value of the melaleuca. Following their inclination, Douglas made the melaleuca her bête noire when she became an environmental activist. While Juanita Greene wrote *Herald* articles about the tree, the ninety-nine-year-old Douglas spearheaded a letter-writing campaign mounted by several South Florida environmental groups to convince state officials, the South Florida congressional delegation, the Environmental Protection Agency, and Nathaniel Reed to urge the U.S. Department of Agriculture to add melaleuca to the federal list of noxious weeds. Florida's Department of Natural Resources considered designating the tree a noxious aquatic plant. Graham, Reed, Governor Bob Martinez, Representative Dante Fascell, and the Environmental Protection Agency did as she asked. Both the Brazilian pepper and the melaleuca made the state list, but Agriculture Department officials told Douglas and the others in essence that melaleuca did not threaten agriculture or public health—notwithstanding respiratory studies to the contrary—and therefore did not qualify for the federal list. In a sympathetic postscript, the department promised to continue participating in interagency and state and federal efforts at eradication.[9]

The state took the lead on exotic-plant control, initiating eradication and spending more money than the federal government. Douglas had always had a stronger working relationship with Tallahassee than with Washington, believing in part that the state had more of a vested interest in its own environmental welfare. Activists such as Joe Browder, by contrast, tended to rely heavily on the federal government, which had more money to do things such as buy land to create nature preserves and which, being more detached from the hornet's nest of local and state politics, could more effectively institute policy that displeased a constituency.

As good as the state had been to her—giving her financial security at the end of her life and showering her with awards and recognition— Douglas often regretted that it sometimes failed to heed her demands. She and the state, for example, never found common ground on the subject of hunting. The state legislature and even the Department of Natural Resources were full of hunters. Governor Chiles was a sportsman who relished being in the great outdoors with a gun cradled in his arms. There was also the incendiary issue of swamp buggies, halftracks, and airboats bearing loads of camouflaged, armed men and women and tearing across the Everglades terrain. Douglas insisted that hunting unsettled ecological balances, especially when whole populations were annihilated. Hunters argued that their activity stabilized balances when development chopped away at habitat areas, and, good conservationists that they were, they stood against the gratuitous destruction of wildlife. But Douglas was old enough to have witnessed the hungry assault on wading birds, and now the same was happening to other nongame animals, such as the Florida bobcat and otter, which were taken under commercial licenses issued by the state. To think of killing as sport was the hunter's most grievous self-delusion. Douglas wrote to Robert Brantly, head of the Florida Game and Freshwater Fish Commission and a hunter, coldly describing hunters as "people dwelling in the habits of the past, an attitude of mind which is nothing short of immature."[10]

Her environmental comrade, Johnny Jones, inevitably got an earful, too, despite their original agreement to disagree over his sport. On one occasion, she wrote to decline with regrets a conservation award from the Florida Wildlife Federation. On another occasion, she became upset with him for backing the Sportsman's Bill of Rights, a law that allowed hunting on land the state had purchased under the Endangered Lands Act and the Conservation and Recreation Lands Act. Their differences boiled down to basics. With measured patience, Jones explained that the federation members were "conservationists," not "preservationists." He believed in managing wildlife and in hunters playing a role; she quite simply did not. "If it had not been for hunting," he told her, "I probably never would have been involved in the conservation movement." He had a point, but she saw it as nothing more than a convenient palliative. The hunted animal over which they repeatedly clashed was the whitetail deer of the Everglades. As long as there had been humans in the region, deer had been the prey of hunters. But the first human inhabitants had stalked the animals for food, raiment, and other essentials, not for sport and not with off-road vehicles that gave modern-day hunters and their scent-crazed dogs access to areas that would have vexed their low-tech predecessors.[11]

Douglas and Jones agreed that nothing imperiled the deer community more than modern technology of another sordid form. Water management and wildlife were ill-suited companions. Contrary to its claims, the SFWMD could not mimic the Everglades' natural wet and dry seasons and still remain obedient to its operational guidelines. "The executive director shall be guided by the standard of public interest," they read, giving a single individual exceptional discretionary power; "users that supply necessities to the population are to be preferred over users not supplying such necessities." In other words, unless animals were harbored in the national park (a slight improvement over the days of the Central and Southern Florida Flood Control District) or considered an essential natural resource—that is, livestock—they failed to rank among the preferred. To keep agriculture quenched during dry times, the district stored water in part of a conservation area that was deer habitat. If conditions were wetter than normal, water was pumped away from agriculture and human dwellings and into, again, deer habitat. In development-obsessed South Florida, that wildlife territory was shrinking with each passing day. Mass drownings of deer often followed. The drownings horrified Douglas; Jones called them "Bambicide." Both blamed insensitive bureaucrats at the SFWMD. Drownings occurred in the early 1970s and again in September 1981 and summer 1982. In the 1980s, animal-rights activists tried with little success to relocate the deer to dry ground. The state's alternative solution was to initiate so-called mercy hunts.[12]

Such hunts reminded Douglas of a state-financed slaughter in 1937, about which she had written in *River of Grass*. South Florida cattle at the time were infested with fever ticks that were preventing the sale of the livestock outside the state. Cattlemen and the state veterinarian believed that the ticks were coming from deer and that the only way to eradicate the ticks was to eradicate the deer. The state livestock sanitary board took charge and hired hunters to do the job. "Everybody killed deer along with the well-paid gangs of deer killers," wrote Douglas. Their diminishing prey ultimately led them deep into the Everglades, where the Miccosukees and Seminoles stopped the hunters from coming onto Indian land. Around the same time, the state supreme court ruled that the sanitary board had to abide by Florida's mandated hunting seasons. An optimistic interpreter of history, Douglas wrote, "It was like the small beginning of new hope, in the century-long history of man's destructiveness here."[13]

Yet the 1970s and 1980s were decades of vanished hope. Douglas shot off a fury of letters to "everyone legally involved" in the mercy hunts. She even testified in court to seek an injunction against the 1982 hunt, which had a target kill of two thousand deer. She proposed eliminating the conservation areas to allow "sheet flow of the Everglades to proceed according to normal and natural methods." That would have solved both the deer problem and the park's perpetual underhydration. But the bureaucrats hastened to dismiss the suggestion. She was all but alone in her desire for complete prohibition of hunting. The Game and Freshwater Fish Commission was in the business of facilitating recreational hunting, and it claimed to have good reason for doing so. The commission determined that Florida's deer population had reached its capacity and that one hundred thousand deer a year died of starvation. A larger number would perish, said one state wildlife expert, if deer were not hunted. Douglas argued that the population, in Mathusian fashion, would eventually find its balance without the help of guns.[14]

Abolishing deer hunting of any kind was a battle Douglas could not win. Her fair-haired governor, Bob Graham, a nonhunter, authorized the 1982 mercy hunt. But she was not one to give up. If for no other reason, she wanted the deer left alone because hunters were depriving the endangered Florida panther of its main food source. Years later, scientists concluded that her argument was wrong. A University of Florida wildlife study showed that during hunting season, deer instinctively increased their nocturnal activity and moved deeper into the brush—that is, into panther areas. They also steered clear of roadways, which likely drew their predators away from the blacktop and consequently death by vehicular traffic. Douglas persisted. She wrote to the head of Save the Florida Panther, on whose advisory board she served, and proposed a program to have schoolchildren "get out letters of protest . . . to stop the killing of the panthers' food." Schoolchildren had a record of influence, she knew. In a recent statewide ballot, they had chosen the panther as the state animal, a selection the legislature made official in 1982.[15]

Of all the wild land animals, the panther received most of her attention. Estimates at the time put its population below fifty, and disease, inbreeding, and the encroaching human population made extinction a likely scenario. The panther was a Florida legend and popular symbol of the state's exotic wild, depicted in paintings by Winslow Homer and others. In one of the historical ironies in the American relationship with nature, the Florida panther, a member of the cougar family, acquired its subspecies identification from Palm Beach socialite and worldly huntsman Charles B. Cory, the nineteenth-century naturalist who enjoyed hunting for sport as much as for science. Panther numbers had already begun falling by the time Cory named *Puma concolor coryi*, which is slightly lighter in weight and darker in color and with longer legs and smaller feet than its seven North American subspecies counterparts. From the beginning and into the mid–twentieth century, Americans stumped for extermination of animals considered vicious or a threat to the business of civilization—the timber wolf, coyote, mountain lion, and others. The panther was an early outlaw. In 1832, the territorial legislature instituted a handsome bounty, and in Cory's day in the 1880s, a hunter could collect five dollars from the state for a panther scalp. Scientists estimated that the number of panthers, which once roamed as far as Arkansas and the Carolinas, had already dropped to 1,360. By the time the animal made the state's list of endangered species in 1958 and the federal list nine years later, some experts believed it no longer existed. Then in 1973, a team of biologists treed and anesthetized a panther, renewing hope for its future.[16]

Killing panthers had long been outlawed when a controversy arose in 1984 after Seminole chairman James E. Billie shot one on the Big Cypress reservation. Eventually charged with violating Florida laws and the federal Endangered Species Act, he defended his actions by arguing that Indians had a right to hunt and pursue traditional medicine practices on Indian land. Seminoles believed that the panther's whiskers contained medicinal powers. Some of Billie's supporters argued that the panther had become an endangered species not because of Indians but because of Tamiami Trail and I-75. Billie did not help his case by having himself photographed, Charles Cory–style, proudly displaying his trophy. Tried in federal and state courts, he faced a deadlocked jury in the first and secured a not-guilty verdict in the other. Douglas, who was sympathetic to Indian rights and rituals, came up with a "bright idea" to serve both interests. She wrote to director Brantly, encouraging the commission to collect for Indian use whiskers from panthers killed by cars.[17]

Her idea was adopted, along with others, in an attempt to save the panther. The state issued a Florida panther automobile license plate to provide proceeds to the Panther Research and Management Trust Fund. It also instituted a multitask recovery plan, which included a controversial collaring and tracking program. The program was controversial because of the criticisms of the state's most visible environmentalist. Douglas chafed against the use of radio-tracking collars, which scientists said were necessary to learn the panthers' demographic habits and hence save them. From watching her cat, Jimmy, she believed she understood a natural fact about panthers: successfully stalking food required precise timing, which could be thrown off by the weight of a collar. Moreover, she deduced from studies of other animals, collars might stop panthers from eating and copulating. All of these contentions rested on shaky ground, but she found firmer footing when she pointed out that chasing down a panther with dogs and shooting it with a tranquilizer dart risked its life. Two treed panthers had fallen to their deaths after being tranquilized, and two wearing collars had drowned. Scientists defended the collaring program, and the game commission defended the scientists. As part of the recovery plan, the federal government set up the Florida Panther National Wildlife Refuge on twenty-six thousand acres in Collier County in 1989, the same year a computer analysis convinced scientists that the animal had a 15 percent chance of averting extinction. That determination led to a captive-breeding program instituted by the U.S. Fish and Wildlife Service. Douglas first shared her "violent opposition" but then suddenly backed off and took a vow of silence on the issue. Her assistant, Sharyn Richardson, had researched the subject and advised that Jimmy was conceivably not the best source from which to judge the science. Six years later, as a component of a genetic restoration program intended to reduce instances of inbreeding, the first cougars from a Texas subspecies were released into the Everglades.[18]

When Douglas turned one hundred, she stepped down as president of Friends of the Everglades, passing the helm to her vice president, Nancy Brown, a past vice president of Tropical Audubon. Although Douglas had never before listened, old age was telling her it was time to retire from heady demands of the feisty activist. She planned to devote her days to finishing the Hudson book. For more than a decade, she had been saying it was one year from completion. Even though she had been careful to set aside at least two days a week for the book, the Everglades consumed too much of her energy.[19]

    She did manage to fit in several research trips, including three to Argentina and seven to England. She had made many of her trips while Carolyn Cole was still alive, sending long, detailed letters describing days sifting through materials at the British Museum; poring over Hudson's

letters at his former publishing house, J. M. Dent; and retracing his footsteps in Hampshire and Cornwall, the home of Douglas's Trefethen ancestors. One of her most memorable trips took her to the long-abandoned
Hudson-family estancia in Argentina, where William had spent an "important ten years" in his youth. That time, Douglas reflected, "gave him
so much understanding of the gauchos and their country." The homestead was owned by a neighbor, now elderly, who offered to drive Douglas
over for a tour of the vacated premises. But the rains had been heavy just
before her visit, and they filled the marsh surrounding the estancia and
flooded the roadway, making it impassable. "So there we were," Douglas wrote to a friend, "standing and looking over longingly at the place I
had come so far to see, and could get no nearer." But as with the deer and
the panther, she persisted, and a subsequent trip under favorable conditions allowed her to walk amid the ombu trees and comb every inch of
the estancia. Said her friend Marilyn Reed, "The only time she stumbles
is when she's involved in 10 projects."[20]

After retiring from Friends, she had only one project, at least officially,
and she could, as she said, finally put the finishing touches on the book
and behold a suitable denouement to her first career. One assistant working with her on the Hudson book died and another moved away, but
Sharyn Richardson, an environmental studies professor at a local university, shifted over from volunteer work for Friends of the Everglades, for
which she had written a pamphlet on water conditions in Lake Okeechobee. In the meantime, Marjory's Army, as her devotees called themselves,
carried on the war. The other veteran organizations, the Florida Audubon and Florida Wildlife Federation, remained very much in the thick
of things, too. There was also the second Everglades Coalition, formed in
1985 by Governor Graham, now an umbrella for twenty-five national and
state organizations. In 1993, the aggressive Everglades Foundation was
founded by George Barley, an Orlando developer and assiduous sportsman, and Paul Tudor Jones, a wealthy commodities trader and longtime
part-time Floridian.[21]

In the end, Douglas never got her two-hundred-thousand-word Hudson manuscript off to a publisher, and she never completely set aside
her environmental work. In January 1992, for example, she held a press

conference outside her Coconut Grove house to denounce a proposal by President George H. W. Bush's administration to redefine wetlands in a way that environmentalists said would lead to the exposure of half the nation's wetlands to development, including thousands of acres in the Everglades, this despite Bush's "no-net-loss" pledge. Douglas told the summoned reporters, "That is a very bad thing indeed. . . . I'm absolutely opposed. . . . We need vociferous action against it." Even while approaching age 102 years, she revealed a glimmer of the spirited fighter.[22]

After more than two decades of environmentalists' hard work, public opinion about the Everglades was shifting toward repair. Any politician wanting to maintain a favorable image therefore had to show some sensitivity to the River of Grass. And if politicians were taking the side of the Everglades, or at least pretending to do so, then environmentalists risked losing the power to make decisions about what was good or bad for the Everglades. The struggle increasingly concerned not whether something should be done but how it should be done, and as before, environmentalists found themselves losing the struggle to special interests that convinced the public that theirs was a more sensible approach than that of the squeamish activists. Environmentalists such as Douglas did not regard a clean and healthy environment as a squeamish concern. Nor did they count their cause as a special interest, instead seeing it as a universal and vital interest. Environmentalists were better organized and better funded in the 1990s than they had been twenty years earlier, even if most activists were volunteers—like Douglas—or low-income staff workers at nonprofit organizations. But in the arena of spending money to promote or lobby for their cause, the environmentalists could not compete with the other side. "For every penny sugar puts into this," said Mary Barley, who assumed command of the Everglades Foundation after her husband, George, died in a plane crash, "they get a return on their investment. For every penny we put in, we'll never see a return to us personally."[23]

Anyone who knew anything about Florida politics knew that the most powerful special interest, next to development, was agriculture. Douglas had formed a "very definite opinion about farmlands in South Florida," as she wrote to Ken Alvarez, the district biologist with the Department of

Natural Resources. She traced all the ecosystem's problems—too much water, too little water, polluted water, the more than three score endangered species, and the invasive flora—to pernicious agriculture, "beginning with the sugar cane fields around the Lake, and the tomato farms in south Dade." The corps was still back pumping into the lake, having raised the water level to store more water for farmers, which meant that avian food sources disappeared, as did large numbers of birds. The Everglades, plain and simple, could not be the real Everglades with agriculture in them. It was the running conflict with agriculture, notably Big Sugar, that pulled her out of her more-or-less retirement, and a dispute between environmentalists and politicians regarding what was best for the Everglades framed her last major public appearance as an activist.[24]

A month after she turned 101, she and Governor Chiles sat at a folding table in the shade of her front yard as the press gathered around. The governor's office had arranged the event. Chiles was there to sign legislation that pledged forty million dollars toward Everglades repair. Much of that money, state officials implied, would come from the pockets of agriculture. Having long said that "it's going to take a lot of money and attention to clean up" South Florida, Douglas had previously rejected a similar ten-million-dollar bill as inadequate. But forty million dollars had the ring of a true commitment. Douglas was flattered when Chiles wrote in her name at the front of the Everglades Protection Act. He then signed the bill and gave her the pen. She called the day "historic."[25]

In a front-yard press conference the previous year, Douglas had endorsed Chiles in the gubernatorial election. Chiles and his running mate, Buddy McKay, were standing beside her. Douglas was no fan of the current governor, Bob Martinez. He was a Republican, which was an automatic strike against him on her scorecard, and no Claude Kirk. Martinez had assured Douglas that "restoration and protection of the Kissimmee River–Lake Okeechobee–Everglades system is a major environmental goal of mine." He also hired Graham's main environmental point person, Estus Whitfield; launched Preservation 2000, a program that sold bonds to generate monies to buy environmentally sensitive lands; and sustained Graham's three "Save Our" programs. But Martinez failed to prioritize environmental protection to a degree that impressed Douglas. "I've talked to him and at him," she insisted. "If he wants to be a two-term governor, he better watch out."[26]

He was not. Chiles defeated him. As a U.S. senator, Chiles had one of the greenest voting records in Congress. He had worked vigorously to secure the Big Cypress National Preserve and had a salubrious relationship with environmentalists. During his previous Senate reelection campaign, Douglas had served, at his request, on his Environmentalists for Lawton Chiles committee. In his run for governor, he had three pet issues: education, children's health, and the environment. Chiles was also one of the smartest campaigners around. As a dark-horse candidate for the Senate in 1970, he had walked 1,033 miles from the Panhandle to Key West, shaking hands with everyone he met. People took to calling him Walkin' Lawton. They liked the folksy manner of the self-described Florida Cracker, and they appreciated his rule against accepting anything more than a one-hundred-dollar campaign donation from a single individual. They also elected him to the Senate three times and made sure he remained an undefeated candidate.[27]

But some of Douglas's friends thought that Chiles was a bit too savvy and that he took advantage of her. As it happened, she had been misinformed about the details of the legislation he signed with great fanfare in her front yard, believing that agriculture would pay for its own mess. But the law set no parameters for who would pay how much; it mentioned no forty-million-dollar spending goal; it made no specific reference to agriculture; and it offered no acknowledgment of existing pollution or the sources of that pollution. It also described its intent not in terms of reparation or pollution reduction but as a "stormwater management system" to be executed by the SFWMD. The law, critics complained, miserably failed to uphold the bold words Chiles had used in a January speech in Miami: "Sugar cane growers and other agricultural interests do not have a right to pollute the Everglades and to avoid compliance with pollution-control laws." Big Sugar would have to stop dumping bad water into the Everglades and would have to pay to clean up its waste. No panel or commission was required to tell him what needed to be done. He was a longtime friend of the Everglades and student of their ecological problems. And if any member of the water district's board of governors got in his way, he would promptly replace that person when the appointments expired in March. Environmentalists stood and applauded.[28]

Chiles had not inked in Douglas's name to a bill simply to hide the bad provisions contained within. Other political calculations were involved. At the time, Florida was entangled in a federal lawsuit claiming that the state had violated its own pollution laws and failed to protect federal property from that pollution. Despite Governor Bob Graham's Save Our Everglades program, initiated eight years earlier, little had changed for the better in the great wetland. State acquisitions of private land for the Kissimmee River restoration proceeded at a funeral's pace, and with each passing year, rising real estate prices increased costs. Beyond restoring the short, experimental leg of the river and observing the results, the corps and the SFWMD had made few other alterations. By some estimates, phosphorous levels were higher than in the past, prompting a sugar-industry spokesperson to comment, "Phosphorous makes things grow" and to call phosphorous "reverse pollution." Federal subsidies had enabled sugar planters to expand profitably into marginal lands. As Charles Lee of Florida Audubon saw it, price supports turned land that would have been unprofitable for farming into highly profitable land. Cheap water further aided the bottom line. According to a Wilderness Society study, South Florida's farmers paid nearly four cents less per acre foot of water than did urban dwellers. Put another way, agriculture paid less than 1.7 percent of the taxes that helped cover the SFWMD's $227 million budget; urban residents paid the rest. And in yet another scenario, agriculture generated around eleven hundred dollars in goods, jobs, and services for each acre foot of water it used, while urban businesses generated around eighty-two thousand dollars.[29]

None of this sat well with U.S. attorney Dexter Lehtinen, who sued the state on behalf of the national park and the Arthur R. Marshall National Wildlife Refuge, downstream recipients of sugar's refuse. A stocky, square-headed, bulldog of an attorney with a combat-scarred face, Lehtinen had been born and raised in south Dade. As an Eagle Scout,

he and his brother, Douglas, had roamed, hunted, and fished the Everglades. Lehtinen was a red-white-and-blue conservative, a decorated and
proud Vietnam veteran who had led a rifle platoon into Laos during the
1971 invasion. He was wicked smart, with degrees from Columbia University and Stanford Law School. As a member of the Florida Legislature, he had been known as a "passionate, militaristic, straight shooter."
Tapped for the U.S. attorney post in 1988, he was chosen, said associate attorney general Frank Keating, precisely because he was the "bright-
est, toughest, meanest scrapper we could find," someone who would not
flinch in the face of South Florida's notorious drug-smuggling and corruption problem. The Justice Department quickly learned what kind of
scrapper Lehtinen could be.[30]

Not long after assuming his new post, he filed the Everglades case,
doing so without clearing his actions with the Justice Department. When
the SFWMD's executive director, John Wodraska, complained to Lehtinen
about the suit, the U.S. attorney told him, "Sugar has walked all over you
guys; you're the handmaidens of agriculture." His bosses promptly summoned him to Washington, and Lehtinen remembered being told that
"Republicans don't file these sorts of lawsuits." The admonishment was
accompanied by a "long debate," which he initiated, "about Theodore
Roosevelt, and what's conservative and what's not." Lehtinen saw the
law in black-and-white, and the state was simply not enforcing its own
water-standard guidelines. In the end, Lehtinen's bosses had to stand behind their upstart. Vice President George H. W. Bush was running for
president, in the process skewering his Democratic opponent, Massachusetts governor Michael Dukakis, for a polluted Boston Harbor.[31]

Environmentalists admired Lehtinen's brassy move. For once, someone
in the federal government outside the Interior Department was standing
up for the park. Three months before he filed the suit, Douglas got wind
of Lehtinen's intentions. "It was with the greatest possible pleasure that I
have just learned that you have taken steps to sue the Board of the South
Florida Water Management District," she wrote to him. She agreed that
the district and the Department of Environmental Regulation had failed
to enforce state laws, something about which activists had complained

for years. "Your effort is the first good news we've had toward the solution of the problem with which we have been faced for so long. You have given us new hope. Let me be one of the great numbers of citizens who are happy to congratulate you for your excellent plans, and pledge to you every possible encouragement and support in carrying them out."[32]

When Chiles launched his campaign for governor two years later, the state was still wrestling with the suit. The SFWMD district had put some five million dollars toward legal fees—money, critics argued, that could have gone toward cleanup or the purchase of Everglades land. Governor Martinez tried to bargain the state out of the lawsuit by offering to donate 17,000 acres of recently purchased state property to the national park. Lehtinen rejected the deal, and Congress expanded the eastern side of the park by 107,000 acres. Countering his gubernatorial opponent, Chiles promised to stop wasting taxpayer money and to use his experience to settle the squabble between the state and the federal government. After taking office, he fired the state's high-priced private attorneys. Then in the best showman fashion, he strode his lanky frame and governorship into the federal district court in Miami and announced that he was now serving as legal counsel for the defense and that he was seeking a one-year stay to give the state a chance to show that it could improve the water quality. Here in his defense strategy was the motivation for signing the Marjory Stoneman Douglas Everglades Protection Act a few days earlier. But Lehtinen did not buy these ploys; sitting next to him in court was a glass of murky Everglades water—the state's water. In the end, Chiles knew he was defeated and theatrically declared, "Your Honor . . . I brought my sword. I want to find out who I can give that sword to and I want to be able to give that sword and have our troups [sic] start the reparation, the clean up."[33]

The cleanup was slow to come, however, and the squabbling slow to end. The agreement reached between Lehtinen and Chiles bound the state to create thirty-five thousand acres of filtering marsh, to bring phosphorous levels down 70 percent, and to meet its water-quality standards by 2002— that is, a reduction in the phosphorus level from 50 parts per billion to 10 parts per billion. This agreement meant that agriculture would have to give up land to the state and spend a lot of money to clean up its water. Instead, agriculture spent a lot of money on lawsuits and scientific research to challenge these requirements. It paid more than seventeen million dollars for a team of scientists, led by Curtis Richardson of Duke University, who concluded that 50 parts per billion was a safe level. Eventually, he revised his figure to 15.6 parts per billion, but a scientific peer-review process questioned even that figure. The SFWMD, which had spent millions fighting a cleanup plan, spent another $2.5 million fighting sugar and defending the cleanup plan. The dispute was finally settled when interior secretary Bruce Babbitt formulated a plan that pleased sugar and that Chiles and the state legislature adopted into law.[34]

Worked over heavily by sugar lobbyists, the law was hailed by Chiles and sugar barons as a model for balancing the scales between environmental protection and business. It called for the development of forty thousand acres of filtering marshes, even though sugar's scientists actually recommended one hundred thousand acres. The measure also extended the court's 2002 deadline for clean water to 2006, offered no clear plan for how to reach that level, and left the standard for water cleaner than 50 parts per billion vague. Finally, agriculture would pay for less than half the estimated seven hundred million dollars in reparation costs. The law was dubbed the Marjory Stoneman Douglas Everglades Forever Act.[35]

This came as news, dramatically shocking news, to the 103-year-old in Coconut Grove. Chiles again exercised astounding presumption: he had not learned from previous experience, and this time he used her name without her consent. Three months after receiving the Presidential Medal of Freedom and less than two months before her 104th birthday, when the bill was still pending, Douglas dispatched a letter to Chiles demanding the removal of her name. "The Act and now the new proposed amendments," she wrote, are a "blunder" and "are directly contrary to the goals and policies of my organization." A press release put out by Friends president Nancy Brown and supported by other environmental organizations, sporting groups, and the Miccosukee Indian Tribe described the bill as an affront to Douglas. Browder couldn't agree more. At a news conference at which Babbitt declared that the "River of Grass has been given a new lease on life," Browder accused the secretary of double-dealing. The Miccosukees leveled their own accusations, charging the state with using their land as a "toilet." Angering Tallahassee policymakers, the Indians set their water standard at 10 parts per billion, an action that they hoped would force the state to follow suit. The Miccosukees and the environmentalists simultaneously encouraged Floridians to support a referendum ballot for a constitutional amendment that would impose on every pound of domestic sugar sold a penny tax to go toward cleanup. By some accounts, the industry spent thirty-five million dollars to defeat the Save Our Everglades Amendment, the campaign launched by the Everglades Foundation. Sugar companies transported farmworkers across the state and dropped them off in middle-class neighborhoods, where they knocked on doors and implored voters to save their jobs. It was a scene reminiscent of the plume-hunting days, when the millinery industry sought to convince the public that wildlife protection undermined the economic interests of hardworking people. At the ballot box, sugar's disingenuous commitment to social justice won out over the activists' genuine commitment to the environment. Within a few years, machines took away the jobs of many of Big Sugar's canvassers.[36]

After setting the record straight on the Everglades Forever Act, Douglas lived on for four more birthdays. She did not live long enough to see a proper resolution in the Everglades or to consummate her relationship with Mr. Hudson. Mentally and physically, she had reached a point in which she "was incapable of holding enough in memory at one time to make decisions about what was relevant to the larger story and what was not," said Richardson. "She tired quickly and was easily distracted." Douglas had gotten her personal life in order, though, ready for the moment when she would not wake. Her papers and literary rights were assigned to the university. A few personal effects would go to friends, and she would leave small sums of money to her nurses and secretaries of the past several years and to William Henry Hudson's Royal Society for the Protection of Birds. Her presidential medal was in residence at Wellesley. The house in which she had lived for more than seventy years was to become a state historical museum and environmental learning center. Her instructions for funerary arrangements and memorial service had been imparted to her estate's administrators.[37]

The century had still been young when she disembarked from the hissing train in her blue wool dress, when she sensed from the lift of the subtropical sun a renewed self and future. Florida indeed allowed her a full life, and a surplus of years. She came of age as a writer and environmental activist. As both she helped usher in the modern era of independent activist organizations and informative ecological science, studies of which stuffed her file cabinet. She never stopped learning. She was a teacher, but she kept herself educated so that she could be a better teacher. Whenever her instincts had been wrong—about collaring panthers, controlling floodwaters, or farming in the Everglades—"she figured things out," Helen Muir said, acknowledging errors and adjusting the course. Douglas wanted those who controlled policy and whose actions disrupted a healthy environment to do the same. She carried this message as she oversaw to a significant degree the emergence of a united and unprecedented effort to try to save and even repair not just a part—a lake, hammock, marsh, or park—but an entire ecosystem. Hers had been the labors not of a single individual but of activists, scientists, right-minded politicians, and good-hearted benefactors; of that, she was faithfully aware and grateful. That the powers of growth would continue to frustrate these powers of a new kind of progress, not chamber of commerce progress but progress in environmental civility, she was also aware. How could she not be when at 103 she felt compelled to dress down a governor. Capable others would have to do that now. They would have to sustain her power as a tocsin, censor, and beacon. She may unwittingly have been referring to herself and her book when she uttered, "No matter what has happened to the state of Florida, the light, thank goodness, they haven't been able to change."[38]

"Without Me"

William "Toby" Muir's wife, Celeste, called him to the phone one afternoon. "Jarjee" wanted to talk to him. Douglas was probably 106 at the time, and Muir surely had not expected a phone call from her. But there on the line was that familiar resonant voice. "Toby," she asked, "do you still have your sailboat?" He did. "It has been a long time since I've been sailing. Would you take me sailing?" He would. "How long is your boat?" Twenty-three feet. "As I remember, it is a sloop, isn't it?" Yes. "Now a sloop has only one mast, isn't that right?" Yes. "It is the ketch and the yawl that have two masts." True. "And it is the yawl that has the mizzenmast behind the rudder." For a half hour, the questions and conversation continued. Marjory Stoneman Douglas still knew a thing or two about boats. She might have been gathering information for a story, except that writing stories was long behind her. She wanted to go sailing, though, and at this moment she was not thinking of the inability of her mostly bedridden body to carry out the vision so clear in her mind. Before hanging up, she told Muir she would have to find her bathing suit or buy a new one. They made a date for the following weekend. But Muir knew that she would soon forget the conversation.[1]

Although Douglas continued to hold occasional press conferences and to make public speeches after she turned one hundred and retired from Friends of the Everglades, she was clearly declining. A few months after Governor Lawton Chiles signed the calamitous Marjory Stoneman Douglas Everglades Protection Act in her front yard, she went into the hospital with swallowing problems. The doctors and nurses believed she was intentionally starving herself, dismissing her as an old woman going out into the woods to die. But they put little effort into trying to communicate with their near-deaf patient. Sharyn Richardson explained to Douglas that she would die if she did not eat. "Well," she responded resolutely, "I certainly don't want to do that." She would have a bowl of vanilla ice cream, which Richardson gladly retrieved from bemused nurses.[2]

After her release from the hospital, she functioned with increasingly impaired mental faculties. A full-time aid, Medina Brown, came to care for her, as did the Wellesley Club and many of her friends. Some stopped coming around after she began spending much of her time in bed and required assistance (fetching her a glass of water or escorting her to the bathroom). One or two trailed off when they realized they no longer had a drinking buddy. Helen Muir wished her friend had been spared the last declining years. Around the time of the telephone conversation with Toby, Helen asked how she was feeling generally. "Like a caged bird, my dear," she said. "Like a caged bird."[3]

Sometimes, though, she got to spread her wings, as in 1993, when she went to the White House to receive the Presidential Medal of Freedom. The year before, Hillary Clinton had come to Miami to campaign for Bill's run for the presidency. The Wellesley Club hosted Clinton, a fellow alumna, and took her to the Stewart Avenue home of the oldest living Wellesley graduate. Clinton was familiar with Douglas and her hard work to protect the Everglades, cheerfully sitting next to her and chatting as she lay in bed. Douglas was an important enough individual that Hillary Clinton sought her endorsement for Bill. And Douglas eventually gave it. The next year, both Clintons came to Miami, and this time Douglas was rallied into evening clothes and a wheelchair to meet the president and First Lady at a reception at the Sheraton Bal Harbor Hotel, the site of

many environmental conferences of years before. Bill knelt next to Douglas, held her hand, and raised his voice above the din to have a short conversation with her. Among other things, he said she should come to the
White House to visit, repeating an invitation Hillary had previously extended. Kathy Gaubatz, one of the Wellesley "mafia" who escorted Douglas that night, saw this as an opportunity. For the next few months, she
and the Miami Wellesley Club delivered a steady stream of letters and
phone calls to the First Lady and her aides.[4]

In November, Douglas traveled to Washington to receive the Presidential Medal of Freedom, along with Joseph Rauh, William Brennan Jr.,
John Minor Wisdom, and the late Thurgood Marshall, and to witness the
signing of the Brady gun-control bill. The trip required a small entourage
to assist the 103-year-old. Plane and taxi travel exhausted her, as did the
three-day stay in the White House, away from familiar surroundings and
the "memory-paths" along which she padded at home. At moments she
looked shockingly cadaverous, an appearance propounded by an untra-
ditional reticence and a slumped-over torpidity. During other moments,
the old glow and a faint reminder of the schoolgirl posture returned. At
the awards ceremony, Douglas was mostly in good form. She wore a dress
borrowed from the mother of Linda Dann, another Wellesley Club member, and a two-hundred-dollar white, narrow-brimmed hat Richardson
bought for the occasion. Douglas was attentive and engaged, although
she delayed the start of the ceremony when she announced at the decibel
level of an elderly deaf person that she needed to excuse herself to the ladies' room. Finally, in her wheelchair, hands folded properly across her
lap, she wore a smile as President Clinton told her, "Mrs. Douglas, the
next time I hear someone mention the timeless wonders and powers of
Mother Nature, I'll be thinking about you."[5]

Douglas lacked something less than the powers of Mother Nature, but
there was certainly a timelessness about her. She was a vintage woman of
the Victorian era who in the budding Internet age advocated for a cause
of contemporary importance, informed by modern science. Although she
was infirm and ebbing mentally, she still had star power. She had become
the spirit of the Everglades, a once destitute wilderness that the American

public announced it wanted to save. No one else had won the Presidential Medal of Freedom for trying to repair the Everglades. No one else had
an Everglades Wilderness Area dedicated in her name. No one else had
written *River of Grass*. She received hundreds of birthday cards each year,
and at public events, politicians scrambled to have their photos taken
with her. Invoking her name in a cabinet meeting, legislative debate, or a
public hearing had meaning.

Her name continued to carry weight after her death. Her ashes had
been drifting in the Everglades for only a month when the Army Corps of
Engineers produced the draft of a comprehensive plan to do what Douglas had demanded into her last days: repair the Everglades. When the U.S.
Senate Committee on Environment and Public Works held hearings in
2000 on the plan, the remarks of several witnesses and committee members quoted Douglas or *River of Grass*. Republican chair Bob Smith of
New Hampshire summed up his opening remarks by repeating a plea
from Douglas: "A century after man first started to dominate the Everglades, the progress has stumbled. Consequences have started to catch up.
It is perhaps an opportunity. The great wet wilderness of South Florida
need not be degraded to a permanent state of mediocrity. If the people
will it, the Everglades can be restored."[6]

Just before the 106th Congress adjourned, lawmakers passed an updated Water Resources Development Act. Title IV of the act, known as
the Comprehensive Everglades Restoration Plan (CERP), stimulated
vigorous across-the-aisle handshaking. Policymakers and the press hailed
the $7.8-billion, thirty-six-year restoration initiative, unprecedented in
spending and scope, as the wave of the new century. With the development of sixty-eight engineering projects, all to create a new and improved
sheet-flow system, the plan promised a trillion gallons a year in additional
water, enough for farmers, city dwellers, the national park, and birds and
alligators. Interior secretary Bruce Babbitt, a stalwart supporter of CERP
from the beginning, said, "It's going to open an entirely new chapter
in conservation history." In a special 2001 issue of *Audubon* magazine,
"The Everglades Rises Again," National Audubon expressed the opinion of other environmentalists, scientists, civic and recreational groups,

industrial and agricultural interests, and former Environmental Protection Agency chief Carol Browner, who grew up next to the Everglades,
when it called CERP a "blueprint for the future," a plan that "will serve as
a road map for the rescue of other battered ecosystems" around the globe.
The plan had its critics, but in the pages of *Audubon* they included only
ranchers and property-rights advocates who thought restoring the Kissimmee River a fool's errand. National Audubon was emerging as the "big
tiger" defending the plan and assuming a take-what-you-can-get attitude
while recognizing some of the plan's flaws. Taxpayers rather than agriculture would be paying the CERP bill; this was regrettable, the special issue
acknowledged, but Audubon was willing to accept this reality. Once the
project was set in motion, the potential for expensive foul-ups and false
starts was another reality. The inchoate science of ecological restoration
demanded both an adaptive-management approach and dogged patience,
and Audubon leaders believed that CERP's on-site architect, the corps,
was equal to the task. Audubon's about-face from opposing restoration
by corps edict grated on Browder. Its solicitous tone was at odds with the
organization that had been in the Everglades trenches since the days of
plume hunting. Notwithstanding his own years in the trenches, the special issue made no mention of Browder or the stalwart Johnny Jones. It
quoted *River of Grass*'s famous opening sentence but otherwise ignored
Douglas's memory. The assembly of CERP critics was more diverse and
their credentials more significant than the magazine suggested.[7]

Before implementation could validate or disprove anyone's claims
about CERP, promising developments were unfolding with the new century. Carrying forward an ongoing project from the 1980s, the corps had
opened up fourteen miles of the old Kissimmee River by the tenth anniversary of Douglas's death. Johnny and Mariana Jones toured part of the
restored river early on and were impressed by nature's ability to rejuve-
nate itself. Under the Everglades Forever Act, vilified by environmentalists, the state had created forty thousand acres of filtering swamps, and
the phosphorus levels in the stored sugar water had declined by more
than half, to around twenty parts per billion. Organized citizens also beat
an airport proposal in South Florida. Once again, the Department of the

Interior defended Everglades and Biscayne National Parks against another federal agency—in this case, the Federal Aviation Administration, which was prepared to approve a plan by a local investment group to refit Homestead Air Force Base, shut down after Hurricane Andrew and lying between the two parks, into a commercial airport. Some Everglades Coalition members who supported CERP refused to stand with the Sierra Club, Natural Resources Defense Council, and Friends of the Everglades against the proposal. Browder himself was having none of another noxious airport scheme in South Florida. He convinced Tropical Audubon to part with the position of National Audubon and the Florida Audubon Society and support the protection of the two parks. But he could not convince the Clinton administration or Democratic candidate Al Gore, in the midst of the turbid 2000 presidential campaign, to do the same. Browder turned to Ralph Nader, the Green Party candidate, "with information he could use about Gore's" unwillingness to acknowledge the airport's potential harm to the environment. Nader publicly accused Gore of environmental double-dealing. Gore lost the Florida vote and the election, and the investment group lost when Air Force officials rejected their proposal. In another familiar saga, Friends, the Florida Wildlife Federation, and the Miccosukees sued the South Florida Water Management District (SFWMD) for back pumping farm water into Lake Okeechobee without obtaining necessary Clean Water Act permits. This time, the environmentalists won. And the Natural Resources Defense Council took legal measures to stop the corps and the Bush administration from allowing a "massive rock mining project" in the Everglades. These efforts and others paid off: in 2006, the Everglades had fifty-five thousand wading-bird nests, up from a low of five thousand in the mid-1980s.[8]

But with the good came plenty of bad. The legislature pushed the Everglades Forever Act's 2006 deadline for reaching ten parts per billion back another ten years, forcing Friends and the Miccosukees to take the state to court. After the corps discovered leaks in its Hoover Dike in 2006, it lowered the level of Lake Okeechobee by a foot as a precaution against a breach; the level was then lowered a few more feet in anticipation of hurricane season. These actions left the canals to the Seminoles' Brighton and Big Cypress Reservations dry, and bureaucrats and engineers attempted to figure out how to get water to the Indians. Friends and the Miccosukees filed another federal suit to stop the SFWMD from pumping agriculture's foul into Conservation Area 3. The conservation area is really the upper reach of Shark River Slough, the park's main water source from the north. Water bureaucrats typically kept the floodgates at Tamiami Trail closed, which meant parkland below remained dangerously dry while Miccosukee territory above remained dangerously wet, a condition that imperiled the Everglades snail kite. Yet letting water flow to avail the indigenous bird created another problem that shared a tragic similarity with that of the kite: engineers would drain water into the park through improperly located canals and risk inundating the endangered Cape Sable seaside sparrow. The ungainly artificial system showed once again the magnitude of its opposition to Nature's providence. Another compromised species, the Florida panther, hit a wall, as the *New York Times* put it. Crossbreeding with the Texas subspecies threatened to overwhelm the Florida subspecies. Equally problematic, an animal that required a roaming range of up to two hundred square miles was unlikely to reach a population of 250, the number scientists estimated the species needed to sustain itself, in a state that would not stop growing and gobbling up habitat. In 2007, a record fifteen panthers were killed on Florida roads. Although Miami–Dade County had stopped a major legal and political effort launched by developers to push into the East Everglades, developers on the west side, in Collier and Lee Counties—panther country—were draining wetland for gated communities of air-conditioned homes on treeless lots and for a state university. Developers were also eying farmland in the Everglades Agricultural Area, where growers, tired of environmentalists and government regulations, were threatening to go into the real estate business. If the real estate boom harkened to days of old, the ghost of Frank Stoneman spoke in 2003 when atmospheric scientists determined that converting wetland to farmland in South Florida had precipitated a number of crop freezes in recent decades, including a 1997 chill that caused three hundred million dollars in damages.[9]

Everglades management seemed as dysfunctional as ever. The state controlled some parts of the Everglades, local governments other parts, and the federal government still others. No consistent water-quality standard existed across the region, and the various governments involved clearly could not agree on what such a standard might be. The corps claimed that under CERP it would be removing hundreds of miles of water-control devices, but it also promised to build new structures that would likely add to rather than diminish the overall size of the water-management system. Meanwhile, experts had revised the estimate of restoration upward from $7.8 billion to more than $10 billon. The federal government had invested only $358 million in CERP, while the state had spent nearly $2 billion. This meant the state was guiding CERP. Governor Jeb Bush, a self-proclaimed champion of restoration, once purportedly told aides, "We don't need [environmentalists'] permission to save the Everglades." But Bush wanted to save the Everglades his way, which included stocking the SFWMD with cronies from among the development, finance, and agriculture industries. They quickly showed their colors and adopted a plan to meet a midcentury forecast for the cities' water supply needs within ten years. The governor's brother, President George W. Bush, angered CERP backers when, around the sixtieth anniversary of the publication of *River of Grass*, he vetoed a spending bill that included $2 billion for Everglades restoration. Congress overrode Bush's veto of the spending bill—the first time it had overridden one of this president's vetoes—but then experts again revised their estimates for CERP costs, pushing the figure up to $20 billion. And for what? An internal Army Corps of Engineers memo revealed that in five years, the corps had not built a single project, though it was somehow $1 billion over budget. Audubon, which had its reputation wrapped up in the project, defended the corps for its candor. All this happened around the time a young assistant secretary of the interior, Todd Willens, engineered the removal of Everglades National Park from the United Nations' list of endangered World Heritage Sites.[10]

Some CERP supporters were beginning to think that the plan's opponents had perhaps been right. But the bipartisan enthusiasm and commitment in resources had made challenging the plan difficult. It had also been made seductive with the suggestion that it would fulfill the legacy of the Everglades' protector-matriarch. At the dedication of the Marjory Stoneman Douglas Wilderness Area in 1997, Vice President Gore used the occasion to announce that a massive Everglades replumbing project sparing no expense would soon be forthcoming. The day after President Clinton signed the plan into law, National Public Radio's *Morning Edition* aired a story about an orchestral tribute that composer Steve Heitzig had written in honor of Douglas; the work used manatee bones, seashells, and sawgrass as percussion instruments. Introducing the story, *Morning Edition* host Bob Edwards indicated that the new restoration plan was the culmination of Douglas's "last project." In light of the new law, Wellesley College officials decided to name Douglas the college's Person of the Week.[11]

But Douglas had not set aside her literary life in 1979 to work toward a plan that failed to make the Everglades whole again, a wholeness to which she originally gave eloquent importance in *River of Grass.* The natural conditions of an ecosystem could not be restored if that ecosystem remained under human control. The natural flow of the River of Grass could not be redeemed if agriculture were allowed to keep its real estate blocking the flow. The dreadful destroyer of the Everglades, the Army Corps of Engineers, could not be their restorer. Browder compared the corps' mandated role as custodian of the Everglades to putting the "Bureau of Reclamation in charge of protecting the Grand Canyon." He was also outraged at the federal government's refusal to consider a scientific peer review of the plan until after the legislation had been passed. In 2003, the National Academy of Sciences released a doleful assessment of CERP, concluding that "restoration goals, objectives, and targets for the Everglades are inadequately defined and are not reconciled with the large-scale forces of change in south Florida." To Browder, CERP amounted to junk science.[12]

That is how the Friends of the Everglades saw things. Two months before Clinton authorized the plan, Friends and the Biodiversity Legal Foundation, a component of the public-interest law firm Earthjustice, sent an eight-page letter to the House Committee on Transportation and Infrastructure detailing objections to CERP. It was clear to Friends investigators that the plan was meant to keep agriculture and cities well fortified with liquid sustenance. Although the descriptive lineage had descended from *drainage* to *flood control* to *water management* to *restoration,* the imperatives in Everglades policy had hardly changed. The plan would produce "insufficient" water for the park and nature, noted the letter, but water aplenty to allow the cities to keep growing. CERP also rejected "biologically friendly, natural-system based restoration for expensive, unproven, high-technology efforts" and "almost completely ignored" the habitat of native species. Finally, it was too damn expensive. The letter, not CERP, honored Douglas's legacy.[13]

In the summer of 2008, Governor Charlie Crist excited international press coverage and streams of e-mail exchanges between environmentalists about the potential for a shift in the dynamics of Everglades restoration when he announced state plans to buy out the properties of U.S. Sugar, 187,000 acres, the largest private landholding in the Everglades Agricultural Area. The implications were enormous. With a closing price of $1.75 billion, likely to represent the largest single expenditure for a conservation land acquisition, the purchase suggested that Big Sugar would no longer be so big or such a burly gorilla in state politics. Piggybacking on Crist's announcement, SFWMD officials conceded something that environmentalists not quoted in the *Audubon* special issue had argued steadily: CERP's water-quality goals using primarily filtering marshes were unrealistic. If engineered properly, restoration of U.S. Sugar land could mean the salubrious segregation of befouled agricultural water within the Everglades Agricultural Area and the partial restoration of natural flows into the conservation areas and national park unencumbered by the resource demands of sugar, vegetable, and grass-sod growers. Friends of the Everglades described the impending purchase (likely to take place in 2014) as "jaw-dropping," a "historic turn in the course of Everglades Restoration." Browder, who as much as anyone retains Douglas's philosophical spirit, believed that she would have heartily applauded the Republican governor's proposal as a "bolder and more fundamental step towards Everglades restoration than any actions since Everglades National Park was established in 1947." Yet ever cautious with enthusiasm, she would have advised taxpayers to ensure that they were buying a package that included reclaiming the "integrity of water flows, natural habitats, and wildlife within the millions of acres of Everglades in down-stream National Park, Miccosukee, and Conservation Area lands."[14]

Two organizations, Friends of the Everglades and the Marjory Stoneman Douglas Biscayne Nature Center, occupied the best position for carrying on Douglas's legacy after her death. With its multi-million-dollar edu-cation and research facility, brightened by approving natural light, the nature center reached young minds and touched the future to an extent Douglas might not have imagined. Friends too had persevered without its founder, with a steady membership of around four thousand. With Browder, Juanita Greene, Johnny Jones, and Nancy Brown on its board of directors, it had the means to retain its historical memory. Still, it had been forced into metamorphosis. It began spending more time on litiga-tion and less time on the hard streets of activism. Douglas had been not only the organization's chief agitator and "elocutor"—or, more precisely, Friends had been the foundation supporting her ferment—but also its identity. Her star appeal could not be replicated. The same was true for the Everglades. No voice had replaced hers; no one individual person-ified the Everglades as had she. Other groups could organize, put up useful Web sites, and lobby the water management district, Tallahassee policymakers, and Congress; other activists could claim a scientific un-derstanding of the Everglades. But Douglas's book first laid out the idea of the necessity of a conjoined Everglades system, a living expanse of not just water but of air, rock, rain, sky, plants, animals, light, and the poetic enunciations of all. Therein lay the difference between Douglas and virtu-ally everyone else who came in contact with or defended the Everglades. Few could master the science and the politics and grasp the poetry too.

The breadth of Douglas's Everglades errand provided the muse for *Voice of the Everglades (Epitaph for Marjory Stoneman Douglas)*. Heitzig had not yet visited the Everglades when he began composing his orchestral piece, but he had read *River of Grass,* and he was touched. An equal part of the appeal was Douglas's political fight. "She was outspoken, she was direct, she had the energy and belief to make the world a better place," he said. The photographs of Clyde Butcher, whose Everglades art reminded people of Ansel Adams in the way it captured the unfolding landscape and cloud mountains, all of which had moved Douglas to literary expression, accompanied the music and Butcher's voice-over narration telling the story of Douglas and the Everglades. "We're trying to wake people up," said Butcher, whose full white beard, large self, and suspenders reminded one of an Old Testament prophet. Following Douglas's example, he and Heitzig were inspired to bring people to "another level of sensitivity that will develop into one more step toward seeing the light."[15]

The other entity that embodied the sum and the spirit of her life was her house. It was to be a museum. Or was it? By the last decade of her life, Coconut Grove was growing less bohemian and more ostentatious. Older, less capacious houses—like hers—were either being razed and replaced with larger homes that poorly mimicked grand architecture or being reconstituted on a larger scale. Such residences had grown up on Stewart Avenue, casting cautionary shadows over her small house. In 2007, the county estimated the market value of her 943-square-foot cottage at six hundred thousand dollars. The houses to each side and the three across the street averaged 6,144 square feet with an average market value of $2.1 million.[16] History had been sacrificed for space. It was perhaps inevitable that the land trust in charge of converting her vacated house into a museum ran into trouble with neighbors. Some accused the trust of neglecting the appearance of the house and yard, although other neighbors said the complainers contributed to the "eyesore" by having their landscaping services dump their yard refuse on Douglas's property. Sallye Jude, the head of the land trust, erupted a firestorm of angry protests when she started talking about rebuilding the Cole house to create an environmental learning center and hosting daily visits by schoolchildren. Neighbors envisioned convoys of yellow school buses rumbling down their narrow street, an endless shuffling of parking cars, and strangers lurking outside their gated compounds. At a public hearing, one neighbor, a realtor named Jeffrey Schottenstein, pursued Jude, a septuagenarian hardly five feet tall, across the room wagging his finger and browbeating her until she cowered and broke into tears. Another neighbor, John Freud, whose 4,900-square-foot home abutted the Cole property, sent a succession of communications to the Division of State Lands on his law firm's letterhead. In one he warned that "litigation will surely result" unless the state terminated the lease with the trust. In another missive, he maintained that museum custodians were willfully attempting "to disrupt and forever alter the essential nature and character of the street and immediate neighborhood where Douglas lived" (overlooking the fact that his neighbors' newer, larger houses had already done that). He described the trust as "power hungry and arrogant" and run by a cadre of "sycophants" motivated "solely by personal gain," while Jude maintained a "'holier than thou' attitude." Even some people who agreed with Jude privately believed that her abrasive manner had inflamed the conflict, and they wanted her out.[17]

By the spring of 2005, the trust had spent eighty-three thousand dollars to put on a new cedar-shingle roof (though not being true to the original), smarten up the exterior, recondition the furniture, and rewax the wood floors. The house had never looked better. Then in the fall, hurricanes ripped through South Florida, and a blue tarpaulin, a familiar after-storm hue in Florida, went atop Douglas's roof. House repairs in the region were backlogged for a year or more, an unpleasant reality for the neighbors. Beleaguered by the opposition and the storms, Jude began thinking that the best solution might be to move the house to Fairchild Garden. Freud and Schottenstein had made a similar suggestion to the state years earlier. There would be a buffer between the house/museum and peaceful neighborhoods and ample parking; equally important, Fairchild had had special meaning to Douglas. Some of her old friends liked the idea, but others were appalled by the thought of cutting Douglas's house in two and uprooting it from the original site. This was her patch of Coconut Grove, where she planted and tended her green garden, where she sat on the back porch and wrote *River of Grass*. A regionalist, she embraced the notion that cultural memory and tradition were grounded in the land as well as buildings. A historian, she understood that a place with no sense of its history had no sense of its self, that it grew impersonal and culturally barren. A culture cannot burrow roots and thrive when the physical setting has little permanence. Too often in her lifetime, change had trumped preservation. Toby Muir shared the foreboding about the past having a stake in Florida's future. "You can't pack history like a suitcase and carry it to another site," he said during the conflict. As the state considered the merits of the relocation, the Coconut Grove Village Council adopted a resolution to keep the house in its place, and the Marching Marjorys, a group of one hundred people dressed in wide-brim hats and big glasses, joined in the King Mango Strut, "Miami's zaniest parade, to protest what a mounting number of Miamians think is a zany idea." The state ultimately decided the half-million-dollar cost of moving the house was impractical. It relieved the trust of its oversight, with no objection from Jude, and put the state Department of Recreation and Parks in charge. A ranger from a nearby historic park took occupancy of the house and cleaned up the grounds. Peace returned to Stewart Avenue. But the future of the museum, like that of the Everglades, remained uncertain.[18]

Two other markers of Douglas's legacy remain. At age 107, she learned that Congress had given her name to the Everglades Wilderness Area, and she was flattered. Here finally was an award that might facilitate her cause. She was even more pleased to learn that the same legislation named a new $2.8-million Everglades National Park visitor center after her old friend and activist inspiration, Ernest Coe. He was finally being properly honored. Both Coe and Douglas loved the park as much as anything else. It preserved the regional heart of South Florida even while the rest of it was disappearing under concrete and artificiality. The wilderness area and visitor center seemed a compact for the park's future.

Anyone unsure of what was required to secure the future of the park and the Everglades needed only to heed the wisdom in *River of Grass:* make them whole again. When the publisher released an anniversary edition in 2007, the book had for sixty years preserved that wisdom. But the architects of CERP had apparently failed to read beyond that most famous opening sentence, "There are no other Everglades in the world." They apparently also had failed to regard closely another oft-quoted line: "The Everglades is a test. If we pass it, we get to keep the planet." These words have been falsely attributed to Douglas. They actually belong to Joe Podgor, but Douglas certainly agreed, and she was hopeful about humanity's ability to pass the test. As she said when at the peak of her influence, "I believe in the endurance of man. I don't despair the human race. How can I? I am a part of it. I believe it will endure. It's going to have to get along without me."[19]

Notes

ABBREVIATIONS

AMP   Arthur R. Marshall Jr. Papers, P. K. Yonge Library of Florida History, Special and Area Studies Collection, University of Florida, Gainesville

CPC   Claude Pepper Collection, Claude Pepper Library, Florida State University, Tallahassee

Florida   Marjory Stoneman Douglas, *Florida: The Long Frontier* (New York: Harper and Row, 1967)

FSA   Florida State Archives, Tallahassee

HMSF   Historical Museum of Southern Florida, Miami

HP   Martha Hubbart Papers, in possession of author

IIF Minutes   *Minutes, Board of Trustees of the Internal Improvement Fund of the State of Florida,* Florida State Archives, Tallahassee

JBP   Joe B. Browder Papers, copy in possession of author

MH   *Miami Herald*

MMJP   May Mann Jennings Papers, P. K. Yonge Library of Florida History, Special and Area Studies Collection, University of Florida, Gainesville

MSD   Marjory Stoneman Douglas

MSDP   Marjory Stoneman Douglas Papers, Archives and Special Collections Department, Otto G. Richter Library, University of Miami, Miami

NYT   *New York Times*

PKY   P. K. Yonge Library of Florida History, Special and Area Studies Collection, University of Florida, Gainesville

River of Grass   Marjory Stoneman Douglas, *The Everglades: River of Grass* (Sarasota, Fla.: Pineapple, 1997)

SEP   *Saturday Evening Post*

SPOHP   Samuel Proctor Oral History Program, University of Florida, Gainesville

SPT   *St. Petersburg Times*

UM   Archives and Special Collections, Otto G. Richter Library, University of Miami, Miami

USF   Special Collections Department, University of South Florida Library, Tampa

Voice   Marjory Stoneman Douglas with John Rothchild, *Marjory Stoneman Douglas: Voice of the River* (Sarasota, Fla.: Pineapple, 1987)

WP   *Washington Post*

CHAPTER ONE: Journey's End

1. Sandy Dayhoff, interview by author, 16 March 2006; *Seminole Tribune*, 5 June 1998.

2. H.R. 136, To Amend the National Parks and Recreation Act of 1978, 105th Cong., 1st sess., 7 January 1997 (copy provided by Sandy Dayhoff); Friends of the Everglades, Miami, Fla., "Marjory Stoneman Douglas Wilderness Act Clears House," press release, 4 November 1997; *NYT,* 26 December 1997.

3. Dayhoff, interview.

4. *River of Grass,* 5; *SPT,* 16 July 2001; *USA Today,* 15 May 1998; Matt Schudel, "Marjory's Place," *Fort Lauderdale Sun-Sentinel,* 2 May 1999, 19; Helen Muir, interview by author, 11 March 1999.

5. Joe Podgor, interview by author, 10 August 2000; Helen Muir, interview; Franklin Adams, interview by author, 8 August 2000; *MH,* 11 June 1920; Al Burt, "The Grande Dame of the Everglades," clipping, MSDP, box 39, folder 11; Al Burt, "The Elocutioner," clipping, MSDP, box 39, folder 12; Joette Lorion, "Ode to Marjory," 14 May 1998, available online at www.everglades.org/memorial (accessed spring 2006); *Fort Lauderdale Sun-Sentinel,* 14 May 1998; *MH,* 19 May 1985; *SPT,*

7 April 1992, 7 April 1994, 15 May 1998; Stephen W. Byers, "Don't Mess with Her Wetlands," *New York Times Magazine,* 3 January 1999, 46; Hampton Dunn, "The Introduction of Marjory Stoneman Douglas," speech, 1 April 1972, Hampton Dunn Collection, MSD folder, USF.

6. Dayhoff, interview; Helen Muir, interview; Schudel, "Marjory's Place," 23.

7. William Muir, interview by author, 8 December 2007; Marjory Stoneman Douglas, death certificate, 14 May 1998, Florida Office of Vital Statistics. The official cause of death was dehydration.

8. Theo Long, interview by author, 23 July 2002; Martha Hubbart, interview by author, 14 August 2002; Lili Krech Neale, interview by author, 18 November 2005; William Muir, interview.

9. Kathy Gaubatz, interview by author, 10 January 2008.

10. Joe Browder, interview by author, 7 August 2002; Nancy Brown, interview by author, 27 August 2000; Hubbart, interview; *MH,* 15 May 1998; *Orlando Sentinel,* 8 June 1996; *SPT,* 8 June 1996.

11. Byers, "Don't Mess with Her Wetlands," 46; Joe Browder to author, 13 October 2005, 14 January 2008; Adams, interview; Browder, interview; Hubbart, interview; Neale, interview; Podgor, interview; William Muir, interview; Dayhoff interview; Juanita Greene, interview by author, 16 March 2006; *MH,* 21 December 1920, 24 May 1998; "Marjory Stoneman Douglas: A Memorial Tribute," Everglades National Park, 23 May 1998 (program provided by Sandy Dayhoff); *NYT,* 15 May 1998; Leslie Poole, "Woman of the Century," *Florida Naturalist* 71 (Summer 1998): 8–9; *USA Today,* 17 May 1998; *MH,* 15, 24 May 1998; *SPT,* 15 May 1998; "Marjory Stoneman Douglas, 1890–1998," 14 May 1998, available online at www .everglades.org (accessed spring 2006).

12. George Rosner, "Meals and Marjory," 22 March 1990, provided to author by Alice Knight; Hubbart, interview.

13. *MH,* 23 October 1922; Sharyn T. Richardson, "Marjory Stoneman Douglas: Her Place on Earth," *Florida Living,* May 1999, 27; John Hicks, "Marjory Stoneman Douglas," *Florida* (*Orlando Sentinel*), 14 October 1979, 7; Helen Muir, interview.

14. *MH,* 15 May 1998; Adams, interview; Browder, interview; Helen Muir, interview; *SPT,* 15 May 1998; *Jacksonville Florida Times-Union,* 6 June 1994; Al Burt, "The Grande Dame of the Everglades," in Al Burt, *Becalmed in the Mullet Latitudes: Al Burt's Florida* (Port Salerno, Fla.: Classics Library, 1983), 131–33; MSD, interview by Lois Knowles, circa 1993, HP; MSD to Nedra, 22 December 1989, HP.

15. *MH,* 16 May 1920; Podgor, interview; Judy Wilson Lawrence, interview by author, 3 November 2005. See also Jack E. Davis, ed., *The Wide Brim: Early Poems and Ponderings of Marjory Stoneman Douglas* (Gainesville: University Press of Florida, 2001).

16. Burt, "Elocutioner"; *Tropic (MH),* 18 March 1984, 4 April 1982; "Honored, Marjory Stoneman Douglas," *Time,* 13 December 1993, 3; Anastasia Toufexis and William McWhirter, "Lady of the Everglades," *Time,* 31 January 1983, 57; MSD, interview; Podgor, interview; Helen Muir, interview.

17. *Voice,* 85, 69, 128, 177; Hicks, "Marjory Stoneman Douglas," 7.

18. *MH,* 15 May 1998; *SPT,* 15 May 1998; *Sarasota Herald-Tribune,* 8 March 1993; *Orlando Sentinel,* 1 April 1990; *Orlando Sentinel Star,* 15 April 1973; *Tampa Tribune,* 15 May 1998; *Voice,* 252–56; MSD to Fred, 29 December 1971, Emma D. Gaylord Papers, MSD folder, Department of Special Collections, Rollins College, Winter Park, Fla.; MSD to A. Esperando Roseberry, 8 September 1986, MSDP, box 46, folder 106; John Doussard, "'It's Never Too Late for Anything,'" clipping, n.d., MSDP, box 11, folder 11; MSD to Robinettes, 18 July 1985, Maud Davis to MSD, 13 November 1984, MSD to Maud Davis, 18 June 1985, all in MSDP, box 40, folder 21; Dava Sobel, "Still Fighting the Good Fight for the Everglades," *Audubon,* July–August 1991, 39; *Great Floridians Film Series: Marjory Stoneman Douglas* (Tallahassee: Museum of Florida History and Florida History Associates, 1990); Hubbart, interview.

19. *Orlando Sentinel Star,* 15 April 1973; Hubbart, interview.

20. William Henry Hudson, *Green Mansions: A Romance of the Tropical Forest* (New York: Modern Library, 1916); Sharyn T. Richardson to Royce Bemis, 23 May 1993, HP; "Abstract," 1993 manuscript of "W. H. Hudson and the Green World," HP; *MH,* 7 April 1980.

21. Marjory Stoneman Douglas, *Nine Florida Stories,* ed. Kevin M. McCarthy (Gainesville: University Press of Florida, 1990); Marjory Stoneman Douglas, *"A River in Flood" and Other Florida Stories,* ed. Kevin M. McCarthy (Gainesville: University Press of Florida, 1998).

22. Browder, interview; *Voice,* 233; Sobel, "Still Fighting," 35; *Tampa Tribune,* 16 May 1981.

23. Adams, interview; Brown, interview; Podgor, interview; *Voice,* 233; *Special Voices, Two Florida Women: Marjorie Carr, Marjory Stoneman Douglas,* video production (Florida Atlantic University/Florida International University, Joint Center for Environmental and Urban Problems, 1985).

24. Roderick Nash, *Wilderness and the American Mind*, 3rd ed. (New Haven: Yale University Press, 1982), 85, 86–88; John Muir, *The Mountains of California* (San Francisco: Sierra Club Books, 1988), 45; Stephen Fox, *The American Conservation Movement: John Muir and His Legacy* (Madison: University of Wisconsin Press, 1981), 84–85; Thomas P. Slaughter, *The Natures of John and William Bartram* (New York: Vintage, 1996); Adams, interview; William Muir, interview; Podgor, interview.

25. *MH*, 21 November 1922. "Writer's notebook" is a reference MSD sometimes used in her daily column to identify specific writings. Many issues of her column, "The Galley," are found in Book of the Galley, MSDP, box 52.

26. *MH*, 6 April 1923.

27. MSD, "River of Grass," *Rotarian*, November 1959, 21.

28. *Voice*, 257–58; "Monism," n.d., MSDP, box 30, folder 97; *Tampa Tribune*, 15 May 1998; *SPT*, 8 April 1995.

29. Douglas's will is less explicit about a religious service but definitive about no service, stating, "No funeral services are to be had" (MSD, last will and testament, 6 November 1994, copy provided to author by William T. Muir).

30. *Fort Lauderdale Sun-Sentinel*, May 14, 1998; *MH*, 14, 15 May 1998; *SPT*, 8 June 1996, 15 May 1998; *Tampa Tribune*, 15 May 1998; *NYT*, 15 May 1998; *USA Today*, 17 May 1998; "Statement by Interior Secretary Bruce Babbitt on the Death of Marjory Stoneman Douglas," Office of the Secretary, 14 May 1998, press release, available online at www.ios.doi.gov/news/douglas.htm (spring 2006).

31. Poole, "Woman of the Century," 8–9; *USA Today*, 17 May 1998; Toufexis and McWhirter, "Lady of the Everglades," 57; *SPT*, 7 April 1994, 15 May 1998.

CHAPTER TWO: River of Life

1. *Voice*, 135–36; MSD, "The Everglades Remembered," *Florida Naturalist* 55 (December 1983): 8; *Special Voices, Two Florida Women: Marjorie Carr, Marjory Stoneman Douglas*, video production (Florida Atlantic University/Florida International University, Joint Center for Environmental and Urban Problems, 1985).

2. Nathaniel P. Reed, "Dare to Save the Everglades," *Park Science* 13 (Summer 1993): 3.

3. William A. Niering, "Human Impacts on the South Florida Wetlands: The Everglades and Big Cypress Swamp," in *The Earth in Transition: Patterns and Processes of Biotic Impoverishment*, ed. George M. Woodwell (New York: Cambridge

University Press, 1990), 463–75; Malcolm G. Scully, "Restoring the Fragile Ever-glades, Evermore," *Chronicle of Higher Education,* 12 January 2001, B14–15; "Liter-ary Snapshot," *Florida (Orlando Sentinel),* 5 May 1991, 4; *SPT,* 7 April, 7 December 1997; Cyril T. Zaneski, "Anatomy of a Deal," *Audubon,* July–August 2001, 50–51.

4. Carole C. McIvor, Janey A. Ley, and Robin D. Bjork, "Changes in Freshwater Inflow from the Everglades to Florida Bay Including Effects on Biota and Bi-otic Processes: A Review," in *Everglades: The Ecosystem and Its Restoration,* ed. Steven M. Davis and John C. Ogden (Delray Beach, Fla.: St. Lucie, 1994), 117–46.

5. *North Miami Sun Reporter,* 18 April 1984.

6. *River of Grass,* 10, emphasis added; Dava Sobel, "Still Fighting the Good Fight for the Everglades," *Audubon,* July–August 1991, 32.

7. *River of Grass,* 5, 10; David McCally, *The Everglades: An Environmental His-tory* (Gainesville: University Press of Florida, 1999), 179–80; Niering, "Human Impacts," 465–66P; MSD, *Alligator Crossing* (1959; reprint, Minneapolis: Milk-weed, 2003), 49.

8. *River of Grass,* 15; Charles M. Brookfield and Oliver Griswold, *They All Called It Tropical: True Tales of the Romantic Everglades National Park, Cape Sable, and the Florida Keys* (Miami, Fla.: Data, 1960), 73.

9. Lance H. Gunderson, "Vegetation of the Everglades: Determinants of Com-munity Composition," in *Everglades,* ed. Davis and Ogden, 323–40; Randolph J. Widmer, *The Evolution of the Calusa: A Nonagricultural Chiefdom on the South-west Florida Coast* (Tuscaloosa: University of Alabama Press, 1988), 104–28; Thomas Barbour, *That Vanishing Eden: A Naturalist's Florida* (Boston: Little, Brown, 1944), 164; *River of Grass,* 10; *The Florida Handbook, 1947–48* (Talla-hassee: Peninsular, 1946), 196; Patricia Caulfield, *Everglades* (New York: Sierra Club/Ballantine, 1970), 35–39; John Kunkel Small and George V. Nash, "Report of Mr. J. K. Small and Mr. G. V. Nash upon a Trip to Florida," *Journal of the New York Botanical Garden* 3 (February 1902): 35; John Kunkel Small, "Report on Exploration in Tropical Florida," *Journal of the New York Botanical Garden* 5 (March 1904): 52–53; John Kunkel Small, *From Eden to Sahara: Florida's Tragedy* (Sanford, Fla.: Seminole Soil and Water Conservation District, 2004), 36; W. S. Blatchley, *In Days Agone: Notes on the Fauna and Flora of Subtropical Florida in the Days When Most of Its Area Was a Primeval Wilderness* (Indianapolis: Nature, 1932), 254–331.

10. The Everglades are so vast that annual precipitation varies from forty-five to fifty inches in the southwest coastal sector to sixty to sixty-five inches in the

east. Widmer, *Evolution of the Calusa,* 99–101; Millicent Todd Bingham, "Miami: A Study in Urban Geography," *Tequesta* 9 (1949): 76, 77, 85; Patrick J. Gleason and Peter Stone, "Age, Origin, and Landscape Evolution of the Everglades Peatland," in *Everglades,* ed. Davis and Ogden, 149–97.

11. M. J. Duever, J. F. Meeder, L. C. Meeder, and J. M. McCollom, "The Climate of South Florida and Its Role in Shaping the Everglades Ecosystem," in *Everglades,* ed. Davis and Ogden, 225–48; James R. Karr and Kathryn E. Freemark, "Disturbance and Vertebrates: An Integrative Perspective," in *The Ecology of Natural Disturbance and Patch Dynamics,* ed. S. T. A. Pickett and P. S. White (Orlando, Fla.: Academic, 1985), 154–55; Niering, "Human Impacts," 467–68; Caulfield, *Everglades,* 37–39; "At Last: Biscayne Aquifer Designated Sole Source by EPA," MSDP, box 30, folder 96; Garald G. Parker, "The Paradox of Florida's Water Supply," *Florida Trend* 15 (February 1973): 31–32; McCally, *Everglades,* 2–30, 37; *River of Grass,* 14–25.

12. *River of Grass,* 25; Garald G. Parker, "Notes on the Geology and Ground Water of the Everglades in Southern Florida," *Soil Science Society of Florida Proceedings* 4-A (1942): 4, 70–71; Thomas E. Lodge, *The Everglades Handbook: Understanding the Ecosystem* (Delray Beach, Fla.: St. Lucie, 1994); Widmer, *Evolution of the Calusa,* 98–104; Howard A. Kelly, "The Everglades National Park," *Journal of the Maryland Academy of Sciences* 2 (January 1931): 37–39; McCally, *Everglades,* 10; Niering, "Human Impacts," 465–66; William B. Robertson Jr., *Everglades: The Park Story* (Coral Gables, Fla.: University of Miami Press, 1959), 5–9.

13. Frank Hamilton Cushing, *The Florida Journals of Frank Hamilton Cushing,* ed. Phyllis E. Kolianos and Brent R. Weisman (Gainesville: University Press of Florida, 2005), 3–4.

14. *River of Grass,* 306; Donald Worster, *A River Running West: The Life of John Wesley Powell* (New York: Oxford University Press, 2001), 405–6.

15. Cushing, *Florida Journals,* 8; *River of Grass,* 308.

16. Thomas P. Slaughter, *The Natures of John and William Bartram* (New York: Vintage, 1996), 202; Kirkpatrick Sales, *The Conquest of Paradise: Christopher Columbus and the Columbian Legacy* (New York: Knopf, 1990).

17. McCally, *Everglades,* 53–57, 60–61; "The Report of Buckingham Smith, Esq.," 1 June 1848, *Report of the Committee on Public Lands,* U.S. Senate, 30th Cong., 1st sess., 1848, Ref. Com. 242, 18–21, 29; John M. Goggin, "The Indians and History of the Matecumbe Region," *Tequesta* 10 (1950): 16–22; Mark Derr, *Some Kind of Paradise: A Chronicle of Man and the Land in Florida* (New York:

Morrow, 1989), 238–43; Charlton W. Tebeau, *Man in the Everglades: 2,000 Years of Human History in the Everglades National Park* (Coral Gables, Fla.: University of Miami Press, 1986), 43–45, 68; Eugene Lyons, "The Enterprise of Florida," *Florida Historical Quarterly* 52 (April 1974): 411–22.

18. *River of Grass,* 147–72, 175, 184; Widmer, *Evolution of the Calusa,* 213–60.

19. Widmer, *Evolution of the Calusa,* 189–213; McCally, *Everglades,* 31–39.

20. Goggin, "Indians and History," 13,–19; Robertson, *Everglades,* 55–60; Tebeau, *Man in the Everglades,* 37–49; Widmer, *Evolution of the Calusa,* 213–60; McCally, *Everglades,* 31–53; *River of Grass,* 67–79.

21. Irving Rouse, "John Mann Goggin, 1916–1963," *American Antiquity* 29 (January 1964): 369–75; William C. Sturtevant, "John Mann Goggin, 1916–1963," *American Anthropologist* 66 (April 1964): 385–93; Brent Richard Weisman, *Pioneer in Space and Time: John Mann Goggin and the Development of Florida Archaeology* (Gainesville: University Press of Florida, 2002); *Voice,* 192, 195, 210.

22. *River of Grass,* 387. Literary scholar Michael P. Branch has made similar observations about *River of Grass* ("Writing the Swamp: Marjory Stoneman Douglas and *The Everglades: River of Grass,*" in *Such News of the Land: U.S. Women Nature Writers,* ed. Thomas S. Edwards and Elizabeth A. De Wolfe [Hanover, N.H.: University Press of New England, 2001], 130, 131).

23. James W. Covington, *The Seminoles of Florida* (Gainesville: University Press of Florida, 1993), 48, 58, 61–63; Kenneth W. Porter, *The Black Seminoles: History of a Freedom-Seeking People* (Gainesville: University Press of Florida, 1996), esp. 4–7, 14–16, 121; Tebeau, *Man in the Everglades,* 49–52; Timothy Silver, *A New Face on the Countryside: Indians, Colonists, and Slaves in South Atlantic Forests, 1500–1800* (New York: Cambridge University Press, 1990), 73, 89, 92, 94; Donald Edward Davis, *Where There Are Mountains: An Environmental History of the Southern Appalachians* (Athens: University of Georgia Press, 2000), 24–25, 75; Albert E. Cowdrey, *This Land, This South: An Environmental History* (Lexington: University Press of Kentucky, 1996), 51–56.

24. *River of Grass,* 185–86.

25. Weisman, *Pioneer in Space and Time,* 136–46.

26. *River of Grass,* 220–45, 255–66; Tebeau, *Man in the Everglades,* 61–62, 69–70; Covington, *Seminoles of Florida,* 50–144; Porter, *Black Seminoles,* 27–29, 39–107; Derr, *Some Kind of Paradise,* 271–93.

27. Nelson M. Blake, *Land into Water—Water into Land: A History of Water Management in Florida* (Tallahassee: Florida State University Press, 1980), 16–17.

28. Hugh Willoughby, *Across the Everglades: A Canoe Journey of Exploration* (Philadelphia: Lippincott, 1900), 120; Alonzo Church, "A Dash through the Everglades," *Tequesta* 9 (1949): 19; *River of Grass*, 6.

CHAPTER THREE: Lineage

1. *Voice*, 85, 128, 187; clipping, July 1957, Mrs. Alfred Peacock Collection, HMSF.

2. Jessie B. Trefethen, *Trefethen: The Family and the Landing* (Portland, Me.: Falmouth, 1959), 5; William J. Curnow, "Cousin Jenny Saved the Everglades," *Cornwall Family History Society* 93 (September 1999): 8–10; M. L. Newson, "Trefethen Family," n.d., MSDP, box 47, folder 118; Clint Trefethen, Trefethen Genealogy, available online at http://homepage.nhvt.net/users/ctref/Genealogy/142 .html (fall 2005).

3. Elias Nason and George J. Varney, *Gazetteer of Massachusetts* (Boston: Russell, 1890); Samuel Hopkins Emery, *History of Taunton, Massachusetts, from Its Settlement to the Present Time* (Westminster, Md.: Heritage, 1992), 665.

4. MSD, "There Was Nothing Odd about Grampa," MSDP, box 35, folder 89.

5. *Voice*, 32–34.

6. Clint Trefethen, Trefethen Genealogy. The Parady family genealogy comes from the FamilySearch Web site hosted by the Church of Jesus Christ of Latter-Day Saints (www.familysearch.org [accessed fall 2005]); Curnow, "Cousin Jenny Saved the Everglades."

7. *Voice*, 34; Jessie B. Trefethen, *Trefethen*, 5; MSD, "There Was Nothing Odd."

8. MSD, "There Was Nothing Odd"; *MH*, 20 March 1921.

9. MSD, "The Stoneman Family—A Memoir," October 1986, HP; *Voice*, 34–35.

10. *Voice*, 35–36; "Ancestors of Alan Barry Wood," http://freepages.genealogy .rootsweb.com/~alanwood/alanc/f653.htm (accessed spring 2006); Carolyn Spence, "Descendants of William Burcham," http://homepages.rootsweb.com/ ~willspnc/burcham/burchamweb.htm (accessed spring 2006); Grayson County, Virginia, Land Tax List, 1799, 1805, and Personal Property Tax List, 1800, 1810, 1813, 1817, 1824, 1835 (electronic versions), New River Notes Web site, http://www .ls.net/~newriver/nrv.htm (accessed spring 2006); Aras B. Cox, *Foot Prints on the Sands of Time: A History of Southwestern Virginia and Northwestern North Carolina* (Sparta, N.C.: Star, 1900), available online at http://www.rootdigger.net/ Chapter_XII.pdf (accessed spring 2006). Douglas said in a 2 February 1941 *MH*

article that her grandfather was named for his maternal grandfather, a fighting Quaker and lieutenant in the Revolutionary War. The name of Mark's maternal grandfather, however, was William, and he was born in 1771, too late to fight in the revolution. His father's name was Thomas; he had no brothers named Mark, and his father was Charles.

11. Douglas speculated, based on family lore, that her grandfather studied medicine in Cincinnati, Ohio (*Voice,* 36; *MH,* 2 February 1941).

12. *Kansas: A Cyclopedia of State History, Embracing Events, Institutions, Industries, Counties, Cities, Towns, Permanent Persons, Etc.,* vol. 3 (Chicago: Standard, 1912), 1475–77, available online at http://lightways.lib.ks.us/genweb/archives/1912/c3/cox_floyd_c.html (accessed spring 2006); Cox, *Foot Prints,* chapter 12. For two fine environmental histories of the region, see Timothy Silver, *A New Face on the Countryside: Indians, Colonists, and Slaves in South Atlantic Forests, 1500–1800* (New York: Cambridge University Press, 1990); Donald Edward Davis, *Where There Are Mountains: An Environmental History of the Southern Appalachians* (Athens: University of Georgia Press, 2000).

13. Stephen B. Weeks, *Southern Quakers and Slavery: A Study in Institutional History* (Baltimore: Johns Hopkins Press, 1896), 70–144; Caroll S. Roller to MSD, 23 February, 10 December 1989, in possession of author; MSD, "Stoneman Family"; U.S. Census, 1870, 1880; "Mark Stoneman," in *Abstracts of the Records of the Society of Friends in Indiana,* part 4, ed. Willard Heiss (Indianapolis: Indiana Historical Society, 1972).

14. Mark D. Stoneman and Aletha C. White marriage certificate, 24 January 1849, Hamilton County Marriage Records, Book A, 1843–57, Indiana State Library, Indianapolis; Caroll S. Roller to MSD, 23 February, 10 December 1989; "Stoneman," in *Abstracts,* part 6, ed. Heiss; Weeks, *Southern Quakers and Slavery,* 47.

15. Larry Dale Gragg, *Migration in Early America: The Virginia Quaker Experience* (Ann Arbor, Mich.: UMI Research Press, 1980), 47–55; Weeks, *Southern Quakers and Slavery,* 251, 268, 284.

16. Stoneman and White marriage certificate; Evan Jessup to Mark Stoneman et al., Hamilton County, Deed Records, 1853–54, Book 5, Indiana State Library, Indianapolis; John F. Haines, *History of Hamilton County, Indiana: Her People, Industries, and Institutions* (Indianapolis: Bowen, 1915), 137; Augustus Finch Shirts, *A History of the Formation, Settlement, and Development of Hamilton County, Indiana, from the Year 1818 to the Close of the Civil War* (n.p., 1901), 212; Le-

anna K. Roberts, Stuart M. Neal, Byron O. Baker, and Joseph G. Roberts, eds., *A History of Westfield and Washington Township* (Noblesville, Ind.: Image Builder/ Rowland, n.d.), 155.

17. Donald Brooks Kelley, "Friends and Nature in America: Toward an Eighteenth-Century Quaker Ecology," *Pennsylvania History* 53 (October 1986): 257–72; Donald Brooks Kelley, "The Evolution of Quaker Theology and the Unfolding of a Distinctive Quaker Ecological Perspective in Eighteenth-Century America," *Pennsylvania History* 52 (October 1985): 242–53; Donald Brooks Kelley, "'A Tender Regard to the Whole Creation': Anthony Benezet and the Emergence of an Eighteenth-Century Quaker Ecology," *Pennsylvania Magazine of History and Biography* 63 (January 1982): 69–88.

18. Gragg, *Migration in Early America*, 57–67; Jean R. Soderlund, *Quakers and Slavery: A Divided Spirit* (Princeton: Princeton University Press, 1985); Weeks, *Southern Quakers and Slavery*, 232.

19. MSD, "Levi Coffin's Road to Freedom," MSDP, box 47, folder 113; *Voice*, 36–39.

20. Roberts et al., *History*, 13–15, 78–79; Haines, *History*, 238, 491; Melvyn Hammarberg, *History of Henry County, Indiana* (Chicago: Inter-State, 1884), 832–33.

21. Historical sources variously give this name as *Lavica, Lovia*, and *Louisa*. Douglas's autobiography uses *Lovica*.

22. *Indianapolis Star*, 4 January 1940; Roberts et al., *History*, 15.

23. *MH*, 2 February 1941; MSD, "Stoneman Family"; *Voice*, 36–37.

24. Thomas E. Drake, *Quakers and Slavery in America* (New Haven: Yale University Press, 1950), 193–200; Weeks, *Southern Quakers and Slavery*, 303–7.

25. Shirts, *History*, 305–7, 358–59.

26. U.S. Census, 1860, 1870; Joseph Stipanovich, *Minneapolis: City of Lakes* (Woodland Hills, Calif.: Windsor, 1982), 3–6.

27. Hammarberg, *History*, 832, 833; U.S. Census, 1870; MSD to Dorothy Vaile, 18 July 1985, MSDP, box 44, folder 78; MSD, "Stoneman Family"; *Voice*, 36–37; *MH*, 20, 21, 22 July 1911.

28. *MH*, 2 February 1941; Doris Ritzinger to MSD, 14 July 1952, MSDP, box 44, folder 78.

29. *The Calendar*, essentially the school's annual, of the 1874–75 academic year listed Benjamin Franklin Stoneman, rather than Frank B. Stoneman, as a previously matriculated student.

30. *MH*, 2 February 1941; *Voice*, 39; Preparatory Department student register, 1874–75, Carleton College, Northfield, Minnesota (Eric Hillemann, e-mail to author, 2 August 2004); Adam Gopnik, "Display Cases: The Man Who Discovered Conspicuous Consumption Is Back in Style," *New Yorker*, April 26–May 3, 1999, 176–79; MSD, "Stoneman Family."

31. *MH*, 2 February 1941; MSD, "Stoneman Family."

32. MSD, "Stoneman Family"; *MH*, 2 February 1941; *Voice*, 37.

33. *MH*, 20, 21, 22 July 1911.

34. MSD, "Stoneman Family"; Jessica L. Harland Jacobs, *Builders of Empire: Freemasons and British Imperialism, 1717–1927* (Chapel Hill: University of North Carolina Press, 2007).

35. *MH*, 2 February 1941; MSD, "Frank Bryant Stoneman," *Tequesta* 4 (November 1944): 5; Doris Ritzinger to MSD, 14 July 1952, MSDP, box 44, folder 78; MSD, "Stoneman Family"; *Voice*, 35–40.

36. *MH*, 2 February 1941; MSD, "Frank Bryant Stoneman," 5; *Minneapolis City Directory*, 1885–88 (Minneapolis: Tribune Company, 1885–88).

37. *MH*, 2 February 1941; MSD, "Frank Bryant Stoneman," 5; *Minneapolis City Directory*, 1885–88.

CHAPTER FOUR: Mr. Smith's "Reconnoissance"

1. *NYT*, 7 January 1871; "Buckingham Smith," www.drbronsontours.com/bronsonbuckinghamsmith.html (accessed spring 2006).

2. "Philanthropy on the First Coast: A Comprehensive Look at Giving and Philanthropy in Metropolitan Jacksonville," November 2004, 28, 34, available online at http://www.dupontfund.org/news/pdfs/sector_philanthropy.pdf (accessed spring 2008).

3. "Report of Secretary of Treasury to Senate," 10 August 1848, *Report of the Committee on Public Lands*, U.S. Senate, 30th Cong., 1st sess., 1848, Ref. Com. 242, 3–4; *River of Grass*, 251–52; Charlton W. Tebeau, *A History of Florida* (Coral Gables, Fla.: University of Miami Press, 1971), 214, 346; Mark Derr, *Some Kind of Paradise: A Chronicle of Man and the Land in Florida* (New York: Morrow, 1989), 153–54.

4. "The Report of Buckingham Smith, Esq.," 1 June 1848, in *Report of the Committee on Public Lands*, 21, 29, 32, 34, 37; Thomas P. Slaughter, *The Natures of John and William Bartram* (New York: Vintage, 1996), 202, 145; *Orlando Sentinel*, 30 August 1986.

5. "Report of Buckingham Smith," 21, 29, 32, 34, 37.

6. D. LeBaron Perrine, "The Remaking of Florida," *Tropic (MH)* 7 (February 1926): 187.

7. MSD, "A Bird Dog in Hand," *SEP,* 12 September 1925, reprinted in *Nine Florida Stories,* ed. Kevin M. McCarthy (Gainesville: University Press of Florida, 1990), 45.

8. J. E. Dovell, "The Everglades—Florida's Frontier, Part 1," *Economic Leaflets* 6 (April 1947): 1–4.

9. Dovell, "Everglades," 15, 17, 33; "Report of Buckingham Smith," 15, 17, 33, 36; Charlton W. Tebeau, *Man in the Everglades: 2,000 Years of Human History in the Everglades National Park* (Coral Gables, Fla.: University of Miami Press, 1986), 70–71.

10. "Report of Secretary of Treasury to Senate," 3–4; "Florida," *Commercial Review* 7 (October 1849): 300.

11. Morgan Dewey Peoples and Edwin Adams Davis, eds., "Across South Central Florida in 1882: The Account of the First New Orleans *Times-Democrat* Exploring Expedition," *Tequesta* 10 (1950): 53; *River of Grass,* 253; Hernando d' Escalante Fontaneda, *Mentoir of Do. d'Escalante Fontaneda Respecting Florida,* translated by Buckingham Smith (1854; reprint, Coral Gables, Fla.: University of Miami and the Historical Association of Southern Florida, 1973).

12. Act of Congress (1850) to Enable States to Reclaim "Swamp Lands," 9 U.S. Statute L., 519, 520, 1850; Ann Vileisis, *Discovering the Unknown Landscape: A History of America's Wetlands* (Washington, D.C.: Island, 1997), 71–78; "Florida," 297–304.

13. Act of Congress (1850) to Enable States to Reclaim "Swamp Lands"; Vileisis, *Discovering the Unknown Landscape,* 71–78; "Florida," 297–304.

14. "Report of Buckingham Smith," 23; "Historical Review of Everglades Development," in *Caloosahatchee River and Lake Okeechobee Drainage Areas, Florida,* U.S. Senate, 71st Cong., 3rd sess., 1930, 9–11; "History of Drainage and Reclamation Work in the Everglades of Florida," in *Everglades of Florida, Acts, Reports, and Other Papers, State and National, Relating to the Everglades of the State of Florida and Their Reclamation,* U.S. Senate, 62nd Cong., 1st sess., 1911, 7–9; *River of Grass,* 258–59; Christopher F. Meindl, "Water, Water Everywhere," in *Paradise Lost? The Environmental History of Florida,* ed. Jack E. Davis and Raymond Arsenault (Gainesville: University Press of Florida, 2005), 122–23; Thomas E. Dahl and Gregory J. Allord, *Technical Aspects of Wetlands: History of Wetlands in the Coterminous United States,* U.S. Geological Survey Water Supply

Paper 2425, available online at http://water.usgs.gov/nwsum/WSP2425/history
.html (accessed winter 2007). Before Alaska became a state, only Michigan was
wetter than Florida.

15. Minnie Moore-Willson, *The Birds of the Everglades and Their Neighbors the
Seminole Indians* (Tampa, Fla.: Tampa Tribune, 1920), 7, available online at http://
webluis.fcla.edu (accessed winter 2007); L. D. Huston to son, 17 March 1874, Miscellaneous Manuscripts, box 7, PKY; Samuel C. Upham, *Notes from Sunland, on
the Manatee River, Gulf Coast of South Florida: Its Climate, Soil, and Productions:
Land of the Orange and Guava, the Pine-Apple, Date, and Cassava* (Philadelphia: Claxton, 1881), available online at http://webluis.fcla.edu (accessed summer
2005); Patricia Clark, ed., "'A Tale to Tell from Paradise Itself': George Bancroft's
Letters from Florida, March 1855," *Florida Historical Quarterly* 48 (January 1970):
268; Daniel F. Tyler, *Where to Go in Florida* (New York: Hopcraft, 1880), n.p.

16. Edward King, *The Great South: A Record of Journeys in Louisiana, Texas,
the Indian Territory, Missouri, Arkansas, Mississippi, Alabama, Georgia, Florida,
South Carolina, North Carolina, Kentucky, Tennessee, Virginia, West Virginia, and
Maryland* (Hartford, Conn.: American, 1875), 403–4, available online at docsouth
.unc.edu/nc/king/menu.html (accessed summer 2005).

17. Jack London, *White Fang*, in *Great Short Works of Jack London* (New York:
Harper and Row, 1970), 99; Hugh Willoughby, *Across the Everglades: A Canoe
Journey of Exploration* (Philadelphia: Lippincott, 1900), 85; Alonzo Church, "A
Dash through the Everglades," *Tequesta* 9 (1949): 16, 29, 21; William J. Krome,
"Railway Location in the Florida Everglades," *Tequesta* 39 (1979): 5.

18. Church, "Dash through the Everglades," 30; *River of Grass*, 292.

19. Morgan Peoples and Edwin Adams Davis, eds. "Across South Central
Florida in 1882: The Account of the First New Orleans *Times-Democrat* Exploring
Expedition," *Tequesta* 10 (1950): 49, 52, 11 (1951): 75–76; Church, "Dash through
the Everglades," 18–19, 25, 27–28; MSD, "The Road to the Horizon," *SEP*, 22 February 1941, reprinted in *Nine Florida Stories*, ed. McCarthy, 186.

20. MSD, "Road to the Horizon," 188, 190, 191–92.

21. J. E. Ingraham Diary, 27 March–1 April 1892, Miscellaneous Manuscripts,
box 26, James E. Ingraham file, PKY; Mary K. Wintringham, ed., "North to
South through the Glades in 1883: The Account of the Second Expedition into
the Florida Everglades by the New Orleans *Times-Democrat*," *Tequesta* 23 (1963):
33–59; Mary K. Wintringham, ed., "North to South through the Glades in 1883:
The Account of the Second Expedition into the Florida Everglades by the New

Orleans *Times-Democrat,* Part II," *Tequesta* 24 (1964): 59–93; Church, "Dash through the Everglades," 26; Edwin Asa Dix and John Nowry MacGonigle, "The Everglades of Florida: A Region of Mystery," *Century,* February 1905, 520; A. W. Dimock, "Crossing the Everglades in a Power-Boat," *Harper's Monthly,* January 1907, 249–50.

22. Church, "Dash through the Everglades," 19; Krome, "Railway Location," 10; Dimock, "Crossing the Everglades," 245.

23. Wintringham, "North to South [Part I]," 46; Krome, "Railway Location," 10; Church, "Dash through the Everglades," 19–26.

24. "Report of Buckingham Smith," 28; Wintringham, "North to South [Part I]," 48; William Todd, "The Maligned Everglades," *Florida East Coast Homeseeker* 22 (April 1910): 121; Willoughby, *Across the Everglades,* 115; Dimock, "Crossing the Everglades," 246–47; Mary Douthit Conrad, "Homesteading in Florida during the 1890s," *Tequesta* 17 (1957): 11; Dix and MacGonigle, "Everglades of Florida," 526; Lieutenant C. R. P. Rodgers to James D. Westcott, 14 February 1848, in *Report of the Committee on Public Lands,* 50–51.

25. Garald G. Parker Sr., abbreviated résumé, Garald G. Parker Collection, USF; Garald G. Parker, "Truth about the Everglades," n.d., MSDP, box 25, folder 27; MSD to Mrs. Parker, MSDP, box 40, folder 21; *River of Grass,* 8–17; Willoughby, *Across the Everglades,* 14.

26. Peoples and Davis, "Across South Central Florida," 53, 50; *River of Grass,* chapter 12; MSD, "Bird Dog in Hand," 48; Church, "Dash through the Everglades," 20, 21.

27. Wintringham, "North to South [Part I]," 35; Wintringham, "North to South, Part II," 93.

28. Dovell, "Everglades," 2–3.

CHAPTER FIVE: Birth and Despair

1. Joseph Stipanovich, *Minneapolis: City of Lakes* (Woodland Hills, Calif.: Windsor, 1982), 7–8; Hanje Richards, *Minneapolis–St. Paul: Then and Now* (San Diego, Calif.: Thunder Bay, 2001), 5; Lucy M. Kane, *The Falls of St. Anthony: The Waterfall That Built Minneapolis* (St. Paul: Minnesota Historical Society Press, 1987), 30–41; William Cronon, *Nature's Metropolis: Chicago and the Great West* (New York: Norton, 1991).

2. Kane, *Falls of St. Anthony,* 42–61.

3. Kane, *Falls of St. Anthony,* 2–3; "Minnesota from the Mississippi," available online at www.tfaoi.com (accessed summer 2005); "Red Wing and the Grand Excursion," available online at www.goodhuehistory.mus.mn.us (accessed summer 2005); "St. Anthony Falls," available online at www.nps.gov/miss/maps/model/ history/stanthony (accessed summer 2005); Stipanovich, *Minneapolis,* 8–9.

4. "St. Anthony Falls"; Stipanovich, *Minneapolis,* 73.

5. E. Bird Johnson, *Forty Years of the University of Minnesota* (Minneapolis: General Alumni Association, 1910), 17, 33, 34–35, 89.

6. Larry Millet, *Twin Cities: Then and Now* (St. Paul: Minnesota Historical Society Press, 1996), 4.

7. Johnson, *Forty Years,* 58–59; MSD, "The Stoneman Family—A Memoir," October 1986, HP; *Minnesota Alumni Weekly,* 13 November 1913; *Voice,* 30, 35.

8. *Minneapolis City Directory,* 1888 (Minneapolis: Tribune Company, 1888); *Minneapolis City Directory,* 1889 (Minneapolis: Tribune Company, 1889); MSD, "Stoneman Family"; MSD to Matilda Woolfolk, 13 March 1989, HP.

9. *Minneapolis City Directory,* 1888, 1889; Clint Trefethen, Trefethen Genealogy, available online at http://homepage.nhvt.net/users/ctref/Genealogy/142 .html (accessed summer 2005).

10. MSD, "Stoneman Family"; *Special Voices, Two Florida Women: Marjorie Carr, Marjory Stoneman Douglas,* video production (Florida Atlantic University/Florida International University, Joint Center for Environmental and Urban Problems, 1985); MSD, speech to Florida Historical Society, Pensacola, 6 May 1978, SPOHP.

11. Mark Derr, *Some Kind of Paradise: A Chronicle of Man and the Land in Florida* (New York: Morrow, 1989), 22, 43, 102–3.

12. MSD, speech to Florida Historical Society; *Voice,* 31; *Special Voices.*

13. MSD to Matilda Woolfolk, 13 March 1989, HP; MSD, "Stoneman Family"; *Great Floridians Film Series: Marjory Stoneman Douglas* (Tallahassee: Museum of Florida History and Florida History Associates, 1990).

14. Lisa Roseman Beade, Donald Breed, Marygael Cullen, and Michelle Green, *The Wealth of Nations: A Peoples' History of Rhode Island* (Providence, R.I.: Community Communications, 1999).

15. MSD (*Voice,* 40, 41) said that Rundell and her father were in the building-and-loan business together in Minneapolis, but no documents support this contention.

16. *Voice,* 41–43.

17. *Providence, Rhode Island Directory, 1896* (Providence: Sampson, Murdock, and Company, 1896), 12; *Voice,* 40–43; MSD, "Stoneman Family"; *Special Voices.*

18. *SPT,* 5 June 1989; *Voice,* 43.

19. MSD, "Stoneman Family"; *Special Voices.*

20. *Voice,* 43.

21. *Voice,* 43, 100; *MH,* 2 February 1941.

22. MSD, "Stoneman Family."

23. *Voice,* 44; *Special Voices.*

24. MSD, "Stoneman Family."

25. MSD, "Stoneman Family."

26. *Voice,* 45.

27. MSD, untitled manuscript, n.d., MSDP, box 48, folder 123; *Voice,* 44–45.

28. *Great Floridians Film Series: Marjory Stoneman Douglas.*

29. *Voice,* 44.

CHAPTER SIX: Suicide

1. Jacob S. Disston Jr., "Henry Disston (1819–1879), Pioneer Industrialist, Inventor, and Good Citizen," speech to Newcomen Society, 17 January 1950, available online at www.disstoninstitute.com/disstonbio.html (accessed summer 2006); "Hamilton Disston Profile," available online at http://members.aol.com/historictacony2/profile hamilton.html (accessed summer 2006).

2. Mark Derr, *Some Kind of Paradise: A Chronicle of Man and the Land in Florida* (New York: Morrow, 1989), 77–78, 87–88; Joe Knetsch, "Hamilton Disston and the Development of Florida," *Sunland Tribune* 24 (1998): 5–6; Pat Dodson, "Hamilton Disston's St. Cloud Sugar Plantation, 1887–1901," *Florida Historical Quarterly* 49 (April 1971): 356–57; *River of Grass,* 282.

3. J. E. Dovell, "The Everglades—Florida's Frontier, Part 1," *Economic Leaflets* 6 (April 1947): 1–4; W. Turner Wallis, "The History of Everglades Drainage and Its Present Status," *Soil Science Society of Florida Proceedings,* 21 April 1942, 29–30; *River of Grass,* 281, 282–83; Derr, *Some Kind of Paradise,* 88–89; *Everglades of Florida, Acts, Reports, and Other Papers, State and National, Relating to the Everglades of the State of Florida and Their Reclamation,* U.S. Senate, 62nd Cong., 1st sess., 1911, 8, 9–10; "Historical Review of Everglades Development," in *Caloosahatchee River and Lake Okeechobee Drainage Areas, Florida,* U.S. Senate, 71st Cong., 3rd sess., 1930, 12.

4. Richard A. Bartlett, *The New Country: A Social History of the American Frontier* (New York: Oxford University Press, 1986), 63–78; Derr, *Some Kind of Paradise,* 281; Charlton W. Tebeau, *A History of Florida* (Coral Gables, Fla.: University of Miami Press, 1971), 142–43, 281–83.

5. William Cronon, *Nature's Metropolis: Chicago and the Great West* (New York: Norton, 1991), 68, 80, 216–17; J. E. Dovell, "A Brief History of the Florida Everglades," *Soil Science Society of Florida Proceedings,* 21 April 1942, 138–39; Wallis, "History," 30–31; John Melvin DeGrove, "The Administration of Internal Improvement Problems in Florida, 1845–1869" (master's thesis, Emory University, 1954), 208–9; Samuel Proctor, *Napoleon Bonaparte Broward: Florida's Fighting Democrat* (Gainesville: University Press of Florida, 1990), 218; R. E. Rose, *The Swamp and Overflow Lands of Florida: The Disston Drainage Company and the Disston Purchase: A Reminiscence* (Tallahassee: n.p., 1916), 2–4, available online at http://webluis.fcla.edu (accessed summer 2006).

6. T. Frederick Davis, "The Disston Land Purchase," *Florida Historical Quarterly* 17 (January 1939): 200–210; *River of Grass,* 281, 282–83; Derr, *Some Kind of Paradise,* 88–89; Dovell, "Everglades"; *Everglades of Florida,* 8, 9–10; "Historical Review of Everglades Development," 12; Wallis, "History," 30.

7. *NYT,* 18 February 1881; Knetsch, "Hamilton Disston," 9; *Florida,* 237; Alfred Jackson Hanna and Kathryn Abbey Hanna, *Lake Okeechobee: Wellspring of the Everglades* (Indianapolis: Bobbs-Merrill, 1948), 95; Junius Elmore Dovell, "A History of the Everglades of Florida" (Ph.D. diss., University of North Carolina at Chapel Hill, 1947), chapter 4.

8. *IIF Minutes,* 26 February 1881, 3:463–70, 1 September 1881, 3:22–23; S. H. Grey to Board of Trustees, 22 November 1881, in *IIF Minutes,* 3:79–80; I. Coryell to W. D. Bloxham, 27 December 1881, in *IIF Minutes,* 3:94; William Wallace Harney, "The Drainage of the Everglades," *Harper's* 58 (March 1884): 598–605.

9. Harney, "Drainage of the Everglades."

10. Dovell, "Brief History," 139; Dodson, "Hamilton Disston's St. Cloud Sugar Plantation," 358; Hanna and Hanna, *Lake Okeechobee,* 173–74; Derr, *Some Kind of Paradise,* 88–90; *River of Grass,* 283; Joe M. Richardson, "The Florida Excursion of President Chester A. Arthur," *Tequesta* 24 (1964): 41–47; *NYT,* 6 May 1883.

11. T. Frederick Davis, "Disston Land Purchase," 209.

12. "Note no. 3—Abstract of Report by J. J. Daniel, W. H. Davison, and John Bradford, Committee Appointed by the Governor of Florida on November 17, 1885," in *Everglades of Florida,* 24; Dodson, "Hamilton Disston's St. Cloud Sugar

Plantation," 359–60, 361, 362–63; Derr, *Some Kind of Paradise*, 90–91; *River of Grass*, 285–86; *MH*, 20, 21, 22 July 1911.

13. Wallis, "History," 30–31; Derr, *Some Kind of Paradise*, 91–92; "Note no. 3," 21–24; Hamilton Disston to E. A. Perry, 10 March 1887, in *IIF Minutes*, 3:447–49; *IIF Minutes*, 25 March 1887, 3:449–51.

14. Dovell, "Brief History," 139–40; Wallis, "History," 30–31.

15. Derr, *Some Kind of Paradise*, 95–96; Dodson, "Hamilton Disston's St. Cloud Sugar Plantation," 364–66; *NYT*, 1, 9, 15 May 1896; *WP*, 1, 9 May 1896. Those who doubt the suicide scenario include Michael Grunwald, *The Swamp: The Everglades, Florida, and the Politics of Paradise* (New York: Simon and Schuster, 2006), 96, who has followed the lead of Knetsch, "Hamilton Disston," 16–17.

16. Aldo Leopold, *A Sand County Almanac and Sketches Here and There* (New York: Oxford University Press, 1987), viii; Roderick Nash, *Wilderness and the American Mind*, 3rd ed. (New Haven: Yale University Press, 1982), 8–43; William Cronon, *Changes in the Land: Indians, Colonists, and the Ecology of New England* (New York: Hill and Wang, 1992); Timothy Silver, *A New Face on the Countryside: Indians, Colonists, and Slaves in South Atlantic Forests, 1500–1800* (New York: Cambridge University Press, 1990).

17. Christopher F. Meindl, "Water, Water Everywhere," in *Paradise Lost? The Environmental History of Florida*, ed. Jack E. Davis and Raymond Arsenault (Gainesville: University Press of Florida, 2005), 131. When Florida became a state in 1821, 54 percent of its surface area was wetland (Thomas E. Dahl, *Wetlands Losses in the United States 1780s to 1980s* [Washington, D.C.: U.S. Department of the Interior, Fish and Wildlife Service, 1990], table 1, available online at http://www.npwrc.usgs.gov/resource/wetlands/wetloss/index.htm [accessed summer 2006]).

CHAPTER SEVEN: Growing Up

1. MSD, "There Was Nothing Odd about Grampa," MSDP, box 35, folder 89.

2. MSD, "There Was Nothing Odd."

3. MSD, "There Was Nothing Odd"; *Voice*, 64.

4. MSD, "Portuguese Pink," *The Archer* 24 (January 1928): 59.

5. *The Book of Taunton* (Taunton, Mass.: Hack, 1907), 7–8, 13–15; Elias Nason and George J. Varney, *Gazetteer of the State of Massachusetts* (Boston: Russell, 1890), 50, 231.

6. *MH*, 20 March 1921. For an illuminating history of the American elm tree, see Thomas J. Campanella, *Republic of Shade: New England and the American Elm* (New Haven: Yale University Press, 2003).

7. MSD, "There Was Nothing Odd."

8. The correct spelling of her name is unclear. Douglas's autobiography spells it *Fanny*, but the volume contains various misspellings and factual errors that were either overlooked and not checked by the editor, John Rothchild. Rothchild composed the book by transcribing recorded interviews with Douglas, who had become too blind to read or write. Census and genealogical records use *Fannie*, the more common spelling.

9. Unless otherwise noted, information about Douglas's early life is taken from her autobiography, *Voice*.

10. MSD, "There Was Nothing Odd."

11. *Voice*, 47.

12. Henry M. Hurd, William F. Drewry, Richard Dewey, Charles W. Pilgrim, G. Alder Blumer, and T. J. W. Burgess, *The Institutional Care of the Insane in the United States and Canada* (Baltimore: Johns Hopkins University Press, 1916), 657–63; Luther V. Bell, "Modern Improvements in the Construction, Ventilation, and Warming of Buildings for the Insane," *American Journal of Insanity* 2 (July 1845): 13–35, available online at http://www.disabilitymuseum.org/lib/docs/1572 .htm?page=1 (accessed summer 2005); Isaac Ray, "Popular Feeling toward Hospitals for the Insane," *American Journal of Insanity* 9 (July 1852): 36–65, available online at http://www.disabilitymuseum.org/lib/docs/1124card.htm (accessed spring 2003).

13. *MH*, 7 April 1980; *Voice*, 46–49; *Special Voices, Two Florida Women: Marjorie Carr, Marjory Stoneman Douglas*, video production (Florida Atlantic University/Florida International University, Joint Center for Environmental and Urban Problems, 1985).

14. *MH*, 7 April 1980; *Voice*, 46–49; *Special Voices*; MSD, "There Was Nothing Odd."

15. *Palm Beach Post-Times*, 26 March 1978.

16. Patricia Ann Palmieri, *In Adamless Eden: The Community of Women Faculty at Wellesley* (New Haven: Yale University Press, 1995), 188–91; *Voice*, 55–56.

17. MSD, "There Was Nothing Odd"; *Coconut Grove Post*, July 1957, Mrs. Alfred Peacock Collection, HMSF; *Special Voices*; MSD, "Portuguese Pink," 60.

18. *Palm Beach Post-Times*, 26 March 1978; *MH*, 15 March 1921; *Special Voices*.

19. *MH*, 11 February 1923.

20. *Old Colony Historical Society Newsletter* 4 (October 1990): n.p.

21. *MH*, 13 April 1920, 23 October 1923; MSD, "A Major in English Composition," circa 1976, in possession of author.

22. St. Nicholas Center Web site, available online at www.stnicholascenter.org (accessed summer 2005); *St. Nicholas: An Illustrated Magazine for Young Folks* 34 (January 1907): 273; Linda Lear, *Rachel Carson: Witness for Nature* (New York: Holt, 1997), 7.

23. Marjory Stoneman, "An Early Morning Paddle," *Boston Herald,* 23 June 1907.

24. *Voice*, 69–70; *Special Voices*; MSD, speech to Florida Historical Society, Pensacola, 6 May 1978, SPOHP.

25. *Taunton High School Journal*, 1908, 22.

26. *Palm Beach Post-Times,* 26 March 1978.

27. Taunton High School English Book, MSD folder, Wellesley College Archives, Wellesley, Mass.; *Taunton High School Journal*, 1908, 28, 38; MSD to Helen Betagh, 6 June 1988, HP.

28. *Taunton High School Journal*, 1908, 19, 28, 30, 38; "For Excellent Short Story," circa 1928, clipping, MSDP, box 33, folder 44; MSD, "Major in English Composition."

29. *Voice*, 65; Taunton High School English Book.

CHAPTER EIGHT: Frank's Journey

1. MSD, "The Stoneman Family—A Memoir," October 1986, HP; Charlton W. Tebeau, *A History of Florida* (Coral Gables, Fla.: University of Miami Press, 1971) 283; Edward N. Akin, *Flagler: Rockefeller Partner and Florida Baron* (Gainesville: University Press of Florida, 1992), 163; John F. Kasson, *Amusing the Million: Coney Island at the Turn of the Century* (New York: Hill and Wang, 1998), 3–9; Christopher F. Meindl, "Past Perceptions of the Great American Wetland: Florida's Everglades during the Early Twentieth Century," *Environmental History* 5 (July 2000): 379; *Special Voices, Two Florida Women: Marjorie Carr, Marjory Stoneman Douglas,* video production (Florida Atlantic University/Florida International University, Joint Center for Environmental and Urban Problems, 1985).

2. Mark Derr, *Some Kind of Paradise: A Chronicle of Man and the Land in Florida* (New York: Morrow, 1989), 81–82, 102–3; Tebeau, *History of Florida, 283;*

Voice, 98; *Great Floridians Film Series: Marjory Stoneman Douglas* (Tallahassee: Museum of Florida History and Florida History Associates, 1990).

3. Lillias's name is spelled differently in various sources, from the U.S. Census to Douglas's autobiography, which uses *Lillius.* MSD was blind at the time she dictated her autobiography to John Rothchild, and it contains many misspellings. I use the spelling listed on Frank and Lillias's marriage certificate, since Lillias would have been present when applying for it. Stoneman's obituary used this spelling as well.

4. *U.S. Census,* 1900; *MH,* 2 February 1941; MSD to Fred, 29 December 1971, Emma D. Gaylord Papers, Correspondence with MSD folder, Department of Special Collections, Rollins College, Winter Park, Fla.

5. In a retrospective newspaper column published in 1940, Frank Stoneman recounted the origins of the Orlando newspaper, calling it the *Evening Record.* Two other sources, including a 1911 feature on Stoneman in the *MH,* list the newspaper as the *Orlando Daily Herald.* Douglas said in her autobiography and elsewhere that her father acquired the printing press in lieu of legal fees, but Stoneman indicated that he and LaSalle purchased the press. *MH,* 20, 21, 22 July 1911, 3 March 1940; Nixon Smiley, ed., *The Miami Herald Front Pages, 1903–1983* (New York: Abrams, 1983), 18; *Voice,* 98–99; MSD, speech to Florida Historical Society, Pensacola, 6 May 1978, SPOHP.

6. MSD to Fred, 29 December 1971, Gaylord Papers, Correspondence with MSD folder; *Florida,* 246.

7. Millicent Todd Bingham, "Miami: A Study in Urban Geography," *Tequesta* 9 (1949): 97.

8. *Miami, Florida: Official Directory of the City of Miami and Nearby Towns,* 1904, available online at http://fcit.usf.edu/florida/docs/m/miami04.htm (accessed summer 2003); Bingham, "Miami," 81, 83, 94, 95, 98, 101–2; F. Page Wilson, "Miami: From Frontier to Metropolis: An Appraisal," *Tequesta* 14 (1954): 27; John C. Gifford, "Some Reflections on South Florida of Long Ago," *Tequesta* 6 (1946) 38–43; Derr, *Some Kind of Paradise,* 53; Akin, *Flagler,* 163; Paul S. George, "The First Hundred Years," *South Florida History Magazine* 24 (Summer 1997): 25; J. K. Dorn, "Recollections of Early Miami," *Tequesta* 9 (1949): 53–54; Ruby Leach Carson, "Miami: 1896 to 1900," *Tequesta* 16 (1956): 9; Will Davenport, "Growing Up, Sort of, in Miami, 1909–1915," *Tequesta* 39 (1979): 7, 9, 10, 13, 18; *MH,* 1 January 1911.

9. Akin, *Flagler,* 163–64, 201; Helen Muir, *Miami, U.S.A.* (Gainesville: University Press of Florida, 2000), 63–65; *Florida,* 246–47, 250–51; *River of Grass,* 290.

10. *Florida*, 251.

11. Derr, *Some Kind of Paradise*, 55–56, 62–63; *Miami, Florida; MH*, 25 February 1940.

12. Hugh Willoughby, *Across the Everglades: A Canoe Journey of Exploration* (Philadelphia: Lippincott, 1900), 62–63; Mary Douthit Conrad, "Homesteading in Florida during the 1890s," *Tequesta* 17 (1957): 4; *MH*, 20, 21, 22 July 1911.

13. *Miami, Florida; MH*, 21 April 1940.

14. *MH*, 27 April 1940.

15. Willoughby, *Across the Everglades*, 62.

16. *Florida*, 251.

17. Linda D. Vance, *May Mann Jennings: Florida's Genteel Activist* (Gainesville: University of Florida Press, 1985), 9–32.

18. W. S. Jennings, "Florida's Public Lands," in *Legislative Blue Book* (Tallahassee, Fla.: Appleyard, 1917), 52–53; J. E. Dovell, "The Everglades—Florida's Frontier, Part 1," *Economic Leaflets* 6 (April 1947): 1–4; W. Turner Wallis, "The History of Everglades Drainage and Its Present Status," *Soil Science Society of Florida Proceedings*, 4-A (1942), 32; *NYT*, 15 March 1925.

19. *IIF Minutes*, 4:40–41, 6:5–6, 32–37, 50–51, 112–18; *Everglades of Florida, Acts, Reports, and Other Papers, State and National, Relating to the Everglades of the State of Florida and Their Reclamation*, U.S. Senate, 62nd Cong., 1st sess., 1911, 13–14; David McCally, *The Everglades: An Environmental History* (Gainesville: University Press of Florida, 1999), 91–93; Christopher F. Meindl, Derek H. Alderman, and Peter Waylen, "On the Importance of Environmental Claims-Making: The Role of James O. Wright in Promoting Drainage of Florida's Everglades in the Early Twentieth Century," *Annals of the Association of American Geographers* 92 (December 2002): 688; Samuel Proctor, *Napoleon Bonaparte Broward: Florida's Fighting Democrat* (Gainesville: University Press of Florida, 1990), 190–91, 195, 259; Joe Knetsch, "Admitting the Obvious: Origins of the Swamplands Patent to the Everglades, Part 2," *Professional Surveyor* 26 (December 2006): 26–29.

20. Model Land Company, Perrine Grant Land Company, Flagler System, memo, 19 February 1949, Gilbert D. Leach to Claude Pepper, 9 March 1949, both in CPC, s201/34D/1.

21. Muir, *Miami, U.S.A.*, 78–79; Derr, *Some Kind of Paradise*, 53, 54; *MH*, 17, 31 December 1939, 28 January, 3, 17 March 1940.

22. *Miami Metropolis*, 24 October 1908; *MH*, 3 March 1940, 15 September 2002; Smiley, *Miami Herald Front Pages*, 18–20; Les Standiford, *Last Train to Paradise:*

Henry Flagler and the Spectacular Rise and Fall of the Railroad That Crossed an Ocean (New York: Crown, 2002), 114; Jeanne Bellamy, "Newspapers of America's Last Frontier," *Tequesta* 12 (1952): 7–9.

23. D. LeBaron Perrine, "The Remaking of Florida," *The Tropic* 7 (February 1926): 187, 192; William Stuart Hill, "Dade County of Today," *Florida Magazine* 1 (September 1922): 24; John Hicks, "Marjory Stoneman Douglas," *Florida* (*Orlando Sentinel*), 14 October 1979, 7; Muir, *Miami, U.S.A.*, 78–79; Smiley, *Miami Herald Front Pages*, 18; *MH*, 15 September 2002; MSD, *Florida*, 7.

CHAPTER NINE: The Sovereign

1. Archie Carr, "The Bird and the Behemoth," in *The Wild Heart of Florida*, ed. Jeff Ripple and Susan Cerulean (Gainesville: University Press of Florida, 1999), 33–42; *IIF Minutes*, 7:281–312; Joe Knetsch, "Governor Broward and the Details of Dredging: 1908," *Broward Legacy* 14 (Winter–Spring 1991): 38–44; Lawrence E. Will, "Everglades Rendezvous," *All Florida* (*Orlando Evening Star*), 23 October 1967, 11–13.

2. *Weekly Miami Metropolis*, 30 August 1907; William Stuart Hill, "Dade County of Today," *The Florida Magazine* 1 (September 1922): 24.

3. *Daily Miami Metropolis*, 29 January 1908.

4. *Weekly Miami Metropolis*, 30 August, 29 November 1907; *Daily Miami Metropolis*, 28, 29 January, 25 September, 24 October, 28 December 1908; *Jacksonville Florida Times-Union*, 18 March, 27 September, 30 December 1908; *MH*, 20, 21, 22 July 1911, 31 December 1939; "Broward in Broward," *Broward Legacy* 22 (Winter–Spring 1999): 12–13, 16–19; *Florida*, 17; Isidor Cohen, *Historical Sketches and Sidelights of Miami, Florida* (n.p., 1925), 166–68.

5. *Miami Morning News-Record*, 9 April 1909.

6. *MH*, 5 February, 18 November 1908, 8, 9 April 1909, 4 June 1916.

7. *Miami Morning News-Record*, 5 February, 4, 18 November 1908, 9 April 1909; *MH*, 31 December 1939; Christopher F. Meindl, "Frank Stoneman and the Florida Everglades during the Early 20th Century," *Florida Geographer* 29 (1998): 52; Helen Muir, *Miami, U.S.A.* (Gainesville: University Press of Florida, 2000), 55; *Florida*, 7; *Voice*, 104, 108, 168.

8. *River of Grass*, 286.

9. "Open Letter of Governor N. B. Broward to the People of Florida," 1906, available online at http://palmm.fcla.edu/fh/ (accessed fall 2003); Eric Frederick

Goldman, *Rendezvous with Destiny: A History of Modern American Reform* (New York: Knopf, 1952), 51; Samuel Proctor, *Napoleon Bonaparte Broward: Florida's Fighting Democrat* (Gainesville: University Press of Florida, 1990), 190; *Tampa Daily Times,* 23 January 1917.

10. Proctor, *Napoleon Bonaparte Broward,* 260.

11. Proctor, *Napoleon Bonaparte Broward,* 49–50, 103–15; Ralph D. Paine, *Roads of Adventure* (n.p., 1922), 176–81; "Napoleon Bonaparte Broward: Candidate for Governor of Florida, Autobiography, Platform, Letter, and Short Story of the Steamer Three Friends, and a Filibustering Trip to Cuba, Part 1," *Broward Legacy* 5 (Winter–Spring 1982): 5–16.

12. *River of Grass,* 312; Proctor, *Napoleon Bonaparte Broward,* 1–30, 50–52, 73, 92–95, 100–111, 160, 165, 178–205; Paine, *Roads of Adventure,* 181–82; "Napoleon Bonaparte Broward," 5–16.

13. "Open Letter of Governor N. B. Broward"; *Message of N. B. Broward, Governor of Florida, to the Legislature, Regular Session of 1907* (Tallahassee, Fla.: Capital, 1907), available online at http://webluis.fcla.edu (accessed fall 2003); *River of Grass,* 312–14; Charlton W. Tebeau, *A History of Florida* (Coral Gables, Fla.: University of Miami Press, 1971), 347–48; Proctor, *Napoleon Bonaparte Broward,* 216–22; Mark Derr, *Some Kind of Paradise: A Chronicle of Man and the Land in Florida* (New York: Morrow, 1989), 157.

14. *Message of N. B. Broward;* Proctor, *Napoleon Bonaparte Broward,* 216–23, 240–45, 259; J. E. Dovell, "The Everglades—Florida's Frontier, Part 1," *Economic Leaflets* 6 (April 1947): 1; W. Turner Wallis, "The History of Everglades Drainage and Its Present Status," Soil Science Society of Florida Proceedings 4-A (1942): 32–33; Derr, *Some Kind of Paradise,* 158–59; David McCally, *The Everglades: An Environmental History* (Gainesville: University Press of Florida, 1999), 92–93; Paine, *Roads of Adventure,* 182.

15. Proctor, *Napoleon Bonaparte Broward,* 259, 264–66, 294; Knetsch, "Governor Broward," 39, 41–42; Donald Worster, *The Wealth of Nature: Environmental History and the Ecological Imagination* (New York: Oxford University Press, 1993), 211–12; Will, "Everglades Rendezvous"; Paine, *Roads of Adventure,* 183–84.

16. *MH,* 31 December 1939.

17. Proctor, *Napoleon Bonaparte Broward,* 243; *MH,* 31 December 1939; F. Page Wilson, "Miami: From Frontier to Metropolis: An Appraisal," *Tequesta* 14 (1954): 32.

18. *Florida,* 7.

19. Meindl, "Frank Stoneman," 48–49; *Miami Evening Record*, 25, 27 October 1906; *Miami Morning News-Record*, 5 February 1908.

20. *Miami Morning News-Record*, 5 February 1908; *River of Grass*, 286; Ann Vileisis, *Discovering the Unknown Landscape: A History of America's Wetlands* (Washington, D.C.: Island, 1997), 143–45.

21. *Miami Metropolis*, 24 October 1908; Jeanne Bellamy, "Newspapers of America's Last Frontier," *Tequesta* 12 (1952): 7–9.

22. Proctor, *Napoleon Bonaparte Broward*, 241–42, 249–50; *Jacksonville Metropolis*, 28 February 1908; *Miami News-Record*, 5 February, 18 November 1908; *Everglades of Florida, no. 1: Hearings before the Committee on Expenditures in the Department of Agriculture* (Washington, D.C.: U.S. Government Printing Office, 1912), 583, 584.

23. Goldman, *Rendezvous with Destiny*, 50–51, 82–83.

24. Quoted in Christopher F. Meindl, Derek H. Alderman, and Peter Waylen, "On the Importance of Environmental Claims-Making: The Role of James O. Wright in Promoting Drainage of Florida's Everglades in the Early Twentieth Century," *Annals of the Association of American Geographers* 92 (December 2002): 688.

25. Nixon Smiley, ed., *The Miami Herald Front Pages, 1903–1983* (New York: Abrams, 1983), 17–19; *Miami Morning News-Record*, 5 February 1908, 18 November 1908; *MH*, 1 January 1911, 2 February 1941; Meindl, "Frank Stoneman," 49, 51, 52; *Voice*, 40, 99; MSD, "Frank Bryant Stoneman," *Tequesta* 4 (November 1944): 7–8; MSD, "When You and I Were Young, Miami," *Tropic (MH)*, 5 November 1967, 17.

CHAPTER TEN: Wellesley

1. *Special Voices, Two Florida Women: Marjorie Carr, Marjory Stoneman Douglas*, video production (Florida Atlantic University/Florida International University, Joint Center for Environmental and Urban Problems, 1985); *Voice*, 68.

2. Patricia Ann Palmieri, *In Adamless Eden: The Community of Women Faculty at Wellesley* (New Haven: Yale University Press, 1995), 206–7.

3. Palmieri, *In Adamless Eden*, 10–12; Florence Converse, *The Story of Wellesley* (Boston: Little, Brown, 1915); *Nineteen Twelver*, February 1977, MSDP, box 31, folder 111.

4. *Voice*, 69–70; MSD, "Perspectives," *Wellesley Alumnae Magazine*, Summer 1977, 22.

5. Palmieri, *In Adamless Eden*, 80, 165.

6. MSD, "Perspectives," 22; *MH*, 7 October 1922; Cathy Shaw, "The Friend of the Everglades," *Wellesley Magazine*, Summer 1983, 15; Palmieri, *In Adamless Eden*, 60; Susan S. Lang, interview transcript and article draft, in Susan S. Lang to MSD, 14 April 1991, HP.

7. MSD, "Perspectives," 22; Nancy Woloch, *Women and the American Experience* (New York: McGraw-Hill, 1984), 276–83; Shaw, "Friend of the Everglades," 15; Palmieri, *In Adamless Eden*, 6, 7, 223–27.

8. "Courses Taken at Wellesley College by Marjory Stoneman, Class of 1912," MSD folder, Wellesley College Archives, Wellesley, Mass.; MSD, "Alumnae Achievement Award," *Wellesley Alumnae Magazine*, Spring 1977, 31; Palmieri, *In Adamless Eden*, 162–66; MSD, "A Major in English Composition," circa 1976, in possession of author.

9. Marjory Stoneman, "The Tree Day Pageant at Wellesley," *Taunton High School Journal* (1909), 41–42; Marjory Stoneman, "Lost Balls," *Wellesley Magazine*, 1 March 1911, 229–35; MSD, "Alumnae Achievement Award"; *Orlando Sentinel Star*, 9 November 1975; Andy Taylor, "Marjory Stoneman Douglas," clipping, Hampton Dunn Collection, MSD folder, USF; MSD, "Major in English Composition."

10. MSD to Robinettes, 18 July 1985, MSDP, box 40, folder 21; "Courses Taken at Wellesley"; MSD, "Major in English Composition"; *Special Voices*; Shaw, "Friend of the Everglades," 15; Palmieri, *In Adamless Eden*, 79, 85.

11. *Palm Beach Post-Times*, 26 March 1978; Al Burt, "The Elocutioner," clipping, MSDP, box 39, folder 12; Palmieri, *In Adamless Eden*, 51, 78.

12. Palmieri, *In Adamless Eden*, 148–60.

13. Mercedes M. Randall, *Improper Bostonian: Emily Greene Balch* (New York: Twayne, 1964); Cindy Miller, "Marjory Stoneman Douglas Spurs 'Grassroots,'" clipping, MSDP, box 39, folder 11; Palmieri, *In Adamless Eden*, 170–71, 238–44; MSD, "Major in English Composition"; *MH*, 19 March 1921.

14. MSD, "Alumnae Achievement Award," 31; Taylor, "Marjory Stoneman Douglas"; *Florida*, 16; *Orlando Sentinel Star*, 9 November 1975; Palmieri, *In Adamless Eden*, 157–58, 182–83.

15. Jean Areson, interview by author, 10 June 2000; Helen Rowley to MSD, 22 January 1948, MSDP, box 42, folder 43.

16. MSD, "Major in English Composition."

17. *Voice*, 78–79, 82; Areson, interview.

18. MSD, "Major in English Composition"; *Voice*, 82.

19. Diary, 31 August 1925, MSDP, box 30; Sharyn T. Richardson, "Marjory Stoneman Douglas: Her Place on Earth," *Florida Living,* May 1999, 26.

CHAPTER ELEVEN: Reports

1. MSD, *Road to the Horizon* (New York: Rinehart, 1952), 6, 9.

2. Samuel Proctor, *Napoleon Bonaparte Broward: Florida's Fighting Democrat* (Gainesville: University Press of Florida, 1990), 247–48; *Everglades of Florida, no. 1: Hearings before the Committee on Expenditures in the Department of Agriculture* (Washington, D.C.: U.S. Government Printing Office, 1912), 581–82, 585; *MH,* 6, 8, 9, 12 November 1915.

3. *Everglades of Florida, no. 1,* 94–97; Aaron D. Purcell, "Plumb Lines, Politics, and Projections: The Florida Everglades and the Wright Report Controversy," *Florida Historical Quarterly* 80 (Fall 2001): 161–97.

4. Purcell, "Plumb Lines, Politics, and Projections," 169; W. Turner Wallis, "The History of Everglades Drainage and Its Present Status," *Soil Science Society of Florida Proceedings,* 4-A (1942): 32; Proctor, *Napoleon Bonaparte Broward,* 224; Christopher F. Meindl, Derek H. Alderman, and Peter Waylen, "On the Importance of Environmental Claims-Making: The Role of James O. Wright in Promoting Drainage of Florida's Everglades in the Early Twentieth Century," *Annals of the Association of American Geographers* 92 (December 2002): 689; David McCally, *The Everglades: An Environmental History* (Gainesville: University Press of Florida, 1999), 90–91; *Everglades of Florida, no. 1,* 822.

5. Purcell, "Plumb Lines, Politics, and Projections," 171; Meindl, Alderman, and Waylen, "On the Importance," 689; Marc Reisner, *Cadillac Desert: The American West and Its Disappearing Water* (New York: Penguin, 1987), 111–15.

6. Ann Vileisis, *Discovering the Unknown Landscape: A History of America's Wetlands* (Washington, D.C.: Island, 1997), 125–27; Hugh Prince, *Wetlands of the American Midwest: A Historical Geography of Changing Attitudes* (Chicago: University of Chicago Press, 1998), 208, 241–42.

7. Meindl, Alderman, and Waylen, "On the Importance," 694–95.

8. *IIF Minutes,* 7:122–25.

9. *WP,* 25 March 1906; Meindl, Alderman, and Waylen, "On the Importance," 695; Charlton W. Tebeau, *A History of Florida* (Coral Gables, Fla.: University of Miami Press, 1971), 349; *Everglades of Florida, no. 1,* 1322–27; Florida Everglades Land Company, "Little Journeys to the Everglades of Florida," n.d., Thomas E. Will Papers, Everglades Publications folder, box 33, PKY.

10. Meindl, Alderman, and Waylen, "On the Importance," 694–95; *Daily Miami Metropolis*, 30 January 1908; Purcell, "Plumb Lines, Politics, and Projections," 173–74.

11. McCally, *Everglades*, 103; Alfred Jackson Hanna and Kathryn Abbey Hanna, *Lake Okeechobee: Wellspring of the Everglades* (Indianapolis: Bobbs-Merrill, 1948), 158–59; Purcell, "Plumb Lines, Politics, and Projections," 191–93.

12. *Miami Morning News-Record*, 5 February 1908.

13. *Miami Morning News-Record*, 6, 8 October 1908; *Miami Metropolis*, 5, 6 October 1908.

14. Meindl, Alderman, and Waylen, "On the Importance," 690–94.

15. *Everglades of Florida, no. 1*, 822–25; Meindl, Alderman, and Waylen, "On the Importance," 690; McCally, *Everglades*, 94–96.

16. J. E. Dovell, "Thomas Elmer Will, Twentieth-Century Pioneer," *Tequesta* 8 (1948): 23, 26, 28–29; *Everglades of Florida, no. 1*, 840–41, 858–59; Hanna and Hanna, *Lake Okeechobee*, 156; Meindl, Alderman, and Waylen, "On the Importance," 690; McCally, *Everglades*, 96; *Boston Evening Tribune*, 13 February 1912.

17. McCally, *Everglades*, 100; Proctor, *Napoleon Bonaparte Broward*, 267–84; Meindl, Alderman, and Waylen, "On the Importance," 69; Purcell, "Plumb Lines, Politics, and Projections," 180.

18. *MH*, 10 December 1920, 1 May 1923; *River of Grass*, 323–24. Not only did she show Will respect, she failed to mention that he had stormed Elliot's office demanding that he retract his circular letter.

19. James O. Wright, "Twenty-five Facts about the Everglades Worth Remembering," 30 December 1911, and "Why Was Wright's Report on the Everglades Suppressed?" 28 December 1911, in *Everglades of Florida, no. 1*; Purcell, "Plumb Lines, Politics, and Projections," 176.

20. *Everglades of Florida, no. 1*, 840; Tebeau, *History of Florida*, 349–50; McCally, *Everglades*, 100–101; Roy Talbert Jr., *FDR's Utopian: Arthur Morgan of the TVA* (Jackson: University Press of Mississippi, 1987), 33–35.

21. *MH*, 20, 21, 22 July 1911, 15 February 1912; *Orlando Sentinel*, 1 January 1984; *WP*, 12 March 1912; *Boston Evening Tribune*, 13 February 1912; Arthur E. Morgan, "The Florida Everglades Incident: Section of Autobiographical Writings of Arthur E. Morgan," Arthur E. Morgan Papers, box 1, PKY; "Digest and Analysis of Senate Bill no. [blank] Relating to Everglades Drainage District," Morgan Papers, box 1; *Everglades of Florida, no. 1*, 856–58; Talbert, *FDR's Utopian*, 33–35; McCally, *Everglades*, 101–2.

22. McCally, *Everglades,* 103; Talbert, *FDR's Utopian,* 35; Purcell, "Plumb Lines, Politics, and Projections," 191–95.

23. Quoted in Meindl, Alderman, and Waylen, "On the Importance," 689; *IIF Minutes,* 8:451.

24. Florida Everglades Reclaimed Land Company, *Florida Everglades,* company pamphlet, n.d., Will Papers, box 33, Everglades Publications folder; *IIF Minutes,* 8:450–51; McCally, *Everglades,* 83–94, 98–100; *Tampa Morning Tribune,* 9 January 1909.

25. *Miami Morning News-Record,* 6, 8, 19 October, 1, 18 November, 31 December 1908; *MH,* 15 February 1912; "Everglades Drainage Notes," 7 December 1931, available online at http://palmm.fcla.edu/index.html (accessed fall 2004).

26. *IIF Minutes,* 448–50; McCally, *Everglades,* 109–14; Meindl, Alderman, and Waylen, "On the Importance," 695.

27. U.S. Congress, Senate, *Florida Everglades: Report of the Florida Everglades Engineering Commission to the Board of Commissioners of the Everglades Drainage District and the Trustees of the Internal Improvement Fund, State of Florida, 1913,* 63rd Cong., 2nd sess., 1914, S. Doc. 379; J. E. Dovell, "The Everglades—Florida's Frontier, Part 1," *Economic Leaflets* 6 (April 1947): 4–10; McCally, *Everglades,* 111–12; Tebeau, *History of Florida,* 349–50; Meindl, Alderman, and Waylen, "On the Importance," 695; Isham Randolph, "Reclaiming the Everglades of Florida," *Journal of the Franklin Institute* 184 (July 1917): 49–72.

28. Proctor, *Napoleon Bonaparte Broward,* 292, 295; McCally, *Everglades,* 93–94.

29. "Broward in Broward," *Broward Legacy* 22 (Winter–Spring 1999): 18; Christopher F. Meindl, "Frank Stoneman and the Florida Everglades during the Early 20th Century," *Florida Geographer* 29 (1998): 52–53; *MH,* 1 January 1911, 15 February 1912, 6, 8, 12 November 1915, 2 February 1941; *Miami Morning News-Record,* 19 August 1908; *Voice,* 167; McCally, *Everglades,* 94, 96–97, 101, 105, 130; Proctor, *Napoleon Bonaparte Broward,* 293–94; Helen Muir, *Miami, U.S.A.* (Gainesville: University Press of Florida, 2000), 78–79; "Why Was Wright's Report on the Everglades Suppressed?"

30. Thomas E. Will, "Conservation in Earnest," n.d., Will Papers, box 33, Everglades folder.

31. Will, "Conservation in Earnest"; Dovell, "Thomas Elmer Will," 23, 26, 28–29.

32. Donald Worster, *The Wealth of Nature: Environmental History and the Ecological Imagination* (New York: Oxford University Press, 1993), 206–13; *River of Grass,* 312.

CHAPTER TWELVE: Marriage

1. MSD, "Alumnae Achievement Award," *Wellesley Alumnae Magazine,* Spring 1977, 31; MSD, "A Major in English Composition," circa 1976, in possession of author; MSD, "Frank Bryant Stoneman," *Tequesta* 4 (November 1944): 7–8; MSD, untitled manuscript, n.d., MSDP, box 48, folder 123; clipping, n.d., Mrs. Alfred Peacock Collection, HMSF.

2. *MH,* 2 February 1913.

3. *Voice,* 82–83; Walter Lord, *A Night to Remember* (New York: Holt, 2005), 5; *NYT,* 18 May 1964.

4. Louis E. Westheimer to MSD, n.d., MSDP, box 46, folder 98; *Newark Evening News,* 4 June 1914.

5. "Old Newark Memories," available online at http://oldnewark.com (accessed fall 2004); Daniel J. Boorstin, *The Americans: The Democratic Experience* (New York: Random House, 1973), 89–164; William R. Leach, *Land of Desire: Merchants, Power, and the Rise of a New American Culture* (New York: Vintage, 1994); Lizabeth Cohen, *A Consumer's Republic: The Politics of Mass Consumption in Postwar America* (New York: Knopf, 2003).

6. *Voice,* 83.

7. Holly Hays, "Marjory Stoneman Douglas: Conservationist of the Century," *Florida Living,* August 1992, 53; *Voice,* 84–85.

8. *Newark Evening News,* 18 April, 15 June 1914; *Miami Metropolis,* 28 April 1914; *Voice,* 85–86.

9. *Voice,* 87–89.

10. *Newark Evening News,* 15 April, 15 June 1914.

11. *Newark Evening News,* 4, 6 June 1914.

12. *Newark Evening News,* 4 June 1914.

13. *Newark Evening News,* 5, 15 June 1914.

14. *Newark Evening News,* 6, 12, 15 June 1914.

15. *Newark Evening News,* 13, 15, 30 June, 2 July, 10 November 1914; MSD, "The Stoneman Family—A Memoir," October 1986, HP.

16. Diary, 11 August 1925, MSDP, box 40.

17. *Voice*, 88–89.

18. *Voice*, 90–92; *MH*, 1 February 1918.

CHAPTER THIRTEEN: By Violence

1. MSD, *Alligator Crossing* (1959; reprint, Minneapolis: Milkweed, 2003), 116–17.

2. *Florida*, 216; MSD, *Alligator Crossing*, 116–17; Anne E. Rowe, *The Idea of Florida in the American Literary Imagination* (Gainesville: University Press of Florida, 1992), 30–43, 56, 58–65; Elliot James Mackle Jr., "The Eden of the South: Florida's Image in American Travel Literature and Painting, 1865–1900" (Ph.D. diss., Emory University, 1977), 115. See also Jack E. Davis, "Alligators and Plume Birds: The Despoliation of Florida's Living Aesthetic," in *Paradise Lost? The Environmental History of Florida*, ed. Jack E. Davis and Raymond Arsenault (Gainesville: University Press of Florida, 2005), 245–59.

3. Quoted in Tom Staley, "Florida Alligator Carvings," *Antiques and Art around Florida*, Winter–Spring 1998, available online at http://aarf.com/fealig98 .htm (accessed summer 2005).

4. George M. Barbour, *Florida for Tourists, Invalids, and Settlers: Containing Practical Information Regarding Climate, Soil, and Productions; Cities, Towns, and People; the Culture of the Orange and Other Tropical Fruits; Farming and Gardening; Scenery and Resorts; Sports; Routes of Travel, etc., etc.* (New York: Appleton, 1884), 285.

5. Frank M. Chapman, *Camps and Cruises of an Ornithologist* (New York: Appleton, 1908), 123; "Buffalo, Wild Pigeons, and Plume Birds," *Forest and Stream*, 4 August 1894, 95; Mark Derr, *Some Kind of Paradise: A Chronicle of Man and the Land in Florida* (New York: Morrow, 1989), 384.

6. Howard A. Kelly, "The Everglades National Park," *Journal of the Maryland Academy of Sciences* 2 (January 1931): 39; Charles B. Cory, "Descriptions of Six Supposed New Species of Birds from the Islands of Old Providence and St. Andrews, Caribbean Sea," *The Auk* 4 (July 1887): 177.

7. John F. Reiger, *American Sportsmen and the Origins of Conservation* (Norman: University of Oklahoma Press, 1986), 19–28; Stephen Fox, *The American Conservation Movement: John Muir and His Legacy* (Madison: University of Wisconsin Press, 1981), 108.

8. *River of Grass,* 280; William Cronon, *Nature's Metropolis: Chicago and the Great West* (New York: Norton, 1991), 216–18; Harriet Beecher Stowe, *Palmetto Leaves* (1873; reprint, Gainesville: University Press of Florida, 1999), 260–61; Minnie Moore-Willson, *The Birds of the Everglades and Their Neighbors the Seminole Indians* (Tampa, Fla.: *Tampa Tribune,* 1920), 17, available online at http://webluis.fcla.edu (accessed summer 2004); John Newhouse, "Pioneering in the Everglades," 1932, 5, Miscellaneous Manuscripts, box 25, John Newhouse file, PKY; Mary K. Wintringham, ed., "North to South through the Everglades in 1883, Part II" (*New Orleans Times-Democrat,* 23 December 1883), *Tequesta* 24 (1964): 66–67.

9. John Whipple Potter Jenks, *Hunting in Florida in 1874* (n.p., 1884), 53–54.

10. Moore-Willson, *Birds of the Everglades,* 17.

11. Moore-Willson, *Birds of the Everglades,* 17.

12. *Florida,* 17; Lawrence Will, *Cracker History of Okeechobee: Custard Apple, Moonvine, Catfish, and Moonshine* (Belle Glade, Fla.: Glades Historical Society, 1977), 91–93; Harry A. Kersey Jr., *Pelts, Plumes, and Hides: White Traders among the Seminole Indians, 1870–1930* (Gainesville: University of Florida Press, 1975), 36–37, 44–45, 49–53, 117, 130–33; Derr, *Some Kind of Paradise,* 133.

13. Richard Rhodes, "The Killing of the Everglades," *Playboy,* January 1972, 114.

14. Fred Whittaker, "Alligator Ike; or, The Secret of the Everglade," *Beadle's New York Dime Library,* 18 July 1883, 1–11; Kirk Munroe, "Catching Alligators," *Harper's,* 12 April 1884, 233; Peter A. Soderbergh, "Florida's Image in Juvenile Fiction, 1909–1914," *Florida Historical Quarterly* 51 (October 1972): 160; John Richard Bothwell, "How an Alligator Sold St. Petersburg," in *Alligator Tales,* ed. Kevin M. McCarthy (Sarasota, Fla.: Pineapple, 1998), 161–64; *NYT,* 13 July 1891.

15. Julian Ralph, *Dixie; or, Southern Scenes and Sketches* (New York: Harper, 1896); Alonzo Church, "A Dash through the Everglades," *Tequesta* 9 (1949): 19; Jenks, *Hunting in Florida in 1874,* 47; Soderbergh, "Florida's Image in Juvenile Fiction," 159–60; *Tampa Morning Tribune,* 20 March 1898; Bothwell, "How an Alligator"; "The Alligator Satchel," *Forest and Stream,* 8 July 1893, 26.

16. Kirk Munroe, "Alligator Hunting with Seminoles," in *Alligator Tales,* ed. McCarthy, 59–67; Kirk Munroe, "Catching Alligators," 233; Hugh Willoughby, *Across the Everglades: A Canoe Journey of Exploration* (Philadelphia: Lippincott, 1900), 81; Kirk Munroe, Miscellaneous Vita, Kirk Munroe Collection, box

2, Special Collections, Rollins College Library, Winter Park, Fla.; Irving Leonard, *The Florida Biography of Kirk Munroe: Narrative and Biographical* (Chuluota, Fla.: Mickler House, 1975), 1–17, 19–32; Jenks, *Hunting in Florida in 1874*, 47. MSD offered a very similar image of a night hunt in *Alligator Crossing*: "The gator's head vanished in foam. For a minute the tail and arms thrashed. Then they were quiet and the lighter belly came up and hung. A redness like smoke spread in the lighted water" (124)

17. Kersey, *Pelts, Plumes, and Hides*, 47, 48, 130, 132; Derr, *Some Kind of Paradise*, 141–42; A. H. Brown, "Haunting Heart of the Everglades," *National Geographic* 93 (February 1948): 152; Clarence B. Moore, "The 'Gator,'" *St. Nicholas: An Illustrated Magazine for Young Folks* 28 (November 1890): 74.

18. "Alligator Satchel," 26; Charlton W. Tebeau, *Man in the Everglades: 2,000 Years of Human History in the Everglades National Park* (Coral Gables, Fla.: University of Miami Press, 1986), 44; "In the 'Glades: Prof. C. B. Cory Tells about What He Saw in the Everglades" (*Tropical Sun*, 23 May 1895), *Broward Legacy* 14 (Winter–Spring 1991): 23; Florida Audubon Society, "Shall We Protect the Pelican?" n.d., Conservation folder, Special Collections, Rollins College Library; Mary Douthit Conrad, "Homesteading in Florida during the 1890s," *Tequesta* 17 (1957): 9; Kersey, *Pelts, Plumes, and Hides*, 47, 48, 130, 132; Derr, *Some Kind of Paradise*, 141–42; A. H. Brown, "Haunting Heart of the Everglades," 152; Thomas Barbour, *That Vanishing Eden: A Naturalist's Florida* (Boston: Little, Brown, 1944), 178, 193; John C. Gifford, *Billy Bowlegs and the Seminole War* (Coconut Grove, Fla.: Triangle, 1925), 24; John C. Jones and Mariana Jones, interview by author, 11 August 2000.

19. A. W. Dimock, "The Passing of the Florida Alligator," in *Alligator Tales*, ed. McCarthy, 96–106; Will, *Cracker History of Okeechobee*, 92–93; Moore, "'Gator'"; "Alligator Satchel"; MSD, *Alligator Crossing*, 128.

20. W. E. D. Scott, "The Present Condition of Some of the Bird Rookeries of the Gulf Coast," *The Auk* 4 (April 1887): 138, 4 (July 1887): 218; Stuart B. McIver, *Death in the Everglades: The Murder of Guy Bradley, America's First Martyr to Environmentalism* (Gainesville: University Press of Florida, 2003), 16–17, 20; Tebeau, *Man in the Everglades*, 75–91.

21. W. E. D. Scott, "The Present Condition of Some of the Bird Rookeries of the Gulf Coast," *The Auk* 4 (October 1887): 282; McIver, *Death in the Everglades*, 18; Tebeau, *Man in the Everglades*, 89.

22. Derr, *Some Kind of Paradise*, 139; Scott, "Present Condition" (October 1887), 281; *River of Grass*, 279; "About the Aigrette," *Bird-Lore* 11 (October 1909): 232; Archie Carr, "The Bird and the Behemoth," in *The Wild Heart of Florida*, ed. Jeff Ripple and Susan Cerulean (Gainesville: University Press of Florida, 1999), 40–42; A. C. Bent, "Nesting Habits of the Herodiones in Florida," *The Auk* 21 (January 1904): 20–29; Lawrence Will, *Dredgeman of Cape Sable* (St. Petersburg, Fla.: Great Outdoors, 1967), 55.

23. Barry Reese, "The Plume Wars," unpublished paper, in possession of the author, 38.

24. Jennifer Price, *Flight Maps: Adventures with Nature in Modern America* (New York: Basic Books, 2000), 81–82; "About the Aigrette," 232; Alfred Jackson Hanna and Kathryn Abbey Hanna, *Lake Okeechobee: Wellspring of the Everglades* (Indianapolis: Bobbs-Merrill, 1948), 340–41.

25. *South Florida Courier*, 17 April 1886; Will, *Cracker History of Okeechobee*, 94; Derr, *Some Kind of Paradise*, 136–37; Barry Reese, "Plume Wars."

26. Gifford, *Billy Bowlegs*, 53; Oscar E. Baynard to A. J. Hanna, 24 September 1947, Alfred J. Hanna Papers, Plume Hunting folder, Special Collections, Rollins College Library; Jean C. Taylor, "The Ox Woman," *Update* 6 (February 1979): 1–3.

27. MSD, "Wings," *SEP*, 14 March 1931, 79; MSD, *Alligator Crossing*, 128; Lucy Worthington Blackman, *The Florida Audubon Society, 1900–1935* (n.p., n.d.), 30–31; *NYT*, 13 July 1891; *MH*, 7 April 1920.

28. Moore-Willson, *Birds of the Everglades*, 7, 8; MSD, "Wings," 78; Lawrence Will, *Okeechobee Boats and Skippers* (St. Petersburg, Fla.: Great Outdoors, 1965), 15–72, 129–42; Kersey, *Pelts, Plumes, and Hides*, 52–63, 75–77, 104–5, 132; "A Heartless Fashion," *Current Literature* 23 (April 1898): 337; *WP*, 3 March 1907, 4 March 1973.

29. *NYT*, 13 July 1891; *WP*, 3 March 1907; *Forest and Stream*, 9 May 1889, 316; Jenks, *Hunting in Florida in 1874*, 53–54; J. A. Allen, "The American Ornithologists' Union," *Bird-Lore* 1 (October 1899): 143–44.

30. "Heartless Fashion"; *River of Grass*, 279.

31. Jim Huffstodt, "The Reign of the Plume Hunter," *Florida Wildlife*, March–April 1992, 3; *American Eagle*, 2 September 1926; Loren G. Brown, *Totch: A Life in the Everglades* (Gainesville: University Press of Florida, 1993), 11; "Autobiography of C. G. McKinney" (1928), 8, in Reclaiming the Everglades, online database

sponsored by the State University System of Florida, available at http://ever
glades.fiu.ed/reclaim (accessed summer 2008); "About the Aigrette," 232; Oliver H. Orr, *Saving American Birds: T. Gilbert Pearson and the Founding of the Audubon Movement* (Gainesville: University Press of Florida, 1992), 30–31; *NYT,*
13 July 1891, 17 April 1898.

32. *MH,* 28 April 1915; *WP,* 7 October 1900, 1 October 1902, 3 March 1907; *NYT,*
8, 13 August 1905; "Heartless Fashion"; "The Plume Bird Traffic," *Forest and Stream,*
27 July 1895, 71; Carol Mattingly, *Appropriate(ing) Dress: Women's Rhetorical Style
in Nineteenth-Century America* (Carbondale: Southern Illinois University Press,
2002); Valerie Steele, *Fashion and Eroticism: The Ideals of Feminine Beauty from
the Victorian Era to the Jazz Age* (New York: Oxford University Press, 1985).

33. "Florida Still Asleep," *Bird-Lore,* February 1, 1916, *NYT,* 13 July 1891; Orr,
Saving American Birds, 237; Will, *Cracker History of Okeechobee,* 93, 95; Fox,
American Conservation Movement, 148–51; *River of Grass,* 279; Scott, "Present
Condition" (April 1887), 135–44; Scott, "Present Condition" (October 1887), 276–
77; Hanna and Hanna, *Lake Okeechobee,* 341; T. Gilbert Pearson to Mrs. W. S.
Jennings, 1 April 1916, MMJP, box 9; Bent, "Nesting Habits," 23–29; Derr, *Some
Kind of Paradise,* 140; Harold H. Bailey, *The Birds of Florida* (Baltimore: Waverly,
1925), 31; Steven Beissinger, "A Faithful, Fickle Hawk," *Natural History,* January
1988, 43–50; Barry Reese, "Plume Wars"; Catherine Beach Fly, "The Vanishing
Flame-Colored Flamingo," *Nature* 5 (January 1925): 11–13.

34. Dimock, "Passing"; Daniel F. Tyler, *Where to Go in Florida* (New York:
Hopcraft, 1880), 20–21; "Buffalo, Wild Pigeons, and Plume Birds"; *MH,* 7 March
1916; Moore-Willson, *Birds of the Everglades,* 7, 17; Elizabeth Ogren Rothra, *Florida's Pioneer Naturalist: The Life of Charles Torrey Simpson* (Gainesville: University Press of Florida, 1995), 182–83; "Impressions of Florida," *The Friend: A Religious and Literary Journal* 64 (30 May 1891): 347.

35. Dimock, "Passing," 106.

CHAPTER FOURTEEN: Killing Mr. Bradley

1. MSD, "Plumes," *SEP,* 14 June 1930, 8–9, 112, 114, 117–18, 121; Mildred Campbell to literary editor, 30 July 1930, MSDP, box 30, folder 46.

2. MSD, "Plumes," 9, 117.

3. Mark Derr, *Some Kind of Paradise: A Chronicle of Man and the Land in
Florida* (New York: Morrow, 1989), 38–41; *River of Grass,* 275; Stuart McIver,

"Death of a Bird Warden," *South Florida History Magazine* 29 (Fall 2001): 21–22; Charlton W. Tebeau, *Man in the Everglades: 2,000 Years of Human History in the Everglades National Park* (Coral Gables, Fla.: University of Miami Press, 1986), 75; Barry Reese, "The Plume Wars," unpublished paper, in possession of the author, 38.

4. Tebeau, *Man in the Everglades,* 91–94; McIver, "Death of a Bird Warden," 21–22; Derr, *Some Kind of Paradise,* 137.

5. MSD, "Plumes," 9, 112.

6. In 1893, the state also passed legislation outlawing the killing of manatee.

7. Robin W. Doughty, *Feather Fashions and Bird Preservation: A Study in Nature Protection* (Berkeley: University of California Press, 1975); Ann Vileisis, *Discovering the Unknown Landscape: A History of America's Wetlands* (Washington, D.C.: Island, 1997), 151–56; Oscar E. Baynard to A. J. Hanna, 24 September 1947, Alfred J. Hanna Papers, Plume Hunting folder, Special Collections, Rollins College Library, Winter Park, Fla.; Lucy Worthington Blackman, *The Florida Audubon Society, 1900–1935* (n.p., n.d.), 21; Alfred Jackson Hanna and Kathryn Abbey Hanna, *Lake Okeechobee: Wellspring of the Everglades* (Indianapolis: Bobbs-Merrill, 1948); Derr, *Some Kind of Paradise,* 136–38; Florida Audubon Society, *Summary of the Bird Laws of Florida and Federal Regulations Applying to Migratory Birds,* 1915–16, A. Gray to A. J. Hanna, 11 September 1947, both in Hanna Papers, Plume Hunting folder; John H. Baker, "Saving Man's Wildlife Heritage," *National Geographic* 106 (November 1954): 584; Emily Perry Dieterich, "Birds of a Feather: The Coconut Grove Audubon Society, 1915–1917," *Tequesta* 45 (1985): 9–10; Frank M. Chapman, *Camps and Cruises of an Ornithologist* (New York: Appleton, 1908), 148; "Florida Plume Birds," *Forest and Stream,* 1 June 1895, 441; Blackman, *Florida Audubon Society,* 26–27; Oliver H. Orr, *Saving American Birds: T. Gilbert Pearson and the Founding of the Audubon Movement* (Gainesville: University Press of Florida, 1992), 1; *NYT,* 27 November 1897; Barry Reese, "Plume Wars," 41, 48.

8. MSD, "Wings," *SEP,* 14 March 1931, 77–78; MSD, "Plumes," 117; *MH,* 12 March 1915, 16, 19 May 1916.

9. "This Is Not a Pretty Story," *Ladies' Home Journal,* February 1914, 5; "Most Beautiful Bird Saved from Extinction by Law," *Popular Mechanics,* August 1930, 210; Baker, "Saving Man's Wildlife Heritage," 584.

10. Blackman, *Florida Audubon Society,* 13, 15, 27; "About the Aigrette," *Bird-Lore* 11 (October 1909): 232–33; *SPT,* 10 January 1915; Leslie Kemp Poole, "The

Women of the Early Florida Audubon Society: Agents of History in the Fight to Save State Birds," *Florida Historical Quarterly* 85 (Winter 2007): 319–20.

11. *Tampa Tribune*, 14 March 2003; William T. Hornaday, *Thirty Years War for Wild Life* (Stamford, Conn.: Permanent Wild Life Protection Fund, 1931), 249; Poole, "Women," 311–12.

12. Blackman, *Florida Audubon Society*, 1–34; Todd Pearson, *The First One Hundred Years: Being a Description of the Origins, History, and Prospects of the Florida Audubon Society and Its Seventy-five Years* (n.p., n.d.), 1–10; Poole, "Women," 303–6.

13. McIver, "Death of a Bird Warden," 24–25; Dieterich, "Birds of a Feather," 6–7.

14. Stuart B. McIver, *Death in the Everglades: The Murder of Guy Bradley, America's First Martyr to Environmentalism* (Gainesville: University Press of Florida, 2003), 97–99.

15. Barry Reese, "Plume Wars," 30–31; *SPT*, 10 January 1915; MSD, "The Mayor of Flamingo," *SEP*, 24 August 1926, in *"A River in Flood" and Other Florida Stories*, ed. Kevin M. McCarthy (Gainesville: University Press of Florida, 1998), 118; McIver, "Death of a Bird Warden," 24; "Warden Guy M. Bradley," *Forest and Stream*, 29 July 1905, 87; Irston R. Barnes, "In the Interest of Conservation," *WP*, 25 March 1973; Poole, "Women," 310; MSD, "Plumes," 117.

16. *MH*, 19 May 1916; *NYT*, 4 December 1977; Frank M. Chapman, *Camps and Cruises*, 135–48; *Fort Myers News Press*, 6 February 1990; "Warden Guy M. Bradley"; Peter Matthiessen, *Killing Mr. Watson* (New York: Vintage, 1991).

17. MSD, "By Violence," *SEP*, 22 November 1930, 6–7, 44, 46, 48, 50, 53; Marjory Stoneman Douglas, *Nine Florida Stories*, ed. Kevin M. McCarthy (Gainesville: University Press of Florida, 1990), xv.

18. McIver, "Death of a Bird Warden," 24–25; Barry Reese, "Plume Wars"; "Warden Guy M. Bradley."

19. Frank M. Chapman, *Camps and Cruises*, 135–36; Baker, "Saving Man's Wildlife Heritage," 584; Barry Reese, "Plume Wars"; McIver, "Death of a Bird Warden," 25; Loren G. Brown, *Totch: A Life in the Everglades* (Gainesville: University Press of Florida, 1993), 12; *WP*, 13 August 1905.

20. Barry Reese, "Plume Wars"; McIver, "Death of a Bird Warden," 22; Jim Huffstodt, "The Reign of the Plume Hunter," *Florida Wildlife*, March–April 1992, 3; McIver, *Death in the Everglades*, 78.

21. *WP*, 13 August 1905; *NYT*, 11 February 1965; McIver, "Death of a Bird Warden," 6; Baker, "Saving Man's Wildlife Heritage," 584; Charles M. Brookfield and

Oliver Griswold, *They All Called It Tropical: True Tales of the Romantic Everglades National Park, Cape Sable, and the Florida Keys* (Miami, Fla.: Data, 1960), 60–63, 65–68; Huffstodt, "Reign," 3–4; MSD, "The Man Who Died for Birds," MSDP, box 82, folder 35; Barry Reese, "Plume Wars."

22. "Warden Guy M. Bradley"; *WP*, 13 August 1905; *NYT*, 13 August 1905; McIver, "Death of a Bird Warden," 27; Blackman, *Florida Audubon Society*, 17.

23. *WP*, 13 August 1905; *NYT*, 8, 13 August 1905; "Warden Guy M. Bradley"; Barry Reese, "Plume Wars," 37, 38; "About the Aigrette," 232–33; William Dutcher, *The Horrors of the Plume Trade* (n.p.: National Association of Audubon Societies, n.d.), 1–2.

24. Mary B. Munroe, "Bird Gossip: Two Plume-Bearing Birds," *The Tropic Magazine* 2 (April 1915): 13; "About the Aigrette," 232–33; Dutcher, *Horrors of the Plume Trade*, 1–2; Baker, "Saving Man's Wildlife Heritage," 584; *Tampa Tribune*, 14 March 2003.

25. "Pioneering Conservation in Florida: How the Egrets Found a Friend," *Florida Game and Fish* 3 (April 1942): 1; Brookfield and Griswold, *They Called It Tropical*, 68; Barry Reese, "Plume Wars," 41, 48; McIver, "Death of a Bird Warden," 24; Huffstodt, "Reign," 4; Stephen Fox, *The American Conservation Movement: John Muir and His Legacy* (Madison: University of Wisconsin Press, 1981), 155, 157; Blackman, *Florida Audubon Society*, 26–27; Orr, *Saving American Birds*, 12.

26. Blackman, *Florida Audubon Society*, 19, 26–27, 28; "Warden Guy M. Bradley"; *WP*, 13 August 1905; *NYT*, 11 February 1965.

27. Lucy Worthington Blackman, *The Women of Florida* (Jacksonville: Southern Historical, 1940), 145; Hanna and Hanna, *Lake Okeechobee*, 342; Harry A. Kersey Jr., *Pelts, Plumes, and Hides: White Traders among the Seminole Indians, 1870–1930* (Gainesville: University of Florida Press, 1975), 81; Barry Reese, "Plume Wars," 52; *Establishment of Everglades National Park: Hearings before the Committee on the Public Lands, House of Representatives*, 71st Cong., 3rd sess. (Washington, D.C.: U.S. Government Printing Office, 1931), 35–36.

28. McIver, *Death in the Everglades*.

CHAPTER FIFTEEN: A New Life

1. Edward N. Akin, *Flagler: Rockefeller Partner and Florida Baron* (Gainesville: University Press of Florida, 1992), 189–200; MSD, "When You and I Were Young, Miami," *Tropic* (*MH*), 5 November 1967, 16–22, 36; *Florida*, 1; Seth Bramson, "The Opening of Rail Service to Miami and Key West," *Update* 2 (April 1975): 8–9;

MH, 28 January 1940; F. Page Wilson, "Miami: From Frontier to Metropolis: An Appraisal," *Tequesta* 14 (1954): 5.

2. *Florida*, 1; MSD, speech to Florida Historical Society, Pensacola, 6 May 1978, SPOHP.

3. *Florida*, 1; MSD, "A Bird Dog in Hand," *SEP*, 12 September 1925, reprinted in *Nine Florida Stories*, ed. Kevin M. McCarthy (Gainesville: University Press of Florida, 1990), 58; John Muir, *A Thousand-Mile Walk to the Gulf* (Boston: Mariner, 1998), 114; Bill Belleville, *River of Lakes: A Journey on Florida's St. Johns River* (Athens: University of Georgia Press, 2000), 143–46.

4. *Florida*, 1–2; *Newark Evening News*, 18 April 1914.

5. Diary, 1 July 1925, MSDP, box 40; Patricia Ann Palmieri, *In Adamless Eden: The Community of Women Faculty at Wellesley* (New Haven: Yale University Press, 1995), 147–54; *Special Voices, Two Florida Women: Marjorie Carr, Marjory Stoneman Douglas*, video production (Florida Atlantic University/Florida International University, Joint Center for Environmental and Urban Problems, 1985). A few years earlier, Kenneth Douglas's second wife, from Toledo, also had moved to Florida to seek a divorce.

6. MSD, speech to Florida Historical Society.

7. MSD, "Mabel White Dorn, 1899–1972," MSDP, box 54, folder 6.

8. F. Page Wilson, "Miami," 30; Will Davenport, "Growing Up, Sort of, in Miami, 1909–1915," *Tequesta* 39 (1979): 29; *Florida*, 1–2; MSD, "When You and I"; MSD, "The Everglades Remembered," *Florida Naturalist* 55 (December 1983): 8; *Voice*, 96.

9. *Florida*, 3–4; *Special Voices*.

10. *Florida*, 3–4; *Voice*, 96–97; MSD, speech to Florida Historical Society.

11. MSD, "The Story of a Homely Woman," *SEP*, 4 December 1931, 10.

12. *Florida*, 3–4; *Voice*, 96.

13. MSD, "When You and I"; *MH*, 29 December 1922.

14. *MH*, 20, 21, 22 July 1911, 26 May 1940; James J. Carney, "Population Growth in Miami and Dade County, Florida," *Tequesta* 6 (1946): 55; MSD, "Pioneers, O, Pioneers!" in possession of author.

15. On the subject of residential segregation in the North and South, see, for example, Thomas W. Hanchett, *Sorting Out the New South City: Race, Class, and Urban Development in Charlotte, 1875–1975* (Chapel Hill: University of North Carolina Press, 1998); Kevin Boyle, *Arc of Justice: A Saga of Race, Civil Rights, and Murder in the Jazz Age* (New York: Holt, 2004).

16. Paul S. George, "The First Hundred Years," *South Florida History Magazine* 24 (Summer 1997): 26–27; Millicent Todd Bingham, "Miami: A Study in Urban Geography," *Tequesta* 9 (1949): 95; F. Page Wilson, "Miami," 31; J. K. Dorn, "Recollections of Early Miami," *Tequesta* 9 (1949): 55; Raymond A. Mohl, "Black Immigrants: Bahamians in Early Twentieth-Century Miami," *Florida Historical Quarterly* 65 (January 1987): 271–97; *MH*, 4 February 1916.

17. Raymond A. Mohl, "Miami: The Ethnic Cauldron," in *Sunbelt Cities: Politics and Growth since World War II*, ed. Richard M. Bernard and Bradley R. Rice (Austin: University of Texas Press, 1983), 59; Bingham, "Miami," 101–2; *MH*, 20, 21, 22 July 1911, 14 April 1940.

18. *MH*, 20, 21, 22 July 1911, 24 March, 5 May 1940; Mark S. Foster, *Castles in the Sand: The Life and Times of Carl Graham Fisher* (Gainesville: University Press of Florida, 2000), 151–71; *Florida*, 5.

19. *Voice; Florida*, 3, 7; 97–99; Gail Fishman, *Journeys through Paradise: Pioneering Naturalists in the Southeast* (Gainesville: University Press of Florida, 2000), 235; *MH*, 20 December 1921.

20. Frank B. Stoneman and Lillias Eleanor Shine, marriage certificate, 19 April 1914, MSDP, box 44, folder 78; *MH*, 2 February 1941; *Voice*, 97, 100, 257; MSD, speech to Florida Historical Society.

21. *Voice*, 98–99; *Special Voices*.

22. MSD to Martha Waters, 9 December 1987, in possession of author; *Florida*, 5; *Voice*, 98–101; *Special Voices*.

23. *Florida*, 7–8; *Voice*, 102–3; MSD, "A Major in English Composition," circa 1976, in possession of author; *Fort Lauderdale News*, 8 June 1979; *MH*, 25 October 1915; Howard Lawrence Preston, *Dirt Roads to Dixie: Accessibility and Modernization in the South, 1885–1935* (Knoxville: University of Tennessee Press, 1991), 60.

24. On women in journalism, see Marion Marzolf, *Up from the Footnote: A History of Women Journalists* (New York: Hastings House, 1977); Nan Robertson, *The Girls in the Balcony: Women, Men, and the New York Times* (New York: Random House, 1992); Robert C. Kochersberger, *More Than a Muckracker: Ida Tarbell's Lifetime in Journalism* (Knoxville: University of Tennessee Press, 1994).

25. MSD, "Major in English Composition"; *Florida*, 6–7.

26. MSD, untitled manuscript, n.d., MSDP, box 48, folder 123.

27. *MH*, 3 March, 24 May, 13 September 1916.

28. *Palm Beach Post*, 26 March 1978; MSD, "Major in English Composition."

CHAPTER SIXTEEN: Conservationists

1. Mary B. Munroe, "Bird Gossip: Two Plume-Bearing Birds," *The Tropic Magazine* 2 (April 1915): 11–13; Mary B. Munroe, "Bird Gossip: Everglade Bird," *The Tropic Magazine* 1 (July 1914): 11–12; *MH*, 12 April 1916, 22 May 1919; Lucy Worthington Blackman, *The Florida Audubon Society, 1900–1935* (n.p., n.d.), 20–21; Emily Perry Dieterich, "Birds of a Feather: The Coconut Grove Audubon Society, 1915–1917," *Tequesta* 45 (1985): 21–22.

2. The Bird Defenders may have been the same group known as the Coconut Grove Rangers, founded in 1906. See Dieterich, "Birds of a Feather," 10.

3. Dieterich, "Birds of a Feather," 10–12, 23, 25–26; Blackman, *Florida Audubon Society*, 22, 33; Lucy Worthington Blackman, *The Women of Florida* (Jacksonville: Southern Historical, 1940), 145; *MH*, 13 January, 12 April 1916; Coconut Grove Audubon Society Minutes, 16 April 1915, "Coconut Grove Audubon Society," clipping, 14 October 1915, "The Coconut Grove Audubon Society," clipping, March 1915, all in Coconut Grove Audubon Society Records, 1915–22, box 3, folder 1, HMSF; *Miami Metropolis*, 14 May 1915.

4. *Christian Science Monitor*, 12 March 1919; *NYT*, 12 March 1919. Carolyn Merchant has been the most prolific author on women and environmental history. See her *Earthcare: Women and the Environment* (New York: Routledge, 1995); *The Death of Nature: Women, Ecology, and the Scientific Revolution* (San Francisco: Harper and Row, 1980); *Ecological Revolutions: Nature, Gender, and Science in New England* (Chapel Hill: University of North Carolina Press, 1989); "Women of the Progressive Conservation Movement, 1900–1916," *Environmental Review* 8 (Spring 1984): 57–86. Other important studies include Vera Norwood, *Made from This Earth: American Women and Nature* (Chapel Hill: University of North Carolina Press, 1993); Glenda Riley, *Women and Nature: Saving the "Wild" West* (Lincoln: University of Nebraska Press, 1999); Angela Gugliotta, "Class, Gender, and Coal Smoke: Gender Ideology and Environmental Injustice in Pittsburgh, 1868–1914," *Environmental History* 5 (April 2000): 165–93; Jan R. McStay and Riley E. Dunlap, "Male-Female Differences in Concern for Environmental Quality," *International Journal of Women's Studies* 16 (September–October 1983): 291–301; Anthony N. Penna, *Nature's Bounty: Historical and Modern Environmental Perspectives* (New York: Sharpe, 1999), 99–101; David Evans, *A History of Nature Conservation in Britain* (London: Routledge, 1997), 38.

5. MSD, "When You and I Were Young, Miami," *Tropic* (*MH*), 5 November 1967, 19–20; *MH,* 3 December 1916; Mrs. William S. Jennings, "Woman's Work in Florida," *The Florida Magazine* 1 (April 1922): 13–14; Linda Gordon, "U.S. Women's History," in *The New American History,* ed. Eric Foner (Philadelphia: Temple University Press, 1990), 185–210; Sara M. Evans, "Women's History and Political Theory: Toward a Feminist Approach to Public Life," in *Visible Women: New Essays on American Activism,* ed. Nancy A. Hewitt and Suzanne Lebsock (Urbana: University of Illinois Press, 1993), 119–39; Dorothy Schneider and Carl J. Schneider, *American Women in the Progressive Era, 1900–1920* (New York: Anchor, 1993); Karen J. Blair, *The Clubwoman as Feminist: True Womanhood Redefined, 1868–1914* (New York: Holmes and Meier, 1980), 83, 103–6; Florida Equal Suffrage Association Letterhead, 1917, Florida Federation of Women's Clubs Letterhead, 1918, both in MMJP, box 12.

6. Florida Audubon Society, *Summary of the Bird Laws of Florida and Federal Regulations Applying to Migratory Birds,* 1915–16; A. Gray to A. J. Hanna, 11 September 1947, both in Alfred J. Hanna Papers, Plume Hunting folder, Special Collections, Rollins College Library, Winter Park, Fla.; Blackman, *Florida Audubon Society,* 21; Merchant, "Women"; Schneider and Schneider, *American Women;* Cameron Binkley, "'No Better Heritage Than Living Trees': Women's Clubs and Early Conservation in Humboldt County," *Western Historical Quarterly* 33 (Summer 2002): 179–204; Riley, *Women and Nature,* 97–113; David Stradling, *Smokestacks and Progress: Environmentalists, Engineers, and Air Quality in America, 1881–1951* (Baltimore: Johns Hopkins University Press, 1999), 52–55, 59, 93; Suellen M. Hoy, "'Municipal Housekeeping': The Role of Women in Improving Urban Sanitation Practices, 1880–1917," in *Pollution and Reform in American Cities, 1870–1930,* ed. Martin V. Melosi (Austin: University of Texas Press, 1980), 173–98; Maureen A. Flanagan, "The City Profitable, the City Livable: Environmental Policy, Gender, and Power in Chicago in the 1910s," *Journal of Urban History* 22 (January 1996): 163–90; Harold L. Platt, "Jane Addams and the Ward Boss Revisited: Class, Politics, and Public Health in Chicago, 1890–1930," *Environmental History* 5 (April 2000): 194–222.

7. Florida Federation of Women's Clubs Letterhead, circa 1915, MMJP, box 6; Linda D. Vance, *May Mann Jennings: Florida's Genteel Activist* (Gainesville: University of Florida Press, 1985), 80, 154–55; *MH,* 24 November 1916; *Tampa Morning Tribune,* 6 December 1908.

8. *MH*, 21 July 1911.

9. Charlton W. Tebeau, *Man in the Everglades: 2,000 Years of Human History in the Everglades National Park* (Coral Gables, Fla.: University of Miami Press, 1986), 167–68.

10. John Kunkel Small and George V. Nash, "Report of Mr. J. K. Small and Mr. G. V. Nash upon a Trip to Florida," *Journal of the New York Botanical Garden* 3 (February 1902): 29–35; John K. Small, "Royal Palm Hammock," *Journal of the New York Botanical Garden* 17 (October 1916): 166, 167–68; Elizabeth Ogren Rothra, *Florida's Pioneer Naturalist: The Life of Charles Torrey Simpson* (Gainesville: University Press of Florida, 1995), 74–75, 84–87; Charles T. Simpson, "Paradise Key," *The Tropic Magazine* 4 (April 1916): 5; Leah La Plante, "The Sage of Biscayne Bay: Charles Torrey Simpson's Love Affair with South Florida," *Tequesta* 55 (1995): 6–7; May Mann Jennings, "Royal Palm State Park," July 1939, MMJP, box 23; "The Alumnus," n.d., Peter Henry Rolfs Collection, box 4, Writings and Speeches, 1899–1920, folder, Special and Area Studies Collection, University of Florida, Gainesville.

11. May Mann Jennings, "Royal Palm State Park," 10–11; Small, "Royal Palm Hammock," 166–67; Gertrude M. Kent, "The Housekeepers' Club of Coconut Grove," *Update* 4 (April 1977): 7; Vance, *May Mann Jennings*, 58; Linda D. Vance, "May Mann Jennings and Royal Palm State Park," *Florida Historical Quarterly* 55 (July 1976): 2; Lucy Worthington Blackman, *The Florida Federation of Women's Clubs, 1895–1939* (Jacksonville: Southern Historical, 1939), 21.

12. *MH*, 12 April, 29 September 1916; Arthur H. Howell, "A List of the Birds of Royal Palm Hammock," *The Auk* 38 (April 1921): 250–53.

13. Vance, *May Mann Jennings*, 1–32.

14. On Indians and national parks, see Mark David Spence, *Dispossessing the Wilderness: Indian Removal and the Making of the National Parks* (New York: Oxford University Press, 1999).

15. May Mann Jennings, "Royal Palm State Park," *The Tropic Magazine* 4 (April 1916): 12–13, 14; Jennings, "Royal Palm State Park," MMJP, box 23; Vance, "May Mann Jennings," 9–10.

16. May Mann Jennings to T. Gilbert Pearson, Adair Edwards to Mrs. W. S. Jennings, 10 June 1915, May Mann Jennings to Mrs. William Hocker, 5 April 1915, all in MMJP, box 6; Elizabeth Hacks to Madame President, n.d., Mary B. Jewett to Mrs. Jennings, 5 December 1914, Kate V. Jackson to Mrs. Jennings, 7 December 1914, all in MMJP, box 5; Leslie Kemp Poole, "The Women of the Early Florida

Audubon Society: Agents of History in the Fight to Save State Birds," *Florida Historical Quarterly* 85 (Winter 2007): 315.

17. John Kunkel Small to Mrs. W. S. Jennings, 31 October, 2 November 1916, John Kunkel Small Papers, box 5, folder H–J, 1914–15, FSA.

18. MSD, "Mabel White Dorn, 1899–1972," MSDP, box 54, folder 6; John C. Gifford, *The Everglades and Other Essays Relating to Southern Florida* (Kansas City, Mo.: Everglade Land Sales, 1911); U.S. Army Corps of Engineers, "Everglades Restoration Critical Projects," available online at http://www.saj.usace .army.mil/projects/index.html (accessed winter 2004); U.S. Army Corps of Engineers and South Florida Water Management District, "Central and Southern Florida Project, Project Management Plan, Melaleuca Eradication and Other Exotic Plants," September 2004, available online at http://www.evergladesplan.org/ pm/program/program_docs/pmp_95_melaleuca/092704_pmp_95_main_body .pdf (accessed summer 2006).

19. Small, "Royal Palm Hammock," 171–72; Rothra, *Florida's Pioneer Naturalist,* 89–91; La Plante, "Sage of Biscayne Bay"; John Kunkel Small, *From Eden to Sahara: Florida's Tragedy* (Sanford, Fla.: Seminole Soil and Water Conservation District, 2004), 111; *MH,* 23 December 1915; John Kunkel Small to Mrs. W. S. Jennings, 31 October, 2 November 1916, Small Papers, box 5, folder H–J, 1914–15.

20. *MH,* 30 March 1923; Simpson, "Paradise Key," 7–8.

21. John C. Gifford, *Billy Bowlegs and the Seminole War* (Coconut Grove, Fla.: Triangle, 1925), 53, 69; "John Clayton Gifford," available online at http://everglades .fiu.edu/reclaim/bios/gifford.html (accessed winter 2004); Small, *From Eden to Sahara,* 111, 113.

22. Rothra, *Florida's Pioneer Naturalist,* 90; Vance, *May Mann Jennings,* 85.

23. On women, gender, and nature, see, for example, Merchant, *Earthcare;* Mary Mellor, "Gender and the Environment," in *Ecofeminism and Globalization: Exploring Culture, Context, and Religion,* ed. Heather Eaton and Lois Ann Lorentzen (Lanham, Md.: Rowman and Littlefield, 2003), 11–22; Annette Kolodny, *The Lay of the Land: Metaphors as Experience in American Life and Letters* (Chapel Hill: University of North Carolina Press, 1975); *Women's Studies* (special issue) 31 (April 2002); Janice Monk, "Approaches to the Study of Women and Landscape," *Environmental Review* 8 (Spring 1984): 23–33; Jennifer Price, *Flight Maps: Adventures with Nature in Modern America* (New York: Basic Books, 2000), 81–82, 88–89; *MH,* 22 May 1919.

24. Kolodny, *Lay of the Land*, 4; E. Anthony Rotundo, *American Manhood: Transformation in Masculinity from the Revolution to the Modern Era* (New York: Basic Books, 1995), 235–36.

25. *MH*, 10 March 1923.

26. Mary B. Munroe, "Bird Gossip: Two Plume-Bearing Birds," 13; *MH*, 30 September 1916.

27. *MH*, 6 January 1917; *River of Grass*, 280; *Florida*, 16, 18, 19.

28. Vance, *May Mann Jennings*, 84–86; Vance, "May Mann Jennings," 10–12; Bryan Jennings to May Jennings, 2 June 1915, William S. Jennings to May Jennings, 3 June 1915, both in MMJP, box 6.

29. May Mann Jennings, "Parks and Natural Scenery," speech, March 1930, MMJP, box 19; Kathryn Wright to Mrs. Jennings, 29 June 1916, May Mann Jennings to Hon. W. W. Blackman, 21 June 1915, May Mann Jennings to W. Stanley Hanson, 21 June 1915, May Mann Jennings to W. F. Bancroft, 21 June 1915, all in MMJP, box 6; May Mann Jennings, "Royal Palm State Park," 16; Vance, "May Mann Jennings," 12–13; "Women Seeking Mile of Dimes for Royal Palm," *Christian Science Monitor*, 21 February 1916; "Annual Meeting Audubon Society Held in Coconut Grove March 6," clipping, 1916, Coconut Grove Audubon Society Records, 1915–22, box 3, folder 1.

30. *MH*, 30 September, 24 November 1916, 17 March 1940; May Mann Jennings, "Royal Palm State Park," 14, 16; Paul S. Sutter, *Driven Wild: How the Fight against Automobiles Launched the Modern Wilderness Movement* (Seattle: University of Washington Press, 2002), 19–53.

31. *MH*, 24 November 1916; Vance, "May Mann Jennings," 13–14; "Florida Club Women Dedicate Park," *Christian Science Monitor*, 4 December 1916.

CHAPTER SEVENTEEN: Rights

1. MSD, "When You and I Were Young, Miami," *Tropic (MH)*, 5 November 1967, 19–20; *Florida*, 9–10; Mrs. William S. Jennings, "Woman's Work in Florida," *The Florida Magazine* 1 (April 1922), 13–14; Jessie Hamm Meyer, *Leading the Way: A Century of Service: The Florida Federation of Women's Clubs, 1895–1995* (Lakeland: Florida Federation of Women's Clubs, 1994), 52–79; Carl Parke, "A Headwaters of Marjory Stoneman Douglas's *River of Grass*: Writings for the *Miami Herald* and *Saturday Evening Post* as Twin Headwaters for Her Later Activism on

Behalf of the Florida Everglades" (seminar paper, University of South Florida, 1998); Mrs. William S. Jennings, "Woman's Work in Florida," 13.

2. *MH*, 15, 16, 18, 29 September 1916.

3. A. Elizabeth Taylor, "The Woman Suffrage Movement in Florida," *Florida Historical Quarterly* 36 (July 1957): 42–44; Florida Constitution, 1885; Edward C. Williamson, "The Constitutional Convention of 1885," *Florida Historical Quarterly* 41 (October 1962): 116–26; Annette Van Howe, "The Women's Suffrage Movement in Broward County and Florida," *Broward Legacy* 14 (Summer–Fall 1991): 38; Kenneth R. Johnson, "The Woman Suffrage Movement in Florida" (Ph.D. diss., Florida State University, 1966), 22–27.

4. Taylor, "Woman Suffrage Movement," 44–46; Johnson, "Woman Suffrage Movement," 29–81.

5. A state literacy test for voting qualifications was also part of the proposed amendment, which, if ratified, would have added to the list of seventeen states (nine outside the South) that used the literacy test as a requirement for voting. The *Guinn* decision came down before Florida voters made their decision about the state amendment, which they ultimately failed to ratify. Dade County voters supported it, however, by a vote of 743 to 419. See Tracy E. Danese, "Disfranchisement, Women's Suffrage, and the Failure of the Florida Grandfather Clause," *Florida Historical Quarterly* 74 (Fall 1995): 117–31.

6. Taylor, "Woman Suffrage Movement," 51; Kathleen Siler Perrucci, "'The Sordid Prizes of Life': The Florida Woman Suffrage Movement, 1869–1920" (master's thesis, University of Florida, 1989), 97–98; *MH*, 24 January, 18 September 1916; *Orlando Sentinel*, 8 April 1990.

7. Linda D. Vance, *May Mann Jennings: Florida's Genteel Activist* (Gainesville: University of Florida Press, 1985), 28, 61, 89–99, 155; Taylor, "Woman Suffrage Movement," 48, 49, 53.

8. *Florida*, 17; MSD, "William Jennings Bryan with Frank B. Stoneman, Long Time Editor of the *Miami Herald*," *Coconut Grove Village Post*, February 1958; *MH*, 28 April, 22 September, 3 November 1940; Paul S. George, "The First Hundred Years," *South Florida History Magazine* 24 (Summer 1997): 28; Lawrence W. Levine, *Defender of the Faith: William Jennings Bryan, the Last Decade, 1915–1925* (Cambridge: Harvard University Press, 1987), 237–40.

9. *MH*, 3 February, 8 March, 3 December 1916; Mrs. William S. Jennings, "Woman's Work in Florida," 14; "Marjory Stoneman Douglas, a List of Achievements

and Honors," in possession of author; Isidor Cohen, *Historical Sketches and Side-lights of Miami, Florida* (n.p., 1925), 156; MSD to Linda Vance, 25 November 1985, MSDP, box 48, folder 123; Sharon Hartman Strom, *Gender, Class, and the Origins of Modern American Office Work, 1900–1930* (Urbana: University of Illinois Press, 1992), 353–55, 397, 398; *A History of the National Federation of Business and Professional Women's Clubs, Inc., 1919–1944* (New York: National Federation of Business and Professional Women's Clubs, 1944).

10. *Florida,* 18–19; Taylor, "Woman Suffrage Movement," 56–58.

11. Mary Bryan to May Mann Jennings (telegram), 13 April 1917, MMJP, box 10, Correspondence file; Van Howe, "Women's Suffrage Movement," 38–39; *Florida,* 18–19.

12. *Florida,* 17–18.

13. No legislative record of these speeches exists. *Florida,* 18–19; MSD, brief vita, MSDP, box 39, file 3; *MH,* 19, 20, 21 April 1917, 18 February 1974, 25 August 1976, 11 November 1985; *Jacksonville Florida Times-Union,* 19 April 1917; *Special Voices, Two Florida Women: Marjorie Carr, Marjory Stoneman Douglas,* video production (Florida Atlantic University/Florida International University, Joint Center for Environmental and Urban Problems, 1985).

14. Unidentified to May Mann Jennings, 2 December 1917, MMJP, box 12, Correspondence file, September–December 1917, January–February 1918; William S. Jennings to May Mann Jennings (telegram), 19 April 1917, May Mann Jennings to Mrs. George M. Wright, 30 April 1917, May Mann Jennings to E. C. Loveland, 30 April 1917, all in MMJP, box 10, Correspondence file; Wayne Flynt, *Cracker Messiah: Governor Sidney J. Catts of Florida* (Baton Rouge: Louisiana State University Press, 1977), 143, 185, 187; Taylor, "Woman Suffrage Movement," 58–60; Van Howe, "Women's Suffrage Movement," 39–40; *MH,* 26 April 1917, 22 April 1922.

15. *Florida,* 18; John Hicks, "Marjory Stoneman Douglas," *Florida (Orlando Sentinel),* 14 October 1979, 10.

16. *MH,* 27 March 1920; *Florida,* 18.

17. For the first six days she served as the society-page editor, MSD used Kenneth's name, but she changed to "Mrs. Marjory Stoneman Douglas" before eventually dropping *Mrs. (MH,* 25, 31 October 1915).

18. Lucy Worthington Blackman, *The Women of Florida* (Jacksonville: Southern Historical, 1940); Meyer, *Leading the Way;* Dava Sobel, "Still Fighting the Good Fight for the Everglades," *Audubon,* July–August 1991, 33.

19. Levine, *Defender of the Faith*, 130; Vance, *May Mann Jennings*, 109; *MH*, 2 December, 27 December 1922, 10 March 1923, 18 February 1974, 25 August 1976, 11 November 1985; *Orlando Sentinel*, 9 November 1975, 30 March 1997; *SPT*, 16 September 1990; James R. McGovern, "Helen Hunt West: Florida's Pioneer for ERA," *Florida Historical Quarterly* 57 (July 1978): 39–53; Catherine E. Rymph, *Republican Women: Feminism and Conservatism from Suffrage to the Rise of the New Right* (Chapel Hill: University of North Carolina Press, 2006), 14–65.

20. Isidor Cohen, *Historical Sketches*, 58–59; *MH*, 11 December 1915, 14 April 1940; May Mann Jennings to E. C. Loveland, 30 April 1917, Mrs. John W. Simmons to the Honorable Members of the 1917 Legislature, 31 March 1917, both in MMJP, box 10, Correspondence file.

21. Vance, *May Mann Jennings*, 128; *Florida Times-Union*, 28 September 1920; Van Howe, "Women's Suffrage Movement," 39; Johnson, "Woman Suffrage Movement," 26; Dewey Grantham, *Southern Progressivism: The Reconciliation of Progress and Tradition* (Knoxville: University of Tennessee Press, 1983); Vance, *May Mann Jennings*, 128; Dorothy Schneider and Carl J. Schneider, *American Women in the Progressive Era, 1900–1920* (New York: Anchor, 1993), 99–100, 126–29, 189; Anne Firor Scott, *Natural Allies: Women's Associations in American History* (Urbana: University of Illinois Press, 1991), 127, 129, 181.

22. *Florida*, 11–12; MSD, "Years I Have Seen: An Epilogue," "1. The Recent Past," *Florida*, Prologue folder (unedited draft for the *Florida* book containing subsequently excised material), MSDP, box 2; *Special Voices*.

23. *MH*, 19 February 1917, 1 October 1922, 5 April 1923; MSD, "The University and the Forgotten Curriculum," *Journal of Social Forces* 1 (March 1923): 235.

CHAPTER EIGHTEEN: World War

1. Horacio Sierra, "Marjory Stoneman Douglas's River of Progress: Modernism, Feminism, and Environmentalism in Her Short Stories" (master's thesis, University of Florida, 2006), 9; Record of Mrs. Marjory S. Douglas, 8 April 1917 to 21 May 1918, Military Personnel Records for Marjory Douglas, National Personnel Records Center, St. Louis, Mo.; MSD, speech to Florida Historical Society, Pensacola, 6 May 1978, SPOHP.

2. "Marjory Conquers the United States Navy," *Update* 1 (April 1974): 10; *Voice*, 112–13; *Florida*, 20; *MH*, 25 November 1917, 31 January 1920; *Special Voices, Two Florida Women: Marjorie Carr, Marjory Stoneman Douglas*, video production

(Florida Atlantic University/Florida International University, Joint Center for Environmental and Urban Problems, 1985).

3. Some Douglas aficionados claim that Douglas was a closet lesbian and that she fabricated Andy to hide her sexuality. But evidence indicates that Andy was fictitious only in name. Claims that Douglas was a lesbian are apparently based on speculation, which is not to say she was not a lesbian. However, no evidence, documented or oral, suggests that she ever had a female lover or was sexually drawn to women.

4. *Voice*, 109–13; "Marjory Stoneman Douglas," clipping, n.d., Hampton Dunn Collection, MSD folder, USF; MSD to commandant, Seventh Naval District, 8 May 1918, Military Personnel Records for Marjory Douglas; *MH*, 1 January 1916, 27 May 1917, 22 March 1920, 23 April 1922; Harry Angevin Rider, *Indiana Book of Merit: Official Individual Decorations and Commendations Awarded to Indiana Men and Women for Services in the World War* (Indianapolis: Historical Bureau, Indiana Library and Historical Department, 1932), 635; Beth Swift to author, e-mail, 22 October 2007.

5. Diary, 1 July 1925, MSDP, box 40; *MH*, 5 December 1916.

6. *MH*, 29 August 1916, 3, 4, 5, 6, 9, 10 March 1917, 23 June 1940.

7. Eunice C. Dessez, *The First Enlisted Women, 1917–1918* (Philadelphia: Dorrance, 1955), 23–24.

8. *MH*, 19, 22, 25, 26, 28, 29 March 1917; U.S. Naval Reserve Force, form N. Nav. 351, 27 March 1917, Military Personnel Records for Marjory Douglas.

9. "Marjory Conquers the United States Navy"; "Application for Adjusted Compensation for Service in U.S. Naval Reserve," 24 October 1934, Military Personnel Records for Marjory Douglas; *MH*, 29 March 1917.

10. Lettie Gavin, *American Women in World War I: They Also Served* (Niwot: University Press of Colorado, 1997), 1–18; *Florida*, 20; *MH*, 4, 12 April 1917, 9 December 1951, Change of Rating, 6 July 1917, Duncan Fletcher to Josephus Daniels, 6 March 1918, Josephus Daniels to Duncan Fletcher, 12 March 1918, M. S. Brown to commandant, Seventh Naval District, 17 May 1918, MSD to section commander, Second Section, 23 February 1918, commandant to secretary of the navy, 26 February 1918, section commander, Second Section, to commandant, 23 February 1918, all in Military Personnel Records for Marjory Douglas.

11. *MH*, 7, 14 December 1915, 16 January, 4, 16 February, 10 December 1916, 20 March, 6 April 1917, 30 June, 7 July 1940; *Florida*, 20.

12. *MH*, 5 December 1916, 11 March, 25 May 1917; MSD, "The Hummingbird Charm," MSDP, box 60.

13. Gavin, *American Women,* 179–99; Susan Zieger, *In Uncle Sam's Service: Women Workers with the American Expeditionary Force, 1917–1919* (Philadelphia: University of Pennsylvania Press, 2004); Judith S. Graham, *"Out Here at the Front": The World War I Letters of Nora Saltonstall* (Boston: Northeastern University Press, 2004), 7; *NYT,* 23 October 1919; "Woman's Part Vividly Told," *Red Cross Bulletin,* 14 July 1919, 7–8.

14. A David Douglas (one of Kenneth's aliases or his real name), age seventy-one (apparently the age of Kenneth Douglas), appears in the 1930 U.S. Federal Census as an inmate at the Rensselaer County Jail in Troy, New York.

15. MSD, "The Story of a Homely Woman," *SEP,* 4 December 1931, 10; *MH,* 1 February, 14 April 1918.

16. MSD, "Athens to Marseilles," *SEP,* 3 September 1938, 8, 9, 65.

17. MSD, "The Hand Is Quicker," *SEP,* 5 March 1938, 13.

18. MSD file, Personnel Files, Hazel Braugh Record Center and Archives, American Red Cross, Falls Church, Va.; MSD, "Far Up the Black Mountain," *SEP,* 7 January 1939, 10.

19. *MH,* 25 October 1918.

20. *MH,* 3 June 1919; *Fort Wayne News and Sentinel,* 1 February 1919; Charles Nordhoff, *The Lafayette Flying Corps* (New York: Houghton Mifflin, 1920), 336.

21. *Voice,* 110, 116–17; *Charlotte Observer,* 30 April 1922; Nordhoff, *Lafayette Flying Corps,* 336, 357.

22. *Voice,* 114–24.

23. *MH,* 6 December 1918, 11 November 1938.

24. MSD, "Athens to Marseilles," 8.

25. MSD, "Story of a Homely Woman," 10; *NYT,* 11 January 1918; *WP,* 11 January, 13 May 1918; *MH,* 12 February 1919.

26. *NYT,* 20 November 1917, 20 April 1918, 30 June, 3, 5, 19, 26 July 1919; *Christian Science Monitor,* 19 April 1918; *WP,* 30 June 1919; *MH,* 13, 23 August 1919, 9 December 1951; "Italian Earthquake Relief," *Red Cross Bulletin,* 21 July 1919, 4; *Special Voices.*

27. *MH,* 8 October 1922; MSD, "A Major in English Composition," circa 1976, in possession of author.

28. *MH,* 13 July 1919, 4 April 1920, 8 October 1922; Daniel T. Rodgers, *Atlantic Crossings: Social Politics in a Progressive Age* (Cambridge: Harvard University Press, 1998), 166–67.

29. "Review of Relief Work Done by Friends," *Red Cross Bulletin,* 21 July 1919, 6–7.

30. *MH,* 21 April, 5 May 1919.

31. MSD to family, 16 November 1919, MSDP, box 42, folder 42; MSD, "Far Up the Black Mountain," 46; "The American Invasion of Serbia," *Red Cross Bulletin,* 7 July 1919, 7; "Pack Donkeys Carry Relief," *Red Cross Bulletin,* 11 August 1919, 7.

32. *WP,* 22 April 1919, made the same comment about Romania.

33. *NYT,* 9 November 1918, 10 March, 13 April, 18, 29 June 1919; *WP,* 3 August 1918, 30 October 1918, 9 January, 1 February, 10 March, 22 April, 5 May, 27 July 1919; *Christian Science Monitor,* 14 October 1918; *MH,* 21 April 1919, 17, 18, 20, 22 February 1920; *Voice,* 121.

34. *NYT,* 9 November 1919; *WP,* 14 August 1919; *MH,* 21 July 1923.

35. MSD to family, 16 November 1919, MSDP, box 42, folder 42; MSD, "Far Up the Black Mountain," 10; MSD, "Athens to Marseilles," 9.

36. MSD to family, 16 November 1919, MSDP, box 42, folder 42; *Voice,* 123–24; MSD, "Major in English Composition."

37. MSD to family, 16 November 1919, MSDP, box 42, folder 42.

CHAPTER NINETEEN: Land Booms

1. F. Scott Fitzgerald, *The Great Gatsby* (New York: Bantam, 1945), 3; MSD, "Bees in the Mango Bloom," *SEP,* 12 December 1931, 13; MSD, "A Bird Dog in Hand," *SEP,* 12 September 1925, reprinted in *Nine Florida Stories,* ed. Kevin M. McCarthy (Gainesville: University Press of Florida, 1990), 6–7, 56, 58, 60, 62; *MH,* 7 November 1922. At one point in "A Bird Dog in Hand," George Henry spouts dialogue that is near verbatim from Henry George. The fictional George says, "It is true that social reform is not to be secured by noise and shouting, but only by making people think." The real-life George said, "Social reform is not to be secured by noise and shouting, by complaints and denunciations, by the formation of parties or the making of revolutions but by the awakening of thought and the progress of ideas" ("Topics of the Day: Illusions of the Landless," *The Freeman,* 22 September 1920, 30). MSD made a note of this quote; see Diary, June–November 1925, MSDP, box 27.

2. William Stuart Hill, "Dade County of Today," *The Florida Magazine* 1 (September 1922): 24; *MH,* 20, 21, 22 July 1911; *Everglades Magazine,* circa 1910, available online at www.evergladesonline.com (accessed winter 2004); *WP,* 12 February 1905.

3. Alfred Jackson Hanna and Kathryn Abbey Hanna, *Lake Okeechobee: Wellspring of the Everglades* (Indianapolis: Bobbs-Merrill, 1948), 137–43; *MH,* 9 April 1917; *NYT,* 12 February 1912.

4. Paul S. George, "Land by the Gallon: The Florida Fruitlands Company and the Progresso Land Lottery of 1911," *South Florida History Magazine* 16 (Spring 1989): 8–9; Hanna and Hanna, *Lake Okeechobee*, 137–43; Nancy Martin Harris and Henry Jurden Martin, "The Story of the Henry Wilson Martin Family: Experiences of Our Family in the Belle Glade Area in Early Days and an Account of the Hurricane of 1926 and 1928," Miscellaneous Manuscripts, PKY.

5. *NYT,* 21, 23 November, 7 December 1913, 27 March 1917; *WP,* 21 November 1913.

6. Hanna and Hanna, *Lake Okeechobee,* 140, 142; *NYT,* 30 April 1911; *WP,* 12 February 1905.

7. J. E. Dovell, "John Newhouse: Upper Everglades Pioneer," *Tequesta* 27 (1967): 23–28; John Newhouse, "1912 Land Buyer's Convention, West Palm Beach, Florida," Miscellaneous Manuscripts, box 26, John Newhouse file, PKY; John Newhouse, "Pioneering in the Everglades," 1932, 13–17, Miscellaneous Manuscripts, box 25, John Newhouse file, PKY; Hanna and Hanna, *Lake Okeechobee,* 164–72.

8. *NYT,* 30 April 1911, 15 March 1925; *WP,* 12 February 1905, 25 March 1906; D. LeBaron Perrine, "The Remaking of Florida," *The Tropic Magazine* 7 (February 1926): 187; Kenneth Ballinger, *Miami Millions: The Dance of the Dollars in the Great Florida Land Boom of 1925* (Miami: Franklin, 1936), 65; Henry Fitzgerald, "A Five Million-Acre Garden," *South,* September 1926, 1.

9. *MH,* 1, 4 June, 16 September 1916, 15 January, 20, 22 February, 16 March, 6, 11 April 1917; "Back to Broward League," 1916, available online at http://purl.fcla .edu/fcla/dl/RTEP00060001.jpg (accessed summer 2005); *New Smyrna News,* 30 March 1917; *Tampa Daily Times,* 23 January 1917.

10. David McCally, *The Everglades: An Environmental History* (Gainesville: University Press of Florida, 1999), 132–33; *Flood Control in Florida and Elsewhere: Hearings before the Committee on Flood Control, House of Representatives,* 70th Cong., 2nd sess., January 10–February 1, 1929 (Washington, D.C.: U.S. Government Printing Office, 1929), 247; MSD, "Bees in the Mango Bloom," 13.

11. David Arnold, *The Problem of Nature: Environment, Culture, and European Expansion* (Oxford, Eng.: Blackwell, 1996), 150; John Newhouse, "Everglades Taxes," Miscellaneous Manuscripts, box 26, John Newhouse file, PKY; *MH,* 17 May, 12, 30, 31 August, 3 September, 12, 27 December 1922. Although submissions were to be sent to the *Herald* editor, Stoneman's involvement in the contest is unclear.

12. C. V. Piper to Dr. Will, 5 August 1919, Scrapbook, Thomas E. Will Papers, box 33, Everglades folder, PKY; *MH,* 2 November 1947; McCally, *Everglades,* 143–

45; *Establishment of Everglades National Park: Hearings before the Committee on the Public Lands, House of Representatives,* 71st Cong., 3rd sess. (Washington, D.C.: U.S. Government Printing Office, 1931), 55; Lawrence E. Will to MSD, 2 December 1947, MSDP, box 42, folder 42; Garald G. Parker Sr., interview by David McCally, 27 February 1992, Oral History Program, University of South Florida Library, Tampa; "The President Reports to You," *Bird-Lore* 41 (September 1939): 305–6; Juanita Greene, "Losing Ground: Soil Subsidence in the Everglades," in *The Book of the Everglades,* ed. Susan Cerulean (Minneapolis: Milkweed, 2002), 80–81.

13. MSD, "Bird Dog in Hand," 46–47; J. E. Dovell, "Thomas Elmer Will, Twentieth-Century Pioneer," *Tequesta* 8 (1948): 41–43; Thomas E. Will, *Settle or Sell,* 24 October 1925, available online at http://purl.fcla.edu/fcla/dl/RTEP00060001.jpg (accessed summer 2005).

14. *Voice,* 174–75; "Biography, Marjory Stoneman Douglas," résumé, HP; H. E. Huttig, "MSD," 31 August 1987, HP; Muriel V. Murrell, *Miami: A Backward Glance* (Sarasota, Fla.: Pineapple, 2003), 75; Bookkeeping Department, Jaundon Realty Company, to MSD, 19 December 1925, Daisy Aldridge to MSD, 16 September 1930, both in Reclaiming the Everglades, online database sponsored by the State University System of Florida, available at http://everglades.fiu.ed/reclaim (accessed summer 2008).

15. *River of Grass,* 334; *NYT,* 15, 22 March 1925; Frank B. Sessa, "Miami in 1926," *Tequesta* 16 (1956): 15–16; Paul S. George, "Brokers, Binders, and Builders: Greater Miami's Boom of the Mid-1920s," *Florida Historical Society* 65 (July 1986): 34; Benedicte Sisto, "Miami's Land Gambling Fever of 1925," *Tequesta* 59 (1999): 55; Vic Knight, "The Florida Land Boom: A Promoter's Dream," *South Florida History Magazine* 23 (Summer 1994): 24; Felix Isman, "Florida's Land Boom," *SEP,* 22 August 1925, 14.

16. *MH,* 20, 21, 22 July 1911, 29 September 1940; Millicent Todd Bingham, "Miami: A Study in Urban Geography," *Tequesta* 9 (1949): 97; Ballinger, *Miami Millions,* 53.

17. Sessa, "Miami in 1926," 23–25; Knight, "Florida Land Boom," 22–27; Helen Muir, *Miami, U.S.A.* (Gainesville: University Press of Florida, 2000), 136, 138; *MH,* 1 September, 13 October 1940; *NYT,* 22 March 1925; Lawrence W. Levine, *Defender of the Faith: William Jennings Bryan, the Last Decade, 1915–1925* (Cambridge: Harvard University Press, 1987), 236; Hampton Dunn, "House Built to Last for Centuries," *Update* 2 (October 1974): 9; Paul S. George, "Brokers, Binders, and Builders," 40; Ballinger, *Miami Millions,* 9.

18. Paul S. George, "Brokers, Binders, and Builders," 40, 44; Sisto, "Miami's Land Gambling Fever," 60; William Frazer and John J. Guthrie, *The Florida Land Boom: Speculation, Money, and the Banks* (Westport, Conn.: Quorum, 1995), 97–102; *MH*, 9 June 1923.

19. MSD, "Bees in the Mango Bloom," 13; Jeanne Bellamy, "Newspapers of America's Last Frontier," *Tequesta* 12 (1952): 12; Ballinger, *Miami Millions*, 6–7, 21–23; *MH*, 20 October 1940; Sisto, "Miami's Land Gambling Fever," 55; Kenneth L. Roberts, "Tropical Growth," *SEP*, April 29, 1922, 9; Jane T. Tolbert, "'Plowing Gold from the Wasteland': Media Portrayal of South Florida's Boom, 1920–25," *Journalism History* 33 (Summer 2007): 113.

20. Emily Perry Dieterich, "Doc Dammers, Super-Salesman," *Update* 15 (August 1988): 4, 5; Paul S. George, "Brokers, Binders, and Builders," 41, 42; *Miami Herald*, 6, 20 October 1940; Muir, *Miami, U.S.A.*, 136; Roberts, "Tropical Growth," 77.

21. *MH*, 9 April 1917, 1, 15, 29 September, 6, 13, 20 October, 13, 16 November 1940; *NYT*, 15 March 1925; Paul S. George, "Brokers, Binders, and Builders," 30–31, 43; Sessa, "Miami in 1926," 16–19, 26; Frank B. Sessa, "Miami on the Eve of the Boom: 1923," *Tequesta* 11 (1951): 11–12; Ballinger, *Miami Millions*, 56; Paul S. George, "Brokers, Binders, and Builders," 39–40; Dieterich, "Doc Dammers, Super-Salesman," 5; Frazer and Guthrie, *Florida Land Boom*, 95–97.

22. *MH*, 6 October, 13 November 1940; Ballinger, *Miami Millions*, 21–23; Frazer and Guthrie, *Florida Land Boom*, 94–95.

23. Ballinger, *Miami Millions*, 65; Paul S. George, "Brokers, Binders, and Builders," 36–37; Knight, "Florida Land Boom," 26; *MH*, 24 March, 3 November 1940.

24. Muir, *Miami, U.S.A.*, 132; Ballinger, *Miami Millions*, 65; Perrine, "Remaking of Florida," 199; *MH*, 18 October, 11 November, 20 December 1922, 24 June 1923, 29 December 1940; *NYT*, 22 March 1925; Roberts, "Tropical Growth," 77.

25. *NYT*, 29 December 1929; *MH*, 9 April 1917, 18, 19 August, 17 September 1925, 5 May 1940; Ballinger, *Miami Millions*, 59; Paul S. George, "Brokers, Binders, and Builders," 47.

26. *MH*, 26 October 1922.

CHAPTER TWENTY: The Galley Slave

1. *Voice*, 124–26.

2. *MH*, 31 January 1920; *Voice*, 125.

3. Donald C. Gaby, *The Miami River and Its Tributaries* (Miami: Historical Association of Southern Florida, 1993), 91–94; *MH*, 24 June 1919, 31 January, 22 March, 30 April 1920, 4 February 1921, 23 April 1922; *Charlotte Observer*, 30 April 1922.

4. MSD, "The Message to Hassan Beg," *SEP*, 11 February 1939, 94.

5. Diary, 12 March 1925, MSDP, box 41. She may have been quoting English historian John Richard Green.

6. *Charlotte Observer*, 14 September 1983; Frederick Erastus Pierce, *Mobilizing the Mid-Brain: The Technique for Utilizing Its Latent Power* (New York: Dutton, 1924), 65; Diary, 10 August 1924, MSDP, box 41; "Our Lady of the 'Glades," *Chicago Tribune*, clipping, n.d., "Marjory Stoneman Douglas," *Miami News*, clipping, ca. 1980, both in MSDP, box 11, folder 39.

7. Harry Angevin Rider, *Indiana Book of Merit: Official Individual Decorations and Commendations Awarded to Indiana Men and Women for Services in the World War* (Indianapolis: Historical Bureau, Indiana Library and Historical Department, 1932), 635; Marjory Rotharmel, telephone interview by author, 18 October 2007.

8. *WP*, 23 December 1917; *MH*, 7 March, 23 April 1920.

9. "Nocturne," the poem that *Scribner's* accepted, was ultimately rejected after the magazine, which had a policy against using previously published work, learned that the poem had been printed in the *MH*. Charles Scribner's Sons to MSD, 27 July, 3 August 1920, George to MSD, 28 September 1920, Mary P. Gould to MSD, 29 September 1920, all in MSDP, box 40, folder 17; John E. Holland to MSD, 22 April 1922, Mary Hoge Wordlaw to MSD, 26 October 1920, both in MSDP, box 40, folder 14.

10. *MH*, 5 June 1920, 19 March, 1 April 1921, 11 October 1922, 10 May 1923.

11. *MH*, 8 April, 20 August, 4 September 1920, 15 December 1921; F. H. Wharton to MSD, 8 December 1931, MSDP, box 39, Correspondence folder, 13 February 1920–3 January 1935.

12. MSD, untitled manuscript, n.d., 31, MSDP, box 48, folder 23; *MH*, 23 February 1923.

13. *MH*, 23 June, 21 July 1923, 22 September 1940; *Florida*, 261.

14. Kip Vought, "Racial Stirrings in Colored Town: The UNIA in Miami during the 1920s," *Tequesta* 60 (2000): 58–59; James J. Carney, "Population Growth in Miami and Dade County, Florida," *Tequesta* 6 (1946): 53–54; *Florida*, 12, 259, 260–61.

15. MSD, "Years I Have Seen: A Prologue," MSDP, box 2, Florida, Prologue folder; *Special Voices, Two Florida Women: Marjorie Carr, Marjory Stoneman Douglas,* video production (Florida Atlantic University/Florida International University, Joint Center for Environmental and Urban Problems, 1985).

16. On Florida convict leasing, see N. Gordon Carper, "Martin Tabert, Martyr of an Era," *Florida Historical Quarterly* 52 (October 1973): 115–31; Jerrell H. Shofner, "Postscript to the Martin Tabert Case: Peonage as Usual in the Florida Turpentine Camps," *Florida Historical Quarterly* 60 (October 1981): 164–66; Jerrell H. Shofner, "Forced Labor in Florida Forests, 1880–1950," *Journal of Forest History* 25 (1981): 18–20; Robert N. Lauriault, "From Can to Can't: The North Florida Turpentine Camp, 1900–1950," *Florida Historical Quarterly* 67 (January 1989): 310–28; J. C. Powell, *The American Siberia; or, Fourteen Years Experience in a Southern Convict Camp* (Chicago: Donohue, Henneberry, 1891); Wayne Flynt, *Cracker Messiah: Governor Sidney J. Catts of Florida* (Baton Rouge: Louisiana State University Press, 1977), 138–39, 238–39. On the subject in the South, see Pete Daniel, *The Shadow of Slavery: Peonage in the South* (Urbana: University of Illinois Press, 1972); Leon F. Litwack, *Trouble in Mind: Black Southerners in the Age of Jim Crow* (New York: Knopf, 1998), 270–76; Paul Ortiz, *Emancipation Betrayed: The Hidden History of Black Organizing and White Violence in Florida from Reconstruction to the Bloody Election of 1920* (Berkeley: University of California Press, 2005), 54.

17. *NYT,* 18 April 1923.

18. *WP,* 21 April, 1, 8, 25 May, 9 July 1923; Robert D. Highfill, "The Effects of News of Crime and Scandal upon Public Opinion," *Journal of the American Institute of Criminal Law and Criminology* 17 (May 1926): 84.

19. *MH,* 20, 25 April 1923; *NYT,* 9, 11, 18 April, 29 November 1923; *Macon Telegraph,* 24 June 1923; *Literary Digest* 77 (12 May 1923): 34. The Tabert family sued Putnam Lumber for fifty thousand dollars and settled for twenty thousand dollars.

20. *MH,* 13 November 1922.

21. *MH,* 1 October 1922.

22. *Voice,* 174–80, 197.

23. MSD, "The Story of a Homely Woman," *SEP,* 4 December 1931, 55; John William Leonard, ed., *Woman's Who's Who of America: A Biographical Dictionary of Contemporary Women of the United States and Canada, 1914–1915* (New York: American Commonwealth, 1914), 737.

24. *MH*, 30 December 1922, 31 January 1923; Katherine Jocher, "Two Decades of Social Forces," *Social Forces* 23 (March 1945): 291–301; Mel Scott, *American City Planning since 1890* (Berkeley: University of California Press, 1969), 2; Daniel Joseph Singal, *The War Within: From Victorian to Modernist Thought in the South, 1919–1945* (Chapel Hill: University of North Carolina Press, 1982), 148–52; Robert L. Dorman, *Revolt of the Provinces: The Regionalism Movement in America, 1920–1945* (Chapel Hill: University of North Carolina Press, 1993), 52–53, 134–35; Howard W. Odum and Harry Estill Moore, *American Regionalism: A Cultural-Historical Approach to National Integration* (New York: Holt, 1938); Donald L. Miller, *Lewis Mumford: A Life* (Pittsburgh: University of Pittsburgh Press, 1989), 51–57. The *Journal of Social Forces* later changed its name to just *Social Forces*.

25. *MH*, 21 October 1920, 17 July 1921, 7 November 1922; *Florida*, 262–63.

26. MSD, "The University and the Forgotten Curriculum," *Journal of Social Forces* 1 (March 1923): 235–37; *MH*, 7 May 1923; Christine Stansell, *American Moderns: Bohemian New York and the Creation of a New Century* (New York: Owl, 2001).

27. Odum and Moore, *American Regionalism*, 277–94; *MH*, 18 October, 11 November, 20, 21 December 1922, 24 June 1923.

28. *MH*, 26 December 1922; "The Galley," clippings, n.d., MSDP, box 39, folder 12.

29. *MH*, 12 October 1922.

30. *MH*, 11 November 1922.

31. *MH*, 14 March, 24 April 1920, 23 October 1922; "As Contemporaries See Us," *The Freeman*, 5 April 1922, 96.

32. MSD, "A Bird Dog in Hand," *SEP*, 12 September 1925, reprinted in *Nine Florida Stories*, ed. Kevin M. McCarthy (Gainesville: University Press of Florida, 1990), 7.

33. *MH*, 22 April, 30 December 1922, 29 January, 8 March, 11 May 1923; Stanley K. Schultz, *Constructing Urban Culture: American Cities and City Planning, 1800–1920* (Philadelphia: Temple University Press, 1989); Diana Balmori, Diane Kostial McGuire, and Eleanor M. McPeck, *Beatrix Farrand's American Landscapes: Her Gardens and Campuses* (Sagaponack, N.Y.: Sagapress, 1985); Vera Norwood, *Made from This Earth: American Women and Nature* (Chapel Hill: University of North Carolina Press, 1993), 110–11, 114–17; R. Bruce Stephenson,

Visions of Eden: Environmentalism, Urban Planning, and City Building in St. Petersburg, Florida, 1900–1995 (Columbus: Ohio State University Press, 1997), vii, 91. On the City Beautiful movement generally, see William H. Wilson, *The City Beautiful Movement* (Baltimore: Johns Hopkins University Press, 1989). On Addams, Hamilton, and other women urban reformers, see Harold L. Platt, "Jane Addams and the Ward Boss Revisited: Class, Politics, and Public Health in Chicago, 1890–1930," *Environmental History* 5 (April 2000): 194–222; Christopher C. Sellers, *Hazards of the Job: From Industrial Disease to Environmental Health Science* (Chapel Hill: University of North Carolina Press, 1997), 69–106; William H. Wilson, *City Beautiful Movement*, 44, 57–58, 126–46.

34. *MH,* 20 April 1917, 13 March 1921; Stephenson, *Visions of Eden,* 30–34.

35. F. H. Wharton to MSD, 8 December 1921, MSDP, box 14, folder 40; MSD, "When You and I Were Young, Miami," *Tropic* (*MH*), 5 November 1967, 17; "The Remarkable Marjory Stoneman Douglas," *Miamian,* September 1970, 62.

36. *MH,* 6 April 1923; *Charlotte Observer,* 14 September 1983; *Chicago Tribune,* clipping, n.d., MSDP, box 11, folder 37; MSD, "The Everglades Remembered," *Tropical Trails,* Spring–Summer 1991, 14.

37. *MH,* 26 October, 21 December 1922; Dorman, *Revolt of the Provinces,* 53, 134–35.

38. David Fairchild, "Some Plant Reminiscences of Southern Florida," *Tequesta* 2 (1942): 8–15; David Fairchild, *The World Grows round My Door: The Story of the Kampong, a Home on the Edge of the Tropics* (New York: Scribner's, 1947), 18–34; Philip J. Pauly, *Biologists and the Promise of American Life: From Meriwether Lewis to Alfred Kinsey* (Princeton: Princeton University Press, 2002), 81–87; *MH,* 21 December 1922.

39. *MH,* 6 February 1917, 14 January, 26 May 1940; "The Original Tamiami Trail Blazer: Fort Myers–Miami, 1923," *South Florida History Magazine* 16 (Winter 1989): 3–5, 12; James Lorenzo Walker, "Dedication of Tamiami Trail Marker," *Tequesta* 19 (1959): 23–28.

40. *MH,* 6 February, 12 September 1916, 16, 18 April 1923; Gary Garrett, "Blasting through Paradise: The Construction and Consequences of the Tamiami Trail," in *Paradise Lost? The Environmental History of Florida,* ed. Jack E. Davis and Raymond Arsenault (Gainesville: University Press of Florida, 2005), 271–73; MSD, "The Cars Pass, but the Everglades Remain," *Sunrise* 1 (November 1931): 48.

41. *MH,* 31 July 1923.

CHAPTER TWENTY-ONE: Hurricanes

1. Eric L. Gross, "Somebody Got Drowned, Lord: Florida and the Great Okeechobee Hurricane Disaster of 1928" (Ph.D. diss., Florida State University, 1995), 216–17; Joe Hugh Reese, *Florida's Great Hurricane* (Miami: General Printing, 1926), 15–16.

2. Gross, "Somebody Got Drowned, Lord," 215; Richard W. Gray, *Florida Hurricanes* (Washington, D.C.: U.S. Government Printing Office, 1936), 2.

3. Richard W. Gray, "Monthly Meteorological Notes at Miami, Fla., September, Thursday, 16th," available online at http://www.srh.noaa.gov/mfl/newpage/ 1926_hurricane_WBO1.jpg (accessed spring 2008).

4. *MH*, 17 September 1926, 1 December 1940; L. F. Reardon, *The Florida Hurricane and Disaster* (Coral Gables, Fla.: Parks, 1986), 4–5; Gross, "Somebody Got Drowned, Lord," 216–17; Jay Barnes, *Florida's Hurricane History*, revised by Grady Norton (Chapel Hill: University of North Carolina Press, 1998), 111–12.

5. Joe Hugh Reese, *Florida's Great Hurricane*, 18; Gross, "Somebody Got Drowned, Lord," 218–20.

6. Fred Pettijohn, *Hurricane 1926* (Fort Lauderdale: Fort Lauderdale Historical Society, 1986), 1–2; Raymond Arsenault, "The Public Storm: Hurricanes and the State in Twentieth-Century America," in *Paradise Lost? The Environmental History of Florida*, ed. Jack E. Davis and Raymond Arsenault (Gainesville: University Press of Florida, 2005), 207–10.

7. Gross, "Somebody Got Drowned, Lord," 222.

8. Pettijohn, *Hurricane 1926*, 2; Gross, "Somebody Got Drowned, Lord," 222; Joe Hugh Reese, *Florida's Great Hurricane*, 17; Richard W. Gray, "Monthly Meteorological Notes at Miami, Fla., September, Saturday 18th," available online at http://www .srh.noaa.gov/mfl/newpage/1926_hurricane_WBO1.jpg (accessed spring 2008).

9. Joe Hugh Reese, *Florida's Great Hurricane*, 20–21; Pettijohn, *Hurricane 1926*, 2–3; Gross, "Somebody Got Drowned, Lord," 222–26; Gray, "Monthly Meteorological Notes, Saturday 18th."

10. Joe Hugh Reese, *Florida's Great Hurricane*, 21; Pettijohn, *Hurricane 1926*, 3–4; Gross, "Somebody Got Drowned, Lord," 226–27.

11. Joe Hugh Reese, *Florida's Great Hurricane*, 19–21; Gross, "Somebody Got Drowned, Lord," 227–28; Gray, "Monthly Meteorological Notes, Saturday 18th."

12. Joe Hugh Reese, *Florida's Great Hurricane*, 21–22; Jay Barnes, *Florida's Hurricane History*, 113–14; Gross, "Somebody Got Drowned, Lord," 229; MSD,

Hurricane (New York: Rinehart, 1958), 262; Gray, "Monthly Meteorological Notes, Saturday 18th."

13. Jay Barnes, *Florida's Hurricane History,* 113, 118–19; Erling Ayars, "The 1926 Hurricane in the Grove," *Update* 5 (August–October 1978): 6–8; *Voice,* 172–73.

14. Gross, "Somebody Got Drowned, Lord," 229–31; Reardon, *Florida Hurricane and Disaster;* Joe Hugh Reese, *Florida's Great Hurricane,* 30–36; Jay Barnes, *Florida's Hurricane History,* 115–17; *NYT,* 21 September, 17 October 1926; *WP,* 23, 24 September 1926; *MH,* 8 December 1940.

15. Ayars, "1926 Hurricane," 6–8; *Voice,* 172–73.

16. Joe Hugh Reese, *Florida's Great Hurricane,* 22; Gross, "Somebody Got Drowned, Lord," 230–32; Reardon, *Florida Hurricane and Disaster,* 4; *NYT,* 29 September 1926; Gray, *Florida Hurricanes,* 3.

17. Reardon, *Florida Hurricane and Disaster,* 73–76; Gross, "Somebody Got Drowned, Lord," 232–38; Joe Hugh Reese, *Florida's Great Hurricane,* 35, 49–58; John Newhouse, "Pioneering in the Everglades," 1932, 44, Miscellaneous Manuscripts, box 25, John Newhouse file, PKY; Nancy Martin Murray and Henry Jurden Martin, "The Story of the Henry Wilson Martin Family: Experiences of Our Family in the Belle Glade Area in Early Days and an Account of the Hurricanes of 1926 and 1928," circa 1978, PKY; *WP,* 23 September 1926; *Flood Control in Florida and Elsewhere: Hearings before the Committee on Flood Control, House of Representatives,* 70th Cong., 2nd sess., January 10–February 1, 1929 (Washington, D.C.: U.S. Government Printing Office, 1929), 247; Juanita Greene, "Losing Ground: Soil Subsidence in the Everglades," in *The Book of the Everglades,* ed. Susan Cerulean (Minneapolis: Milkweed, 2002), 79–80.

18. *NYT,* 21, 22, 23, 24, 28, 29 September, 6 November 1926; *WP,* 24, 28 September 1926; *MH,* 27 October 1940; Ted Steinberg, *Acts of God: The Unnatural History of Natural Disaster in America* (New York: Oxford University Press, 2000), 33–42; Cynthia Barnett, *Mirage: Florida and the Vanishing Water of the Eastern U.S.* (Ann Arbor: University of Michigan Press, 2007), 65.

19. Gross, "Somebody Got Drowned, Lord," 240–41; *NYT,* 17 October 1926.

20. Frank B. Sessa, "Miami in 1926," *Tequesta* 16 (1956): 28–29, 30; William Frazer and John J. Guthrie, *The Florida Land Boom: Speculation, Money, and the Banks* (Westport, Conn.: Quorum, 1995), 63, 69–75; Gross, "Somebody Got Drowned, Lord," 240; Paul S. George, "Brokers, Binders, and Builders: Greater Miami's Boom of the Mid-1920s," *Florida Historical Society* 65 (July 1986) 47; *MH,* 24 November 1940.

21. *NYT,* 21, 27 September 1926; Steinberg, *Acts of God;* Eliot Kleinberg, *Black Cloud: The Deadly Hurricane of 1928* (New York: Carroll and Graf, 2004), cover.

22. *NYT,* 27 September 1926; *MH,* 8 December 1940. Peay signed into law the "monkey" bill, which outlawed the teaching of evolution in public schools and was the law under which the schoolteacher John Scopes was tried, with William Jennings Bryan assisting the prosecution and Clarence Darrow the defense.

23. Steinberg, *Acts of God,* xix; MSD, *Hurricane,* 6.

24. MSD, "The Thirty," *Sunrise* 1 (May 1932): 5–6; MSD, "September—Remember," *SEP,* 7 December 1935, 12–13, 39–40, 42, 46; MSD, *Hurricane,* 272; Phil Scott, *Hemingway's Hurricane: The Great Labor Day Storm of 1935* (New York: Ragged Mountain, 2005).

25. Marguerite J. Reese to MSD, 9 September 1958, MSDP, box 47, folder 110; MSD to Archie Carr, 9 August 1956, Archie F. Carr Jr. Papers, box 18, PKY. The principal academic book on hurricanes at the time was Ivan Ray Tannehill, *Hurricanes: Their Nature and History, Particularly Those in the West Indies and the Southern Coasts of the United States* (Princeton: Princeton University Press, 1956).

26. Miscellaneous clippings, MSDP, box 44, folder 82; Holt, Rinehart and Winston, Inc., Publishers, royalty statements for *Hurricane,* 1 July, 21 December 1962, Agreement, Rinehart and Company, Inc., and MSD, 25 February 1955, Stanley M. Rinehart to MSD, 5 December 1955, all in MSDP, box 47, folder 110; *NYT,* 27 October 1958; *WP,* 26 October 1958.

27. Randolph J. Widmer, *The Evolution of the Calusa: A Non-Agricultural Chiefdom on the Southwest Florida Coast* (Tuscaloosa: University of Alabama Press, 1988), 267; Darcie A. MacMahon and William H. Marquardt, *The Calusa and Their Legacy: South Florida People and Their Environments* (Gainesville: University Press of Florida, 2004), 96; Sherry Johnson, "The St. Augustine Hurricane of 1811: Disaster and Political Unrest on the Florida Frontier during the Age of Revolution," paper presented at the Southern Historical Association Meeting, 5 November 2004, Memphis, Tenn.; MSD, *Hurricane,* 37–42, 73–78.

28. MSD, *Hurricane,* 153–74, 217.

29. Arsenault, "Public Storm," 205–6.

30. MSD, *Hurricane,* 249–58; Arsenault, "Public Storm," 208–9; Eric Larson, *Isaac's Storm: A Man, a Time, and the Deadliest Hurricane in History* (New York: Vintage, 2000).

31. MSD, *Hurricane,* 6.

32. Sessa, "Miami in 1926," 30; *NYT*, 17 October 1926.

33. William G. Shepard, "Beating the Hurricane," *Collier's*, 17 November 1928, 9, 40; Kleinberg, *Black Cloud*, 35–56; Jay Barnes, *Florida's Hurricane History*, 127–29; MSD, *Hurricane*, 169.

34. Shepard, "Beating the Hurricane," 40; Kleinberg, *Black Cloud*, 57–68; Robert Mykle, *Killer 'Cane: The Deadly Hurricane of 1928* (New York: Cooper Square, 2002), 136.

35. Kleinberg, *Black Cloud*, 60–61, 68–85.

36. Jay Barnes, *Florida's Hurricane History*, 130.

37. Zora Neale Hurston, *Their Eyes Were Watching God* (New York: Quality, 1990), 146–47.

38. Jay Barnes, *Florida's Hurricane History*, 130; Kleinberg, *Black Cloud*, 71; Mykle, *Killer 'Cane*, 132–33; Hurston, *Their Eyes Were Watching God*, 154.

39. Hurston, *Their Eyes Were Watching God*, 151; Jay Barnes, *Florida's Hurricane History*, 132; Kleinberg, *Black Cloud*, 95–111; Lawrence E. Will, *Okeechobee Hurricane and the Hoover Dike* (St. Petersburg, Fla.: Great Outdoors, 1961), 9–55; Murray and Martin, "Story," 12–22; Mykle, *Killer 'Cane*, 134–89.

40. Unofficially, the death toll has been set at between twenty-three hundred and thirty-five hundred (Jay Barnes, *Florida's Hurricane History*, 127).

41. Hurston, *Their Eyes Were Watching God*, 160, 163; *WP*, 19 September 1918; *NYT*, 20, 21, 23, 24, 25 September 1928; Jay Barnes, *Florida's Hurricane History*, 137–28; "The Hurricane's Tragic Toll," *Literary Digest* 99 (6 October 1928): 13–14.

42. *Christian Science Monitor*, 11 October 1928; *WP*, 21, 22, 27 September, 24 October, 11 November 1928; *NYT*, 17, 18, 20, 22, 23, 24, 25, 26, 27 September, 14 October, 18 November, 6 December 1928; Shepard, "Beating the Hurricane"; Arsenault, "Public Storm," 212; Jay Barnes, *Florida's Hurricane History*, 139–40; MSD, *Hurricane*, 270–71.

CHAPTER TWENTY-TWO: Stories

1. MSD, "From the Terror by Night," *SEP*, 1 August 1936, 75; *Voice*, 118.

2. Donald C. Gaby, *The Miami River and Its Tributaries* (Miami: Historical Association of Southern Florida, 1993), 91–93.

3. *Voice*, 169; *Palm Beach Post*, 26 March 1978.

4. Sharon Hamilton, "The First *New Yorker*? The Smart Set Magazine, 1900–1924," *Serials Librarian* 37 (October 1999): 89–104; manuscript fact sheet, "White

Midnight," MSDP, box 35, folder 97; MSD, "White Midnight," *Black Mask*, 15 March 1924, 51; MSD, "Painkiller," *Ainslee's,* February 1924, 83–93; MSD, "Hibiscus Red," *Ainslee's,* June 1924, 41–49.

5. Jeffrey Meyers, *Scott Fitzgerald: A Biography* (New York: HarperCollins, 1994), 48, 80.

6. Jan Cohn, *Creating America: George Horace Lorimer and the* Saturday Evening Post (Pittsburgh: University of Pittsburgh Press, 1989), 28, 165–217.

7. MSD, "At Home on the Marcel Waves," *SEP,* 14 June 1924, 12–13, 48, 50, 52, 54, 56, 58.

8. Robert Gottlieb, *Forcing the Spring: The Transformation of the American Environmental Movement* (Washington, D.C.: Island, 1993), 27–28.

9. MSD, "By Violence," *SEP,* 22 November 1930, 6–7, 44, 46, 48, 50, 53.

10. *MH,* 3 April 1923.

11. MSD, "Bees in the Mango Bloom," *SEP,* 12 December 1931, 12–13, 102, 104, 105; Susan A. Eacker, "Gender in Paradise: Harriet Beecher Stowe and Postbellum Prose on Florida," *Journal of Southern History* 64 (August 1998): 496–97.

12. MSD, "From the Terror by Night," 18–19, 74–76, 78. See also MSD's character, Margaret Murray, in "Adventuress," *Household Magazine,* February 1933, 1–2, 40, March 1933, 4–5, 19, 20.

13. The youngest Charles was actually a junior, though he was sometimes identified as a III. His grandfather was Charles August Lindbergh, and his father, the famed aviator, Charles Augustus Lindbergh. See Joyce Milton, *Loss of Eden: A Biography of Charles and Anne Morrow Lindbergh* (New York: HarperCollins, 1993), 6–7, 197,

14. MSD, "From the Terror by Night," 75, 76.

15. Diary, 27 July, 9 March 1927, MSDP, box 27; Diary, 10 January, 15 April 1930, MSDP, box 40; "Re: Her Short Stories," n.d., MSDP, box 39, folder 12; George Horace Lorimer to MSD, 7 April 1927, MSDP, box 10, folder 54.

16. MSD, "Along the Grove Road," *Coconut Grove Village Post* 2 (April 1958): 2–3; *MH,* 6 November, 3 December 1922; MSD, "The Everglades Remembered," *Tropical Trails,* Spring–Summer 1991, 14; Arva Moore Parks, "Coconut Grove before the Railroad," *Update* 3 (December 1975): 7–8.

17. *MH,* 15 February 1953; Matt Schudel, "Marjory's Place," *Fort Lauderdale Sun-Sentinel,* 2 May 1999, 10–11.

18. *MH,* 11 March 1973; Stephen W. Byers, "Don't Mess with Her Wetlands," *New York Times Magazine,* 3 January 1999, 46; Schudel, "Marjory's Place," 10–11;

Sharyn T. Richardson, "Marjory Stoneman Douglas: Her Place on Earth," *Florida Living,* May 1999, 24–28; Holly Hays, "Marjory Stoneman Douglas: Conservationist of the Century," *Florida Living,* August 1992, 54; Dava Sobel, "Still Fighting the Good Fight for the Everglades," *Audubon,* July–August 1991, 34, 35; George Rosner, "MSD, a House of My Own," 1990, HP.

19. Diary, 1 February 1926, MSDP, box 27.

20. "A Simple Solution," clipping, n.d., MSDP, box 39, Clippings folder; Rosner, "MSD, a House of My Own"; Schudel, Marjory's Place," 10–11; William Muir to author, e-mail, 26 December 2007.

21. *MH,* 11 March 1973; "History Was Real," Miami-Dade Community College clipping, n.d., Mrs. Alfred Peacock Collection, HMSF; Hays, "Marjory Stoneman Douglas," 54; Kathryn Schuller to MSD, 19 May 1949, MSDP, box 42, folder 43.

22. MSD, "Along the Grove Road"; Schudel, "Marjory's Place," 10–11; MSD, speech to Florida Historical Society, Pensacola, 6 May 1978, SPOHP.

23. Doubleday, Doran, and Company to MSD, 26 November 1928, MSDP, box 33, folder 44; *NYT,* 29 January 1928; *WP,* 2 December 1928. The other O. Henry story is "He Man," published in *O. Henry Memorial Award Prize Stories of 1927* (Garden City, N.Y.: Doubleday, Doran, 1928), 149–74. "Peculiar Treasure of Kings" was published in *Great American Short Stories: O. Henry Memorial Prize Winning Stories, 1919–1934* (Garden City, N.Y.: Doubleday, Doran, 1935), 500–527. The "peculiar treasure of kings" meant, according to a handwritten notation in the margin of Douglas's copy of the story, "pride" (Douglas's copy found in HP).

24. William G. B. Carson to MSD, 20 February 1933, Louis E. Westheimer to MSD, n.d., 23 February 1933, Adelaide Tarrant to MSD, 14 March 1933, All State Little Theatre Tournament program, Tampa, Fla., 14, 15 July 1930, Civic Theater of Greater Miami program, 10 June 1930, various undated clippings, all in MSDP, box 46, folder 98; MSD, *The Gallows Gate* (Boston: Baker, 1931).

25. *MH,* 15 February 1953.

26. MSD, "Goodness Gracious, Agnes," *SEP,* 17 October 1925, 12–13, 201–2, 205–6, 209–21.

27. Walter Prescott Webb, *The Great Plains* (Boston: Ginn, 1931), 167–78.

28. *MH,* 9 December 1951; MSD, "Solid Mahogany," *SEP,* 20 June 1925, 24–25, 62, 67; MSD, "Pineland," *SEP,* 15 August 1925, 14–15, 115, 118, 121; MSD, "The Woman of It," *SEP,* 21 November 1925, 12–13, 165–66, 169–70, 172; MSD, "The Mayor of Flamingo," *SEP,* 14 April 1926, 30–31, 209–10, 213–14, 217–19; MSD, "Charcoal," *SEP,* 11 January 1930, 16–17, 88, 91, 95; MSD, "Wind before Morning,"

SEP, 8 June 1935, 18–19, 50, 52, 53; MSD, "September—Remember," *SEP,* 7 December 1935, 12–13, 39–40, 42, 46; MSD, "A Mountain in the Sea," *SEP,* 30 October 1937, 14–15, 82, 84, 89, 91; MSD, "Volcano," *SEP,* 25 December 1937, 8–9, 58–59, 61–62; MSD, "Road to the Horizon," *SEP,* 22 February 1941, 14–15, 60, 62–63, 67.

29. Kevin M. McCarthy, "How Marjory Stoneman Douglas Crusaded for South Florida in Her Short Stories," *Marjorie Kinnan Rawlings Journal of Florida Literature* 8 (special issue 1997): 15–21; MSD to Mrs. Moore, 27 July 1976, HP; MSD, "A Flight of Ibis," *SEP,* 21 December 1935, 12–13, 69–70, 72.

30. Vera Norwood, *Made from This Earth: American Women and Nature* (Chapel Hill: University of North Carolina Press, 1993); Michael P. Branch, "Writing the Swamp: Marjory Stoneman Douglas and *The Everglades: River of Grass,*" in *Such News of the Land: U.S. Women Nature Writers,* ed. Thomas S. Edwards and Elizabeth A. De Wolfe (Hanover, N.H.: University Press of New England, 2001), 125–35; Melissa Walker, "Marjory Stoneman Douglas," in *American Nature Writers,* ed. John Elder (New York: Scribner's, 1996), 1:231–45; MSD, "Pineland," 115.

31. *MH,* 21 December 1922, 7 May 1923.

32. *MH,* 15 February 1953; MSD, "Far Up the Black Mountain," *SEP,* 7 January 1939, 10.

33. Mabel White Dorn and MSD, *The Book of Twelve for South Florida Gardens* (Miami: South Florida, 1928); MSD, "Mabel White Dorn, 1899–1972," MSDP, box 54, folder 6.

CHAPTER TWENTY-THREE: The Proposal

1. In MSD's and Coe's day, the Caribbean pine and Dade County pine were considered the same tree. But the two actually have separate botanical designations, *Pinus elliottii* var. *densa* for the Dade County pine, and *Pinus caribaea* for the Caribbean. See Thomas E. Lodge, *The Everglades Handbook: Understanding the Ecosystem* (Delray Beach, Fla.: St. Lucie, 1994), 63.

2. Lynn McMillin (granddaughter of Ted Smallwood), telephone interview by Gary Garrett, 21 April 2005; Charlton W. Tebeau, *The Story of the Chokoloskee Bay Country* (Coral Gables, Fla.: University of Miami Press, 1955), 51–87; MSD, "The Forgotten Man Who Saved the Everglades," *Audubon,* September 1971, 79; Charlton W. Tebeau, *Man in the Everglades: 2,000 Years of Human History in the Everglades National Park* (Coral Gables, Fla.: University of Miami Press, 1986), 86, 88, 166.

3. MSD, "Forgotten Man," 79–80; Cesar A. Becerra, "Birth of Everglades National Park," *South Florida History Magazine* 25 (Fall 1997): 15; Ernest F. Coe to B. F. Asch, 25 October 1928, in Reclaiming the Everglades, online database sponsored by the State University System of Florida, available at http://everglades.fiu .ed/reclaim (accessed summer 2008); Theodore Pratt, "Papa of the Everglades National Park," *SEP,* 9 August 1947, 32–33; Mary Stockly to MSD, 12 September 1971, MSDP, box 40, folder 22; Daniel B. Beard, "Let 'er Burn?" *Everglades Natural History Journal* 2 (March 1954): 3.

4. Harold H. Bailey, *The Birds of Florida* (Baltimore: Waverly, 1925); Tebeau, *Man in the Everglades,* 175; Becerra, "Birth of Everglades National Park," 15.

5. Tebeau, *Man in the Everglades,* 174–75; MSD, "Forgotten Man," 82; Becerra, "Birth of Everglades National Park," 15; "Find Process to Make Paper Out of Peat," n.d., in Reclaiming the Everglades.

6. Ales Hrdlicka to Ernest Coe, 8 December 1932, in Reclaiming the Everglades; Tebeau, *Man in the Everglades,* 170–71.

7. "Grande Dame of the Everglades," *MH* clipping, n.d., MSDP, box 11, folder 39; *MH,* 25 May 1930; Tebeau, *Man in the Everglades,* 170–71; Pratt, "Papa"; "Death Takes Mrs. E. F. Coe," clipping, July 1940, Spessard L. Holland Collection, box 136, Everglades National Park folder, PKY.

8. MSD, "Forgotten Man," 79; Pratt, "Papa"; *MH,* 2 April 1933; Beard, "Let 'er Burn?" 3.

9. John M. Barry, *Rising Tide: The Great Mississippi Flood of 1927 and How It Changed America* (New York: Simon and Schuster, 1997), 363–426; Raymond Arsenault, "The Public Storm: Hurricanes and the State in Twentieth-Century America," in *Paradise Lost? The Environmental History of Florida,* ed. Jack E. Davis and Raymond Arsenault (Gainesville: University Press of Florida, 2005), 211–12.

10. Lawrence E. Will, *Okeechobee Hurricane and the Hoover Dike* (St. Petersburg, Fla.: Great Outdoors, 1961), 100–101, 105–7; Florida, *Minutes of the Board of Commissioners of the Okeechobee Flood Control District, 1929–1943* (West Palm Beach, Fla.: Office of the Secretary of the Board, n.d.), 8–12; *Flood Control in Florida and Elsewhere: Hearings before the Committee on Flood Control, House of Representatives,* 70th Cong., 2nd sess., January 10–February 1, 1929 (Washington, D.C.: U.S. Government Printing Office, 1929), 2–3, 29, 37; George B. Hills, "Everglades of Florida," *Municipal Record* 8 (December 1930): 10; *MH,* 26 May 1929.

11. MSD, "Forgotten Man," 86; Pratt, "Papa"; Tebeau, *Man in the Everglades,* 171; Becerra, "Birth of Everglades National Park," 15; Ernest F. Coe to "Dear Friend," 5 June 1928, in Reclaiming the Everglades.

12. Alfred Runte, *National Parks: The American Experience* (Lincoln: University of Nebraska Press, 1929), 48–64.

13. *History of the Everglades National Park Project,* n.d., Mary McDouglas Axelson Papers, box 41, folder 9, UM; "Everglades National Park Project," 30 November 1937, G. O. Palmer, "Brief: Proposed Everglades National Park," 22 July 1938, both in Holland Collection, box 136, Everglades National Park folder.

14. "The Everglades National Park Bill," May 1934, J. Hardin Peterson Collection, box 55, Everglades National Park folder, PKY; Palmer, "Brief," 2–3; "Proposed Tropic Everglades National Park Location the Cape-Sable Region of South Florida," 25 October 1928, in Reclaiming the Everglades; "Everglades National Park Project"; Pratt, "Papa"; *WP,* 1 December 1929; Tropic Everglades Park Association, Bulletins 14 and 15, 13 January 1930, in Reclaiming the Everglades; "Everglades National Park Bill"; A. B. Cammerer to David Fairchild, 23 January 1929, in Reclaiming the Everglades; David Arnold, *The Problem of Nature: Environment, Culture, and European Expansion* (Oxford, Eng.: Blackwell, 1996), 141–68; Nancy Leys Stephan, *Picturing Tropical Nature* (Ithaca: Cornell University Press, 2001).

15. Florida Federation of Women's Clubs Annual Report, 1923–24, 38–39, MMJP, box 19; May Mann Jennings, "Royal Palm Park," March 1929, MMJP, box 23; Linda D. Vance, *May Mann Jennings: Florida's Genteel Activist* (Gainesville: University of Florida Press, 1985), 129–30.

16. Tropic Everglades Park Association, Bulletin 14, 13 January 1930; *Tropic Everglades National Park: Letter from the Secretary of the Interior,* House Doc. 654, 71st Cong., 3rd sess., 3 December 1930; MSD, "Forgotten Man," 88; Pratt, "Papa"; *Christian Science Monitor,* 11 February 1930; David Fairchild to Ruth Bryan Owen, February 1930, in Reclaiming the Everglades; May Mann Jennings, "Royal Palm State Park," July 1939, MMJP, box 23.

17. *MH,* 12 October 1922; Ernest F. Coe to "Dear Friend," 5 June 1928, Ernest F. Coe to MSD, 30 December 1947, both in MSDP, box 40, Correspondence 1930–45 folder; Robert Kelley, interview by author, 17 March 2006; Helen Muir, interview by author, 11 March 1999; MSD, "Forgotten Man," 86–87; MSD, draft of introduction for Lodge, *Everglades Handbook,* HP.

18. Runte, *National Parks,* 132; MSD, "Forgotten Man," 88.

19. MSD, "Wings," *SEP,* 14 March 1931, 10; MSD, "Forgotten Man," 88, 90; *Christian Science Monitor,* 23 September 1970.

20. MSD, "Wings," 10–11; *Establishment of Everglades National Park: Hearings before the Committee on the Public Lands, House of Representatives,* 71st Cong., 3rd sess. (Washington, D.C.: U.S. Government Printing Office, 1931), 35–36; *Special Voices, Two Florida Women: Marjorie Carr, Marjory Stoneman Douglas,* video production (Florida Atlantic University/Florida International University, Joint Center for Environmental and Urban Problems, 1985).

21. MSD, "Wings," 10–11; MSD, "Forgotten Man," 90, 92; Becerra, "Birth of Everglades National Park," 15; *Establishment of Everglades National Park* (1931), 34; *Special Voices.*

22. MSD, "Wings," 11, 74; Stephen Fox, *The American Conservation Movement: John Muir and His Legacy* (Madison: University of Wisconsin Press, 1981), 155–59; *NYT,* 31 January 1932; *Establishment of Everglades National Park* (1931), 32–33.

23. Pratt, "Papa"; *History of the Everglades National Park Project; MH,* 25 May 1930; *Christian Science Monitor,* 11 February 1930; *NYT,* 6 June 1930; *WP,* 7 September 1930; Ernest F. Coe to Clayton Cooper, 17 October 1920, in Reclaiming the Everglades; Runte, *National Parks,* 131; Tropic Everglades Park Association, Bulletin 16, 17 January 1930, in Reclaiming the Everglades; *Tropic Everglades National Park.*

24. Ernest F. Coe to Ruth Bryan Owen, 23 October 1930, in Reclaiming the Everglades; Sally Vickers, "Ruth Bryan Owen: Florida's First Congresswoman and Lifetime Activist," in *Making Waves: Female Activists in Twentieth-Century Florida,* ed. Jack E. Davis and Kari Frederickson (Gainesville: University Press of Florida, 2003), 23–55.

25. *NYT,* 16, 17 December 1930; *WP,* 20 October 1929; *Christian Science Monitor,* 17 December 1930; Charles M. Brookfield and Oliver Griswold, "The Founding of Everglades National Park," available online at www.historical-museum .org/history/tacit/tacit.htm (accessed fall 2006); *Establishment of Everglades National Park, House of Representatives,* 73rd Cong., 1st sess., 14 June 1933, 54–59.

26. *WP,* 25 December 1930; Horace M. Albright to Gerald P. Nye, 20 December 1930, A. B. Cammerer to David Fairchild, 23, 26 December 1930, unsigned to David Fairchild, 26 December 1930, Ernest F. Coe to David Fairchild, 23, 25 December 1930, Ernest F. Coe to Ruth Bryan Owen, 4 March 1931, Ernest F. Coe to Caspar Hodgson, 4 January 1931, all in Reclaiming the Everglades.

27. Vickers, "Ruth Bryan Owen," 42–43; Ernest F. Coe to Frank A. [*sic*] Stoneman, 11 March 1933, Ernest F. Coe to David Sholtz, 30 May 1933, both in Peterson Collection, box 55, Correspondence folder; Ernest F. Coe to Doyle E. Carlton, 21 December 1931, Ernest F. Coe to A. H. Andrews, 27 February 1931, both in Reclaiming the Everglades.

28. MSD and Ralph Stoutamire, *The Parks and Playgrounds of Florida* (Tallahassee: Florida Department of Agriculture, 1932); Ernest F. Coe to members of the Seventy-third Congress, 25 April 1934, Peterson Collection, box 55, Correspondence folder; "Another Important Wild Life Conservation Organization Passes Resolutions Favoring the Everglades National Project," press release, 5 October 1932, "Another Important Wild Life Conservation Organization Passes Resolution Favoring the Everglades National Project," 14 November 1932, both in Reclaiming the Everglades; Sam Houston and MSD, "Florida Parks," *Sunrise* 1 (January 1933): 5–6, 20.

29. Ernest F. Coe to J. Hardin Peterson, 6 July 1933, Ernest F. Coe to Edward W. Pou, 16 February 1933, both in Peterson Collection, box 55, Correspondence folder; *MH,* 24 June 1923; Ernest F. Coe to David Sholtz, 30 May 1933, Ernest F. Coe to J. K. Small, 6 November 1929, Ernest F. Coe to Ruth Bryan Owen, 23 October 1930, all in Reclaiming the Everglades; Betty Anholt to MSD, 10 February 1990, HP; MSD, "I Am the Mangrove," available online at http://purl.fcla.edu/fcla/dl/RTMD00460100.jpg (accessed spring 2008).

30. Frederick Law Olmsted Jr. and William P. Wharton, "The Florida Everglades: Where the Mangrove Forests Meet the Storm Waves of a Thousand Miles of Water," *American Forests* 38 (March 1932): 142–47, 192; *The Proposed Everglades National Park: Report of a Special Committee of the National Parks Association Appointed to Study All the Features in Connection with the Proposed Everglades National Park in the State of Florida,* 72nd Cong., 1st sess. (Washington, D.C.: U.S. Government Printing Office, 1932); *History of the Everglades National Park Project.*

31. Ernest F. Coe to members, 28 September 1932, in Reclaiming the Everglades; Runte, *National Parks,* 115–17; Ray Lyman Wilbur to Director Albright, 7 January 1933, in *Establishment of Everglades National Park* (1933), 43.

32. *MH,* 25 May 1934; Mrs. W. S. Jennings to J. Hardin Peterson, 29 May 1934, Peterson Collection, box 55, Everglades National Park Correspondence folder; *History of the Everglades National Park Project;* "From President Roosevelt's Address at Glacier National Park," Everglades National Park Association, memorandum, 5 August 1934, in Reclaiming the Everglades.

33. Palmer, "Brief"; Tebeau, *Man in the Everglades,* 178–79; Vance, *May Mann Jennings,* 130–31; Pratt, "Papa."

CHAPTER TWENTY-FOUR: The Book Idea

1. *MH,* 2 February 1941.

2. *MH,* 2 February 1941.

3. *MH,* 2 February 1941; "Uniformed Members of Masonic Orders in Crowd," clipping, n.d., Miami Scrapbooks, 1939–47, HMSF; MSD, "Frank Bryant Stoneman," *Tequesta* 4 (November 1944): 9–11.

4. *MH,* 3 March 1940, 2 February 1941, 15 September 2002; "Uniformed Members of Masonic Orders."

5. Undated clipping, Frank Stoneman scrapbook, MSDP, box 53; *Voice,* 186–89; *Great Floridians Film Series: Marjory Stoneman Douglas* (Tallahassee: Museum of Florida History and Florida History Associates, 1990).

6. *Voice,* 174–75; "Biography, Marjory Stoneman Douglas," résumé, HP; H. E. Huttig, "MSD," 31 August 1987, HP; Muriel V. Murrell, *Miami: A Backward Glance* (Sarasota, Fla.: Pineapple, 2003), 75; Bookkeeping Department, Jaundon Realty Company, to MSD, 19 December 1925, Daisy Aldridge to MSD, 16 September 1930, in Reclaiming the Everglades, online database sponsored by the State University System of Florida, available at http://everglades.fiu.ed/reclaim (accessed summer 2008).

7. MSD, *An Argument for a Botanical Garden in South Florida to Be Called the Fairchild Tropical Garden* (Coral Gables, Fla.: Craftsmen of Kells, 1937); *Fort Lauderdale Sun-Sentinel,* 27 December 2006; MSD, *Dedication of the Fairchild Tropical Botanic Garden, March 23, 1938* (Coral Gables, Fla.: Fairchild Gardens, 1938).

8. *Voice,* 188–89; MSD, "The Road to the Horizon," *SEP,* 22 February 1941, 14–15, 60, 62–63. 67.

9. Diary, 21 June 1926, MSDP, box 27; Doubleday, Doran, and Company to MSD, 26 November 1928, MSDP, box 33, folder 44; *Orlando Morning Sentinel,* 4 March 1944; *MH,* 11 June 1944; Helen Muir, interview by author, 11 March 1999.

10. Gary R. Mormino, "World War II," in *The New History of Florida,* edited by Michael Gannon (Gainesville: University Press of Florida, 1996), 323–43; Christian Warren, "'Nature's Navel': An Overview of the Many Environmental Histories of Florida Citrus," in *Paradise Lost? The Environmental History of Florida,* ed.

Jack E. Davis and Raymond Arsenault (Gainesville: University Press of Florida, 2005), 201–33; Garald G. Parker Sr., interview by David McCally, 27 February 1992, Oral History Program, University of South Florida Library, Tampa.

11. *MH,* 28 March 1923, 2 November 1947; *Orlando Morning Sentinel,* 4 March 1944; Stuart E. Knee, *Hervey Allen, 1889–1949: A Literary Historian in America* (Lewiston, N.Y.: Mellen, 1988); "Fact Sheet" (Marjory Stoneman Douglas), 8 November 1983, HP.

12. Jean Barman, *Constance Lindsay Skinner: Writing on the Frontier* (Toronto: University of Toronto Press, 2002); Jack C. Lane, "Constructing *The St. Johns:* History as Literary Narrative," *Florida Historical Quarterly* 80 (Winter 2002): 312–13; Carol Fitzgerald, *The Rivers of America: A Descriptive Biography* (New Castle, Del.: Oak Knoll, 2001), 1:xxi–xxii, xlix–lii.

13. Cecile H. Matschat, *Suwannee River: Strange Green Land* (New York: Literary Guild of America, 1938); Branch Cabell and A. J. Hanna, *The St. Johns, a Paradise of Diversity* (New York: Farrar and Rinehart, 1943).

14. *Voice,* 190; agreement, Farrar and Rinehart and MSD, 23 November 1943, MSDP, box 47, folder 110; draft acknowledgments, 1947 edition of *The Everglades: River of Grass,* MSDP, box 42, folder 54; Carol Fitzgerald, *Rivers of America,* 1:li–lii, lv–lvii.

15. Science historian Sharon E. Kingsland offers a slightly different version of the origins of ecology, arguing that "the New York Botanical Garden served as midwife for the emergence of ecology in the United States" (*The Evolution of American Ecology, 1890–2000* [Baltimore: Johns Hopkins University Press, 2005], 5).

16. Robert A. Croker, *Stephen Forbes and the Rise of American Ecology* (Washington, D.C.: Smithsonian Institution Press, 2001), 3–4, 129; Joel B. Hagen, *An Entangled Bank: The Origins of Ecosystem Ecology* (New Brunswick, N.J.: Rutgers University Press, 1992), 7–9; Robert P. McIntosh, "Ecology since 1900," in *History of American Ecology* (New York: Arno, 1977), 353; Daniel W. Schneider, "Local Knowledge, Environmental Politics, and the Founding of Ecology in the United States: Stephen Forbes and 'The Lake as a Microcosm' (1887)," *Ibis* 91 (December 2000): 681–86.

17. McIntosh, "Ecology since 1900," 353–56; Roscoe Pound, "Frederic E. Clements as I Knew Him," *Ecology* 35 (April 1954): 112–14; Hagen, *Entangled Bank,* 20–22, 172; Paul B. Sears, "Some Notes on the Ecology of Ecologists," *Scientific Monthly* 83 (July 1956): 24–25; Kingsland, *Evolution of American Ecology,* 145–46,

138, 140; Croker, *Stephen Forbes,* 125; Eric Enno Tamm, *Beyond the Outer Shores: The Untold Odyssey of Ed Ricketts, the Pioneering Ecologist Who Inspired John Steinbeck and Joseph Campbell* (New York: Thunder's Mouth, 2005), 8.

18. McIntosh, "Ecology since 1900," 354–55; W. F. Ganong, "The Cardinal Principles of Ecology," *Science* 19 (25 March 1904): 493, 494; Donald Worster, *Nature's Economy: The Roots of Ecology* (San Francisco: Sierra Club Books, 1977), 191–93, 203; R. Goodland, "Review: History of 'Ecology,'" *Science* 188 (25 April 1975): 313; G. E. Nichols, "Plant Ecology," *Ecology* 3 (July 1928): 267–70; Sears, "Some Notes," 23, 24; Kingsland, *Evolution of American Ecology,* 128–32.

19. McIntosh, "Ecology since 1900," 359–60; Hagen, *Entangled Bank,* 50–51, 74–77, 99, 122–23; Betty Jean Craige, *Eugene Odum: Ecosystem Ecologist and Environmentalist* (Athens: University of Georgia Press, 2001), 24–27; Robert A. Croker, *Pioneer Ecologist: The Life and Work of Victor Ernest Shelford, 1877–1968* (Washington, D.C.: Smithsonian Institution Press, 1991), 45–90; Kingsland, *Evolution of American Ecology,* 129–32, 165, 186–89.

20. Char Miller, *Gifford Pinchot and the Making of Modern Environmentalism* (Washington, D.C.: Island, 2001), 336–38; Donald Worster, *Dust Bowl: The Southern Plains in the 1930s* (New York: Oxford University Press, 1979), 198–209; Donald Worster, *The Wealth of Nature: Environmental History and the Ecological Imagination* (New York: Oxford University Press, 1993), 71–83; Kingsland, *Evolution of American Ecology,* 149.

21. Worster, *Nature's Economy,* 232; Robert Gottlieb, *Forcing the Spring: The Transformation of the American Environmental Movement* (Washington, D.C.: Island, 1993), 19–43; McIntosh, "Ecology since 1900," 360–61; Kingsland, *Evolution of American Ecology,* 132.

22. Alton A. Lindsey, "A History of American Conservation," *Ecology* 63 (April 1982): 604; McIntosh, "Ecology since 1900," 360; Worster, *Dust Bowl,* 207–9; Paul B. Sears, "Ecology: A Subversive Subject," *Bioscience* 14 (July 1964): 11–13; Sears, "Some Notes," 27; Kingsland, *Evolution of American Ecology,* 200–201.

23. MSD, "How I Wrote My Everglades Book," in *The Book Lover's Guide to Florida,* ed. Kevin M. McCarthy (Sarasota, Fla.: Pineapple, 1992), 318–19

24. *MH,* 27 April 1923.

25. "Marjory Stoneman Douglas: Crusading Friend of the Everglades," *IMC Journal* 2 (Autumn 1984): 18; MSD to Mrs. Parker, 11 June 1985, MSDP, box 40, folder 21; Garald G. Parker, "Truth about the Everglades," speech, n.d., MSDP, box 25, folder 27; *MH,* 7 April 1990.

26. Parker, interview; Garald G. Parker Sr., abbreviated résumé, 26 June 1991, Garald G. Parker Collection, USF; *Brandon Times,* 8 October 2004.

27. Parker, interview; *MH,* 7 April 1990.

28. Parker, interview; David McCally, *The Everglades: An Environmental History* (Gainesville: University Press of Florida, 1999), 146–47; "The Proposed Everglades National Park," *Science* 77 (17 February 1933): 185; G. G. Parker, *Interim Report on the Investigations of Water Resources in Southeastern Florida with Special Reference to the Miami Area in Dade County* (Tallahassee: Florida Geological Survey, 1944).

29. Parker, interview; McCally, *Everglades,* 146–47; "Proposed Everglades National Park," 185; Parker, *Interim Report;* "The Paradox of Florida's Water Supply," *Florida Trend* 16 (February 1973): 28–29, 31–32, 34, 36, 38, 40, 42, 44, 46.

30. Parker, "Truth about the Everglades"; Parker, interview.

31. MSD to Mrs. Parker, 11 June 1985, MSDP, box 40, folder 21; Parker, interview.

32. John H. Davis Jr. to MSD, 6, 13 December 1943, "Some References on the Everglades," 1943, both in MSDP, box 42, folder 45; draft acknowledgments, 1947 edition of *The Everglades: River of Grass,* MSDP, box 42, folder 54; MSD, "How I Wrote My Everglades Book," in *The Book Lover's Guide to Florida,* ed. Kevin M. McCarthy (Sarasota, Fla.: Pineapple, 1992), 318–19.

33. MSD to Mrs. Parker, 11 June 1985, MSDP, box 40, folder 21.

34. Parker, interview; Hugh Willoughby, *Across the Everglades: A Canoe Journey of Exploration* (Philadelphia: Lippincott, 1900), 14; *North Miami Sun Reporter,* 18 April 1984; *Special Voices, Two Florida Women: Marjorie Carr, Marjory Stoneman Douglas,* video production (Florida Atlantic University/Florida International University, Joint Center for Environmental and Urban Problems, 1985).

35. Carol Fitzgerald, *Rivers of America,* 1:169; "60th Anniversary of 'Rivers of America' Book Series Celebrated at the Library of Congress on April 9 and 10, 1997," *News from the Library of Congress,* 7 April 1997, available online at http://www.loc.gov/today/pr/1997/97-067.html (accessed winter 2004); *River of Grass,* 10; Carol Fitzgerald to MSD, 25 September 1989, HP.

36. Michael P. Branch, "Writing the Swamp: Marjory Stoneman Douglas and *The Everglades: River of Grass,*" in *Such News of the Land: U.S. Women Nature Writers,* ed. Thomas S. Edwards and Elizabeth A. De Wolfe (Hanover, N.H.: University Press of New England, 2001), 130.

37. *River of Grass,* 92.

38. Frances Fitzgerald, *America Revised* (Boston: Little, Brown, 1979), 92–105.

39. Melville J. Herskovits to MSD, 13 July 1944, 25 April 1946, MSDP, box 42, folder 49; Lydia Parrish to MSD, 22 September 1945, box 42, folder 42; Howard Sharp to MSD, 27 January 1947, MSDP, box 40, folder 15; *River of Grass,* 387; Carol Fitzgerald, *Rivers of America,* 1:194.

CHAPTER TWENTY-FIVE: The Park Idea

1. John C. Paige, *The Civilian Conservation Corps and the National Park Service, 1933–1942* (Washington, D.C.: National Park Service, 1985), 1–19; Linda Flint McClelland, *Presenting Nature: The Historic Landscape Design of the National Park Service, 1916 to 1942* (Washington, D.C.: National Park Service, 1993), 195, 200–203; A. L. Riesch Owen, *Conservation under F.D.R.* (New York: Praeger, 1983), 1–37; Leslie Alexander Lacy, *The Soil Soldiers: The Civilian Conservation Corps in the Great Depression* (Radnor, Pa.: Chilton, 1976), 10–21.

2. Perry H. Merrill, *Roosevelt's Forest Army: A History of the Civilian Conservation Corps, 1933–1942* (Montpelier, Vt.: Merrill, 1981), 120–22; Dave Nelson, "'Improving' Paradise: The Civilian Conservation Corps and Environmental Change in Florida," in *Paradise Lost? The Environmental History of Florida,* ed. Jack E. Davis and Raymond Arsenault (Gainesville: University Press of Florida, 2005), 92–112. The seven include Highlands Hammock, Myakka River, Hillsborough River, Fort Clinch, Goldhead Branch, Florida Caverns, and Torreya State Parks.

3. Dave Nelson to author, 17 May 2005; Nelson, "'Improving' Paradise." See also David J. Nelson, "Relief and Recreation: The Civilian Conservation Corps and the Florida Park Service, 1935–1942" (master's thesis, Florida State University, 2002).

4. Jay Barnes, *Florida's Hurricane History,* revised by Grady Norton (Chapel Hill: University of North Carolina Press, 1998), 140–42; May Mann Jennings, "Royal Palm State Park," July 1939, MMJP, box 23; Mrs. W. S. Jennings to Mr. E. E. Atkinson, 28 October 1933, 10 May 1934, May Mann Jennings, "Royal Palm State Park, C.C.C. Camp Work," n.d., George W. Davis, "A Message to the Florida Federation of Women's Clubs from the Florida Conservation Committee," n.d., Mrs. W. S. Jennings to Mr. Robert M. Shearer, 23 April 1934, Mrs. W. S. Jennings to Governor Dave Sholtz, 28 October 1933, all in MMJP, box 19.

5. Nelson, "'Improving' Paradise."

6. Nelson, "'Improving' Paradise."

7. Paige, *Civilian Conservation Corps,* 103–5, 117–20; McClelland, *Presenting Nature,* 97, 195–226; "From President Roosevelt's Address at Glacier National Park," Everglades National Park Association, memorandum, 5 August 1934, in Reclaiming the Everglades, online database sponsored by the State University System of Florida, available at http://everglades.fiu.ed/reclaim (accessed summer 2008).

8. *MH,* 25 May 1930; Ernest F. Coe, "America's Tropical Frontier: A Park," *Landscape Architecture* 27 (October 1936): 6–11.

9. Paul S. Sutter, *Driven Wild: How the Fight against Automobiles Launched the Modern Wilderness Movement* (Seattle: University of Washington Press, 2002), 100–141; "A Change of Policy for the National Parks," *Ecology* 7 (January 1926): 112; Robert Sterling Yard, "Reorganization of the National Parks Association," *Science* 73 (January 1931): 33–34; Henry Baldwin Ward, "Maintaining the Standards and the Scientific Usefulness of the National Parks," *Science* 69 (January 1929): 14–15.

10. *MH,* 22 October 1939; Alfred Runte, *National Parks: The American Experience* (Lincoln: University of Nebraska Press, 1929), 1332–33; Sutter, *Driven Wild,* 131–34; "Change of Policy"; "Minutes of Meeting of Executive Committee, Everglades National Park Commission," Jacksonville, Florida, 21 October 1946, 4–41, 42–43, Everglades National Park Commission Papers, Special Collections, Robert Manning Strozier Library, Florida State University, Tallahassee.

11. Victor E. Shelford, "The Preservation of Natural Biotic Communities," *Ecology* 14 (April 1933): 240–45; Victor E. Shelford, "Nature Sanctuaries—A Means of Saving Natural Biotic Communities," *Science* 77 (17 March 1933): 281–82; V. E. Shelford, "Conservation versus Preservation," *Science* 77 (2 June 1933): 535; "A Scientist on Park Standards," *Regional Review* 1 (November 1938): 20; Mark A. Harwell, "Science and Environmental Decision Making in South Florida," *Ecological Applications* 8 (August 1998): 583–84; Michael Soulé and Reed Noss, "Rewilding and Biodiversity: Complementary Goals for Conservation," *Wild Earth* 8 (Fall 1998): 3–4; Craig L. Shafer, "Conservation Biology Trailblazers: George Wright, Ben Thompson, and Joseph Dixon," *Conservation Biology* 15 (April 2001): 332–44; George W. Wright, Joseph S. Dixon, and Ben H. Thompson, *Fauna of the National Parks of the United States: A Preliminary Survey of Fauna Relations in National Parks* (Washington, D.C.: U.S. Government Printing Office, 1933).

12. Sutter, *Driven Wild,* 132–33; Robert A. Croker, *Pioneer Ecologist: The Life and Work of Victor Ernest Shelford, 1877–1968* (Washington, D.C.: Smithsonian Institution Press, 1991), 120–44.

13. Runte, *National Parks,* 131.

14. *MH,* 25 May 1930; *Establishment of Everglades National Park: Hearings before the Committee on the Public Lands, House of Representatives,* 71st Cong., 3rd sess. (Washington, D.C.: U.S. Government Publishing Office, 1931), 25, 29, 44; Howard A. Kelly, "The Everglades National Park," *Journal of the Maryland Academy of Sciences* 2 (January 1931): 42; Tropic Everglades National Park Association, Bulletin 4-D, 18 March 1932, in Reclaiming the Everglades.

15. David Fairchild, "The Unique Everglades," 20 December 1933, in Reclaiming the Everglades; Coe, "America's Tropical Frontier"; Everglades National Park Association, "Attributes," 17 January 1936, in Reclaiming the Everglades; *Tropic Everglades National Park: Letter from the Secretary of the Interior,* House Doc. 654, 71st Cong., 3rd sess., 3 December 1930, 22; Ernest F. Coe to Harold L. Ickes, 17 May 1933, "Striking Features of the Proposed Everglades National Park," press release, 20 May 1933, Ernest F. Coe to Director, 1 August 1934, all in J. Hardin Peterson Collection, box 55, Everglades National Park Correspondence folder, PKY.

16. Ernest F. Coe, "Re-Proposed Tropic Everglades National Park: Location the Cape-Sable Region of South Florida," 25 October 1928, in Reclaiming the Everglades; Ernest F. Coe to Edward W. Pou, 16 February 1933, Peterson Collection, box 55, Everglades National Park Correspondence folder; *Establishment of Everglades National Park* (1931), 26–27.

17. "Scientist on Park Standards," 20; "Proposed Everglades National Park," 2–3, 6–7; *Establishment of Everglades National Park* (1931), 25; Frederic E. Clements, "Nature and Structure of the Climax," *Journal of Ecology* 24 (February 1936): 256.

18. *WP,* 1 December 1929; Ernest F. Coe to Harold L. Ickes, 17 May 1933, Peterson Collection, box 55, Everglades National Park Correspondence folder; Wright, Dixon, and Thompson, *Fauna;* Runte, *National Parks,* 132–35, 139; Sutter, *Driven Wild,* 134–35.

19. Daniel B. Beard, "Diversity in the Everglades," *Regional Review* 1 (August 1938): 25; Daniel B. Beard, *Wildlife Reconnaissance: Everglades National Park Project* (Washington, D.C.: U.S. Government Printing Office, 1938); *Orlando Sunday Sentinel-Star,* 9 March 1947.

20. Runte, *National Parks,* 108, 130, 135; *Zephyrhills News,* 27 June 1947; Soulé and Noss, "Rewilding and Biodoversity," 3.

21. *WP,* 17, 20, 21 March 1935; *NYT,* 17 March 1935; U.S. Congress, Senate, *Distribution of Seminole Judgment Funds, Hearings before the U.S. Senate Select Committee on Indian Affairs,* 2 March 1978, 95th Cong., 2nd sess. (Washington, D.C.: U.S. Government Printing Office, 1978), 147.

22. Harry A. Kersey Jr., *The Florida Seminoles and the New Deal, 1933–1942* (Boca Raton: Florida Atlantic University Press, 1989), 75–77; *River of Grass,* 372; Patsy West, *The Enduring Seminoles: From Alligator Wrestling to Ecotourism* (Gainesville: University Press of Florida, 1998), 54–55; U.S. Congress, Senate, *Distribution of Seminole Judgment Funds,* 166–67.

23. Kersey, *Florida Seminoles,* 69–72, 77, 78, 89–90; Fergus M. Bordewich, *Killing the White Man's Indian: Reinventing Native Americans at the End of the Twentieth Century* (New York: Anchor, 1996), 71–72, 121–23; *River of Grass,* 373.

24. For an excellent study of the relationship between Indians and national parks, see Mark David Spence, *Dispossessing the Wilderness: Indian Removal and the Making of the National Parks* (New York: Oxford University Press, 1999).

25. Kersey, *Florida Seminoles,* 6–7; *Florida,* 12–13; *MH,* 10 March 1940; Millicent Todd Bingham, "Miami: A Study in Urban Geography," *Tequesta* 9 (1949): 92–93; U.S. Congress, Senate, *Distribution of Seminole Judgment Funds,* 150.

26. Harry A. Kersey Jr., *The Stranahans of Fort Lauderdale: A Pioneer Family of New River* (Gainesville: University Press of Florida, 2003), 130–45; Kersey, *Florida Seminoles,* 9–10, 12, 38, 56; *MH,* 28 December 1915, 13 April, 5 June 1916; Gale Butler, "Stranahan Recalls Early Lauderdale," *Update* 15 (August 1988): 11; Karen Davis, *Public Faces—Private Lives: Women in South Florida, 1870s–1910s* (Miami: Pickering, 1990), 148.

27. Minnie Moore-Willson, "The Seminole Indians of Florida," *Florida Historical Quarterly* 7 (July 1928): 86–87; Harry A. Kersey Jr., "The 'Friends of the Florida Seminoles' Society: 1899–1926," *Tequesta* 24 (1974): 3–18; Minnie Moore-Willson, "Royal Palm Hammock: To the Club Women of Florida," circa 1915, in Reclaiming the Everglades; Minnie Moore-Willson to Stephen Cochran Singleton, 14 January 1929, in Reclaiming the Everglades; Kersey, *Florida Seminoles,* 56; Claud F. Johnson, *Florida Seminoles Will Have a Home at Last,* 1917, in Reclaiming the Everglades.

28. U.S. Congress, Senate, *Distribution of Seminole Judgment Funds,* 187; *Tampa Tribune,* 5 March 1915; Kersey, *Stranahans of Fort Lauderdale,* 133–34; May M. Jennings to Minnie Moore-Willson, 12 May 1915, Minnie Moore-Willson Papers, box 1, folder 14, UM; Mrs. Frank Jennings to Minnie Moore-Willson, 29 April 1916, Minnie Moore-Willson to Mrs. Jennings, 6 May, 22 March 1916, Moore-Willson Papers, box 1, folder 15; Minnie Moore-Willson to Mrs. Jennings, 4, 6 December 1928, Moore-Willson Papers, box 2, folder 3.

29. Minnie Moore-Willson to MSD, 6 December 1928, Moore-Willson Papers, box 2, folder 3; Minnie Moore-Willson to MSD, 28 August 1925, Moore-Willson

Papers, box 1, folder 24; Ernest F. Coe to Minnie Moore-Willson, 13 April 1932, in Reclaiming the Everglades; Ernest F. Coe to John Collier, 27 March 1935, Mary McDouglas Axelson Papers, box 40, folder 345, UM; Ernest F. Coe to Spessard L. Holland, 2 July 1940, Spessard L. Holland Collection, box 136, Everglades National Park folder, PKY; *MH*, 13 January 1929, 2 April 1933; U.S. Congress, Senate, *Distribution of Seminole Judgment Funds*, 190–91, 194–95, 196–97. It is unclear whether Douglas responded to Moore-Willson's requests for help.

30. U.S. Congress, Senate, *Distribution of Seminole Judgment Funds*, 202–3, 204–5; Minnie Moore-Willson to S. C. Singleton, 24 February 1930, Minnie Moore-Willson to Ruth Bryan Owen, 20 February 1920, both in Miscellaneous Manuscripts, box 7, Stephen C. Singleton folder, PKY.

31. Kersey, *Florida Seminoles*, 94–96; *MH*, 7 April 1990; Robert H. Keller and Michael F. Turek, *American Indians and National Parks* (Tucson: University of Arizona Press, 1999), 227–30.

CHAPTER TWENTY-SIX: Dedications

1. Diary, June 1947, MSDP, box 27; *Voice*, 197.

2. Carol Fitzgerald, *The Rivers of America: A Descriptive Biography* (New Castle, Del.: Oak Knoll, 2001), 1:170, 191–93; Dava Sobel, "Still Fighting the Good Fight for the Everglades," *Audubon*, July–August 1991, 38.

3. Fitzgerald, *Rivers of America*, 1:170–71.

4. *MH*, 15, 24 December 1940; "National Park Project Is Under Way," clipping, n.d., Spessard L. Holland Collection, box 136, PKY.

5. *Orlando Sentinel-Star*, 16 March 1947; *MH*, 22 October 1947; "Everglades National Park Commission," unpublished list, MMJP, box 22; Theodore Pratt, "Papa of the Everglades National Park," *SEP*, 9 August 1947, 32–33; MSD, "The Forgotten Man Who Saved the Everglades," *Audubon*, September 1971, 94–95, MMJP; "Official Meeting of the Executive Committee of the Everglades National Park Commission at the Lunsford Lodge on Windley Island," 15 June 1946, Everglades National Park Commission Papers, Special Collections, Robert Manning Strozier Library, Florida State University, Tallahassee; Ernest F. Coe to Members, 1 February 1940, "Death Takes Mrs. F. F. Coe," clipping, July 1940, "Notes on Conference between Ernest F. Coe and Spessard L. Holland," 15 August 1940, G. O. Palmer, 27 August 1940, all in Holland Collection, box 136, Everglades National Park folder.

6. Arthur E. Chapman, "John D. Pennekamp," *South Florida History* 28 (Winter 2000): 12–14; "Address by John D. Pennekamp, Legislative Chairman,

Everglades National Park Commission, before the Florida Retail Merchants Association, Orange Court Hotel, Orlando, Florida," 29 October 1947, J. Hardin Peterson Collection, box 56, Everglades National Park Federal and State: Reports, Statements, and Hearings folder, PKY; MSD, "Forgotten Man," 94.

7. "Minutes of Meeting of Executive Committee, Everglades National Park Commission," Jacksonville, Florida, 21 October 1946, 2–4, Everglades National Park Commission Papers; *Orlando Morning Sentinel,* 22 October 1946; "The President's Report to You," *Audubon,* January 1945, 45–52; "The Director Reports to You," *Bird-Lore* 41 (September 1939): 306–7; John H. Baker, "Wildlife Preservation in the Glades," *Soil Science Society of Florida Proceedings* 5-A (1943): 11–15.

8. "The Everglades," *Economic Geography* 20 (April 1944): n.p.; David McCally, *The Everglades: An Environmental History* (Gainesville: University Press of Florida, 1999), 161–64; Alfred Jackson Hanna and Kathryn Abbey Hanna, *Lake Okeechobee: Wellspring of the Everglades* (Indianapolis: Bobbs-Merrill, 1948), 303; Victor H. Cahalane, "The Everglades—Yesterday, Today and Tomorrow," *Nature* 40 (December 1947): 513.

9. McCally, *Everglades,* 158–59; Hanna and Hanna, *Lake Okeechobee,* 292, 294; R. V. Allison, "The Soil and Water Conservation Problem in the Everglades," *Soil Science Society of Florida Proceedings* 1 (1939): 35–58.

10. Hanna and Hanna, *Lake Okeechobee,* 293, 340.

11. Humble added ten thousand dollars to the prize and donated the money evenly to the University of Florida and the Florida State College for Women.

12. "Minutes," 22; "Address by John D. Pennekamp," 6–8; "Director Reports to You," 305–6; Everglades National Park Landowners Association, "A Short Summary of the Issues Involved in H.R. 4029 (S 285)," July 1949, Mary McDougal Axelson Collection, box 41, folder 354, UM; Hanna and Hanna, *Lake Okeechobee,* 345; "Discovering Florida's First Oil Well," available online at http://www.aoghs .org/DiscoveringFlorida.asp (accessed fall 2006).

13. *Authorizing the Secretary of the Interior to Procure Land for the Everglades National Park, Fla.,* 81st Cong., 1st sess., Senate Report 968, 2 June 1949, 3; R. T. Spangler to W. R. Fokes, 20 August 1943, CPC, s201/35/1A; *MH,* 23 July 1947; *Miami News,* 13 August 1947; Gilbert D. Leach to Claude Pepper, 9 March 1949, CPC, s201/34D/1; Carl W. Hawkins to John D. Pennekamp, 19 February 1949, CPC, s201/34D/1; "Short Summary of the Issues."

14. *NYT,* 20 April 1947; *MH,* 22 July 1947; "Statement of John D. Pennekamp, Legislative Chairman, the Everglades National Park Commission, in Support of

Senate Bill 1212 and House Bill 3378," 14 July 1947, CPC, 5201/34/2; *Authorizing the Secretary of the Interior,* 5–7.

15. "Minutes of Meeting of Landowners of the Everglades Park Area," 18 December 1947, Axelson Collection, box 40, folder 346; "Statement of Ivar Axelson on H.R. 3378 at the Hearing July 14, 1947," Axelson Collection, box 41, folder 355; "Short Summary of the Issues."

16. *MH,* 22, 24 July, 22 October 1947; "Address by John D. Pennekamp," 5–7; "Statement of John D. Pennekamp"; *J. Tom Watson v. J. Edwin Larson,* Motion of Defendant to Dismiss Bill of Complaint, n.d., Chancery Court, Leon County, Fla., no. 9743, *J. Tom Watson v. J. Edwin Larson,* Notice of Hearing, 18 June 1947, Chancery Court, Leon County, Fla., no. 9743, *J. Tom Watson v. Millard Caldwell,* Bill of Complaint, n.d., Chancery Court, Leon County, Fla., *J. Tom Watson v. J. Edwin Larson,* Final Orders, 19 June 1947, Chancery Court, Leon County, Fla., no. 9743, all in National Park Service Records, 1933–44, RG 79, box 900, National Archives and Records Administration, College Park, Maryland.

17. MSD, *Hurricane* (New York: Rinehart, 1958), 291–92; Jay Barnes, *Florida's Hurricane History,* revised by Grady Norton (Chapel Hill: University of North Carolina Press, 1998), 170–74; "Hurricane: Life and Death of Cyclops," *Newsweek,* 29 September 1947, 27–28; *MH,* 17, 18, 19, 20, 21, 29; R. A. Wheeler to Secretary of the Army, "Report on Central and Southern Florida for Flood Control and Other Purposes," CPC, s201/33/11.

18. Jay Barnes, *Florida's Hurricane History,* 176; *WP,* 20 January 1948.

19. Jay Barnes, *Florida's Hurricane History,* 176–78; MSD, *Hurricane,* 292; *MH,* 21 September 1947; Marjorie Dickey Parsons, "The October 1947 Hurricane: Disaster on Top of Disaster," *Broward Legacy* 14 (Summer–Fall 1991): 31–32.

20. *MH,* 19, 20, 21, 22, 23, 24, 25, 26, 27 September, 2 November 1947; *WP,* 18 September 1947; *Wall Street Journal,* 14 October 1947; *NYT,* 14 November 1947; K. M. Throop to Claude Pepper, 7 February 1948, CPC, s201/34/1; J. R. Brennan to O. T. Ray, "Status of Equipment Furnished under Public Law 233," CPC, s201/33/1; Claude Pepper to Millard F. Caldwell, 21 March 1947, CPC, s201/33/1; Paul Rardin to Claude Pepper, 21 March 1947, CPC, s201/33/1; "Estimate of Agricultural Losses in Broward County from Storms of September 21 and October 5, 1948, and Resulting High Waters," Holland Collection, box 287, Flood Control Permanent folder. For letters and resolutions supporting flood control, see Holland Collection, box 287, Flood Control Permanent folder; CPC, box 33.

21. Walter A. Rosenbaum, *The Politics of Environmental Concern* (New York: Praeger, 1977), 170–73; John M. Barry, *Rising Tide: The Great Mississippi Flood*

of 1927 and How It Changed America (New York: Simon and Schuster, 1997); *Christian Science Monitor,* 26 November 1947; *The History of the U.S. Army Corps of Engineers* (Alexandria, Va.: Office of History, U.S. Army Corps of Engineers, 1998), 17–63.

22. *Comprehensive Report on Central and Southern Florida for Flood Control and Other Purposes,* 80th Cong., 2nd sess., House Doc. 643 (Washington, D.C.: U.S. Government Printing Office, 1949); "Department of the Army Corps of Engineers, Public Notice," 31 December 1947, A. G. Mathews, "Chief Engineer, Florida State Board of Conservation, Report," 10 March 1949, both in CPC, 201/1/34; Board of Commissioners, Everglades Drainage District, "Conservation Areas in the Everglades," 25 February 1947, Holland Collection, box 287, Flood Control Permanent folder; Millard F. Caldwell, "Water Conservation," speech before State Cattlemen's Association, St. Petersburg, Fla., 12 November 1947, Millard F. Caldwell Collection, box 10, Speeches Delivered April–October 1947 folder, PKY; *NYT,* 21 December 1947; *Christian Science Monitor,* 26 November 1947.

23. Claude Pepper to Associated Press, 25 May 1949, CPC, s201/34/1; John H. Banks to Spessard Holland, 12 July 1948, Holland Collection, box 287, Flood Control Hearing folder; *Tampa Tribune,* 2 November 1947.

24. Michael Grunwald, *The Swamp: The Everglades, Florida, and the Politics of Paradise* (New York: Simon and Schuster, 2006), 228–29; Nelson M. Blake, *Land into Water—Water into Land: A History of Water Management in Florida* (Tallahassee: Florida State University Press, 1980), 179.

25. *WP,* 20 January 1952, 12 July 1957; David McCally, "The Everglades and the Florida Dream," in *Paradise Lost? The Environmental History of Florida,* ed. Jack E. Davis and Raymond Arsenault (Gainesville: University Press of Florida, 2005), 153; Blake, *Land into Water,* 153, 263.

26. Florida Department of State, *Waters of Destiny* (Atlanta: International Sound Films, 1955).

27. Big Bend and Olympic National Parks were authorized after but dedicated before Everglades.

28. "The President's Third Visit to Key West," Log 3, 14–15, 3–8 December 1947, available online at www.trumanlittlewhitehouse.com (accessed fall 2006); *NYT,* 7 December 1947; *WP,* 22 June 1947.

29. Spessard L. Holland to John D. Pennekamp, 19 November 1947, CPC, s201/34A/1; John H. Baker to MSD, 21 November 1947, MSDP, box 42, folder 42; U.S. Department of the Interior, "Invitations," 28 October 1947, National Park Service

Records, 1933–49, RG 79, box 902; Diary, 6 December 1947, MSDP, box 27; *Authorizing the Secretary of the Interior,* 6; reserved seat invitation to Everglades National Park dedication, MSDP, box 42, folder 41; Harold L. Ickes to Mr. Coe, 8 January 1946, Peterson Collection, box 55, Everglades National Park Correspondence folder; Ernest F. Coe to Director Drury, 10 December 1947, National Park Service Records, 1933–49, RG 79, box 902; J. D. Coffman to Ernest F. Coe, 26 July 1947, National Park Service Records, 1933–49, RG 79, box 900; Pratt, "Papa"; MSD, "Forgotten Man," 95.

30. "Dedication Ceremonies for Everglades National Park, Everglades, Florida, December 6, 1947," program and speeches, 3–10, MMJP, box 22; "President's Third Visit," 12; *Florida,* 282.

31. "Dedication Ceremonies," 10–13; *NYT,* 7 December 1947; "Glistening River," clipping, n.d., "A Great Day for Florida," clipping, n.d., both in CPC, 201/35/1; *MH,* 7 December 1947; *Fort Myers News-Press,* 7 December 1947.

32. Grunwald, *Swamp,* 230.

33. MSD to Marjorie Kinnan Rawlings, 8 December 1947, Douglas, Marjory-ALS-MKR, 1947, December 8, folder, Marjorie Kinnan Rawlings Papers, box 1, PKY; *MH,* 2 November 1947.

34. *NYT,* 23, 30 November 1947; *New York Herald Tribune,* 7 December 1947; first-day cover for commemorative stamp and accompanying card, 5 December 1947, in Reclaiming the Everglades, online database sponsored by the State University System of Florida, available at http://everglades.fiu.edu/reclaim (accessed summer 2008); Harnett T. Kane, draft review of *The Everglades: River of Grass,* MSDP, box 2, folder 48; Russell Kay to MSD, 2 January 1948, MSDP, box 42, folder 41; John Selby to MSD, 12 December 1947, MSDP, box 47, folder 110; George O'Hara to MSD, 19 December 1947, MSDP, box 42, folder 42; miscellaneous clippings, MSDP, box 42, folder 41.

35. Junius Elmore Dovell, "A History of the Everglades of Florida" (Ph.D. diss., University of North Carolina at Chapel Hill, 1947); J. E. Dovell, review of *The Everglades: River of Grass,* by MSD, *Florida Historical Quarterly* 26 (January 1948): 275–78; Carol Fitzgerald, *Rivers of America,* 1:193.

36. MSD to Marjorie Kinnan Rawlings, 8 December 1947, Rawlings Papers; John D. Pennekamp to Claude Pepper, 1 July 1947, CPC, s201/34/2; Newton B. Drury to MSD, 9 December 1947, Herbert Evison to MSD, 9 December 1947, both in MSDP, box 42, folder 43; Margaret MacGready to MSD, 11 November 1947, Lawrence E. Will to MSD, 2 December 1947, MSDP, box 42, folder 42;

Ernest F. Coe to MSD, 30 December 1947, MSDP, box 40, Correspondence, 1930–45 folder.

37. MSD, "The Everglades Face the Future," *Trailways* 9 (Fall 1944): 9–10, 26, 28; *River of Grass,* 381–85.

38. MSD, "What Are They Doing to the Everglades?" circa 1948, in Reclaiming the Everglades; Garald G. Parker, "Truth about the Everglades," speech, n.d., MSDP, box 25, folder 27; Garald G. Parker Sr., interview by David McCally, 27 February 1992, Oral History Program, University of South Florida Library, Tampa.

39. *River of Grass,* 24–25, 286.

40. Marian Murray, "Prophetess in Prose," *Florida Speaks* 4 (April 1952): 75; John H. Baker to MSD, 21 November 1947, MSDP, box 42, folder 42; Norman S. Giles, review, *The Everglades: River of Grass, Quarterly Review of Biology* 23 (December 1948): 346. For an interpretation of metaphor and a natural place, see Deborah E. Popper and Frank J. Popper, "The Buffalo Commons: Metaphor as Method," *Geographical Review* 89 (October 1999): 491–510.

41. MSD, speech to Florida Historical Society.

CHAPTER TWENTY-SEVEN: An Unnecessary Drought

1. Alfred Runte, *National Parks: The American Experience* (Lincoln: University of Nebraska Press, 1929), 146, 187; Marc Reisner, *Cadillac Desert: The American West and Its Disappearing Water* (New York: Penguin, 1987), 284–85; Wallace Stegner, ed., *This Is Dinosaur: Echo Park Country and Its Magic Rivers* (New York: Knopf, 1955); *NYT,* 21 March 1954.

2. *NYT,* 4 September 1960; *WP,* 20 January 1952, 12 July 1957.

3. Peter Farb, "Disaster Threatens the Everglades," *Audubon,* September–October 1965, 302–7; Wallace Stegner, "Last Chance for the Everglades," *Saturday Review,* 6 May 1967, 22–23, 72–73.

4. Daniel B. Beard, *Wildlife Reconnaissance: Everglades National Park Project* (Washington, D.C.: U.S. Government Printing Office, 1938); *Fort Myers News-Press,* 3 June 1962; "The Vanishing Everglades," clipping, 1964, Conservation folder, Special Collections, Rollins College, Winter Park, Fla.; *Christian Science Monitor,* 5 February, 23 June 1965; *NYT,* 28 November 1965; *Orlando Evening Star,* 10 October 1967.

5. Edwin A. Roberts Jr., "Disaster Stalks Florida's Everglades," *Florida* (*Orlando Sentinel*), clipping, circa 1965, Conservation folder, Special Collections, Rollins College; Gene Marine, "Algae and Aerojet," in *The Environmental Destruction of South Florida: A Handbook for Citizens,* ed. William Ross McCluney (Coral Gables, Fla.: University of Miami Press, 1971), 30–32; United Nations Educational, Scientific, and Cultural Organization, "Convention Concerning the Protection of the World Cultural and Natural Heritage, World Heritage List; Nomination Submitted by the United States of America, Everglades National Park," 3 February 1979, 10, HP.

6. Stegner, "Last Chance for the Everglades," 22–23; Farb, "Disaster Threatens the Everglades," 306–7; *Christian Science Monitor,* 23 June 1965; *NYT,* 5 June 1961, 28 November 1965; *Fort Myers News-Press,* 3 June 1962.

7. *NYT,* 16 June 1968; Farb, "Disaster Threatens the Everglades," 306–8; Stegner, "Last Chance for the Everglades," 72; Nelson M. Blake, *Land into Water—Water into Land: A History of Water Management in Florida* (Tallahassee: Florida State University Press, 1980), 184.

8. S. H. DuBon to "Dear Congressman," 19 October 1965, CPC, s301/613/4; Allen Beck to "Dear Sir," 24 May 1965, CPC, s301/613/5; Lisa Klein to Claude Pepper, 10 May 1967, CPC, s301/767/2; Barney H. Spivey to Claude D. Pepper, 19 October 1965, CPC, s301/613/4; Lila A. Livingston to Dante Fascell, 25 May 1965, CPC, s301/613/5; W. C. Kiss Jr. to Claude D. Pepper, 21 October 1965, CPC, s301/613/4; W. D. Mitchell to Dante Fascell, 17 April 1966, CPC, s301/767/2; Richard Rhodes, "The Killing of the Everglades," *Playboy,* January 1972, 154.

9. U.S. Army Corps of Engineers, *Water Resources for Central and Southern Florida,* 90th Cong., 2nd sess., House Doc. 369 (Washington, D.C.: U.S. Government Printing Office, 1968), 20, 31–32, 36, 37; "Statement Concerning Levee 67 Extension of the Central and Southern Florida Project," 27 October 1965, CPC, 301/613/4; U.S. Congress, House, *River Basin Monetary Authorizations and Miscellaneous Civil Works Amendments,* 26 May 1970, 91st Cong., 2nd sess., Report 91-895; "House OKs $1.5 Million to Ease Everglades Woes," clipping, n.d., CPC, s301/770/2; *WP,* 14 November 1968; *Christian Science Monitor,* 15 November 1968.

10. Farb, "Disaster Threatens the Everglades," 308–10; *NYT,* 16 June 1968; Reisner, *Cadillac Desert,* 181; Stegner, "Last Chance for the Everglades," 73; Jackson E. Price to Claude Pepper, 3 June 1966, CPC, s301/767/2; Department of the Army,

Office of Chief of Engineers, press release, 14 April 1966, CPC, s301/613/4; William O. Douglas, "The Public Be Damned," *Playboy*, July 1969, 143, 186–87.

11. Lizabeth Cohen, *A Consumer's Republic: The Politics of Mass Consumption in Postwar America* (New York: Knopf, 2003); Adam Rome, *The Bulldozer in the Countryside: Suburban Sprawl and the Rise of American Environmentalism* (New York: Cambridge University Press, 2001); Robert Gottlieb, *Forcing the Spring: The Transformation of the American Environmental Movement* (Washington, D.C.: Island, 1993), 75–80.

12. *NYT*, 21 December 1953, 5 January, 21 March 1954, 1 January 1956; Linda Lear, *Rachel Carson: The Life of the Author of Silent Spring* (New York: Holt, 1997), 257; Roy E. Huffman, "The Role of Private Enterprise in Water Resources Development," *Land and Contemporary Problems* 22 (Summer 1957): 433–43; Elmo Richardson, "The Interior Secretary as Conservation Villain: The Notorious Case of Douglas 'Giveaway' McKay," *Pacific Historical Review* 41 (August 1972): 333–45.

13. Lynne Page Snyder, "'The Death-Dealing Smog over Donora, Pennsylvania': Industrial Air Pollution, Public Health, and Federal Policy, 1915–1963" (Ph.D. diss., University of Pennsylvania, 1994); *Christian Science Monitor*, 4 November 1954; Scott H. Dewey, "The Fickle Finger of Phosphate: Central Florida Air Pollution and the Failure of Environmental Policy, 1957–1970," *Journal of Southern History* 65 (August 1999): 568; Stephen Fox, *The American Conservation Movement: John Muir and His Legacy* (Madison: University of Wisconsin Press, 1981), 303.

14. *NYT*, 1 January 1956; *Christian Science Monitor*, 4 November 1954.

15. James C. Cobb, *The Selling of the South: The Southern Crusade for Industrial Development, 1936–1980* (Baton Rouge: Louisiana State University Press, 1982); Scott Hamilton Dewey, "'Is This What We Came to Florida For?': Florida Women and the Fight against Air Pollution in the 1960s," in *Making Waves: Female Activists in Twentieth-Century Florida*, ed. Jack E. Davis and Kari Frederickson (Gainesville: University Press of Florida, 2003), 199–201; June Cleo and Hank Mesouf, *Florida's Polluted Paradise* (Philadelphia: Chilton, 1964); Charles Irvin Harding, Samuel B. McKee, and J. J. Schueneman, *A Report on Florida's Air Resources* (Jacksonville: Florida State Board of Health, 1961), 28–29, 31.

16. Fox, *American Conservation Movement*, 272–90; Gottlieb, *Forcing the Spring*, 81–86; Philip Shabecoff, *A Fierce Green Fire: The American Environmental Movement* (New York: Hill and Wang, 1993), 103–4. The legal defense funds

were created as separate entities in part so that the parent organizations could retain their tax-exempt status. Lawmakers and others who objected to the political activities of the parent organizations tried to silence them by insisting that they should relinquish their tax-exempt status if they engaged in lobbying practices.

17. Betty Jean Craige, *Eugene Odum: Ecosystem Ecologist and Environmentalist* (Athens: University of Georgia Press, 2001), 8–44; Joel B. Hagen, *An Entangled Bank: The Origins of Ecosystem Ecology* (New Brunswick, N.J.: Rutgers University Press, 1992), 122–45; Robert P. McIntosh, "Ecology since 1900," in *History of American Ecology* (New York: Arno, 1977), 361–68.

18. Robert A. Croker, *Pioneer Ecologist: The Life and Work of Victor Ernest Shelford, 1877–1968* (Washington, D.C.: Smithsonian Institution Press, 1991), 144–46; McIntosh, "Ecology since 1900," 368–69; Angus M. Woodbury, "Colorado Dam Controversy," *Scientific Monthly*, June 1956, 304–13.

19. Susan L. Flader, *Thinking like a Mountain: Aldo Leopold and the Evolution of an Ecological Attitude toward Deer, Wolves, and Forests* (Columbia: University of Missouri Press, 1974), 1–35; Fox, *American Conservation Movement*, 244–49; Gottlieb, *Forcing the Spring*, 33–35; McIntosh, "Ecology since 1900," 361; Aldo Leopold, "Wilderness as a Form of Land Use," *Journal of Land and Public Utility Economics* 1 (October 1925): 398–404; Aldo Leopold, *A Sand County Almanac and Sketches Here and There* (New York: Oxford University Press, 1987).

20. *NYT*, 18 December 1949; *MH*, 21 October 1984; Paul B. Sears, "Ecology: A Subversive Subject," *Bioscience* 14 (July 1964): 11–13; Leopold, *Sand County Almanac*, 204.

21. A few predecessors to *Silent Spring* include Fairfield Osborn, *Our Plundered Planet* (Boston: Little, Brown, 1948); William Voght, *Road to Survival* (New York: Sloane, 1948); Murray Bookchin, *Our Synthetic Environment* (New York: Knopf, 1962).

22. Paul Brooks, *The House of Life: Rachel Carson at Work* (Boston: Houghton Mifflin, 1989), xi.

23. Lear, *Rachel Carson*, 166–67; Brooks, *House of Life*, 81–83; Glen Simmons and Laura Ogden, *Gladesmen: Gator Hunters, Moonshiners, and Skiffers* (Gainesville: University Press of Florida, 1998), 148.

24. Joan Gill Blank, *Key Biscayne: A History of Miami's Tropical Island and the Cape Florida Lighthouse* (Sarasota, Fla.: Pineapple, 1996), xi.

25. Fox, *American Conservation Movement*, 292–99; Lear, *Rachel Carson*, 396–456.

26. Kirkpatrick Sale, *The Green Revolution: The American Environmental Movement, 1962–1992* (New York: Hill and Wang, 1993), 3–5; Gottlieb, *Forcing the Spring,* 86.

27. Herbert R. Mills, "Broadcasting DDT," *Florida Naturalist* 19 (July 1946): 57–62; Herbert R. Mills, "Another Look at DDT," *Florida Naturalist* 22 (July 1949): 71–78; Dewey, "'Is This What We Came to Florida For?'" 205–11; Dewey, "Fickle Finger of Phosphate," 565–603; Harding, McKee, and Schueneman, *Report,* 22–28, 51–53; David M. Oshinsky, *Polio: An American Story* (New York: Oxford University Press, 2005), 2–3, 162.

28. Raymond Arsenault, *St. Petersburg and the Florida Dream, 1888–1950* (Norfolk, Va.: Donning, 1988), 88; *Christian Science Monitor,* 6 December 1957; *NYT,* 30 November 1958.

29. Bruce Stephenson, "A 'Monstrous Desecration': Dredge and Fill in Boca Ciega Bay," in *Paradise Lost? The Environmental History of Florida,* ed. Jack E. Davis and Raymond Arsenault (Gainesville: University Press of Florida, 2005), 326–49.

30. Stegner, "Last Chance for the Everglades," 73.

CHAPTER TWENTY-EIGHT: Perishing and Publishing

1. "Herald Founder's Widow Dies" and "Mrs. Frank Stoneman Is Dead at Age of 89," clippings, n.d., Mrs. Alfred Peacock Collection, HMSF.

2. Rhode Island Historical Cemeteries Transcription Project Index, available online at www.rootsweb.com/~rigenweb/cemetery/cemetery362.html (accessed summer 2005); *Voice,* 195–97, 219; Helen Muir, interview by author, 11 March 1999; MSD to Hannah Kahn, Hannah Kahn Papers, UM; MSD, "Mabel White Dorn, 1899–1972," MSDP, box 54, folder 6.

3. Al Burt, *Becalmed in the Mullet Latitudes: Al Burt's Florida* (Port Salerno, Fla.: Classics Library, 1983), 132; MSD, "The Forgotten Man Who Saved the Everglades," *Audubon,* September 1971, 78–79; *MH,* 2 January 1951; *Orlando Sentinel,* 24 February 1950.

4. Jean Areson, interview by author, 10 June 2000; Julia Allen Field, interview by author, 15 August 2002.

5. Rinehart and Company, tax forms, 1948, 1949, 1952, Rinehart and Company, royalty statements, 1 July, 31 December 1952, 1 January, 30 June 1953, 1 July 1957, 31 December 1958, 17 April 1959, Stanley M. Rinehart Jr. to MSD, 5 December

1955, 19, 24 February 1959, Jean Crawford to MSD, 12 March 1954, 30 September 1957, all in MSDP, box 47, folder 110; *NYT,* 3 September 1950.

6. *New York Herald-Tribune,* 6 January 1952; *NYT,* 6 January 1952; *Sarasota Herald-Tribune,* 6 January 1952; "Poetry, Fiction, and Drama" (review of MSD, *Road to the Sun), College English* 13 (April 1952): 414; Rinehart and Company, royalty statements, 1 January–30 June 1952, agreement between Rinehart and Company and MSD, 1 December 1949, all in MSDP, box 47, folder 110; Marjorie Kinnan Rawlings to MSD, 26 January 1952, MSDP, box 22, folder 205; B. F. Ashe to MSD, 2 May 1952, MSDP, box 40, folder 17.

7. MSD, *Road to the Sun* (New York: Rinehart, 1951), 3; Marc Reisner, *Cadillac Desert: The American West and Its Disappearing Water* (New York: Penguin, 1987), 61–93.

8. Erick Berry to MSD, 29 November 1951, MSDP, box 22, folder 206; Erick Berry to MSD, 10 January 1952, MSDP, box 47, folder 12; Stanley M. Rinehart Jr. to MSD, 13, 22 August 1952, MSDP, box 47, folder 110.

9. *NYT,* 12 November 1952; Alice Dalgliesh to MSD, 18 November 1953, "New Series Fiction about Each State," *New York Herald-Tribune* clipping, n.d., both in MSDP, box 47, folder 112.

10. Erick Berry to MSD, 29 November 1951, MSDP, box 22, folder 206; MSD, *Freedom River* (Miami: Valiant, 1994). For a more comprehensive interpretation of *Freedom River,* see Melissa Walker, "*Freedom River:* A Book for the Next Millennium," *Marjory Kinnan Rawlings Journal of Florida Literature* 8 (Special Issue 1997): 35–44.

11. Marian Murray, "Prophetess in Prose," *Florida Speaks* 4 (April 1952): 75.

12. Donald O. Cowgill and Mary S. Cowgill, "An Index of Segregation Based on Block Statistics," *American Sociological Review* 16 (December 1951): 828–29, 830; Raymond A. Mohl, "Shadows in the Sunshine: Race and Ethnicity in Miami," *Tequesta* 49 (1989): 66–70; Raymond A. Mohl, "Elizabeth Virrick and the 'Concrete Monsters': Housing Reform in Postwar Miami," *Tequesta* 61 (2001): 12–13.

13. Laura Breckenridge Danahy, "Elizabeth Virrick, the Maverick of Miami Slum Clearance," in *Making Waves: Female Activists in Twentieth-Century Florida,* ed. Jack E. Davis and Kari Frederickson (Gainesville: University Press of Florida, 2003), 250 55.

14. Mohl, "Elizabeth Virrick"; Raymond A. Mohl, "Trouble in Paradise: Race and Housing in Miami during the New Deal Era," *Prologue: The Journal of the National Archives* 19 (Spring 1987): 3–21; Danahy, "Elizabeth Virrick," 250–61;

MSD, "Slum Clearance, Community Style," n.d., Elizabeth Virrick Collection, box 2, HMSF; *MH,* 15 September 2002.

15. Mohl, "Elizabeth Virrick"; Danahy, "Elizabeth Virrick"; MSD, "Slum Clearance, Community Style."

16. MSD, "Cities Face Their Slums," *Ladies' Home Journal,* October 1950, 23, 224–25; Burt to MSD, 2 July 1953, Elizabeth Virrick to MSD, September 27, 1951, MSD and Elizabeth Virrick, "People against Slums," book prospectus, n.d., MSD and Elizabeth Virrick, "Who Wants Slums?" n.d., all in Virrick Collection, box 2.

17. *MH,* 21 November 1922.

18. Cindy Thorner, interview by author, 25 July 2002; Mildred Cowan, interview by author, 16 August 2002; Howard Dixon, interview by author, 16 August 2002; *MH* 16, 18, 21, 23 July 1954; *Miami Daily News,* 6, 10 July 1954; "The Report of the Nominating Committee of the Greater Miami Chapter of the American Civil Liberties Union," February 1956, Cindy Thorner Papers, in possession of author; Leslie B. Bain, "Red Hunt in Miami: Who Formed the Posse?" *Nation,* 7 August 1954, 110–12.

19. List, box 12, Organizations List—Dade County Individuals Belonging to Various Groups folder, Florida Legislative Investigation Committee Collection, FSA.

20. "Constitutional Defense Letter," circa 1954, Thorner Papers; "Velde Rushes to Save Miami McCarthyites," *Daily Worker,* September–October 1958, Thorner Papers; "Miami 'Contempt' Sentences Rise to 28; No End Yet in Sight," clipping, n.d., Thorner Papers; *MH,* 20 November 1954; *National Guardian,* 29 November 1954; Robert M. Thorner to American Civil Liberties Union, 27 June, 27 July 1954, Thorner Papers; list, box 12, Organizations List—Dade County Individuals Belonging to Various Groups folder, Florida Legislative Investigation Committee Collection; Greater Miami Chapter, American Civil Liberties Union, "Dear Friend" circular signed by Arnold M. Greenfield, n.d., box 17, Publications—ACLU folder, Florida Legislative Investigation Committee Collection; Application for Charter, American Civil Liberties Union of Greater Miami, Dade County, Florida, 22 July 1955, American Civil Liberties Union of Greater Miami, 1955–59, box 1, folder 1, American Civil Liberties Union of Florida Records, PKY; Florence Morgenroth, "Organization and Activities of the American Civil Liberties Union in Miami, 1955–1966" (master's thesis, University of Miami, 1966).

21. MSD, "Famous Trial Recalled," *Coconut Grove Village Post,* February 1958, 1, 4 March 1958, 1.

22. Agreement between J. B. Lippincott Company and MSD, 8 July 1959, J. B. Lippincott Company, royalty statement, 31 December 1967, both in MSDP, box 45, folder 60; *MH*, 1, 29 November 1959.

. 23. MSD, *Alligator Crossing* (1959; reprint, Minneapolis: Milkweed, 2003), 130; Melissa Walker, "Marjory Stoneman Douglas," in *American Nature Writers,* ed. John Elder (New York: Scribner's, 1996), 1:241–43.

24. MSD to Mrs. Kelly Cole, 23, 26, 27 May, 1, 3, 27 June 1963, MSDP, box 40, folder 18; *Coconut Grove Village Post,* 8 March 1964; Holly Hays, "Marjory Stoneman Douglas: Conservationist of the Century," *Florida Living,* August 1992, 55; "Biography, Marjory Stoneman Douglas," HP; *Voice,* 208–9; Areson, interview; A. A. McDonald to MSD, 14 July 1957, MSD to John T. McGovern, 30 May 1963, William L. Rothenberg to MSD, 25 June 1963, William A. Shaver to Carnegie Fund for Authors, 10 June 1963, all in MSDP, box 39, folder 7.

25. Areson, interview; Helen Muir, interview; MSD to Mrs. Freeman, 7 October 1963, MSDP, box 43, folder 62; *Voice,* 250; *Miami News,* 20 May 1963; Eric C. Van Enter to Sallye Jude, 3 November 1989, HP.

26. Hays, "Marjory Stoneman Douglas," 55; "Biography, Marjory Stoneman Douglas," "Vita, Marjory Stoneman Douglas," both in HP; MSD to John T. McGovern, 30 May 1963, MSDP, box 39, folder 7; Helen Muir, interview.

27. MSD to Fred J. Hanna, 24 June 1969, Emma D. Gaylord: Correspondence with MSD folder, Special Collections, Rollins College, Winter Park, Fla.; *MH*, 24 April 1974. The source of the start-up capital for Hurricane House is unknown. The copyright page of the 1978 Banyan Books edition of *River of Grass* and the subsequent Pineapple Press editions incorrectly list a 1962 printing (Carol Fitzgerald, *The Rivers of America: A Descriptive Biography* [New Castle, Del.: Oak Knoll, 2001], 1:174–75).

28. MSD, *Adventures in a Green World: The Story of David Fairchild and Barbour Lathrop* (Coconut Grove, Fla.: Field Research Projects, 1973); "Seventy-sixth Annual Meeting," *Florida Historical Quarterly* 57 (October 1978): 251, 253, 257; MSD, speech to Florida Historical Society, Pensacola, 6 May 1978, SPOHP; *MH*, 13 November 1922; *Florida.*

29. "The Remarkable World of Marjory Stoneman Douglas," part 1, *Miamian,* September 1970, 30; "'History Was Real,' Marjorie [*sic*] Stoneman Douglas," *Catalyst,* 6 September 1967, 21; *MH*, 26 March 1991; *Asbury Park Press,* 9 November 1967; "A Brief Autobiography by Marjory Stoneman Douglas Written in March 1987," HP; William R. Spear, "New Book on Florida Has Many Errors,"

clipping, n.d., "Florida: Story of the Long Frontier," clipping, n.d., LeRoy Collins to MSD, 28 November 1967, 4 March 1968, all in MSDP, box 42, folder 50; Carl Carmer to MSD, 29 February 1960, M. S. Wyeth Jr. to MSD, 28 March, 25 July 1960, 9 July 1963, 19 March 1968, all in MSDP, box 59, folder 7.

30. "The Winner of the Horton-Hallowell Fellowship," *Wellesley Alumnae Magazine*, January 1967, 32, 38; Cathy Shaw, "The Friend of the Everglades," *Wellesley Magazine*, Summer 1983, 14–16; *Orlando Sentinel*, 1 April 1990; *MH*, 30 June 1967; MSD to Gilly, 13 January 1986, MSD to Roy Bazire, 24 June 1985, both in MSDP, box 40, folder 21; Bill Cairnes to MSD, 26 July 1967, MSDP, box 40, folder 22; "Birds Have Personality," clipping, n.d., MSDP, box 39, folder 11; Frank M. Chapman, "William Henry Hudson, American," *Audubon*, September–October 1943, 264–67; William Henry Hudson, *A Traveler in Little Things* (New York: Dutton, 1923), vii–xiii.

31. Hudson, *Traveler in Little Things*, 1–3, 247; "Abstract," 1993 manuscript of "W. H. Hudson and the Green World," HP; Andy Taylor, "Marjory Stoneman Douglas," *Tropic* (*MH*), 23 December 1979, 15; Shaw, "Friend of the Everglades," 16; William C. Sturtevant to MSD, 5 November 1968, MSD Correspondence folder, HMSF; "Marjory Stoneman Douglas: 'It's Never Too Late for Anything,'" *Miami News* clipping, circa 1980, MSDP, box 11, folder 39.

CHAPTER TWENTY-NINE: Grassroots

1. Luther J. Carter, "Dade County: The Politics of Managing Urban Growth," *Science*, 4 June 1976, 982; *MH*, 11 February 1923; MSD, "When You and I Were Young, Miami," *Tropic* (*MH*), 5 November 1967, 18.

2. Scott Hamilton Dewey, "'Is This What We Came to Florida For?': Florida Women and the Fight against Air Pollution in the 1960s," in *Making Waves: Female Activists in Twentieth-Century Florida*, ed. Jack E. Davis and Kari Frederickson (Gainesville: University Press of Florida, 2003), 213–14; Charles Irvin Harding, Samuel B. McKee, and J. J. Schueneman, *A Report on Florida's Air Resources* (Jacksonville: Florida State Board of Health, 1961), 35–37, 44–45; Juanita Greene, "How the Automobile Multiplies the Problems of Dade County," in *The Environmental Destruction of South Florida: A Handbook for Citizens*, ed. William Ross McCluney (Coral Gables, Fla.: University of Miami Press, 1971), 69; William Ross McCluney, "Air Pollution Problems in South Florida," in *Environmental Destruction of South Florida*, ed. McCluney, 54–63; E. R. Rich, "The Population

Explosion in Dade County," in *Environmental Destruction of South Florida*, ed. McCluney, 41–43; *NYT*, 29 December 1968; Robert B. Rackleff, *Close to Crisis: Florida's Environmental Problems* (Tallahassee, Fla.: New Issues, 1972), 16.

3. J. Walter Dineen to MSD, 3 August 1982, MSDP, box 24, folder 21–22; *Chicago Tribune*, 26 March 1986; MSD, "River of Grass," *The Rotarian* 95 (November 1959): 22–24.

4. Dewey, "'Is This What We Came to Florida For?'" 214–15; *Christian Science Monitor*, 26 February 1964; John Edwin Leaird, "The Politics of Arrogance: A Case Study of the Controversy over the Proposed Everglades Jetport, 1967–1970" (master's thesis, University of Florida, 1972), 118.

5. Polly Redford, "Small Rebellion in Miami," *Harper's*, February 1964, 96–97; *Christian Science Monitor*, 26 February 1964; Dewey, "'Is This What We Came to Florida For?'" 213–14; Martha Munzer, "The Everglades and a Few Friends," *South Florida History Magazine* 23 (Winter 1995): 10.

6. Lloyd Miller to Dante Fascell, 11 February 1992, Dante Fascell Papers, box 2779–83, Biscayne National Monument folder, UM; Redford, "Small Rebellion in Miami," 100–101.

7. Redford, "Small Rebellion in Miami," 100–101; Helen Muir, *Miami, U.S.A.* (Gainesville: University Press of Florida, 2000), 202, 218; McCluney, "Air Pollution," 55–56; Rackleff, *Close to Crisis*, 70–71; Munzer, "Everglades and a Few Friends," 9–10; Polly Redford to Mrs. Morrison, 31 July ?, Polly Redford, "Exhausting Administrative Remedy—Before It Exhausts You," n.d., Polly Redford, "Keys to Biscayne Bay," *Izaak Walton Magazine*, December 1965, 14–15, all in AMP, box 7, folder 18; Luther J. Carter, *The Florida Experience: Land and Water Policy in a Growth State* (Baltimore: Johns Hopkins University Press, 1974), 158–59; Hoover Environmental Legal Defense Fund, "Results of the Coliform Sampling Program for Biscayne Bay," 7 December 1969, available online at www .aoml.noaa.gov/general/lib/cedar5.pdf (accessed winter 2007).

8. *Christian Science Monitor*, 26 February 1964; McCluney, "Air Pollution," 55–56; Redford, "Small Rebellion in Miami," 96–102; Polly Redford, *Raccoons and Eagles: Two Views of American Wildlife* (New York: Dutton, 1963); *NYT*, 25 June 1965; Joe Browder, interview by author, 7 August 2002.

9. *Christian Science Monitor*, 7 September 1960, 4 February 1961; *NYT*, 2, 9 September 1960, 10 February 1964; *WP*, 7 October 1962.

10. Redford, "Small Rebellion in Miami," 99–101; Dewey, "'Is This What We Came to Florida For?'" 214; Carter, *Florida Experience*, 160.

11. Redford, "Small Rebellion in Miami," 98–101; "'Is This What We Came to Florida For?'" 214, 215.

12. Redford, "Small Rebellion in Miami," 98–101; Dewey, "'Is This What We Came to Florida For?'" 214–15; *Christian Science Monitor,* 16 February 1964.

13. *NYT,* 15 January 1967.

14. Jennifer Brown Leynes and David Cullison, *Biscayne National Park Historic Resource Study* (Atlanta: National Park Service Southeast Region, 1998), 1–2; *WP,* 13 September 1966, 5 October 1968, 12 January 1969; *NYT,* 1 June 1969; Redford, "Small Rebellion in Miami," 102; Carter, *Florida Experience,* 159–60.

15. Carter, *Florida Experience,* 147, 161; Joe Browder to author, 18 September 2005; *NYT,* 15 January 1967; Hardy Matheson, interview by Lili Krech, 21 May 1969, provided to author by Lili Krech Neale.

16. Joe Browder to author, 19 September 2005; *Wall Street Journal,* 27 December 1968.

17. *Proposed Biscayne National Monument: Master Plan Brief* (n.p.: U.S. National Park Service, 1968), 6, 10–11; *Biscayne National Monument: A Proposal* (Washington, D.C.: U.S. National Park Service, 1960), 8, 16; Thomas W. Bilhorn, *Biscayne Bay and Its Environs: An Analysis of Its Present and Future Uses for Metropolitan Dade County* (Coral Gables, Fla.: Information Services, Sea Grant Program, University of Miami, 1976), 7.

18. McCluney, *Environmental Destruction of South Florida.*

19. *MH,* February 24, 1970, 24 April 1991; "Luncheon, Scholarship to Recognize Audubon Leaders of Service," 5 September 1989, JBP, Alice Wainwright, 1991 folder.

20. *WP,* 21 April 1968; *NYT,* 2 April 1967; *Christian Science Monitor,* 27 January 1967; Joe Browder to author, 12 September 2005; "Statement by McGregor Smith, before President's Water Pollution Control Advisory Board, Turkey Point, Fla.," 6 December 1968, in Lili Krech, Senior Independent Project notebook, April 28–May 28, 1969, provided to author by Lili Krech Neale.

21. Gilbert L. Voss, *Coral Reefs of Florida* (Sarasota, Fla.: Pineapple, 1988), 9–10.

22. Carter, *Florida Experience,* 6–7, 163–65; *WP,* 22 February 1970; "Report of the Committee on Inshore and Estuarine Pollution," 13 March 1969, Krech, Senior Independent Project notebook.

23. James A. Kushlan, "In Memoriam: Oscar T. Owre, 1917–1990," *The Auk* 108 (July 1991): 705; "In Memoriam: Oscar T. Owre, a Teacher of Ornithology,"

Florida Field Naturalist 19 (November 1990): 122–24; Joe Browder to author, 1, 12 September 2005; "Statement by McGregor Smith."

24. *MH,* 24 February 1970; Carter, *Florida Experience,* 165–66.

25. Browder, interview; Juanita Greene, interview by author, 16 March 2006.

26. *MH,* 24, 25, 26 February 1970; "Statement by A. M. Davis, before President's Water Pollution Control Board, Turkey Point, Fla.," 6 December 1968, Krech, Senior Independent Project notebook.

27. *MH,* 24, 25, 26 February 1970; *WP,* 22 February, 2 March 1970; Redford, "Exhausting Administrative Remedy."

28. Peter Farb, "Save the Everglades!" *Reader's Digest,* November 1965, 245–46; *NYT,* 12 September 1971; Carter, *Florida Experience,* 166–67.

29. *Gainesville Sun,* 28 July 1971; *River of Grass,* 25; MSD to John D. MacDonald, 14 September 1968, John D. MacDonald Collection, box 68, folder 1, PKY.

30. U.S. Congress, House, *River Basin Monetary Authorizations and Miscellaneous Civil Works Amendments,* 26 May 1970, 91st Cong., 2nd sess., Report 91-895; "House OKs $1.5 Million to Ease Everglades Woes," clipping, n.d., CPC, s301/770/2; Carter, *Florida Experience,* 123–24; *Florida Water Conservation News,* January 1971, Edmund S. Muskie Collection, box 1603, folder 6, Edmund S. Muskie Archives and Special Collections, Bates College, Lewiston, Me.; Anthony Wayne Smith to Edmund S. Muskie, 13 April 1970, Muskie Collection, box 1205, folder 7; *MH,* 9 April 1970; *Gainesville Sun,* 28 July 1971; Rackleff, *Close to Crisis,* 132.

31. *MH,* 31 July 1923.

CHAPTER THIRTY: The Jetport

1. Joe Browder to author, 18 September 2005.

2. Joe Browder, interview by author, 7 August 2002; Joe Browder to author, 18 September 2005.

3. Browder, interview.

4. Browder, interview; Joe Browder to author, 10, 18 September 2005; *Tampa Sunday Tribune,* 2 August 1954, 22 July 1956; Alexander "Sandy" Sprunt Jr., "Emerald Kingdom," *Audubon,* January 1961, 24–40; Carl W. Buchheister, "The Acquisition and Development of the Corkscrew Swamp Sanctuary, 1952–1967," available online at http://www.audubon.org/local/sanctuary/corkscrew/Information/Information.html (accessed fall 2005).

5. Browder, interview.

6. Joe Browder to author, 30, 31 August 2005; Robert S. Gilmour and John McCauley, "Environmental Preservation and Politics: The Significance of 'Everglades Jetport,'" *Political Science Quarterly* 90 (Winter 1975–76): 723; *SPT*, 30 April 1969; "Miami Jetport and Interstate 75, Everglades National Park," circa 1968, document provided to author by Lili Krech Neale.

7. Browder, interview; Walter A. Rosenbaum, *The Politics of Environmental Concern* (New York: Praeger, 1977), 168–69; *WP*, 16 October 1968; *NYT*, 12 June 1969; Marquis Childs, "The Everglades in an Era of Reprieve," *Smithsonian* 1 (June 1970): 6; *MH*, 31 August 1969; Dan Paul to Frank Hatch Jr., 22 May 1975, JBP, Dan Paul folder. The land area in Miami was 35.7 square miles; the jetport was 39 square miles.

8. John Edwin Leaird, "The Politics of Arrogance: A Case Study of the Controversy over the Proposed Everglades Jetport, 1967–1970" (master's thesis, University of Florida, 1972), 12–22, 45, 50; Rosenbaum, *Politics of Environmental Concern*, 168–69; Browder, interview; *MH*, 26 May 1929; Gilmour and McCauley, "Environmental Preservation and Politics," 722–23.

9. Leaird, "Politics of Arrogance," 47–48, 53–54; Browder, interview; Childs, "Everglades," 6–7; *MH*, 21 August 1969; Howard V. Bloomfield, "Everglades: Pregnant with Risks," *American Forests* 76 (May 1970): 52.

10. *SPT*, 30 May 2004; Nathaniel Reed, interview by Julian Pleasants, 18 December 2000, SPOHP, 30; "Biographical Information, Nathaniel P. Reed," Nathaniel P. Reed Everglades Papers, 1983–2000, box 1, folder 1, PKY; Jean George, "Victory in the Everglades," *Reader's Digest*, August 1970, 75; Nathaniel Pryor Reed, speech to Sierra Club annual meeting, 2 May 1981, JBP, Nat v Watt folder.

11. *NYT*, 14 March 1969; Leaird, "Politics of Arrogance," 66–67; Joe Browder, "Decision-Making in the White House," in *Nixon and the Environment: The Politics of Devastation*, ed. James Rathlesberger (New York: Village Voice, 1972), 258.

12. James A. Kuslan, "Observations on the Role of the American Alligator (Alligator Mississippiensis) in the Southern Florida Wetlands," *Copeia*, 31 December 1974, 993–96; James W. Fourqurean and Michael B. Robblee, "Florida Bay: A History of Recent Ecological Changes," *Estuaries* 22 (June 1999): 345–57.

13. *NYT*, 11 January, 9, 14, 16 March, 21 December 1969; *Washington Times-Herald*, 14, 15 March 1969; *Christian Science Monitor*, 15 March 1969; Leaird, "Politics of Arrogance," 66–67; Browder, "Decision-Making," 258–59; Reed, interview.

14. Ben Herr to Frank E. Maloney, 5 November 1969, Frank E. Maloney to Ben Herr, 17 November 1969, Harold Turk to Claude Pepper, 11 March 1970, all in CPC, 301/801/6.

15. Claude Kirk, "The Everglades," *Natural History* 80 (January 1971): 78; "Jetport Comes before Glades," clipping, n.d., David O. True Collection, box 25, Everglades folder, PKY; Leaird, "Politics of Arrogance," 111; *NYT*, 9, 16 March 1969.

16. Leaird, "Politics of Arrogance," 124–25; Joe Browder to Charles Lee, 27 May 1998, JBP, Dade folder; Dale Crider to Joe Browder, 23 July 1998, JBP, Dale Hunt folder; Joe Browder to Everglades Restoration, 24 September 1998, JBP, evhsb folder; Izaak Walton League of America, Florida Division, typed statement, circa May 1969, Lili Krech, Senior Independent Project notebook, April 28–May 28, 1969, provided to author by Lili Krech Neale.

17. Mariana Jones to MSD, 8 July 1976, MSDP, box 3, folder 110.

18. Johnny Jones and Mariana Jones, interview by author, 11 August 2000; *Tallahassee Democrat*, 19 May 1981; *MH*, 15 August 1982; Johnny Jones, interview by Brian Gridley, 23 May 2001, SPOHP.

19. Charles Lee, interview by author, 23 November 2005.

20. Browder, interview; Lee, interview; Joe Browder to author, 31 August 2005; Juliana Field, interview by author, 2 November 2005; Frank Tamen to Claude Pepper, 1 May 1971, CPC, 301/746/2.

21. Joe Browder to author, 3 November 2005; December Duke McSherry, interview by author, 19 November 2005; Judy Wilson Lawrence, interview by author, 5 November 2005.

22. Mrs. Alden Hine to Ed Adair, 13 May 1969, Krech, Senior Independent Project notebook; Luther Gerlach to author, 30 November 2005, 26 January 2006; Luther P. Gerlach and Virginia H. Hine, *People, Power, Change: Movements of Social Transformation* (Indianapolis: Bobbs-Merrill, 1970), xi–xxiii, 203; Luther P. Gerlach and Virginia H. Hine, *Lifeway Leap: The Dynamics of Change in America* (Minneapolis: University of Minnesota Press, 1973), 193–94.

23. December Duke McSherry to author, 23 November 2005; Mrs. Alden Hine to Ed Adair, 13 May 1969, Krech, Senior Independent Project notebook; Gerlach and Hine, *People, Power, Change*, 203; Lili Krech Neale, interview by author, 18 November 2005; McSherry, interview; December Duke and Lili Krech, "Thermal Pollution: Man's Blindness toward the Consequences of His Actions," May 1969, Lili Krech, Independent Project notebook.

24. Miami-Dade Water and Sewer, available online at http://www.miamidade
.gov/wasd/facts_glance.asp (accessed fall 2006).

25. *SPT,* 22 August 1971; Diary, 19 May 1969, Krech, Senior Independent Project
notebook; Neale, interview; McSherry, interview; "People Eco-Action from *Lifeway Leap,*" documentary provided by Luther Gerlach.

26. Patsy West, *The Enduring Seminoles: From Alligator Wrestling to Ecotourism*
(Gainesville: University Press of Florida, 1998), 113; Buffalo Tiger and Harry A.
Kersey Jr., *Buffalo Tiger: A Life in the Everglades* (Lincoln: University of Nebraska
Press, 2002), 13–32, 108; *NYT,* 11 August 1969; *Christian Science Monitor,* 25 April
1969, 2 June 1970; *Washington Times-Herald,* 26 April 1969; Bloomfield, "Ever-
glades," 54; Joe Browder to author, 28 September 2005.

27. *Florida,* 283.

CHAPTER THIRTY-ONE: The Conversion

1. Joe Browder, interview by author, 7 August 2002; Judy Wilson Lawrence, interview by author, 3 November 2005; *Florida,* 281, 283; *Voice,* 224–25; *MH,* 6 April
1975.

2. Joe Browder to author, 29, 30, 31 August, 1 September 2005; Juliana Field,
interview by author, 2 November 2005; Julia Allen Field, interview by author,
15 August 2002; Lawrence interview; Juliana Field to author, 1 November 2005;
Florida Naturalist 39 (April 1966): 49; Henry Field, *The Track of Man: Adventures
of an Anthropologist* (New York: Doubleday, 1953).

3. Lawrence, interview; *MH,* 6 April 1975.

4. Lawrence, interview.

5. Robert Kelley, interview by author, 17 March 2006; Charles Lee, interview
by author, 23 November 2005; Juanita Greene, interview by author, 16 March
2006.

6. George Rosner, "MSD, a House of My Own," 1990, HP; Browder, interview.

7. *Gainesville Sun,* 26 February 1989.

8. Browder, interview; Lawrence, interview; *Lakeland Ledger,* 24 March 1996.

9. *NYT,* 6 November 1966, 7 January 1968, 9 March, 3 August, 29 December
1969.

10. Browder, interview; Martha Munzer, "The Everglades and a Few Friends,"
South Florida History Magazine 23 (Winter 1995): 11–12; Judith Bauer Stamper,
Save the Everglades (Austin, Tex.: Steck-Vaughn, 1993), 31–36.

11. Michael Chenoweth, interview by author, 9 August 2000; Browder, interview.

12. *SPT,* 25 April 1991; *Voice,* 226; *Christian Science Monitor,* 23 September 1970; *Gainesville Sun,* 26 February 1989; Franklin Adams, interview by author, 8 August 2000; Joe Podgor, interview by author, 10 August 2000.

13. MSD to Fred Hanna, 17 December 1971, Emma D. Gaylord: Correspondence with Marjory Stoneman Douglas folder, Special Collections, Rollins College, Winter Park, Fla.

14. *Rocky Mountain News,* 22 July 1970; Lee, interview; December Duke McSherry, interview by author, 19 November 2005; Podgor, interview; Lili Krech Neale, interview by author, 18 November 2005.

15. Adams, interview; Chenoweth, interview; Lawrence, interview; Martha Hubbart, interview by author, 14 August 2002; Podgor, interview; Pam Pierce, interview by author, 9 August 2000; Nancy Brown, interview by author, 27 August 2000; *Orlando Sentinel Star,* 15 April 1973.

16. *MH,* 11 November 1922, 31 January 1923; Adams, interview.

17. *Tampa Tribune,* 24 April 1988; Michael P. Branch, "Writing the Swamp: Marjory Stoneman Douglas and *The Everglades: River of Grass,*" in *Such News of the Land: U.S. Women Nature Writers,* ed. Thomas S. Edwards and Elizabeth A. De Wolfe (Hanover, N.H.: University Press of New England, 2001), 131–33 (Branch emphasizes *River of Grass*'s similarity to *A Sand County Almanac* and *Silent Spring*); *River of Grass,* 286, 279.

18. "The Fort Myers Story," *Florida Naturalist* 39 (July 1966): 105; "Marjorie Stoneman Douglas," *Florida Audubon,* April 1966, 47.

19. Nathaniel Pryor Reed, "Memories of Marjory Stoneman Douglas and Her Everglades Crusade," *Foresight* 10 (Fall 1998), available online at http://www .1000friendsofflorida.org/Natural_Resources/Marjory_Stoneman_Douglas.asp (accessed fall 2006).

20. Carol Fitzgerald, *The Rivers of America: A Descriptive Biography* (New Castle, Del.: Oak Knoll, 2001), 1:176–77; *Orlando Sentinel,* 1 January 1984; Adams, interview; Lawrence interview.

21. Browder, interview; Joe Browder to author, 13 October 2005.

22. *MH,* 24, 25, 26 April 1991; *Jacksonville Florida Times-Union,* 25 April 1963.

23. MSD to Ms. Roseberry, 8 September 1986, MSDP, box 46, folder 106; MSD to Mrs. Woodhead, 22 May 1985, MSDP, 22 May 1985; *Fort Lauderdale Sun-Sentinel,* 14 September 1986.

24. Luther J. Carter, *The Florida Experience: Land and Water Policy in a Growth State* (Baltimore: Johns Hopkins University Press, 1974), 198.

25. Joe Browder to author, 29, 30 August 2005; Browder, interview; Carter, *Florida Experience,* 200–201; Nelson M. Blake, *Land into Water—Water into Land: A History of Water Management in Florida* (Tallahassee: Florida State University Press, 1980), 219–20; *SPT,* 30 April 1969; J. Brooks Flippen, *Conservative Conservationist: Russell E. Train and the Emergence of American Environmentalism* (Baton Rouge: Louisiana State University Press, 2006), 55, 82, 218.

26. Joe Browder to author, 29, 30 August 2005; Juliana Field, interview; Lee, interview; Lawrence, interview; Muriel V. Murrell, *Miami: A Backward Glance* (Sarasota, Fla.: Pineapple, 2003), 92–93.

27. J. Brooks Flippen, *Nixon and the Environment* (Albuquerque: University of New Mexico Press, 2000), 39; John Edwin Leaird, "The Politics of Arrogance: A Case Study of the Controversy over the Proposed Everglades Jetport, 1967–1970" (master's thesis, University of Florida, 1972), 70–71; Jean George, "Victory in the Everglades," *Reader's Digest,* August 1970, 75–76; *NYT,* 11, 31 August 1969; Blake, *Land into Water,* 220; Carter, *Florida Experience,* 207; Marti Mueller, "Everglades Jetport: Academy Prepares a Model," *Science,* 10 October 1969, 202–3.

28. Jean George, "Victory in the Everglades," 73–76; Richard Rhodes, "The Killing of the Everglades," *Playboy,* January 1972, 112–16, 154, 278–82; Marquis Childs, "The Everglades in an Era of Reprieve," *Smithsonian* 1 (June 1970): 4–13; Howard V. Bloomfield, "Everglades: Pregnant with Risks," *American Forests* 76 (May 1970): 24–27, 52–54; *NYT,* 11 January, 12 June, 11, 31 August, 5 September 1969; Leaird, "Politics of Arrogance," 78–80; "Conservation: Jets v. Everglades," *Time,* 22 August 1969, 42–43; Wilbur F. McIntyre to Edmund Muskie, 3 September 1969, Joan C. Zimber to "Dear Sirs," 8 November 1969, Joan Carroll Wood to Richard M. Nixon, 16 September 1969, all in Edmund S. Muskie Collection, box 1742, folder 7, Edmund S. Muskie Archives and Special Collections, Bates College, Lewiston, Me.; Craig Fisher, *The Everglades* (NBC News Production, transcript, 16 February 1971), Muskie Collection, box 1823, folder 6.

29. This observation was reminiscent of MSD'S 1925 "A Bird Dog in Hand," when George Henry, believing he can drain the lower Everglades into civilized living, remarks to a doubting Pomona Brown, "You've heard of Holland, of course" (MSD, "A Bird Dog in Hand," *SEP,* 12 September 1925, reprinted in *Nine Florida Stories,* ed. Kevin M. McCarthy [Gainesville: University Press of Florida, 1990], 46).

30. Rhodes, "Killing of the Everglades," 280; MSD, "Bird Dog in Hand," 60; Bloomfield, "Everglades," 27; *NYT,* 11 January 1969; *MH,* 31 August 1969; Leaird, "Politics of Arrogance," 109, 113.

31. *MH,* 1 August 1973; U.S. Federal Aviation Agency, *Replacing the Everglades Jetport: An Executive Summary* (Washington, D.C.: Federal Aviation Agency, 1976), 9; Bill Christofferson, *The Man from Clear Lake: Earth Day Founder Senator Gaylord Nelson* (Madison: University of Wisconsin Press, 2004), 173–74, 332–33; Blake, *Land into Water,* 220–21; Carter, *Florida Experience,* 200–208; *Environmental Impact of the Big Cypress Swamp Jetport* (Washington, D.C.: U.S. Department of the Interior, September 1969), 2; Joe Browder to author, 28 December 2007.

32. *Washington Times-Herald,* 11 September 1969; *NYT,* 12 June, 11, 31 August, 5 September 1969, 1 February 1970; Flippen, *Nixon and the Environment,* 59.

33. Scott Hamilton Dewey, *Don't Breathe the Air: Air Pollution and U.S. Environmental Politics, 1945–1970* (College Station: Texas A & M University Press, 2000), 74–77, 242–44; Childs, "Everglades," 8–9; Bloomfield, "Everglades," 53–54; Christofferson, *Man from Clear Lake,* 302–12; Fisher, *Everglades.* For a comprehensive study of Nixon's significant part in this new age of environmentalism, see Flippen, *Nixon and the Environment.*

CHAPTER THIRTY-TWO: Regionalism and Environmentalism

1. *Myrtle Beach (South Carolina) Sun News,* 6 August 1978; Gordon E. Harvey, "'We Must Free Ourselves . . . from the Tattered Fetters of the Booster Mentality': Big Cypress Swamp and the Politics of Environmental Protection in 1970s Florida," in *Paradise Lost? The Environmental History of Florida,* ed. Jack E. Davis and Raymond Arsenault (Gainesville: University Press of Florida, 2005), 351; Cynthia Barnett, *Mirage: Florida and the Vanishing Water of the Eastern U.S.* (Ann Arbor: University of Michigan Press, 2007), 54; "Governors' Conference on Water Management in South Florida, September 22, 23, 24, [1971], Long Term Problems," AMP, box 6, folder 4.

2. Richard Stone to Robert Pittman, 14 November 1973, Department of State, Secretary (Richard) Stone, Acc. P77-502, box 9, Correspondence from Secretary Stone, FSA; *MH,* 24 November 1973; *Miami Daily News,* 21 November 1973; *Sarasota Herald-Tribune,* 18 February 1974; *Tampa Tribune,* 25 February 1974; Robert B. Rackleff, *Close to Crisis: Florida's Environmental Problems* (Tallahassee,

Fla.: New Issues, 1972), 112–13; S. V. Dáte, *Quiet Passion: A Biography of Senator Bob Graham* (New York: Tarcher/Penguin, 2004), 65.

3. *Sarasota Herald-Tribune,* 18 February 1974; *MH,* 17 January 1974.

4. Howard V. Bloomfield, "Everglades: Pregnant with Risks," *American Forests* 76 (May 1970): 52; *Florida Conservation News* (November 1975): 5.

5. Charles Lee, interview by author, 23 November 2005; Claude Kirk to "Ladies and Gentlemen," circa 1969, AMP, box 2, folder 6; Luther J. Carter, "Dade County: The Politics of Managing Urban Growth," *Science,* 4 June 1976, 982, 985.

6. Carter, "Dade County," 983; Rackleff, *Close to Crisis,* 3.

7. Frank C. Craighead, *The Trees of South Florida* (Coral Gables, Fla.: University of Miami Press, 1971).

8. "Everglades Conference at Miami, February 26–28, 1970," program, Final List of Registrants of the Everglades Conference at Miami, 26–28 February 1970, both in Garald G. Parker Collection, Everglades folder, USF; *MH,* 27 February 1970; Rackleff, *Close to Crisis,* 18.

9. *Florida Conservation Digest* 55 (1 October 1975): 21; "Governor's Conference Report in This Issue," *Water Management Bulletin* 5 (December–January 1971– 72): 3–4; *MH,* 23, 25 September 1971; *Myrtle Beach (South Carolina) Sun News,* 6 August 1978; "Governors' Conference on Water Management in South Florida"; Harvey, "'We Must Free Ourselves,'" 355–56.

10. *Stuart News,* 1 March 1974; *Sarasota Herald Tribune,* 30 January 1974; MSD, speech to Florida Historical Society, Pensacola, 6 May 1978, SPOHP.

11. Jean Areson, interview by author, 10 June 2000; Franklin Adams, interview by author, 8 August 2000; Helen Muir, interview by author, 11 March 1999.

12. *Sarasota Herald-Tribune,* 30 January 1974; *MH,* 14 April 1974; Areson, interview.

13. *Sarasota Herald-Tribune,* 30 January 1974; *MH,* 14 April 1974; Areson, interview; Joe Browder, interview by author, 7 August 2002; MSD, "The Everglades," *The Rotarian,* November 1959, 24; *Fort Lauderdale News,* 4 November 1971.

14. *Sarasota Herald-Tribune,* 30 January 1974.

15. Nelson M. Blake, *Land into Water—Water into Land: A History of Water Management in Florida* (Tallahassee: Florida State University Press, 1980), 228–30.

16. "Governor's Conference Report," 5–6; *Florida Conservation Digest,* 5; *Sarasota Herald-Tribune,* 30 January, 18 February 1974; *Clewiston News,* 7 March 1974; *Stuart News,* 1, 10 March 1974; "Distinguished Visitor," *Marie Selby Botanical*

Gardens Bulletin, August 1978, 29, Hampton Dunn Collection, USF; Rackleff, *Close to Crisis,* 59; MSD, draft foreword, MSDP, box 23, folder 23.

17. Steve Yates, "Marjory Stoneman Douglas and the Glades Crusade," *Audubon,* March 1983, 126; MSD, "The Everglades Remembered," *Florida Naturalist* 55 (December 1983): 15; MSD, "Wings," *SEP,* 14 March 1931, 3; MSD, "The Forgotten Man Who Saved the Everglades," *Audubon,* September 1971, 90; *Florida,* 281–82; Jeffrey Kahn, "Restoring the Everglades," *Sierra* 71 (September–October 1986): 41; James A. Kuahlan, "The Sandhill Crane in the Everglades," *Anhinga Newsletter* (Everglades Natural History Association), 1 June 1982, 2.

18. *Chicago Tribune,* 26 March 1986.

19. Christopher F. Meindl, "Water, Water Everywhere," in *Paradise Lost?* ed. Davis and Arsenault, 113–37; Nano Riley, "Lake Apopka: From Natural Wonder to Unnatural Disaster," in *Paradise Lost?* ed. Davis and Arsenault, 280–93; Lee Irby, "'The Big Ditch': The Rise and Fall of the Cross-Florida Barge Canal," in *Paradise Lost?* ed. Davis and Arsenault, 375–97; *NYT,* 13 February 1972; *MH,* 22 August 1986; Mark Derr, *Some Kind of Paradise: A Chronicle of Man and the Land in Florida* (New York: Morrow, 1989), 204, 366–67; Waldo Proffitt, "Eventually, Why Not Now?" speech to Tampa Bay Regional Planning Council, 30 July 1971, HP; Rackleff, *Close to Crisis,* 40–41.

20. Lee Irby, "A Passion for Wild Things: Marjorie Harris Carr and the Fight to Free a River," in *Making Waves: Female Activists in Twentieth-Century Florida,* ed. Jack E. Davis and Kari Frederickson (Gainesville: University Press of Florida, 2003), 177–96; Thomas T. Ankersen, "Law, Science, and Little Old Ladies: The Many Hands That Made a Movement," *Forum,* Summer 1995, 29; Archie Carr, *The Everglades* (New York: Time-Life, 1973); Proffitt, "Eventually"; *NYT,* 13 February 1972; Kathryn Ziewitz and June Wiaz, *Green Empire: The St. Joe Company and the Remaking of Florida's Panhandle* (Gainesville: University Press of Florida, 2004), 130–31; Derr, *Some Kind of Paradise,* 317, 360–73; John D. MacDonald, "Last Chance to Save the Everglades: Threatened America," *Life,* 5 September 1969, 58–64; Jim Harrison, *Just before Dark* (New York: Mariner, 1999), 248; John D. MacDonald to Pat Hunt, 28 July 1969, John D. MacDonald Collection, box 48, folder 2, PKY.

21. *NYT,* 1, 29 March, 21, 22, 23 April 1970; *Christian Science Monitor,* 20 January 1970; *Wall Street Journal,* 23 February 1970; *WP,* 15 March, 14, 21 April 1970.

22. Luther P. Gerlach and Virginia H. Hine, *Lifeway Leap: The Dynamics of Change in America* (Minneapolis: University of Minnesota Press, 1973), 205–10; *MH,* 22, 23 April 1970.

23. *MH,* 23 April 1970.

24. James H. Hartwell, Arthur R. Marshall, Frank C. Craighead, William B. Robertson Jr., and Bernard J. Yokel, *Statement to Subcommittee on National Parks and Recreation of the Committee on Interior and Insular Affairs,* House of Representatives, 15 February 1972, Fort Myers, Florida, Everglades Digital Library, Arthur R. Marshall Collection, 5; Stuart D. Strahl, interview by Julian Pleasants, 22 February 2001, SPOHP; Estus Whitfield, interview by Brian Gridley, 15 May 2001, SPOHP; Harvey, "'We Must Free Ourselves,'" 362, 363.

25. Derr, *Some Kind of Paradise,* 116, 131, 342; *River of Grass,* 49.

26. *MH,* 12, 14 November 1954; *Tampa Sunday Tribune,* 2 August 1954, 22 July 1956; Ernest Taylor, "The 'Trek' into the Big Cypress Swamp, Lee and Collier Counties," Ernest Taylor Papers, PKY.

27. Browder, interview; Joe Browder to author, 28 November 2005; Harvey, "'We Must Free Ourselves,'" 366; Joe Browder to Ted Levine, 12 August 1998, JBP, JBPEvHistory folder; Office of the Secretary, Department of the Interior, news release, 20 May 1971, JBP, DOI Land Use folder; Michael McCloskey to Joseph Browder, 7 August 1972, JBP, JBP sc re Jackson folder; *MH,* 6 May 1971; Hartwell et al., *Statement,* 5; U.S. Congress, House, *Big Cypress Preserve, Florida: Hearings before the Subcommittee on National Parks and Recreation of the Committee on Interior and Insular Affairs, House of Representatives,* Fort Myers, Fla., 15 February 1972 (Washington, D.C.: U.S. Government Printing Office, 1972).

28. *Naples Star,* 24 August 1973; *Naples Daily News,* 7 September, 12 November 1973; *MH,* 1 March 1970, 23 September, 25 November 1973; *Fort Lauderdale News,* 4 November 1971; *Sarasota Herald-Tribune,* 18 February 1974; *Okeechobee News,* 11 July 1974; East Collier County Land Owners Improvement Committee pamphlet, JBP, Land of Dreams folder; Joe Browder, statement to Senate Subcommittee on Interior and Insular Affairs, 21 March 1974, JBP, JBP BigC testimony folder.

29. "Regarding Death for Those Leading the Fight to Steal Our Land," 25 July 1975, JBP, Death Threat folder; "Why Should Innocent People Be Punished for the Crime Committed by Senator Jackson, Governor Askew, Senator Graham, Joe Browder, and Three Collier County Commissioners," JBP, Death to JBB folder; Joe Browder to Everglades Restoration, 12 July 1998, JBP, Gator Bill folder; Nathaniel Reed to Joe Browder, 12 July 1998, Joe Browder to Nathaniel Reed, both in JBP, Nat Threats folder; Browder, statement to Senate Subcommittee on Interior and Insular Affairs.

30. Friends of the Everglades postcard, 12 October 1970, MSDP, box 23, folder 2; Niki Butcher, "History of the Big Cypress National Preserve," available online at www.friendsofbigcypress.org/history/htm (accessed fall 2006); "Big Cypress Watershed," *ENFO Newsletter* (June 1971): 1–7; "Exxon Applications for Drilling at Sites 32-4 and 33-4, Big Cypress," Hal Scott to MSD, 17 July 1976, both in MSDP, box 31, folder 110; MSD to Joe Browder, 29 August 1977, JBP, MSD to jbbtxt folder; Joe Browder to Dan Paul, 2 September 1972, JBP, Dan Paul folder.

31. Harvey, "'We Must Free Ourselves,'" 350–51; Marquis Childs, "The Everglades in an Era of Reprieve," *Smithsonian* 1 (June 1970): 9; Cesar A. Becerra, "Giants of the Swamp: The Story of South Florida's Logging Industry," *South Florida History Magazine* 22 (Winter 1994): 16–25; *Naples Daily News,* 13 November 1973; *MH,* 14 November 1973; Butcher, "History"; F. C. Craighead to Joe Browder, 26 August 1975, JBP, Craighead BigC folder.

32. Harvey, "'We Must Free Ourselves,'" 362–66; Blake, *Land into Water,* 231–35; *WP,* 23 February 1973; *Wall Street Journal,* 30 March 1973; Rackleff, *Close to Crisis,* 106–9, 111–12.

33. "Floor Statement by Senator Edmund Muskie announcing cosponsoring of S. 2465, a bill to establish the Everglades–Big Cypress National Recreational Area in Florida," Edmund S. Muskie Collection, box 1894, folder 38, Edmund S. Muskie Archives and Special Collections, Bates College, Lewiston, Me.; *MH,* 5 February 1971, 2 August 1973, 15 August 1974; *Naples Daily News,* 17 August, 4 October 1973; *Naples Star,* 28 September, 2 November 1973; *WP,* 10 July 1973.

34. Johnny Jones, interview by Brian Gridley, 23 May 2001, SPOHP; "Exxon Applications"; Joel Kuperberg to Joe Browder, 10 July 1998, JBP, Joel Hntrs folder; Joe Browder to Clyde Butcher, 22 June 1998, JBP, ClydEvHist folder; Joe Browder to Nat Reed, 8 October 1975, JBP, NatBgCyp folder; W. Richard West Jr. and Joe Browder to James A. Haley, 31 July 1973, JBP, jb to Haley BigC folder; undated clipping, JBP, Seminoles Sue folder.

35. Johnny Jones and Mariana Jones, interview by author, 11 August 2000; *Fort Lauderdale News,* 4 November 1971; "Member Organizations," Coalition for Water Resources, MSDP, box 23, folder 8.

36. Jones and Jones, interview.

37. *Palatka Daily News,* 1 November 1984; *Lakeland Ledger,* 24 March 1996; *MH,* 28 February 1970, 21 October 1984; Final List of Registrants; Estus Whitfield to author, 28 March 2006.

38. MSD to Arthur Marshall, 5 February 1971, AMP, box 1, folder 28; news release, 22 October 1970, "Arthur R. Marshall," award letter, Governor's Conservation Award Recipients, all in AMP, box 2, folder 6.

39. Albert R. Veri, Arthur R. Marshall, Susan Uhl Wilson, James H. Hartwell, Peter Rosendahl, and Thomas Mumford, *The Resource Buffer Plan: A Conceptual Land Use Study* (Washington, D.C.: Conservation Foundation, 1973); Arthur R. Marshall, "The Future of South Florida's Salt and Freshwater Resources," in *The Environmental Destruction of South Florida: A Handbook for Citizens,* ed. William Ross McCluney (Coral Gables, Fla.: University of Miami Press, 1971), 17–24; Arthur R. Marshall, "Statement for Presentation to the Governor and Cabinet of Florida," 13 April 1971, Charles M. Loveless, "Report of the Special Study Team on the Florida Everglades," August 1970, both in Friends of the Everglades Papers, box 1, HMSF; Arthur R. Marshall to Nathaniel P. Reed, 21 July 1971, AMP, box 1, folder 43; Reubin Askew to Arthur R. Marshall, 13 September 1971, AMP, box 6, folder 4.

40. "Marjory Stoneman Douglas: Crusading Friend of the Everglades," *IMC Journal* 2 (Autumn 1984): 19; Anastasia Toufexis and William McWhirter, "Lady of the Everglades," *Time,* 31 January 1983, 57; MSD, "An Ominous Cloud over the Everglades," *Florida Trend* 30 (Spring 1988): 17–18.

41. *Palm Beach Post,* 10 September 1984; *MH,* 20 February 1984; *Voice,* 226–27; Joe Browder to author, 22 April 2008.

CHAPTER THIRTY-THREE: The Kissimmee

1. *Sarasota Herald-Tribune,* 28 November 1982; *MH,* 2 December 1951; Joe Podgor, interview by author, 10 August 2000.

2. *Sarasota Herald-Tribune,* 30 January 1974; *MH,* 1 February 1987.

3. Steve Yates, "Marjory Stoneman Douglas and the Glades Crusade," *Audubon,* March 1983, 119; Robert B. Rackleff, *Close to Crisis: Florida's Environmental Problems* (Tallahassee, Fla.: New Issues, 1972), 59, 64; A. H. "Gus" Craig to Lawton Chiles, 24 January 1978, Nathaniel P. Reed to Arthur Marshall, 13 September 1983, both in MSDP, box 27, folder 61.

4. Garald G. Parker to Dale H. Twachtmann, 3 October 1972, Garald G. Parker Collection, USF.

5. *MH,* 14 August 1971, *St. Petersburg Independent,* 17 August 1971, clippings provided by Joe Browder.

6. Martin Reuss, *Shaping Environmental Awareness: The United States Army Corps of Engineers Environmental Advisory Board, 1970–1980* (Alexandria, Va.: Historical Division, Office of Administrative Services, Office of the Chief of Engineers, 1983), 1–6; Raymond H. Merritt, *The Corps, the Environment and the Upper Mississippi River Basin* (Alexandria, Va.: Historical Division, Office of Administrative Services, Office of the Chief of Engineers, 1984), 91–92; Martin Reuss, *Designing the Bayous: The Control of Water in the Atchafalaya Basin, 1800–1995* (Alexandria, Va.: Office of History, U.S. Army Corps of Engineers, 1998), 277–78.

7. R. Bruce Stephenson, *Visions of Eden: Environmentalism, Urban Planning, and City Building in St. Petersburg, Florida, 1900–1995* (Columbus: Ohio State University Press, 1997), 140–41; Reuss, *Shaping Environmental Awareness*, 6; *Christian Science Monitor*, 30 November 1964; *NYT*, 21 July 1970.

8. Reuss, *Shaping Environmental Awareness*, 6; Reuss, *Designing the Bayous*, 278–79.

9. *Jacksonville Florida Times-Union*, 21 August 1971, clipping provided by Joe Browder; "Comments of Sierra Club and Friends of the Earth on the Army Corps of Engineers Draft Environmental Impact Statement for the Central and Southern Florida Flood Control District," 7 January 1972, JBP, Corps NEPA folder.

10. *MH*, 14 April 1974.

11. Mary Schmich, "Our Lady of the 'Glades," *Chicago Tribune* clipping, n.d., MSDP, box 11, folder 37; *Sarasota Herald-Tribune*, 30 January, 18 February 1974; *Stuart News*, 10 March 1974; *MH*, 14 April 1974; *Myrtle Beach (South Carolina) Sun News*, 6 August 1978; Joe Browder, interview by author, 7 August 2002; Nathaniel Reed, interview by Julian Pleasants, 18 December 2000, SPOHP; Nathaniel P. Reed to Joe Browder, 21 October 1975, JBP, Lnpn c111 folder.

12. Robert P. McIntosh, "Ecology since 1900," in *History of American Ecology* (New York: Arno, 1977), 368–69.

13. Browder, interview; Johnny Jones and Mariana Jones, interview by author, 11 August 2000; Johnny Jones, interview by Brian Gridley, 23 May 2001, SPOHP; Arthur R. Marshall to Nathaniel P. Reed, July 1976, AMP, box 1, folder 43.

14. *Lakeland Ledger*, 24 March 1996; "State of Florida, Certificate of Incorporation, WATER! Inc.," 24 August 1976, MSDP, box 23, folder 8; "Corporation Annual Report, 1977," Coalition for WATER! Inc., AMP, box 3, folder 25; MSD to Arthur R. Marshall, 2 December 1976, AMP, box 1, folder 28; press release, 13 February 1976, "'WATER!' Coalition Formed," news release, circa October 1975, both

in MSDP, box 31, folder 110; WATER! Program, 22 February 1976, Marge Zapoleon to Wesley Sarvis, 10 November 1975, both in MSDP, box 23, folder 8.

15. Untitled draft petition, 23 January 1976, MSDP, box 3, folder 110; WATER! program, 22 February 1976, MSDP, box 23, folder 8; Lawton Chiles to Ann M. Gorsuch, 12 May 1982, AMP, box 3, folder 19; John C. Jones to Barbara Blum, 28 September 1979, John C. White to MSD, 25 October 1979, "At Last: Biscayne Aquifer Designated Sole Source by EPA," n.d., all in MSDP, box 30, folder 96; *NYT,* 26 August 1979.

16. Browder, interview; Arthur R. Marshall to Nathaniel P. Reed, July 1976, AMP, box 1, folder 43.

17. *Wall Street Journal,* 14 September 1979; Friends of the Everglades, "For the Future of Florida, Repair the Everglades," 1981, HP.

18. *Gainesville Sun,* 26 February 1989; Leonard Pardue, Jessie Freeling, L. J. Greenfield, and P. T. Gannon Jr., *Who Knows the Rain? Nature and Origin of Rainfall in South Florida* (Coconut Grove, Fla.: Friends of the Everglades, 1982), 61.

19. *Tallahassee Democrat,* 19 May 1981; *Sarasota Herald-Tribune,* 28 November 1982; MSD and Arthur R. Marshall to Guy Spicola and William E. Fulford, 23 February 1976, MSDP, box 31, folder 110; Allan Dodds Frank, "Without Water, Everything Stops," *Forbes,* 2 December 1984, 63–64, 68, 72; Yates, "Marjory Stoneman Douglas," 118; Pardue et al., *Who Knows the Rain?* 5; *River of Grass,* 16; John Kunkel Small, *From Eden to Sahara: Florida's Tragedy* (Sanford, Fla.: Seminole Soil and Water Conservation District, 2004), 63.

20. Arthur R. Marshall, "A Critique of Water Management in South Florida," presented to the South Florida Water Management District, 20–21 November 1980, Everglades Digital Library, Arthur R. Marshall Collection; Arthur Marshall to MSD, 3 October 1976, MSDP, box 23, folder 8; *Palm Beach Post,* 10 September 1984.

21. Arthur R. Marshall, "Statement for Presentation to the Governor and Cabinet of Florida," 13 April 1971, Friends of the Everglades Papers, box 1, HMSF; "Repairing the Florida Everglades," 1 April 1983, "Florida Must Dechannelize the Lower Kissimmee River," 2 April 1983, both in AMP, box 1, folder 5; Arthur R. Marshall to MSD, 24 November 1975, MSDP, box 31, folder 110; Jones, interview by Gridley.

22. MSD to Arthur R. Marshall, 22 July 1971, 1 December 1976, 10 September 1978, AMP, box 1, folder 28; Garald G. Parker Sr., interview by David McCally, 27 February 1992, Oral History Program, University of South Florida Library,

Tampa; Yates, "Marjory Stoneman Douglas," 127; *Palm Beach Post,* 10 September 1984; *HMSF,* 20 February 1985.

23. MSD to Joe Browder, 22 August 1977, JBP, MSD to jbbtxt folder.

24. Yates, "Marjory Stoneman Douglas," 118–19, 121; Arthur R. Marshall, "Statement to Governing Board, South Florida Water Management District," 11 June 1981, AMP; William V. Storch, *Some Environmental Effects of Drainage in Florida* (n.p.: Central and Southern Florida Flood Control District, 1968).

25. Jones, interview by Gridley; Pardue et al., *Who Knows the Rain?* 5; John Hicks, "Marjory Stoneman Douglas," *Florida* (*Orlando Sentinel*), 14 October 1979, 7; Stuart D. Strahl, interview by Julian Pleasants, 22 February 2001, SPOHP; MSD to Arthur R. Marshall, 27 June 1978, 10 September 1978, AMP, box 1, folder 28; Yates, "Marjory Stoneman Douglas," 118.

26. "Kissimmee River Valley Restoration Resolution," presented in Tallahassee to Chairman Jay Landers (DER), by MSD, 2 February 1977, MSDP, box 23, folder 8; *Florida Wildlife Federation et al. v. State of Florida Department of Environmental Regulation et al.,* DOAH Case 79-256, MSDP, box 23, folder 1; Barry Lessinger to MSD, 1 April 1977, MSDP, box 23, folder 8; MSD to Alan G. Greer, 21 October 1977, Scott D. Sheftall to MSD, 20 November 1977, both in MSDP, box 27, folder 64; *MH,* 10 June 1979, 24 May 1998; MSD to Arthur R. Marshall, 24, 27 March 1977, AMP, box 1, folder 28.

27. *Florida Wildlife Federation et al. v. State of Florida Department of Environmental Regulation et al.; MH,* 10 June 1979.

28. *Florida Wildlife Federation et al. v. State of Florida Department of Environmental Regulation, et al.,* Petitioners' Motion/Affidavit for Disqualification of Hearing Officer, DOAH Case 79-256, 11 June 1979, Scott D. Sheftall to MSD, 29 November 1979, South Florida Water Management District, "Temporary Operating Permit for Lake Okeechobee," February 1980, all in MSDP, box 27, folder 64.

29. *MH,* 6 April 1975; "Minutes of a Regulatory Meeting of the Governing Board of the Central and Southern Florida Flood Control District," 9 September 1976, document provided by the South Florida Water Management District; "Minutes of a Regional Meeting of the Governing Board of the South Florida Water Management District," 11 June 1981, document provided by the South Florida Water Management District; "Resolution: Restoration of the Kissimmee River, circa post-1976, MSDP, box 23, folder 8; "Kissimmee River Valley Restoration Resolution"; resolutions for dechannelization and restoration of the

Kissimmee River Valley, presented in Tallahassee, 28 April 1977, by MSD, AMP, box 3, folder 25; Friends of the Everglades, "For the Future of Florida"; "Restoration Alternatives," *ENFO Newsletter,* February 1977, 6.

30. Al Burt, *Becalmed in the Mullet Latitudes: Al Burt's Florida* (Port Salerno, Fla.: Classics Library, 1983), 131–33; Estus Whitfield to author, 28 March 2006.

CHAPTER THIRTY-FOUR: Grande Dame

1. MSD, "How You Can Protect the Environment," *Geojourney* 1 (October 1980): 13.

2. *Chicago Tribune,* 26 March 1986.

3. *MH,* 7 April 1985; Joe Podgor, interview by author, 10 August 2000; Sharyn Richardson, interview by author, 28 December 2007.

4. Al Burt, "The Grande Dame of the Everglades," 30, clipping, MSDP, box 39, folder 11; Dava Sobel, "Still Fighting the Good Fight for the Everglades," *Audubon,* July–August 1991, 31; Anastasia Toufexis and William McWhirter, "Lady of the Everglades," *Time,* 31 January 1983, 57; Podgor, interview; *Great Floridians Film Series: Marjory Stoneman Douglas* (Tallahassee: Museum of Florida History and Florida History Associates, 1990).

5. John Hicks, "Marjory Stoneman Douglas," *Florida* (*Orlando Sentinel*), 14 October 1979, 7, 10. The Curtis H. Stanton Energy Center protected the groundwater, becoming one of the first power plants to use reclaimed water from the local wastewater treatment facility to cool its generators and to significantly reduce its dependence on water from the Floridan Aquifer. In the area of greenhouse emissions, however, the Orlando-area facility made it to the top list of polluters after adding a second plant and increasing emissions by 140 percent between 1995 and 2003 (Jill Krueger, "Local Power Plants Get Dirtier, Report Says," *Orlando Business Journal,* 5 April 2002, available online at http://www .bizjournals.com/orlando/stories/2002/04/01/daily37.html [accessed fall 2007]); U.S. Public Interest Research Group Education Fund, "Pollution on the Rise: Local Trends in Power Plant Pollution," available online at http://www.cleartheair.org/ reports/pollution_on_the_rise.pdf (accessed fall 2007).

6. *MH,* 17 July 1974, 20 February 1975, 11 August 1986; William Roy Shelton, *Land of the Everglades: Southern Tropical Florida* (Tallahassee: Florida Department of Agriculture), 42; Luther J. Carter, "Dade County: The Politics of Managing Urban Growth," *Science,* 4 June 1976, 985; "Here's One Plane Trip," *MH*

clipping, n.d., HP; "A WPLG Editorial," 15 January 1975, JBP, Dade Zoning folder; Hicks, "Marjory Stoneman Douglas," 7; MSD to South Florida Water Management District, 1 October 1984, MSDP, box 26, folder 50; MSD to anonymous, 19 October 1981, MSD to Robert Graham, 27 September 1984, MSD to Kathy, 8 June 1985, Bob Graham to MSD, 2 September 1983, all in MSDP, box 24, folder 21–22; Michael Grunwald, *The Swamp: The Everglades, Florida, and the Politics of Paradise* (New York: Simon and Schuster, 2006), 232.

7. "'It's Never Too Late for Anything," *MH* clipping, n.d., MSDP, box 39, folder 11; "The Elocutioner," *MH* clipping, n.d., MSDP, box 39, folder 12; Podgor, interview; "Marjory Stoneman Douglas: Crusading Friend of the Everglades," *IMC Journal* 2 (Autumn 1984): 18. A similar rendition of this event appears in what is perhaps the most insightful popular article on Douglas and the Everglades, Steve Yates, "Marjory Stoneman Douglas and the Glades Crusade," *Audubon,* March 1983, 112–27; Nancy Brown, interview by author, 27 August 2000.

8. Juanita Greene to MSD, n.d., MSD to James C. Cato, 6 November 1986, James C. Cato to MSD, 6 January 1987, all in MSDP, box 28, folder 73; Howard C. Forman to MSD, 29 August 1984, MSDP, box 26, folder 42; MSD to William G. Gordon, 7 July 1986, Marjorie H. Carr to William G. Gordon, 26 June 1986, both in MSDP, box 31, folder 107; MSD to Bob Graham, 4 August 1982, Leo Chappell to MSD, n.d., Bob Graham to MSD, 30 August 1982, all in MSD, box 25, folder 39; Friends of Fort George Island, "Rezoning Would Destroy Fort George Island," August 1982, MSDP, box 25, folder 39; David Ettman to MSD, n.d., Linda J. Hardin to Metro-Dade County, 17 October 1984, Anthony J. Clemente to Linda Hardin, all in MSDP, box 31, folder 103; *Florida Times-Union,* 22 July, 6 August, 15 September 1982; *NYT,* 22 January 2006; *Sarasota Herald-Tribune,* 28 November 1982.

9. Podgor, interview; "Environmental Information News Service," undated announcements, AMP, box 1, folder 28; *MH,* 14 April 1974; MSD to Arthur R. Marshall, 10 September 1978, AMP, box 1, folder 28; *Christian Science Monitor,* 23 September 1970; *Sarasota Herald-Tribune,* 18 February 1974.

10. Robert M. Judge to MSD, 24 September 1982, MSDP, box 26, folder 57; MSD to "Mayor Neu and Honorable Members," 22 January 1980, MSD to James W. R. Adams, 25 March 1980, both in MSDP, box 43, folder 65; Bill Gunter to MSD, 14 December 1983, John M. De Grove to MSD, 23 December 1983, Friends of the Everglades to Bob Graham, 11 December 1983, all in MSDP, box 43, folder 69; MSD to Bob Graham, 30 July 1984, MSDP, box 44, folder 75; "Project Summary:

Biscayne Bay Environmental Evaluation Project," n.d., MSD to Gloria Lemeske, n.d., both in MSDP, box 25, folder 25; *Florida Times-Union,* 6 August 1982; *Tampa Tribune,* 27 June 1982; *MH,* 20 May 1973, 14 April 1974; *Miami News,* 21, 22 May 1973; Hicks, "Marjory Stoneman Douglas," 6.

11. Daniel A. Mica to MSD, 25 February 1980, MSDP, box 44, folder 75; MSD to Arthur R. Marshall, 24 March 1977, AMP, box 1, folder 28; Peter Rhoades Mott to John Morehead, 20 May 1981, CPC, 5301/319/6; Central and Southern Florida Flood Control District News Release, 12 July 1974, Garald G. Parker Collection, Everglades folder, USF; *MH,* 23 September 1971, 12 August 1973, 14, 27 August 1974; Alice Wainwright to Hal, 14 January 1975, JBP, FAS jetport folder; *Florida Conservation News* 12 (August 1976): 12.

12. United Nations Educational, Scientific, and Cultural Organization, "Convention Concerning the Protection of the World Cultural and Natural Heritage, World Heritage List; Nomination Submitted by the United States of America, Everglades National Park," 3 February 1979, 15, HP; *WP,* 14 November 1976; "Everglades: Biosphere Reserve and World Heritage Site," *National Park Service Courier,* November 1982, 2; Yates, "Marjory Stoneman Douglas," 127.

13. Podgor, interview; Franklin Adams, interview by author, 8 August 2000; Holly Hays, "Marjory Stoneman Douglas: Conservationist of the Century," *Florida Living,* August 1992, 54; *SPT,* 5 June 1989; *Orlando Sentinel,* 26 May 1986; *MH,* 26 April 1920, 21 May 1983; *Fort Lauderdale Sun-Sentinel,* 14 May 1998; *Voice,* 232.

14. Podgor, interview.

15. Podgor, interview.

16. S. V. Dáte, *Quiet Passion: A Biography of Senator Bob Graham* (New York: Tarcher/Penguin, 2004), 57, 64–67; *Voice,* 245–46; Podgor, interview; *WP,* 15 March 1964; MSD to Robert Graham, 27 September 1984, MSDP, box 24, folder 21.

17. Dáte, *Quiet Passion,* 164–65; David McCally, "The Everglades and the Florida Dream," in *Paradise Lost? The Environmental History of Florida,* ed. Jack E. Davis and Raymond Arsenault (Gainesville: University Press of Florida, 2005), 153; Nelson M. Blake, *Land into Water—Water into Land: A History of Water Management in Florida* (Tallahassee: Florida State University Press, 1980), 153, 263; Howard Kohn and Vicki Monks, "Greetings from the Everglades," *Mother Jones,* December 1987, 20, 22; William Graham, "The Pennsuco Sugar Experiment," *Tequesta* 11 (1952): 27–50; Herbert Bowerman to Manuel Rionda, 11 January 1921,

in Sugar Cane in the Everglades, 1922, Miscellaneous Manuscripts, box 83, PKY; Leonard Collins, "Our New National Sugar Bowl," *South* 2 (March–April–May–June 1926): 12–13, 26.

18. Dáte, *Quiet Passion*, 160, 161; Kohn and Monks, "Greetings from the Everglades," 22, 44.

19. Dáte, *Quiet Passion*, 63–96, 124–27, 168–69; Lester Collins, *Inisfree: An American Garden* (New York: Abrams, 1994); Kohn and Monks, "Greetings from the Everglades," 49; Bob Graham, *Workdays* (Miami: Banyan, 1978).

20. "Seventh Annual Members' Reception and Dinner Honorary Committee, National Parks and Conservation Association," 11 November 1986, MSD to Paul Pritchard, 11 November 1986, both in MSDP, box 46, folder 106.

21. Luther J. Carter, "Carter Places Environment High on the Agenda," *Science*, 3 June 1977, 1065; A. H. "Gus" Craig to Lawton Chiles, 24 January 1978, MSDP, box 27, folder 64.

22. *Tampa Tribune*, 2 November 1987; Nathaniel Pryor Reed, "An Address to the Sierra Club's 1981 Annual Meeting at the Empress of China, San Francisco," 2 May 1981, JBP, Nat v Watt folder; MSD to Jerry and Lucile, 26 February 1986, MSDP, box 40, folder 21; MSD to Arthur R. Marshall, 1 December 1976, AMP, box 1, folder 28; *San Francisco Chronicle*, 15 April 2007.

23. Ted Steinberg, *Down to Earth: Nature's Role in American History* (New York: Oxford University Press, 2002), 249; Ann Vileisis, *Discovering the Unknown Landscape: A History of America's Wetlands* (Washington, D.C.: Island, 1997), 252, 264, 273, 274–75; *Tampa Tribune*, 16 May 1981; *Sarasota Herald-Tribune*, 28 November 1982; *SPT*, 16 May 1981, 25 January 1987; *WP*, 9 March 1984; *NYT*, 26 August 1979; MSD to "My Dear Turners," 2 July 1982, MSDP, box 43, folder 68.

24. Bill Gunter to MSD, 10 August 1983, HP; Kohn and Monks, "Greetings from the Everglades," 46; Cabinet Tape Log, 3 August 1983, tape 1, Department of State, Cabinet Meeting Official Records, July 19, 1983–September 6, 1983, s. 184, Tape Log folder, FSA.

25. Bob Graham to MSD, 27 June 1996, HP; *Voice*, 246; Michael Chenoweth, interview by author, 9 August 2000; Pam Pierce, interview by author, 9 August 2000; *Tampa Tribune*, 3 January 1986.

26. Lawton Chiles to Ann M. Gorsuch, 12 May 1982, Charles R. Jeter to MSD, 26 August 1982, both in AMP, box 2, folder 19; Bob Graham to MSD, 5 May 1980, MSD to Elton Gissendanner, 15 July 1985, Arthur R. Marshall to John, 8 August 1979, MSDP, box 26, folder 56; *Christian Science Monitor*, 18 April 1973; Joe

Browder, interview by author, 7 August 2002; Joe Browder to author, 22 February 2006; *SPT,* 16 May 1981; I-75 Construction/Big Cypress Acquisition: Save Our Everglades, 10 June 1985 (n.p.), Estus Whitfield to MSD, 24 June 1985, C. W. Bill Young to MSD, 31 March 1987, MSD to John C. Jones, 20 July 1983, all in HP.

27. Johnny Jones, interview by Brian Gridley, 23 May 2001, SPOHP; Estus Whitfield, interview by Brian Gridley, 15 May 2001, SPOHP; *For the Future of Florida, Repair the Everglades* (n.p.: Friends of the Everglades, 1982), Everglades Digital Library, Arthur R. Marshall Collection; Art Marshall, "A Report Card," *Florida Angler,* AMP, box 1, folder 5; *NYT,* 10 September 1983; *Christian Science Monitor,* 12 August 1983, 21 March 1984; *WP,* 15 February 1985; Rose Mary Mechem, "There's Trouble in Paradise," *Sports Illustrated,* 9 February 1981, 82–96. The author of the *Sports Illustrated* article wrote a similar piece for *National Wildlife.* See Mary Rose Mechem, "Florida: The Grass Is No Longer Greener," *National Wildlife,* October–November 1982, 50–55.

28. Estus Whitfield to author, 28 March 2006; Bob Graham to MSD, 5 July, 2 September 1983, MSD to Bob Graham, 2 August 1983, all provided to author by Estus Whitfield.

29. "Graham Announces Save Our Everglades Program," press release, 9 August 1983, Governor Robert Graham Papers, box 44, FSA; "Save Our Everglades," governor's statement, 9 August 1983, MSDP, box 27, folder 60.

30. *Gainesville Sun,* 18 February 1985; Dáte, *Quiet Passion,* 126, 174; *Save Our Everglades Second Anniversary Report Card,* 9 August 1985, Nathaniel Reed Papers, box 1, folder 2, PKY.

31. MSD, "An Article for Raconteur Magazine, March 1989," draft, 6–7, HP; Duke Cullimore, "Restoration of a River," *Sierra,* September–October 1985, 23–24.

32. MSD to Robinettes, 18 July 1985, MSDP, box 40, folder 21; MSD to Robert Graham, 8 July 1985, MSDP, box 25, folder 37; MSD to Bob Graham, 30 July 1984, MSDP, box 44, folder 75; MSD, "Article for Raconteur Magazine," 7; *Chicago Tribune,* 26 March 1986; *Fort Myers News-Press,* 7 July 1984; Estus Whitfield to author, 28 March 2006; Bob Graham, interview by author, 10 March 2006; Bob Graham, Governor's Notebooks, log 7/85G, 27 July 1985, Robert D. Graham Papers, PKY.

33. Arthur R. Marshall to MSD, 21 March 1977, MSDP, box 27, folder 61; Arthur R. Marshall memorial program, 18 February 1985, MSDP, box 28, folder 71; *Gainesville Sun,* 20 February 1985; "Graham Issues Statement on Art Marshall,"

press release, 19 February 1985, document provided to author by Estus Whitfield; Bob Graham to Arthur R. Marshall III, 1 August 1984, provided to author by Estus Whitfield; Bob Graham to Jere Moore, Ken Woodburn, and Estus Whitfield, 29 August 1984, provided to author by Estus Whitfield.

CHAPTER THIRTY-FIVE: Justice and Equality

1. Charles Flowers, "Starting over in the Everglades: A Look to Restore This Precious Wild Land through the Eyes of Four Uncommon People," *National Wildlife,* April–May 1985, 60; *SPT,* 5 June 1989; George Rosner, "MSD, a House of My Own," 1990, HP; Nancy Brown, interview by author, 27 August 2000; Martha Hubbart, interview by author, 14 August 2002; Sallye Jude, interview by author, 16 August 2002; Sharyn Richardson, interview by author, 28 December 2007; Lili Krech Neale, interview by author, 18 November 2005; George Rosner, interview by Sharyn Richardson, May 1999, February 2000, provided to author by Sharyn Richardson.

2. *Lakeland Ledger,* 24 March 1996; "Directory, Class of 1912," 30 June 1987, HP; MSD to Robinettes, 18 July 1985, MSDP, box 40, folder 21; Hubbart, interview.

3. MSD, "Five-Year Diary," 1987–91, HP.

4. *Chicago Tribune,* 26 March 1986.

5. *Voice,* 14–15; *MH,* 19 October 1984; *Fort Lauderdale News,* 4 November 1971; "Marjory Stoneman Douglas: A List of Achievements and Honors," HP.

6. *Voice,* 16–18.

7. "Hall of Fame," *Rolling Stone,* 3 May 1990, 59–63; *MH,* 23 January 1987; *SPT,* 25 January 1987; Mrs. R. L. Bisplinghoff to Wellesley College Alumni Office, 10 April 1982, MSDP, box 31, folder 111; Holly Hays, "Marjory Stoneman Douglas: Conservationist of the Century," *Florida Living,* August 1992, 52; MSD to Nedra, 22 December 1989, HP; Henry Truby, "Henry Field, DSC: 1902–1986," MSDP, box 25, folder 31; Valerie Gladstone, "Marjory Stoneman Douglas," *Ms.,* January–February 1989, 68–71; "Marjory Stoneman Douglas: A List of Her Achievements and Honors," HP; Hubbart, interview.

8. Sev Sunseri, "A Dream for DNR Becomes a Reality," *Geojourney* 15 (February 1980): 10–13.

9. *Tallahassee Democrat,* 19 May 1981; *NYT,* 22 October 1984; *Tampa Tribune,* 16 May 1981; *MH,* 19 October 1984, 23 January 1987; Estus Whitfield to author, 28 March 2006; Bob Graham, Governor's Notebooks, log 5/81c, 8 May 1981, log

5/81D, 12 May 1981, Robert D. Graham Papers, PKY; Sandy Dayhoff, interview by author, 16 March 2006; Hubbart, interview.

10. *Voice,* 23; *MH,* 25 August 1976; Cindy Miller, "Marjory Douglas Spurs 'Grassroots,'" *Orlando Sentinel,* 9 November 1975; *SPT,* 16 September 1990; *Lakeland Ledger,* 24 March 1996.

11. *Countdown,* directed by Carl Kesser (Coconut Grove, Fla.: Kesser Productions, 1981); Carl Kesser, interview by author, 2 December 2007; *NYT,* 10 October 1981; *Christian Science Monitor,* 20 October 1981.

12. "Bart vs. Thanksgiving," *The Simpsons* (Twentieth Century Fox, 1989).

13. *Countdown; Orlando Sentinel,* 9 November 1975; *Princeton Packet,* 3 October 1989; *Daily Princetonian,* 3 October 1989; *Princeton (New Jersey) Times,* 3 October 1989; *Princeton University News and Notes,* 29 September 1989, 1.

14. *Charlotte Observer,* 14 September 1983.

15. MSD to Robinettes, 18 July 1985, MSD to Maud, 18 July 1985, MSDP, box 40, folder 21; Maud H. Chapman to Walter Sullivan, 29 August 1984, Miami Wellesley Club Newsletter, both in MSDP, box 31, folder 111; *MH,* 19 October 1984; *NYT,* 10 March 1995; "Recipients of Wellesley Alumnae Achievement Awards," *Wellesley,* Fall 1994, 1; R. Steven Schiavo to MSD, 15 September 1994, HP; Alice Knight, interview by author, 23 August 2006.

16. *NYT,* 6 November 1991; *MH,* 18 February 1974, 9 November 1991; *Sarasota Herald-Tribune,* 18 February 1974; Anastasia Toufexis and William McWhirter, "Lady of the Everglades," *Time,* 31 January 1983. On strands of ecofeminist thought, see Mary Mellow, "Gender and the Environment," in *Ecofeminism and Globalization: Exploring Culture, Context, and Religion,* ed. Heather Eaton and Lois Ann Lorentzen (Lanham, Md.: Rowman and Littlefield, 2003), 11–22.

17. *MH,* 9 November 1991; Richardson, interview.

18. *NYT,* 6 November 1991; *MH,* 7 April 1990; *Chicago Tribune,* 26 March 1986; *Daily Princetonian,* 3 October 1989; "Marjory Stoneman Douglas: Crusading Friend of the Everglades," *IMC Journal* 2 (Autumn 1984): 18; Myra Farr to MSD, 1 April 1992, HP.

19. Myra Farr to MSD, 1 April 1992, HP; "Mission Statement of the Dade County Women's Coalition for a Healthy Planet," January 1992, HP; *Tampa Tribune,* 16 May 1981; "Voice of the Everglades: Marjory Stoneman Douglas," *Calypso Log* 17 (August 1990): 10; Melanie M. Pratt to MSD, 20 February, 2 June 1985, *NYT* clipping, n.d., all in MSDP, box 25, folder 35; Joe Browder, interview by author, 7 August 2002.

20. December Duke McSherry, interview by author, 19 November 2005; Browder, interview; Neale, interview; Judy Wilson Lawrence, interview by author, 3 November 2005; Nancy Brown, interview; Juanita Greene, interview by author, 16 March 2006.

21. *NYT*, 26 November, 4 December 1960, 23, 24 March 1961, 29 August 1977; *MH*, 5 April 1923; *WP*, 11 March 1976; "The Harvester," *Time*, 31 March 1961, 99; Cindy Hahamovitch, *The Fruits of Their Labor: Atlantic Coast Farmworkers and the Making of Migrant Poverty, 1870–1945* (Chapel Hill: University of North Carolina Press, 1997), 113–37; David McCally, *The Everglades: An Environmental History* (Gainesville: University Press of Florida, 1999), 164–70; Jacqueline Jones, *The Dispossessed: America's Underclasses from the Civil War to the Present* (New York: Basic Books, 1992), 167–70, 181–89; J. Carlyle Sitterson, *Sugar Country: The Cane Sugar Industry in the South, 1753–1950* (Lexington: University of Kentucky Press, 1953), 376.

22. *NYT*, 24 March 1961.

23. Browder, interview. For an excellent study on the Cuban migration to South Florida, see Maria Christina Garcia, *Havana U.S.A.: Cuban Exiles and Cuban Americans in Miami, Florida, 1959–1994* (Berkeley: University of California Press, 1997).

24. F. W. Kettle, "Extract from Chapter 23, History of the Everglades of Florida," Thomas E. Will Papers, box 33, Everglades Publications folder, PKY; P. H. Rolfs, "Sugar Cane: The Ideal Crop for Florida," speech transcript, n.d., Peter Henry Rolfs Collection, box 4, Writings and Speeches, 1899–1920, folder, Special and Area Studies Collection, University of Florida, Gainesville; *MH*, 19 February 1917, 10 October 1988; B. Braga Rionda to Manuel Rionda, 4 January 1922, Miscellaneous Manuscripts, box 83, PKY; Terry L. McCoy and Charles H. Wood, "Caribbean Workers in the Florida Sugar Cane Industry," December 1982, Center for Latin American Studies, University of Florida, George E. Smathers Library Collection, University of Florida, Gainesville; Sheila Kaplan, "A Sweet Deal," *Common Cause*, May–June 1986, 24–29; Thomas K. Billington, "The Unsweetened Truth about Sugar Subsidies," *Reader's Digest*, August 1987, 51–54; Sitterson, *Sugar Country*, 361–78.

25. McCally, *Everglades*, 1/2–73; *Florida Sugar Industry* (Clewiston: Florida Sugar League, 1975); Leonard Collins, "Our Newest National Sugar Bowl," *South* 2 (March–April–May–June 1926): 12; Steve Yates, "Marjory Stoneman Douglas and the Glades Crusade," *Audubon*, March 1983, 119.

26. U.S. Congress, Senate, Subcommittee on Immigration, Committee on the Judiciary, *The West Indies (BWI) Temporary Alien Labor Program: 1943–1977,* 95th Cong., 2nd sess. (Washington, D.C.: U.S. Government Printing Office, 1978), 1–2, 4–5, 23–25; *Florida Sugar Industry; MH,* 29 September 1982; *WP,* 11 March 1976; U.S. Congress, House, Subcommittee on Labor Standards, Committee on Education and Labor, *Job Rights of Domestic Workers: The Florida Sugar Cane Industry,* 98th Cong., 1st sess. (Washington, D.C.: U.S. Government Printing Office, 1983), 5–6.

27. U.S. Congress, House, Subcommittee on Labor Standards, Committee on Education and Labor, *Job Rights,* 5–40; McCally, *Everglades,* 164–70; Alec Wilkinson, *Big Sugar: Seasons in the Cane Fields of Florida* (New York: Knopf, 1989).

28. U.S. Congress, House, Subcommittee on Labor Standards, Committee on Education and Labor, *Job Rights,* 4; U.S. Congress, Senate, Committee on Labor and Human Resources, Migrant and Seasonal Farmworker Powerlessness, *Who Is Responsible? Hearings before the Subcommittee on Migratory Labor,* 91st Cong., 2nd sess., 1, 20, 21, 24 July 1970, 4979–80, 4982; *Florida Sugar Industry;* McCoy and Wood, "Caribbean Workers," 11–12; McCally, *Everglades,* 169–70.

29. Jimmie Darrell Phaup, "The Politics of Poverty: Controversy in Three South Florida Migrant Programs" (Ph.D. diss., University of Arizona, 1975), 1–5, 152–273, 331–62; "Sugar Cane Workers Get Raise," *MH* clipping, n.d., Friends of the Everglades Scrapbook, July–August 1974, HMSF; *NYT,* 7 October 1972, 6 April 1975.

30. Greene, interview; Phaup, "Politics of Poverty," 15–16.

31. Sidney W. Mintz, *Sweetness and Power: The Place of Sugar in Modern History* (New York: Penguin, 1986), xx, 188–89; MSD to Kathy Abrams, 8 June 1985, MSDP, box 24, folder 21; B. F. Ashe to Ward S. Canaday, 6 November 1952, MSDP, box 40, folder 17; "Marjory Stoneman Douglas: Crusading Friend of the Everglades," 20; MSD, "A Mountain in the Sea," *SEP,* 30 October 1937, 14–15, 82, 84, 89, 91; MSD, "A Hill in Haiti," *Cosmopolitan,* July 1939, 32–35, 86–92; MSD, "Caribbean Cauldron," *Saturday Review,* 13 December 1952, 32–33; MSD, "On the Discovery and Enjoyment of Certain West Indies Islands," n.d., MSDP, box 35, folder 85; *Orlando Sentinel,* 1 January 1984; *Voice,* 183–84; MSD to Charles Scribner Jr., 21 June 1987, HP.

32. Rob Williams, interview by author, 1 June 2006; Greene, interview; *WP,* 13 March, 22 April, 23 June 1976.

33. Greene, interview; Williams, interview; MSD to Robert Graham, 17 October 1985, Rob Williams to MSD, 24 June 1986, Bob Graham to MSD, 16 July 1982, David A. Pasquarelli to MSD, all in MSDP, box 26, folder 47; U.S. Congress,

Senate, Subcommittee on Immigration and Refugee Policy, Committee on the Judiciary, *The H-2 Program and Nonimmigrants,* 97th Cong., 1st sess., 30 November 1981 (Washington, D.C.: U.S. Government Printing Office, 1982), 9–12; U.S. Congress, House, Subcommittee on Labor Standards, Committee on Education and Labor, *Job Rights,* 5–40.

34. Williams, interview; S. V. Dáte, *Quiet Passion: A Biography of Senator Bob Graham* (New York: Tarcher/Penguin, 2004), 171–73; Greene, interview; Kaplan, "Sweet Deal," 25; Nano Riley, *Florida's Farmworkers in the Twenty-first Century* (Gainesville: University Press of Florida, 2002).

35. "Florida: Sugar, Tomatoes, Housing," *Rural Migration News* 12 (April 2006), available online at http://migration.ucdavis.edu/rmn/more.php?id=453_0_3_0 (accessed fall 2006); *NYT,* 22 March 2004.

CHAPTER THIRTY-SIX: The Gathering Twilight

1. Helen Muir, *Miami, U.S.A.* (Gainesville: University Press of Florida, 2000), 33; Theo Long, interview by author, 23 July 2002; Joan Gill Blank, *Key Biscayne: A History of Miami's Tropical Island and the Cape Florida Lighthouse* (Sarasota, Fla.: Pineapple, 1996), x–xii.

2. Long, interview; MSD to Bob Martinez, 13 April 1989, William E. Sadowski to John Cosgrove, 6 April 1989, MSD Biscayne Nature Center, Mission Statement, 22 March 1989, Joseph A. Fernandez to William A. Sadowski, 31 October 1988, Robert W. Jensen to Mary-Therese Delate, 14 December 1988, all in HP.

3. Sarah Cussen, "Voice of Wellesley: Marjory Stoneman Douglas Revolutionized Environmentalism," *Counterpoint* 17 (October 1999): 11; "Marjory Stoneman Douglas Centennial, April 7, 1990" program, "Famous Centenarian," clipping, n.d., both in HP; *Florida Today,* 7 April 1990; *WP,* 3 April 1990; *NYT,* 8 April 1990.

4. *Orlando Sentinel,* 13 April, 28 April 1990; *SPT,* 13 April 1990; "Marjory Stoneman Douglas Recognition/100th Birthday Celebration," Bob Graham to MSD, 2 May 1990, HP; H.R. 136, To Amend the National Parks and Recreation Area Act of 1978, 105th Cong., 1st sess., 7 January 1997.

5. Martha Hubbart, interview by author, 14 August 2002; Sallye Jude, interview by author, 16 August 2002; *MH,* 30 July 1994, 17 February 2000, 28 March 2001, 30 May 2006; MSD to Mr. and Mrs. Crane, 9 September 1988, HP; MSD to Charles Scribner Jr., 21 June 1987, HP; Minutes, Board of Trustees, Cabinet

Meeting, 28 February 1991, item 6, p. 5, Florida Department of Natural Resources, provided to author by Joe Knetsch; Florida Department of Natural Resources contract review form, DNR contract SL126, 2 June 1994, provided to author by Joe Knetsch; *Don Dehut v. Marjory Stoneman Douglas*, 21 June 1991, Dade County Court, case 9021053, provided to author by Joe Knetsch.

6. *NYT*, 18 May 1991; *MH*, 1 May 1991; Muir, *Miami, U.S.A.*, 109–10; Dava Sobel, "Still Fighting the Good Fight for the Everglades," *Audubon*, July–August 1991, 34; Hubbart, interview; Jude, interview.

7. "Advocate Celebrates Her Birthday," clipping, 7 April 1992, HP; *MH*, 9 November 1922; *SPT*, 9 February 2000; *Tampa Tribune*, 27 February 2006; Connie Toops, "The Tree That's Changing the Everglades," *American Forests* 55 (February 1986): 26; Frank C. Craighead, *The Trees of South Florida* (Coral Gables, Fla.: University of Miami Press, 1971), 147–48; Lloyd L. Loope and Vicki L. Dunevitz, *Impact of Fire Exclusion and Invasion of* Schinus Terebinthifolius *on Limestone Rockland Pine Forests of Southeastern Florida* (Homestead, Fla.: National Park Service, South Florida Research Center, 1981), 2.

8. *MH*, 2 April 1933, 31 August 1947; John C. Gifford, *The Everglades and Other Essays Relating to Southern Florida* (Kansas City, Mo.: Everglade Land Sales, 1911), 102; David Fairchild, "Some Plant Reminiscences of Southern Florida," *Tequesta* 2 (1942): 8–15; John C. Gifford, "Trees of South Florida. I. Five Naturalized Exotic Forest Trees," *Scientific Monthly*, July 1944, 21–28; "Another Invader: Melaleuca," *American Forests* 55 (February 1986): 25; Ronald L. Meyers, "Site Susceptibility to the Invasion of the Exotic Tree Melaleuca Quinquennervia in Southern Florida," *Journal of Applied Ecology* 20 (August 1983): 645–58.

9. *MH*, 17 October 1959; Robert L. Williamson to MSD, 7 July 1989, MSD to Bob Graham, n.d., MSD to E. Clay Shaw, n.d., MSD to Dante Fascell, n.d., MSD to Nathaniel P. Reed, n.d., MSD to Robert Martinez, n.d., MSD to Clayton K. Yeutter, n.d., Nathaniel P. Reed to MSD, 9 August 1999, all in HP.

10. *Christian Science Monitor*, 6 July 1968; MSD to Robert Brantly, 7 March 1986, MSDP, box 29, folder 81; MSD to Ken Morrison, 30 April 1983, MSD to Lawton Chiles, 2 July 1984, MSD to J. Jeffrey Campbell, n.d., MSD to Don Ashley, 15 September 1984, all in MSDP, box 26, folder 51.

11. Juanita Greene, "The Everglades: Deer vs. Sugar," clipping, *MH*, n.d., Friends of the Everglades Scrapbook, HMSF; John C. Jones to MSD, 20 February 1982, MSDP, box 26, folder 51.

12. *Orlando Sentinel,* 15 March 1964; *MH,* 21 July, 15 August 1982; Randy Loftis, "Unlikely Allies to Team Up to Offer Proposal to Ease Hendry Flooding," *MH* clipping, n.d., John D. West to Robert Ellis, 30 September 1981, Gun Hunt to Robert Ellis, 9 February 1982, all in MSDP, box 24, folder 16; John C. Jones to MSD, 20 February 1982, 2 June 1982, MSDP, box 26, folder 51; MSD to Johnny Jones, 8 February 1982, MSDP, box 28, folder 51; *SPT,* 18 June 1982; John C. Jones to Nathaniel P. Reed, 21 July 1982, MSDP, box 25, folder 27.

13. *River of Grass,* 363–68; *Tampa Tribune,* 4 April 1937.

14. Bob Graham to MSD, 5 July 1983, provided to author by Estus Whitfield; MSD to Lawton Chiles, 28 January 1980, MSDP, box 44, folder 75; Juanita Greene, "Disease, Hunger Kill 100,000 Deer Yearly, Expert Says," *MH* clipping, n.d., MSDP, box 24, folder 16.

15. John C. Kilgo, Ronald F. Labisky, and Duane E. Fritzen, "Influences of Hunting on the Behavior of White-Tailed Deer: Implications for Conservation of the Florida Panther," *Conservation Biology* 12 (December 1998): 1359–64; Howard Kohn and Vicki Monks, "Greetings from the Everglades," *Mother Jones,* December 1987, 6; *Fort Lauderdale Sun-Sentinel,* 10 March 1982; MSD to Bob Graham, 4 July 1986, Bob Graham to MSD, 15 August 1986, MSD to Mary E. White, 8 September 1986, all in HP.

16. Charles Fergus, *Swamp Screamer: At Large with the Florida Panther* (Gainesville: University Press of Florida, 1998); Chuck Fergus, "The Panther Verges on Extinction," *Science,* 8 March 1991, 1178–80; David S. Maehr, *The Florida Panther: Life and Death of a Vanishing Carnivore* (Washington, D.C.: Island, 1997); Jon T. Coleman, *Vicious: Wolves and Men in America* (New Haven: Yale University Press, 2004).

17. MSD to Robert Brantly, 16 June 1986, MSDP, box 29, folder 81; *Seminole Tribune,* 4 May, 8, 19 September, 19 October, 2 November 1987.

18. A. C. Alvarez to Bernard Yokel, 28 June 1985, MSDP, box 28, folder 78; Ken Alvarez to MSD, 31 May 1985, MSD to Robert Jantzen, 1 May 1985, both in MSDP, box 30, folder 84; Robert M. Brantly to MSD, 21 March 1983, MSDP, box 29, folder 80; MSD to Robert M. Brantly, 30 July 1984, MSDP, box 29, folder 81; MSD to Desmond Morris, 8 July 1988, HP; *MH,* 7 April 1983; "Radio-Tracking the Florida Panther: Will It Help Save Him?" clipping, n.d., HP; *Voice,* 239; Sharyn Richardson, interview by author, 28 December 2007.

19. Nancy Brown, interview by author, 27 August 2000.

20. MSD to Gilly, 13 January 1986, MSDP, box 40, folder 21; MSD to Carolyn Cole, 27 September 1967, 22 June 1971, MSDP, box 40, folder 18; John Hicks, "Marjory Stoneman Douglas," *Florida* (*Orlando Sentinel*), 14 October 1979, 6.

21. Allan L. Egbert to MSD, 21 November 1984, MSDP, box 28, folder 77; *MH*, 1 April 1990; MSD to Sue, 30 September 1989, HP; MSD to Robinettes, 30 April 1986, MSDP, box 40, folder 21; Martha Hubbart to Mrs. Dewar, 22 September 1992, Bob Graham to MSD, 19 March 1987, both in HP; Richardson, interview.

22. *NYT*, 4 July 1992; *SPT*, 22 January 1992.

23. Daniel Glick, "Big Sugar vs. the Everglades," *Rolling Stone*, 2 May 1996, 64.

24. MSD to K. C. Alvarez, 14 March 1985, MSDP, box 29, folder 81; MSD to Bob Graham, 27 September 1984, MSDP, box 24, folders 21–22.

25. *SPT*, 21 December 1987, 8 May 1991; Marjory Stoneman Douglas Everglades Protection Act, Fla. Stat. § 373.4592 (1991); Hubbart, interview.

26. Estus Whitfield, interview by Brian Gridley, 15 May 2001, SPOHP; Bob Martinez to MSD, 25 February 1988, HP; *Tampa Tribune*, 17 October 1986; *Orlando Sentinel*, 13 January 1988, 13 April 1990; *SPT*, 25 January 1987, 5 July 1989, 13 April 1990; *Jacksonville Florida Times-Union*, 1 April 1990.

27. MSD to "Dear Friend" (form letter for Lawton Chiles Campaign Committee), n.d., Lawton Chiles to MSD, 7, 24 July 1987, all in HP; *SPT*, 13 June 1990.

28. Marjory Stoneman Douglas Everglades Protection Act; *NYT*, 12 January 1991; *Orlando Sentinel*, 11, 14 January 1991.

29. John R. Wodraska to Lawton M. Chiles, 29 July 1987, HP; "Restoration of the Kissimmee River," *Florida Defenders of the Environment Bulletin* 17 (September–October 1986): 3; *Orlando Sentinel*, 11 January 1991; *MH*, 21 March 2002; *NYT*, 1 April 1989; James R. Hagy, "Watergate," *Florida Trend* 35 (March 1993): 34.

30. *Miami News-Times*, 22 May 2003; Hagy, "Watergate," 33.

31. Nathaniel Reed, interview by Julian Pleasants, 18 December 2000, SPOHP; *Wall Street Journal*, 26 September, 13 October 1988.

32. MSD to Dexter Lehtinen, 28 July 1988, HP.

33. *United States vs. SFWMD et al.*, Case 88-1886-CIV-Hoeveler, 21 May 1991, Hearing Transcript, 7; Everglades National Park Protection and Expansion Act 1989, Public Law 101-229, 101st Cong.; Hagy, "Watergate," 34; *Orlando Sentinel*, 23, 24 January 1988, 25 October, 11 November 1990; *SPT*, 23 May 1991.

34. Keith Rizzardi, "Translating Science into Law: Phosphorous Standards in the Everglades," *Journal of Land Use and Environmental Law* 17 (2001): 153–56; Hagy, "Watergate," 32–36; *NYT*, 12 July 1991; *Orlando Sentinel* 11, 12 July 1991;

Michael Grunwald, *The Swamp: The Everglades, Florida, and the Politics of Paradise* (New York: Simon and Schuster, 2006), 421 n. 289; Settlement Agreement, 26 July 1991, docket 980, *United States v. South Florida Water Management District, et al.*, Case. 88-1886-CIV-Hoeveler.

35. *MH*, 16 April 1994; *NYT*, 11 March 1991, 4 May 1994; "Notes on the National Scene: Everglades Restoration Law Passed," *Nonpoint Source News-Notes* (U.S. Environmental Protection Agency) 37 (July–August 1994): 1–5.

36. Friends of the Everglades et al., "Media Advisory, Everglades," 3 March 1994, JBP, MSD vs. EFA folder; MSD to Lawton Chiles, 26 February 1994, JBP, Douglas ltr EFA folder; *Tampa Tribune*, 8 March 1994; *NYT*, 15 July 1993; *MH*, 7 November 1996; "Federal Court Decision Causes EPA to Review Florida's Everglades Forever Act," *Section Reporter*, March 1998, www.eluls.org/mar1998 (accessed winter 2007).

37. Sharyn Richardson to author, 7 January 2008; MSD, revocable trust agreement, 6 November 1994, copy provided to author by William T. Muir.

38. Helen Muir, interview by author, 11 March 1999; MSD, speech to Florida Historical Society, Pensacola, 6 May 1978, SPOHP.

EPILOGUE: "Without Me"

1. I am indebted to Toby Muir for constructing this paragraph.

2. Ann Peyton to MSD, 20 August 1990, Leslie Riviera to MSD, 4 October 1990, both in HP; Sharyn Richardson, interview by author, 28 December 2007.

3. Helen Muir, interview by author, 11 March 1999; William Muir, interview by author, 8 December 2007.

4. Kathy Gaubatz, interview by author, 10 January 2008; Richardson, interview.

5. Gaubatz, interview; Richardson, interview; "Remarks by the President in Ceremony Honoring Medal of Freedom Recipients," 30 November 1993, available online at http://medaloffreedom.com/1993Recipients.htm (accessed winter 2008).

6. U.S. Congress, Senate, *Hearings before the Subcommittee on Transportation and Infrastructure and the Committee on Environment and Public Works,* 106th Cong., 2nd sess., 2000, S. Hrg. 106-729 (Washington, D.C.: U.S. Government Printing Office, 2000), 5.

7. *SPT*, 20 October 2000; Cyril T. Zaneski, "Anatomy of a Deal," *Audubon*, July–August 2001, 50–53; Jon R. Luoma, "Blueprint for the Future," *Audubon*,

July August 2001, 66; John Flicker, "Audubonview," *Audubon,* July–August 2001, 10; Ted Williams, "Big Water Blues," *Audubon,* July–August 2001, 108–9.

8. "Homestead Airport Plan: National Parks Face Grave Danger," *Everglades Reporter,* Spring 2000, 2; *WP,* 23 June 2003; *SPT,* 2 August 2000, 17 January 2001; "Sierra Director Blasts Homestead Plans," *Pelican* 30 (Summer 1998): 1; "NRDC Blocks Disastrous Everglades Mining Scheme," nrdc.org e-mail bulletin, 31 March 2006; *South Florida Sun-Sentinel,* 11 January 2004; *MH,* 25 October 2006; *Naples News,* 22 October 2007; Joe Browder to author, 16 January 2008; Juanita Greene, "Friends of the Everglades in Federal Court," *Everglades Reporter,* Spring 2006, 2–3. At the time of this writing, the case against the SFWMD remains on appeal.

9. *NYT,* 15 October 2002, 25 November 2003; *Tampa Tribune,* 27 February 2003; *South Florida Sun-Sentinel,* 22 March 2004, 25 October 2007; Stuart L. Pimm and Oron L. Bass Jr., "Cape Sable Seaside Sparrow Report for 2004," available online at http://www.nicholas.duke.edu/people/faculty/pimm/cssp/cssspdf/2004report.pdf (accessed winter 2008); *MH,* 6 July 2008. The suit regarding the Everglades Forever Act deadline is pending.

10. *South Florida Sun-Sentinel,* 28 March 2007; *NYT,* 2 November 2007; "The Everglades: Water, Bird, and Man," *Economist,* 8 October 2005, 29–30, 33.

11. "Person of the Week: Marjory Stoneman Douglas," 11 December 2000, available online at http://www.wellesley.edu/Anniversary/douglas.html (accessed winter 2008); *SPT,* 19 November 2000; MH, 2 December 2007; "Tribute to Marjory Stoneman Douglas," transcript, 12 December 2000, available online at http://www.npr.org/templates/story/story.php?storyId=1115372 (accessed winter 2001).

12. Joe Browder to author, 16 January 2008; Committee on Restoration of the Greater Everglades Ecosystem et al., *Adaptive Monitoring and Assessment for the Comprehensive Everglades Restoration Plan* (Washington, D.C.: National Academies Press, 2003), 51.

13. Friends of the Everglades and Biodiversity Legal Foundation to Bud Shuster, 2 October 2000, provided to author by Friends of the Everglades.

14. *SPT,* 28 June, 9 July 2008; *Palm Beach Post,* 28 June 2008; *South Florida Sun-Sentinel,* 9 July 2008; *MH,* 29 June 2008; BBC News online, http://news.bbc.co.uk/2/hi/americas/7472760.stm (accessed summer 2008); Friends of the Everglades Web site, http://www.everglades.org/ (accessed summer 2008); Joe Browder to author, 12, 13 July 2008.

15. *SPT,* 19 November 2000.

16. These figures were compiled from public information obtainable at the property appraiser's Web page at miamidade.gov.

17. John S. Freud to Mark Glisson, 10 January, 30 January, 1 February 2001, 19 February 2003, provided to author by Joe Knetsch; *Miami News-Times,* 17 February 2001; Sallye Jude, interview by author, 16 August 2002; William Muir, interview; *MH,* 11 February 2007; Jeffrey Schottenstein to Ron Krongold, 19 January 2000, provided to author by Joe Knetsch.

18. *MH,* 3 January, 29 March, 27 May 2007; *Orlando Sentinel,* 27 December 2006.

19. Andy Taylor, "Marjory Stoneman Douglas," *Tropic* (*Miami Herald*), 23 December 1979, 10.

Index